Human Development Report 2010

20th Anniversary Edition

The Real Wealth of Nations:
Pathways to Human Development

Published for the
United Nations
Development
Programme
(UNDP)

ISBN: 9780230284456 90101

Palgrave Macmillan
Houndmills, Basingstoke, Hampshire RG21 6XS and
175 Fifth Avenue, New York, NY 10010

Companies and representatives throughout the world

Palgrave Macmillan in the UK is an imprint of Macmillan Publishers Limited,
registered in England, company number 785998, of Houndmills, Basingstoke,
Hampshire RG21 6XS.

Palgrave Macmillan in the US is a division of St Martin's Press LLC,
175 Fifth Avenue, New York, NY 10010.

Palgrave Macmillan is the global academic imprint of the above companies
and has companies and representatives throughout the world.

Palgrave® and Macmillan® are registered trademarks in the United States,
the United Kingdom, Europe and other countries.

A catalogue record for this book is available from the British Library and the Library of Congress.

Printed in the United States by Consolidated Graphics. Cover is printed on Tembec's 12 pt Kallima coated-one-side
paper. Text pages are printed on Cascades Mills' 60# Rolland Opaque Smooth text that is 50% de-inked post-
consumer recycled fibre. Both sheets are Forest Stewardship Council Certified, elemental chlorine-free papers and
will be printed with vegetable-based inks and produced by means of environmentally compatible technology.
Please recycle the shrinkwrapping.

Mixed Sources
Product group from well-managed
forests, controlled sources and
recycled wood or fiber
www.fsc.org Cert no. BV-COC-080214
© 1996 Forest Stewardship Council

Editing and production: Communications Development Incorporated, Washington D.C.
Design: Bounford.com

For a list of any errors or omissions found subsequent to printing please visit our
website at http://hdr.undp.org

Human Development Report 2010 team

The UNDP Human Development Report Office

The *Human Development Report* is the product of a collective effort under the guidance of the Director, with research, statistics, communications and production staff, and a team supporting National Human Development Reports. Operations and administration colleagues facilitate the work of the office.

Director and lead author

Jeni Klugman

Research

Francisco Rodríguez (Head of Research), Hyung-Jin Choi, Beth Osborne Daponte, Ricardo Fuentes-Nieva, Mamaye Gebretsadik, Zachary Gidwitz, Martin Heger, Difei Hu, Isabel Medalho Pereira, Emily Newman, José Pineda, Emma Samman and Sarah Twigg

Statistics

Milorad Kovacevic (Head of Statistics), Astra Bonini, Liliana Carvajal, Amie Gaye, Melissa Hernandez, Shreyasi Jha, Alison Kennedy (Head of Statistics until June 2010) and Andrew Thornton

National HDRs support

Eva Jespersen (Deputy Director), Mary Ann Mwangi, Paola Pagliani and Timothy Scott

Communications and production

William Orme (Head of Communications), Carlotta Aiello, Ekaterina Berman, Wynne Boelt, Jean-Yves Hamel and Roy Laishley

Operations and administration

Sarantuya Mend (Operations Manager), Oscar Bernal, Fe Juarez-Shanahan and Myint Myint Than

Foreword

In 1990 UNDP published its first *Human Development Report,* with its newly devised Human Development Index. The premise of the HDI, considered radical at the time, was elegantly simple: national development should be measured not simply by national income, as had long been the practice, but also by life expectancy and literacy.

The new HDI had its shortcomings, as the Report's authors forthrightly acknowledged, including a reliance on national averages, which concealed skewed distribution, and the absence of "a quantitative measure of human freedom." Yet it successfully advanced the Report's central thesis, stated succinctly in its first sentence: "People are the real wealth of a nation."

Twenty years later the conceptual brilliance and continuing relevance of that original human development paradigm are indisputable. It is now almost universally accepted that a country's success or an individual's well-being cannot be evaluated by money alone. Income is of course crucial: without resources, any progress is difficult. Yet we must also gauge whether people can lead long and healthy lives, whether they have the opportunity to be educated and whether they are free to use their knowledge and talents to shape their own destinies.

That was the original vision and remains the great achievement of the creators of the *Human Development Reports,* Mahbub ul-Haq of Pakistan and his close friend and collaborator, Amartya Sen of India, working with other leading development thinkers. Their concept has guided not just 20 years of global *Human Development Reports,* but more than 600 National Human Development Reports—all researched, written and published in their respective countries—as well as the many provocative regionally focused reports supported by UNDP's regional bureaus.

Perhaps most important, the human development approach has profoundly affected an entire generation of policy-makers and development specialists around the world—including thousands within UNDP itself and elsewhere in the UN system.

This 20th anniversary milestone presents an opportunity to review human development achievements and challenges systematically at both the global and national levels—a task not attempted since the first Report—and to analyse their implications for policy and future research.

On one crucial point the evidence is compelling and clear: there is much that countries can do to improve the quality of people's lives even under adverse circumstances. Many countries have made great gains in health and education despite only modest growth in income, while some countries with strong economic performance over the decades have failed to make similarly impressive progress in life expectancy, schooling and overall living standards. Improvements are never automatic—they require political will, courageous leadership and the continuing commitment of the international community.

Data from the past 40 years also reveal an enormous diversity of pathways to human development achievement: there is no single model or uniform prescription for success.

This Report shows significant progress by most countries in most areas, with the poorest countries often showing the largest gains. While perhaps not a surprise to statisticians, it was far from universally assumed four decades ago that most low-income nations would make the strong strides forward that the record now shows in health, education and (to a lesser extent) income.

Not all the trends are positive, as we know too well. Sadly, several countries have moved backwards in absolute HDI achievement since the 1990 Report. These countries offer lessons on the devastating impact of conflict, the AIDS epidemic and economic and political mismanagement. Most suffered from more than one if not all these factors.

I especially welcome the continuation of the *Human Development Report* tradition of measurement innovation. Three new measures—capturing multidimensional inequality, gender disparities and extreme deprivation—are introduced in this year's Report. The Inequality-adjusted HDI, Gender Inequality Index and Multidimensional Poverty Index, building on innovations in the field and advances in theory and data, are applied to most countries in the world and provide important new insights.

These new measurement tools reinforce the continuing validity of the original human development vision. Going forward, future Reports will have to grapple with even more difficult issues, including the increasingly critical area of sustainability, as well as inequality and broader notions of empowerment. Many of the analytical and statistical challenges identified in the original 1990 Report continue to confront us today.

UNDP can take appropriate pride in its backing of this intellectually independent and innovative Report for the past two decades, but *Human Development Reports* have never been a UNDP product alone. The Reports rely heavily on knowledge and insights from sister UN agencies, national governments and hundreds of scholars from around the world, and we have always been grateful for that collaboration. As this year's 20th anniversary edition persuasively demonstrates, we can and should continue to be guided by the *Human Development Report's* values and findings for the next 20 years—and beyond.

Helen Clark
Administrator
United Nations Development Programme

The analysis and policy recommendations of this Report do not necessarily reflect the views of the United Nations Development Programme or its Executive Board. The Report is an independent publication commissioned by UNDP. The research and writing of the Report was a collaborative effort by the Human Development Report team and a group of eminent advisors led by Jeni Klugman, Director of the Human Development Report Office.

Introduction by Amartya Sen

In 1990 public understanding of development was galvanized by the appearance of the first *Human Development Report*. Led by the visionary Mahbub ul Haq, it had a profound effect on the way policy-makers, public officials and the news media, as well as economists and other social scientists, view societal advancement. Rather than concentrating on only a few traditional indicators of economic progress (such as gross national product per capita), "human development" accounting proposed a systematic examination of a wealth of information about how human beings in each society live and what substantive freedoms they enjoy.

At the time Mahbub ul Haq became the pioneering leader of the human development approach, several voices of discontent were demanding an approach broader than standard economic measurements provided and were proposing constructive departures. With remarkable insight Mahbub saw the possibility of harnessing these initiatives towards the development of a capacious alternative outlook that would be at once practical and inclusive. The *Human Development Reports* made room for a rich variety of information and analyses related to different aspects of human life.

The difficulty, however, of replacing a simple number like GNP with an avalanche of tables (and a large set of related analyses) is that the latter lacks the handy usability of the crude GNP. So a simple index, the Human Development Index (HDI), was devised explicitly as a rival to GNP and concentrating only on longevity, basic education and minimal income. Not surprisingly, the HDI, which proved very popular in public discussion, has a crudeness that is somewhat similar to that of the GNP. This diagnosis is not meant as an "unkind" description. As someone who was privileged to work with Mahbub in devising the HDI, I would claim that the crude HDI did what it was expected to do: work as a simple measure like GNP but, unlike GNP, without being oblivious of everything other than incomes and commodities. However, the huge breadth of the human development approach must not be confused, as it sometimes is, with the slender limits of the HDI.

The world has moved on since 1990. There have been many gains (in literacy for example), but the human development approach is motivationally committed to concentrating on what remains undone—what demands most attention in the contemporary world—from poverty and deprivation to inequality and insecurity. New tables continue to appear in the steady stream of *Human Development Reports,* and new indices have been devised to supplement the HDI and enrich our evaluation.

As it happens, the new challenges we face have also intensified—for example, those surrounding the conservation of our environment and the sustainability of our well-being and substantive freedoms. The human development approach is flexible enough to take note of the future prospects of human lives on the planet, including the prospects of those features of the world that we value, whether related to our own welfare or not (for example, we can be committed to the survival of threatened animal species on grounds that transcend our own well-being). It would be a great mistake to cram more and more considerations into one number like the HDI, but the human development approach is sophisticated enough to accommodate new concerns and considerations of future prospects (including forecasts of future levels of the HDI) without muddled attempts at injecting more and more into one aggregate measure.

Twenty years after the appearance of the first *Human Development Report,* there is much to celebrate in what has been achieved. But we also have to be alive to ways of improving the assessment of old adversities and of recognizing—and responding to—new threats that endanger human well-being and freedom. That continuing commitment is indeed a part of the large vision of Mahbub ul Haq. The need for that commitment has not diminished over time.

Acknowledgements

This Report is the fruit of the advice, contributions and support of many people. Preparation of any global *Human Development Report (HDR)* is a daunting task—and especially so on such an auspicious anniversary. I would like to especially thank Amartya Sen for his strategic advice and wisdom and Sakiko Fukuda-Parr, Frances Stewart and Michael Walton for their helpful intellectual inputs and feedback. My family, Ema, Josh and Billy, were patient and supportive throughout. The *HDR* depends on the dedication and hard work of the research team and the staff of the Human Development Report Office (HDRO). The continued success of the Report owes much to the support of UNDP Administrator Helen Clark.

An academic advisory panel provided valuable guidance. The panel comprised Bina Agarwal, Philippe Aghion, Arjun Appadurai, Anthony Atkinson, François Bourguinon, Simon Commander, Ariel Fiszbein, Nancy Folbre, Sakiko Fukuda-Parr, Stephen Gelb, Enrico Giovannini, Heba Handoussa, Richard Jolly, Ravi Kanbur, Mwangi Kimenyi, Deepak Nayyar, Lant Pritchett, Gustav Ranis, Henry Richardson, Dani Rodrik, José Salazar-Xirinachs, Hadi Salehi-Esfahani, Timothy Smeeding, Frances Stewart, Jan Svejnar, Michael Walton and Tarik Yousef.

More than 25 consultations were held between September 2008 and June 2010 to help inform preparation of the Report—including in Brussels, Busan, Cambridge (United Kingdom), Cambridge (United States), Canberra, Geneva, Istanbul, Johannesburg, Lima, London, Melbourne, Nairobi, New Delhi, New York, Oxford, Paris, Rabat, Rio de Janeiro, Sydney and Washington, D.C.—involving some 400 experts and practitioners, with the support of UNDP country and regional offices. Key partners hosting the consultations included the Center for Global Development, the European Commission, Harvard University's Center for International Development, the Human Development and Capability Association, the Organisation for Economic Co-operation and Development Development Center and the UNDP Civil Society Advisory Group.

Background research, commissioned on a range of thematic issues, is available online in our Human Development Research Papers series and listed in *References*. Intensive collaboration with the Oxford Poverty and Human Development Initiative, led by Sabina Alkire and involving a wide range of researchers, was extremely fruitful in pushing forward the conceptual and measurement agendas. Special thanks also go to James Foster of George Washington University, Stephan Klasen of Goettingen University and Lant Pritchett of Harvard University for their timely advice on a variety of measurement and empirical issues.

The statistics used in this Report rely on various databases. We are particularly grateful to the International Labour Organization, the Inter-Parliamentary Union, Jong-Wha Lee, the Luxembourg Income Study, the Polity IV Project, the Stockholm International Peace Research Institute, the UN Department of Economic and Social Affairs, the United

Educational, Scientific and Cultural Organization Institute for Statistics, the UN Refugee Agency, the United Nations Children's Fund, Uppsala University's Conflict Data Program and the World Bank. Claudio Montenegro conducted the analysis on the World Bank's International Income Distribution Database needed to construct the Inequality-adjusted Human Development Index. Eduardo Zambrano of California Polytechnic State University advised on the construction of the Gender Inequality Index. The advice of the Experts' Group of the United Nations Statistical Commission is gratefully acknowledged.

A UNDP Readers Group, representing all the regional and policy bureaus, and a number of other colleagues, too numerous to list, provided valuable advice throughout preparation of the Report, although special thanks go to Abdoulaye Mar Dieye, Chief of Staff. The HD Network, which comprises some 1,400 UNDP staff, academics and nongovernmental organizations, generated a range of useful ideas and feedback through online discussions. Solaiman Al-Rifai and Martha Mai of the UN Office for Project Services provided administrative support.

Several interns worked with HDRO over the course of the year: Kevin Chua, Zaynab El-Bernoussi, Jennifer Escobar, Rebecca Funk, Georgios Georgiadis, Saad Gulzar, Francesca Rappocciolo, Thomas Roca, Sandra Scharf, Fredrik Sjoberg and Seol Yoo. Namsuk Kim was seconded from UNDP's Office of Development Studies.

A team at Communications Development Incorporated, led by Bruce Ross-Larson, did a fabulous job editing and laying out the Report, and Bounford.com carried out the design work. Cesar Hidalgo provided valuable ideas for the visualization of human development concepts and trends.

We thank all of those involved directly or indirectly in contributing to our efforts, while acknowledging sole responsibility for errors of commission and omission.

Jeni Klugman
Director
Human Development Report 2010

Abbreviations

GDP	gross domestic product
GII	Gender Inequality Index
GNI	gross national income
HDI	Human Development Index
HDR	Human Development Report
HPI	Human Poverty Index
IHDI	Inequality-adjusted HDI
MPI	Multidimensional Poverty Index
OECD	Organisation for Economic Co-operation and Development
PPP	purchasing power parity
UNDP	United Nations Development Programme

Contents

FIGURES

TABLES

Overview

"People are the real wealth of a nation." With these words the 1990 *Human Development Report* (*HDR*) began a forceful case for a new approach to thinking about development. That the objective of development should be to create an enabling environment for people to enjoy long, healthy and creative lives may appear self-evident today. But that has not always been the case. A central objective of the *HDR* for the past 20 years has been to emphasize that development is primarily and fundamentally about people.

This year's Report celebrates the contributions of the human development approach, which is as relevant as ever to making sense of our changing world and finding ways to improve people's well-being. Indeed, human development is an evolving idea—not a fixed, static set of precepts—and as the world changes, analytical tools and concepts evolve. So this Report is also about how the human development approach can adjust to meet the challenges of the new millennium.

The past 20 years have seen substantial progress in many aspects of human development. Most people today are healthier, live longer, are more educated and have more access to goods and services. Even in countries facing adverse economic conditions, people's health and education have greatly improved. And there has been progress not only in improving health and education and raising income, but also in expanding people's power to select leaders, influence public decisions and share knowledge.

Yet not all sides of the story are positive. These years have also seen increasing inequality—both within and across countries—as well as production and consumption patterns that have increasingly been revealed as unsustainable. Progress has varied, and people in some regions—such as Southern Africa and the former Soviet Union—have experienced periods of regress, especially in health. New vulnerabilities require innovative public policies to confront risk and inequalities while harnessing dynamic market forces for the benefit of all.

Addressing these issues requires new tools. In this Report we introduce three measures to the *HDR* family of indices—the Inequality-adjusted Human Development Index, the Gender Inequality Index and the Multidimensional Poverty Index. These state-of-the-art measures incorporate recent advances in theory and measurement and support the centrality of inequality and poverty in the human development framework. We introduce these experimental series with the intention of stimulating reasoned public debate beyond the traditional focus on aggregates.

Today's challenges also require a new policy outlook. While there are no silver bullets or magic potions for human development, some policy implications are clear. First, we cannot assume that future development will mimic past advances: opportunities today and in the future are greater in many respects. Second, varied experiences and specific contexts preclude overarching policy prescriptions and point towards more general principles and guidelines. Third, major new challenges must be addressed—most prominently, climate change.

Many challenges lie ahead. Some are related to policy: development policies must be based on the local context and sound overarching principles; numerous problems go beyond the capacity of individual states and require democratically accountable global institutions. There are also implications for research: deeper analysis of the surprisingly weak relationship between economic growth and improvements in health and education and careful consideration of how the multidimensionality of development objectives affects development thinking are just two examples.

Celebrating 20 years of human development

Twenty years ago the world had just experienced a decade of debt, adjustment and austerity, and a host of political transformations were under way. With eloquence and humanity the first *HDR* called for a different approach to economics and development—one that put people at the centre. The approach was anchored in a new vision of development, inspired by the creative passion and vision of Mahbub ul Haq, the lead author of the early *HDRs*, and the groundbreaking work of Amartya Sen.

In this, the 20th edition of the *HDR*, we reaffirm human development's enduring relevance. We show how the human development approach has been ahead of the curve—how its concepts, measures and policies produced important insights about patterns of progress and how it can help chart a course for people-centred development.

The 1990 *HDR* began with a clear definition of human development as a process of "enlarging people's choices," emphasizing the freedom to be healthy, to be educated and to enjoy a decent standard of living. But it also stressed that human development and well-being went far beyond these dimensions to encompass a much broader range of capabilities, including political freedoms, human rights and, echoing Adam Smith, "the ability to go about without shame." Its enthusiastic reception by governments, civil society, researchers and the media demonstrated the deep resonance of this innovative approach in the development community and beyond.

A reaffirmation

Although the first *HDR* was careful in presenting a nuanced vision of human development, over time the short-hand description of "enlarging people's choices" became widely used. This description is fundamental—but not enough. Human development is about sustaining positive outcomes steadily over time and combating processes that impoverish people or underpin oppression and structural injustice. Plural principles such as equity, sustainability and respect for human rights are thus key.

Inherent in the human development tradition is that the approach be dynamic, not calcified. We propose a reaffirmation consistent with development practice on the ground and with the academic literature on human development and capabilities:

> Human development is the expansion of people's freedoms to live long, healthy and creative lives; to advance other goals they have reason to value; and to engage actively in shaping development equitably and sustainably on a shared planet. People are both the beneficiaries and the drivers of human development, as individuals and in groups.

This reaffirmation underlines the core of human development—its themes of sustainability, equity and empowerment and its inherent flexibility. Because gains might be fragile and vulnerable to reversal and because future generations must be treated justly, special efforts are needed to ensure that human development endures—that it is sustainable. Human development is also about addressing structural disparities—it must be equitable. And it is about enabling people to exercise individual choice and to participate in, shape and benefit from processes at the household, community and national levels—to be empowered.

Human development insists on deliberation and debate and on leaving the ends of development open to discussion. People, individually and in groups, shape these processes. The human development framework applies to all countries, rich and poor, and to all people. It is sufficiently open ended, robust and vibrant to provide a paradigm for the new century.

The evolution of well-being: an uneven ascent

A major contribution of this Report is the systematic assessment of trends in key components of human development over the past 40 years. This retrospective assessment, an important objective for the 20th anniversary, is the most comprehensive analysis of the *HDR* to date and yields important new insights.

In some basic respects the world is a much better place today than it was in 1990—or in 1970. Over the past 20 years many people around the world have experienced dramatic improvements in key aspects of their lives. Overall, they are healthier, more educated and wealthier and have more power to appoint and hold their leaders accountable than ever before. Witness, for example, the increases in our summary measure of development—the Human Development Index (HDI), which combines information on life expectancy, schooling and income in a simple composite measure. The world's average HDI has increased 18 percent since 1990 (and 41 percent since 1970), reflecting large aggregate improvements in life expectancy, school enrolment, literacy and income. But there has also been considerable variability in experience and much volatility, themes to which we return below.

Almost all countries have benefited from this progress. Of 135 countries in our sample for 1970–2010, with 92 percent of the world's people, only 3—the Democratic Republic of the Congo, Zambia and Zimbabwe—have a lower HDI today than in 1970.

Overall, poor countries are catching up with rich countries in the HDI. This convergence paints a far more optimistic picture than a perspective limited to trends in income, where divergence has continued. But not all countries have seen rapid progress, and the variations are

striking. Those experiencing the slowest progress are countries in Sub-Saharan Africa struck by the HIV epidemic and countries in the former Soviet Union suffering increased adult mortality.

The top HDI movers (countries that have made the greatest progress in improving the HDI) include well known income "growth miracles" such as China, Indonesia and South Korea. But they include others—such as Nepal, Oman and Tunisia—where progress in the nonincome dimensions of human development has been equally remarkable. It is striking that the top 10 list contains several countries not typically described as top performers. And Ethiopia comes in 11th, with three other Sub-Saharan African countries (Botswana, Benin and Burkina Faso) in the top 25.

Thus, the broader human development perspective provides an assessment of success very different from, say, that of the Spence Commission on Growth and Development. This perspective reveals that progress in health and education can drive success in human development—in fact, 7 countries enter the top 10 list thanks to their high achievements in health and education, in some cases even with unexceptional growth.

Not all countries have progressed rapidly, and the variation is striking. Over the past 40 years a quarter of developing countries saw their HDI increase less than 20 percent, another quarter, more than 65 percent. These differences partly reflect different starting points—less developed countries have on average faster progress in health and education than more developed ones do. But half the variation in HDI performance is unexplained by initial HDI, and countries with similar starting points experience remarkably different evolutions, suggesting that country factors such as policies, institutions and geography are important.

Health advances have been large but are slowing. The slowdown in aggregate progress is due largely to dramatic reversals in 19 countries. In nine of them—six in Sub-Saharan Africa and three in the former Soviet Union—life expectancy has fallen below 1970 levels. The causes of these declines are the HIV epidemic and increased adult mortality in transition countries.

A major contribution of this Report is the systematic assessment of trends in key components of human development over the past 40 years

Progress in education has been substantial and widespread, reflecting not only improvements in the quantity of schooling but also in the equity of access to education for girls and boys. To a large extent this progress reflects greater state involvement, which is often characterized more by getting children into school than by imparting a high-quality education.

Progress in income varies much more. Despite aggregate progress, there is no convergence in income—in contrast to health and education—because on average rich countries have grown faster than poor ones over the past 40 years. The divide between developed and developing countries persists: a small subset of countries has remained at the top of the world income distribution, and only a handful of countries that started out poor have joined that high-income group.

In sum, we see great advances, but changes over the past few decades have by no means been wholly positive. Some countries have suffered serious setbacks—particularly in health—sometimes erasing in a few years the gains of several decades. Economic growth has been extremely unequal—both in countries experiencing fast growth and in groups benefiting from national progress. And the gaps in human development across the world, while narrowing, remain huge.

Understanding the patterns and drivers of human development

Global progress has coincided with substantial variability across countries. This suggests that global forces have made progress more feasible for countries at all levels of development but that countries differ in how they take advantage of the opportunities.

One of the most surprising results of human development research in recent years, confirmed in this Report, is the lack of a significant correlation between economic growth and improvements in health and education. Our research shows that this relationship is particularly weak at low and medium levels of the HDI. This is traceable to changes in how people become healthier and more educated. The correlation in

levels today, which contrasts with the absence of correlation in changes over time, is a snapshot that reflects historical patterns, as countries that became rich were the only ones able to pay for costly advances in health and education. But technological improvements and changes in societal structures allow even poorer countries today to realize significant gains.

The unprecedented flows of ideas across countries in recent times—ranging from health-saving technologies to political ideals and to productive practices—have been transformative. Many innovations have allowed countries to improve health and education at very low cost—which explains why the association between the income and nonincome dimensions of human development has weakened over time.

Income and growth remain vital. To conclude otherwise is to ignore the importance of income in expanding people's freedoms. Income is critical in determining people's command over the resources necessary to gain access to food, shelter and clothing and in making possible much broader options—such as working in meaningful and intrinsically rewarding activities or spending more time with loved ones. Income growth can indicate that opportunities for decent work are expanding—though this is not always so—and economic contractions and associated job losses are bad news for people around the world. Income is also the source of the taxes and other revenues that governments need in order to provide services and undertake redistributive programs. Thus, increasing income on a broad basis remains an important policy priority.

Nor do our results negate the importance of higher income for increasing poor people's access to social services, a relationship supported by extensive microeconomic evidence. The strong correlation between socioeconomic status and health often reflects wealthier people's relative advantage in gaining access to health services. But the analysis in this Report sheds doubt on whether economywide income growth is sufficient to further health and education in low and medium HDI countries. And that is good news, at least insofar as sustained growth has often been elusive.

> Our research shows that the relationship between economic growth and improvements in health and education is weak in low and medium HDI countries

Our results also confirm, with new data and analysis, two central contentions of the *HDR* from the outset: that human development is different from economic growth and that substantial achievements are possible even without fast growth. Early *HDRs* pointed to the Indian state of Kerala and countries such as Costa Rica, Cuba and Sri Lanka that attained much higher human development than other countries at their incomes. These achievements were possible because growth had decoupled from the processes determining progress in the non-income dimensions of human development.

How institutions matter

The policies and reforms compatible with progress vary widely across institutional settings and depend on structural and political constraints. Attempts to transplant institutional and policy solutions across countries with different conditions often fail. And policies typically must be informed by the prevailing institutional setting to bring about change. For instance, economic liberalization in India sought to ease an overly restrictive and family-dominated business environment by reducing regulation and introducing more competition. In short, while institutions are a key determinant of human development, how they interact with their context merits careful investigation.

One important aspect is how relationships between markets and states are organized. Governments have addressed, in a range of ways, the tension between the need for markets to generate income and dynamism and the need to deal with market failures. Markets may be necessary for sustained economic dynamism, but they do not automatically bring progress in other dimensions of human development. Development that overly favours rapid economic growth is rarely sustainable. In other words, a market economy is necessary, but not enough.

These observations hark back to Karl Polanyi's brilliant exposition more than 60 years ago of the myth of the self-regulating market—the idea that markets could exist in a political and institutional vacuum. Generally, markets are very bad at ensuring the provision of public goods, such as security, stability, health and education. For example, firms that produce cheap labour-intensive goods or that exploit natural resources may not want a more educated workforce and may care little about their workers' health if there is an abundant pool of labour. Without complementary societal and state action, markets can be weak on environmental sustainability, creating the conditions for environmental degradation, even for such disasters as mud flows in Java and oil spills in the Gulf of Mexico.

Regulation, however, requires a capable state as well as political commitment, and state capability is often in short supply. Some developing country governments have tried to mimic the actions of a modern developed state without having the resources or the capacity to do so. For example, import substitution regimes in many Latin American countries floundered when countries tried to develop a targeted industrial policy. In contrast, an important lesson of the East Asian successes was that a capable, focused state can help drive development and the growth of markets. What is possible and appropriate is context specific. Beyond the state, civil society actors have demonstrated the potential to curb the excesses of both the market and the state, though governments seeking to control dissent can restrict civil society activity.

The dynamics can be virtuous when countries transition to both inclusive market institutions and inclusive political institutions. But this is difficult and rare. Oligarchic capitalism tends to spell its own demise, either because it stifles the productive engines of innovation—as in the failed import substitution regimes of Latin America and the Caribbean—or because material progress increases people's aspirations and challenges the narrow elite's grip on power, as in Brazil, Indonesia and South Korea since the 1990s.

Good things don't always come together

Human development is not only about health, education and income—it is also about people's

Attempts to transplant policy solutions across countries with different conditions often fail: policies must be grounded in the prevailing institutional setting to bring about change

active engagement in shaping development, equity and sustainability, intrinsic aspects of the freedom people have to lead lives they have reason to value. There is less consensus about what progress on these fronts entails, and measures are also lacking. But lack of quantification is no reason to neglect or ignore them.

Even when countries progress in the HDI, they do not necessarily excel in the broader dimensions. It is possible to have a high HDI and be unsustainable, undemocratic and unequal just as it is possible to have a low HDI and be relatively sustainable, democratic and equal. These patterns pose important challenges for how we think about human development, its measurement and the policies to improve outcomes and processes over time.

There is no straightforward pattern relating the HDI to other dimensions of human development such as sustainability and empowerment. An exception is inequality, which is negatively related to the value of the HDI, but even that relationship shows wide variation. The lack of correlation can be seen in the large number of countries that have high HDI values but perform poorly on the other variables: about a quarter of countries have a high HDI but low sustainability; we can see a similar though less marked picture for political freedoms.

Trends conducive to empowerment include the vast increases in literacy and educational attainment in many parts of the world that have strengthened people's ability to make informed choices and hold governments accountable. The scope for empowerment and its expression have broadened, through both technology and institutions. In particular, the proliferation of mobile telephony and satellite television and increased access to the Internet have vastly increased the availability of information and the ability to voice opinions.

The share of formal democracies has increased from fewer than a third of countries in 1970 to half in the mid-1990s and to three-fifths in 2008. Many hybrid forms of political organization have emerged. While real change and healthy political functioning have varied, and many formal democracies are flawed and fragile, policy-making is much better informed by the views and concerns of citizens. Local democratic processes are deepening. Political struggles have led to substantial change in many countries, greatly expanding the representation of traditionally marginalized people, including women, the poor, indigenous groups, refugees and sexual minorities.

But averages can be misleading. Since the 1980s, income inequality has risen in many more countries than it has fallen. For every country where inequality has improved in the past 30 years, in more than two it has worsened, most markedly in countries of the former Soviet Union. Most countries in East Asia and the Pacific also have higher income inequality today than a few decades ago. Latin America and the Caribbean is an important recent exception: long the region with the widest income and asset disparities, major recent improvements have led to more progressive public spending and targeted social policies.

Recent years have also exposed the fragility of some of our achievements—perhaps best illustrated by the biggest financial crisis in several decades, which caused 34 million people to lose their jobs and 64 million more people to fall below the $1.25 a day income poverty threshold. The risk of a "double-dip" recession remains, and a full recovery could take years.

But perhaps the greatest challenge to maintaining progress in human development comes from the unsustainability of production and consumption patterns. For human development to become truly sustainable, the close link between economic growth and greenhouse gas emissions needs to be severed. Some developed countries have begun to alleviate the worst effects through recycling and investment in public transport and infrastructure. But most developing countries are hampered by the high costs and low availability of clean energy.

New measures for an evolving reality

Pushing the frontiers of measurement has always been a cornerstone of the human development approach. But it has never been measurement for the sake of measurement. The HDI has enabled innovative thinking about progress by capturing the simple yet powerful idea that development is about much more than income. Over the years the *HDR* has introduced new measures to evaluate progress in reducing poverty and empowering women. But lack of reliable data has been a major constraint.

This year we introduce three new indices to capture important aspects of the distribution of well-being for inequality, gender equity and poverty. They reflect advances in methods and better data availability. We also present a refined version of the HDI, with its same three dimensions, but that addresses valid criticisms and uses indicators more pertinent for evaluating future progress.

Adjusting the Human Development Index for inequality. Reflecting inequality in each dimension of the HDI addresses an objective first stated in the 1990 *HDR*. This Report introduces the Inequality-adjusted HDI (IHDI), a measure of the level of human development of people in a society that accounts for inequality. Under perfect equality the HDI and the IHDI are equal. When there is inequality in the distribution of health, education and income, the HDI of an average person in a society is less than the aggregate HDI; the lower the IHDI (and the greater the difference between it and the HDI), the greater the inequality. We apply this measure to 139 countries. Some findings:

- The average loss in the HDI due to inequality is about 22 percent—that is, adjusted for inequality, the global HDI of 0.62 in 2010 would fall to 0.49, which represents a drop from the high to the medium HDI category. Losses range from 6 percent (Czech Republic) to 45 percent (Mozambique), with four-fifths of countries losing more than 10 percent, and almost two-fifths of countries losing more than 25 percent.
- Countries with less human development tend to have greater inequality in more dimensions—and thus larger losses in human development. People in Namibia lost 44 percent, in Central African Republic 42 percent and in Haiti 41 percent because of multidimensional inequality.

- People in Sub-Saharan Africa suffer the largest HDI losses because of substantial inequality across all three dimensions. In other regions the losses are more directly attributable to inequality in a single dimension—as for health in South Asia.

A new measure of gender inequality. The disadvantages facing women and girls are a major source of inequality. All too often, women and girls are discriminated against in health, education and the labour market—with negative repercussions for their freedoms. We introduce a new measure of these inequalities built on the same framework as the HDI and the IHDI—to better expose differences in the distribution of achievements between women and men. The Gender Inequality Index shows that:

- Gender inequality varies tremendously across countries—the losses in achievement due to gender inequality (not directly comparable to total inequality losses because different variables are used) range from 17 percent to 85 percent. The Netherlands tops the list of the most gender-equal countries, followed by Denmark, Sweden and Switzerland.
- Countries with unequal distribution of human development also experience high inequality between women and men, and countries with high gender inequality also experience unequal distribution of human development. Among the countries doing very badly on both fronts are Central African Republic, Haiti and Mozambique.

A multidimensional measure of poverty. Like development, poverty is multidimensional—but this is traditionally ignored by headline figures. This year's Report introduces the Multidimensional Poverty Index (MPI), which complements money-based measures by considering multiple deprivations and their overlap. The index identifies deprivations across the same three dimensions as the HDI and shows the number of people who are poor (suffering a given number of deprivations) and the number of deprivations with which poor households typically contend. It can be deconstructed by region, ethnicity and other groupings as well as

> We introduce three new indices to capture multidimensional aspects of well-being for inequality, gender equity and poverty that reflect advances in methods and better data availability

by dimension, making it an apt tool for policy-makers. Some findings:

- About 1.75 billion people in the 104 countries covered by the MPI—a third of their population—live in multidimensional poverty—that is, with at least 30 percent of the indicators reflecting acute deprivation in health, education and standard of living. This exceeds the estimated 1.44 billion people in those countries who live on $1.25 a day or less (though it is below the share who live on $2 or less). The patterns of deprivation also differ from those of income poverty in important ways: in many countries—including Ethiopia and Guatemala—the number of people who are multidimensionally poor is higher. However, in about a fourth of the countries for which both estimates are available—including China, Tanzania and Uzbekistan—rates of income poverty are higher.
- Sub-Saharan Africa has the highest incidence of multidimensional poverty. The level ranges from a low of 3 percent in South Africa to a massive 93 percent in Niger; the average share of deprivations ranges from about 45 percent (in Gabon, Lesotho and Swaziland) to 69 percent (in Niger). Yet half the world's multidimensionally poor live in South Asia (844 million people), and more than a quarter live in Africa (458 million).

*　　　*　　　*

These new measures yield many other novel results—and insights—that can guide development policy debates and designs. Large HDI losses due to inequality indicate that society has much to gain from concentrating its efforts on equity-improving reforms. And a high MPI coinciding with low income poverty suggests that there is much to gain from improving the delivery of basic public services. The measures open exciting new possibilities for research, allowing us to tackle critical questions. Which countries are most successful in lowering inequality in human development? Are advances in gender equity a cause or a reflection of broader development trends? Does reduced income poverty bring about reduced multidimensional poverty, or vice versa?

Guiding the way to future human development

What are the implications for the policy agenda, both national and international? The story is encouraging but also cautionary. Progress is possible even without massive resources: the lives of people can be improved through means already at the disposal of most countries. But success is not guaranteed, and the pathways to advancing human development are varied and specific to a country's historical, political and institutional conditions.

Much development discourse has looked for uniform policy prescriptions that can be applied across the vast majority of countries. The shortcomings of that intellectual project are now evident and widely accepted. They underline the need to recognize the individuality of countries and communities alongside the basic principles that can inform development strategies and policies in different settings. A global report like this one can draw general lessons and push the research and policy agenda and discussions into complementary domains.

If one size fits all solutions are inherently misguided, how do we guide policy-making? Policies are being devised and implemented every day around the world, and concrete advice is sought from development institutions and researchers. Some basic ideas:

- *Think of principles first.* Asking whether a particular policy is a general prescription for human development is not the best approach, because many policies work well in some settings but not in others. We must ask what principles we can use to evaluate alternative policies. Examples include putting equity and poverty at the forefront of policy and designing institutions to manage conflict and resolve disputes. How this translates into specific policies will vary by setting. Careful consideration of experience and of institutional, structural and political constraints is vital.

These new measures yield many novel results—and insights—that can help guide development policy debates and designs

HUMAN DEVELOPMENT REPORT **2010**

- *Take context seriously.* State capacity and political constraints are examples of why and how context matters. A common cause of failure is assuming that a well functioning state and regulatory system already exist or can be readily transplanted or created. Similarly, national policies ignore the broader political economy at their peril. Policy design that is not rooted in an understanding of these institutional realities is likely to be irrelevant.

- *Shift global policies.* Numerous challenges such as international migration, effective and equitable trade and investment rules, and global threats such as climate change, are beyond the capacity of individual states. A global governance system that promotes democratic accountability, transparency and inclusion of the least developed countries—and that seeks a stable and sustainable global economic environment—should be broadly applied to such challenges.

The impacts of the *HDR* have illustrated that policy thinking can be informed and stimulated by deeper exploration into key dimensions of human development. An important element of this tradition is a rich agenda of research and analysis. This Report suggests ways to move this agenda forward through better data and trend analysis. But much is left to do. Three priorities: improving data and analysis to inform debates, providing an alternative to conventional approaches to studying development, and increasing our understanding of inequality, empowerment, vulnerability and sustainability.

The economics of growth and its relationship with development, in particular, require radical rethinking. A vast theoretical and empirical literature almost uniformly equates economic growth with development. Its models typically assume that people care only about consumption; its empirical applications concentrate almost exclusively on the effect of policies and institutions on economic growth.

The central contention of the human development approach, by contrast, is that well-being is about much more than money: it is about the possibilities that people have to fulfil the life plans they have reason to choose and pursue. Thus, our call for a new economics—an economics of human development—in which the objective is to further human well-being and in which growth and other policies are evaluated and pursued vigorously insofar as they advance human development in the short and long term.

"Human progress," wrote Martin Luther King, Jr., "never rolls in on wheels of inevitability. It comes through tireless efforts and persistent work. . . . Without this hard work, time itself becomes an ally of the forces of social stagnation." The idea of human development exemplifies these efforts, brought about by a committed group of intellectuals and practitioners who want to change the way we think about the progress of societies.

But fully realizing the human development agenda requires going further. Putting people at the centre of development is much more than an intellectual exercise. It means making progress equitable and broad-based, enabling people to be active participants in change and ensuring that current achievements are not attained at the expense of future generations. Meeting these challenges is not only possible—it is necessary. And it is more urgent than ever.

> Putting people at the centre of development means making progress equitable, enabling people to be active participants in change and ensuring that current achievements are not attained at the expense of future generations

1 Reaffirming human development

The United Nations Development Programme (UNDP) launched the *Human Development Report (HDR)* in 1990. It is worth recalling the broader context. The Berlin Wall was crumbling, and the Soviet Union would soon dissolve. The apartheid regime in South Africa had just released Nelson Mandela from prison. Iraq was about to invade Kuwait. Augusto Pinochet had left the presidency of Chile, replaced by a new democratic regime. The Sandinistas were voted out of office in Nicaragua. Aung San Suu Kyi's National League for Democracy Party won Myanmar's national elections. Students were demonstrating for political reform in Beijing. The Shanghai and Shenzhen stock exchanges opened. Margaret Thatcher had ruled the United Kingdom for more than a decade. The term "Washington Consensus" had just been coined.

In this climate the first *HDR* stood out, calling with eloquence and humanity for a different approach to economics and to development. These calls have continued to resonate around the world and have gained renewed prominence with recent investigations into measuring people's well-being and remarkable advances in data and knowledge.[1] Box 1.1 traces these recent calls back to earlier decades and introduces Mahbub ul Haq, the visionary Pakistani economist who pioneered the *HDR*.

Today, 20 years later, the world faces new as well as perennial challenges. Meeting the Millennium Development Goals has assumed greater urgency. Prominent concerns threatening future progress include mounting environmental damage that imperils the planet and has harmful consequences for the poor. Uncertainty prevails about economic stability and global security. The political balance has shifted from domination by two major powers to multiple sources of influence and greater complexity.

Today, as in 1990, we begin the first chapter of this Report with an examination of the concept. And today, as in 1990, the concept of human development has particular relevance.[2] Benefiting from hindsight and experience, we examine its intellectual and policy motivations, as well as its evolution, highlighting the work of Amartya Sen.[3] We look at broader shifts in development policy thinking. And we reaffirm the concept of human development, underscoring sustainability, equality and empowerment. The aim is to understand patterns of human development and the ways societies allow and enable people to lead lives they value. That is the best way of thinking about human progress.

The original statement

The 1990 *HDR* clearly articulated the concept of human development. The first chapter, "Defining and Measuring Human Development," opened with the forthright statement that:

> People are the real wealth of a nation. The basic objective of development is to create an enabling environment for people to live long, healthy and creative lives. This may appear to be a simple truth. But it is often forgotten in the immediate concern with the accumulation of commodities and financial wealth.

This objective was not new. Thinkers from Aristotle on have voiced similar positions. The Report argued for renewed attention to people in the light of countries' uneven progress in human development in the 1980s, a decade of economic crisis, stabilization and adjustment.

The succinct section on "Defining human development" began with what came to be a standard formulation:

> Human development is a process of enlarging people's choices. The most critical ones are to lead a long and healthy life, to be educated and to enjoy a decent standard of living. Additional choices include political freedom, guaranteed human rights and self-respect—what Adam Smith called the ability to mix with others without being "ashamed to appear in public."

The 1990 *HDR* emphasized that development is about freedom, both human choice (opportunity freedoms) and a participatory process (process freedoms).[4] It underscored the fact that human development, because of its breadth and generality, pertains to all countries:

> Human development . . . brings together the production and distribution of commodities and the expansion and use of human capabilities. It also focuses on choices—on what people should have, be and do to be able to ensure their own livelihood. Human development is, moreover, concerned not only with basic needs satisfaction but also with human development as a participatory and dynamic process. It applies equally to less developed and highly developed countries.

As Sen so eloquently put it, "the twin recognition that human beings can (1) fare far better and (2) do much more to bring this about,

---

BOX 1.1 From Karachi to the Sorbonne—Mahbub ul Haq and the idea of human development

Hearing French President Nicolas Sarkozy's impassioned speech in 2009 calling for fundamental reforms in how we measure progress and criticizing the focus on gross domestic product (GDP) in evaluating well-being, one might be forgiven for believing this to be the latest crowning achievement in Western thought about development. Speaking in Paris from the podium of the Grand Amphitheatre of the Sorbonne, before larger than life statues of Pascal and Descartes, Sarkozy introduced the work of a commission of eminent economists. They called for broader measures of progress that take into account inequality, environmental sustainability, nonmarket production and quality of life.

In fact, the talking points for Sarkozy's speech began to be written more than 40 years ago, almost 4,000 miles from the City of Light. In 1968 Mahbub ul Haq, then Chief Economist of Pakistan's Planning Commission, spoke in Karachi on his country's economic development. The economy had been growing at more than 6 percent a year for a decade, and many of those gathered expected to hear a comprehensive exposition of the success of government policies by ul Haq, one of Pakistan's brightest minds and the author of the Five-Year Plan that generated this economic boom.

The young economist shocked his audience by delivering a stinging indictment of Pakistan's development strategy. During the period that the government called the "decade of development," income differences between East and West Pakistan had more than doubled, and industrial wages had slumped by a third. The country's foreign exchange earnings went to satisfy the demands of the elite. Twenty-two families controlled two-thirds of industrial assets and four-fifths of banking and insurance. Stellar economic growth gave an utterly distorted picture of what this period meant for ordinary Pakistanis.

Some years later ul Haq convinced the United Nations Development Programme (UNDP) to produce a report by independent researchers that would offer an alternative to the single-minded concentration on GDP so prevalent among international organizations and economists—the *Human Development Report (HDR)*. The idea that the United Nations would assess the economic and social progress of countries was so controversial that some countries threatened to boycott the enterprise. However, UNDP has held fast to its commitment to preserve the autonomy and academic integrity of the *HDR*, all the way through to this, the 20th anniversary edition.

Source: Haq and Ponzio 2008; ul Haq 1973; Jolly, Emmerij, and Weiss 2009.

---

may sensibly be seen as the two central theses of the human development approach."[5] From the outset, the human development approach was oriented towards practical analyses and policies to advance well-being, emphasizing local and national public debates of alternative policy options.

Powerful related themes enunciated in the initial statements addressed deprivation, inequality and empowerment. The 1990 *HDR* described the considerable inequalities within countries that mask the continuing severe deprivation of many people. It highlighted differences between rural and urban dwellers, men and women, rich and poor people. And at its core was a strong emphasis on political freedom, voice, accountability and democratic practice.[6] These are early examples of the *HDR* being ahead of the curve, an attribute that continues to characterize the Report.

The Human Development Index

The Human Development Index (HDI) was a strategic element in the new approach. It symbolizes the shift in thinking, even if not fully capturing human development's richness. As a composite measure of health, education and income, the HDI assesses levels and progress using a concept of development much broader than that allowed by income alone (figure 1.1). And as with any aggregate measure and international comparison, it simplifies and captures only part of what human development entails.

Over the past 20 years the HDI has received its share of criticism. Some take issue with its construction and composition. Others suggest that it be expanded to include more dimensions, ranging from gender equity to biodiversity. Many concerns are valid. But the objective is not to build an unassailable indicator of well-being—it is to redirect attention towards human-centred development and to promote debate over how we advance the progress of societies. The more we discuss what should or should not be included in the HDI—whether it makes sense to lump distinct categories together, how much importance to accord to each category, how to obtain more and better data—the more the debate moves away from the single-minded focus on growth that pervaded thinking about development.

FIGURE **1.1**   **Components of the Human Development Index**

The HDI—three dimensions and four indicators

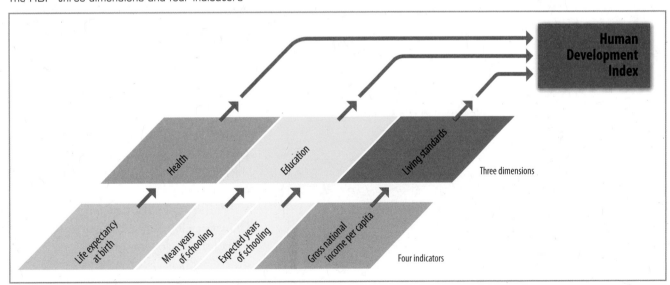

Note: The indicators presented in this figure follow the new methodology, as defined in box 1.2.

Source: HDRO.

As an alternative to a narrow focus on income, the HDI has proved hugely successful. As *The Economist* wrote in 1990: "Moses made the first recorded attempt; Plato, Rousseau and Marx had shots at it. The United Nations Development Programme had high standards to match in trying, as it does in a new report, to define and measure 'human development.'"[7] In 1991 that same news magazine wrote, "the heart of the report is a simple but ingenious index designed to measure the relative attainments of nations more subtly than the annual income rankings that the World Bank provides."[8]

The HDI has been the hallmark of the *HDR,* a major factor in its continuing success. Since the HDI's release, it has attracted the attention of the media, the general public, civil society organizations, researchers and governments around the world. After the 2009 *HDR* was launched, the *HDR* website was visited nearly 3 million times, and almost half a million copies were downloaded (figure 1.2). The pattern shows a large spike in interest each year with the release of the HDI and the *HDR.*

This year's Report introduces some careful innovations to the HDI, while retaining its simplicity and familiarity (box 1.2).

Growing media attention

The HDI's strengths—particularly its transparency, simplicity and popular resonance around the world—have kept it at the forefront of the growing array of alternatives to gross domestic product (GDP) in measuring well-being.[9] As the *New York Times* wrote on 10 May 2010, "So far only one measure has succeeded in challenging the hegemony of growth-centric thinking. This is known as the HDI, which turns 20 this year."[10] Politically and rhetorically powerful, the HDI is a valuable counterpoint to measures of development that focus exclusively on monetary indicators.

Media coverage over the years illustrates the power of the concept of human development and the HDI. In 1990 the *Financial Times* wrote about "a strongly worded report that is likely to ignite political controversies,"[11] while the UK's *Guardian* predicted that "people in the centre of development" will surely become one of the catch phrases of the 1990s.[12] By 1999 Singapore's *Straits Times* described the *HDR* as the "benchmark for judging universal human development standards."[13] The HDI was the "global standard," according to Lebanon's *Daily Star* in 2005.[14] From the very first *HDR,* when the *Straits Times* used Singapore's lower HDI ranking relative to South Korea's to urge the government to focus more on higher education and skills development, advocates and activists have compared performance across countries to stimulate policy responses.[15] Analysis of media coverage in the 2000s shows a significant increase in the use of the HDI to challenge—and to praise—government performance.

This Report reaffirms the concept of human development and enhances the family of measures that stimulate debate and thinking around human development. Before doing so, we highlight the myriad ways that *HDRs* have led development thinking and influenced development discourse.

FIGURE 1.2 **Popularity of the *Human Development Report* and the Human Development Index**

Frequency of Google searches for the *Human Development Report,* Human Development Index and *World Development Report,* 2006–2010

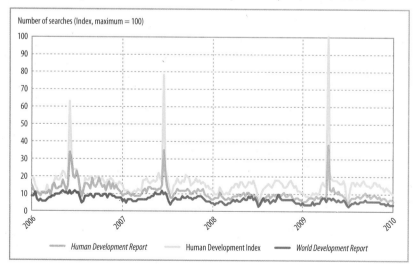

Note: The left axis presents the number of searches expressed as a percentage of the highest number attained by any of the three series.

Source: Generated from Google Insights, accessed 9 August 2010.

BOX 1.2   Refining the Human Development Index

The Human Development Index (HDI) remains an aggregate measure of progress in three dimensions—health, education and income. But in this Report we modify the indicators used to measure progress in education and income, and we change the way they are aggregated.

In the knowledge dimension mean years of schooling replaces literacy, and gross enrolment is recast as expected years of schooling—the years of schooling that a child can expect to receive given current enrolment rates. Mean years of schooling is estimated more frequently for more countries and can discriminate better among countries, while expected years of schooling is consistent with the reframing of this dimension in terms of years. Ideally, measures of the knowledge dimension would go beyond estimating quantity to assessing quality, as several National and Regional Human Development Reports (HDRs) have done. For example, the 2003 Arab States HDR constructed a measure that captures both the quantity and quality of education, adjusting mean years of schooling with average test scores and including indicators related to media, communication and scientists trained. But good measures of education quality do not exist for enough countries—cross-national assessments of science, mathematics and reading levels of young people are valuable but scarce in coverage and irregular in frequency. We also investigated alternative measures of the ability to enjoy a healthy life but found no viable and better alternative to life expectancy at birth.

To measure the standard of living, gross national income (GNI) per capita replaces gross domestic product (GDP) per capita. In a globalized world differences are often large between the income of a country's residents and its domestic production. Some of the income residents earn is sent abroad, some residents receive international remittances and some countries receive sizeable aid flows. For example, because of large remittances from abroad, GNI in the Philippines greatly exceeds GDP, and because of international aid, Timor-Leste's GNI is many times domestic output.

We also reconsidered how to aggregate the three dimensions. A key change was to shift to a geometric mean (which measures the typical value of a set of numbers): thus in 2010 the HDI is the geometric mean of the three dimension indices. Poor performance in any dimension is now directly reflected in the HDI, and there is no longer perfect substitutability across dimensions. This method captures how well rounded a country's performance is across the three dimensions. As a basis for comparisons of achievement, this method is also more respectful of the intrinsic differences in the dimensions than a simple average is. It recognizes that health, education and income are all important, but also that it is hard to compare these different dimensions of well-being and that we should not let changes in any of them go unnoticed.

We maintain the practice of using the log of income: income is instrumental to human development but higher incomes have a declining contribution to human development. And we have shifted the maximum values in each dimension to the observed maximum, rather than a predefined cut-off beyond which achievements are ignored.

Note: For further details, see *Readers guide* and *Technical note 1.*

Source: Kovacevic 2010b.

Human Development Reports—ahead of the curve

The 1990 *HDR* was launched following a period of deep economic and debt crises, when policy thinking was dominated by notions of stabilization and adjustment. Many developing countries faced declining export earnings, dwindling capital inflows, rising interest rates and mounting foreign debt. Countries were forced to turn outward for financial help—typically from the international financial institutions in a package that demanded stabilization measures and structural adjustment reforms aimed at very low inflation, a reduced role for the state and an outward orientation—the Washington Consensus. This response was not universal, as more heterodox ideas, particularly those favouring stronger state-led approaches, were still being pursued—most evidently in China, India and Viet Nam.

But by the early 1990s the Washington Consensus had attained near hegemony, and mainstream development thinking held that the best payoffs would come from hewing to its key tenets of economic liberalization and deregulation.[16] Many Western countries were also reducing the role of the public sector in the economy and lightening regulation. Privatization affected rail and postal services, airlines, banking and even utility networks.

From the outset the *HDR* explicitly challenged this orthodoxy and established a tradition that would be applied to a range of issues important to development policy. Mahbub ul Haq brought together a group of leading development thinkers to pioneer the human development approach at UNDP, building on several movements defying conventional economic approaches to development. These included an influential group concerned with basic needs, advocates of a focus on children, and a range of activists concerned with hunger and social justice more broadly.[17]

Amartya Sen's capability approach provided the philosophical foundations of human development, drawing on a long and august lineage of influential thinkers. Human development attracted interest and adherents with its criticism of GDP and its clear yet open-ended ethical orientation. A dynamic academic discourse emerged (box 1.3), encouraged by an emphasis on the centrality of enlightened public discussion that kept the door open for revisions and improvements over time.

Contributions to development discourse

As independent global reports, the *HDRs* have challenged mainstream thinking. They have pioneered ideas, some of them controversial at the time, that have been ahead of the curve but that have since become more widely accepted.

The Millennium Development Goals

> Human development needs its own specific goals like literacy or basic education for all. And it needs to be an overall goal—the main focus of development.
>
> —*Human Development Report 1991*: 178

The 1990–1994 *HDRs* called for poverty-focused international development agendas based on a compact between developed and developing countries. This compact was to have more operational goals, that is, "global targets for human development," including halving income poverty and similar goals for basic education, primary healthcare, safe water and malnutrition.[18] These *HDRs* also advocated participatory national development strategies grounded in realistic budgets to achieve these goals—and in different ways heralded the *Poverty Reduction Strategy Papers*, the Millennium Declaration and the Millennium Development Goals that emerged at the end of the decade.

In September 2000, 189 heads of state and government adopted the UN Millennium Declaration—with commitments for international cooperation on peace, security and disarmament; development and poverty eradication; environmental protection; and human rights, democracy and good governance, based on a set of fundamental values including freedom, equality, solidarity, tolerance, respect for nature and shared responsibility.[19]

As a means to promote development and poverty eradication, the declaration laid out a series of objectives that became the Millennium Development Goals and that have galvanized broad international support with the active engagement of key institutional actors and civil society.[20] The goals and associated targets and indicators denote commitments related to extreme hunger and income poverty; primary education; gender equity; child mortality; maternal health; HIV and AIDS, malaria and

---

BOX 1.3

Human development and capabilities: intellectual foundations and evolution

Since 1990 writings on the capability approach have blossomed, alongside the annual global *Human Development Report (HDR)* and more than 700 National and Regional HDRs. A large literature has emerged on the finer aspects of theory and measurement. For example, work on education and capabilities clarified distinctions between policies to promote human capital and those to advance education for human development. The approach has been applied to human rights, disability, health, growth, democratic practice and disadvantaged groups.

Amartya Sen's 2009 book, *The Idea of Justice*, perhaps his most important recent work, is a trenchant critique of a dominant idea in current political philosophy, exemplified by Rawls's assertion that it is possible to secure agreement on what constitutes a just society and its associated rules and institutions. Sen argues that differences in reasonable people's outlooks make perfect agreement unfeasible—but more important, he says, it is not necessary either. We can agree that some states of affairs are better than others. We can identify clear injustices that people and societies must remove. So we need not agree on the lineaments of a perfectly just society, because these principles give us enough information to reduce injustice: "What tends to 'inflame the minds' of suffering humanity cannot but be of immediate interest both to policy-making and to the diagnosis of injustice."

As with *HDRs* generally, Sen's perspective deeply informs this Report—notably, our emphasis on comparing better and lesser performers in human development and our focus on key injustices. We also draw on the powerful notion that not being able to realize a perfect world should not distract from doing what is possible to bring about change. That notion has important and practical implications for policy.

Source: ul Haq 1995; Sen 1985a, 1999, 2009b; Jolly, Emmerij, and Weiss 2009; Fukuda-Parr 2003; Rawls 1971.

other diseases; environmental sustainability and global partnerships for development.[21]

Conceptually, the Millennium Development Goals articulate and quantify some core human development priorities focused on minimum levels of achievement. They reflect the possibilities and limits of a consensus decision by the international community at the time, and they largely overlook, among other important dimensions, inequality and process freedoms.[22] Human development is a broader framework that includes the Millennium Development Goals, with an emphasis on broader principles of human rights, democracy and participation to shape pathways for change. The widespread support mobilized by the Millennium Development Goals stimulates debate and drives advances in core human development priorities.

Human security

In the final analysis, human security is a child who did not die, a disease that did not spread, a job that was not cut, an ethnic tension that did not explode in violence, a dissident who was not silenced. Human security is not a concern with weapons—it is a concern with human life and dignity.

—*Human Development Report 1994*: 22

The 1994 *HDR* introduced and defined the concept of human security as "freedom from fear and freedom from want" and "safety from chronic threats such as hunger, disease and repression as well as protection from sudden and harmful disruptions in the patterns of daily life—whether in homes, in jobs or in communities." This concept of human security was a radical shift in thinking on peace and conflict prevention. That *HDR* also advocated creating a global fund to address the common threats to human security and supported the "Tobin tax" on foreign exchange transactions as a way to finance development.

This idea of human security directly parallels that of human development, and the 1994 *HDR* was instrumental in bringing the two agendas together.[23] As that *HDR* explained, human development and human security are distinct concepts—the first relating to expanding people's freedoms and the second to ensuring against threats to those freedoms. Human security demands attention to all risks to human development, not just situations of conflict and post-conflict and fragile states. It encompasses safety from chronic threats such as hunger, disease and repression, and protection from sudden and hurtful disruptions in patterns of daily life—whether from violence, earthquakes or financial crises.[24]

This broad concept of human security contrasts with an older, narrower approach whose key audiences were the military and humanitarian workers. The traditional paradigm framed security as the protection of a country's territorial boundaries, and the focal variable was territorial aggression. The new human security paradigm shifts the unit of analysis from territories to the people dwelling in them and looks at the multiple threats that could undermine their security, dignity and livelihoods. It looks at all threats to human development, including violence, and studies how poverty causes violence and how violence, or the threat of violence, contributes to poverty. It also considers the trade-offs between investments in the military and investments in people's survival, livelihoods and dignity. Human security is not an alternative to human development—it is a critical part of it that focuses on creating a minimum set of capabilities and protecting them from pervasive threats.

This concept of human security has since become central to several global initiatives,[25] has been picked up by national governments[26] and is reflected in the agendas and policy debates of regional intergovernmental organizations.[27] The concept continues to be influential, most recently through the 2010 Report of the Secretary-General and its debate in the UN General Assembly.[28]

Human rights

Human rights are the rights possessed by all persons, by virtue of their

As independent global reports, the *HDRs* have pioneered ideas that have been ahead of the curve and that have since become more widely accepted

common humanity, to live a life of freedom and dignity. They give all people moral claims on the behaviour of individuals and on the design of social arrangements—and are universal, inalienable and indivisible.

—Human Development Report 2000: 16

Human development focuses on individual and group empowerment; human rights, on structural safeguards

The 2000 *HDR* offered an intellectual framework for the human rights community to engage more effectively with "development." It argued that a decent standard of living, adequate nutrition, healthcare, education and protection against calamities are all human rights, not just development goals, and that poverty is a human rights challenge.

Human rights and human development have much in common.[29] Since the 1948 Universal Declaration of Human Rights, defending human rights has had a broad influence in protecting people's lives. International conventions and protocols, and associated codifications in national laws, have given legal status to normative claims. Human rights are also politically appealing, and many civil society groups have mobilized to protect and advance them.[30] Principles of human rights complement human development by providing absolute safeguards or prohibitions against violations, such as those affecting minority communities.

Human development focuses on individual and group empowerment; human rights, on structural safeguards. Over time national and global citizen action has broadened the parameters of human rights, as with the global movements that led to the UN Declaration for the Elimination of Violence against Women and the campaigns for conventions to regulate landmines.[31]

Human rights include economic, social and cultural rights, as well as civil and political liberties. Human development also encompasses this broad agenda. The realization of human rights evolves by setting baselines and progressive goals, devising implementation and monitoring strategies, and updating legislation. Human development thus complements the realization of human rights through ongoing

attention to the interconnections among objectives, priorities and strategic trade-offs. This complementary strength of human development lies in responding to differing and evolving contexts, identifying barriers to human progress and opportunities for synergies, and stimulating local solutions.

Sustainable development

There is no tension between human development and sustainable development. Both are based on the universalism of life claims.

—Human Development Report 1994: 19

Early *HDRs* drew attention to environmental threats, including the global water crisis and climate change. The first *HDR* already highlighted a safe environment—"clean water, food and air"—in people's freedoms. The 1994 *HDR* discussed environmental security, and as early as 1998 the *HDR* recognized the unfairness associated with environmental degradation—acid rain, ozone depletion and climate change—with the poor suffering most.

The 2006 *HDR* exposed the unfairness in the use of water and its implications for human development: it showed that people in slums in Sub-Saharan Africa pay more for their drinking water than do residents of New York and Paris. The 2007/2008 *HDR* applied a human development lens to highlight the costs of climate change, including cross-generational poverty traps caused by climate shocks and the phenomenon of "adaptation apartheid." It was the first major development report to explore the implications of climbing world temperatures, reflected in melting ice caps, changing patterns of local rainfall, rising sea levels and forced adaptation by some of the world's most vulnerable groups.

Around the world people now see global warming as a serious threat to their well-being.[32] It is more widely accepted that the earth faces one of the largest challenges in its history—the threat of human-induced climate change, with potentially catastrophic consequences, largely unforeseen in 1990. Various *HDRs* have contributed, alongside other major reports, to transforming the policy landscape and expanding recognition of the environment and sustainability, including climate change.

Human development and sustainable human development cannot be separated.[33] Universalism, traceable to Immanuel Kant, is at the heart of human development; it requires granting future generations the same attention as the current one.[34] Human development is about enabling people to lead long, healthy, educated and fulfilling lives. Sustainable human development is about making sure that future generations can do the same. Human development, if not sustainable, is not true human development.

The most commonly cited definition of sustainable development is "development that satisfies the needs of the present without compromising the ability of future generations to meet their own needs."[35] But in practice some discussions about sustainability focus on future growth and consumption, others seek to ensure the survival of the species despite climate change and some give the ecosystem intrinsic importance. Essential aspects of human development, such as education, are sometimes treated merely as instrumental, as capital for producing future flows of utility.

Human development's emphasis on multidimensionality complements conventional approaches to sustainability, reminding us that the debate about what should be sustained is as important as how to sustain it. Human development requires that people have the freedoms and choices to fulfil their needs, desires and wants. Of course, people still unborn cannot make decisions for themselves—but we can preserve the conditions of their future agency. Human development also signals that intragenerational equity is as important as intergenerational equity.[36]

* * *

This discussion has highlighted examples of how global *HDRs*, by applying a human development lens, have generated concepts,

measures and policies that were ahead of their time. We return to many more instances later in this Report. These include the 1995 *HDR*, which presented a range of innovative proposals for gender equity and women's empowerment, recognizing in particular the significance of unpaid work and offering the first global estimate of the value of nonmonetized production by women and men in economic and household activities.[37] Likewise, the 1997 *HDR* distinguished multidimensional poverty from income poverty and drew attention to political power as a driver of poverty trends—a precursor to the broadening of thinking about these issues in international development discourse and to the World Bank's 2000/2001 *World Development Report* on attacking poverty.[38] And as discussed below, several *HDRs*, including the 1993 and 2002 *HDRs*, have explored the intrinsic value of political freedom. They argued not simply for "good governance" or governance of markets, but also for more inclusive democratic governance as a policy priority.

Shifts in development discourse

Karl Polanyi's 1944 characterization of policy change in motion is evident today in important ways. In the sweep of history in now-developed countries, he discerned long swings from state regulation to markets and back again, as the consequences of one regime led to political reactions and policy reversals. More recent analysis shows that this pendulum has continued to swing throughout the 20th and the early 21st centuries. Polanyi's concept provides a useful lens for viewing developing country policy-making.[39]

Development thinking has changed considerably over time: starting with the idea that capital investment equals growth and development, moving on successively to the role of human capital, the role of markets and policies, the role of institutions and more recently the role of individual and group empowerment and country ownership.[40]

Today, there is no consensus about development policy.[41] But new trends are emerging.

HDRs have expanded recognition of the environment and sustainability, including climate change, and signalled that intragenerational equity is as important as intergenerational equity

Many people have interpreted the financial crisis, symbolized by the collapse of the US financial giant, Lehman Brothers, as a sharp reminder of the hazards of unmitigated liberalization. The crisis's impact on development thinking is not yet clear, but in ways explored throughout this Report the pendulum is swinging back towards a more active role for public policy and a more humane development objective. The seeds of the next "big idea" are already visible and warrant further exploration, as we argue in chapter 6.

Competing and complementary strands

The conventional development package—the Washington Consensus—has increasingly been regarded as untenable as a set of universal prescriptions, though it still holds sway in many places. There are competing strands in current thinking about development, not all of them new, and some complementarities. Their influence on practice has varied across countries. Several reflect the influence of the human development approach:

- Recognizing the need for public action in regulating the economy, protecting vulnerable groups and producing public goods—both traditional (health, education, infrastructure) and new (overcoming threats posed by climate change).
- Operationalizing the many dimensions of well-being—going beyond average income and monetary measures of poverty—and including vulnerability to risk and shocks. With better data and techniques to capture the "missing" dimensions, doing this is increasingly feasible.[42]
- Seeing poverty, growth and inequality as essentially indivisible—with poverty reduction depending not only on the rate of growth but also on levels and changes in income distribution.[43] Rapid growth should not be the sole policy goal because it ignores the distribution of income and neglects (and can undermine) the sustainability of growth.
- Paying more explicit attention to the risks posed by climate change, put most forcefully by the Stern Report[44] and the 2007/2008 HDR, which called for strong and early

international action that builds on national and regional efforts.

The new strands in development thinking recognize that one size does not fit all, that the payoffs to policy reform differ with circumstances and that appropriate strategies need to be identified and developed locally.[45] Country ownership is seen as critical, because without it reforms would not be sustained and because the lack of country engagement in formulating policy means that the policy was inherently inappropriate. The limitations of external assistance are better recognized, alongside the potentially negative effects where it is inappropriately designed and implemented.

All these strands have been associated with attempts to better understand the richness and multidimensionality of experience and the importance of local context, brought to life by such path-breaking studies as *Voices of the Poor*[46] and by many Local, National and Regional HDRs (box 1.4).

Contexts influence institutions

The centrality of institutions has been increasingly stressed—though which aspects matter remains contested. The new institutional economics stresses property rights and the rule of law, as well as the more instrumental effects of participation and accountability. Alongside this has come recognition that context affects which institutional forms and functions are appropriate—and that mimicking or transplanting best practice is unlikely to yield the expected returns.[47] This recent literature has rediscovered some of the core principles of the institutionalist tradition: that all economies are embedded in social institutions and that a self-regulating market system independent of these institutions does not exist.[48]

Several contributions in the mid-2000s articulated this new heterodoxy. The 2004 Barcelona Development Agenda, drafted by a mixed group of development economists from developed and developing countries, emphasized key lessons from the last two decades. They highlighted good institutions, greater equity, prudent fiscal policy and an appropriate balance between market and state. They called

The new strands in development thinking recognize that one size does not fit all, that the payoffs to policy reform differ with circumstances and that appropriate strategies need to be identified and developed locally for an enabling environment that allowed for experimentation and for the adaptation of policies to overcome different sets of obstacles at the country level.

Soon thereafter, the World Bank published *Economic Growth in the 1990s*, a major reappraisal of approaches to policy reform. The report emphasized the variation in growth outcomes among countries with similar policy regimes, marking a major departure from the one size fits all approach of the Washington Consensus.[49] In 2008 the Spence Commission on Growth and Development—supported by the World Bank and several developed country governments—echoed these findings, stating that for sustained growth, "no generic formula exists. Each country has specific characteristics and historical experiences that must be reflected in its growth strategy."[50] The recent economic successes of Brazil, China and India attest to this new heterodoxy.

Moves towards greater accountability

Over time, the focus on monitoring has grown, linked to a movement supporting greater state and donor accountability. Results-based management, including using performance information in making budget allocations, has featured in several public sector reforms. The PARIS21 Consortium, launched in 1999 by the United Nations and other international agencies, supports investments in data collection and promotes a culture of evidence-based policy-making, monitoring and evaluation. The European Union's Social Inclusion Strategy, agreed to in Laeken, Brussels, in 2001, applies a set of 14 headline indicators (including those related to income poverty and inequality, work and social programmes) to benchmark and monitor national plans.[51]

Supporting the explosion in data on public sector activities and performance in developed and developing countries is the greater reach of the Internet and web-based data systems. This allows a better understanding of links among inputs, outputs, outcomes and impacts—such as spending on education, number of pupils, how much graduates have learned and what difference their education makes to their personal opportunities and to broader society. In

---

BOX 1.4

Human development in action: regional, national and local

In 1992 a team of academics, civil society representatives and the United Nations broke new ground by producing the first National Human Development Report (HDR) in Bangladesh. They set an example—soon followed in other countries, in many cases supported by local United Nations Development Programme offices. To date, some 700 Regional, National and Local HDRs have been produced—taking cues from the global *HDRs*, from each other and from regional and local development discourse. These reports actively engage governments and other stakeholders, ranging from opinion leaders to those who have had little voice. Focus group discussions and ad hoc surveys yield new and critical insights. And engaging networks of local scholars contributes to the strength and credibility of the reports.

The reports have explored the role of the state and the synergy between individual and collective dimensions of human development. For example, the 2005 Guatemala HDR and the 2008 Lebanon HDR tackled the sensitive issues of citizenship and diversity in societies scarred by deep-rooted tensions. The 2009 Bosnia and Herzegovina HDR framed these issues in the light of rebuilding social capital. In addition, as part of the 2009–2010 Brazil HDR, broad national debates in the media sought to build a shared vision for society.

Regional and National HDRs have often explored the barriers to full participation in society facing vulnerable groups, including people with disability, those living with HIV and AIDS, youth, the elderly and minorities. Examples include Regional HDRs on Roma and on social inclusion, and the 2008 Swaziland HDR on HIV and AIDS.

A recent stream of reports focuses on environmental change. The 2009 Croatia HDR considered the potential adverse impacts on fishing, agriculture and tourism. The 2010 China HDR highlights possible responses, such as building new low-carbon communities for the millions of people who continue to flock to urban centres.

Regional HDRs have tackled critical governance issues with cross-border relevance. The 2009 Arab States HDR considered human security threats across the region. The 2008 Asia-Pacific HDR recognized the disproportionate effect of corruption on the poor and considered codes of conduct for the public and private sectors and the role of citizen groups to monitor accountability.

In practice the reports need the support of the government, but governments can and often do object to the sensitive issues addressed.

Source: Pagliani 2010. See also www.hdr.undp.org/en/nhdr/.

1996, for example, nearly all European countries shifted to directly measuring public sector outputs, which had a noticeable effect on measured growth. Improved information and analysis have informed policy discussions, debates and decisions about government priorities, although as this Report shows, the data constraints remain large.

Discussions about program effectiveness are now often better informed by the findings of careful randomized and controlled experiments, though these provide precise, albeit robust, answers only to specific questions, such as what is the effect of an intervention to reduce teacher absenteeism in rural villages in

Rajasthan, India?[52] This approach has the disadvantage of overlooking the broader structural questions and often the underlying mechanisms generating the outcomes.[53] The policy influence of such evaluations has been limited by their deliberately narrow focus.

Happiness and subjective well-being

Finally and briefly, we highlight the surge in interest in happiness and subjective well-being.[54] This new interest has been stimulated by the finding that happiness is not fully explained by income or, as we found in background research for this Report, by the HDI.[55] Subjective measures have broad appeal and are fairly easy to collect. A growing body of evidence suggests that happiness is experienced along a good-bad continuum and can be measured through a single question.[56] Subjective states have clear intrinsic and instrumental value and may provide compelling insights into the value that people place on other aspects of life. However, as we argue further below, happiness is best thought of as complementing other measures of well-being, not as a sole measure.

Human development remains as vibrant as ever

The concept of human development is deliberately open ended—and sufficiently robust and vibrant to provide a paradigm for the new century. As the discussion here suggests and the chapters that follow show, human development is relevant across years, ideologies, cultures and classes. Yet it always needs to be specified by context, as in the Local, National and Regional HDRs, and subjected to scrutiny and public debate.

Describing human development as enlarging people's choices is fundamental—but not enough. Plural principles such as equity, sustainability and respect for human rights are key. Human development is about steadily sustaining positive outcomes and combating processes that impoverish people or underpin oppression and structural injustice. Because gains can be fragile and vulnerable to reversal, special efforts can ensure that human development endures for individuals, groups and nations.

HDRs since 1990 have highlighted different aspects of human development, often linked to the annual theme and taking advantage of the flexibility of the capability approach. As stressed above, inherent in the human development tradition is that the approach be dynamic, not calcified. We can see from the local, national and regional experiences, as well as the global *HDRs*, that what we mean by human development has varied by time and place while maintaining an underlying coherence. We propose a reaffirmation consistent with the human development tradition, with development practice on the ground and with the academic literature on human development and capabilities. We propose the following statement as a short definition of human development:

> Human development is the expansion of people's freedoms to live long, healthy and creative lives; to advance other goals they have reason to value; and to engage actively in shaping development equitably and sustainably on a shared planet. People are both the beneficiaries and drivers of human development, as individuals and in groups.

Thus stated, human development has three components:
- *Well-being:* expanding people's real freedoms—so that people can flourish.
- *Empowerment and agency:* enabling people and groups to act—to drive valuable outcomes.
- *Justice:* expanding equity, sustaining outcomes over time and respecting human rights and other goals of society.

There are always policy choices, though the choices are not unconstrained. Some are better for poverty reduction, for human rights and for sustainability—while others favour elites, dismiss freedom of association and deplete natural resources. Principles of justice need to be explicit—to identify trade-offs among them, such as between equity and sustainability, so that public debates and decisions are well informed.

When human development is successful, people can be creative and enjoy activities and states of being that they value. Human development is concerned not only with freedoms on paper. The capability to enjoy healthcare requires that health clinics exist, that they are staffed, that staff come to work, that medical supplies are stocked and that people are not refused treatment because they cannot pay or because of their gender, race or religion. That is why capabilities are called "real" freedoms. Resources, income and institutions are all vitally important means and policy goals; yet success ultimately is evaluated in terms of the lives people can lead and enjoy.

Process freedoms involve empowerment and democratic practices at different levels. Individuals are not only the beneficiaries of development. Their vision, ingenuity and strength are vital to advancing their own and others' well-being. If the right to free speech is enshrined in the constitution but violated in practice, there is no such capability. Human development views people as the architects of their own development, both personally in families and communities and collectively in public debate, shared action and democratic practice.

People who are empowered are able to bring about change, be it in their own lives at home or at work, in their communities or on a wider scale. A concern with people's ability to shape their own destinies—what Sen calls their "agency"—is at the core of the capability approach and its strong association with freedom.[57] Empowerment requires both agency and supportive institutional structures. People can be empowered at home and at work, in politics, in the community and in society. Empowerment is about people as individuals and acting in groups—be they local cooperatives, trade unions or national political movements lobbying for change.

Political freedoms—such as democracy and civil liberties—have intrinsic value and are important in at least two additional respects.[58] First, as shown by a review of the evidence commissioned for this Report, democratic governments are in general best able to advance human development goals,[59] such as lowering child mortality and raising education levels, in part because they are more accountable. Accountability is needed to translate democracy into human development, and elections alone do not provide enough accountability to empower the poor. Second, political freedoms allow people to participate actively in discussions about goals and policy priorities. At the same time, as we discuss in chapter 4, even though democratic accountability influences human development, it is no guarantee, and material prosperity and good achievements in health and education can coexist with nondemocratic practices.

Concerns about equity in human development translate directly into an explicit focus on inequality. This Report explores inequality in various aspects of human development—since income is an inadequate measure of the full array of human flourishing, broader measures of distribution are needed. The Report builds on recent analytical advances and better data to explore inequalities in health and education—alongside income—and their evolution over time.

Nearly 7 billion people now inhabit the earth. Some live in extreme poverty—others in gracious luxury. The limits of our planet will shape human development more sharply in the coming years than during the first 20 years of the *HDR*. As recognized in the chapters that follow, the reality of climate change requires a fundamental reshaping of the behaviours and aspirations of many people and institutions around the world, a challenge that has yet to be tackled.

The richness of the concept of human development is graphically illustrated in figure 1.3, which depicts the three components of capabilities. These are related to people's opportunities, process freedoms (affecting people's ability to shape their lives) and key principles of justice that shape processes and outcomes across people, time and space. These components are

> Human development carries the melody of the culture, values and current priorities of countries, communities and individuals in a way that reflects inclusive democratic choices

FIGURE 1.3

The human development concept—on a shared planet

Conceptual framework for human development

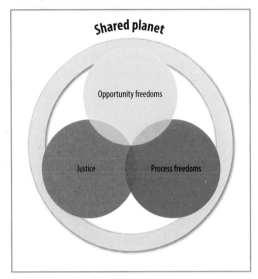

Source: HDRO based on Alkire 2010.

all embedded within a green band to acknowledge the shared environment. These freedoms are interlocking, and their expansion must be achieved within the bounds set by the sharing of the earth's limited resources.

Different countries, communities and individuals will emphasize different dimensions and principles. Human development carries the melody of their culture, values and current priorities in a way that reflects inclusive democratic choices. Many people—activists, leaders, intellectuals and many others—help articulate human development in diverse contexts, as with the Local and National HDRs, offering people more opportunities while fostering their ability to shape their lives and advance justice across society, now and into the future.

*　　　*　　　*

Subsequent chapters demonstrate the value and insights to be gained from a human development perspective. People around the world have achieved much in the past two decades, and we now face new and urgent challenges—the products of social, economic and political transformations that accelerated towards the end of the 20th century. These challenges must be addressed. Whether and how we do so will define human development in the 21st century.

The advance of people

Thinking clearly about the future requires looking critically at the past. In this chapter and the next we assess the evolution of the dimensions of development included in the Human Development Index (HDI; health, education and income) and identify advances and setbacks. We find substantial progress but also considerable variability across countries and time. Progress has been extensive for education, somewhat less so for health and much more variable for income. Despite advances, serious inequalities remain. The gulf separating developed and developing countries is still huge, and some key aspects show no sign of closing.

As stressed in chapter 1, human development encompasses more than health, education and income. The chance to lead a meaningful life depends on the conditions people face, including the distribution of advantages in their society, the possibilities for participating in decision-making and the way choices affect the well-being of future generations. These dimensions merit their own exploration—and receive it in chapter 4.

Trends since publication of the first *Human Development Report (HDR)* reflect longer run processes, so this chapter extends the period of the review. We investigate a specially created dataset covering HDI trends for 135 countries since 1970. We summarize the broad patterns and then discuss progress in each of the three HDI dimensions.

Recent trends in human development: through the lens of the Human Development Index

The HDI is a central contribution of the *HDR*. Intended as a simple measure of development and as an alternative to gross domestic product (GDP), it captures progress in three basic capabilities: to live a long and healthy life, to be educated and knowledgeable and to enjoy a decent standard of living. In the words of the *HDR*'s founder, Mahbub ul Haq, it shares many of the flaws of GDP but is more relevant to people's lives.[1]

The HDI helps answer some basic questions about the progress of societies, such as which countries have progressed faster and whether poor countries are catching up with

rich ones. Such questions are often addressed using income. However, a much clearer picture of development comes from measures that consider progress more broadly.

Since its inception, the HDI has been revised several times to address major criticisms.[2] This 20th anniversary is an opportunity to reinforce the HDI's credibility and ensure its continuing relevance, building on key strengths and learning from major recent initiatives that are similar in spirit. Among them are the Global Project on Measuring the Progress of Societies, hosted by the Organisation for Economic Co-operation Development, and the Stiglitz-Sen-Fitoussi

Commission. In this Report, we introduce several improvements to the indicators and the construction of the HDI (see box 1.2 in chapter 1 and *Technical note 1* for details).[3]

As described in chapter 1, this Report introduces new indicators into the HDI to exploit the greater availability of data, especially as some indicators—such as the literacy rate—have become less useful precisely because of the progress observed. However, this chapter and the next are about measuring the past, not just the present. For such a historical assessment, data for the original indicators (life expectancy, literacy rate, gross enrolment and per capita GDP) are more broadly available and remain meaningful. Therefore, this chapter and the next use a combination of the original HDI and the new—the original indicators and the new functional form—in what we call a hybrid HDI.[4] (Box 2.1 defines the HDI, the hybrid HDI and other basic terms used in this Report.) For simplicity, we refer to this as the HDI in these two chapters.

Overall patterns

For the first time since 1990, this Report provides a systematic review of patterns and trends in human development; previous efforts were hampered by sparse data.[5] The analysis is based on a new dataset of human development trends since 1970, covering 135 countries that account for 92 percent of the world's population.[6]

Measured in terms of the HDI, progress around the world has been impressive (figure 2.1). The world average HDI rose to 0.68 in 2010 from 0.57 in 1990, continuing the upward trend from 1970, when it stood at 0.48 (table 2.1).[7] This increase reflects aggregate expansions of about a fourth in the health and education indicators and a doubling of income per capita.[8]

The aggregate global measures are strongly influenced by the most populous countries—China and India. Even so, global figures unweighted by population (and thus reflecting average country performance) show similar progress.[9]

BOX 2.1 Basic terms used in this Report

Convergence. A narrowing over time of the gap between countries for a particular indicator.

Country. A shorthand term used to refer to countries or territories, including provinces and special administrative regions that directly report data to international statistical agencies.

Developed/developing. Countries in the very high HDI category (see below) are referred to as developed, and countries not in this group are referred to as developing. The terms are used for convenience only, to distinguish countries that have attained the highest HDI levels.

Deviation from fit. A measure of progress that captures changes in a country's indicators relative to the average change for countries starting from the same point.

Gender Inequality Index (GII). A measure that captures the loss in achievements due to gender disparities in the dimensions of reproductive health, empowerment and labour force participation. Values range from 0 (perfect equality) to 1 (total inequality).

Human Development Index (HDI). A composite measure of achievements in three basic dimensions of human development—a long and healthy life, access to education and a decent standard of living. For ease of comparability, the average value of achievements in these three dimensions is put on a scale of 0 to 1, where greater is better, and these indicators are aggregated using geometric means (see box 1.2 in chapter 1).

Hybrid HDI. HDI calculated using the new functional form described in chapter 1 and the indicators used up through the 2009 *Human*

Development Report (HDR): life expectancy, literacy rate, gross enrolment and per capita GDP. For reasons that include greater data availability, this method is more suitable to the exploration of long-term trends presented in chapters 2 and 3.

Inequality-adjusted HDI (IHDI). A measure of the average level of human development of people in a society once inequality is taken into account. It captures the HDI of the average person in society, which is less than the aggregate HDI when there is inequality in the distribution of health, education and income. Under perfect equality, the HDI and IHDI are equal; the greater the difference between the two, the greater the inequality.

Multidimensional Poverty Index (MPI). A measure of serious deprivations in the dimensions of health, education and living standards that combines the number of deprived and the intensity of their deprivation.

Top/bottom movers. The countries that have made the greatest or least progress in improving their HDI, as measured by the deviation from fit criterion.

Very high, high, medium, low HDI groups. Country classifications based on HDI quartiles. A country is in the very high group if its HDI is in the top quartile, in the high group if its HDI is in percentiles 51–75, in the medium group if its HDI is in percentiles 26–50 and in the low group if its HDI is in the bottom quartile. Earlier *HDRs* used absolute rather than relative thresholds.

Note: See chapter 5 and *Technical notes 1–4* for details on the new indices.

Advances in the HDI have occurred across all regions and almost all countries (see table 2.1). The fastest progress has been in East Asia and the Pacific, followed by South Asia, then the Arab States. All but 3 of the 135 countries have a higher level of human development today than in 1970—the exceptions are the Democratic Republic of the Congo, Zambia and Zimbabwe.

Which countries have been most successful in furthering the human development of their people? Table 2.2 shows the top 10 movers—the countries with fastest HDI increase in our sample. These new results offer some interesting insights—and unexpected contrasts.

A country's progress in human development can be measured in various ways, and which countries are classed as top movers depends on the standard used to judge change.[10] This Report uses the deviation from fit—the country's deviation from its expected improvement given its initial HDI and the improvement of countries at a similar starting point—as the measure of country progress over time.[11] Figure 2.2 illustrates how the method works: it selects the countries whose improvement is farthest above or below what would be expected given their initial level of development. This measure builds on earlier research by Gustav Ranis and Frances Stewart, who assessed a country's progress in relation to its HDI group.[12]

The top movers include several countries in East and South Asia and the Arab States (both from North Africa and the oil-rich Gulf region). Oman—a country that benefited from oil discoveries at the beginning of the period—tops the list, followed by China, Nepal and Indonesia. Since the method used to evaluate progress compares countries with similar initial HDI levels, some countries experiencing rapid progress from low starting points—such as Nepal and Lao PDR—are on the list. A more in-depth discussion of some of these cases—as well as of others with more disappointing experiences—is provided in box 2.2 and box 3.3 in chapter 3.

Strikingly, this list contains several countries not typically described as success stories. This is because several countries make it into

FIGURE **2.1**

Overall progress, significant variability

Worldwide trends in the Human Development Index, 1970–2010

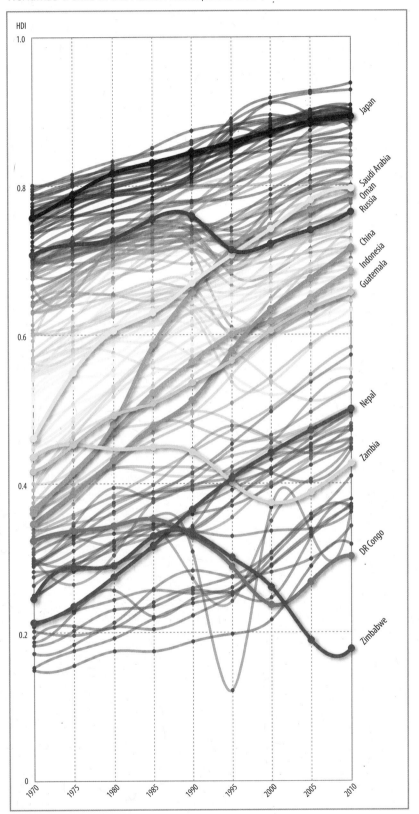

Note: Results are for a sample of 135 countries based on the hybrid HDI described in box 2.1. The top movers (as defined in box 2.1) are Oman, China, Nepal, Indonesia and Saudi Arabia; the bottom movers are DR Congo, Zambia and Zimbabwe.

Source: Hidalgo (2010) based on HDRO calculations using data from the HDRO database.

TABLE 2.1

Widespread improvements in the Human Development Index since 1970

Trends in the hybrid HDI and components by regional and HDI groups, 135 countries, 1970–2010

	Hybrid HDI			Life expectancy			Literacy			Gross enrolment			Income		
	Value	% change		Value	% change		Value	% change		Value	% change		Value	% change	
	2010	1970–2010	1990–2010	2010	1970–2010	1990–2010	2010	1970–2010	1990–2010	2010	1970–2010	1990–2010	2010	1970–2010	1990–2010
Regional groups															
Developing countries	0.64	57	23	68	21	8	81	61	21	66	28	24	5,873	184	89
Arab States	0.66	65	20	70	37	10	74	149	41	64	89	22	8,603	66	44
East Asia and the Pacific	0.71	96	35	73	23	9	94	76	18	69	7	31	6,504	1,183	352
Europe and Central Asia	0.75	13	4	69	3	2	97	7	2	82	17	7	11,866	120	20
Latin America and the Caribbean	0.77	32	12	74	24	9	92	27	10	83	59	16	11,092	88	42
South Asia	0.57	72	31	65	33	12	66	113	46	59	64	29	3,398	162	119
Sub-Saharan Africa	0.43	53	21	52	19	7	65	183	43	54	109	42	1,466	20	28
Developed countries	0.89	18	7	80	13	6	99	2	1	92	33	14	37,185	126	38
OECD	0.89	18	7	80	13	6	99	2	1	93	33	14	37,105	125	38
Non-OECD	0.86	24	9	80	14	7	96	13	6	79	29	10	40,043	263	58
HDI groups															
Low	0.44	61	27	55	27	11	63	180	48	52	98	43	1,434	33	44
Medium	0.65	83	31	69	25	9	82	79	24	65	21	28	5,010	606	237
High	0.77	24	9	73	15	7	93	20	8	82	38	13	12,610	94	35
Very high	0.89	18	7	80	13	6	99	2	1	92	33	14	37,185	126	38
1970 hybrid HDI quartiles															
1 (lowest)	0.60	82	32	66	22	8	76	96	29	61	23	33	4,323	560	250
2	0.69	51	16	71	34	11	88	53	15	74	55	16	7,334	110	53
3	0.79	24	9	75	15	6	96	11	4	85	36	16	14,486	152	54
4 (highest)	0.88	16	6	79	11	5	99	1	0	91	29	11	34,585	122	36
World average	**0.68**	**41**	**18**	**70**	**18**	**7**	**83**	**39**	**15**	**70**	**26**	**20**	**10,645**	**107**	**47**

Note: All values are population weighted. Life expectancy is in years, literacy and gross enrolment are in percentages and income is in purchasing power parity 2008 US dollars. See *Definitions of statistical terms* for more detailed descriptions. The sample covers 135 countries, and thus the group aggregates may differ from those presented in statistical tables 1–17. The hybrid HDI is distinct from the 2010 HDI reported in statistical tables 1 and 2: it uses the same functional form but a different set of indicators that are available over a longer time period (see box 2.1). HDI groups are based on the 2010 HDI.

Source: HDRO calculations using data from the HDRO database.

our top 10 list thanks to their high achievements in health and education, in some cases even with unexceptional growth performance. Thus, our list is very different from, say, that presented by the Spence Commission on Growth and Development.[13]

Also remarkable is the general lack of overlap between top performers in growth and those in health and education. Only Indonesia and South Korea are in the top 10 for both income and nonincome dimensions. Of the remaining eight countries, five enter the list through higher levels of health and education; only one (China) enters solely through its growth performance. The new HDI functional form recognizes balanced development, so that two countries with moderately high progress on both income and nonincome dimensions (Lao PDR and Morocco) make it into the top movers.

Although no countries from Sub-Saharan Africa are in the top 10, Ethiopia comes in at 11, and several African countries are in the top 25 (see box 2.2). Perhaps most notable is the absence of any Latin American country—the top mover there, Guatemala, comes in 22nd. Even so, the top performers are diverse not only in regional origin but in how they achieve success.

| TABLE 2.2 | **Fastest progress in human development comes in different ways** |

Top movers in HDI, nonincome HDI and GDP, 1970–2010

		Improvements in	
Rank	HDI	Nonincome HDI	Income
1	**Oman**	Oman	China
2	**China**	Nepal	Botswana
3	**Nepal**	Saudi Arabia	South Korea
4	**Indonesia**	Libya	Hong Kong, China
5	**Saudi Arabia**	Algeria	Malaysia
6	**Lao PDR**	Tunisia	Indonesia
7	**Tunisia**	Iran	Malta
8	**South Korea**	Ethiopia	Viet Nam
9	**Algeria**	South Korea	Mauritius
10	**Morocco**	Indonesia	India

Note: Improvements in HDI and nonincome HDI are measured by the deviation from fit—how well a country does relative to other countries starting from the same point (see box 2.1). Improvements in income are measured by the annual percentage growth rate in per capita GDP.

Source: HDRO calculations using data from the HDRO database.

Convergence—big time

The HDI can help assess whether poor countries are closing the gap with rich countries. This question is generally answered by looking at some measure of difference in a specific indicator between poor and rich countries or by assessing whether less developed countries are advancing more rapidly than more developed ones. Many researchers have investigated this question using GDP as a measure of development. They have generally concluded that the gap is widening.[14]

Catching up
But the HDI tells a more optimistic story. Overall, poor countries are catching up with rich countries in the HDI (see table 2.1). The HDI gap between developing and developed countries narrowed by about a fifth between 1990 and 2010 (and by about a fourth since 1970). For example, the HDI more than doubled for Mali (from 0.17 to 0.37), Nepal (from 0.22 to 0.50) and Oman (from 0.36 to 0.79). Good news indeed, this occurred despite the large divergence in incomes.[15]

One might suspect that this convergence is an artefact of the HDI being bounded at 1

or of some indicators—like the literacy rate—having natural upper bounds.[16] While these factors contribute to convergence, they are not the only explanation. Dispersion fell significantly for all the health and education variables that go into the HDI—including those for which the existence of an upper bound is debatable.[17] In contrast, incomes show increased divergence. Statistical tests confirm that upper bounds on these variables do not generate the convergence.[18] But even if the bounds contribute to the convergence, the substantive result—that health and education outcomes are becoming more alike in poor and rich countries—still holds.[19]

Consider life expectancy. Someone born in The Gambia in 1970 could expect to live to age 41—some 33 years fewer than someone born in Norway. By 2010 life expectancy in The Gambia had increased by 16 years (to 57) but in Norway by only 7 years. Thus, while the gap in life expectancy between Norway and The Gambia is still huge (24 years), it has shrunk by more than a fourth.

On average then, living in a developing country today is more similar—at least for these basic health and education indicators—to living in a developed country than was the case 40 or even 20 years ago. However, this is not true for all developing countries.

| FIGURE 2.2 | **Top movers vary across regions, but bottom movers are concentrated in Africa** |

Top and bottom movers as measured by deviation from fit, 1970–2010

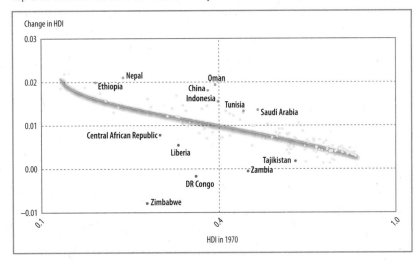

Note: HDI values in 1970 are in logarithmic scale.

Source: HDRO calculations using data from the HDRO database.

BOX **2.2** **Contrasting stories from Africa**

Sub-Saharan Africa is typically considered the region facing the greatest challenges in human development. Across all dimensions, it has the lowest Human Development Index (HDI) indicators of any region. However, several African countries have registered substantial progress in improving human development. Ethiopia ranks 11th in progress over time; Botswana, Benin and Burkina Faso are also among the top 25 countries with the fastest progress in human development.

Consider Burkina Faso. That it is a top mover may seem surprising: it ranks 126th on the HDI of the 135 countries in our sample. But the country has achieved major strides on the HDI since 1970, when it ranked 134th.

Public policies certainly helped—it ranked sixth among countries with the fastest growth in access to an improved water source since 1970. Access to basic services spread, with primary school enrolment rising from 44 percent in 1999 to 67 percent in 2007. Despite rapid demographic change, income poverty (measured by the share of the population living below $1.25 a day) declined 14 percentage points to 57 percent between 1994 and 2003.

That Burkina Faso is among the top movers illustrates how our method for assessing progress—which compares countries to those with a similar starting point—works. In fact, other countries with similar starting points experienced economic and social implosions, while Burkina Faso more than doubled its HDI. Our results also shed light on the debate about the "Burkina paradox"—low human development performance despite growth and macroeconomic stability. When progress is evaluated through changes over time and compared with that of countries with similar starting points, the paradox disappears.

By contrast, some African countries have seen dramatic setbacks in human development. The region is home to the only three countries whose HDI is lower today than in 1970: the Democratic Republic of the Congo, Zambia and Zimbabwe.

Zambia experienced declines in life expectancy, gross enrolment and income—for many reasons. The collapse of copper prices in 1980 sparked a protracted depression that shrank the economy by a third. Incomes have yet to return to previous levels. It also suffered from waves of refugees fleeing civil wars in neighbouring Angola and Mozambique and from the HIV epidemic, which gave the country the fifth highest HIV prevalence in the world. The lack of resources and the HIV epidemic hurt the provision of public services. Chapter 4 shows that 63 percent of Zambians suffer poverty in multiple dimensions, similar to the share living below $1.25 a day.

Zimbabwe was often praised for the progressive social policies adopted after the overthrow of minority White rule. In the 1980s public spending on health and education, especially for rural health centres, water, sanitation and rural schools, rose rapidly. Infant mortality rates were halved between 1980 and 1993, and child immunization rates rose from 25 percent to 80 percent. However, the government faced challenges in sustaining expansion, especially when the economy collapsed because of poor economic management. The HDI fell from 0.34 in 1990 to 0.26 in 2000, driven by a contraction of three of the four indicators used to calculate the HDI—the literacy rate was the exception. Income poverty increased, and people coped in part by moving to towns and neighbouring countries. The HIV epidemic was a further shock, compounding the strains on public services. The income poverty rate is now around 62 percent (up from 42 percent in 1995).

Source: World Bank 2009a, 2010g; Grimm and Günther 2004; UNDP Zambia 1997; UNDP 1998; WHO 2010b; Mwabu and Fosu 2010.

In several countries—mainly in Southern Africa and the former Soviet Union—life expectancy has declined. A handful of countries—including, perhaps most strikingly, China—have also seen drops in gross enrolment.[20] Moreover, in several more cases of some absolute improvements—such as for Armenia and Trinidad and Tobago—these have not been sufficient to narrow the gap with developed countries. In general, however, most developing countries have enjoyed rapid and significant progress in health and education.

A concern more difficult to address due to lack of data is the possibility that the quality of both healthcare and education could be diverging between developing and developed countries.[21] This concern underlines the importance of the measurement agenda in chapter 6.

Local variability

Not all countries have seen rapid progress, and the variation is striking. Over the past four decades a fourth of developing countries saw their HDI increase less than 20 percent, while another fourth experienced a more than 65 percent increase. Since 1990, 10 countries have seen no overall improvement in the HDI.[22] The recent global financial crisis and the East Asian financial crisis of 1997–1998 remind us that progress is not linear, even for countries that perform well. Economic crises can throw countries off track. So can shocks that affect health and education directly, such as epidemics and natural disasters.

To some extent, these differences in rates of progress reflect different starting points—convergence means that less developed countries tend, on average, to improve more rapidly

FIGURE **2.3**   **Diversity of paths**

Evolution of the HDI from similar starting points in 1970

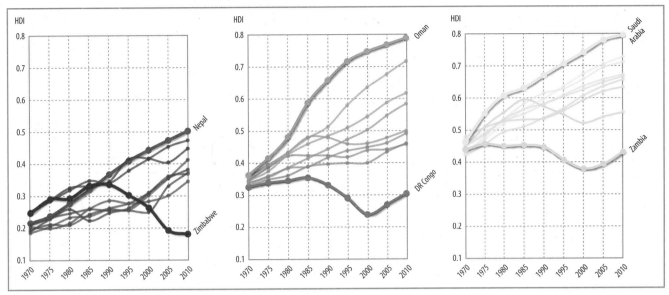

Source: HDRO calculations using data from the HDRO database.

than more developed ones. However, half the variation in HDI progress is unexplained by initial HDI level, and countries with similar starting points experience remarkably different evolutions over time (figure 2.3). This evidence suggests that country factors such as institutions, geography and policies—and even pure luck (good and bad)—are important in determining outcomes.

Take Morocco and Côte d'Ivoire. Measured by the variables that go into the HDI, they had similar levels of development in 1970 and so might be expected to have followed similar development paths. However, their human development trajectories diverged widely. Over the 40 years to 2010, life expectancy rose

20 years in Morocco but just 11 years in Côte d'Ivoire. Today, 61 percent of Moroccan children are enrolled in schools, far more than the 38 percent in Côte d'Ivoire, and Morocco's per capita income is 2.7 times Côte d'Ivoire's.

There is a story behind these differences. Political instability and a protracted civil war held back Côte d'Ivoire, and active social policies appear to have made a big difference in Morocco. Understanding the causes of these variations is of major policy relevance, and we explore them in detail in the next chapter.

By design, the HDI gives only a summary assessment of progress. We need to look at what happened in each of the relevant dimensions—and we do so in turn in the following sections.

Longer lives, better health

Many countries have achieved large gains in life expectancy. A baby born today in almost any country can expect to live longer than at any time in history. Life expectancy has risen most in the Arab States, by more than 18 years since 1970 (just more than a third). Even in Sub-Saharan Africa, life expectancy is more

than eight years longer than in 1970. And increases in longevity were more than twice as rapid in the bottom quarter of countries in the 1970 HDI distribution than in the top quarter. In several developing countries—including Chile and Malaysia—mortality rates are about 60 percent what they were 30 years ago.

Figure 2.4 illustrates the extent and breadth of this progress. Alongside the country values of life expectancy represented in the left panel, we introduce a "thermal image" graph in the right panel that helps us see where countries are clustering in the distribution of health achievements. The "hotter" areas—those shaded red and yellow—show that many countries cluster at high life expectancy levels, with very few still at the lower levels (green and blue). This pattern of clustering at high levels is striking for health and education but not, as we will see below, for income (see figures 2.7 and 2.10 later in the chapter).[23] But while life expectancy increased in most countries, some saw precipitous declines. This is also well captured by the thermal graph, which shows some areas of "heat" (shaded yellow) towards the bottom of the right panel.

What accounts for this progress? Mortality rates have fallen faster in infants and children than in adults. If children were still dying at the higher rates prevalent in the late 1970s, 6.7 million more children would die each year.[24] Absolute progress has been fastest in developing countries from the 1970s to the 2000s (figure 2.5). From 1970 to 2005, for example, infant mortality declined by 59 per 1,000 live births in developing countries, almost four times the decline of 16 per 1,000 in developed countries. However, the percentage decline continues to be faster in developed countries (77 percent) than in developing countries (59 percent).[25] And huge health gaps remain, with eight times more infant deaths per 1,000 live births in developing countries than in developed countries. Less than 1 percent of child deaths occur in developed countries.[26]

Maternal mortality ratios have also fallen, though by how much is uncertain. UN estimates show a modest 5 percent decline since 1990—from 430 deaths per 100,000 live births to 400.[27] A recent study using vital registration data, censuses, surveys and verbal autopsy studies found lower levels of maternal mortality and a somewhat faster decline of 22 percent (from 320 per 100,000 to 251) in the same period.[28] These data indicate that even the bottom five countries—Mauritania, Eritrea, Angola, Sierra Leone and

Guinea-Bissau—reduced maternal mortality (from 1,159 per 100,000 live births to 711). Alternative estimates coincide in one basic assessment: progress is far slower than needed to reach the Millennium Development Goal target of reducing maternal deaths by three-fourths between 1990 and 2015.[29]

Progress has slowed

Health progress has slowed since 1990. Average life spans rose about six years between the 1970s and 1990s, but only four years in the subsequent two decades.[30] Adult mortality since the 1990s has fallen 23 percent for women and 6 percent for men, much slower than the declines of 27 percent and 26 percent in the previous two decades. Infant mortality rates also fell more slowly.

This slowdown in aggregate progress is due largely to dramatic reversals in 19 countries (home to about 6 percent of the world's people) that experienced declines in life expectancy in the past two decades. In nine countries life expectancy fell below 1970 levels: six in Africa (the Democratic Republic of the Congo, Lesotho, South Africa, Swaziland, Zambia and Zimbabwe) and three in the former Soviet Union (Belarus, the Russian Federation and Ukraine). Driving these declines are the HIV epidemic and the mortality reversal in transition economies. These phenomena have partially offset the convergence in health outcomes observed since 1990, though some convergence—albeit slow—is observed between the rest of developing countries and developed ones (figure 2.6).[31]

The decline in several Sub-Saharan African countries can be clearly linked to the HIV epidemic. Since the 1980s AIDS has slashed life expectancy in Southern Africa, where adult HIV prevalence rates still exceed 15 percent.[32] In the most affected countries life expectancy is now below 51 years; in Lesotho it stands at 46—similar to that in England before the Industrial Revolution. Since 2000 HIV prevalence rates appear to have been stabilizing (though in some cases at very high levels), and most of Southern Africa has seen some recent

If children were still dying at the higher rates prevalent in the late 1970s, 6.7 million more children would die each year

FIGURE **2.4**   **Progress in health**

Worldwide trends in life expectancy, 1970–2010

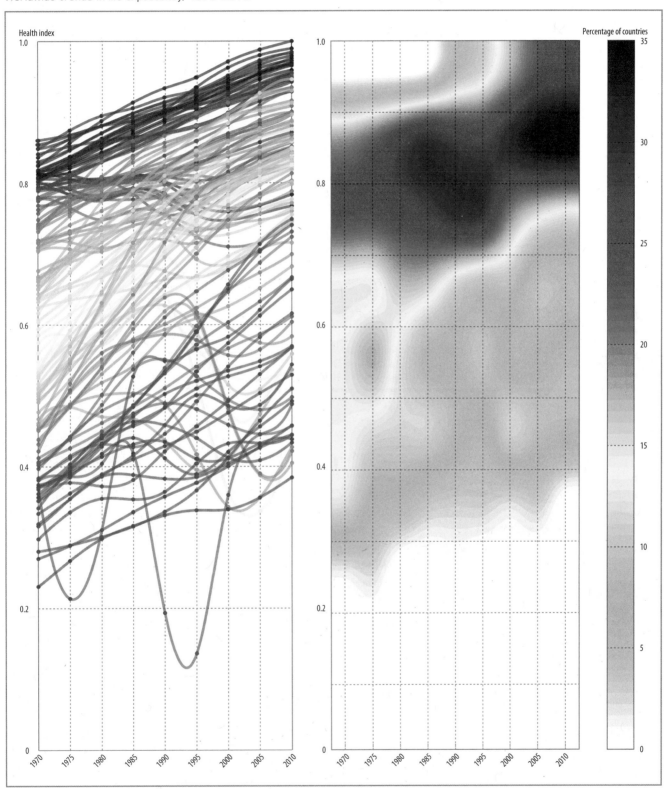

Health index

Percentage of countries

Note: Results are for a sample of 135 countries based on the hybrid HDI described in box 2.1. The health index is calculated applying the methodology presented in *Technical note 1* to life expectancy and thus represents the contribution of the health dimension to both the hybrid HDI and the HDI. The left panel shows the time series for each country; the right panel represents the relative distribution of countries, with colours closer to red denoting a higher share of countries in the corresponding area.

Source: Hidalgo (2010) based on HDRO calculations using data from the HDRO database.

FIGURE **2.5**

Progress in key health indicators, but developing countries still lag

Selected health indicators, 1970s and 2000s

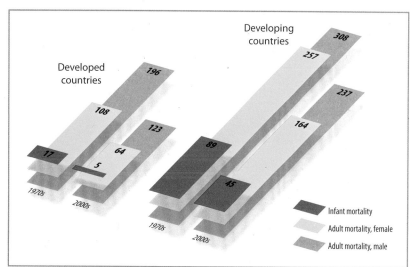

Note: Infant mortality is the number of deaths per 1,000 live births; adult mortality is the number of deaths per 1,000 adults.

Source: HDRO calculations using data from World Bank (2010g).

FIGURE **2.6**

Declines in life expectancy for the former Soviet Union and countries severely affected by HIV

Trends in life expectancy around the world, 1970–2010

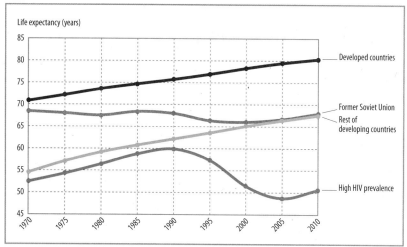

Note: A country is considered to have a high HIV prevalence if the rate exceeds 15 percent, which is the case for seven countries in our sample (Botswana, Lesotho, Namibia, South Africa, Swaziland, Zambia and Zimbabwe).

Source: HDRO calculations using data from the HDRO database.

recovery in life expectancy. The exceptions: Lesotho, South Africa and Swaziland, which suffered further declines (of about four years) over the last decade.

The declines in life expectancy in the former Soviet Union were concentrated among

men. In the Russian Federation male life expectancy plummeted by seven years from 1989 to 1994. There is considerable debate over the causes.[33] Alcohol consumption and, after 1990, stress during the transition to a market economy—with high inflation, unemployment and uncertainty—appear to be important in explaining the trends, though disentangling the effects is not easy.[34] One study found that 21 percent of 25,000 men autopsied in Siberia between 1990 and 2004 whose deaths were attributed to circulatory diseases had lethal or near-lethal ethanol concentrations in their blood.[35]

Yet one cannot simply conclude that the transition to a market economy was the main driver of higher mortality. Some transition economies with a similar initial worsening in mortality—including Kyrgyzstan and Montenegro—saw a rapid recovery beginning in the early 2000s. In addition, the decline in life expectancy in the former Soviet Union had started before the transition—it fell by 1 year in the 1970s, a time when life expectancy in the world was increasing by 3.5 years.[36]

Many factors other than disease affect mortality trends. Public sector involvement has been important, with notable changes over time and across countries. Health service fees were introduced in Africa in the late 1980s and subsequently challenged for several reasons, including the limited revenue raised.[37] Several countries in East and Southern Africa have recently abolished fees for some preventive health services for pregnant women, infants and young children. There is evidence of immediate positive effects, with more use of healthcare services among young children. After Uganda abolished fees in 2001, new cases treated rose 19 percent for children under age five, and in the following two years use of government health units in rural areas rose 77 percent.[38]

Health is also affected by conflict, which not only results in deaths and injuries but strains weak public health systems, destroys the infrastructure to deliver medicine and immunizations and makes populations vulnerable to disease and worse.[39] Widespread conflict—as in Afghanistan (1979–1989; 2001–today), Cambodia (1967–1999) and Mozambique

(1975–1992)—can inflict immense damage on people's health.[40]

Yet stories vary across countries, depending on the nature and intensity of the conflict and the humanitarian response. Conflicts in more isolated areas have not adversely affected nationally measured outcomes (such as Uganda's northern insurgency), while some countries have even made health advances despite conflict, thanks to extensive humanitarian efforts to deliver basic services. This was the case, for example, in Afghanistan, which saw infant and under-five mortality rates drop by a fourth from 2002 to 2004, thanks to major efforts in constructing health centres and district hospitals, training community health workers and applying simple technologies such as standardized drug kits.[41]

Hunger—the many-headed monster

Mortality data measure one key—if dramatic—aspect of well-being. However, surviving is just one part of leading a long and healthy life. Being well nourished is another. Those who survive need to be sufficiently well nourished to live decently and fulfil their life plans. Going to bed hungry—or falling asleep due to lack of energy—is one of the most tangible deprivations that people can face.

Nutrition is an aspect of health where income matters—hungry people who have more money are likely to spend it on food. And as famously illustrated by Amartya Sen's ground-breaking work on famines, hunger often reflects the lack of means to acquire food rather than general food scarcity.[42] However, more income does not always guarantee proper nutrition, and people who are not poor can still go hungry.

In fact, differences persist between numbers of poor people—estimated by dollar a day thresholds—and numbers of hungry people. This variation reflects differences in how the two states are measured differently as well as weaknesses in the data.[43] It also reflects influences other than income on the nutritional outcomes of family members—such as maternal health and education, and feeding and hygiene practices in the home. Researchers in India have highlighted women's health and feeding practices and the limited reach of public health services as key factors.[44] A study in East Africa commissioned for this Report found that vaccinations and medical care during birth reduce child malnutrition, as does women's education.[45]

Inadequate nutrition also affects the way people—particularly children—acquire knowledge and participate in society. It hampers the ability to work and be productive and thus limits the ability to earn the income needed to lead a decent life. And the irreversibility of some health consequences of malnutrition—blindness from vitamin A deficiency, physical stunting from protein shortages—reinforces the urgency of eradicating hunger.[46]

Jean Drèze and Amartya Sen wrote that "hunger is a many-headed monster," highlighting the many ways a lack of food can affect people's freedoms.[47] Hunger is also a behemoth—and a stubborn one. Hunger persists despite the remarkable boost in food production brought about by the green revolution between the early 1960s and the early 1980s. By 2000 further gains in food production had contributed to lower prices for most staples. The share of undernourished people in developing countries fell from 25 percent in 1980 to 16 percent in 2005.

According to the most recent data used to monitor progress towards the hunger Millennium Development Goal, there have been encouraging advances in reducing the rate of malnourishment. But the absolute number of malnourished people—defined by minimal energy consumption—hardly budged from 850 million since 1980, although it spiked recently to around 1 billion. Of these, 63 percent are in Asia and the Pacific, 26 percent in Sub-Saharan Africa and 1 percent in developed countries.[48]

While many millions of people have too little to eat, millions eat too much. The recent rise in obesity, especially in children, jeopardizes advances in the care of cardiovascular disease, stroke and diabetes. Severe obesity can reduce life by 5–20 years, leading some specialists to conclude that life expectancy in the United

Going to bed hungry—or falling asleep due to lack of energy—is one of the most tangible deprivations that people can face

States is likely to level off and may even fall by 2050.[49] These risks are the result not just of higher income but also of cultural influences that can be transmitted across borders. Mexico, where people's incomes average only a fifth those of the United States, has shares of obese and overweight people similar to those in the United States.[50]

Knowledge expands possibilities

No country has seen declines in literacy or years of schooling since 1970

Knowledge expands people's possibilities. It promotes creativity and imagination.[51] In addition to its intrinsic value, it has substantial instrumental value in expanding other freedoms. Being educated empowers people to advance their interests and resist exploitation.[52] Educated people are more aware of how to avoid health risks and to live longer and more comfortable lives.[53] They also tend to earn higher wages and have better jobs. Many uneducated parents value schooling because they believe education will enable their sons and daughters to overcome the indignities their families face.

Progress in education has been substantial and widespread, reflecting improvements in the quantity of schooling and in equity of access for girls and boys. To a large extent, this reflects greater state involvement, though many developing countries have proven more capable of putting children in school than of giving them a high quality education.

Education levels higher than ever

People around the world today have much higher levels of education than ever before—a result that holds across many different measures of education. Take years of schooling: an average person age 15 or older in 1960 had fewer than 4 years of schooling—by 2010 this number had doubled globally and more than tripled in developing countries (from 1.9 years to 6.4). Since the first *HDR* in 1990 average years of schooling have risen by two years and gross enrolment ratios by 12 percentage points—while literacy rates have risen from 73 percent to 84 percent.

Progress has been widespread. No country has seen declines in literacy or years of schooling since 1970. And education has been extended to many more people: since 1960 the proportion of people who attended school has risen from 57 percent to 85 percent. This means that many countries have achieved success in education, at least as measured by the conventional HDI indicator—one of our key motivations for the refinements discussed in box 1.2 in chapter 1.

The average education index used in the HDI, which combines information on enrolment and literacy, captures this general picture of widespread progress (figure 2.7). As in health, the thermal graph in the right hand panel signals a strong concentration at the top of the distribution.

Even these increases may underestimate progress. Literacy and years of schooling reflect past access to education (or lack of it) by people who are adults today; thus, measured progress may not reflect recent advances in schooling for the young population. People who have not been in school tend to be older: in developing countries almost 36 percent of people ages 65–74 never attended school compared with only 7 percent of those ages 15–24. The youth literacy rate now exceeds 95 percent in 63 of the 104 countries with data and is 99 percent in 35 (including such medium HDI countries as Moldova and Samoa). This suggests that lack of basic writing skills will cease to be a major constraint on access to knowledge.

Enrolment ratios and expected years of schooling—the number of years of schooling that today's children can expect to have once they grow up, given current enrolment ratios—give a better picture of children's current access to education. Average world enrolment ratios are now 100 percent or higher for primary education in both developed and developing

FIGURE 2.7

Progress in education

Worldwide trends in education levels, 1970–2010

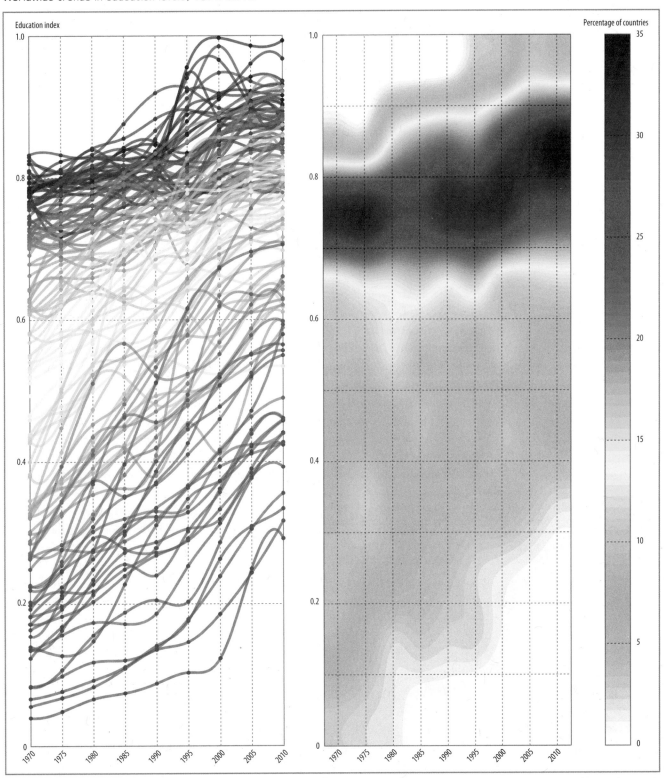

Note: Results are for a sample of 135 countries based on the hybrid HDI described in box 2.1. The education index is calculated applying the methodology presented in *Technical note 1* to the country's rate of adult literacy and combined primary, secondary and tertiary gross enrolment ratios and thus represents the contribution of the education dimension to the hybrid HDI. The left panel shows the time series for each country; the right panel represents the relative distribution of countries, with colours closer to red denoting a higher share of countries in the corresponding area.

Source: Hidalgo (2010) based on HDRO calculations using data from the HDRO database.

countries, and both groups have made substantial strides in higher levels of education as well—though developing countries still have large gaps to close (figure 2.8).[54] Not only are more children going to school—but more of those who go are finishing: primary completion rates have risen from 84 percent to 94 percent since 1991. Increased enrolment is reflected in expected years of schooling, which has risen from 9 years in 1980 to 11 years today and from 5 years to 8 years for low HDI countries.

Gender differences narrowing

Enrolments have increased faster for girls than for boys over the past few decades, and from 1991 to 2007 the ratio of female to male primary enrolment rose in all regions. Both primary and secondary school completion rates have improved more rapidly for girls.

On average between 1991 and 2007, girls' completion rates rose 29 points, to 87 percent; boys' rates rose 17 points, to more than 90 percent.[55] Improvements in girls' rates are reflected in the progress in secondary school enrolment. In 79 of the 134 countries with data—including Bangladesh and Lesotho—secondary school enrolment of women relative to men exceeds 98 percent. In another 17 countries

the female to male enrolment ratio is at least 95 percent.

However, there is still plenty of room for improvement: of the 156 countries with data, only 87 have primary school enrolment ratios for girls close to or above those for boys.[56] While gender gaps are small on average for young children in developing countries, they remain pronounced for older children in rural areas. In Bolivia 35 percent of rural girls and 71 percent of urban boys are enrolled in school. In Guinea the rates are 37 percent and 84 percent.

In contrast, women's enrolment in higher education, also on the rise, exceeds that of men in many parts of the world. In the Arab States, for example, where enrolment in higher education rose 45 percentage points, the average is now 132 women for every 100 men. Lagging are South Asia and Sub-Saharan Africa, with female to male ratios of 75 percent and 51 percent. Among the countries farthest behind are Guinea and Niger, where three men for every woman are enrolled in higher education.

Summary measures of educational attainment (such as mean years of schooling or population with at least secondary education) thus show remarkable increases across the board for both men and women, though the gap is still large in many developing countries (see statistical table 4). In the Arab States and South Asia the gender gap in years of education has narrowed by 33–40 percentage points since 1970; in Sub-Saharan Africa, by 26 points (figure 2.9). But in eight countries—Afghanistan, Benin, Central African Republic, Haiti, Liberia, Mozambique, Niger and Togo—women have fewer than half the years of schooling of men.

Public sector involvement has grown

Expanded schooling is associated with increased public funding in much of the world. Students attend mainly public schools, especially at the primary (92 percent) and secondary (85 percent) levels.[57] Public spending on education averaged 5.1 percent of GDP in 2006, up from 3.9 percent of GDP in 1970.[58]

FIGURE 2.8 **More children attend school, but there is room for improvement in secondary and higher education**

Gross enrolment ratios by level of schooling, 1970–2007

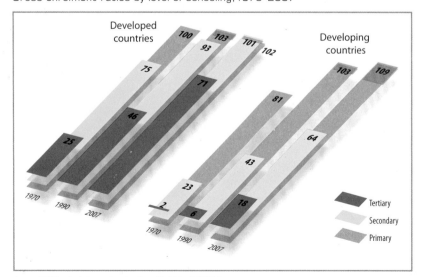

Source: HDRO calculations using data from World Bank (2010g).

As we discuss in chapter 3, this increase continues a longer trend, with education spending around 1 percent of GDP a century ago.[59]

The resources devoted to educating each student have also increased, rising 43 percent since 1990. And pupil–teacher ratios declined.[60] But disparities in spending are enormous. The annual average is nearly $4,611 per pupil worldwide,[61] but only $184 in Sub-Saharan Africa—even after increasing 15 percent since 1990—roughly an eighth that in Latin America and less than one fortieth that in developed countries. And the gap in spending per pupil is widening.

A number of countries have worked hard to get more children into school. Yet there have been reversals. As in health services, user fees were heavily promoted by the World Bank and others in the 1980s and early 1990s as a means of cost recovery for government services. Several studies found highly adverse impacts on access. By the late 1980s it was evident that cost recovery was not compatible with education objectives. In one southern Nigerian state primary enrolment plummeted from 90 percent to 60 percent in 18 months following the introduction of school fees in the 1980s.[62]

Many countries later abolished school fees for primary schools. Among them were Ethiopia, Malawi and Uganda in the 1990s and Cambodia, Kenya and Tanzania in the early 2000s. As attendance surged, challenges emerged in seat availability and education quality. In Malawi, a forerunner in abolishing fees in 1994, primary school enrolment grew 97 percent between 1990 and 1995; and in Uganda it grew 72 percent between 1995 and 2000. In Latin America conditional cash transfer programmes were introduced with the explicit aim of increasing school attendance, as with Brazil's Bolsa Escola and Bolsa Familia, Mexico's Oportunidades and Chile's Chile Solidario (see box 3.7 in chapter 3).[63]

But many children are not learning

Higher spending and enrolment do not necessarily mean better schooling. The gaps in school

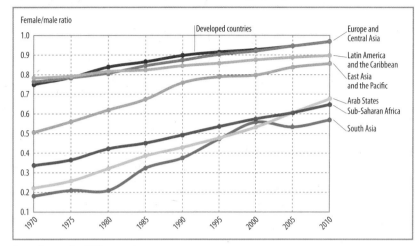

FIGURE 2.9 **Progress in gender equity in education, but gaps remain**

Ratio of female to male mean years of schooling by region, 1970–2010

Source: Barro and Lee 2010.

quality are huge, although whether schooling has improved or deteriorated over time is hard to tell due to lack of data. In general, children in developing countries learn far less than children schooled for the same number of years in developed countries.[64] Children at the same education level in developing countries as their counterparts in developed countries score on average about 20 percent lower on standardized tests—about a three-grade difference.[65] Average math scores were as high in South Korea and Malaysia as in developed countries, but abysmally low in South Africa, for example. In some cases the differences reflect inefficiencies as much as low spending. For example, grade 8 students in Indonesia scored at least as high as those in many Latin American countries, with an eighth of the spending per capita.[66]

Fiji, despite universal primary education, illustrates some of the challenges. Recent focus groups of children revealed corporal punishment, unprofessional teacher behaviour and sexual harassment of female students as driving secondary school dropout rates and other adverse outcomes. As one 17-year-old girl noted, "When children don't do anything at all, or they start talking or something, that's when they [teachers] start hitting. I think that should be stopped." A similar study in Indonesia found that poor students were often singled out for ridicule when they could not pay for uniforms or school supplies, often leading to their exclusion. Asked why he dropped out of school, an 11-year-old boy responded: "I often feel embarrassed. When I didn't wear shoes, the teacher pointed to my feet, and said, 'This is not the way to come to school.'"[67]

Case studies in poorer developing countries paint an even bleaker picture. Sixth graders in Ghana had an average score of 25 percent on a multiple-choice test—no different from what they would score by choosing answers randomly. More than half of 11-year-olds in Bangladesh could not write basic letters or numerals.[68] In Timor-Leste more than 70 percent of students at the end of grade 1 could not read even one word when shown a simple text passage.[69]

The difficulties in improving education quality illustrate the varying effectiveness of state involvement—at least as traditionally conceived. Decisions to expand schools usually come from the top down, supported by politically aligned teachers unions and contractors. It is much harder to get motivated teachers to impart real learning skills. Solving incentive problems for managers and workers, always difficult, is especially challenging when the state is embedded in patronage-based mechanisms of channelling goods and services to core

supporters, creating new entrenched groups along the way.[70] Almost a decade after De and Drèze's *Public Report on Basic Education in India* exposed teacher absenteeism of 48 percent, high rates have persisted, despite major budget and management reforms and infrastructure improvements in the interim.[71]

Low quality education in developing countries does not necessarily imply that deterioration has occurred. Data are inadequate for reaching firm conclusions about long- or even medium-term trends in quality. Moreover, test scores depend on many factors, particularly students' socioeconomic background. Children from well-off families are likely to be better nourished and healthier and have more access to materials than poorer children, and their parents can do more to help them.[72] So as school expansions bring in more disadvantaged students, average test scores will tend to drop even if education quality does not change.[73]

The picture is thus of poor countries rapidly catching up on aggregate educational attainment and gender equity but not necessarily on quality. There are also major disparities between groups within countries, as explored in chapter 4. Thus, while the advances of the past decades are substantial, there is still a long way to go towards equity in access to knowledge.

> While the advances of the past decades are substantial, there is still a long way to go towards equity in access to knowledge

Rising standards of living

Income has many shortcomings as a summary measure of development—a central message of *HDRs* for the past 20 years. Among its flaws is the neglect of inequality in distribution and of the unsustainability of current production. However, money is an important means of expanding choice, especially poor people's choices, and average income does proxy for a society's overall command of resources. The evolution of income is thus of great interest.

However, the story is not just one of overall increases—it is also one of widening disparities and a persistent divide between developed countries and the rest of the world. Since 1970, 155 countries—home to 95 percent of the world's people—have experienced increases in

real per capita income (figure 2.10). The annual average today is $10,760, almost 1.5 times its level 20 years ago and twice its level 40 years ago. People in all regions have seen substantial increases in average income, though patterns vary.[74] And the range, amount and quality of goods and services available to people today is unprecedented.

The thermal graph on the right panel of figure 2.10 shows that the world distribution of income is far more dispersed than that of health and education. The corresponding figures for health (see figure 2.4) and education (see figure 2.7) showed a "hot" red area towards the top where many countries were converging. This is not the case for income, which

FIGURE **2.10** | **Progress in living standards**

Worldwide trends in GDP, 1970–2010

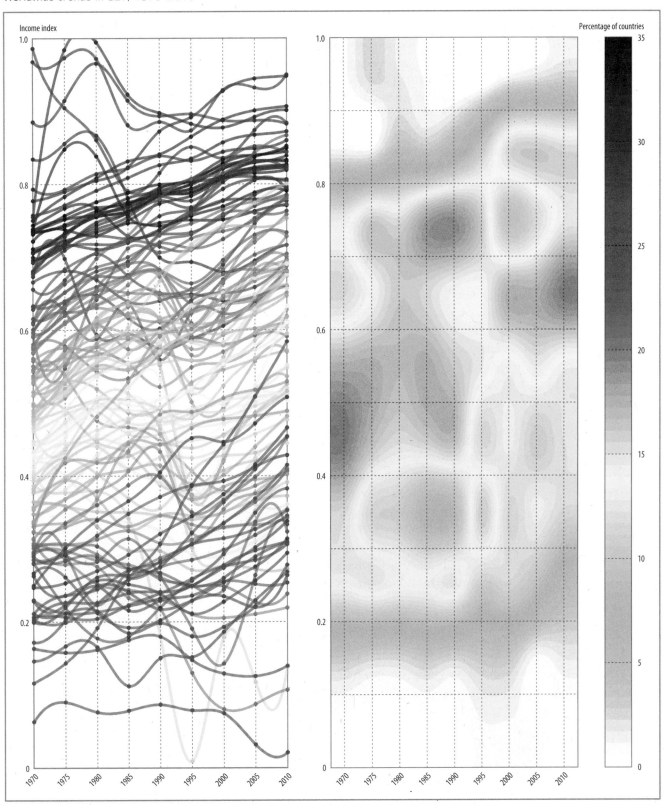

Income index

Percentage of countries

Note: Results are for a sample of 135 countries based on the hybrid HDI described in box 2.1. The income index is calculated applying the methodology presented in *Technical note 1* to the country's per capita GDP in purchasing power parity adjusted US dollars and thus represents the contribution of the income dimension to the hybrid HDI. The left panel shows the time series for each country; the right panel represents the relative distribution of countries, with colours closer to red denoting a higher share of countries in the corresponding area.

Source: Hidalgo (2010) based on HDRO calculations using data from the HDRO database.

illustrates the fact that the world distribution of income is much more unequal than that of health and education.

Divergent progress

The gap in incomes between developed and developing countries has continued to widen

Unlike in health and education, there has been substantial divergence in income across countries. From 1970 to 2010 per capita income in developed countries increased 2.3 percent a year on average, compared with 1.5 percent for developing countries.[75] In 1970 the average income of a country in the top quarter of the world income distribution was 23 times that of a country in the bottom quarter. By 2010 it approached 29 times. Divergence among developing countries has become more marked as well. Some developing countries—including Botswana, China, Malaysia and Thailand—have grown faster since the 1970s than any rich country.[76] At the same time, the income of several other countries—including Comoros, Iran and Senegal—has stagnated. Still other countries, such as Côte d'Ivoire, Madagascar and Zimbabwe, have suffered economic collapses.

Developing countries' growth performance has improved over time, both in absolute levels and relative to developed countries. This was particularly evident during the global financial crisis, when many developing countries were able to maintain strong growth. Nevertheless, even over the past 20 years, the gap between developed and developing countries has continued to widen. One important question is whether developing countries will be able to grow at the relatively faster average rates attained over the past five years.[77]

The distance between the richest and poorest countries has widened to a gulf. The richest country today (Liechtenstein) is three times richer than the richest country in 1970.[78] The poorest country today (Zimbabwe) is about 25 percent poorer than the poorest country in 1970 (also Zimbabwe). It is sobering to see, amid enormous material prosperity in developed countries, that the real average income of people in 13 countries in the bottom quarter of today's world income distribution is lower than in 1970.[79]

Few countries cross the threshold

Economic growth has been spectacular in some developing countries. Between 1970 and 2010, China's per capita income rose twenty-one-fold, Botswana's more than ninefold and Malaysia's and Thailand's more than fivefold.[80] But these countries have far to go before they cross the divide: China's per capita income is only a fifth the average for developed countries. Botswana, Malaysia and Thailand are also far from this mark.

Will these countries continue to grow until they cross the threshold to developed countries? History suggests that growth cannot be taken for granted. Many countries grew impressively over long periods only to stagnate. For example, between 1950 and 1980 Brazil's per capita economic growth was almost 5 percent a year—similar to recent growth in Botswana, Singapore and Thailand—but its economy collapsed in the 1980s and has only recently started to recover. Argentina's collapse was even more dramatic, from a per capita GDP in 1913 that exceeded the European average,[81] to one in 2007 that was just a fifth of Western Europe's.

These cases illustrate how hard it is to cross the great income divide. Of the 108 countries with incomes below $7,000 per capita in 1970, only 4 moved up to the World Bank's high-income classification in 2010. Three are small island economies (Antigua and Barbuda, Equatorial Guinea and Malta), one with abundant oil. The fourth—South Korea—remains an important exception. Estonia and Slovakia did not exist as independent countries in 1970, but both achieved growth that moved them up into the high-income group.

*　　　　*　　　　*

In important respects, the world is a better place today than it was in 1990. Many people live longer, children spend more time in school and people have access to many more goods—including food, housing, clothing and other necessities for a decent life—than at any time in history. The major convergence of countries in the HDI, documented systematically for the first time in this Report, has been a huge achievement. As we discuss in chapter 4, these advances extend to other dimensions of human development, notably to political freedoms.

Yet the assessment of the past few decades is by no means wholly positive. Some countries have suffered grave setbacks—particularly in health—sometimes erasing in a few years the gains of several decades. Patterns of economic growth have been extremely unequal—both in the countries experiencing fast growth and, as we explore in chapter 4, in the groups benefiting from national progress.

And despite convergent trends in health and education, gaps in human development are huge. A person born in Niger can expect to live 26 fewer years, to have 9 fewer years of education and to consume 53 times fewer goods than a person born in Denmark. While the Danes have elected their parliament in free and open elections since 1849, Niger's president dissolved parliament and Supreme Court in 2009—and was then ousted in a military coup. More than 7 of 10 people surveyed in Niger say there were times in the past year when they did not have enough money to buy food for their families. Very few Danes would be in such straits.

CHAPTER 3

Diverse paths to progress

We have seen that many people around the world are healthier, wealthier and more educated than ever before. But progress over the past 40 years has been uneven, with people in some countries and regions experiencing far slower advances, and, in a few places, deteriorations.

The progress has occurred against a backdrop of growing formal democratization but also of increasing inequalities within and across countries in some dimensions of human development. Many people remain politically disempowered, and the sustainability of today's patterns of production and consumption is shaky. These observations—explored in chapter 4—seriously qualify any conclusion of global progress.

Even so, the advances in health, education and income have expanded the freedoms of billions of people to lead lives they have reason to value. This chapter seeks to deepen our understanding of the causes of that progress.

Chapter 2 emphasized two key characteristics of the evolution of human development over the past 40 years. First, progress has been almost universal—only 3 countries in our sample of 135 have a lower Human Development Index (HDI) than in 1970. Second, variability in outcomes across countries has been enormous, with some countries progressing rapidly and others attaining much smaller gains. The concurrence of these two trends rules out some explanations. For example, if countries with similar starting points had progressed at the same rate, this would suggest that common global forces have dominated. Alternatively, if some countries had improved while others deteriorated but average global achievements had not changed, this would suggest that only national forces—such as different policies or institutional reforms—were the key drivers.

Experience thus suggests that global forces have made progress more feasible for countries at all levels of development but that not all countries take advantage of these opportunities in the same way. The obvious question then is why some countries succeed and others fail in grasping global opportunities. This chapter provides some answers to this vital question.

The chapter is also about making sense of one of the most surprising results to come out of human development research in the past few years: the lack of a significant correlation between economic growth and improvements in health and education. Understanding this result is enormously important for development policy.

Our explanation emphasizes the unprecedented increase in the cross-country flow of ideas—ideas ranging from health-saving technologies to democratic political ideals and more efficient production practices. We argue that many innovations have enabled countries to improve health and education outcomes at low cost—explaining the weakening association between growth and the nonincome dimensions of human development. In other words, over time progress has come to depend more on how countries exploited these ideas—with differences among countries traceable, in part, to variations in institutions and in the underlying social contract.

Nothing in our argument implies that growth is unimportant. The human development approach recognizes the contribution of income to greater command over resources and the effect that this has in expanding people's capabilities through nourishment, shelter and broader opportunities. The centrality of income is recognized by including it as one of the three basic dimensions in the HDI, along with health and education.

This chapter analyses the determinants of progress in those three dimensions. Politics, inequality and institutions, among others, join the story insofar as they help explain progress in health, education and income. But we do not attempt to explain why democracy has spread or why production has become progressively unsustainable. These vital questions merit in-depth investigations, to be taken up in future Reports.

Countries became top performers on the HDI through two broad routes, but more often through exceptional progress in health and education than through growth

We start by highlighting some of the most remarkable aspects of human development in the past 40 years, focusing on global progress alongside local variability and on the lack of correlation between improvements in the income and nonincome dimensions of human development. We then examine the key drivers of global trends in each of the three HDI components as well as the country-specific factors determining performance. The chapter culminates in an analysis of how the findings fit into the broader story of interactions between markets and states.

The puzzle of economic growth and human development

Alongside findings of global progress and local variability, chapter 2 identified how achievements in income growth related to progress in other HDI dimensions. We found that average income growth has been high but that it has been variable across countries, while progress has been more consistent for health and education. Many developing countries have attained levels of health and education similar to those in developed countries, but crossing the divide that separates income-poor from income-rich countries is much harder. Therefore, countries became top performers on the HDI through two broad routes: fast income growth or exceptional progress in health and education.

These findings suggest that over the past 40 years the forces driving improvements in health and education are different from those driving improvements in income. Had these processes had the same drivers, the processes would have broadly coincided. But we show that they did not. We now explore in more detail the growth–human development link.

Economic growth and human development do not always coincide

What does the evidence from the past 40 years tell us about the relationship between growth and changes in human development?

Figure 3.1 presents the basic result. The left panel shows a positive association—though with substantial variation—suggesting that growth and improvements in human development are positively associated.[1]

Remember, however, that income is part of the HDI; thus, by construction, a third of the changes in the HDI come from economic growth, guaranteeing a positive association. A more useful exercise is to compare income growth with changes in the nonincome dimensions of human development. We do this using an index similar to the HDI but calculated with only the health and education indicators of the HDI to compare its changes with economic growth. The nonincome HDI is presented in the right panel of figure 3.1. The correlation is remarkably weak and statistically insignificant.[2]

Previous studies have found the same result. One of the first scholars to study this link systematically was US demographer Samuel Preston, whose landmark 1975 article showed that the correlation between changes in income and changes in life expectancy over 30 years for 30 countries was not statistically significant.[3]

As more data became available, other researchers obtained the same result. In a 1999 article, "Life during Growth," William Easterly found a remarkably weak association between growth and quality of life indicators such as health, education, political freedom,

FIGURE **3.1**

Weak relationship between economic growth and changes in health and education

Relationship between economic growth and the HDI and its nonincome components, 1970–2010

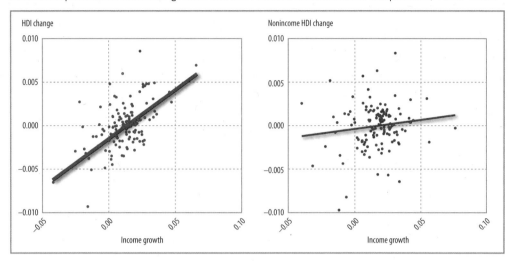

Note: Based on the analysis of deviation from fit (see box 2.1 in chapter 2 and *Technical note 1*). Income is per capita GDP. Thicker regression line indicates relationship is statistically significant.

Source: HDRO calculations using data from the HDRO database.

conflict and inequality.[4] François Bourguignon, director of the Paris School of Economics, and several African and European colleagues concluded that "the correlation between GDP per capita growth and nonincome [Millennium Development Goals] is practically zero."[5] World Bank economist Charles Kenny recently confirmed the lack of correlation between improvements in life expectancy and growth, using both a large sample of countries over 25 years and a smaller sample covering a much longer period.[6]

Many examples illustrate this result. Take a revealing comparison between China—the world's fastest growing economy in the past 30 years—and Tunisia. In 1970 a baby girl born in Tunisia could expect to live 55 years; one born in China, 63 years. Since then, China's per capita GDP has grown at a breakneck pace of 8 percent annually, while Tunisia's has grown at 3 percent. But a girl born today in Tunisia can expect to live 76 years, a year longer than a girl born in China. And while only 52 percent of Tunisian children were enrolled in school in 1970, today's gross enrolment ratio is 78 percent, considerably higher than China's 68 percent.

Other interesting examples come from countries whose economies have contracted over the past 40 years. If economic growth was indispensable for progress in health and education, countries with falling GDP would not be progressing in health and education. But this is not the case: Iran, Togo and Venezuela experienced income declines, yet their life expectancy has risen an average of 14 years and their gross school enrolment an average of 31 percentage points since 1970.[7]

This result is about the lack of relationship between *changes* in income (growth) and *changes* in the nonincome dimensions of human development. It thus does not negate a basic fact, which is that *levels* of income and *levels* of health and education are positively and significantly correlated. We now turn to discuss the ways in which these two facts can be reconciled.

Explaining the puzzle

A puzzle remains. While there is little correlation between income growth and changes in health and education, there is a strong correlation between national levels of income and national levels of health and education. This is also true at the individual and household levels, as scores of studies have found. How do we reconcile this with the finding of no correlation between changes over time?

First, correlation does not imply causation in a specific direction.[8] Even if there is a causal relation, the direction is unknown: higher incomes could improve quality of life, or improvements in health and education could make societies more productive.

Second, the absence of a correlation in changes casts doubt on whether a snapshot of the world at a given moment accurately reflects the relationship between the variables. We can shed some light on the puzzle by observing that over time, the relationship between the income and nonincome dimensions of human development has shifted up (figure 3.2). So while people in richer countries are healthier and more educated on average, people in countries at all levels of income have experienced progress through improving health and education levels. In addition to moving up, these relationships have flattened, meaning that poorer countries have enjoyed faster improvements in health and education than have richer countries.

One explanation of the puzzle could be that there are long and variable lags in translating greater wealth into better health and education outcomes.[9] This would account for the weak correlation, as not enough time may have elapsed for the changes in income to lead to improvements in other dimensions of human development. However, this explanation is much less tenable over longer periods. Figure 3.1 shows that the lack of correlation holds for a large sample of 135 countries over 40 years, a long enough time, surely, for income growth to translate into health and education improvements at the national level and for income deteriorations to be reflected in worsening health and education outcomes.

Another explanation is that the processes through which people became healthier and more educated in countries that are rich today differ from those in developing countries today. The hypothesis of a changing development process suggests that the correlation in levels is a snapshot that reflects a past when countries that became rich were the only ones able to pay for costly advances in health and education. But technological improvements and changes in societal structures, discussed below, make it easier today even for poorer countries to realize substantial gains.

We tested several possible explanations for the changes in health and income over the

There is surprisingly little correlation between income growth and changes in health and education over time

FIGURE **3.2**   **Better health and more education are possible today for all countries**

Changing relationships between income and life expectancy and schooling, 1970–2010

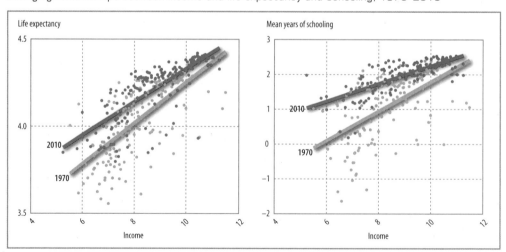

Note: All data are in natural logs.

Source: HDRO calculations using data from the HDRO database.

48   HUMAN DEVELOPMENT REPORT **2010**

past 40 years (box 3.1). The findings suggest that countries with low and medium levels of human development could attain higher levels of health through inexpensive interventions. But as countries attain higher levels of development, improvements rely on costlier technologies, and income starts to matter again. Thus the results are compatible with the hypotheses of changing development opportunities and processes.

What our results mean

These results do not mean that growth is unimportant. Income is a summary indicator capturing access to resources important for developing capabilities and expanding people's freedoms—and should remain an important policy goal. Income increases people's command over the resources necessary to gain access to food, shelter, clothing and broader options in life. Such resources also make it possible to advance people's life plans without being unduly constrained by material necessities—such as working in meaningful and intrinsically rewarding activities or spending more time with loved ones.[10] Income growth can indicate that opportunities for decent work are expanding—though this is not always the case.

Nor do our results negate the importance of higher income for increasing poor people's access to health and education services, a result documented extensively in the microeconomic literature. The strong correlation between socioeconomic status and health within a society often reflects the relative advantage of wealthier people in gaining access to health services. High or rising inequalities can occur alongside a rise in aggregate income, as China's recent experience shows (see box 6.1 in chapter 6).

However, the evidence does cast doubt on whether economywide income growth is instrumental in furthering health and education at low and medium levels of human development. And as we explore below, high rates of growth can coincide with environmental degradation and worsening income distribution, which are grave concerns.

Countries with higher per capita income have longer life expectancy on average. But the positive and significant correlation between income and life expectancy does not hold for changes over the past 40 years. What could be behind this apparent contradiction?

Several explanations have been proposed. The changes over time could be dominated by short-run factors, if health reacts only slowly to changes in income. But the lack of correlation extends over 40 years, which should be long enough to feel the effect of higher income on health. Alternatively, it could be that the positive association between income and life expectancy has broken down, so that the evolution of life expectancy is now independent of that of income. Background research for this Report systematically investigated alternative explanations.

We first conducted two simulations to investigate what type of model could replicate the main features of the data: one in which the conventional relationship holds and one in which it breaks down. The evidence was mixed: the "wealthier is healthier" hypothesis could explain the levels at specific points in time but not the changes. The breakdown hypothesis explained the changes but not the levels.

Next, we considered a different hypothesis: what if "wealthier is healthier" holds only for countries that achieve a sufficiently high level of development, while the breakdown hypothesis holds for less developed countries? This mixed hypothesis, which distinguishes between countries below and above a threshold Human Development Index of around 0.5, explained both the association in levels and the lack of association in changes over time.

Source: Georgiadis, Pineda, and Rodríguez 2010; Pritchett and Summers 1996; Pritchett and Viarengo 2010.

Using a new dataset and analysis, our results also confirm a central contention of the *Human Development Reports* (*HDRs*) from the outset: that human development is different from economic growth and that great achievements are possible even without fast growth. The first *HDR* pointed to countries such as Costa Rica, Cuba and Sri Lanka, which had attained much higher human development than other countries at the same income levels. These achievements were possible because growth had become decoupled from the processes determining progress in other dimensions of human development.

These results also respond to one of the criticisms often levelled at the HDI. From the outset some economists have regarded the nonincome components as redundant, because the snapshot of development that the HDI reveals is not systematically different from that emerging from comparing income levels.[11] But the HDI gives a very different picture from GDP when we look at changes over time—and in the end these are precisely the changes that development policy tries to influence.

The implications for development policy could be far-reaching. Much development policy-making assumes that economic growth is indispensable to achievements in health and education. Our results suggest that this is not the case. This does not mean that countries can forget about growth—we have underlined that growth generates important possibilities. Rather, the results imply that countries do not have to solve the difficult problem of generating growth in order to tackle many problems on the health and education fronts. This is good news.

More fundamentally, because development processes and the possibilities facing poor countries today are so different from those that once faced the now-developed countries, development is not so much about copying the experiences of developed countries as about finding new paths to progress in today's world.

But if growth does not explain progress in health and education, what does? The next two sections tackle these questions, looking first at understanding global progress and then at accounting for national variability.

Global advance: the role of ideas and innovation

A vast literature has examined the determinants of progress in health and education—from a human development perspective and others.[12] Here we provide a brief overview, with a focus on the factors that led to widespread global advances.

Catching up in health

In 1651 English philosopher Thomas Hobbes described life in the state of nature as "poor, nasty, brutish and short."[13] He was describing what the world would look like without governments, but perhaps inadvertently he was also describing life in his time: life expectancy was 40 years in England and as low as 20 years in many other places.[14] But this was starting to change, as people in Western countries improved their health and lifespans in the centuries that followed. Mortality rates fell as communicable diseases among the young, such as smallpox, diphtheria and whooping cough, were brought under control. A decline in respiratory diseases also affecting mainly the young, such as tuberculosis and influenza, followed.[15] Hygiene and other public health practices played a part, as did better nutrition.[16]

These declines occurred much later in developing countries—but progress was much faster. In 1950 life expectancy in Africa, the Arab States and Asia averaged 39 years, roughly the same as in Hobbes's England and 20 years less than in developed countries at the time.[17] Developing countries have increased life expectancy as much in half a century as now-developed countries did in 300 years. The processes were similar in many ways as countries experienced an epidemiological transition—a change in the prevalence of different types of diseases along country development trajectories.

But in some ways the experience of developing countries was very different. Innovations in medicine and interventions in public health flowed more quickly to many developing countries, benefiting millions of people. Improvements in water supply, sewerage and immunizations took many years in the West and were initially very costly. Effective means of prevention were often discovered fairly late. For example, the tuberculosis vaccine was never used routinely in the United States because it was discovered in 1927, after the disease had been all but eradicated.[18] Poor countries benefited from the rapid spread of these improvements when the cost had fallen dramatically: one study found that some 85 percent of mortality reductions in a sample of 68 countries since 1950 could be explained by global progress.[19]

Concerted international action mattered. The UN Expanded Programme on Immunization subsidized large-scale immunization programmes, as did the Pan American Health Organization's Revolving Fund for Vaccine Procurement.[20] Immunization rates soared in countries reached by these programmes, virtually

Much policy-making assumes that economic growth is indispensable to achievements in health and education. Our results suggest that this is not the case

eradicating polio from the Americas in 1994 and boosting immunization rates for the six target diseases (tuberculosis, diphtheria, neonatal tetanus, whooping cough, poliomyelitis and measles) from 5 percent of the world's newborns to more than 80 percent.[21] Eradicating smallpox, a disease that killed some 2 million people annually in the 1960s, cost only $300 million, the price of three fighter jets at the time.[22]

But cooperation and technology are not the only explanations. Education and public awareness also raised demand for health improvements. Information on breastfeeding, hand washing and sugar-salt rehydration solutions can spread without an advanced health system. Recent research covering 278,000 children in 45 developing countries shows that actions by parents, such as providing fluids during episodes of diarrhoea, are the main factor reducing the prevalence of common diseases that kill children.[23]

Some country differences can be traced to the negative shocks of the HIV epidemic and higher mortality rates in the former Soviet Union. But more generally, national health policies played a key role. Greater use of maternal and infant care services—oral rehydration, immunization, breastfeeding and complementary feeding—is associated with lower infant and child mortality.[24] The Brazilian state of Ceará and the Indian state of Kerala have demonstrated the rapid gains possible through extensive public provision of such services. A free press, contested politics and a culture of public debate of social problems all help in pushing through major reforms.[25]

Many interventions in developing countries to reduce mortality and improve health are not costly. A package of six vaccines assembled by the World Health Organization costs less than $1, and deworming (which can increase school attendance) costs just 50 cents a year.[26] That the most efficient health interventions are inexpensive helps explain the lack of correlation between their provision and aggregate health expenditures.[27] It also helps explain why we find little correlation between health improvements and economic growth, particularly in low HDI countries: lack of resources is not always the most important constraint in delivering these services (see box 3.1).[28]

This macro evidence is not inconsistent with individual and household studies by Angus Deaton and others, which show that people with higher socioeconomic status are generally also healthier.[29] This is because drivers of health improvements at the national level can and often do differ from drivers at the individual level. A new vaccine, for example, can benefit everyone in a society simultaneously and therefore not affect the impact of income on health status in that society. The individual relationship reflects the fact that wealthy people are more likely to have access to healthcare than are poor people. Thus wealthy people in a country tend to have longer life expectancy than do poor people, while changes in the average wealth of the country may not cause general improvements in life expectancy.[30]

Why don't all governments deliver low-cost interventions to improve health? Politics is part of the answer. There is growing evidence that health services are better provided when governments are more democratic. A recent study estimated that a transition to democracy reduces infant mortality by 5 deaths per 1,000.[31] Research also finds that democracy predicts longer life expectancy and a lower probability of women dying in childbirth.[32] While the mechanisms at work require further investigation, evidence suggests that accountability is key—and that information availability, popular participation and politician credibility may contribute.[33] But even without fully competitive national elections, local mechanisms that increase access and thus the provision of public goods can operate effectively, as shown by Ethiopia's expansion of clinics and schools over the past decade. And the fact that some democracies—such as the United States—are particularly ineffective in providing public health services suggests that formal democratic institutions are at best necessary but not sufficient.

Education: parents, states or both?

As in health, the story in education is one of rapid progress and convergence between poor

> Poor countries benefited from the rapid spread of innovations in medicine and interventions in public health, when the cost had fallen dramatically

countries and rich countries. Since 1970 the number of students has risen from 550 million to more than 1 billion, and the number of teachers has risen even faster.[34] But there is a striking difference between education and health: no major technological advances can explain the patterns in education. The basic technologies for delivering schooling are no different today from what they were 40 years ago: buildings, blackboards and books are provided to teachers who are paid to convey knowledge to children.

Why, then, have education levels risen? One explanation emphasizes economic changes—such as the shift from agriculture to industrial and service production—that raise the returns to investing in education and thus boost demand. Extensive micro evidence finds that family income and parental education determine most schooling decisions.[35]

Yet the link between education expansion and income growth is weak. Over 1970–2010 the average increase in enrolment was almost the same in countries with negative economic growth as in countries with positive growth.[36] There also appears to be little relationship between returns to schooling and the expansion of school enrolment, arguing against explanations limited to demand.[37]

Ample historical and contemporary evidence points to a range of motivations, including but not limited to popular pressure, for states and political actors to expand education provision. States have massively expanded education when consolidating political power, reducing the influence of competing institutions and forging a national identity. Examples of politically driven expansions of education abound, ranging from Prussia's national education system under King Frederick II to Turkey's massive secularization of schooling in the 1920s.[38] The objective of promoting a national ideology through state-run schools may also explain why governments provide education directly rather than subsidize families to allow children to attend private schools and why they enforce compulsory education laws.

But it is not always easy to identify political drivers. Independence has been singled out as a potent force, particularly in Africa and Asia. But it is at best a partial explanation:

Democratization may have the strongest effects on primary education; decentralization can have stronger effects on higher levels of schooling

most Latin American countries gained independence in the early 19th century, but they did not expand education on a wide scale until well into the 20th century. International pressure may have had a role, particularly after the 1948 Universal Declaration of Human Rights, but the growth of a global consensus for universal education likely reflected deeper political processes at home.[39]

Political economy factors are clearly important. Government actions reflect people's preferences. Indonesia's Sekolah Dasar INPRES programme, which massively expanded schooling in the 1970s, was part of the Suharto regime's attempt to bolster its legitimacy after wresting power from a communist-backed government.[40]

Expansion of education has often accompanied expansion of the voting franchise and the growth of redistributive taxes and transfers. Democratization appears to drive numerous indicators of education: the educational attainment of adults—though this changes slowly—as well as enrolment, literacy and public education spending, which are more immediately amenable to institutional change.[41] While democratization may have the strongest effects on primary education, decentralization can have stronger effects on higher levels of schooling (see box 3.2 on decentralization and human development).[42] Nondemocratic states can also expand schooling—the Soviet Union in the 1920s and Peru under Velasco Alvarado are among many examples—but this often occurs as part of broad-ranging redistributive strategies.[43] Not all nondemocratic states are created equal: some seize power to avoid the expropriation of elites—others, to carry it out.

Differences and commonalities in advances in health and education

In health the key drivers of improvements were innovation and technology; in education these were at best minor factors. But the two stories reflect similar underlying processes. In both, the transmission of ideas across countries enabled improvements. Broadly understood, ideas encompass technologies and productive

Is decentralization good for human development?

Decentralization of responsibility for government services provision has gone hand in hand with other efforts to make local governments more responsive. Notable examples include participatory budgeting initiatives, which originated in Porto Alegre, Brazil, and numerous monitoring initiatives, such as social audits and community score cards. One such initiative collects data on achieving the Millennium Development Goals at the local level in 16 countries in East Asia, South Asia and Sub-Saharan Africa and uses the data to pressure local governments to meet the identified needs. There has been a surge of interest in nongovernmental organizations (NGOs) providing information to the public to improve services. The Tanzanian NGO Twaweza provides information through mass media, mobile phones, religious groups and consumer goods throughout East Africa to empower people to hold their government accountable and to bring about change in their communities.

Not all decentralization is effective or transformative. The impact on human development depends on the local social and political context and on country conditions, especially institutions and management capacity, and on the causes and patterns of inequality and poverty. Some evidence suggests remarkably positive effects: following reforms in 1994 in Bolivia, decentralization shifted public investment strongly in favour of education, water, sanitation and other community-identified needs. But in Sub-Saharan Africa the devolution of funds to local communities has often reinforced inequality.

A recent study of seven developing countries found unequivocal improvements in health and education but also increased inequality. More generally, because some empowerment is a precondition for grass-roots development schemes, communities that lack the capacity to identify and act on their needs may remain disempowered, which means that a vicious cycle can persist. Political decentralization, on the whole, seems to benefit the poor, while fiscal decentralization has more muted effects. Fiscal decentralization requires appropriate mechanisms to ensure reporting and transparency, as well as resources. Effective decentralization also requires transferring power and responsibility rather than simply implementing policy formulated at higher levels. In Armenia the central government transferred school management to local councils in the early 2000s, but management remained highly centralized, and many people were unaware of the reform. Compounding the problems were fiscal shortcomings: money was transferred to the councils without adequate controls or reporting.

Source: Abraham and Platteau (2004), cited in Walton (2010): 29; Andrews 2008: 395; UNDP Armenia 2007; Faguet 2002; Mansuri and Rao 2010; Thede 2009; Twaweza 2010; Von Braun and Grote 2000: 25.

practices as well as political ideals and principles about a society's organization. While in health the major influence was the transmission of technological innovations such as vaccinations and public health practices, in education it was ideals about what societies—and governments—should do and about what goals parents aspire to for their children.

Large expansions in health and education became feasible even for developing countries. In health once-costly innovations became available at low cost. In education even poor countries could afford to expand the key inputs, teachers and buildings, since neither has to be imported from abroad. This contrasts with setting up a manufacturing plant, which requires access to foreign exchange, a limited resource in many poor countries, to import machinery.

None of this detracts from the importance of capacity or foreign assistance. As discussed below, the substantial differences in rates of progress across countries can be traced to multiple factors, including the organization of the state, the quality of public service provision and the extent of development assistance. Easing financial constraints through aid frees up resources for social expenditures, still abysmally low in most developing countries.

People's aspirations and expectations of government make a difference. Rising demand for quality services has been important in both health and education, especially in democratic transitions. But the growth in demand often reflects broader social processes that are affected by the spread of ideas, such as changes in attitudes towards personal hygiene.

The role of institutions, policies and equity

The spread of ideas and the relatively low costs of delivering basic services explain widespread advances in health and education. So why are there still such large differences across countries? And why have so many countries with similar starting points traversed such different development paths? Many answers are country specific—we explore both successful and unsuccessful cases in box 3.3 and box 3.6 later in the chapter—but there are also some general patterns.

Countries with the fastest progress can be split broadly into two groups—those that did well in economic growth and those that did well in human development. Few countries did well in both (among the top 10 movers, Indonesia and South Korea were the only countries to make it into the top 10 in both the income and nonincome dimensions of the HDI; see table 2.2 in chapter 2). So, there are different pathways to development, some emphasizing the expansion of material living standards, and others, health and education.

Different country trajectories

Some development strategies have concentrated on expanding wealth, seeing possible adverse consequences for other aspects of human development as necessary "social costs." But more inclusive development strategies have greatly improved material conditions without neglecting other dimensions.

Country trajectories can be characterized in a typology of success and failure in human development with four groups: countries with high growth and high human development ("virtuous" development processes), those with neither high growth nor high human development ("vicious" processes), and those

---

BOX 3.3 **Three success stories in advancing the Human Development Index**

Some countries have succeeded in achieving high human development following different pathways.

Nepal—major public policy push. That Nepal is one of the fastest movers in the Human Development Index (HDI) since 1970 is perhaps surprising in light of the country's difficult circumstances and record of conflict. Nepal's impressive progress in health and education can be traced to major public policy efforts. Free primary education for all children was legislated in 1971 and extended to secondary education in 2007. Gross enrolment rates soared, as did literacy later on. Remarkable reductions in infant mortality reflect more general successes in health following the extension of primary healthcare through community participation, local mobilization of resources and decentralization. The gap between Nepal's life expectancy and the world average has narrowed by 87 percent over the past 40 years. By contrast, economic growth was modest, and the lack of jobs led many Nepalese to seek opportunities abroad.

Nepal is still a poor country, with enormous scope to improve human development. It ranks 138th of 169 countries in the HDI. Large disparities in school attendance and the quality of education persist, particularly between urban and rural areas and across ethnic groups. Major health challenges remain, related to communicable diseases and malnutrition. Large disparities separate regions and groups, with a quasi-feudal oligarchic system and caste-based discrimination continuing to marginalize some groups. Inequality is high: according to our new Inequality-adjusted HDI, Nepal's human development is almost a third lower than it would be were it more equally distributed (see chapter 5).

Oman—converting oil to health and education. Oman has had the fastest progress in the HDI. Abundant oil and gas were discovered in the late 1960s, so our data capture the evolution from a very poor to a very rich country, showing a quadrupling of gross enrolment and literacy rates and a 27-year increase in life expectancy.

But even in Oman economic growth is not the whole story. Although first in HDI progress, it ranks 26th in economic growth since 1970, when it had three primary schools and one vocational institute. Its initiatives to convert oil wealth into education included expanding access and adopting policies to match skills to labour market needs. Health services also improved: from 1970 to 2000 government spending on health rose almost sixfold—much faster than GDP.

Tunisia—education a policy focus. Tunisia's success extends to all three dimensions of the HDI, with education a major policy focus. School enrolment has risen substantially, particularly after the country legislated 10 years of compulsory education in 1991. There has also been some progress in gender equity: about 6 of 10 university students are women. But large inequalities persist, as Tunisia's modest (56th of 138 countries) ranking on our new Gender Inequality Index demonstrates. Rapid decline in fertility and high vaccination rates for measles and tuberculosis have yielded successes in health, as has eradication of polio, cholera, diphtheria and malaria. Annual per capita income growth has been around 3 percent over the past 40 years, linked to fiscal and monetary prudence and investment in transport and communication infrastructure.

Political freedom lags. Progress in these countries has lagged on one critical dimension of human development: political freedom. During most of the period discussed here, Nepal was ruled by a monarchy. A decade of civil war and profound political transformations culminated in a peace agreement and interim constitution. Abolition of the monarchy in 2008, establishment of a federal democratic system and subsequent elections have opened new opportunities for participation. Oman remains a sultanate, with a nonelected executive, a nonpartisan legislature and a ban on all political parties. Tunisia, despite its formal multiparty system, has yet to see a peaceful transfer of power.

Source: Oman Ministry of National Economy 2003; UNDP Nepal 2002, 2004, 2009; PNUD Tunisie 2001.

---

successful in pursuing one objective but not both. This characterization echoes Jean Drèze and Amartya Sen's distinction among "growth-mediated security" (growth with broad-based social provisioning), "support-led security" (where direct social action took precedence over growth) and "unaimed opulence" (where growth was the priority).[44]

Most virtuous development processes involve managing distributive conflict; building adequate state and business capacity, with the state having sufficient countervailing power to limit abuse of market power by powerful capitalist groups and resolving sociopolitical contests in favour of broad-based provisioning.[45] Countries on this path include most of the East Asian successes and the more stable Latin American countries such as Brazil. The vicious processes group includes some countries in Sub-Saharan Africa, such as Côte d'Ivoire, and some countries with higher initial human development, such as the Russian Federation.

Countries that succeeded in promoting health and education but not in generating growth displayed a range of patterns. In some, major distributive conflicts eventually led to a democratic transition with associated pushes towards social provisioning. This group includes poorer Latin American economies such as Bolivia and El Salvador. Nondemocratic states, such as Iran and Libya, have also delivered services to middle and lower socioeconomic groups.

Correlates and causes of progress

Which countries succeeded—and which failed—in promoting human development? Background research for this Report on the frequency of underperformance in HDI trends (countries whose progress on the HDI is significantly below that predicted by their initial stage of development) found some interesting regional patterns. Underperformance was highest in Europe and Central Asia, with deterioration on several fronts in the first decade of transition. By 2000 more than two-thirds of countries were doing significantly worse than would be expected given their starting point. Even in 2006–2010 more than half the countries in the region have been underperforming—as have more than 4 in 10 countries in Sub-Saharan Africa, 1 in 3 in East Asia and the Pacific, 1 in 4 in the Arab States and 1 in 7 in Latin America and the Caribbean. No South Asian country was underperforming in these terms in 2010.

The underperforming countries had similar initial levels of human development. They diverge from the better performers because of their slower rate of change (table 3.1). On average, they spend less on health and education and tend to be less democratic. They have high HIV prevalence rates—a result related to the high incidence of underperformance in Southern Africa (see chapter 2). Possibly contrary to expectations, poor performers are on average less endowed than other countries with natural resources, suggesting that the "resource curse" may not apply to human development, a result confirmed by more systematic research.[46] Underperforming countries have a higher incidence of civil war, although this difference is not statistically significant, likely because of the heterogeneity of civil war experiences (box 3.4).[47]

We also find that underperfoming countries receive more aid on average, a result that may appear puzzling but likely reflects the fact that aid is directed towards lagging countries. This and the other results in table 3.1 reflect the average characteristics of countries and do not necessarily imply causality, which is very difficult to establish.[48]

Dramatic successes or failures—outliers—also provide insights into divergent trajectories. Background research for this Report looked at the main characteristics of the best and worst performers.[49] It found few universally applicable results but some interesting patterns that suggest complex interactions for income inequality, social expenditures and initial development. For example, countries with high average income succeeded despite an unequal income distribution when social expenditures were good or moderate. Examples include Chile, Mexico and Panama.[50] But some

TABLE 3.1

TABLE 3.1 Many factors are associated with underperformance

Correlates of underperformance, average period conditions, 1970–2010

Characteristic	Country groups		
	Underperformers[a]	Others	Difference
Human Development Index value, 1970	0.54	0.53	0.01
Public health spending (% of GDP)	3.0	3.6	−0.6*
Public education spending (% of total budget)	9.7	12.3	−2.6*
Democracies with alternation[b]	0.4	0.5	−0.1*
HIV prevalence rate	2.9	1.3	1.6*
Value of natural resources exports (US$ per worker)	0.9	1.8	−0.9*
Civil war (% of countries)	28	18	10
Aid received (% of GNI)	7.3	5.0	2.3*
Total public spending (% of GDP)	23.3	25.1	−1.8
Number of countries	46	89	

* The difference is statistically significant at the 5 percent level.

a. Countries whose HDI value is significantly lower than would be expected from historical trends for countries with similar starting points. See Gidwitz and others (2010) for details.

b. Democracies that have alternated power following an electoral loss (see chapter 4).

Source: HDRO calculations using data from the HDRO database, World Bank (2010g), UN Statistics Division (2010), UCDP and PRIO (2009), and Cheibub, Gandhi, and Vreeland (2009).

BOX 3.4 Conflict and human development

Conflict has devastating repercussions for many people, though countrywide effects vary. Some countries, like Colombia, have lived through prolonged conflicts while still achieving good progress in human development—although less than they would likely have achieved otherwise.

The impact of conflict depends on its nature, intensity and duration. Several countries that performed poorly relative to their starting points have been affected by conflict—including the Democratic Republic of the Congo and Côte d'Ivoire. The impacts are felt by individuals, families, communities and countries: higher mortality, productive resources diverted to destruction, losses of economic infrastructure and social capital, and insecurity and uncertainty.

In some countries economic decline is most readily associated with armed conflict, though the causality is difficult to establish. The intensity of conflict varies enormously across countries, ranging from the Basque region of Spain to Burundi, Liberia and Sierra Leone. Paul Collier and Anke Hoeffler estimated that it takes an average of 21 years to reach the GDP that would have prevailed without conflict. The people of Sierra Leone suffered a halving of incomes over the 11-year conflict, while in Liberia the estimated decline was 80 percent. The mechanisms include high inflation, capital flight, a loss of trust in institutions and reduced international trade.

These effects can persist even after hostilities end. Economic disruptions and slowdowns cause people to lose their livelihoods, increasing already high unemployment. In Bosnia and Herzegovina 18 months after the Dayton Peace Agreement unemployment was 65–75 percent.

Source: Collier and Hoeffler 2007; Davies 2007; Fallon and others 2004; Imai and Weinstein 2000; McLeod and Dávalos 2008; Oxfam International 2007; Staines 2004; UNDP 2008; UNHCR 1997.

low-income countries seemed to overcome adverse conditions through economic growth, even if social spending was not high, as in Bangladesh and Lao PDR. Among middle-income countries, both routes seemed feasible: Tunisia improved its HDI despite moderate income growth, while Indonesia relied primarily on growth and less on social spending.

It is much easier to identify the correlates of successful or unsuccessful development experiences than to establish causality. This problem has plagued the empirical analysis of economic growth based on cross-country regressions. This literature has been harshly criticized for, among other things, coming to such an array of conclusions.[51] Recent work reviving an earlier tradition of case study approaches underlines the heterogeneity in growth experiences, suggesting that the effects of policies and institutions vary systematically for countries according to their historical, political and structural conditions.[52] This work builds on advances in macro- and microeconomic analysis for understanding an economy's growth and combines the strengths of quantitative analysis with the nuanced explanations of the older case study tradition (box 3.5).[53]

Cross-country statistical analysis can be taken too far, but it can also reveal useful insights. In background research for this Report we analyzed the determinants of human development using a sample of 111 countries over 40 years.[54] We dealt with the empirical problems of quantitative cross-country analysis by distinguishing between long-run and short-run effects and considering the country-specific dynamics of human development and the influence of key preconditions—including institutional development, religion, political development, gender inequality and income inequality. By allowing the effects of policies to differ according to country preconditions, this framework frees the analysis from the constraints of the one size fits all approach of many previous studies.

Three key findings emerged. First, the determinants of economic growth are not necessarily the same as those of human development—variables such as trade, foreign investment and institutions tend to have different effects on

| BOX 3.5 | Insights from analytic growth studies |

A new approach to studying economic growth relies on evidence for individual countries, systematically combining microeconomic data, macroeconomic time series analysis and investigations of political economy dynamics. These growth narratives have started to yield useful insights. Consider three examples.

Botswana—strong institutions and strong growth. Botswana had the third highest growth rate in gross national income per capita over the past 30 years worldwide, behind only China and South Korea. Abundant diamond resources financed investment in infrastructure, health and education. But many countries have had abundant natural resources and done poorly. Botswana's success appears to have benefited from strong institutions. Although the size of government—at 40 percent of GDP—is high even for Africa, patronage and graft are relatively low, and spending on education and health has been high since independence. These beneficial policies were aided by high levels of public participation and constraints on political leaders, which stemmed from tribal institutions that had not been eroded during British colonization and subsequent independence. An example is the reforms adopted in the early 1990s in response to incidents of corruption, which included the creation of an independent ombuds office.

Mauritius—export success. Trade was important in Mauritius's success, but not in the conventional way. Mauritius was a highly protectionist country—the International Monetary Fund classified its trade policies in the most restrictive category in the 1990s. Yet the country achieved high export growth relying on export processing zones with duty-free access to imported inputs, tax incentives that subsidized exports, and a labour market that segmented exports from the rest of the economy. Unlike many other governments, Mauritius did not tax agriculture excessively. Instead, it reached a compromise with sugar owners that generated enough revenue to finance a well trained civil service and a generous system of social protection. The social consensus allowed the government to adjust to changing conditions.

Venezuela—lack of economic diversification. Towards the end of the 1970s Venezuela's economy experienced a stunning reversal, with non-oil output per worker falling 36 percent. Weak institutions, inefficient governments and the "resource curse" have all been invoked, but they do not explain how Venezuela managed to achieve the fastest growth in Latin America before 1970 with broadly similar institutions and policies. One explanation is that Venezuela's pattern of specialization was especially sensitive to negative shocks such as the decline in oil prices of the early 1980s, because the skills needed to produce oil are not easily transferable to other industries. Countries with low export flexibility— little capacity to shift to other activities when demand drops—can perform reasonably well under stable export prices but can go into a tailspin when export and fiscal revenues collapse and standard reforms prove ineffective in generating alternative sources of growth.

Source: Hausmann and Rodríguez forthcoming; Subramanian and Devesh 2003; Frankel 2010; Leith 2005; Acemoglu, Johnson, and Robinson 2003; Adamolekun, Lusignan, and Atomate 1997.

economic growth than on human development more broadly. Second, the effect of these determinants differs significantly depending on a country's structural and institutional preconditions. Third, there are multiple feedback loops among the components of the HDI that influence the effectiveness of policies.

Urbanization emerged as a key positive influence on changes in education and income, confirming an established finding on the vital role of cities in transmitting ideas and mobilizing political action. Trade had no significant effect on income but a positive correlation with some health and education indicators, supporting the hypothesis that transmitting knowledge and ideas affects the nonincome dimensions of human development. Institutional variables, such as the constraints on executive power, had positive effects on education and income but not on health.[55]

Policies to improve gender equity can also affect human development. Because women have poorer health and lower educational attainment than men, policies to redress such disparity would contribute to human development. A study commissioned for this Report found that introducing gender quotas for the lower house of provincial legislatures during the 1990s significantly lowered infant mortality rates in Argentinean provinces.[56] And numerous studies link gender equity to economic growth. Closing the gender gap in schooling has also been linked to higher growth.[57]

A large body of evidence suggests that women have a higher marginal propensity to invest in their children than do men, so policies to empower women should improve health and education outcomes for children. One recent study drawing on rich data collected over 35 years in Guatemala finds that a mother's educational attainment, cognitive skills and nutritional status have large impacts on children's human capital and nutrition.[58] In South Africa grandmothers who received a pension had better nourished granddaughters, while pensions given to men did not affect their grandchildren's nutrition.[59] And in China mother's schooling had an important effect on child health for natural born and adopted children.[60]

Our research also found that a country's preconditions affected which policies were conducive to human development. For example, in a regime with strong institutions (measured using a composite index of corruption, rule of law, quality of bureaucracy, investment profile and internal conflict), higher government spending on wages and goods and services was conducive to faster progress in the HDI. But at low levels of institutional development, higher public capital investment was associated with less long-run progress in the HDI.[61]

The analysis confirmed some expected relationships among dimensions of human development. Progress in literacy, for example, improved progress in life expectancy and income, while progress in health predicted future progress in gross enrolment. But economic growth was not positively associated with future progress in the nonincome

dimensions of human development.[62] These results confirm that the lack of correlation between changes in income and in nonincome dimensions of human development is robust to the use of a more complex modelling framework that controls for causality and other intervening factors. One topic that requires further analysis is the costs of instability and shocks to human development (box 3.6).

Progress through equity

There is a strong negative relationship between inequality and human development. Inequality in health, education and income is negatively related to the HDI, with the relationship much stronger for education and income (figure 3.3). This result suggests that reducing inequality can significantly improve human development.

These strong relationships are not difficult to understand. Progress in health and education commonly comes from increasing access to services for disadvantaged groups. In almost any society today the children of elites finish school and have access to care that allows them to grow up healthy. This is not the case for the poor. But as access to health and education is broadened to include them, human development improves and inequalities level out.

What do we know about the policies that can reduce inequality? Fiscal policy can be a vital lever for greater equity, with spending much more powerful than taxation. Public spending on services and social protection improves income distribution—and among publicly provided services, healthcare and primary and secondary education have the biggest impacts.

A recurring theme in the *HDRs* since 1990 is the need for public resources, both domestic and international, to support human development. Yet governments are often constrained by politics, influential groups and low state capacity in taxing income and wealth and allocating spending.

Countries need to generate income and grow, and governments need to raise revenues before spending them. Developing countries, while limited by a small tax base, have

---

BOX 3.6 **Patterns of unsteady ascent**

Development is neither linear nor stable. Progress that comes through technological innovations is intermittent, with periods of acceleration and deceleration. The spread of ideas and technologies across countries is a key explanation for progress in economic growth and in health and education, as shown in this chapter. Scholars such as Samuel Huntington have argued that democratization occurs in waves, with many countries undergoing similar changes in political institutions.

Downward volatility is costly. Collapses in economic growth are common, particularly in developing countries. A recent study found that more than a quarter of recessions in developing countries involved per capita income losses exceeding 15 percent, many lasting more than a decade. While collapses are less frequent in life expectancy or education than in growth, they do occur: 27 countries suffered declines of more than 15 percent in gross enrolment rate, and 7 faced similar collapses in life expectancy during the past 40 years.

Even in societies not experiencing collapses, insecurity affects millions of people. Insecurity can be economic or personal—as explored in box 3.4 on conflict. But people's exposure to insecurity depends on policies and institutions. For example, policies to promote youth employment can reduce social tensions and the likelihood of conflict by improving job opportunities for young people.

The most disappointing performers were all hit by shocks for which they were unprepared, while the best performers emphasized investments in people. But while success can lead to greater democratization, as in Nepal, this has not been a universal trend. And even economies that are not mismanaged, such as Zambia, can suffer "perfect storms" of shocks on several fronts.

Source: Helpman 1998; Huntington 1991; Hausmann, Rodríguez, and Wagner 2008; UNDESA 2004.

FIGURE **3.3**   **More human development is associated with less inequality**

Relationship between inequality in health, education and income and HDI levels, 2010

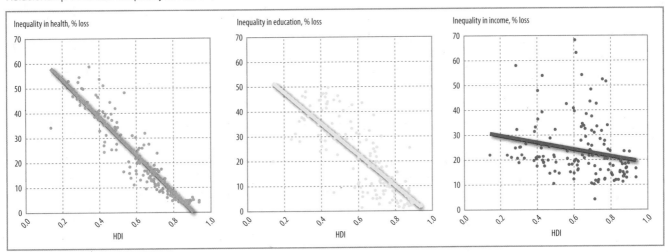

Note: The percentage loss associated with inequality in each dimension is defined in chapter 5. See *Technical note 2* for details on measuring multidimensional inequality.

Source: HDRO calculations using data from the HDRO database.

considerable scope to increase their tax efforts. Income taxes, fairly progressive in their incidence, account for only a minor share of government revenue. A recent study of Central American countries, for example, found that income taxes were generally progressive but accounted for only a quarter of the tax intake; regressive taxes—such as sales, excise and value added taxes—dominated. There are also severe political economy constraints on the rates and coverage of personal income and corporate taxation—and on implementation—especially where economic elites dominate policymaking. Nonetheless, reform is possible, as shown by the recent tax reforms undertaken by Cameroon and Nicaragua.

What about spending patterns? Since 1990 there has been considerable contraction in the size of the state around the world: the average share of public spending in GDP shrank from 29 percent to 26 percent for the 92 countries with data for 1990–2008. Among developing countries, the levels vary by region, but the trend is downward. The largest contraction was in Sub-Saharan Africa, where public spending as a share of GDP fell from 26 percent to 21 percent. East Asia and the Pacific's average remained at 19 percent. A welcome trend in all regions has been the large decline in military spending as a share of GDP—in Sub-Saharan Africa, for example, military spending shrank by about a third, from 2.8 percent to 1.8 percent of GDP.

Health and education spending in developing countries increased as a share of GDP by an average of 16 percent and 19 percent over 1990–2006. South Asia and Sub-Saharan Africa had the biggest increases in health spending, associated with debt relief in several countries.[63] But 57 of 104 developing countries saw declines in either health or education spending as a share of national income from 1990 to 2005.

The differences in how countries mobilize and use public resources to pursue human development are remarkable. Thailand, despite low revenues, introduced health insurance for the poor, while Senegal pushed through comprehensive tax reforms to increase revenues.[64] In Venezuela, by contrast, higher oil revenues led to lower domestic tax rates and no increase in spending on human development priorities.[65] Among many developed countries, public cash transfers through pensions, housing and family cash benefits, and disability and unemployment benefits supplement household income. The cash benefits are typically greatest for retirees and smaller for households with working-age heads.[66]

Spending on basic social services has well known progressive impacts. Costa Rica and El Salvador both direct more than 25 percent of public spending on health to the poorest fifth of the population and more than 70 percent to the bottom three-fifths.[67] In South Africa social spending and taxation have been associated with reduced inequality—with an estimated 10–20 point drop in the Gini coefficient of income inequality in the early 1990s.[68] In the European Union highly progressive social spending has a much larger distributional impact than do taxes.[69]

But redistributive taxation and widespread transfers are not the only ways to tackle inequality and income poverty. Some Latin American countries and more recently other countries as diverse as Nigeria, Pakistan and Turkey have introduced targeted micro-based interventions, such as conditional cash transfers (box 3.7).[70] Unconditional programmes of social assistance have also gained popularity. While helpful, more structural reforms may be needed when communities and groups are systematically excluded from power and decision-making.

The processes for budget allocation and monitoring are also key. There have been major improvements in fiscal transparency—giving people a better idea about what money the government is collecting and how it is being spent and, in several countries, more opportunities to engage in the process. Efforts have also been made to address underlying disparities—looking at allocations by region and gender.[71]

The confirmation of positive synergies between equity-promoting policies and human development is good news.[72] We know the types of policies needed to increase equity—reorienting spending priorities, lowering barriers to entry and ensuring that the rich carry their share of the tax burden. How to achieve this will vary by setting—raising tax rates, for example, can be self-defeating in countries with a large informal economy. But the basic principle that policies to reduce inequalities also work to enhance human development can guide policy formulation in very different settings.

BOX 3.7

Cash transfers and social protection

Cash transfers to poor households are well established in many developed countries, to provide income maintenance following adverse shocks—such as unemployment, disability or sickness—or to redistribute income. Their importance varies across Organisation for Economic Co-operation and Development (OECD) countries. For example, in the mid-2000s New Zealand's cash transfers accounted for around 13 percent of household disposable income and Sweden's more than 32 percent. A recent OECD review underlined the effects of such redistributive efforts on income inequality.

Conditional cash transfers to assist poor families have also become popular since emerging in Brazil and Mexico in the late 1990s. Cash payments are made to poor households that meet behavioural requirements, generally related to household investments in child schooling and health. Today, more than 30 countries have some kind of conditional cash transfer programme, many national in coverage.

Such programmes cannot succeed on their own, however. The benefits depend on the availability and quality of services. Higher service use alone may not translate into better outcomes, as demonstrated in Cambodia and Mexico, where higher school enrolment rates were not matched by better performance on tests. The programmes can also be administratively demanding—targeting households and monitoring compliance are data intensive and require extensive coordination across agencies and levels of government.

Mexico's Progresa programme (now called Oportunidades) relies on central capacities to select beneficiaries and manage finances, while the local health and education ministries monitor compliance. External evaluation helped prevent the programme's becoming too closely associated with one political party. When the ruling party lost the election in 2000 after 70 years in power, the incoming government took over the programme, renaming and expanding it.

Governments and international communities are also increasingly recognizing the value of unconditional cash transfers for providing access to food and other basic necessities. In Africa there is evidence that unconditional transfers may be more appropriate because of inadequate supplies of basic services and more limited capacity to implement and enforce conditions on transfers. Participants in the Mchinji Social Cash Transfer Pilot, part of a wider Malawi Growth and Development Strategy in 2006, had documented gains in school enrolment; better protection against economic, demographic and seasonal shocks; improved basic nutrition; and higher expenditures on basic necessities.

Source: Miller 2008; OECD 2008b; Fiszbein and others 2009; World Bank 2009b, 2010g; López-Calva and Lustig 2010.

The deeper story: markets, states and the social contract

Markets exhibit enormous diversity. There is no single type of market system just as there is no single type of state. The interactions of individuals, firms and institutions of the state can be organized in different ways. The foundational understandings for these arrangements—the mechanisms of accountability and enforcement that they embody and the norms and expectations to which they give rise—can be viewed as a social contract. State institutions generally provide some goods and services and shape the framework for markets to operate along the lines of the social contract and its associated norms and practices.[73]

What is most remarkable about successful development experiences is their heterogeneity. France, Germany, Japan and the United States all generate abundant goods and services enabling material prosperity for their people. And they have among the highest levels of health, education and political freedoms in the world today. But how the state interacts with the private sector in these countries differs considerably. Take the financial sector. German banks often own and operate firms, Japanese firms tend to own banks and US firms were prohibited from uniting with banks until 1999.[74] Or consider education. In France the national government manages education centrally, in Germany state governments take the lead and in the United States local governments control schooling decisions.

Differences are even more marked in the institutional structures that govern markets. In Chile competitive elections determine transfers of power, the state has little involvement in the production of goods (except copper) and the market determines the allocation of pension investments and schooling. Under one-party rule, China's state owns a large part of the economy, including almost all the banking sector; denies access of its migrant population to basic services; and limits the formation of independent unions. In Thailand there is continuing political instability and some involvement

of the military in political affairs, while economic, financial and political power are concentrated in a small business elite.[75]

The variance in institutions is even larger for some countries that have been most successful in furthering health and education. Tunisia has had the same president for the past 23 years, while Nepal just abolished its monarchy after protracted political conflict. Indonesia and Oman made much of their progress in health and education under authoritarian rule. In Bangladesh, despite several governance setbacks since independence in the early 1970s, an extensive set of enterprising actors outside government (BRAC and Grameen Bank stand out) extended credit to millions of poor people and supported the provision of key services.[76] This is just one example of how innovative practices can reshape the relationship between the private and public sectors in the development process (box 3.8).

Clearly, an amazing variety of institutions are compatible with human progress. We can try to understand how they organize relationships between markets and states. Markets—understood as a form of organizing production that involves extensive private ownership—may be an indispensable component of any economic system capable of supporting the sustained dynamism necessary for transformative changes in most dimensions of human development. But markets do not bring progress in other dimensions of human development, and the evidence suggests that markets are necessary but certainly not enough.

These observations hark back to Karl Polanyi's exposition more than 60 years ago of the myth of the self-regulating market—the idea that market relationships can exist in a political and institutional vacuum. Markets can be very bad at providing public goods, such as security, stability, health and education. For example, firms focused on producing cheap labour-intensive goods or exploiting natural resources may not want a more educated workforce. And if there is an abundant pool of

> An amazing variety of institutions are compatible with human progress

The private sector is pivotal for human development. A new conceptual framework on the role of the private sector in development has emerged recently among development institutions that recognizes the role of markets in extending choices and opportunities to poor people and households as producers, consumers and wage earners. Described variously as inclusive market development, pro-poor private sector development and making markets work for the poor, its central precept is inclusiveness.

While the individual incomes of poor people are low, their aggregate buying power is large. The average per capita income of villagers in rural Bangladesh, for instance, is less than $200 a year, but as a group they are huge consumers of telecommunication services. Across the globe—in Bangladesh, India, Kenya and the Philippines—cellular phone services have become more accessible to poor people as competition and technological advances have brought down prices. Access to phone services enhances poor people's lives, enabling them to communicate over long distances and assisting them in their work. Cellular phones have also given many poor people access to basic financial services. For example, M-PESA, a cell phone service offered by Safaricom, gives Kenyans a fast, safe and affordable way to deposit and transfer money anywhere in the country and now provides service to about 25 percent of the population.

The private sector often provides services to poor people in areas the government fails to reach, as in water and telecommunication services. Where public schools are inadequate, many families, even poor families, have turned to private schools. In Lahore, Pakistan, for example, 37 percent of children in the lowest income group attend private schools. Credit is another example. Bangladesh's Grameen Bank model of microfinance has been replicated around the world.

Public-private partnerships are also growing, as in the GAVI Alliance, a global public-private health partnership that has expanded vaccination coverage across 72 developing countries. Social insurance is another example of public-private partnerships helping fill a void in public provision of services. In Colombia the Family Compensation Fund of Antioquia (COMFAMA), a nonprofit social enterprise, provides health, education, housing, credit, job training and other social services to vulnerable middle- and lower middle-class families in cooperation with international organizations.

Source: Alderman, Orazem, and Paterno 2001; Prahalad 2004; Nelson and Prescott 2008.

---

labour to draw on, firms may care little about worker health. We see this today in lax occupational safety standards in many developing countries. A shift from the institutions of reciprocity that hold sway in traditional societies to market relations can weaken the human and social ties that bind communities.[77]

Furthermore, without complementary societal and state action, markets are particularly weak in environmental protection. Poorly regulated markets can create the conditions for environmental degradation, even disaster. A recent example is the oil leak in the Gulf of Mexico in 2010. Such leaks are common: over the past decade there was an average of three or four large oil spills a year, spewing more than 1.5 million barrels of oil.[78] And recorded spills account for only about a tenth of petroleum waste that ends up in the ocean each year.[79] In the Niger Delta endemic oil spills, waste dumping and gas flaring have destroyed ecologically sensitive wetlands, clogged waterways, killed wildlife and damaged the soil and air quality over the past 50 years—ruining the lives of people in the region.[80]

Another example comes from Indonesia, where a massive mud flow that followed an explosion in a natural gas exploration site in 2006 engulfed thousands of hectares of land, affecting dozens of villages. An independent investigation concluded that the mud eruption was due to drilling, but the company denied responsibility and refused to adequately compensate the people affected.[81] The mud flow is expected to continue for 30 years.

Every society needs to define basic rules for relations among businesses, workers, communities and the state, ensuring basic property rights and upholding the rule of law—and determining whose property is protected and what laws rule. Societies need institutions to manage conflicts between groups and individuals and to resolve disputes in an orderly way. Many types of institutions can support equitable and sustainable human development—and many others can fail to do so.

Market structures, especially when dominated by a political-economic elite or when open and participatory, help explain whether markets are inclusive. Oligarchic markets—embedded in state institutions—are often bad for growth in the long run, even if they extract rents for the influential in the short run. Inclusive markets and social contracts that set human development as a priority are more dynamic and more consistent, with greater equity and security.

Some arrangements reflect concentrated political power together with considerable economic competition—as many have characterized the Chinese experience.[82] Such arrangements tend to generate high inequality. When the state is not inclusive, it is hard for institutions of accountability to temper the destructive effects of unbridled markets on other dimensions of well-being. A recent Chinese study found a positive relationship between worker fatalities and industrial growth, suggesting that, in China, slower growth could literally save lives.[83]

Regulation requires a capable state, and state capability is often in short supply. At times, developing country governments have tried to mimic the behaviour of a modern developed state without having the resources or capacity. For example, many Latin American countries failed in efforts to develop a targeted industrial policy to support policies encouraging domestic production over imports.[84] In contrast, an important lesson of the East Asian successes was that a focused, capable state can help drive development and the growth of markets.

Civil society organizations can also curb the excesses of markets and the state. In Indonesia nongovernmental organizations (NGOs), the press and trade unions pressured the state to expand political freedoms and deliver poverty reduction programmes after the 1997 financial crisis. But governments seeking to control dissent can restrict civil society activity. In 2009, for instance, the Ethiopian government passed a law forbidding NGOs with more than 10 percent foreign funding to engage in any activities relating to democracy, justice or human rights.

External factors—such as terms of trade shocks or a threat of invasion—can prompt policy shifts that have positive long-run effects. For example, some of the most successful growth experiences include Chile, South Korea and Taiwan Province of China, where economic elites faced the threat of extinction through takeovers by left-wing regimes. Business leaders allowed policy-makers to exercise enough autonomy to ensure economic success,

a precondition for the survival of the ruling class.[85]

Internal factors can also provoke policy shifts. The breakdown of the power of the robber barons by US President Theodore Roosevelt, Mexico's move to liberalize and enter the North American Free Trade Agreement after the debt crisis and the move to democratic dynamism in Spain after Franco's death are three examples.[86] But the equilibrium is far from optimal when oligarchs can continue to benefit from the regulatory and judicial weaknesses of the state. In Mexico privatization of natural monopolies opened up lucrative opportunities for politically connected business groups, creating some of the world's largest individual fortunes.

The dynamics can be virtuous when countries make the transition to inclusive market institutions and competitive political institutions—though this is difficult and rare. But even in highly unequal societies, as the example of post-apartheid South Africa shows, governments can encourage widespread participation without sacrificing needed reforms—though challenges in including the poor and unorganized persist.[87] Ultimately, oligarchic forms of capitalism tend to contain the seeds of their own demise, either because they stifle innovation—as in the failed import substitution regimes of Latin America—or because material progress broadens people's aspirations so that maintaining power becomes more difficult.

*   *   *

This chapter set out to explain global progress and local variability and the absence of a systematic relationship between economic growth and progress in other dimensions of human development. Our story has highlighted the transmission of ideas and technologies. Money matters—but the evidence shows overwhelmingly that great improvements can be achieved in other aspects of human development without going flat out for economic growth. The diversity of paths and outcomes is traceable to differences in the structure of markets and their interplay with the state and institutions,

> Money matters, but the evidence shows overwhelmingly that great improvements can be achieved in other aspects of human development without going flat out for economic growth

with a key role for the inclusiveness of the political system.

What do these results tell us about the future policy agenda, both national and international? We have identified some correlates of progress—or its absence—and reached some tentative conclusions about which are most important. But for the most part the evidence suggests that different combinations of policies may result in different outcomes depending on the institutional setting and structural constraints.

The story is encouraging but cautionary. Encouraging because progress is possible even without massive resources: most countries have the means to improve people's lives. Cautionary because success is not guaranteed, because routes to success vary and are specific to a country's institutional, political and historical conditions.

Rather than thinking about uniform policy prescriptions, we can apply key principles to inform thinking about development strategies and policies. We illustrate this in our discussion of redistributive policies; policies to promote equity are also likely to foster human development, even if the policies differ from one country to another. Further principles to guide policy are presented in chapter 6.

An approach to policy focused on basic principles rather than blanket recommendations parallels the approach to thinking about justice presented in chapter 1, showing that it is possible to identify possibilities for progress in improving people's lives without full agreement on exactly what an ideal society would look like.

CHAPTER 4

Good things don't always come together

Chapters 2 and 3 surveyed human development over the past 40 years, highlighting global progress and local variability in the three dimensions of the Human Development Index (HDI): health, education and income. But the scope of this survey was incomplete because human development is much broader. Empowerment, equity and sustainability are among the intrinsic parts of people's freedom to lead lives they have reason to value.

This chapter is about understanding what has happened to these dimensions of human development, which are just as important as those covered by the HDI. There is less agreement about what progress on these fronts entails, and measures are lacking. But the lack of quantification is not a reason to ignore them.

The key finding: even when countries make progress in the HDI, they do not always do well in the broader dimensions. Countries may have a high HDI and be undemocratic, unequitable and unsustainable—just as they may have a low HDI and be relatively democratic, equitable and sustainable. This reminds us of the breadth and complexity of the human development agenda: we cannot assume that good things always come together. These patterns challenge the way we think about human development, its measures and the policies to improve outcomes and processes over time—issues we discuss in chapter 6.

The broader dimensions of human development

Norway and the United States are pretty good places to be born for the most part. The HDI captures this well, ranking them first and fourth globally. The comparative assessment holds true for what we measure in the HDI (life expectancy, schooling and income) and for some other dimensions of well-being not included in the HDI. These countries are robust democracies, with effective separation of powers, respect for the rule of law and guarantees of citizens' civil and political rights.

But they do not do well in all dimensions—most notably in environmental sustainability.[1] The ecological footprint of consumption—which measures the area of biologically productive land and sea needed to regenerate the resources that a country consumes—suggests that the United States consumes 4.5 times what would be consistent with global environmental sustainability and Norway, 3.1 times.

Figure 4.1 illustrates the relationship between the HDI and empowerment, inequality and sustainability using a measure of political freedom, the inequality loss in HDI and a measure of sustainability.[2]

Except for inequality, the pattern is not straightforward. There is no statistically significant relationship between sustainability and the HDI. Democracy is on average positively related to the HDI, but the variation around this relationship is much greater than it is for inequality. The lack of correlation can be seen in the large number of countries that have a high HDI but perform poorly on the

Correlation between the HDI and broader dimensions of human development, 2010

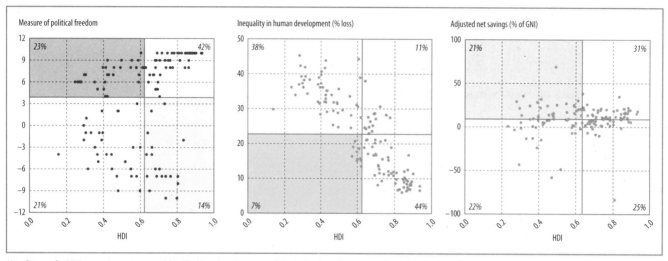

Note: Data are for 2010 or most recent year available. The lines show the means of the distributions. The *percent* values reflect the share of countries in each quadrant. See chapter 5 for construction and results of inequality measures.

Source: HDRO calculations using data from World Bank (2010g) and Marshall and Jaggers (2010).

other variables—depicted in the lighter shaded areas of figure 4.1. About a fourth of countries have a high HDI but low sustainability; a similar though less marked picture emerges for democracy.

These simple correlations are a crude depiction of a far more complex reality. There has been extensive debate about the links between democracy and economic and social development, for example, and about the role of equity in development.[3] It is reasonable to think that there are positive synergies, and we survey strong evidence to this effect below. But we cannot be sure that increases in the HDI will be accompanied by improvements in the broader dimensions of human development or that improvements in those dimensions will yield increases in the HDI.

We next assess trends in the broader dimensions of human development, the extent to which these trends qualify conclusions about progress, and the policy implications.

Empowerment

The opening sentence of the preamble to the UN charter anchors progress in the broader context of "larger freedom." Empowerment—an increase in people's ability to bring about change—is central to the capability approach. It emphasizes the ability of individuals and groups to engage with, shape and benefit from political and other development processes in households, communities and countries. Valuable intrinsically, empowerment has also been linked to many development outcomes. But it is difficult to quantify levels and trends, given differences in views about what is important and the paucity of internationally comparable measures. We focus on the best available indicators, mindful that they present only "simple windows on complex realities"[4]—and limited ones at that.

Empowerment has been recognized since the inception of the *Human Development Report* (*HDR*). The overview to the 1990 *HDR* states: "Human freedom is vital for human development. People must be free to exercise their choices in properly functioning markets, and they must have a decisive voice in shaping their political frameworks."[5] It pointed to the need to measure political freedoms, because "the valuation given to similar human development achievements is quite different depending on whether they were accomplished in a democratic or an authoritarian framework." The 1993 *HDR* on participation was the first to directly address empowerment, which also underpinned the 2000 *HDR* on human rights, the 2002 *HDR* on democracy and the 2004 *HDR* on cultural liberties.[6] Several recent National HDRs have also focused on empowerment, with many producing innovative measures. A Nepal HDR introduced an index to capture the social and political exclusion of different population groups, revealing considerable geographic disparities and lack of correlation with the HDI. A Chile HDR constructed an index of people's power based on information gathered through perception surveys, which probed access to social networks, access to public goods and services, and attitudes towards power. And Dominican Republic HDRs have examined dimensions of empowerment and developed a new index with both individual and collective components.[7]

A change in expectations

Fundamental contextual factors—most important, the vast increases in literacy and educational attainment in many parts of the world—have strengthened people's ability to make informed choices and hold governments accountable. There has also been a sea change in norms and expectations in many places, though it is a slow process.

The technological revolution coupled with globalization has transformed the political landscape. The proliferation of cell phones and satellite television, alongside widening access to the Internet, has vastly increased the availability of information and the ability to voice opinions. Use of these technologies is very high in developed countries—by 2008, 70 percent of people were using the Internet, and phone subscriptions had reached

1.5 per capita—but still low in low HDI countries (figure 4.2). But growth over the past decade has been striking: in low HDI countries Internet use soared more than 4,000 percent, and the share of people with phone subscriptions by close to 3,500 percent.[8] New technology can give voice to marginalized people, though some contend that such innovations consolidate the power of people who already have some resources.[9]

The dramatic increases in Internet coverage and mobile telephone use have occurred despite structural constraints. For example, the average rate of electrification in developing countries in 2008 was still only 70 percent. It was only 59 percent in rural areas and much lower still— 21 percent—in low HDI countries.[10]

Globalization has propelled domestic issues onto the international stage. One expression of this trend is the upsurge of global and transnational civil society: the number of

FIGURE 4.2 Fast growth in communication technologies, but still low access in the poorest countries

Number of people using the Internet and with phone subscriptions, per 100 people, by level of human development, 2000–2008

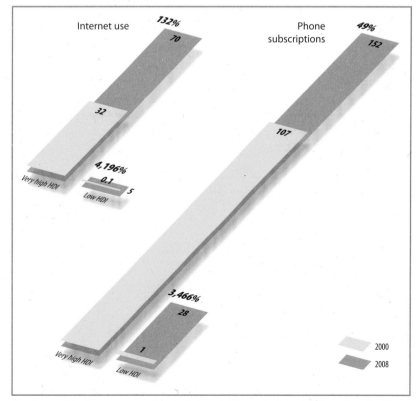

Note: Numbers above bars are percentage growth over the period. Phone subscriptions include mobile and fixed line.

Source: ITU 2009.

international organizations increased more than fivefold from 1970 to 2010, to an estimated 25,000.[11] Protests often have an international dimension—as attested by boycotts of the apartheid regime in South Africa, mobilizations seeking to end the conflict in Darfur, and support, often in Western countries, for pro-democracy protesters in Iran and Myanmar.

Democracy and the freedom to choose

Against this backdrop there has been wide-ranging democratization and an increase in people's perceived freedom to choose.[12] At the national level we see the spread of formal procedural democracy, and at the subnational level the rise of local participatory processes in different forms—with greater possibilities for accountability. There have been some improvements in the protection of human rights—and some setbacks. Identity-based groups that have historically faced exclusion and deprivation have become more visibly engaged in political and social action, though inequalities persist.

Survey evidence suggests that most people around the world feel free to make choices and are satisfied with this freedom.[13] Current satisfaction varies by region: people are most satisfied in developed countries (80 percent), followed by East Asia and the Pacific (77 percent), and least satisfied in Europe and Central Asia (50 percent), which may reflect the upheavals of transition or underlying differences in outlook. Reported trends in freedom of choice, available for 66 countries, suggest general improvement over time.

In 1970 some 30 countries denied full suffrage and rights to stand for election, discriminating mainly against women—with the notable exception of South Africa, where the majority Black and Indian populations were denied the right to vote. These restrictions have been almost entirely lifted.[14] While voting rights are now close to universal, the share of offices filled by election varies markedly, and some countries, such as Saudi Arabia, still restrict women's voting rights.

Democratic government and the protection of human rights are cornerstones of political freedom. But the difference between democratic and nondemocratic states is not always stark, and in practice autocratic, democratic and transitional states exhibit more diversity and fluidity than simple categorizations might suggest. That said, the share of democracies increased from less than a third of countries in the early 1970s to more than half in 1996 and to three-fifths in 2008 (figure 4.3).[15] When including states that are democratic in form but where the ruling party has yet to lose an election and thus hand over power,[16] the share exceeds four-fifths.

Most countries in the very high HDI group are democracies. The low HDI countries have registered the sharpest advances in democratization: none was democratic in 1991, compared with about a third in 2008.

The most dramatic advances were in Europe and Central Asia, followed by Latin America and the Caribbean. Among developing countries in Europe and Central Asia the only democratic country in 1988 was Turkey. Over the following three years 11 of the 23 countries in the region became democracies, with 2 more turning democratic since 1991. In Latin America and the Caribbean most

FIGURE 4.3   More countries adopt democracy

Trends in democracy, by HDI level and overall, 1971–2008

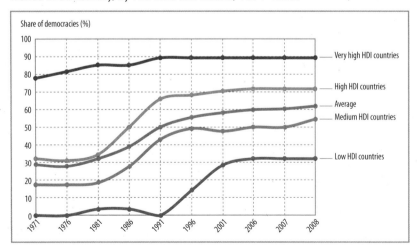

Note: Data are calculated as the number of democracies with alternation of ruling parties as a share of the number of nondemocratic governments plus democracies with no alternation.

Source: HDRO calculations using data from Cheibub, Gandhi, and Vreeland (2009).

countries were not democratic in 1971, and several democracies reverted to authoritarianism during the 1970s.[17] Following a subsequent wave of political change, almost 80 percent of the countries were democratic by 1990. By 2008, with regime changes in Ecuador and Peru, the share reached 87 percent. East Asia and the Pacific and Sub-Saharan Africa also reflect reforms—just 6 percent of governments in both regions were democratic in 1970; by 2008 the share had risen to 44 percent in East Asia and the Pacific and 38 percent in Sub-Saharan Africa. Only the Arab States show few signs of in-depth democratization (box 4.1).

In many cases, including Nepal and Pakistan recently, crises of legitimacy have prompted transitions from authoritarian states. But consolidating democratic practices has proven more difficult. Many national elections have been marred by widespread voter intimidation and fraud, such as those held recently in Afghanistan, Kenya and Nicaragua. And the official results of even peaceful elections have been vigorously contested, including those in the United States in 2000 and Mexico in 2006.

Some nondemocratic governments have taken steps towards democratization, such as the several "unity governments" in Sub-Saharan Africa—as in the case of Sudan. Although negotiated power sharing may avoid or help end conflict, cycles of protest and repression may follow. Other governments have faced the threat of popular movements using democratic mechanisms to roll back democracy.[18] A pro-Taliban Islamist coalition explicitly sought electoral victory in key provinces of Pakistan as a step towards theocracy.[19]

These diverse experiences underline the fact that democracy embraces an array of institutional arrangements and power configurations—and that autocracies are not monolithic either. Processes are open-ended, typically nonlinear and subject to divergent trajectories as well as to partial reversals and protracted uncertainty.[20]

The trend of democratization is evident not just in national elections but also in regional and local elections. The rise of local participatory processes has taken different forms, including decentralization to subnational governmental units, as in many parts of Latin

---

BOX 4.1   The democratic deficit in the Arab States

The 2009 Arab States Human Development Report illustrated vivid contrasts between actual practice and formal support for democracy, human rights and the rule of law. Some of the countries have a multiparty system—including Algeria, Egypt, Jordan, Tunisia and Yemen—while Lebanon and Morocco stand out since their independence for accommodating political pluralism. Yet many governments continue to restrict political freedoms—all the Gulf States except Bahrain, for instance, ban political organizations.

There has been a recent spate of democratic reforms in the region, many offset by countermeasures limiting citizen rights in other respects. Positive steps include the establishment of representative assemblies in Oman, Qatar and the United Arab Emirates, the return of an elected president in Bahrain and the holding of multicandidate presidential elections in Egypt in 2005. Local elections were held in Saudi Arabia in 2006, but voting was limited to male citizens.

To date these reforms "have not changed the structural basis of power in the Arab States, where the executive branch still dominates, unchecked by any form of accountability" (p. 69). For instance, along with Iraq's new constitution came an extended security state that permits the suspension of constitutional freedoms. Egypt amended its constitution to permit multiple candidates in presidential elections but followed with a law limiting this right to existing parties. Algeria's Charter for Peace and National Reconciliation was quickly followed by an extension of the presidential term in office, the removal of term limits and the continuation of the ban on the Islamic Salvation Front. Similar patterns are evident in Qatar, Saudi Arabia, Sudan, Tunisia and the United Arab Emirates.

Many governments in the region seem to have been able to resist pluralist tendencies because of the enormous rents and control bestowed by oil. The political economy allows the state to insulate itself through far-reaching patronage networks and a weighty security apparatus. Oil rents remove the need to levy taxes, thereby reducing accountability. For countries without oil—Jordan, Morocco and Tunisia—foreign aid arguably plays a similar role. Compared with other economies at similar incomes, the business sector is relatively weak, as is civil society. All countries in the region except Libya permit civil organizations, but laws and regulations restrain their activities. Consequently, "few Arabs feel they have any power to change current conditions in their country through political participation" (p. 73).

Source: UNDP 2009.

America and in the *panchayati raj* system of rural India. This has accompanied and at times prompted a powerful narrative in the development community about citizen participation at the front lines of service delivery.

Although difficult to compare across countries, decentralization has generally increased in most parts of the world. In 2009, 95 of 120 countries (about 80 percent) had local governments in which at least the legislature was elected, and in half these both the executive and legislature were elected.[21] Data on fiscal decentralization—very patchy—suggest that for countries reporting data, about 25 percent of spending took place subnationally.

Empowerment in the political arena can be threatened by elite capture of key institutions,[22] though some evidence suggests that opening political systems can beget more equitable decision-making even if elites participate more than others.[23] This depends in part on institutional structures and on the behaviour of elites—whether they seek to extract rents or to voice local community preferences—which in turn can be influenced by average education in the community.[24]

Increased democratization and globalization appear to be associated with the better standing of many identity-based groups that have traditionally encountered exclusion and deprivation.[25] Notable instances include the transition from apartheid in South Africa; the rise (or re-emergence) of indigenous movements in Latin America and the Caribbean, with political parties associated with these movements assuming power in Bolivia; and the growing importance of lower caste politics at the state level in India. Most such advances have occurred under democratic auspices or during democratic transitions. As with democratic transitions, the empowerment of disadvantaged groups has been most successful when it has arisen from their political mobilization.

Efforts have also been made to redress the position of indigenous peoples through political forums and other consultative institutions that seek to incorporate their voices and through a strengthening of traditional mechanisms for local governance and justice. But such consultative mechanisms have been criticized for limiting people's participation to discussion of predetermined issues rather than allowing people to participate meaningfully. Lack of voice also afflicts refugees and migrants, who must often endure long periods in limbo, no longer part of their country of origin and unable to participate politically in their country of residence.[26]

Women have made some major strides in filling political office, becoming heads of state and high-ranking legislators. About one in five countries has a quota imposed by law or the constitution reserving a percentage of parliamentary seats for women, contributing to a rise in women's share from less than 11 percent in 1975 to 19 percent in 2010 (see chapter 5). And in some cases the prominence of gender issues has risen in tandem.[27]

But evidence suggests low female participation at the local level—for instance, in both Latin America and Europe women held about a tenth of mayoralties and less than a fourth of local council seats.[28] An exception is India, where 30 percent of local government (panchayat) seats are reserved for women—with evident effects on patterns of social spending.[29]

Civil and political rights

Civil and political rights are cornerstones of empowerment, but their cross-country patterns and trends are difficult to assess. Reported rights violations may be misleading—because the most repressive regimes may be those where reporting is most difficult—and quantifying human rights abuses is difficult in any context. We carefully considered the existing data sources and determined that it would be inappropriate to use government data or any data from a nongovernmental organization close to a government. The patterns presented below and in statistical table 6 draw on a scale developed to code country human rights practices on the basis of Amnesty International reports.[30]

In 2008 the lowest average human rights violations were reported in developed countries, while the highest were in the Arab

> Most improvements in the standing of traditionally excluded and deprived identity-based groups have occurred under democratic auspices or during democratic transitions

States and in South Asia, which is consistent with regional assessments. The Arab Organization for Human Rights reported that torture was officially practiced in 8 Arab states and illegal detention in 11.[31] And the Asian Human Rights Commission provides evidence of endemic abuses in most countries in that region.[32]

Reported levels of human rights violations have remained virtually unchanged globally over the past 40 years.[33] But over the past decade there has been a slight worsening in developed countries, owing in part to measures taken in the wake of the September 11, 2001, attacks on the United States. The ill treatment of prisoners by the U.S. government at the Guantanamo Bay detention camps has been documented by the Red Cross and other human rights groups. And several countries now have stringent anti-terror laws. For instance, Australia's 2005 Anti-Terror Act permits the government to detain, limit the movement of and request information about any potential suspect without cause—and curtails freedom of expression.

Democratization is expected to improve accountability, though this is not guaranteed, particularly where information is limited and opportunities for public engagement are lacking.[34] Perhaps the most fundamental aspect of accountability is government protection of people's basic civil liberties and responsiveness to minority groups. Over the last several decades more governments have committed to UN conventions and covenants, and national institutions have evolved to safeguard human rights.[35]

But many countries continue to violate basic human rights, notwithstanding these protections. In 2009, 26 countries imprisoned journalists whose views they found threatening. And 58 countries retained the death penalty, though most did not use it.[36] Not only are abuses of human rights prevalent, but in many countries people feel that they cannot express themselves freely: in about a third of 142 countries polled between 2006 and 2009, mostly in Sub-Saharan Africa but also in much of Latin America and the Caribbean, at least 25 percent of respondents felt that "most people" in their country were afraid to openly express their political views.[37] In all but two countries, Botswana and Ireland, fewer than half the respondents felt that "no one is afraid" to express political views.

Finally, there has been marked international progress in recognizing the rights of sexual minorities in recent years, notably the 2008 UN General Assembly Declaration in support of decriminalizing homosexuality, signed by 60 countries to date. Yet barriers continue in national law and practice. In 2009 homosexuality was illegal in 76 countries, with punishments ranging from several years to life imprisonment. In Iran, Mauritania, Saudi Arabia, Sudan and Yemen (as well as in parts of Nigeria and Somalia), it was punishable by death.[38] In 2009 the Ugandan Parliament debated a bill that proposed lifetime imprisonment—and the death penalty in some cases—for engaging in homosexual acts.[39]

*　　　*　　　*

Overall, the evidence suggests a rise in empowerment—both in people's ability to voice their opinions and act in line with their values and in the institutions that enable the exercise of power. Most people now live in democratic states, and decentralization has increased apace, notably in India and Latin America and the Caribbean. However, many factors still constrain participation, and progress in protecting human rights has been limited—democratization and decentralization notwithstanding. Continued dissatisfaction with the ability to choose and with the responsiveness of state institutions suggests the need for a stronger focus on mechanisms of accountability.

> The evidence suggests a rise in empowerment—both in people's ability to voice their opinions and in the institutions that enable the exercise of power

Inequality

Human development cannot be built on exploitation of some groups by others or on greater access to resources and power by some groups. Inequitable development is not human development.

From the outset *HDRs* have focused extensively on deprivation and inequality. Early *HDRs* adjusted the income dimension of the HDI for inequality. Human poverty indices were introduced in the 1997 and 1998 *HDRs*, and the 2005 *HDR* explored inequalities in human development.[40] Many National HDRs, including those for the Russian Federation (1998) and Mongolia (2007), have also explored poverty and inequality at the local level.

Equity and the HDI are systematically related: countries that do well on the HDI tend to be more equitable. This result is consistent with research that shows how reducing inequality—both in the population as a whole and across gender and other groups—can improve overall outcomes in health and education, as well as economic growth.[41]

But considerable variation around the HDI-inequality relationship remains, especially in low and medium HDI countries. For example, inequality is almost three times greater in Namibia than in Kyrgyzstan, countries that both have an HDI of 0.6.[42] Furthermore, as chapters 1–3 have illustrated, the correlation of two variables at a given time does not ensure that progress in the variables will always go hand in hand. In fact, evidence for the income dimension shows a worsening of inequalities within countries.

Rising income inequality

Because income averages can be misleading, especially when inequality is high, the Stiglitz-Sen-Fitoussi Commission recommended using medians to reveal the situation of a "typical" person. In the United States, for instance, mean income is almost a third higher than median income, and the gap is growing—a topic for debate among policy-makers and academics alike.[43] Other developed countries, such as Italy and New Zealand, have similar gaps. And the gap is often large in developing countries as well: more than 50 percent in Côte d'Ivoire and 60 percent in Liberia and Zambia.

The gap between mean and median income is not the best measure of inequality among all people in society, however, as it ignores how income is concentrated at different points in the distribution.[44] The most popular alternative is the Gini coefficient. Within countries rising income inequality is the norm: more countries have a higher Gini coefficient now than in the 1980s.[45] For each country where inequality has improved in the last 20–30 years, it has worsened in more than two.

The worsening is especially marked in countries that were part of the former Soviet Union—which still have relatively low Gini coefficients because they started with low inequality. Transition has eroded employment guarantees and ended extensive state employment. Before the fall of the Berlin Wall, 9 of 10 people in socialist countries were employed by the state, compared with 2 of 10 in Organisation for Economic Co-operation and Development economies.[46] While the privileged elite (the *nomenklatura*) often attained higher material well-being, the measured differences in income were narrow.[47]

Most countries in East Asia and the Pacific also have higher income inequality today than a few decades ago.[48] This is explained partly by growing gaps between urban and rural areas due to rapid industrial growth, though the slow growth of agriculture and increasing returns to higher levels of schooling have also contributed. In formerly centrally planned economies such as those of China and Viet Nam, trends again reflect increases from low levels under central planning. But Mongolia shows that the transition to markets need not be accompanied by greater income disparity.

In Sub-Saharan Africa inequality generally worsened during the economically difficult 1980s then improved substantially during the

> Equity and the HDI are systematically related, but considerable variation remains, especially in low and medium HDI countries

growth period of the late 1990s and 2000s.[49] In Latin America and the Caribbean historically high inequality has been linked to unequal distribution of land and education, higher returns to skilled workers, high fertility in poorer households and regressive public spending. But several countries—among them Brazil, Ecuador and Paraguay—have begun to successfully tackle this inequality. Since the late 1990s progressive policies seem to have resulted in better wages for people with lower education and in higher transfers through targeted social policy.[50] In many developed countries greater inequality in pretax income has been offset by state redistribution (see chapter 3).

For most people around the world the largest components of income are wages and earnings. Income from capital, by contrast, is often highly concentrated among the wealthiest. The relative shares of labour and capital income are thus of interest in any discussion of inequality. Research for this Report found a decline in labour shares in 65 of 110 countries (roughly 60 percent) over the past two decades, contrary to the previous assumption of stable labour shares over time.[51] Some large countries—notably India, the Russian Federation and the United States—saw substantial declines, of up to 5 percentage points, from 1990 to 2008, driving a drop in the average world labour share of 2 percentage points.

The declines coincide with decreased unionization and increased trade and financial openness in most developed countries since 1970. In some cases the drop in the share of union members among total employees has been large: from 22 percent to 8 percent in France and from 63 percent to 35 percent in Austria.[52] But the share of workers covered by collective agreements is often much higher—95 percent in France and 80–95 percent in much of Western Europe, except Germany (63 percent) and the United Kingdom (35 percent).

Global inequality is also relevant when examining distributive justice in the world as a whole,[53] a traditional position of the *HDRs*. Trend estimates for global income inequality are both mixed and controversial.[54] One estimate shows a significant decline in income inequality, with the world Gini coefficient falling from 0.68 to 0.61 over 1970–2006, driven by China. But estimates with different time frames show a different pattern. According to one study, the world Gini coefficient has worsened since 1988 and now stands at a startling 0.71. Yet others find that the improvement or worsening of global income inequality is not robust to the use of different estimation methods and datasets. It is hard to make sense of the competing findings, but they coincide on one fundamental point: income inequality among the world's population is very high.

Overlapping and systemic disparities

Inequalities can be reinforcing. In the end unequal societies—democratic or not—are societies where power is more concentrated in the hands of elites, so it is not surprising that economic and political institutions work in their favour. A study of attitudes towards education among Brazilian elites during the 1990s found that elites were often reluctant to broaden education opportunities on the grounds that educated workers would be more difficult to manage. Government policymakers worried that a more expensive labour force would reduce the country's comparative advantage in labour-intensive goods. Such thinking impedes human development by leading to lower investment in human capital and public goods, less redistribution and more political instability.[55]

Joint deprivations come about where inequality in health and education coincide with inequality in income—which in turn may overlap with ethnicity and gender.[56] Better data for developing countries have improved understanding of joint deprivations, while analysis in developed countries has exposed similar patterns, despite better overall access to services.

Access to public services according to a person's position in the distribution of income reflects the multiple deprivations of households in the bottom of the distribution. The data on trends in inequality in nonincome dimensions are scant, but general patterns emerge. The

> Joint deprivations come about where inequalities in health, education and income overlap—which may in turn interact with ethnicity and gender

good news on trends is that expanded access to education has typically benefited worse off groups. But their children are still more likely to die young and have poorer health, less education and less access to basic services. And the quality of services that poor people can afford or are publicly provided is worse than that available for people who are better off.

For health, trends are mixed. A study of 24 developing countries found widening gaps in child mortality between the extremes of the wealth distribution in 11 countries, narrowing gaps in only 3 and persistent gaps in the rest.[57] And in developed countries recent increases in life expectancy have benefited people who are older, wealthier and more educated—partly because of more effective healthcare interventions and better health-related behaviour, such as less smoking and more exercise.[58]

Overall, the gaps in health between high- and low-income groups tend to be large, especially in developing countries. Infant mortality, for example, is far more frequent among the poorest households across all regions. In the Arab States, East Asia and the Pacific and Latin America and the Caribbean infant mortality roughly doubles in the bottom fifth of the income distribution (figure 4.4). And in Indonesia and Nicaragua infant deaths are more

than three times more common in the poorest fifth than in the richest.[59]

A study using Demographic and Health Survey data for 55 countries in all developing country regions found that only two-fifths of children in poor households received full vaccination treatment, compared with almost two-thirds of children in households at the top of the distribution.[60] Another recent study of 45 countries found large inequalities in maternal and child healthcare by income group and by rural-urban zone: in Bolivia and Peru the richest fifth had almost universal access to a skilled attendant at birth, while only 10–15 percent of the poorest fifth did. Women in poor rural households accounted for some two-thirds of unattended births.[61]

In most developing countries average improvements in education have extended access to children who would not otherwise have attended school—suggesting reduced inequality over the long term. In Egypt between 1995 and 2000 school participation increased by 18 percentage points for girls in the poorest fifth of the income distribution, and by only 5 percentage points for girls in the richest fifth. And in five years the gains were 8 percentage points higher in Nepal and 4 percentage points higher in Viet Nam for those in

FIGURE 4.4 Children of poor households are more likely to die

Infant deaths per 1,000 births, by wealth quintile, 1990–2005

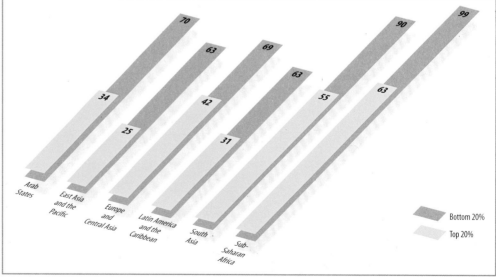

Source: Gwatkin and others 2007.

the bottom of the income distribution.[62] This tendency towards less inequality is reflected in the average Gini coefficient in education, which fell from 0.46 in 1960 to 0.31 in 2000, with steady improvements in all regions since 1970 (despite stalling in East Asia and the Pacific in the 1990s).[63] And, as we saw in chapter 2, the dispersion across countries in health and education has declined.

To investigate the differences across income groups more systematically, a study for this Report estimated the HDI at the household level in 15 countries.[64] The distribution across income deciles shows the expected pattern—the top 10 percent has a much higher HDI than does the bottom, ranging from 20 percent greater in Armenia to 160 percent greater in Nigeria.

When the HDI is calculated for different population groups, some clear patterns emerge:

- Rural households and households with low education consistently have a lower HDI than their urban and higher educated counterparts do. The differences are not due simply to education being part of the HDI: the life expectancy and income indices also show a bias against households with no education.

- For Burkina Faso, Ethiopia and Senegal—countries with low average HDI—HDIs are 33–40 percent lower in rural areas than in urban areas.

- Somewhat surprisingly, no clear distributional pattern emerges between male- and female-headed households. In some countries HDI outcomes are higher for female-headed households (Ethiopia), while in others male-headed households show an advantage (Egypt).

This analysis also examined how different groups' HDIs compare internationally. In more than half the countries analysed the difference between more highly educated households and those without schooling exceeded 50 percent—and reached nearly 90 percent in Burkina Faso—a gap that would amount to 40 positions in the international HDI rankings.[65] The differences are smaller in formerly Communist countries such as Armenia and Kyrgyzstan and

larger in Latin American and the Caribbean countries—Bolivia, Nicaragua and Peru—and Sub-Saharan Africa.

Groups identified by location, ethnicity, gender and other characteristics often face systematic disadvantages that indicate differences in opportunities between groups of people who should have equal chances.[66] These are also referred to as horizontal inequalities.

Examples of group disadvantages abound.[67] The HDI for Roma people in Romania is well below the national average and similar to Botswana's—despite Romania ranking almost 50 places higher than Botswana in the HDI. The Roma people's income is a third the national average, and their infant mortality rates are three times higher.[68] In Pakistan more than 50 percent of young people speaking Baluchi or Saraiki have less than four years of education, in contrast to roughly 10 percent of Urdu-speaking youth.[69] Indigenous peoples also lag on most indicators of human development, even in rich countries (box 4.2).

BOX 4.2 Indigenous peoples and inequality in human development

An estimated 300 million indigenous peoples from more than 5,000 groups live in more than 70 countries. Some two-thirds reside in China.[1] Indigenous peoples often face structural disadvantages and have worse human development outcomes in key respects. For example, recent Mexican government analyses show that while extreme multidimensional poverty is 10.5 percent nationally, it exceeds 39 percent among indigenous Mexicans.

When the Human Development Index (HDI) is calculated for aboriginal and non-aboriginal people in Australia, Canada, New Zealand and the United States, there is a consistent gap of 6–18 percent. Indigenous peoples in these countries have lower life expectancy, poorer education outcomes and smaller incomes. In India 92 percent of people of Scheduled Tribes live in rural areas, 47 percent of them in poverty. In Chhattisgarh, with a sizeable share of Scheduled Tribes, the statewide literacy rate is 64 percent—but that of tribal peoples is only 22 percent.

Some evidence suggests that a schooling gap between indigenous and nonindigenous peoples remains. In China, India and Lao PDR geography, climate and discrimination based on ethnicity make it difficult to deliver basic infrastructure to remote areas, where many indigenous peoples and ethnic minorities live.

Work in Latin America and the Caribbean exploring access to land and this aspect of discrimination shows that a focus on broad-based economic growth can benefit indigenous peoples but is unlikely to be enough to close the gap. More targeted strategies are needed, as proposed by indigenous peoples and as informed by their views and priorities.

1. According to official Chinese policy, there are no indigenous peoples in the country; the term used is "ethnic minorities."

Source: Alkire and Santos 2010; Cooke and others 2007; Burd-Sharps, Lewis, and Martins 2008; Hall and Patrinos 2010; UNDP 2003; Kumar 2010.

BOX **4.3**   **More missing women**

"Missing women" refers to mortality patterns and sex ratios at birth (the ratio of male births to female births) that disadvantage women. According to UN estimates, the sex ratio at birth has increased globally from a stable 1.05 in the early 1970s to a recent peak of 1.07.

Contributing to this global trend has been the preference for boys in China, where the sex ratio rose from 1.07 in the early 1970s to 1.2 recently, despite the country's official ban on prenatal sex determinations since 1989 and on sex-selective abortion since 1994. In India the sex ratio has risen from 1.06 in the early 1970s to 1.08 today, with rates as high as 1.26 in Delhi, Gujarat, Harayana and Punjab. And Armenia's sex ratio at birth rose from 1.07 through the late 1990s to 1.17 today.

By contrast, Africa's sex ratio at birth fell, from 1.04 in the early 1970s to 1.03 today. And among other countries with a stable sex ratio since 1970 is Mongolia.

Since banning sex-specific abortions has not worked, China and India are pursuing other approaches to combat this discrimination. For example, the "Care for Girls" campaign in China sends positive messages about girls, encourages matrilineal marriages with cash incentives and gives pension payments to rural families with daughters once parents reach age 60.

Source: UNDESA 2009c; Ganatra 2008; Sen 2003; *The Economist* 2010; Narayana 2008

In developed countries group disadvantages affect some migrant groups as well as specific minority and indigenous peoples. In the European Union migrants make up about an eighth of the working-age population and are sometimes engaged in low-paid jobs that do not use their skills.[70] Having the "wrong" ethnicity can also undermine job prospects. One study found that 68 percent of applicants with a traditional British name were granted an interview compared with only 39 percent of applicants with names associated with ethnic minority groups.[71] Some minorities fare worse than others: African Americans in the United States live 13 years less than Asian Americans, and Native Americans in South Dakota have shorter lifespans today than the average U.S. citizen did more than 50 years ago.[72]

We turn now to one major horizontal inequality for which the universal distinction between groups and peoples allows cross-national comparisons: the disadvantages facing women and girls.

Gender disparities

Traditionally, gender differences in human development have been acute. All too often, women and girls are discriminated against in health, education and jobs—with a range of detrimental repercussions for their freedoms. Despite important gains over time—particularly for education, as recounted above—women still fare poorly in several respects. Here we look at some broader structural and other dimensions of disadvantage, analysed more systematically in chapter 5.

The most glaring discrimination is evident in women's low relative share in the population, a key aspect of recent demographic trends in several countries.[73] We have updated Sen's earlier estimates of "missing women," which compared the variation in sex ratios across the world.[74] Using the same simplifying assumptions, we found more than 134 million missing women in 2010—almost a third more than previous estimates.[75] Box 4.3 reviews what is driving this deterioration—much of it traceable to China.

There is also evidence of reversals in women's empowerment. In the Caucasus and Central Asia some local government leaders have called for a return to a more "traditional" society. And many reports suggest an upsurge of traditionalism, with consequences for women's disempowerment (box 4.4).

Many women continue to face substantial disempowerment in the household, evident in data on violence against women.[76] Recent surveys from 13 developing countries suggest that an average of 20 percent of women had suffered domestic violence within the past year, and surveys of developed countries also record substantial abuse.[77] Most countries protect women against rape, trafficking and domestic violence through legislation or equivalent nonstatutory protection but do not offer similar protection against sexual harassment and marital rape.[78]

Women are often disempowered in other ways. In many countries women are far less likely and less able to own property and other assets than men are, with negative implications for their absolute and relative status and likelihood of experiencing marital violence.[79] Surveys in five countries in Latin America and the Caribbean found that only 11–27 percent of landowners were women.[80] In Uganda women account for most agricultural production but own 5 percent of the land, and their tenure is highly insecure. The formalization of tenure sometimes excludes women from claiming property they have traditionally used.[81]

BOX **4.4** | **Changing gender relations in the former Soviet Union**

Prior to Soviet rule much of the Caucasus and Central Asia was inhabited by traditional agricultural societies that prescribed limited roles for women outside the household. Predominantly Muslim countries such as Azerbaijan, Tajikistan and Uzbekistan practiced patrilocality, in which a wife joins her husband's extended family following marriage. This system provided little incentive to invest in daughters, since a married woman's contribution accrued to the husband's family rather than to her parents.

Under Soviet rule and its official policy of atheism, the government discouraged many traditional customs favouring men over women: it promoted the nuclear family, banned arranged marriages and polygamy, unveiled women and required girls to attend school. This changed the incentives for parents to invest in girls and—with the greater availability of childcare, healthcare and pensions—opened opportunities for women to work outside the home.

The collapse of Soviet rule has led some local government leaders in the region to call for a return to a more "traditional" society. Among the many reports suggesting an upsurge of traditionalism, some mention Kazakhstan, Kyrgyzstan and Uzbekistan, where there have been calls to re-establish polygamy and to change the law to make it more difficult for women to initiate divorce. Arranged marriages have increased, and bride payments and bride-napping have re-emerged in some countries. The possible deterioration of women's status within the household, little researched, is of growing concern.

Source: Brainerd 2010.

Namibia, Rwanda and Tanzania are among countries that have passed land reforms that include gender parity in ownership of communal land.[82] And several countries have adopted joint ownership and spousal consent on property issues. In Maharashtra, India, the Laxmi Mukti program transferred property to women or instituted joint ownership. But even when legal reforms allow for asset ownership by women, religious beliefs and customary laws can undermine advances. Community-based mobilization may be necessary to enable women to negotiate repeal of religious and customary laws that block their access to assets.[83]

Access to full and decent employment remains a challenge for many women who have to work in insecure, low-paying jobs while bearing a disproportionate burden of unpaid care (see box 5.2 in chapter 5). Women are poorly represented outside agriculture in Sub-Saharan Africa, with only 36 percent working outside the sector. Of working-age women in the region, 55 percent are employed, but 82 percent are in vulnerable jobs.[84] Labour regulations contribute to women's exclusion in some countries: in Egypt, Jamaica and Pakistan women are not allowed to work at night or in certain industries.[85]

The gender wage gap, though slowly narrowing, remains wide. Comparable data are not available for many countries, but in 33 mainly developed countries, women's wages averaged 69 percent of men's in 1998–2002, rising to 74 percent in 2003–2006.[86] The gap was almost 50 percent in 2006 in South Korea.[87] The country in the sample closest to parity is Colombia, with only a 2 percent wage gap in 2004.

Some 61 countries have statutory retirement ages that force women to retire earlier than men, typically five years earlier, despite women's longer life expectancy. Among them are very high HDI countries, such as Austria, Italy and the United Kingdom, as well as Algeria, Panama, the Russian Federation and Sri Lanka. Such discriminatory policies can be a disincentive to hire, promote and invest in women.[88]

*   *   *

Progress in reducing inequalities around the world has been limited, with some serious reversals. Income inequality is increasing in most countries, except in Latin America and the Caribbean, and while the evidence on trends is sketchier for other dimensions, very large gaps remain. Poor people experience deprivations in many dimensions at once, and gender differences remain acute. Perpetuating these inequalities impedes progress in human development.

Vulnerability and sustainability

Economic and social integration have increased the chance of global shocks, but some risks remain localized

Vulnerability means different things to different people—and the meaning changes with the context. *Vulnerare,* the Latin root of *vulnerability*, means "to wound," and the basic conceptual association between vulnerability and injury—as a decline in well-being—remains. In the context of human development vulnerability is associated with the possibility of a decline in human development. Countries and people are vulnerable when their human development is threatened by various risks (aggregate shocks or individual accidents).[89]

Shocks arise in different ways—as economic crises, human-caused or natural disasters, illnesses and accidents. Droughts, floods and earthquakes have occurred since time immemorial—the Epic of Gilgamesh, one of the earliest works of literature, describes a massive flood and the subsequent suffering in ancient Mesopotamia—and financial crises have occurred for centuries.

Economic and social integration have increased the chance of global shocks, but some risks remain localized. The most pervasive and frequent risks occur at the individual and family levels. A basic typology has been used to understand risk and vulnerability: risks may affect individuals, such as the loss of life or the job of the breadwinner or a sudden disability; communities, such as natural disasters; and countries, such as financial crises and macroeconomic shocks.[90]

Vulnerability is intimately linked to sustainability. Sustainability implies that improvements in human development can be sustained. In 1987 the Brundtland Commission defined sustainable development as "progress that meets the needs of the present without compromising the ability of future generations to meet their own needs."[91] When the needs of the future are compromised by the way we are meeting our needs in the present, future generations are exposed to possibly catastrophic losses in human development.

We cannot do justice to vulnerability and sustainability here. That requires a much more dedicated effort, which we propose to undertake for next year's *HDR*. The focus in this section is limited to two aspects of paramount importance—economic insecurity and climate change—and how they have evolved over the recent past.

Job insecurity and shocks

Most people depend on their jobs for their livelihood and that of their families—for many, losing their job is the single most important event (apart from death) that can erode their human development. Employment status also affects people's subjective sense of well-being. Any analysis of vulnerability should thus carefully consider job insecurity and the sources of economic instability, especially important now as the world economy struggles to emerge from the deepest recession in decades and the loss of millions of jobs.

The global financial crisis
International Labour Organization estimates show stability and improvement in most countries from the late 1990s through the late 2000s.[92] Spikes in unemployment commonly result from a macroeconomic shock—a financial or exchange rate crisis. This was definitely the case in the global financial crisis, which involved a sharp spike in layoffs and large rises in unemployment, especially in developed countries and Europe and Central Asia (figure 4.5).

The global financial crisis was precipitated by the bursting of the housing price bubble and banking collapses in the United States, which rapidly spread to most of the world. It was the worst financial crisis since the Great Depression—at least in developed countries.[93] And it certainly will not be the last.[94]

Unemployment and poverty worsened sharply: 34 million people lost their jobs, and 64 million more people fell under the $1.25 a day poverty threshold.[95] This stands on top of the 160–200 million people who fell into poverty as a result of higher commodity prices in the preceding years.[96] In 2010 unemployment averaged 9 percent in developed countries and reached 10 percent in the United States and 20 percent in Spain.

Recovery started in 2009 but is by no means assured: the risk of a "double-dip" recession remains, and a full recovery could take years. Imaginative policy interventions and huge fiscal stimuli in many countries, combined with rapid global coordination, helped avoid a bigger crisis.[97] In the developing countries that had managed economic bonanzas well, the impact of the crisis was milder. Several governments sustained or increased social expenditures, in contrast to the late 1990s after the East Asian and Russian crises.[98]

The consequences of crises can persist even after growth returns because the labour market typically lags behind output in a recovery. The International Labour Organization predicts that 43 million people who lost their job during the global financial crisis through 2009 risk entering long-term unemployment. And some people become discouraged and leave the labour market altogether. Parallels can be drawn to the East Asian crisis in the late 1990s, where participation rates in the workforce never recovered.[99]

But new risks have emerged, as concerns about fiscal sustainability have been raised for some developed countries (such as Greece), and the spectre of contagion remains. Generally, economies growing faster in the 2000s were hit hardest—though Australia and China are just two among the exceptions. In Latin America and the Caribbean GDP growth declined, with significant drops in Chile, Mexico and Peru. Sub-Saharan Africa sustained growth, though at the much lower rate of about 2 percent in 2009, down from more than 5 percent in 2008. In developed countries annual growth fell about 6 percentage points to −3.4 percent in 2009. Some countries in Europe and Central Asia appear to have been hardest hit: the economies of the former Soviet Union went from more than 5 percent growth in 2008 to a contraction of almost 7 percent in 2009, with poverty increasing markedly.[100]

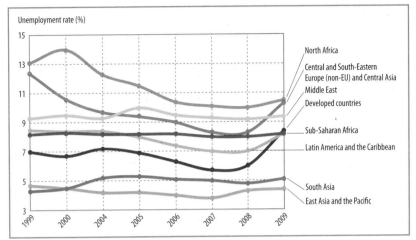

FIGURE 4.5 **Reversal of unemployment declines since 2008**

Trends in unemployment over the past decade

Note: Regions are International Labour Organization classifications.

Source: ILO 2010b.

While developed countries were hit hardest by the crisis, the capacity of some developing countries to deal with its effects is more constrained. Some 40 percent of countries facing a growth slowdown already had high poverty in 2009 and limited fiscal and institutional capacities to cope with economic volatility.[101]

Policy responses

Employment and income fluctuate in all economies, but how well insurance and other mechanisms address such fluctuations varies widely. The US system of unemployment insurance differs from Europe's. What is common, however, is that as countries become richer, social protection increases, with a larger role for public insurance and action. Dani Rodrik has argued that larger governments have been a corollary of the increase in risk from globalization.[102] We can see this during the recent crisis: almost half the Group of 20 countries extended the duration of unemployment benefits in 2009–2010, and more than a third extended the coverage.[103]

A review of international experience suggests that it is impossible to identify a configuration of rules and institutions that will lower unemployment.[104] This agnostic conclusion contrasts with the strong presumptions about the sort of labour market institutions and labour market flexibility that would be optimal as, for example, in the World Bank's *Doing Business* indicators.[105]

At the same time, more governments are addressing employment volatility and youth unemployment—for example in the Arab States, where such problems preceded the recent global crisis. The challenges can be traced not only to rapid labour force growth and economic growth that is not pro-poor but also to the limits on new job creation resulting from employment protection, especially in the public sector.[106]

Designing policy responses that are both financially and institutionally feasible and that avoid the pitfalls in developed countries is a major challenge. In countries with large informal sectors and often weak institutions, a mix of public insurance and self-insurance seems appropriate (box 4.5).[107]

How crises affect human development

Large increases in poverty are common in financial crises. The East Asian financial crisis in the late 1990s cast 19 million Indonesians and 1.1 million Thais into poverty. The Argentine financial crisis in 2001 increased the national poverty rate by 15 percentage points, and the 1998 crisis in Ecuador increased poverty by 13 percentage points.[108]

The impacts on income depend on whether adequate unemployment schemes are in place. Concerns about employment security and job loss have led most governments to address unemployment, although coverage and benefits are often partial and inadequate (see box 4.5). When social protection is lacking, people who lose their jobs must transition to the informal economy, where wages are lower and vulnerability is higher.[109]

The effects of crises on human development obviously go beyond income and can last longer. For example, poor families may decide to take their children out of school, to the detriment of children's future opportunities.[110] Crises also increase infant mortality and malnutrition, with severe long-run costs from stunting.[111] Estimates suggest that in Africa at least 30,000–50,000 children will die because of the recent financial crisis.[112] Damaging effects can extend to increases in the number of street children,[113] in suicide and crime rates, in abuse and domestic violence and in

---

BOX 4.5   Directions in employment protection

Today, about 150 countries operate some form of unemployment compensation program. In many developed countries the risk of unemployment has been widely addressed—particularly in Western Europe—through a variety of welfare programs, most notably unemployment insurance. Spending on social protection in most Western European countries is now 25–30 percent of GDP. While the architecture and coverage of such programs have remained much leaner in the United States, the trend has been towards providing more fall-backs in case of job loss. Discretionary social spending—including unemployment benefits—has accounted for nearly 40 percent of additional fiscal stimulus spending, although less than half the unemployed in the United States receive benefits.

But in developing countries even fewer of the unemployed receive benefits. One estimate suggests that just one unemployed person in five in Latin America and the Caribbean receives some form of unemployment compensation. This proportion falls to 1 in 33–50 in the Arab States and Sub-Saharan Africa. Argentina, Brazil, South Africa and Turkey have unemployment coverage in the range of 7–12 percent, while coverage is about 25 percent in the Russian Federation. Where coverage is available, the value of benefits is low. The average benefit remains at about 10 percent of wage loss replacement. Self-insurance and other informal coping mechanisms continue to be the dominant way for people to deal with job loss in developing countries.

Some countries, most notably Chile, have mandatory individual savings accounts requiring employers and sometimes workers to deposit 3–9 percent of earnings. While such schemes can be motivated on both macroeconomic (boosting savings rates) and incentive grounds, they raise design and capacity challenges as well as equity concerns. Some workers may not accumulate enough savings to draw on during an unemployment spell, particularly young workers and low-wage earners in the informal sector.

Publicly subsidized insurance schemes have become more widespread. For example, South Korea and Turkey have compulsory unemployment insurance. Workers must make a specified contribution and meet eligibility requirements, with benefits payable for 7–10 months. In China unemployment benefits are available for a small share of the urban labour force, with benefits set by local governments at below the local minimum wage.

Source: Commander 2010; Blanchard 2008; Salehi-Isfahani 2010; Freeman 1998; Rodrik 1998; ILO 2010a; Vroman and Brsusentsev 2009; Robalino, Vodopivec, and Bodor 2009.

ethnic tensions.[114] Recent evidence suggests that increases in unemployment will outlast declines in output.[115]

The impact of crises on child mortality is often worse for girls. Evidence from 1.7 million births in 59 developing countries for 1975–2004 showed that a 1 percent drop in GDP was associated with an increase in average infant mortality of 7.4 deaths per 1,000 births for girls and 1.5 for boys.[116]

Some developing countries have protected their social sector budgets this time around.[117] South Africa allocated 56 percent of its stimulus to social protection. But in the Democratic Republic of the Congo and Myanmar the real wages of teachers fell as much as 40 percent, and in Madagascar, Sudan and Yemen they fell 20–30 percent. In many Sub-Saharan African countries payments to teachers and health workers were delayed.[118] Sometimes budget cuts are deemed necessary to respond to falling revenues, but many developing countries now have much more space to carry out countercyclical fiscal policy.[119]

Crises are often disequalizing. While millions have been laid off, others, like some investors, are protected by deposit insurance or benefit from bailouts. Those who gain—relatively and sometimes absolutely—are generally those with more assets, better information and greater financial agility—and those with influence.[120]

A long-run perspective

Despite the harsh effects, it is important to keep the current crisis in long-run perspective. This crisis was the worst since the Great Depression only for developed countries. Most developing countries saw much worse declines in the early 1980s, and some—like China and India—have continued to grow robustly. Indeed, world output is projected to be 1 percent higher at the end of 2010 than before the crisis. Our estimates also indicate that life expectancy and enrolment continued to increase, yielding a world HDI in 2010 of 0.68, 2 percent higher than in 2007. In developed countries, however, the HDI has grown only slightly, as large drops in income have offset gains in health and education.

At the same time the crisis brought market regulation into much sharper focus and raised major questions about the sustainability of the model and approaches underpinning the economic boom of the 2000s. Earlier this year, the United States approved a major reform of its financial regulatory system, increasing the number of financial firms subject to oversight, regulating many of the derivative contracts that were at the root of the crisis and creating a regulatory body to protect consumers of financial services. We return to the broader implications in chapter 6.

The threat of climate change

The main threat to maintaining progress in human development comes from the increasingly evident unsustainability of production and consumption patterns. Current production models rely heavily on fossil fuels. We now know that this is unsustainable—because the resources are finite and their impacts dangerous. The close link between economic growth and greenhouse gas emissions needs to be severed for human development to become truly sustainable. Some developed countries have begun to alleviate the worst effects by expanding recycling and investing in public transport and infrastructure. But most developing countries are hampered by the high costs and low availability of clean energy sources. Developed countries need to blaze the trail on decoupling and support developing countries' transition to sustainable human development.[121]

Early *HDRs* addressed environmental threats, and more recent *HDRs* have tackled climate change and water scarcity. National and Regional HDRs have addressed these same issues, some from a national perspective (climate change in China and Croatia) and some focusing on topics of local significance (energy in the Russian Federation and water resources in Tajikistan). But the broader issue of sustainability—related to the use and distribution of financial and natural resources across individuals and generations—warrants much more attention in the face of current threats.

> The main threat to maintaining progress in human development comes from the unsustainability of production and consumption patterns

The conceptual questions of what sustainability means for human development—and how to assess and measure it—are not yet well understood. How can the observed divergence between increases in the HDI and environmental indicators be addressed? What is needed for the green economy and green growth, and how can they support and accelerate human development? How do we evaluate trade-offs? How can policy prescriptions for the green economy adequately consider the development and distributional implications? These basic questions require careful answers.

Part of the challenge in addressing sustainability at the global and national levels relates to measurement. But there is little consensus. Some analysts advocate a comprehensive measure of sustainability, which takes stock of whether the economy is depleting both natural and physical assets, and others believe in separating environmental sustainability from other types of sustainability. At a more philosophical level people disagree on whether an accumulation of physical assets can compensate for environmental degradation.

Existing measures reflect different positions. The World Bank's adjusted net savings rate is based on a comprehensive measure of capital that aggregates all types of assets and thus assumes that we can substitute some for others. The Global Footprint Network's ecological and carbon footprints and Yale University's environmental sustainability index focus solely on the environment.

All these alternative indicators nonetheless show that the world has become less sustainable. From 1970 to 2008 world-adjusted net savings fell by more than half, from 19 percent of gross national income to 7 percent, while total carbon dioxide emissions more than doubled (figure 4.6). Underlying these global trends are huge regional variations, though the pattern differs depending on the measure.[122]

This situation poses enormous challenges. It is imperative that low HDI countries attain high income growth—but as we have seen in other spheres, the spread of new ideas and technological innovations will be key to allowing countries to achieve green growth.

The consequences of environmentally unsustainable production are already visible. Increased exposure to drought, floods and environmental stress is a major impediment to realizing people's aspirations. The disappointing results of recent international climate change negotiations suggest that greater commitment from all countries is necessary if we are to face up to what may be the most serious threat the world has ever faced. As the 2007/2008 *HDR* emphasized, the world needs a binding international agreement to cut greenhouse gas emissions over a long time horizon that recognizes the imperatives of continuing poverty reduction and differing circumstances and capabilities. Even if we cut back emissions, we must also adapt to the higher temperatures that the world is already experiencing and that can be reversed only in the medium term.

In sum, two decades after the first *HDR* there is little evidence of progress in making the world more sustainable or in effectively protecting vulnerable people against shocks. The effects of the largest financial crisis in decades can still be felt, and the continuing reliance on fossil fuels is threatening irreparable damage to our environment and to the human development of future generations. These developments pose serious questions about the long-run feasibility of the world's current production and consumption patterns.

FIGURE 4.6 The world is becoming less sustainable

Trends in key measures of sustainability, 1970–2010

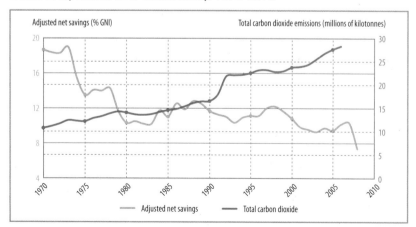

Note: Adjusted net savings excludes particulate emissions damage.

Source: World Bank 2010g.

*   *   *

This chapter has examined trends in empowerment, inequality, and vulnerability and sustainability to contribute to a fuller assessment of human development over the past 40 years.

The picture is mixed:

- Democratic processes have spread around most of the world, at the national and subnational levels, and there have been clear advances in the empowerment of some disadvantaged groups.

- Higher levels of the HDI are associated with greater equality—but inequalities within countries persist and income disparities are rising in many places.

- The spectre of global macroeconomic instability continues to hover over the world, and there is gaining evidence and recognition of the unsustainability of the world's current production and consumption patterns, an unaddressed challenge.

All these results underline the main message of this chapter—that all good things don't always come together. Thinking about human development involves broad objectives that go beyond monetary achievements. Bringing empowerment, inequality, and vulnerability and sustainability into the human development story implies reposing key questions about the direction of development policies and strategies. It highlights the need to assess the models of material progress that have generated some advances but are consistent with exclusionary and unsustainable political and productive practices. We discuss these implications in chapter 6.

Being able to better measure these dimensions would help deepen analysis and understanding of their role in our assessment of development. Chapter 5 presents key innovations to this end, related to the distribution of health, education and income—and casts more light on the nature and extent of absolute deprivation.

5 Innovations in measuring inequality and poverty

Human development is an expansion of the real freedoms of people to pursue lives that they value and have reason to value. The Human Development Index (HDI), launched in 1990, was a pioneering measure that went beyond income to reflect health and education. The 1990 *Human Development Report* (*HDR*) recognized that the HDI "captures a few of people's choices and leaves out many that people may value highly—economic, social and political freedom, and protection against violence, insecurity and discrimination, to name but a few." This gap has been highlighted in subsequent investigations of well-being.[1] Regional and National HDRs have created innovative measures of human development in a wide variety of ways, and a sizeable academic literature has emerged around the HDI and related topics.

To obtain a full picture of the evolution of human development, we must go beyond the dimensions in the HDI. Significant aggregate progress in health, education and income is qualified by high and persistent inequality, unsustainable production patterns and disempowerment of large groups of people around the world. This chapter and chapter 6 review the implications of this broader vision for measuring human development and designing development policies and strategies.

A simple matrix shows how the HDI covers an important core of human development, complemented by the new measures introduced here and presented in the statistical annex (table 5.1). The columns list the components (health, education, material goods, political participation and social cohesion), and the rows list the empirical measures of those components (deprivation, average level, vulnerability and inequality). Environmental sustainability, for example, is captured by vulnerability, which relates to human development prospects and risks. The table displays the areas with advances in measurement this year (stronger colours) and the areas to be pursued in future *HDRs*.

TABLE 5.1 Measuring human development

Towards a new human development dashboard

| Empirical measure | Components of Human Development | | | | |
	Health	Education	Material goods	Political	Social
Average level	Human Development Index			Empowerment indicators	
Deprivation	Multidimensional Poverty Index				
Vulnerability	Indicators of environmental sustainability, human security, well-being, decent work				
Inequality	Inequality-adjusted HDI				
	Gender Inequality Index				

Source: HDRO based on Pritchett (2010).

Three new multidimensional measures

In the most notable innovations in this 20th anniversary year, we introduce three multidimensional measures of inequality and poverty to the *HDR* family of measures:

- The Inequality-adjusted HDI (IHDI), estimated for 139 countries, captures the losses in human development due to inequality in health, education and income. Losses in the three dimensions vary across countries, ranging from 1 percent in education (Czech Republic) to 68 percent in income (Namibia), and tend to be largest in low HDI countries.
- The Gender Inequality Index (GII), estimated for 138 countries, reveals gender disparities in reproductive health, empowerment and labour market participation. The losses in these achievements due to gender inequality, as expressed by the GII, range from 17 percent to 85 percent, with larger losses concentrated in the Arab States and South Asia.[2]
- The Multidimensional Poverty Index (MPI) identifies overlapping deprivations suffered by households in health, education and living standards. An estimated one-third of the population in 104 developing countries, or about 1.75 billion people, experience multidimensional poverty. More than half live in South Asia, though rates are highest in Sub-Saharan Africa, with significant variation across regions, groups and indigenous peoples.

As described in box 1.2 in chapter 1, the HDI is a summary aggregate of progress in health, education and income, and improvements are regularly made in its indicators and functional specifications. The reforms reinforce its value and centrality as an approach to thinking about development.

Our approach is informed by the many National HDRs that have expanded methods of analysing human development. Indeed, measurement innovations have been spawned nationally and locally. Most of them are highly context driven and may not be practical or relevant across countries due to data constraints. Even so, these local adaptations provide valuable insights (box 5.1).

Advances in knowledge and data allow for innovations in measuring multidimensional inequality and poverty, which can be applied globally to enable comparisons and provide new insights.

BOX 5.1

Innovations in measurement: the Human Development Index in action

Several National Human Development Reports (HDRs) have assessed broader aspects of well-being at the national level by extending and adapting the standard Human Development Index (HDI):

- A Bosnia and Herzegovina report examined social exclusion as a multidimensional concept in the shift from socialism and in the wake of conflict. It measured political participation in elections and civil society, access to services, and extreme and long-term exclusion and found that half the population suffers social exclusion, which disproportionately affects rural residents, the poor, the elderly, young people and children with special needs.
- A Colombia report demonstrated the effects of armed conflict on people's lives, using data on homicide, displacement, war

degradation (crimes committed under conflict circumstances), governability and violence. Drawing on social dialogues with communities across the country, it analysed the underlying causes of conflict and identified enhancing freedoms and addressing inequalities as solutions. It pointed to a range of policies beyond military action to complement high-level peace negotiations.
- A Costa Rica report explored the relationship between citizen insecurity and human development. It introduced new tools to measure citizen insecurity at the district level, including security (especially violence and theft), perceptions of insecurity and individual liberties. It discounted the conventional HDI values and redrew the map of Costa Rica based on broader notions of well-being.

Source: Based on Gaye and Jha (2010). See www.hdr.undp.org/en/nhdr/.

Measuring multidimensional inequality—the Inequality-adjusted HDI

The HDI presents averages, concealing wide disparities in human development across people in a country. Previous *HDR* estimates of inequality have been partial (such as income only) or have covered just a few countries (15 in 2006). Building on an innovation in the 2002 Mexico HDR that was recently extended in a Regional HDR for Latin America,[3] this Report constructs the IHDI to be directly comparable to the HDI, reflecting inequality in each dimension of the HDI for a large number of countries. The IHDI has desirable statistical properties for cross-country estimates and enables combining data from different sources—such as health data from life tables and income data from household surveys.[4] A full set of estimates related to the IHDI for all the countries for which data are available is in statistical table 3.

The IHDI takes into account not only a country's average human development, as measured by health, education and income indicators, but also how it is distributed. We can think of each individual in a society as having a "personal HDI." If everyone had the same life expectancy, schooling and income, and hence the average societal level of each variable, the HDI for this society would be the same as each personal HDI level and hence the HDI of the "average person." In practice, of course, there are differences across people, and the average HDI differs from personal HDI levels. The IHDI accounts for inequalities in life expectancy, schooling and income, by "discounting" each dimension's average value according to its level of inequality. The IHDI will be equal to the HDI when there is no inequality across people, but falls further below the HDI as inequality rises. In this sense, the HDI can be viewed as an index of "potential" human development (or the maximum IHDI that could be achieved if there were no inequality), while the IHDI is the actual level of human development (accounting for inequality). The difference between the HDI and the IHDI measures the "loss" in potential human development due to inequality.[5]

Varying losses in human development due to inequality

We estimate the total loss in human development due to multidimensional inequalities, the loss in each dimension and the effects of inequality on country HDI rank.[6] The average loss in HDI is about 22 percent—ranging from 6 percent (Czech Republic) to 45 percent (Mozambique). More than 80 percent of countries lose more than 10 percent, and almost 40 percent lose more than 25 percent (see statistical table 3).

Generally, countries with less human development have more multidimensional inequality—and thus larger losses in human development—though there is significant variation. Figure 5.1 shows the largest and smallest losses across HDI groups and the patterns of losses. For instance, among the low HDI countries, Mozambique loses more than 45 percent of its HDI value whereas Ghana loses 25 percent. Among the high HDI countries Peru loses 31 percent compared with 8 percent for Ukraine. The highest loss among developed countries is for South Korea, which loses almost 17 percent.

People in Sub-Saharan Africa suffer the largest HDI losses because of substantial inequality across all three dimensions, followed by South Asia and the Arab States (figure 5.2). South Asia shows high inequality in health and education: India's loss in HDI is 41 percent in education and 31 percent in health. Considerable losses in the Arab States can generally be traced to the unequal distribution of education. Egypt and Morocco, for example, each lose 28 percent of their HDI largely because of inequality in education. In other regions the losses are more directly attributable to inequality in a single dimension.

People in developed countries experience the least inequality in human development. East Asia and the Pacific also does well, particularly in access to healthcare and education, and formerly socialist countries in Europe and

> The IHDI takes into account not only a country's average human development but also how it is distributed

FIGURE 5.1

FIGURE 5.1   **Inequality has large impacts on human development**

Loss in HDI due to multidimensional inequality

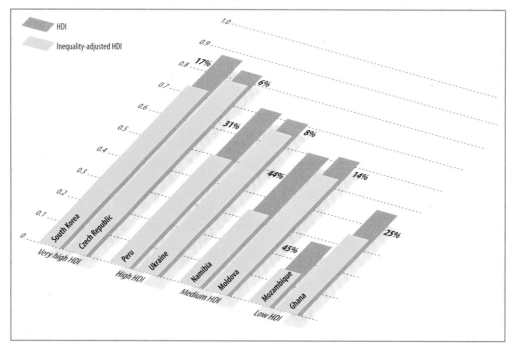

Note: Numbers beside bars are percentage loss due to multidimensional inequality (see statistical table 5).

Source: HDRO calculations using data from the HDRO database.

FIGURE 5.2   **People in Sub-Saharan Africa, South Asia and Arab States lose most from inequality in human development**

Loss in the HDI and its components due to inequality, by region

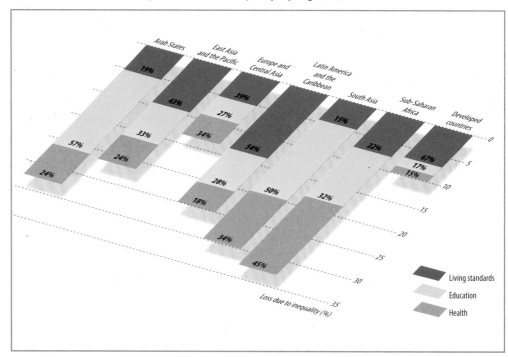

Note: Numbers inside bars are the percentage share of total losses due to inequality attributable to each HDI component.

Source: HDRO calculations using data from the HDRO database.

Central Asia still have relatively egalitarian distributions across all three dimensions.

By calculating the IHDI at different points in time, changes in different aspects of inequality can be estimated and compared. For example, between 2000 and 2005 Brazil's HDI losses due to inequality fell from about 31 percent to 28.5 percent, given declines in inequality across all the dimensions, falling by 3 percentage points in health and 2 percentage points in education and income.

Losses often greater in health and education than in income

In more than a third of countries inequality in health, education or both exceeds that in income. The range of loss is from 4 percent (Iceland) to 59 percent (Afghanistan) in health, from 1 percent (Czech Republic) to 50 percent (Yemen) in education and from 4 percent (Azerbaijan) to 68 percent (Namibia) in income.

Both income and nonincome inequality tend to be greater in low HDI countries. The relationship between inequality and the HDI, however, is stronger for inequality in the nonincome dimensions than in income (see chapter 3). Overall, there is a negative correlation between achievement and inequality, but with great variation: some countries with below average years of schooling are no less equitable than countries with above average attainment.

Mean years of schooling are far lower in Brazil (7 years) than in South Korea (12 years), but the two countries have similar inequality loss in education (about 26 percent). Countries with similar life expectancy can also have very different inequality—for example, Pakistan (33 percent loss in health), Mongolia (23 percent) and the Russian Federation (12 percent). Inequality in life expectancy at birth is driven mainly by infant and child mortality.

These findings show the value of a truly multidimensional measure of inequality and point to potential policies. Dispersion in health and education is a major challenge for policymakers. For health, programmes are needed to reduce the gap in access to public services—such as vaccination programmes—between the rich and the poor.[7] And, as seen in chapter 2, most schooling is publicly provided, so stronger efforts are needed to promote equitable access.

Limitations of the Inequality-adjusted HDI

The IHDI captures the inequality that the HDI does not measure. But due to data and technical issues, it does not yet capture overlapping inequalities—whether the same people experience one or multiple deprivations.[8] As an experimental series, it will be improved over time in response to feedback and greater data availability.

> In more than a third of countries inequality in health, education or both exceeds that in income

Measuring gender inequality—the Gender Inequality Index

Gender inequality remains a major barrier to human development. Girls and women have made major strides since 1990, but they have not yet gained gender equity. In this section we review ways to measure and monitor gender inequality, and we extend the methods applied to measuring multidimensional inequality to gender. The GII, introduced as another experimental series, is unique in including educational attainment, economic and political participation and female-specific health issues

and in accounting for overlapping inequalities at the national level. It is thus an important advance on existing global measures of gender equity. A full set of GII estimates for all the countries for which data are available is in statistical table 4.

Measures of the disadvantages for women raise awareness of problems, permit monitoring of progress towards gender equity objectives and keep governments accountable. Thanks to collective efforts by governments, civil society and international agencies—including the International Labour Organization, the Organisation for Economic Co-operation and Development, the World Bank and the World Economic Forum—the amount of published data that incorporate a gender perspective has increased considerably since 1990.

The first global gender indices were launched in the 1995 *HDR*—the Gender-related Development Index (GDI) and the Gender Empowerment Measure (GEM)—just before the Fourth World Conference on Women, held in Beijing. The GDI considered inequalities by gender in the HDI dimensions.[9] The GEM focused on political participation (measured by women's shares of parliamentary seats), economic participation (shares of high-level and professional positions) and power over economic resources (income gaps). These two pioneering efforts gained some public visibility, supported by annual reporting, and signalled the importance of collecting and analysing gender-disaggregated data. Both the GDI and the GEM provoked debate about how to construct a valid and reliable gender index.[10]

Critics have noted three key drawbacks of the GDI and GEM.[11]

- The measures combine absolute and relative achievements. Thus, a country with low absolute income scores poorly, even with perfect gender equity. The GDI adjusts the HDI for gender inequalities, thereby measuring both total achievements and disparities—though it is often misinterpreted as reflecting only the latter.
- Extensive imputations were needed to fill in missing data. For the relative income shares in both indices, more than three-fourths of country estimates were partly imputed. With income the most important driver of the wedge between the HDI and the GDI, this imputation was particularly problematic.
- Nearly all indicators in the GEM arguably reflect a strong urban elite bias and use some indicators more relevant to developed countries.

These problems partly reflect severe data limitations, which still exist, but the GII addresses the key criticisms. It does not rely on imputations. It includes three critical dimensions for women—reproductive health, empowerment and labour market participation. It captures these dimensions in one synthetic index, since joint consideration of empowerment and development reflects important complementarities.[12] And none of the underlying measures pertains to a country's general level of development, so developing countries can perform relatively well if gender disadvantages are limited.

The approach is consistent with that for inequality—comparing two groups, women and men, and considering only inequalities between them, at the country level (see *Technical note 3* for more details). Like the IHDI, the GII captures the loss of achievement in key dimensions due to gender inequality. It ranges from 0 (no inequality in the included dimensions) to 1 (complete inequality).

The GII increases when disadvantages across dimensions are associated—that is, the more correlated the disparities between genders across dimensions, the higher the index.[13] This recognizes that the dimensions are complementary and that inequality in schooling tends to be correlated with, say, access to work opportunities and maternal mortality.[14] Overlapping disadvantages are an important aspect of gender inequality, and capturing them is a major advantage of the GII. This contrasts with the IHDI, for which data limitations impede capturing associations across dimensions. The method also ensures that low achievement in one dimension cannot be totally compensated for by high achievement in another.

Dimensions and indicators

Figure 5.3 summarizes the dimensions and indicators of the GII and suggests the huge data limitations in measuring how women and girls fare across the globe. We briefly discuss each in turn.

Reproductive health

Two indicators measure women's reproductive health: the maternal mortality ratio and adolescent fertility rates.[15] The well-being

FIGURE **5.3**   **Components of the Gender Inequality Index**

GII—three dimensions and five indicators

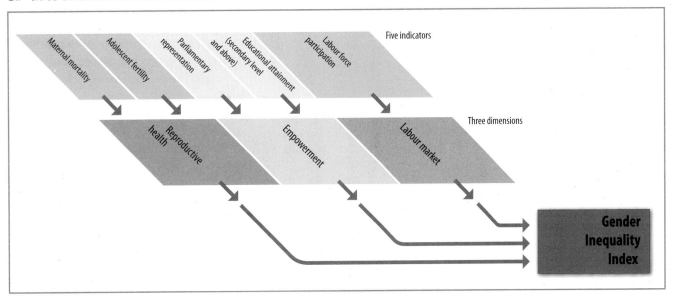

Note: The size of the boxes reflects the relative weights of the indicators and dimensions.

Source: HDRO.

of women during childbirth is intrinsically important and a clear signal of women's status in society. The risk of death in childbirth is reduced through basic education, adequate nutrition, and access to contraceptives, antenatal health services and skilled attendants at birth. However, such services are still denied to too many women, even though many services are inexpensive.

Countries exhibit enormous variation in maternal mortality ratios, even countries at similar incomes. Iran enjoys a higher per capita income than Costa Rica, but Iran's maternal mortality ratio is 4.5 times Costa Rica's. Indonesia's per capita income is slightly higher than Mongolia's, but its maternal mortality ratio is more than 9 times higher. Maternal mortality in the United States is 11 times that of Ireland, the leading country on this front.

Reproduction is not only risky—it often begins too early, compromising health and limiting future opportunities. Early childbearing, as measured by the adolescent fertility rate, is associated with greater health risks for mother and baby and tends to prevent young women from going to school, often destining them to low-skilled jobs at best.[16]

Empowerment

Women have traditionally been disadvantaged in the political arena at all levels of government. To capture this disadvantage, we use the ratio of female to male representatives in parliament. National parliamentary representation, which reflects women's visibility in political leadership and in society more generally, has been increasing over time—though the global average is still only 16 percent. In 2008 Rwanda's parliament became the first to have a majority of women.

Higher educational attainment expands women's freedoms by strengthening their capacity to question, reflect and act on their condition and by increasing their access to information. Educated women are more likely to enjoy satisfying work, participate in public debate, care for their and their family's health and take other initiatives. We focus on differences in secondary and higher educational attainment.

Labour market

Female labour force participation, which includes both the employed and unemployed (actively looking for work) as well as those

Important gender issues not included due to data constraints

Gender roles influence how men and women spend their time. In addition to working in the labour force, many women have the additional burden of care giving and housekeeping, which cut into leisure time and increase stress and exhaustion. While better understanding is emerging of how time use affects well-being, this information is not generally available or regularly collected and thus cannot be included in global measures.

Information about the ownership of economic assets by women, either alone or co-owned with a spouse, is crucial; immovable assets are especially important. However, data are not widely available. The Food and Agriculture Organization of the United Nations has a new database on gender and land rights that covers six topics—legal framework, land tenure, international treaties, customary laws, civil society organizations and land use statistics—but for fewer than 100 countries.

Violence against women is sadly very prevalent but not documented in an internationally comparable way. The World Health Organization estimates that the share of women who have experienced physical or sexual violence is as high as 71 percent in some countries.

For participation in decision-making, community-level indicators would be valuable—for example, on representation and leadership, which have become more important in many countries, including India. However, comparable data are available for only a few countries. Data on the gender breakdown of electoral turnout are equally scarce.

Source: Agarwal 2003; UNDESA-DAW-CSW 2010; Desai 2010.

seeking part-time work, stagnated at around 51 percent in 2008.[17] Women in the Arab States increased their participation by about 9 percentage points since 1980, to 27 percent in 2008, which is still only about half the global average.[18]

While useful, labour force participation neglects occupational segregation in the labour market and the gender wage gap (see chapter 4). Direct measures of income disaggregated by sex are not available for a sufficiently large number of countries.[19]

Unmeasured dimensions

Other important issues are relevant to women's well-being, such as time use, access to assets, domestic violence and local-level empowerment, but reliable and timely data are lacking (box 5.2). These concerns must inform renewed efforts to improve the information base to support greater awareness, public discussion and policy-making (chapter 6).

Large losses due to gender inequality across the HDI spectrum

Loss in achievement due to gender inequality, selected countries

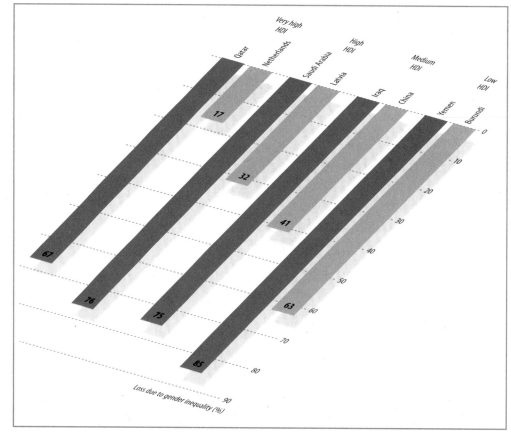

Source: HDRO calculations using data from the HDRO database.

Tremendous variation in gender inequality

The GII ranges from 0.17 to 0.85 (reflecting percentage losses in achievement of 17 percent to 85 percent). Figure 5.4 shows the largest and smallest losses by HDI classification. The Netherlands tops the list as the closest to gender equality, followed by Denmark, Sweden and Switzerland. The average GII for the 10 countries closest to gender equality is 0.23. The Netherlands has very low maternal mortality, has among the world's lowest adolescent fertility rate and is close to parity in educational attainment, political participation and employment. Qatar is the farthest from gender equality among the developed countries, while Saudi Arabia, Iraq and Yemen are farthest from parity in their HDI groups. Burundi emerges as the closest to gender equality among the low HDI countries, as does China among the medium HDI group.

The bottom 10 countries (in descending order) are Cameroon, Côte d'Ivoire, Liberia, Central African Republic, Papua New Guinea, Afghanistan, Mali, Niger, the Democratic Republic of the Congo and Yemen, with an average GII of 0.79. Other countries with high gender inequality are Benin, Malawi, Saudi Arabia and Sierra Leone. Saudi Arabia shows high human development, with a global HDI ranking of 55, an HDI of 0.75 and income per capita of nearly $25,000. However, despite good female educational attainment, women are nearly absent from parliament, and female labour force participation rates are only one-fourth those of men, giving the country a GII value of 0.76 and ranking it 128th of 138 countries.

Regional patterns reveal that reproductive health is the largest contributor to gender inequality around the world (figure 5.5). The Arab States and South Asia are both characterized by relatively weak female empowerment. Women are also affected by unequal labour force participation in the Arab States. Women's political participation is greater in Sub-Saharan Africa than in the Arab States, Europe and Central Asia, and South Asia, but

FIGURE 5.5 **Reproductive health is the largest contributor to gender inequality**

Loss due to gender inequality, by region

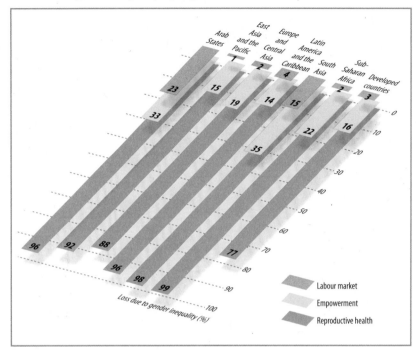

Source: HDRO calculations using data from the HDRO database.

empowerment is offset by disparities in education. Countries in Europe and Central Asia have few women in parliament, though they are close to parity in educational attainment and employment, and they have low maternal mortality ratios.

More generally, the bottom-ranked countries all have appalling records on multiple dimensions of women's well-being. For the bottom 20 the average maternal mortality ratio is about 915 deaths per 100,000 live births, and the adolescent fertility rate is 111 births per 1,000 women ages 15–19, both well above the global averages of 273 deaths and 54 births. Moreover, there is only one woman for every eight men in parliament.

The correlation is strong (0.87) between gender inequality and the loss due to inequality in the distribution of the HDI. This suggests that countries with an unequal distribution of human development also experience high inequality between women and men and that countries with high gender inequality also have an unequal distribution of human development (figure 5.6).[20]

FIGURE 5.6 Comparing inequality losses in human development

Losses due to gender inequality compared with multidimensional inequality

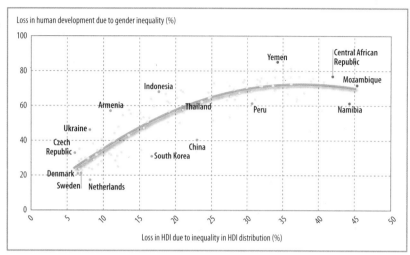

Source: HDRO calculations using data from the HDRO database.

and 70 percent (gender). Countries in the middle of the distribution—with inequality loss of about 21 percent and gender loss of about 58 percent—include Mexico and Thailand. Countries doing the best on both fronts—inequality loss of less than 10 percent and gender loss of less than 22 percent—include Denmark, the Netherlands and Sweden.

Limitations of the Gender Inequality Index

The GII is not perfect. Among its shortcomings is the bias towards elites that remains in some indicators (such as parliamentary representation). Even so, the inequality adjustments cast important new light on the position of women in almost 140 countries.[21] Yielding insights on gender gaps in well-being and empowerment, it also underlines the importance of proactive public policy to overcome systemic disadvantages.

Among the countries doing very badly on both fronts are the Central African Republic, Haiti, Mozambique and Namibia, each with losses of more than 40 percent (inequality)

Measuring poverty— the Multidimensional Poverty Index

A focus on deprivation is fundamental to human development. The dimensions of poverty go far beyond inadequate income—to poor health and nutrition, low education and skills, inadequate livelihoods, bad housing conditions, social exclusion and lack of participation. Experienced by people around the world and brought into vivid relief by the fieldwork that informs this Report (box 5.3), poverty is multifaceted and thus multidimensional.

Money-based measures are obviously important, but deprivations in other dimensions and their overlap also need to be considered, especially because households facing multiple deprivations are likely to be in worse situations than income poverty measures suggest.[22]

The MPI is grounded in the capability approach. It includes an array of dimensions from participatory exercises among

poor communities and an emerging international consensus. However, because the measure requires that all data pertain to the same household, the options of dimensions for the measure were limited. For example, surveys that collect the information necessary to assess other important dimensions have insufficient data on work, empowerment and consumption. Better data are needed in such core areas as informal work, empowerment, safety from violence, and human relationships (social capital and respect)—a theme we revisit in chapter 6.

The MPI, simple and policy relevant, complements monetary-based methods by taking a broader approach.[23] It identifies overlapping deprivations at the household level across the same three dimensions as the HDI and shows the average number of poor people and deprivations with which poor households contend. A

Jiyem, 70, lives near Jenar in Indonesia, with her husband, son, daughter-in-law and grandchild. Jiyem's husband, Djojo, is blind and cannot work. Her son, Paninyo, has a mental disability and works as a harvester, earning about $1.10 a day. Jiyem used to work on a farm, but now she just collects the remains of the rice harvests, which brings her no money but provides some food. No member of Jiyem's household has completed primary school. They are deprived in several indicators of standard of living—they have a dirt floor and no electricity, running water or adequate cooking fuel—as well as in nutrition.

Salome, 30 years old, lives with her husband and six daughters in the Lunga Lunga slum in Nairobi. Her husband can work only when jobs are available in the surrounding industry park, which is not often. She cannot work because she has to take care of their children, but she earns a little money from other households by delivering water. The family has no electricity, running water or adequate sanitation facilities. Salome has given birth to seven children, one of whom passed away a few years ago at 4 months of age. Merah, 6 years old, should already be enrolled in school with her older sisters, but Salome and her husband cannot afford the registration fee of 300 Ksh ($4). The other children range in age from 3 months to 14 years. Salome and her husband sometimes

cannot provide meals for the family, so they rely on other community members. "I am worried about not being able to feed my children," she says. Salome's household is deprived in health, education and standard of living.

Lydia, 35, lives in Manarintsoa, one of the poorest districts of Antananarivo, Madagascar. She lives in a small makeshift cabin, with a dirt floor and no water or electricity, built by her brother on a plot of land that she rents for $2.30 a month. A single parent since her husband left four years ago, Lydia lives with her four children and one grandchild. She earns $0.31–$0.63 a day by selling salvaged garbage, such as plastic bottles, cans, shoes and rags. On a typical day she rises at 5 a.m. to secure a stall in the market to sell the goods she salvages. She then goes home to have breakfast with her children, usually coffee and sometimes some bread, before returning to her stall. Hasina, her eldest daughter, does household chores while Lydia works. The family's main meal is dinner; they usually buy lunch only on holidays. Her youngest children, ages 4 and 6, also collect scrap metal for resale or beg in order to buy food. Lydia's household is deprived in several standard of living indicators—they have a dirt floor and no electricity, toilet or running water—as well as in education and nutrition.

Source: Field studies conducted as part of *Human Development Report* background research; see Alkire and Santos (2010).

full set of estimates related to the MPI for all the countries for which data are publicly available is in statistical table 5.

This new measure replaces the Human Poverty Index (HPI), published since 1997.[24] Pioneering in its day, the HPI used country averages to reflect aggregate deprivations in health, education and standard of living. It could not identify specific individuals, households or larger groups of people as jointly deprived.[25] The MPI addresses this shortcoming by capturing how many people experience overlapping deprivations and how many deprivations they face on average. It can be broken down by dimension to show how the composition of multidimensional poverty changes in incidence and intensity for different regions, ethnic groups and so on—with useful implications for policy.

Overall patterns of multidimensional poverty

The MPI is the product of the multidimensional poverty headcount (the share of

people who are multidimensionally poor) and the average number of deprivations each multidimensionally poor household experiences (the intensity of their poverty). It has three dimensions mirroring the HDI—health, education and living standards—which are reflected in 10 indicators, each with equal weight within its dimension (figure 5.7). A household is multidimensionally poor if it is deprived in at least two to six indicators (the cut-off depends on the weight of the specific indicator in the overall measure; see *Technical note 4*). The cut-offs are austere, reflecting acute deprivations, and most are linked to the Millennium Development Goals.

Immediately apparent is that the MPI is most appropriate for less developed countries. It captures the widespread deprivations in South Asia and Sub-Saharan Africa and in the poorest Latin American countries. It reveals the magnitude of poverty beyond monetary measures—an important accomplishment. In short, it helps capture and vividly convey overlapping deprivations—building on international consensus, captured in the Millennium Development Goals, about the

FIGURE **5.7** **Components of the Multidimensional Poverty Index**

MPI—three dimensions and 10 indicators

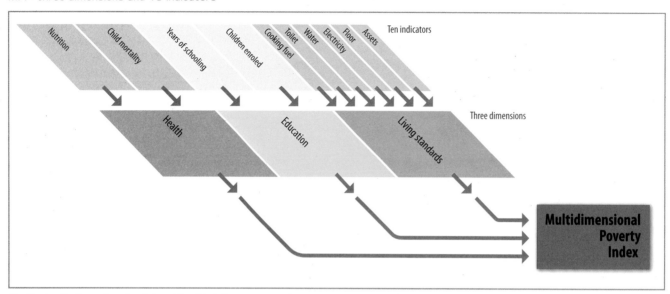

Note: The size of the boxes reflects the relative weights of the indicators.

Source: Alkire and Santos 2010.

dimensions of serious, and indeed unacceptable, disadvantage.

In sum, we estimate that about a third of the population in 104 countries, or almost 1.75 billion people, experience multidimensional poverty.[26] For example, they might live in a household that has a member who is undernourished, that has experienced a child death or that has no member with five years of education and no school-age children who are enroled in school. Or they might live in a household deprived of cooking fuel, sanitation facilities, water, electricity, floor and assets.

Today, the most widely used measure of poverty is income poverty, using either a national poverty line or an international standard. Preliminary analysis suggests that the MPI captures overlapping but still distinct aspects of poverty. Plotting the national headcounts of those who are income poor (using the $1.25 a day poverty line) against those who are multidimensionally poor shows that in most countries—including Ethiopia, Guatemala and Morocco—the number of people who are multidimensionally poor is higher. Figure 5.8 highlights the pattern for selected countries, with the full set of results presented

in statistical table 5. In 19 of the 72 countries in the sample that have both the MPI and the income poverty measure—including China, Sri Lanka, Tanzania and Uzbekistan—the headcount rate for income poverty is higher than that for multidimensional poverty. In general, the lower the national HDI, the more likely that multidimensional poverty exceeds income poverty.[27]

Our aggregate estimate of 1.75 billion multidimensionally poor people exceeds the 1.44 billion people estimated to be living on less than $1.25 a day in the same countries, but it is below the 2.6 billion people estimated to be living on less than $2 a day.[28] For most countries the estimates differ, for several reasons. First, the measures capture different concepts, so they would not be expected to fully converge. Second, in many developing countries income and consumption are difficult to measure, especially because of the size of the informal sector and home-produced consumption. Third, in some countries the resources measured by the MPI are provided free or at low cost; in others, they are out of reach even for working people—hence we see that countries with relatively good access to services have

FIGURE **5.8** | **Comparing multidimensional and income poverty**

Percentage of people living in poverty: MPI and income poverty, selected countries

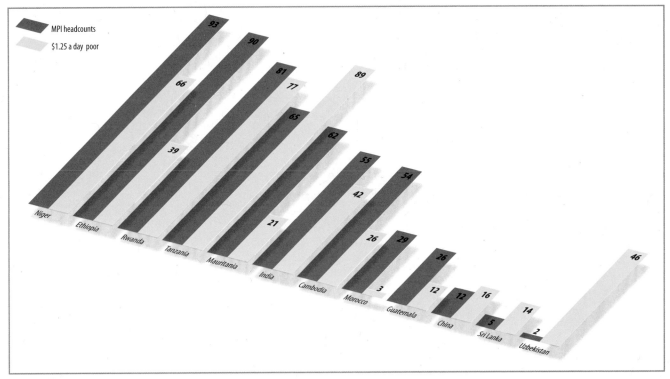

MPI headcounts

$1.25 a day poor

Niger 93, 66
Ethiopia 90, 39
Rwanda 81, 77
Tanzania 65
Mauritania 62, 21
India 55, 42
Cambodia 54, 26
Morocco 29, 3
Guatemala 12
China 12, 26
Sri Lanka 5, 16
Uzbekistan 2, 14
89, 46

Source: HDRO calculations using data from Alkire and Santos (2010).

an MPI that is significantly lower than monetary-based estimates—for example, Sri Lanka, Tanzania and Uzbekistan. This is not the case in countries such as Ethiopia and Niger, where deprivations beyond inadequate income are even worse. Moreover, at the individual and household levels people have different abilities to convert income into nutrition or education gains—for example, in households where there are people with disabilities or special needs. The MPI is thus intended to complement monetary measures of poverty, including $1.25 a day estimates. The relationship between these measures, as well as their policy implications and methodological improvement, are priorities for further research.

How are the multidimensional poverty headcount and its intensity related? The relationship is surprisingly consistent: countries with higher multidimensional poverty headcounts tend to have more deprivations (figure 5.9). At the same time, interesting outliers emerge—countries with a low poverty headcount but high intensity of poverty (such as Myanmar, Philippines and Viet Nam) and countries with a high headcount but low intensity of poverty (such as Bangladesh, Cambodia and the Democratic Republic of the Congo).

Multidimensional poverty by region and country

The regional rates of multidimensional poverty vary from around 3 percent in Europe and Central Asia to 65 percent in Sub-Saharan Africa. South Asia is home to the largest number of people living in multidimensional poverty, followed by Sub-Saharan Africa (figure 5.10).

- Sub-Saharan Africa has the highest incidence of multidimensional poverty, with considerable variation across the 37 African countries in our sample—from a low of 3 percent in South Africa to a massive 93 percent in Niger—while the average

FIGURE 5.9

Countries with higher multidimensional poverty headcounts often have higher intensity of deprivation

Average intensity of poverty relative to share of population considered poor

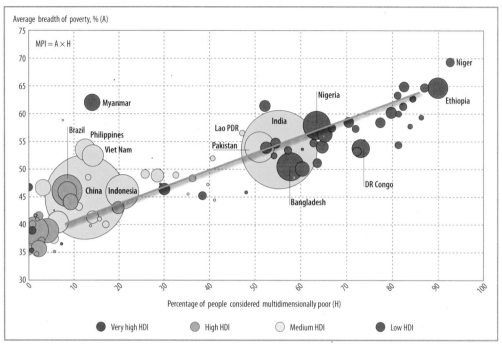

Note: The size of the circles represents the population in each country.

Source: HDRO calculations using data from Alkire and Santos (2010).

FIGURE 5.10

Most of the world's multidimensional poor live in South Asia and Sub-Saharan Africa

Distribution of the world's multidimensional poor living in developing countries

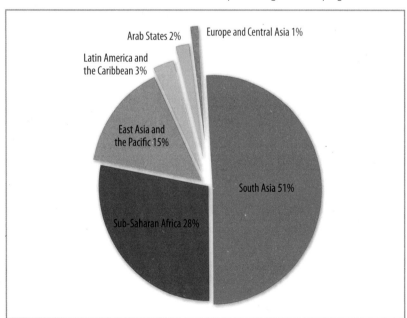

Note: The sample includes 98 developing countries covering 92 percent of the population in developing countries.

Source: HDRO calculations using data from Alkire and Santos (2010).

share of deprivations ranges from about 45 percent (in Gabon, Lesotho and Swaziland) to 69 percent (in Niger). In Guinea, Mali and Niger more than half the population is poor and has experienced a child death. In those countries as well as Burkina Faso, Burundi, Ethiopia and Mozambique more than half the population is poor and lives in a household where no one has completed primary school.

- Eight Indian states, with poverty as acute as the 26 poorest African countries, are home to 421 million multidimensionally poor people, more than the 410 million people living in those African countries combined. Thus, the MPI starkly exposes the intensity and incidence of multidimensional poverty in South Asia as greater than in any other region.

- In most of East Asia and the Pacific, including China and Thailand, rates of multidimensional poverty are relatively low. But more than half of Cambodians are estimated to be multidimensionally poor, mostly because of a lack of electricity, sanitation and cooking fuel.

- In Latin America and the Caribbean multidimensional poverty affects from 2 percent of the population (Uruguay) to 57 percent (Haiti, even before the devastating earthquake in 2010).
- The Arab States constitute a highly heterogeneous group of countries. The incidence of multidimensional poverty is generally below 7 percent—for example, the United Arab Emirates and Tunisia—but the rate rises to more than 14 percent in Iraq, to 28 percent in Morocco and 29 percent in Djibouti, and up to 52 percent in Yemen and 81 percent in Somalia.
- In Europe and Central Asia the levels of poverty estimated with the MPI are very low. The rates are close to zero in several countries, with the higher rates—5–7 percent—in Azerbaijan, Estonia, Kyrgyzstan and Turkey and the highest estimated rate, 17 percent, in Tajikistan. These figures reflect the limitations of using the austere MPI thresholds in countries that have fairly good access to basic services and should not be taken to imply that hardship does not exist in Europe and Central Asia.

Within-country variation is of great policy interest. In India Delhi's rate of multidimensional poverty is close to Iraq's and Viet Nam's (about 14 percent), while the state of Bihar's is similar to Sierra Leone's and Guinea's (about 81 percent). Figure 5.11 shows a decomposition in Kenya by province, and within the poorest and central provinces by urban and rural areas, relative to selected countries. Nairobi's MPI is slightly higher than Brazil's, while that for northeastern rural Kenya is worse than that of Niger, the poorest country in the sample.

Poverty can be investigated by ethnicity, religious affiliation and caste. Mexico's national multidimensional poverty measure, launched in 2009, highlighted poverty among indigenous peoples (see box 6.4 in chapter 6). In Bolivia poverty was 27 percent among Mestizos, but 1.6 times higher among the indigenous Quechua. In India 81 percent of people of Scheduled Tribes are multidimensionally poor,

alongside 66 percent of those of Scheduled Castes and 58 percent of those of Other Backward Castes.[29] About a third of other Indian households are multidimensionally poor, with an MPI just below that of Honduras.

Limitations of the Multidimensional Poverty Index

Like the GII, the MPI has some drawbacks, due mainly to data constraints. First, the indicators include both outputs (such as years of schooling) and inputs (such as cooking fuel) as well as one stock indicator (child mortality, which could reflect a death that was recent or long ago), because flow data are not available for all dimensions. Second, the health data are relatively weak or have poor coverage, especially for nutrition, though the patterns that emerge are plausible and familiar. Third, in some cases careful judgements were needed

FIGURE 5.11 Huge within-country differences in multidimensional poverty: the case of Kenya

Multidimensional Poverty Index: Kenya's provinces compared with other countries

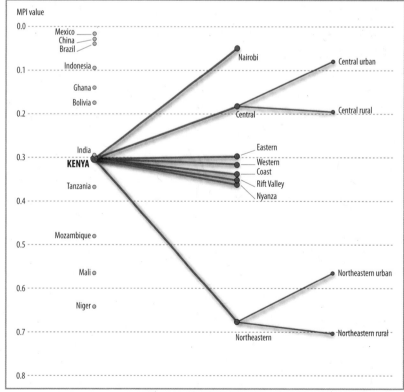

Source: Alkire and Santos 2010.

to address missing data. But to be considered multidimensionally poor, households must be deprived in at least six standard of living indicators or in three standard of living indicators and one health or education indicator. This requirement makes the MPI less sensitive to minor inaccuracies. Fourth, as is well known, intrahousehold inequalities may be severe, but these could not be reflected. Fifth, while the MPI goes well beyond a headcount to include the intensity of poverty experienced, it does not measure inequality among the poor.[30] Finally, the estimates presented here are based on publicly available data and cover various years between 2000 and 2008, which limits direct cross-country comparability.

Among the medium HDI group (Thailand, transition economies and some richer Latin American countries), the deprivations measured by the MPI are much less prevalent. But the low reported MPIs in these countries do not imply that there is no real poverty. While not well captured by the MPI, we know from the field and from complementary sources—including monetary-based estimates of poverty—that the suffering of poor people in these countries is real and that multidimensional inequality is often large.

*   *   *

This year's Report advances the measurement agenda for human development. Building on many years of research and critiques, it introduces new measures for multidimensional inequality—overall and by gender—and for poverty. It underlines the fundamental robustness of the HDI while introducing carefully conceived refinements. With the surge of interest in alternative measures of well-being, the HDI is assuming even greater prominence. It will remain a pillar of the HDR. Despite improvements in data availability and quality since 1990, huge gaps and shortcomings remain. Still lacking are good summary measures of critical aspects of well-being—most notably, empowerment. And more conceptual and empirical work is needed to bring the environmental sustainability and human development measurement agendas together. We return to these challenges in the forward-looking agenda outlined in chapter 6.

CHAPTER 6
The agenda beyond 2010

This Report opened by reaffirming the enduring relevance of human development in the 21st century. We have assembled a range of evidence and examined current thinking to inform and help chart the way ahead. This evidence has shown that people's lives can be improved through means already at the disposal of most countries, though progress is not guaranteed. Pathways to advancing human development are varied and specific to a country's historical, political and institutional conditions.

This Report has reached several conclusions about trends and patterns in the core measurable dimensions of human development:

- People in most, but not all, countries have made steady, long-term advances in health and education over recent decades.
- There has been no general convergence in income across countries, despite major growth surges in East Asia and the Pacific and India.
- The correlation between *changes* in income and *changes* in health and education over the last 40 years is weak. The most plausible explanation is that developing countries today face different opportunities and processes than those prevailing in the past.
- This does not mean that growth is unimportant—command over resources is still key to expanding many capabilities. It does mean that progress in health and education is attainable even when growth proves elusive.
- Global knowledge and technology are opening new options and paths and reducing the costs of basic achievements, putting a greater premium on policies that take strategic advantage of opportunities.
- The paths to success are diverse, with enormous variation in outcomes for countries with similar initial conditions. Many countries have done well in the long term by emphasizing health and education; oth-

ers have strived for rapid economic growth, though sometimes with a high cost to environmental sustainability.

- The policies and reforms compatible with progress vary widely across institutional settings and depend on structural and political constraints. Attempts at transplanting institutional and policy solutions across countries with different conditions often fail.

We also reviewed trends in dimensions of human development that are less commonly measured but no less important than those included in the Human Development Index (HDI). This review showed that:

- Formal processes of democracy have proliferated at national levels, so that most people now live in democratic societies and have the chance to vote in local elections as well—though democracy does not always ensure accountability.
- International, intergroup and interpersonal inequalities remain huge in all dimensions of well-being, and income disparities are on the rise.
- There is increasing evidence that the world's current production and consumption patterns are environmentally unsustainable.

The Report has also introduced key innovations in measurement. The classic HDI has been refined and complemented by new measures of inequality in the HDI, of gender disparities and of multidimensional poverty. While these innovations draw on newly available data and technical advances, the new series have been introduced on an experimental basis and will be reviewed in the light of discussion and feedback and future improvements in data.

These findings carry implications for the future human development agenda. While there are no silver bullets or magic potions for human development, three messages for policy emerge. First, we cannot assume that future development will mimic past advances: in many respects, opportunities are greater today and will continue to be so in the future. Second, varying experiences and specific contexts preclude making overarching policy prescriptions and favour more general guidelines instead. Third, major new challenges must be addressed—most prominently climate change.

Progress and the threat of climate change

Just as the past has been complex and nonlinear, any projections of the future are uncertain. In background research for this Report the average future trajectory of countries was modelled as following the path taken by more developed countries that started from similar initial HDI levels.[1] Such projections suggest that at lower levels of human development, substantial progress can be made in the coming decades. Based on past progress, a country would take around 70 years to move from, say, the Philippines' HDI to Spain's. To move from Niger's HDI to Madagascar's or from Cameroon's to Botswana's would take 25 years, or about a generation.[2] Alternative income scenarios generated by researchers around the world typically project that Asian countries, particularly China and India, will continue to converge with developed countries, while Latin America and the Caribbean and Sub-Saharan Africa will continue to lag.[3]

The underlying models do not anticipate events substantially more adverse, or more favourable, than those in the past. But unanticipated negative shocks—such as wars, epidemics and environmental calamities—would impair future human development. Positive shocks—such as cures for malaria and HIV and AIDS and the cessation of conflict—would push advances.

World population is forecast to reach 9 billion by 2050, with almost all the growth in developing countries. Without migration the population of developed countries would peak in 2020 and shrink somewhat over the following three decades. These changing demographics, along with rising incomes, will have consequences for natural resources and the environment. Climate change may be the single factor that makes the future very different, impeding the continuing progress in human development that history would lead us to expect. While international agreements have been difficult to achieve and policy responses have been generally slow, the broad consensus is clear: climate change is happening, and it can derail human development. It is expected to significantly affect sea levels and weather patterns and possibly human settlement and agricultural productivity.

One estimate suggests that by mid-century the adverse effects of climate change on grain yields will push prices up—more than doubling the price of wheat—with massive repercussions. In a worst case scenario, by 2050 per capita consumption of cereals falls by a fifth, leaving 25 million additional children malnourished, with South Asia the worst affected.[4] Long-term effects on agricultural productivity vary by region—generally adverse in arid and tropical regions, mainly developing countries, and positive in some colder parts of the world, including Canada and the Russian Federation.[5]

With greater recognition of the enormous risks, in some cases threatening the existence of island countries, thinking about climate change has been evolving rapidly. Climate change poses an enormous test for the international community—and the stakes are extremely high. Global and mostly irreversible, climate change is a matter of cross-country and intergenerational distributive justice, affecting the billions of people who will live in the rest of this century and beyond.

The challenge is to consider the policies and strategies that would be good for human development over time, so that improvements exceed those of the past and ensure that previously disadvantaged groups are included in future expansions of freedom. This must be done in ways that overcome the limits of carbon-intensive growth so that human development is truly sustainable.

An agenda for policy

Determining the policy drivers of human development is difficult because the questions are complex, the data sparse and the methods limited. The problems are perhaps best illustrated by the criticisms showered on statistical comparisons across countries (so-called cross-country regressions), criticism so extensive that scarcely any result on the relationship between policies and growth is uncontroversial.[6]

But other methods have shortcomings too. For example, while careful evaluations can yield precise answers to specific questions, many results of randomized trials of programme interventions cannot be extended beyond the experimental setting.[7] Similarly, in-depth country case studies do not necessarily apply across countries or even to the same country across periods, though case studies can provide valuable insights into the complexity and richness of local political, cultural and anthropological conditions.

Policies are devised and implemented every day around the world, and concrete advice is sought from development institutions and researchers. Thinking about development is a contested space where alternative ideas, interpretations and conceptions vie for acceptance. We have offered an interpretation of trends and patterns based on a close reading of history and empirical evidence as well as the basic normative ideals of the human development approach, helping us sketch a vision of the way forward and an agenda for change.

Because fast growth, even when sustained, has not automatically ushered in strong gains for broader aspects of human development, policies must be designed to advance income and other objectives together. Policy-makers can have several variables in view. While economic growth cannot be presumed to lead inevitably to human development and to less poverty, many countries have achieved both. The policies that advance economic growth and the nonincome aspects of human development differ—but they also overlap. We must pay more attention to these overlaps and the potential synergies.

Chapter 3 explored the centrality of how markets and states function in determining success and failure in human development. These forces are shaped by the underlying social contract—by norms and expectations about the roles and responsibilities of the state and the mechanisms of accountability and enforcement. Paths vary with the social contract between political and economic elites and social groups—affecting how the state delivers policies and public goods and services to expand opportunities and freedoms for all. This points to the need to take context seriously in thinking about the policies and programmes most likely to accelerate human development— a particularly relevant point for development partners seeking to provide support.

We do not conclude, however, that all institutions and policies are totally endogenous and captive to events occurring centuries ago. This would imply that policy choices are entirely preordained and that the scope for change— particularly for progressive reform—is inherently severely limited. Fortunately, the evidence does not support such pessimism. Case studies, historical evidence, cross-national empirics and experimental evidence are all pieces of the puzzle. At times they allow us to identify policies expected to promote human development, if

> The policies that advance economic growth and the nonincome aspects of human development differ—but they also overlap. We must pay more attention to these overlaps

at fairly high levels of generality. This evidence must be considered, developed and adapted nationally and locally.

For example, the capacity of state actors influences what can be done and whether politically supported objectives are distorted when implemented, especially in countries with low human development. The capacity of individuals and groups is critically conditioned by the way power is distributed in a society and its institutions, in part a legacy of persisting inequalities.

This brings us back to the recurring theme that no single strategy works well in all cases. Context clearly matters. Consensus is growing that the same policies can have different effects in different contexts.[8] What has worked in one place may not work in another. For example, both Mauritius and Haiti are island economies that created export-processing zones; these were highly successful in Mauritius but failures in Haiti.

Our review of human development over the past 40 years demonstrates that it is not useful for a global report to issue universal prescriptions. More useful is to push the policy and research agendas and discussions into several complementary domains. What are the more direct policy implications that emerge from this approach? We lay these out under three headings: key principles, context and global forces.

Considering principles to inform policy-making

Individuals, groups and leaders who promote human development operate under strong institutional, structural and political constraints that affect policy options. But experience suggests broad principles for shaping an appropriate agenda for human development.

One important finding from several decades of human development experience is that focusing exclusively on economic growth is problematic. While we have good knowledge about how to advance health and education, the causes of growth are much less certain and growth is often elusive.[9] Further,

an unbalanced emphasis on growth is often associated with negative environmental consequences and adverse distributional effects. The experience of China, with its impressive growth record, reflects these broader concerns (box 6.1) and underlines the importance of balanced approaches that emphasize investments in the nonincome aspects of human development, for both instrumental and intrinsic reasons.

Moreover, if growth is a means to various ends—as is now broadly accepted—"success" in growth must be evaluated for the broader human development goals that growth aims to advance. All the relevant variables have to be on the table, in view, at the same time.

Development goals should be discussed and defined through the public exchange of ideas in participatory deliberative forums. In this sense, ends and means come together. As Elinor Ostrom and others have emphasized, capability-enhancing services are always co-produced by people—children do not "receive" education, they use the infrastructure and inputs provided by the state to enhance their knowledge. Likewise, people need to co-produce their own health.[10] This underscores the point of Sen and others that people should be active participants in development, implementing development projects, rather than being treated as passive beneficiaries.[11]

In this light, we suggest several considerations to inform public debate about policy priorities and options:

- Equity and poverty reduction must be at the forefront of policy design, not add-ons. For example, policy-makers need to consider the likely beneficiaries of measures to promote employment, growth and access to public services. A recent example of a pro-poor employment policy is India's National Rural Employment Guarantee Act, which ensures 100 days of paid wage employment a year for any adult representing a rural household (box 6.2).

- All societies need institutions to manage conflict, resolve disputes and address ethnic, racial and class differences. Supporting such institutions requires a social contract to which most groups subscribe. Policies can

BOX 6.1   Development as freedom and China's changing view of development

When Deng Xiaoping stated in the 1980s that "development is the hard truth," he was speaking against the ideology of the Maoist era, when egalitarianism was emphasized at the expense of economic growth. China was one of the world's poorest countries, and rapid growth was viewed as the way to pull it out of poverty and strengthen it economically and on the global political stage. Thirty years later China is realizing these ambitions. But it has also incurred costs, which it is beginning to address.

China began its economic reforms in the late 1970s, adopting a development strategy that can be described as single-minded pursuit of economic growth. The government machinery became the agent of growth. To appraise the performance of different levels of government and key officials, a single criterion was proposed: the rate of a region's economic growth.

China explicitly bucked much of the conventional wisdom about how to manage the transition to markets. It prioritized economic over political reforms, and reforms proceeded without complete liberalization or privatization. Contrary to popular opinion, foreign direct investment and export growth have not been major drivers. Instead, much of China's growth occurred through township and village enterprises, businesses owned and operated by local governments.

The economy grew at a phenomenal 8 percent a year for three decades, and monetary poverty measures fell more than 80 percent between 1981 and 2005. Yet this success was not matched by performance in other dimensions of human development. China ranks first in economic growth since 1970, but 79th of 135 countries in improving education and health. In fact, China is 1 of only 10 countries in the 135 country sample to have a lower gross enrolment ratio now than in the 1970s. Slow progress was associated with decentralizing the financing of basic services without providing adequate national support or increasing the fees levied on families. Public social services deteriorated and in some places even collapsed.

The costs of single-minded pursuit of economic growth also became apparent in other dimensions. Escalating environmental pollution threatened many land, water and air systems that people depended on for their livelihoods, sometimes with global implications. Income inequalities worsened. By 2008 per capita household consumption in the coastal region of Guangdong was more than four times that in Tibet.

China adopted this pursuit of economic growth around the same time that Amartya Sen, and subsequently the *Human Development Report*, had begun to question this mode of thinking. Viewed through a capability lens, the problems China was experiencing called into question the very meaning and value of such income-based development.

In 2002 Sen's *Development as Freedom* was translated into Chinese and published by the People's University Press in China; it has been reprinted several times. An anecdote suggests that it might have had a significant impact, at least in some circles. At the height of the healthcare system reform in China in 2005, when the Ministry of Health convened an expert group meeting, each member was given a copy of *Development as Freedom*.

Reducing social imbalances is now a priority in the five-year plan. China has also recently launched major new policy initiatives aiming to develop a low-carbon economy and expand adoption of climate-friendly technologies. In 2009 it approved a national target for increasing the use of renewable sources to 15 percent of energy use and committed to lowering carbon dioxide emissions by 40–45 percent of 2005 levels by 2020. The success of such reforms in the world's most populous country has enormous implications for human development globally.

Source: UNDP China and China Institute for Reform and Development 2008; UNDP China and Renmin University of China 2010; Chen and Ravallion 2008; Liu 2010; Qian 2003; China NDRC 2006.

include redistributing income, addressing sources of vulnerability facing workers and families and striking a balance between promoting competition and enabling opportunities for profit that stimulate investment. Some rents are necessary for investment and innovation, as in patent protection, and the private sector can be a powerful partner in advancing development, as we saw in chapter 3.

- Domestic investment, private and public, is crucial. Few countries have progressed far solely on foreign investment and development assistance. Mobilizing domestic investment and entrepreneurship implies fostering a conducive climate, with some framework for protecting property rights. But again, case studies reveal diverse suc-

cessful approaches. Some countries have relied more on strategic bargains between the business elite and governments than on general institutional or legal reforms. Financing domestic public investment requires sufficient revenues, collected in ways seen as fair and transparent.

- Global integration into world markets, an important lever for growth, offers opportunities for increasing income. But countries can manage integration into the global economy in many ways that do not require full trade liberalization, thus allowing space for domestic industrial policies.

- Addressing the environmental risks should be integral to policy choices and regulatory design. Policies for adapting to climate change and fostering low-carbon

BOX 6.2   **India's National Rural Employment Guarantee Act**

India's National Rural Employment Guarantee Act (NREGA) of 2005, the world's largest public works programme ever, provides basic social security for rural workers: a universal and legally enforceable right to 100 days of employment per rural household on local public works at minimum wage. Labourers who are not given work within 15 days of asking for it are entitled to unemployment benefits.

The act has other noteworthy features:

- *Encouraging women's participation.* A third of employment generated is to be set aside for women and provided within 5 kilometres of their village; child care facilities (if required) must be provided at the worksite.
- *Decentralizing planning and implementation.* At least half of allocated funds are to be spent by elected local councils; village assemblies are to select and prioritize projects.
- *Creating rural assets.* People are to be employed to create public assets (such as roads and check-dams) as well as assets on private lands (such as land improvement and wells).
- *Imposing strict norms for transparency and accountability.* All documents are to be publicly available, with proactive disclosure of essential documents (such as attendance records), and periodic audits are to be carried out by village representatives.

In fiscal year 2009/2010 India spent almost $10 billion (approximately 1 percent of GDP) on the programme, and 53 million households participated. On average, each participating household worked for 54 days. Disadvantaged groups joined in large numbers; a majority of workers were members of Scheduled Castes or Scheduled Tribes, and more than half were women.

Payment of minimum wages and improved work conditions at NREGA worksites have created pressure for similar improvements in the private labour market, benefiting all rural workers. Distress migration to urban areas has slowed. And for many rural women programme earnings are an important source of economic independence. As Haski, a tribal woman from Rajasthan, said when asked who decided how programme wages should be spent: *"Main ghar ki mukhiya hoon"* (I am the head of the household).

Implementation has been challenging. Awareness is higher than for most pieces of legislation. "NREGA" has become a household word, and even school children can answer questions about workers' rights. But it takes time to understand the notion of "work on demand" as a legal entitlement, awareness that is crucial for NREGA to become a step towards the right to work or even an effective social security measure.

Other challenges include preventing corruption, ensuring accountability and enhancing people's participation in planning. Many of these challenges reflect the conflicts that play out when pro-poor legislation is implemented by inefficient state machinery that is often hostile to poor people. When the rules changed so that NREGA wages were paid through banks instead of government officials and intermediaries to prevent embezzlement, many government functionaries who had benefited from earlier leaks lost interest. This led to long delays in wage payments, causing great hardship.

NREGA's value for rural workers is evident in conversations with tribal members from Surguja District. Some had invested their NREGA earnings (such as in a bullock or bicycle), others used them to repay debts or for their child's education or to meet social obligations (such as wedding expenses). Field levelling undertaken through NREGA was also favourably received by farmers, who felt that they could double their crop yields as a result. Such responses are not uncommon and help validate the battle for employment guarantees.

Source: Written by Jean Drèze and Reetika Khera drawing on Drèze and Khera (2010).

development include promoting climate-resilient varieties of crops and livestock and financing low-carbon development initiatives.[12]

Strategies may yield good results in some contexts but not others, making flexibility a critical aspect of policy and institutional design. Governments that have generated short-term improvements in human development have not always sustained them over the long term, especially where improvements have not been translated into more inclusive political and market systems by addressing deeper issues around the social contract and distributive conflicts.

It is clear that different regime types have pursued effective human development strategies. In many countries alliances between business and political interests can advance the goal of human development.[13] Greater opportunities are opening up with advances in technology and global knowledge, but these also mean that the state's role in human development will be even more challenging. Because of the uncertainty over which policies and approaches are most likely to pay off for human development—and the risks—there is a premium on experimentation and learning by doing, with systematic monitoring and feedback.[14] Local capacity is as important as central capacity—the administrative elite may not have much influence in enabling access to services at the frontline.

As the set of actors continues to widen, information about preferences and possibilities for implementation must be gathered from diverse and less organized groups—from a broad cross-section of civil society.[15] Institutions of deliberative democracy, expanding globally, should be the main route to enabling engagement, though many countries have seen growing distrust of government institutions and antipathy towards the state.

Taking context seriously

Development thinking has to contemplate more systematically how different contexts matter and what makes some policies viable in some contexts but not in others. We consider two different yet related aspects of context: state capacity and political opportunities and constraints.

Capacity and progress

All policies and programmes require effective state capacity. Our review of the evidence on capacity found that its determinants and drivers remain poorly understood. Many officials face hard trade-offs every day, working in difficult, uncertain and under-resourced circumstances and bearing responsibility for controversial outcomes. This is true at the frontline—for nurses and teachers—and at higher levels of policy-making.

Beyond skill and infrastructure, capacity also reflects less tangible factors. It is shaped by the levels and types of power and organizational ability of people and institutions. It also reflects how people accept or resist the status quo and how institutions support or constrain a desire for change and the spread of information and open, critical debate.

This recognition takes us directly to a critique of two common approaches to policy design: the technocratic fix, which assumes a well functioning state and regulatory system, and the transplanted-institution solution, which assumes that successful institutions in developed countries can be transplanted to developing countries. In both cases institutions are likely to be distorted by prevailing social and political forces, and neither approach is likely to succeed.[16] The history of development projects that have pursued these routes shows a high likelihood of failure (box 6.3).

As illustrated in chapter 3, there are many ways to conduct institutional functions, and no single intervention is likely to have the power and traction to shift a complex system. There are limits to how quickly capacity can be developed and increased, and attempting to drive changes faster than the underlying consensus will support can provoke social and political resistance. This is particularly so when trying to redress power imbalances in favour of marginalized individuals and groups.

Organizations and institutions tend to evolve at different speeds through phases and in patterns that shape their capacity. This may conflict with donor timelines and the need to show results. Optimistic goals may be set without considering baseline capacity (which is assumed to exist or to be quickly created). Countries may attempt difficult tasks before they have the capacity to do so, which can slow the expansion of capacity.[17] A better understanding of local specificities and local power structures and of appropriate designs and timelines can help avoid such missteps.

BOX 6.3 **Case studies and some lessons of project implementation failures**

Hundreds if not thousands of project evaluations have documented implementation problems. Often such projects have world-class design—drawing on approaches that have worked elsewhere—and involve large investments of time and money. Yet the impacts have been weak. Consider two examples.

Mozambique, since emerging from conflict nearly two decades ago, has effected far-reaching changes to its governance systems. Its impressive progress is reflected in multiple peaceful elections and in a 54 percent increase in its Human Development Index since 1990. Public financial management reforms strengthened budget processes and budget documents, but budget execution is still largely a black box. Asked about this, officials complained that the new laws and systems are part of the problem. Transplanted best practices may look impressive but may not fit agency needs, match management capacities or reflect political and organizational realities. The officials noted that they were never asked about what kind of system they needed.

Peru in the early 2000s received support from the United Nations Development Programme to reform its judicial system. The initiative created new institutions and strengthened old ones, but the complexity of reforming the entire judicial system, coupled with structural inertia and local resistance, inhibited transformational change.

Many development projects—like the two cited here—deal with functions widely regarded as core government responsibilities. Achieving objectives requires not just "good policy" but also transaction-intensive policy implementation. And that requires supporting approaches that respond to local needs, engage local stakeholders and fully consider structural constraints and local complexities.

Source: Andrews and others 2010; UNDP Evaluation Office 2009.

Aligning policy and the political economy

Societies can go through major transitions because of external shocks or the cumulative effect of internal processes of social and political change. Transitions to democracy and resolutions of conflict are examples of the latter. Since the first *Human Development Report (HDR),* important changes of this type have taken place, notably in South Africa with the ending of apartheid; in Indonesia and Mexico, with the transition to democracy; in Nepal, after the accord with the Maoists and the removal of the monarchy; and in Guatemala, after the peace accords. Less dramatic shifts can occur through normal electoral transitions—such as the election of Evo Morales in Bolivia on a platform supporting the rights and interests of indigenous peoples and the election of the coalition formed by the Congress Party in India, with its support for expanding the provision of social services.

While major changes present opportunities, policy-making during transitions can be complex. Vested interests can regroup, new actors can move into influential positions and organizational responses can be unpredictable. For example, the post-1990 "big bang" reforms in former Soviet bloc countries yielded mixed results, illustrating the hazards of radical policy shifts in transitional institutions.

While major critical junctures can provide opportunities to rewrite the social contract, even during more ordinary times there is scope for policy reform that influences the dynamics of human development. But to be workable, policy proposals should be aligned with local capacities and the domestic social contract. Opportunities to effect gradual change can enable major reforms over time. Several examples highlight how major changes can affect the development trajectory—or fail to get off the ground.

- *India's deregulation since the early 1990s.* India has a long tradition of entrepreneurial activity, with well established business families and networks. Many business families supported the independence movement and were politically aligned with post-independence governments. The extensive regulations during the first few decades

after independence restricted corporate activities but did not threaten domestic business interests. The 1990s liberalization removed restrictions on corporate activity and steadily opened the economy to foreign competition—in effect, reducing regulatory burdens in return for greater efficiency. The evidence on business development in new sectors and on entrepreneurs emerging from different socioeconomic groups suggests a new dynamism.[18] But there is intense debate about rising inequality, the need for complementary social actions, and problems with specific aspects of corporate governance and state-business relations.

- *Ethiopia's strides in key aspects of human development.* Primary school enrolment in Ethiopia rose from 33 percent in 1991 to 95 percent in 2007, astounding for a country with a per capita income of less than $1,000. Indeed, since 1990 Ethiopia has the 14th highest rate of progress in improving health and education and the 11th fastest upward move overall. How did this come about? In 1991 the Ethiopian People's Revolutionary Democratic Front, a Marxist, pro-peasant movement toppled the dictatorship, and the new government focused on ethnic federalism and socioeconomic development to consolidate its base of support.[19] Education became a national priority in an effort to boost enrolment, which had been stagnant or even declining for decades. Federal, regional and local governments assumed joint responsibility for implementing reforms, supported by large increases in domestic financing and external support.[20] The scale-up has also strained the education system, as evidenced by high dropout rates, overcrowding and rising student–teacher ratios—but the overall achievements in delivering basic services are nonetheless impressive.

- *The United States' passage of healthcare reform in 2010.* Progressive healthcare reforms, intended mainly to increase equity of access, were narrowly endorsed by a sharply divided Congress despite unanimous opposition from the conservative Republican Party. Reformers sought to confront escalating costs and declining coverage in a political

> There are many ways to conduct institutional functions, and no single intervention is likely to have the power and traction to shift a complex system

climate that became acrimonious. They faced strong opposition from vested interests, not least the private insurance companies, antiabortion groups and a coalition of medical interests.[21] Although President Barack Obama was elected on a platform of change, reform sentiments were diminishing rapidly. Strategic compromises brought the bill to fruition.[22] Some people expressed frustration that the bill did not provide a public pillar or universal access, and others were concerned about costs. But the legislation is expected to expand health insurance coverage to 32 million more people.

- *Argentina's fight against corruption in the health sector.* Political economy constraints can undermine even effective policies. In 1997 the government of the city of Buenos Aires ordered the managers of 33 publicly owned hospitals to report the prices they were paying for comparable inputs. The city government processed the information and sent it back to all participant hospitals, identifying the managers who were paying the highest prices. Average prices paid fell 10–15 percent as a result of these disclosures, but the policy was soon abandoned because of intense opposition from organized groups. The poor people who used public healthcare did not protest the policy's reversal, perhaps reflecting their disempowerment.[23]

The policy and political texture of these stories is denser and more complex than these summaries can convey. And in each of these countries there are counter-examples of resistance to or adoption of progressive reforms. But the point remains that some policy changes, even if not prompted by major transitions, can contribute to a process that alters the social contract itself as well as the level and distribution of wealth creation and opportunities for human development. India's policy moves were consistent with a long-term shift towards a more open and dynamic capitalism. While oligarchic forms of capitalism could still undercut the dynamic form, the policy moves clearly changed the state-business relationship.[24]

Other measures—to strengthen competition and regulation—seek to shift the functioning of markets and the state more directly. Regulatory attempts can be contested, shaped by those they are meant to control or overshoot—as with financial re-regulation in Europe and the United States in the wake of the recent global financial crisis. Success or failure likely depends on the political equilibrium and the policies themselves. Similarly, actions to increase the public's access to information—embodied in right to information laws that have spread around the world in developed and developing countries alike (including India and Mexico)—are good examples of this type of opening up.

The way the two most important drivers of change—markets and the state—work needs to be understood in terms of the underlying social contract. Social contracts evolve, especially in response to the pressures of domestic groups. Policy design that ignores such institutional processes is likely to be irrelevant.

Shifting global policy

Global forces also create and constrain opportunities for human development. We focus on two crucial dimensions: the need for stronger, principle-based global governance and for aid and partnerships among countries that are sensitive to the principles outlined above.

Global governance
Some problems are beyond the capacity of individual states to deal with effectively, such as international migration, equitable trade and investment rules, and international threats, most notably climate change. These require a global governance system.

Two elements of global governance critical to human development are democratic accountability and institutional experimentation.[25] Democratic accountability requires that global institutions adequately represent the views of people and countries around the world and do not reinforce the deep inequalities in the distribution of economic and political power. It requires broader representation of developing countries in the governance of international financial institutions, perhaps through double

> How the two most important drivers of change, markets and the state, work needs to be understood in terms of the underlying social contract; otherwise, policy is likely to be ineffective or irrelevant

majorities (requiring approval by a majority of votes and voting shares).[26] Institutional experimentation means opening up policy and institutional spaces to allow people and societies to adjust, adapt and frame their own development strategies. It involves rethinking the frameworks of conditionality premised on ineffective one size fits all approaches to policy-making.

Solutions must of course be adapted to the institutions needing reform and the problems being addressed. Yet the basic principles can be broadly applied: a global governance system that promotes democratic accountability, transparency and inclusion of the least developed countries; a stable and sustainable global economic climate; and financial stability.

We illustrate these principles for climate change, an important issue for global debate and governance because the actions (and inaction) of any one country can have implications beyond its borders. For human development to be sustainable, the link between fossil fuels and economic growth has to be severed, beginning in the developed countries, which are responsible for a disproportionate share of damaging emissions. Development strategies need to incorporate low-carbon patterns of economic activity and increase resilience to climate-related shocks. Individual initiatives alone cannot halt climate change: to prevent greenhouse gases from reaching dangerous concentrations, national governments need to modify the energy matrix, and that requires incorporating the environmental cost of using fossil fuels in the price of energy. The point of price realignment is not only to cover these costs but also to change consumer behaviour as people come to recognize that energy waste (through inefficient appliances or fuel-inefficient cars) has dire implications for current and future generations.

For developing countries substantial new financing for environmental policies is becoming available through emerging carbon markets. The World Bank recently estimated that carbon markets mobilized $144 billion in 2009 and that more than 60 countries now participate in the Clean Development Mechanism of the Kyoto Protocol.[27] More research and development—and an international mechanism for jointly developing and transferring clean technology across countries—are also needed, as are more efficient agricultural practices to meet expected higher demand for grain and water.

Current responses to climate change consist largely of uncoordinated local, national and international efforts. Local efforts include regulations to "green" cities and to use low-carbon fuel in public transport (as in New Delhi). National efforts include voluntary commitments to reduce emissions. And international efforts include limited financing to reduce greenhouse gas emissions, such as the Clean Development Mechanism. Such limited and uncoordinated approaches are unlikely to halt—much less reverse—global climate change.

The global governance system needs to step into the breach—but national governments have failed to enable such action. The 2009 UN Climate Conference in Copenhagen delivered very little agreement on actionable items. Some of this failure can be traced to an absence of democratic accountability and deliberation. Uneven representation in global forums that favours developed countries impedes progress in reducing greenhouse gas emissions. Developing countries also lack capacity and negotiating strength, which limits their ability to participate fully in deliberations. Meeting the challenges of climate change will require addressing both democratic accountability and institutional experimentation.

Without major reforms and initiatives, prospects are bleak: global greenhouse gas emissions are rising, and 1.6 billion people still lack access to modern energy services. One hopeful sign is the United Nations Collaborative Programme on Reducing Emissions from Deforestation and Forest Degradation (REDD) in developing countries, which was launched in 2008 to help developing countries prepare and implement national REDD+ strategies and which builds on the convening power and expertise of several UN agencies. To date 12 developed countries have pledged $4 billion to "slow, halt and eventually reverse" deforestation in developing countries—a significant step forward that also incorporates the needs of people who depend on forests for their livelihood.[28]

For human development to be sustainable, the link between fossil fuels and economic growth has to be severed

Aid and partnerships

So, politics are important. Local context and ownership matter. And there is no one size fits all or single best practice to follow. What, then, are the implications for aid and partnerships?

A recurring theme in *HDRs* since 1990 is the need for public resources, both domestic and international, to support human development. We apply a similar lens to our analysis of aid, stressing the need for targeting support to health, education and growth and the importance of the transmission of ideas.

Low HDI countries received aid approaching 15 percent of their gross national income (GNI) in 2007. In Sub-Saharan Africa aid averages 44 percent of government budgets. It reaches as much as 89 percent in Lao PDR and 81 percent in Ethiopia, both among the top 11 HDI movers.[29] Aid can also help avert deteriorations in human development, as in the massive effort to provide antiretroviral treatment to people with HIV or AIDS, which expanded treatment coverage rates from 300,000 people in 2002 to 3.7 million in 2009 and has been enormously important in forestalling what could have been an even more dramatic drop in life expectancy (see chapter 2).[30]

Recent research confirms significant positive effects for aid targeted to health and education.[31] The success of the UN Expanded Programme on Immunization and the Pan American Health Organization's Revolving Fund for Vaccine Procurement in promoting large-scale vaccination programmes was discussed in chapter 3. The eradication of polio in Latin America, the bridling of the AIDS epidemic in Thailand, the marginalization of river blindness in West Africa and the improved capacity to keep mothers from dying during childbirth in Sri Lanka are just a few of the successes of development aid.[32] They suggest that while resources matter, more vital are how aid is targeted, how it is combined with technical assistance and how it supports human development priorities.

But resources are necessary—and scarce. There has been little progress towards the Millennium Development Goal target of increasing aid to 0.7 percent of donors' GNI: official development assistance currently stands at 0.31 percent,[33] lower than in 1990 (0.34 percent).

Debates on aid effectiveness in policy and academic circles have become increasingly polarized. Supporters argue that massive aid is needed to pull countries out of poverty traps and that aid has a strong positive effect on long-run growth—while acknowledging that the type of aid is also important.[34] Opponents argue that aid is seldom spent productively, that progress depends on policies and institutions rather than foreign assistance and that initial returns to aid diminish rapidly over time. They also highlight the risks of neocolonialism disguised as bilateral aid.[35] This debate is useful in highlighting weaknesses in traditional approaches but counterproductive to the extent that it undermines and diminishes partnerships.

The Paris Declaration goal that at least half of technical assistance projects be aligned with country programmes was achieved in 2008. The quality of systems for managing public funds has improved in many developing countries.[36] Aid disbursements have become more predictable.[37] And initiatives supported by a range of governments and stakeholders are improving aid effectiveness through better transparency and accountability.[38] Looking ahead, long-term partnerships and flexibility will remain critical for enabling development assistance to expand people's freedoms.

> Recent research confirms significant positive effects for aid targeted to health and education

An agenda for research

The 1990 *HDR* and subsequent editions have spawned a rich agenda of research and analysis on human development. This has been fostered at the country level by National HDRs that have explored a diverse range of topics—from empowerment and decentralization to gender and climate change and to policy implications. Universities around the world offer courses in human development. And a rich and growing body of research has informed policy-makers and policy activists around the world.[39] Here we point to three key priorities. How can we improve the data and analysis to inform debate? How should we rethink conventional approaches to studying development to ensure a people-centred vision? And how can the vision of human development help frame a better understanding of the dimensions of empowerment, equity and sustainability that are vital to expanding people's freedoms?

Improving data and analysis to inform debates

Data and measurement have real world consequences. Consider poverty. We know that poverty is unique in each region, group, family and individual. For instance, in Mexico the poverty endured by a young boy in Juarez differs from that experienced by a Mixteca weaver in the Sierra Madre de Oaxaca. But capturing these realities requires appropriate data and measures as well as institutional and political commitment. By adopting measures flexible and rigorous enough to comprehend poverty's many dimensions, the Mexican government has increased policy awareness of the breadth and depth of deprivation and informed policy priorities (box 6.4).

Policy-making is becoming more evidence-based. Data today are better than in 1990, and the value of data analysis, monitoring and evaluation are increasingly well recognized. Through international conventions most governments are committed to monitoring economic, social, cultural, civil and political rights—including those of women, people with disabilities, indigenous peoples and children—in ways that meaningfully assess equitable progress. International agencies and initiatives have supported and helped set standards for data gathering, notably the UN Statistics Division, the United Nations Educational, Scientific and Cultural Organization and the World Bank. In addition to official data collection, many nongovernmental bodies—such as universities, civil society groups and commercial firms—are collecting data that contribute to assessing human development.

But the quality, timeliness, relevance and accessibility of data remain perennial obstacles for policy-making, research and international assistance. These shortcomings affect both administrative data (school enrolment, causes of death) and survey information on individuals, households and firms. It is astounding, for example, that in 2010 there are still no comparable country data for maternal mortality over time. Widening the scope of data collection and improving the quality and timeliness of existing data are dual imperatives. Broadening access to the data of commercial data collectors is another issue to resolve.

Micro and household survey data have improved greatly since 1990—enabling us to use our new measures to estimate inequality and multidimensional poverty.[40] But country coverage and frequency remain low. Complex household surveys can reveal the connections among indicators, but they are costly and time-consuming. Lighter surveys also make valuable contributions. Good internationally comparable data are lacking in such critical areas as informal work, empowerment, protection from violence, and social and community relations.[41] Work is needed to integrate measurement of economic aggregates like GNI and their distribution—now based on different sources. Gender-disaggregated data on time use, control

---

BOX 6.4   Mexico's new multidimensional poverty measure

In 2009 Mexico became the first country to adopt a multidimensional poverty measure reflecting the multiple deprivations households face. The National Council for the Evaluation of Social Policy (CONEVAL) used a measure similar to the Multidimensional Poverty Index that we apply to more than 100 countries in this Report.

CONEVAL's approach addresses mandates in Mexico's Constitution and the 2004 General Law on Social Development. Individuals are considered multidimensionally poor when their income is too low to purchase the goods and services they need and when they are deprived in at least one of six dimensions: education, healthcare, social security, housing quality, basic household utilities and access to food. CONEVAL uses a biennial survey, in place since 1984, to track trends in multidimensional poverty and identify the number of dimensions in which households are deprived and the contribution of each deprivation to the intensity of poverty. Charged with monitoring the effectiveness of national social assistance programmes, CONEVAL can chart people's well-being in relation to a range of social deprivations.

Source: Alkire and Santos 2010.

of economic assets, decision-making and violence are scarce, with neglect of unpaid work a major issue (box 6.5).

For emerging measures of well-being, broad conventions are needed for defining indicators. One initiative encouraging debate on these issues is the Organisation for Economic Cooperation and Development Global Project on Measuring the Progress of Societies.[42]

Towards a new economics of human development

The weak long-term association between income growth and changes in education and health is an important finding and requires vigorous exploration.[43] Economists and social scientists need to better understand the dynamics and interconnections. Such studies would complement the extensive literature on economic growth and create a richer awareness of what advances human development alongside growth.

The economics of growth and its relationship with the study of development requires radical rethinking. A vast theoretical and empirical literature almost uniformly equates economic growth with economic development. Its theoretical models typically assume that people care only about consumption, and the analysis of optimal policies follows the same route.[44] The bias is extended to growth

---

BOX 6.5   The need to recognize unpaid work

Unpaid work, including housework and care of children and the elderly in homes and communities, contributes to well-being and to economic growth by producing a labour force that is fit, productive, knowledgeable and creative. Yet national statistics, including gross domestic product (GDP) and gross national income (GNI), ignore the home production activities carried out mainly by women in all economies and cultures (see figure). Similarly, despite the importance of unpaid care work to meeting many of the Millennium Development Goals, the goals do not mention it.

GDP neglects a disproportionate amount of women's work

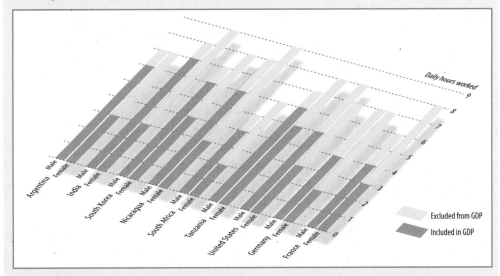

Source: Budlender 2008; Stiglitz, Sen, and Fitoussi 2009.

The omission of unpaid care work from national accounts leads to sizeable undercounts in all countries. By applying the wage rate of a general household worker to the number of hours that people spend on housework, the United Nations Research Institute for Social Development estimates that the omissions equal 10–39 percent of GDP. Incorporating unpaid work in national accounts would better reflect the realities of time use, especially for women.

Source: Stiglitz, Sen, and Fitoussi 2009; UNRISD 2010.

econometrics, where estimates of the growth effects of policies are the basis of policy recommendations. The assumption—often explicit—is that maximizing growth should be the policy-maker's objective.

The central contention of the human development approach, by contrast, is that well-being is about much more than money. We care about the possibilities that people have to advance life plans they have reason to value—income is critical but so are having access to education and being able to lead a long and healthy life, to influence the decisions of society and to live in a society that respects and values everyone. A vast array of evidence supports this view that people care about much more than income or consumption.[45] Theoretical and empirical models that assume that people aim only to maximize consumption are clearly deficient for studying human development. For example, the sustainability indicators discussed in chapter 4 are largely based on models in which agents care only about consumption now and in the future; still unexplored are the consequences of introducing education and health as objectives.[46]

Precisely because we care about so many different aspects of life we need an economics of development that explicitly recognizes its multidimensionality. This statement applies as much to the normative assessment of policies as it does to the models used to analyse and understand development progress. Our understanding of the complex connections between growth and the nonincome dimensions of human development is rudimentary. Human development goals need to be integrated into a framework that supports growth with equity and into well designed sectoral policies. We need to avoid the old discourse of being "for" or "against" growth. What is crucial is the expansion of people's real freedoms, and the greater command over goods and services made possible by rising income is important in facilitating the expansion of freedoms. But trade-offs can arise between multiple objectives and need to be carefully assessed, just as positive synergies need to be identified and exploited.

The potential distortions from elevating growth above all other dimensions of human

development are perhaps best illustrated by considering environmental degradation. Over the past 20 years, since the first Earth Summit in Rio de Janeiro, the importance of natural resources and the environment in development has become very clear. We face enormous challenges with water reserves, land degradation, climate change and the widespread loss of biological diversity and ecological services—challenges that impose new hurdles to promoting growth and broader progress in human development. Weak management of natural resources and the environment creates a heavier burden for poor people, who are usually more reliant on these resources for their livelihoods and who lack the assets to adapt to these changes or to absorb the additional cost. And poverty and low human development can lead to environmental degradation—for example, lack of secure land tenure often results in overfarming and land degradation.[47]

Environmental damage is not an isolated example. In chapters 3 and 4 we showed that high GDP growth does not necessarily mean progress in health, education or other dimensions of human development. Thus the factors and policies that foster high growth are not always the same as those that advance human development. The cross-country research discussed in chapter 3 found very different effects from such variables as urbanization, trade, democracy and institutions on growth and nonincome HDI. Our discussion of health and education improvements showed that the international transmission of ideas and technologies was a key factor in advances in these dimensions—in contrast to income growth, where productivity differences are vast and persistent.[48] Likewise, our case studies of successful performers often point—in contrast to the growth literature—to large public health and education initiatives.[49] The implication of these results is not that growth and human development cannot advance together but that it is a serious mistake to judge policies and institutional reforms solely on their effect on income, as much of the applied growth literature does.

Thus our call for a new economics of human development. The objective of this new framework would be goals related to well-being. Growth and other policies would be evaluated and pursued vigorously insofar as they advanced human development in the short and long term. The analysis would be relevant for developed and developing countries alike. Creating such a framework would be a demanding and complex undertaking—particularly if framed, as it must be, to recognize the sensitivity of climate to patterns of human activity. This research agenda would build on the work of research groups that have already made valuable contributions in these areas and on the research applying quantitative and qualitative interdisciplinary analysis of the relationships between growth and human development.

Research directions

Just as human development is about much more than income, so too is it about much more than the three components included in the HDI—health, education and income. In our reaffirmation of the human development concept, we stressed the need to consider how opportunities are distributed, how much power people have to shape their future and how today's choices affect the future. Past *HDRs* have greatly advanced our understanding of these dimensions, such as democracy, cultural liberties and climate change. Yet much more can be done to deepen our understanding of the relationship between human development and these broader dimensions—as highlighted below.

Empowerment
The ability of individuals and groups to engage with, shape and benefit from political and other development processes in households, communities and countries is a vital component of people's freedoms. As we showed in chapter 3, empowerment has been linked with positive outcomes in health, education and other dimensions of human development. The outcomes that individuals and groups can bring about depend largely on power relations in society, both in the public sphere (political institutions and the market) and the private (gender relations within households).[50]

Empowerment is closely associated with participation: the possibility for all people, including poor and marginalized people, to have their voices heard and to participate meaningfully in shaping debates that affect their lives. This notion has broad resonance, especially among civil society. In a survey of civil society organizations for this Report,[51] three-quarters of respondents agreed "to the highest extent" that empowerment was integral to human development (box 6.6).

While the Political Freedom Index of the 1991 *HDR* created an uproar (the index was subsequently withdrawn), the issue of political freedom has surfaced repeatedly in global and National HDRs. Yet in research for this year's Report, it once again became clear that this is highly contentious terrain. Article 21 of the Universal Declaration of Human Rights enshrines the right to "periodic and genuine elections which shall be by universal and equal suffrage and shall be held by secret vote or by equivalent free voting procedures." But in practice the political institutions of government are very heterogeneous.

Chapter 4 considered several existing measures of empowerment, underlining the scope for further research and debate and building on national and local discussions, such

---

BOX 6.6 **Some views from civil society on human development and empowerment**

In background research for this Report, we conducted an Internet-based survey of civil society organizations to learn their views. Respondents represented organizations ranging in size from 1 to 12,000 staff and volunteers working in a wide range of countries. Nearly all (94 percent) believed that having the opportunity to participate in societal decision-making is a critical aspect of development, and 76 percent agreed "to the highest extent" that empowerment is an integral component of human development. The most important dimensions of empowerment were identified as literacy and education, the right to vote and freedom of expression (see table).

Civil society views on most important dimensions of empowerment

Dimension	Most important (%)	Dimension	Most important (%)
Literacy and education	66	Decision-making in home	29
Right to vote	54	Joining voice with others	27
Freedom of expression	52	Protesting	19
Choosing one's own destiny	35	Standing or running for elected office	18
Making personal choices	33	Group identity	12

Source: Civil society organization survey conducted by HDRO staff.

as the recent National HDRs. Given that the measures used are so often contested, we are exploring new ways to develop a measure that highlights areas of consensus. For example, the theory of partial orderings can be used to build comparisons across countries that are robust to the weights used for each component—thus less vulnerable to disagreements on the relative relevance of each of them.

Participation is essential in defining the objectives of development and influencing decisions through engagement and dialogue. But meaningful participatory processes are complex. The national dialogue that fed into Bolivia's Poverty Reduction Strategy Paper is widely acknowledged to have tipped the balance of power towards disadvantaged groups.[52] However, other participation mechanisms, such as government-led consultations on religious arbitration in Canada and on secularism in France, have been criticized for allowing participation only on predefined themes.[53] Fruitful areas for research include the effects of national and local democratic structures on the forms of people's engagement, national and international policies to protect civil liberties, and community initiatives to monitor and hold governments accountable.

To move beyond mere formal consultation, people need the capabilities, information and institutional structures to advance claims effectively (see chapter 4). Democratic structures provide the preconditions for human development, but governments need to be fully accountable to their people in promoting the expansion of freedoms. A human development approach takes these antecedents very seriously while also considering a broader range of societal structures and institutions that are more (or less) conducive to process freedoms and mechanisms that support individual and group empowerment.

Inequality

Inequality in a range of dimensions and across groups—including women and men and poor and affluent—is a growing challenge to progress in human development. This Report has documented how multidimensional and gender inequality erode human development. And

many Regional, National and Local HDRs have investigated inequality in income and other human development outcomes.[54] Persistent inequalities, often structural, affect the opportunities available to people. Gender inequality, and its impact on human development, has received particular attention.[55]

Today, we know a lot more about the multiple dimensions of inequality, but we still have only a limited understanding of their evolution and key drivers.[56] We need to know more about how inequality interacts with structural forces, particularly with political economy factors and inequality in empowerment.[57] Various social and economic policies have addressed inequalities, while other policies, though not specifically aimed at equity effects, have nonetheless improved equity. We need a better sense of when and how progressive policies have played out in practice.

Research on inequality could systematically address the multiple manifestations of inequality and its underlying drivers. Chapter 5 gives us a snapshot of these differences and provides a fuller characterization of inequalities than was previously available. Priorities for analysis include the overlapping inequalities faced by specific groups—including women and girls, some ethnic groups and indigenous peoples—and how disadvantages interact and reinforce each other. Economic opportunities, legal guarantees, political participation and spatial inequalities should be jointly explored. Innovations in mapping techniques could visually display the distribution of human development nationally and regionally. Case studies of successful initiatives to address inequalities can suggest possible entry points for change.

Policy recommendations to reduce inequality have typically focused on redistributing income, promoting access to services and, to less extent, introducing progressive taxation. The *HDR* research agenda builds on these efforts to explore reforms aimed at addressing structural inequalities, which may relate in turn to political empowerment of disadvantaged groups and institutional change. The role of the state in eliminating barriers to empowerment and inclusion is a major theme.

> Priorities for research include the overlapping inequalities faced by specific groups and how to overcome disadvantages

Vulnerability and sustainability

Human development is about more than achieving desirable outcomes—it is also about securing these achievements against present or future threats. Previous *HDRs*, including the 1994 *HDR* on human security and the 2007/2008 *HDR* on climate change, have studied vulnerability and security at multiple levels—individual, national and global.

The relationships between progress in human development and risk warrant deeper investigation. This Report has made the case that all good things do not always come together. Advances in some aspects of well-being may be possible only at the cost of higher individual and collective risk. This is illustrated by the former Soviet bloc countries, whose centrally planned economies generated stable outcomes for many of their citizens but were not able to produce strong, sustained economic progress.[58] Innovation and efficiency require at least some degree of competition, although competition can also breed some uncertainty and risk.[59]

How does the human development approach help us think about trade-offs between risk and progress? In a general sense the answer is obvious: we should search for solutions that mitigate risk without sacrificing broad-based advances in well-being. But this is not always possible, and when it is not, societies need to confront hard choices. The pendulum seems to have swung too far in the direction of ignoring insecurity and vulnerability. Perhaps this is why, despite the advances documented in chapter 2, opinion surveys consistently show widespread dissatisfaction with key aspects of life—including those linked with security.[60] A reassessment is in order.

Consider again the dangers of catastrophic climate change, the cumulative effect of concentrating exclusively on economic growth and callously disregarding the warning signs of the resulting damage to the planet. But there are numerous other examples, as when liberalization leads to both increased income and lower job stability or when financial deregulation leads to higher growth but increased risk of crises.[61]

Measuring risk and vulnerability is difficult.[62] Policy-makers have an array of data for measuring aggregates—be they health, education, income or other quantifiable indictors of progress—but much weaker information about the risk of say, losing one's job, falling into recession or experiencing a natural disaster. This is partly because risk involves uncertainty. But it is also because we lack good measures of the risks we have faced in the past.

Risk raises concerns about sustainability. Since we are never certain what will happen in the future, all plans involve some degree of risk and vulnerability. But the trade-offs become different when we compare across generations and have to evaluate the effect of today's decisions on people who have not been born. Neoclassical economists would define a discount rate to trade off well-being across generations. But assigning weights to different generations raises serious ethical dilemmas: discounting the well-being of future generations just because they are not yet born seems unjustified, but sustainable human development cannot be isolated from concerns about poverty and inequality in the current generation.[63] Deeper conceptual thinking is necessary to work out alternative principles.

Measuring sustainability also requires considerably more work—many current measures differ radically in their conceptual basis and conclusions. A sound measure of sustainable human development, for example, should reflect how societies use various resources over time and judgements about which resources are substitutes or complements. This approach would differ from existing measures in considering not only the sustainability of consumption and production but also that of human development more broadly—including health, education, equity and empowerment.

Addressing sustainability increases tensions between intragenerational and intergenerational equity because not every policy will benefit poor people today as well as future generations. Key policy questions relate to the transition to renewable energy, development links with the green economy and green growth, and other market mechanisms, such as green taxes, cap and trade schemes for the environment, and regulatory frameworks to prevent

> This Report has made the case that all good things do not always come together

unsustainable use of resources—including property rights and financial oversight.

The risks inherent in climate change demand decisive action. In recognition, the 2011 *HDR* will focus on vulnerability and sustainability. A new global *HDR* on sustainability can broaden the debate on what should be sustained and what steps are needed to protect the world's most vulnerable people. Releasing the sustainability *HDR* in advance of the next Earth Summit in Rio de Janeiro in 2012 can influence the debate as the 1992 *HDR* did before the first Earth Summit.[64] A frank and open discussion of links, conflicts and complementarities will also help clarify the concept of sustainable human development.

* * *

This Report has underlined the value and robustness of the human development approach in thinking about and addressing the challenges of the 21st century.

The review of experience was broad, highlighting new findings that deserve further attention. People around the world have experienced dramatic improvements in some key aspects of their lives. They are healthier, more educated and wealthier and have greater power to select their leaders than at any other time in history. As a result, they have expanded their capabilities to lead better lives.

But we have also seen that the pace of progress is highly variable and that people in some countries and regions have experienced far slower improvements. Stark inequalities and vulnerabilities remain and are increasing in many places, giving rise to—and reflecting—acute power imbalances. And serious questions are being raised about the sustainability of current patterns of production and consumption.

We cast new light on some perennial challenges, not least the many dimensions of poverty and inequality. We identified persistent—and in some areas growing—inequalities in a range of dimensions across various groups as major challenges to progress in human development. The investigation of gender disparities revealed that some countries have achieved good outcomes in important areas but that gaps remain unacceptably large. A new measure of multidimensional poverty showed the intensity and reach of serious deprivation for more than 100 countries.

This final chapter proposed an agenda for expanding human development. Drawing on the rich legacy of thinking in this and related traditions, it focused on policies and research. On the policy front we identified the need for a principle-based approach to policy guidance; the importance of local context, particularly state capacity and the social contract within a country; and the importance of global forces, notably global governance and aid and partnerships. On the research front we highlighted the needs for collecting better data on the dimensions of human development, rethinking the conceptual basis for the study of development and investigating how the human development vision can better inform our understanding of the broader dimensions that are vital to our understanding of human development.

"Human progress," wrote Martin Luther King, Jr., "never rolls in on wheels of inevitability. It comes through tireless efforts and persistent work. . . . [W]ithout this hard work, time itself becomes an ally of the forces of social stagnation."[65] The human development idea exemplifies these efforts, carried out by a committed group of thinkers and practitioners who wanted to change the way we think about the progress of societies. But fully realizing the human development agenda requires going much further. Putting people at the centre of development is more than an intellectual exercise—it means making progress equitable and broad-based, enabling people to become active participants in change and ensuring that achievements are not attained at the expense of future generations. Meeting these challenges is not only possible but necessary—and more urgent than ever.

Notes

Chapter 1

1 Among recent efforts are the Stiglitz-Sen-Fitoussi Commission (www.stiglitz-sen-fitoussi.fr), the Organisation for Economic Co-operation and Development project on measuring well-being (www.oecd.org/progress) and the European Union framework for multidimensional indicators (www.ec.europa.eu/social/).

2 UNDP–HDRO 1990–2009; see inside back cover for a list of *HDRs*.

3 The literature and experience are vast; see Alkire (2010) for a review.

4 Sen 2002: 585.

5 Sen 2009a.

6 Crocker 2007; Narayan and Petesch 2007; Richardson 2006.

7 *The Economist* 1990.

8 *The Economist* 1991. The World Bank subsequently dropped the income-based ranking in 1998 and now presents countries alphabetically.

9 Anand and Sen 2000c.

10 Gertner 2010.

11 Kaletsky 1990.

12 Gittings 1990.

13 Seneviratne 1999.

14 Chahine 2005.

15 *The Straits Times* 1990.

16 John Williamson (1989) coined the term "Washington Consensus" to describe the policy prescriptions that the International Monetary Fund, World Bank and US Department of the Treasury promoted for developing countries hit by the economic crises of the 1980s. Key prescriptions were cutting government spending, reducing inflation, selling state enterprises, opening to trade and liberalizing exchange and interest rates.

17 See Nayyar (2008) for a review of the evolution of development thinking. On basic needs, see Ghai and others (1980).

18 The 1990 *HDR* (UNDP–HDRO 1990: 67; see inside back cover for a list of *HDRs*) included a chapter on development strategies that argued for "more realistic and operational" targets. The 1991 *HDR* developed these points, as did the 1994 *HDR*, which carried the global compact idea forward. Key conferences and summits over the period related to education (Jomtien 1990), children (New York 1990), environment (Rio de Janeiro 1992), population (Cairo 1994), social development (Copenhagen 1995) and women (Beijing 1995).

19 UN 2000.

20 Hulme and Fukuda-Parr 2009: 4.

21 UNDP 2010.

22 New indicators have been added over time to address some of these dimensions, as in 2005 when a target on access to reproductive health was added.

23 This is clearly indicated in a box authored by Sen as co-chair of the Commission on Human Security (2003). See also Alkire (2003), Gasper (2005), ul Haq (1995) and Tajbakhsh and Chenoy (2007).

24 *Journal of Human Development and Capabilities* 2003; Gasper 2005.

25 International Commission on Intervention and State Sovereignty, the 2003 Commission of Human Security, the 2004 High-Level Panel on Threats, Challenges and Change. See Jolly, Emmerij, and Weiss (2009).

26 Including Canada, Japan, Norway and Switzerland.

27 African Union, European Union, Association of Southeast Asian Nations, Organization of American States and League of Arab States. See UN (2010a).

28 UN 2010a.

29 Anand and Sen 2000b; Osmani 2005; Sen 2004, 2005.

30 Vizard 2006.

31 Edwards and Gaventa 2001: 277.

32 The Gallup World Poll asked respondents who had heard of global warming whether they perceived it to be a serious threat. On average, more than three-quarters of respondents in 126 countries described it as serious.

33 Neumayer 2010a.

34 Kant 1785; *HDR* 1994 (UNDP–HDRO 1994: 13; see inside back cover for a list of *HDRs*); Anand and Sen 2000a: 2030.

35 WCED 1987: 43.

36 *HDR* 1994 (UNDP–HDRO 1994; see inside back cover for a list of *HDRs*); Anand and Sen 2000a.

37 Jolly, Emmerij, and Weiss 2009.

38 World Bank 2000; Fukuda-Parr 2007.

39 F. Stewart 2010.

40 For a useful review see Nayyar (2008).

41 Lindauer and Pritchett 2002.

42 Alkire 2007; OECD 2008b.

43 Bourguignon 2004.

44 Stern 2006.

45 Rodrik 2006.

46 Narayan and others 1999.

47 Acemoglu, Johnson, and Robinson 2001; Bardhan 2006; Pritchett, Woolcock, and Andrews 2010.

48 Polanyi 2002. See also Veblen (2007) and Myrdal (1957). Discussions about participatory development and management of common resources also go back several decades; see Agarwal (2001) for a useful review of participation, and Baland and Platteau (1996) on property rights.

49 Rodrik (2006) provides an excellent review of the report.

50 Commission on Growth and Development 2008: 2.

51 The indicator set is updated over time, most recently in 2009, when material deprivation and housing were added; see www.peer-review-social-inclusion.eu/.

52 Duflo, Hanna, and Ryan 2009.

53 Mookherjee 2005; see also Deaton (2009) and Cartwright (2009).

54 Seminal work is associated with Kahneman, Diener, and Schwarz (1999) and Kahneman and Krueger (2006).

55 The well known paradox noted by Easterlin (1995) points out that while richer people are happier than poorer people within countries, there is no systemic relationship between income and happiness above a certain income threshold either between countries or over time (see Graham 2010). This paradox has been challenged of late (see Stevenson and Wolfers 2008 and Deaton 2008) but not yet fully repudiated (see Krueger 2008).

56 Kahneman 1999. See also Diener and others (2009).

57 Sen (1985b) provides a thorough analysis of agency and its importance.

58 Sen (1999: 157) argues that the significance of democracy lies "in three distinct virtues: (i) its *intrinsic importance*, (ii) its *instrumental contributions* and (iii) its *constructive* role in the creation of values and norms [emphasis in original]."

59 Harding and Wantchekon 2010. See also Barbone and others (2007).

Chapter 2

1 Gertner 2010.

2 See Raworth and Stewart (2002) for a survey.

3 For country-level values of the HDI and its components, see statistical table 1.

4 There are no major differences in the results when the new HDI indicators are used; see Gidwitz and others (2010).

5 The analysis in this chapter and chapter 3 covers the 40-year period since 1970. In many cases comparisons over such a long period require restricting the sample to countries for which data are available. For this reason, some of the aggregates presented in these chapters differ from those presented in the statistical tables.

6 Sixty countries are not covered by our sample. On average, they are somewhat less developed than countries in the sample: life expectancy is three years shorter, literacy is similar but gross enrolment is 6 percentage points lower, and per capita income is $2,785 lower. This does not mean that all countries excluded from the hybrid HDI sample are poor: eight (including Germany and Singapore) are classified today as developed according to the new HDI reported in statistical table 1. Their annual economic growth and changes in health were slightly higher than in the rest of the sample, while changes in gross enrolment and literacy were similar. Obviously, this evidence is only partial because the data are incomplete, but it suggests that the omission of these countries does not systematically bias the picture of progress that emerges from our analysis.

7 We start with 1970 because that is the first year for which we can calculate the HDI for a sufficiently large number of countries.

8 Unless otherwise noted, all dollar figures in this Report refer to purchasing power parity–adjusted 2008 dollars.

9 Since the HDI is about people, we use averages weighted by population, unless otherwise noted. The main exception relates to policy indicators such as those discussed in chapter 3, where the country is the relevant unit of observation. Unweighted averages give a better sense of average country performance and show an increase in the HDI from 0.53 in 1970, to 0.62 in 1990 and to 0.69 in 2010.

10 Similarly, Easterly (2009) shows that choices about how to measure and set Millennium Development Goal targets significantly affect which countries and regions are progressing most and which are failing.

11 Specifically, the deviation from fit is the residual from a regression of changes in the HDI on the initial HDI level.

12 Common alternatives to the deviation from fit are the absolute change in the HDI, the HDI growth rate and the percentage reduction of the shortfall from the maximum level. The four methods applied coincide broadly in identifying the bottom movers, which include such countries as the Democratic Republic of the Congo, Moldova, Zambia and Zimbabwe. But the shortfall reduction method comes out with different top performers: 9 of the top 10 are developed countries, in contrast to at most 1 in the other three methods. China, Lao PDR, Nepal, Oman, Saudi Arabia and South Korea are consistently among the top performers regardless of method. See also Gray and Purser (2010) and Ranis and Stewart (2010) for a comparison of alternative methods.

13 The Spence Commission on Growth and Development examined 13 success stories of countries that experienced high growth over sustained periods since 1950. Of these, only four (China, Indonesia, Oman and South Korea) coincide with our group of top movers.

14 Pritchett 1997; UNDESA 2006; Ocampo, Vos, and Sundaram 2007.

15 Pritchett 1997.

16 The HDI upper bound is the result of a normalization that has no effect on rates of change (see *Technical note 1*); thus, it is not true in general that the functional form imposes a constraint on progress at the top. On convergence caused by natural upper bounds, see endnote 18.

17 Take, for example, the case of life expectancy. Although one might expect that there is an upper limit, this is not generally accepted by longevity researchers. Oeppen and Vaupel (2002) show that female life expectancy in the top-ranked country has advanced at a steady annual pace of three more months a year over the past 160 years, with no deceleration over time.

18 To evaluate whether this generates the convergence, we unbounded the variables through a logit transformation

$$lx = \ln\left(\frac{x}{\bar{x}-x}\right),$$

where x is the variable in question and $\bar{x}$ denotes its upper bound and confirmed the convergence results. Beta convergence tests (see Barro and Sala-i-Martin 2003) associated with the logit transform of literacy, gross enrolment and mean years of schooling reject the hypothesis of no convergence with p-values of less than 1 percent for all three variables. A statistically significant decline in the relationship between initial levels and log changes was found for all variables except income, both in levels and in the logit transform. Alternative indicators (among them years of tertiary schooling and undernourishment) confirm the convergence—albeit for shorter time spans and fewer countries. For all nonincome variables except life expectancy, the beta convergence effect weakens after 1990.

19 Proposals have been put forward to create a separate index for developed countries to better distinguish among them; see Herrero, Martínez, and Villar (2010).

20 China's gross enrolment ratio fell from 69 percent in 1976 to 50 percent in 1990 and has recovered to 68 percent today.

21 We created an indicator of quality-adjusted years of schooling for 13 countries for which the dispersion fell from 1995 to 2007, a suggestive but not conclusive result given the small sample size.

22 Namely, the Congo, the Democratic Republic of the Congo, Georgia, Kyrgyzstan, Moldova, Swaziland, Tajikistan, Ukraine, Zambia and Zimbabwe.

23 Note, however, that the clustering does not occur at the top of the scale in either figure 2.4 or figure 2.7, suggesting that it is not due to countries hitting an upper bound.

24 WHO 2008: 2.

25 This is consistent with a faster increase in longevity in developing countries as the higher absolute reductions in infant mortality have a significant effect on life expectancy. Also note that

these values differ from those presented in figure 2.5, as the figure uses decade averages from 1970s and 2000s.

26 Rajaratnam and others 2010.

27 UNICEF 2008.

28 Hogan and others 2010. These results have already sparked some controversy, however; see Graham, Braunholtz, and Campbell (2010).

29 UNICEF 2008.

30 For this as well as several other comparisons presented below, we use decadal averages rather than specific years in order to increase the size of the sample over which the comparison is carried out.

31 Background research prepared for this Report suggests that these phenomena may have contributed to a dual convergence, with different sets of countries converging to different levels of life expectancy. Countries whose life expectancy exceeded 55 years in 1965 continued converging to low mortality. However, only a few countries with initial life expectancy below 55 years made the transition. See Canning (2010).

32 UNAIDS 2008: 39.

33 For alternative views see Treisman (2010); Brainerd and Cutler (2005); and World Bank (2010g).

34 Brainerd 2010.

35 Zaridze and others 2009.

36 Watson 1995.

37 Yates 2006.

38 Ridde and Diarra 2009; Yates 2006.

39 Daponte and Garfield 2000.

40 Brown, Langer, and Stewart 2008.

41 UNDP 2010.

42 Sen 1983.

43 An interesting potential research question, which could be explored in future reports, is whether the correlation of hunger is greater with multidimensional poverty than with income poverty.

44 Shiva Kumar 2007.

45 Kasirye 2010.

46 Barrett and Maxwell 2005.

47 Drèze and Sen 1989.

48 FAO 2010b. Data on undernourishment and food deprivation are also in statistical table 8.

49 Olshansky and others 2005.

50 Strauss and Thomas 1998.

51 Nussbaum 2000.

52 Education is a consistent correlate of empowerment: in Bangladesh, see Kamal and Zunaid (2006); in Ethiopia, Legovini (2006); in India, Gupta and Yesudian (2006); in Nepal, Allendorf (2007); and in the Russian Federation, Lokshin and Ravallion (2005).

53 The positive effect of education on longevity has been found for many countries, including Bangladesh (see Hurt, Ronsmans, and Saha 2004), South Korea (see Khang, Lynch, and Kaplan 2004) and the United States (see Cutler and Lleras-Muney 2006).

54 The gross enrolment ratio captures a country's enrolment as a share of the corresponding school-age population. Gross enrolment ratios can exceed 100 percent when students are enrolled who are not in the school-age population—due to grade repetition or late school entry. The net enrolment ratio covers only children who are in the age subgroup corresponding to a particular level of education—but such data are more limited and ignore the benefits of education for those outside the "appropriate" age group.

55 World Bank 2010g.

56 We say that the female gross enrolment ratio is close to or greater than the male ratio when it exceeds 98 percent; see UN (2009).

57 UNESCO 2010, tables 5 and 8.

58 World Bank 2010g.

59 See Tanzi and Schuknecht (2000), which covers a sample of now-developed countries. There are no systematic data on spending on schooling in developing countries at the turn of the 19th century, but the existing evidence indicates that it was likely even less (Gargarella 2002).

60 The pupil–teacher ratio fell from 37 in 1990 to 35 in 2007 (in 1970, it stood at 36) in all regions except Sub-Saharan Africa. Teachers are also typically better educated now than they were in the past—the ratio of teachers with training now stands at 80 percent for developing countries.

61 The average for 2005–2009 for countries with available data.

62 Nielson 2009.

63 Hanlon, Barrientos, and Hulme 2010.

64 Hanushek 1995; Glewwe 1999.

65 The test is the Trends in International Mathematics and Science Study—see Glewwe and Kremer (2006).

66 Comparison based on the latest available year of data from Trends in International Mathematics and Science Study for the test scores and World Bank (2010g) for spending.

67 Bessell 2009a, b.

68 Greaney, Khandker, and Alam 1999.

69 World Bank 2009d.

70 Pritchett and Murgai 2007; Walton 2010.

71 Pritchett, Woolcock, and Andrews 2010; De and Drèze 1999.

72 The most recent Trends in International Mathematics and Science Study found that higher levels of parents' education (and assets and services at home, such as computers and access to the Internet) were associated with higher average math achievement in almost all countries. Similar patterns exist in developing countries (see Ishida, Muller, and Ridge 1995; Maundu 1988). This gap often remains large even after adjusting for student and family characteristics such as gender, age, number of parents and siblings (see Ma 2001; Caldas 1993; Schultz 1993).

73 Time series data for four developing countries show a decline of 9 percent in test scores from 1995 to 2007, even though these countries also greatly increased gross enrolment (by an average of 14 percent) over the same period. See also UNESCO (2004).

74 The assessment depends on whether the income figures are weighted by population or unweighted—that is, whether one thinks of the income of the average person or the average country. Because of China's size and rapid growth, the income of the average person in East Asia and the Pacific has grown 1,000 percent since 1970—but that of the average country in the region rose 344 percent. Likewise, the income of the average person in Sub-Saharan Africa increased only 17 percent, but that of the average African country, 93 percent. This reflects the weak overall growth records of the Democratic Republic of the Congo, Ethiopia and Nigeria, where 311 million people live.

75 This comparison refers to unweighted averages, which are typically used to evaluate convergence across countries. As shown in table 2.1, the conclusion is reversed if we use weighted averages because of the influence of China and India on the weighted figures. We return to this issue in our discussion of global inequality in chapter 4.

76 That is, than of any country in the top quarter of the world income distribution in 1970.

77 While from 1990 to 2010 differences in per capita income growth rates narrowed—developed countries grew 1.9 percent a year on average, compared with 1.8 percent in developing countries—the gap between the two continued to grow, although much more slowly than in the previous two decades. During 2005–2010 developing countries grew much faster than developed countries (an average of 3 percent a year, compared with 1.2 percent).

78 This comparison excludes oil-producing countries. For countries that are monoexporters and subject to high price fluctuations, per capita GDP at constant prices may not be the best indicator

for assessing long-run performance; see Rodríguez (2006) for a discussion.

79 Namely Burundi, Central African Republic, the Democratic Republic of the Congo, Côte d'Ivoire, Djibouti, Haiti, Liberia, Madagascar, Niger, Somalia, Togo, Zambia and Zimbabwe.

80 Equatorial Guinea's growth was similar to that of China, fuelled by oil. However, the use of base year prices to value growth in oil-abundant economies tends to distort the results from purchasing power parity–adjusted GDP series over long periods; see endnote 78.

81 della Paolera and Taylor 2003: 5.

Chapter 3

1 Improvements in human development are measured using the deviation from fit criterion presented in chapter 2.

2 The nonincome HDI comprises the health and education indices, equally weighted. The correlation between changes in the non-income HDI and economic growth is negative (−0.30) and statistically significant at the 1 percent level. However, this measure may be biased by the fact that less developed countries tend to have faster rates of improvement in the HDI. Thus in figure 3.1 we use the deviation from fit measure to account for different HDI starting points (see box 2.1 in chapter 2). The corresponding correlation is 0.13 and is not statistically significant. This robust finding does not depend on the specific indicators used to calculate nonincome human development.

3 Preston (1975), however, also showed that a snapshot relationship between *levels* of income and life expectancy did yield a significant relationship, a fact to which we return.

4 Easterly 1999. See also Cutler, Deaton, and Lleras-Muney (2006) and Kenny (2009).

5 Bourguignon and others 2008.

6 Kenny 2009.

7 On average, countries with negative economic growth over 1970–2010 experienced an increase of 11 years in life expectancy, 22 percentage points in gross enrolment and 40 percentage points in literacy.

8 See, for example, the discussion in Wooldridge (2002).

9 Easterly 1999.

10 Anand and Sen 2000c. People in high-income economies, however, may not use higher incomes to attain higher functioning. Examples are the high rates of obesity and the decline of leisure time in the United States (see Schor 1992; Cook and Daponte 2008) and more recently in Qatar. Within five years, Qatar's obesity rate is projected to be 70 percent (see WHO 2010).

11 Srinivasan 1994; Wolfers 2009.

12 HDR 1997 and HDR 2003 (UNDP–HDRO 1997, 2003; see inside back cover for a list of HDRs); Casabonne and Kenny 2009; Kenny 2008; Pritchett 2006; Glewwe and Kremer 2006; Strauss and Thomas 2008; Riley 2001; Benavot and Resnik 2006.

13 Hobbes 1651.

14 Wrigley and Schofield 1989: 230; Riley 2001: 33.

15 Some countries in northwestern Europe passed through an earlier health transition by reducing health crises caused by epidemics, wars and harvest failures. See Riley (2001): 20.

16 Soares 2007; Cutler and Miller 2005; Fogel 2004; Cutler, Deaton, and Lleras-Muney 2006.

17 Latin America and the Caribbean and Europe and Central Asia had life expectancies of 51 years and 60 years, still lower than the 65 years in developed countries.

18 Cutler, Deaton, and Lleras-Muney 2006; Cutler and Miller 2005.

19 Kenny forthcoming; Cutler, Deaton, and Lleras-Muney 2006: 108.

20 de Quadros and others 1998.

21 Soares 2007.

22 Jolly 2010.

23 See Kenny (forthcoming) and Boone and Zhan (2006).

24 Bryce and others 2003; Gauri 2002; Jones and others 2003.

25 Drèze and Sen 1989; McGuire 2010.

26 Miguel and Kremer 2004.

27 Cross-country studies examining aggregate measures of expenditures (such as public health spending as a share of GDP) or inputs (hospital beds or nurses per capita) tend to blur the distinctions between diverse programmes and inputs of varying quality and effectiveness and reach mixed conclusions: see Filmer and Prichett (1999); McGuire (2010); Gupta, Verhoeven, and Tiongson (2003); Kruk and others (2007); and Gauri and Khaleghian (2002).

28 For more statistics on health, see statistical table 14.

29 Deaton 2002.

30 Kenny forthcoming: chapters 6 and 7.

31 Lake and Baum 2001. Kudamatsu (2007) used individual-level data from 28 African countries and found that children were more likely to survive after democratization. This analysis examined children born to the same mother before and after democratization to control for familial differences.

32 On mortality and risk of dying in childbirth, see Przeworski (2004); on life expectancy, see Lake and Baum (2001); Franco, Alvarez-Dardet, and Ruiz (2004); and Vollmer and Ziegler (2009).

33 Harding and Wantchekon 2010.

34 This expansion involved an increase in the public provision of education, often while private education was marginalized; UNESCO (2006). See Pritchett (2002).

35 Tansel 2002; Edmonds 2005; Clemens 2004.

36 The increase over 1970–2007 was 22 and 23 percentage points, and the difference was not statistically significant. For more information about levels and trends in education enrolment, see statistical table 13.

37 For a sample of 48 countries the correlation between skill premiums and rate of growth of schooling over 1970–2010 is 0.14 and is not statistically significant.

38 Pritchett 2002.

39 Many governments came under intense international pressure to require universal primary education. The United Nations Educational, Scientific and Cultural Organization convened regional conferences on free and compulsory education (Bombay 1952; Cairo 1955; Lima 1956).

40 Elson 2001. Studies of the programme have shown significant effects on schooling and later on wages compared with people who did not participate; see Duflo (2001).

41 On years of education, see Tavares and Wacziarg (2001); on enrolment and literacy, see Lake and Baum (2001); Tsai (2006); and Vollmer and Ziegler (2009).

42 Expanding enrolment at higher levels requires meeting at least some basic efficiency and quality thresholds. Decentralization of school management at the local level has been found to be positively and significantly associated with efficiency and education quality; see Gallego (2010); Fuchs and Woessmann (2007); Stasavage (2005); and Tsai (2006).

43 See Walton (2010).

44 Drèze and Sen 1989. On typologies of human development, see Ranis and Stewart (2000, 2010).

45 Walton 2010.

46 Pineda and Rodríguez 2010.

47 Data on conflict from UCDP and PRIO (2009). We define as conflicts those that involve two parties, of which one is the government of a state, and that result in at least 1,000 battle-related deaths in one year, and exclude interstate armed conflicts between two or more states, so that our variable covers only "civil" conflicts. Some countries experiencing conflict in this database are Afghanistan (1990–2001, 2003–2008), India (1990–2006), Rwanda (1990–1993, 1997–1998, 2001–2002) and Turkey (1992–1998).

48 Causality in the relation between aid and development has been explored by, among others, Rajan and Subramanian (2008) and Minoiu and Reddy (2007).

49 Ranis and Stewart 2010.

50 Olavarria-Gambi 2003.

51 Durlauf, Johnson, and Temple 2005. See also Barro and Sala-i-Martin (2003) and Rodríguez (2007).

52 Rodrik 2007; Hausmann, Rodrik, and Velasco 2008.

53 Rodrik 2007; Hausmann and Rodríguez forthcoming; Denison 1967; Bhagwati and Desai 1970; Little, Scitovsky, and Scott 1970.

54 Binder and Georgiadis 2010; Gray and Purser 2010; Mayer-Foulkes 2010.

55 Mayer-Foulkes 2010.

56 McGuire 2010.

57 Klasen 2000.

58 Behrman and others 2009.

59 Duflo 2003.

60 Chen and Li 2009.

61 Binder and Georgiadis 2010.

62 Mayer-Foulkes 2010.

63 Moreno-Lopez and others 2009.

64 Brun, Chambas, and Mourji 2009; Diaw, Guérineau, and Jeanneney 2009.

65 Moreno and Rodríguez 2009.

66 OECD 2008b.

67 Cubero and Hollar 2010.

68 Nattrass and Seekings 2001.

69 OECD 2008b.

70 Fiszbein and others 2009.

71 Prasad 2008; HDR 1990 (UNDP–HDRO 1990; see inside back cover for a list of HDRs); OECD 2008b; Nattrass and Seekings 2001; Johannes, Akwi, and Anzah 2006; Cubero and Hollar 2010.

72 World Bank 2005b.

73 This section draws heavily on Walton (2010).

74 The Glass-Steagall Act was repealed in 1999. On the comparative evolution of financial systems regulation in Japan and Germany, see Vitols (2003) and Bebehroth, Dietrich, and Vollmer (2009).

75 Charumilind, Kali, and Wiwattanakantang 2006.

76 Hulme and Moore 2008; Nath, Sylva, and Grimes 1997; Bornstein 2005.

77 Marglin 2008.

78 ITOPF 2010.

79 NOIA 2006; EEA 2008.

80 Amnesty International 2009a.

81 The Economist 2007; Davies and others 2008.

82 However, in recent years, China has erected more barriers to entry and competition; see Bradsher (2010).

83 Li and Meng 2005.

84 Di John 2009.

85 For South Korea and Taiwan Province of China, Wade (1992: 314) noted that "whereas the governments of most other developing countries know that they can fail economically and not risk invasion, the governments and elites of these countries knew that without fast economic growth and social stability this could well happen. This led them to make an unusually close coupling of national security and economic strength."

86 Walton 2010.

87 Friedman 2006.

Chapter 4

1 Fuentes-Nieva and Pereira 2010.

2 In figure 4.1 the measure of political freedom we use is Polity IV because it varies across a greater range and thus can be more easily graphed; the results are similar if we use the democracy measure described later in this chapter; see also statistical

table 6. For the measure of inequality loss in HDI, see chapter 5. The measure of sustainability is adjusted net savings from the World Bank.

3 Harding and Wantchekon 2010; World Bank 2005b; Przeworski and others 2000; Cornia and Court 2001; Eicher and Turnovsky 2003.

4 Kabeer 1999: 447.

5 HDR 1990 (UNDP–HDRO 1990; see inside back cover for a list of HDRs).

6 HDR 1993, 2000, 2002 and 2004 (UNDP–HDRO 1993, 2000, 2002, 2004; see inside back cover for a list of HDRs).

7 Gaye and Jha 2010.

8 Hamel 2010.

9 See discussion in Donner (2008).

10 IEA 2009.

11 UIA 2010.

12 Walton 2010: 22.

13 The World Values Survey asks respondents how much freedom they have over their lives. For 87 countries the average was 7 on a 10-point scale, with a range of 5–8. The Gallup World Poll asks respondents whether they are satisfied with their freedom to choose. This freedom at the individual level does not appear to be connected with democracy at the national level.

14 . Since 1990 Kuwait and Samoa have extended the right to vote to women, and South Africa to Blacks.

15 We present a measure that defines democracy on a minimalist basis (see Cheibub 2010, building on Alvarez and others 1996). Countries are classified as democratic if the chief executive and legislature are elected, more than one political party competes in elections and a party has transferred power in the event of a loss; otherwise, countries are identified as dictatorships. Democracies with no alternation of parties are countries that formally meet the conditions for democracy but where the ruling party has yet to lose an election and thus relinquish power. This simple measure has gained broad endorsement in the comparative political literature (see Munck and Verkuilen 2002).

16 This category consists of countries that have not met the alternation rule; see the previous endnote.

17 Coups took place in Honduras (1972), Chile and Uruguay (1973), Argentina (1976), Bolivia (1980) and Guatemala (1982).

18 See UNDP (2009: 71), which describes political movements using this tactic.

19 The Mutahidda Majlis-i-Amal (United Action Council), a coalition of religious parties, won 19 percent of national assembly seats and made greater inroads in Khyber Pakhutunkhwa and Balochistan.

20 Whitehead 2002.

21 Calculated from Database of Political Institutions (updated 2010) as described in Beck and others (2001).

22 Bardhan and Mookherjee 2000; Abraham and Platteau 2004.

23 See, for example, Besley, Pande, and Rao (2005) and Dasgupta and Beard (2007).

24 Mansuri and Rao (2010), which synthesizes the results of research on the conceptual foundations and the efficacy of initiatives to foster citizen participation.

25 See the 2004 HDR (UNDP–HDRO 2004; see inside back cover for a list of HDRs).

26 On the limits of consultation and the problems of refugee status, see Bassel (2010).

27 See Elson (2006) and O'Brien (2010). For example, Elson (2006) cites gender budget initiatives in Australia, France, Mexico, South Africa and Uganda.

28 Council of Europe CDEG 2009: 41, 43; ECLAC 2010.

29 Chattopadhyay and Duflo 2004.

30 Gibney, Cornett, and Wood 2010.

31 UNDP 2009: 6.

32 ACHR 2008.

33 Trends are assessed using an annual measure (created by Gibney, Cornett, and Wood 2010) based on human rights violations, as reported by Amnesty International. The measure uses a broad notion of the state, including agents that are not officially recognized as agents of the government and areas where quasi-state or extra-state entities are acting in place of a weak or fragmented central government. Countries are coded from 1 (secure rule of law prevails) to 5 (widespread political fear) based on expert assessment of the scope (type of violence), intensity (frequency) and range (share of the population targeted or selectivity) of violations. For 101 countries the median level of abuses was 3.

34 Harding and Wantchekon 2010.

35 See the 2000 HDR on human rights (UNDP–HDRO 2000; see inside back cover for a list of HDRs).

36 Data from Amnesty International (2009b).

37 Data from Gallup World Poll (2010).

38 Ottoson 2009: 5.

39 Amnesty International 2010.

40 HDR 1997, 1998 and 2005 (UNDP–HDRO 1997, 1998, 2005; see inside back cover for a list of HDRs).

41 World Bank 2005b.

42 This calculation uses the loss from the Inequality-adjusted HDI presented in chapter 5.

43 Paul Krugman has often referred to this fact as evidence of increasing inequality in the United States (see, for example, Krugman 2007); United States Census Bureau 2008.

44 World Bank 2005b.

45 Results using data from World Bank (2010g) showed a similar pattern with a smaller sample.

46 Milanovic 1998.

47 Atkinson and Micklewright 1992.

48 ADB 2007; Liu 2010; The broad picture is consistent with the Kuznets (1955) hypothesis that inequality would increase at the initial stages of economic development and then decline, but the empirical evidence is mixed.

49 Pinkovskiy and Sala-i-Martin 2010.

50 López-Calva and Lustig 2010; Cornia 2010.

51 Jayadev and Rodríguez 2010. These results are robust to adjusting for the contribution of self-employment to capital income.

52 Commander 2010. The exceptions are the Scandinavian countries and Belgium.

53 There is considerable debate in the literature on ethics and justice on whether the fairness of distributive arrangements should be evaluated at the global or national level. If the justice of institutions is to be judged at the level at which the social contract is conceptualized, the national level is appropriate, while a cosmopolitan position would suggest that the global level is the relevant one for assessment. See Risse (2009) for a discussion of these issues for international migration.

54 Pinkovskiy and Sala-i-Martin 2009; Milanovic 2009; Anand and Segal 2008. See the 2009 HDR (UNDP–HDRO 2009; see inside back cover for a list of HDRs).

55 Pineda and Rodríguez 2006; Bénabou 2000; Alesina and others 1996.

56 Deaton 2007; Sen, Iyer, and Mukherjee 2009.

57 Narayana 2008; Minujina and Delamonica 2003; see also Cornia, Rosignoli, and Tiberti (2007).

58 K. Stewart 2010.

59 Joe, Mishra, and Navaneetham 2009.

60 Gwatkin and others 2007.

61 Houweling and others 2007.

62 Measure DHS 2010.

63 Thomas, Wang, and Fan (2001), and personal communication with Robert Barro and Jong-Wha Lee.

64 Harttgen and Klasen 2010.

65 Considering the 2003 HDI ranking as presented in the 2005 HDR (UNDP–HDRO 2005; see inside back cover for a list of HDRs) since the Demographic and Health Survey for Burkina Faso used in the example is for 2003.

66 See Stewart, Brown, and Mancini (2005), Roemer (1998), and Barros and others (2008).

67 Stewart 2009.

68 UNDP 2003.

69 UNESCO 2009: 64, 65.

70 See the 2009 HDR (UNDP–HDRO 2009; see inside back cover for a list of HDRs).

71 K. Stewart 2010; Wood and others 2009.

72 Burd-Sharps and others 2010.

73 Sen 2003; The Economist 2010.

74 We follow the more recent practice in these estimates of treating sex-selective abortions as female deaths. This differs from the practice of demographers who distinguish foetal deaths from mortality (for example, Shryock and Siegel 1980). An alternative approach would consider the ramifications of gender discrimination for mortality across genders and age groups. To the best of our knowledge the implications of such an approach have yet to be worked out. See also Coale (1991).

75 This calculation assumes that in the absence of sex-selective abortions a woman would have an equal probability of giving birth to a girl or a boy. See also Klasen and Wink (2009).

76 Nussbaum 2005.

77 WHO 2005.

78 Desai 2010.

79 Agarwal and Panda 2007.

80 UNIFEM 2010.

81 UNIFEM 2010.

82 UNDESA-DAW-CSW 2010.

83 Cuno and Desai 2009.

84 UN 2009.

85 World Bank 2010f.

86 LIS 2009.

87 OECD 2009.

88 UNDESA 2009a.

89 Fuentes-Nieva and Seck 2010.

90 Skoufias 2003.

91 WCED 1987.

92 Information about global employment trends is weak outside developed countries because of differences in definition and data collection methods and lags. Official estimates of unemployment are especially problematic in countries with extensive informal sectors and no formal safety nets. See ILO (2009b).

93 See IMF (2009) for a comparison between the crises.

94 Reinhart and Rogoff 2009.

95 ILO 2010b; World Bank 2010b.

96 World Bank 2009c.

97 One example of how policy intervention and good initial conditions enabled some countries to overcome the negative impacts of the crisis is China, whose growth is high (8.7 percent for 2009 and an expected 10 percent for 2010), driven mostly by infrastructure lending. See IMF (2010b).

98 This was a common pattern in past crises: Thailand reduced its health spending 9 percent and education spending 6 percent in response to the East Asian crisis in 1998; health expenditures in Mexico fell 15 percent during the Tequila crisis (see Calvo 2010).

99 ILO 2009.

100 IMF 2009; Horváth, Ivanov, and Peleah 2010.

101 Cord and others 2009; Marone, Thelen, and Gulasan 2009.

102 Rodrik 1998.

103 Commander 2010.

104 Commander 2010; Freeman 1998.

105 See www.doingbusiness.org/.

106 Salehi-Isfahani 2010.

107 Blanchard 2008; Commander 2010.

108 Sirimanne 2009: 4.

109 ILO 2009.

110 Ablett and Slengesol 2000.

111 Walker and others 2007.

112 Ferreira and Schady 2008; FAO 2010a.

113 Harper and others 2009.

114 Heyzer and Khor 1999; Knowles, Pernia, and Racelis 1999.

115 van der Hoeven 2010.

116 Baird, Friedman, and Schady 2007: 26.

117 Calvo 2010.

118 UNICEF 2010a.

119 UNICEF 2010b.

120 Walton 2010; Lustig 2000.

121 UN 2010b.

122 Fuentes-Nieva and Pereira 2010.

Chapter 5

1 See for example, Narayan and others (2000) and UNDESA (2009b).

2 Because the aspects of well-being and inequality measured by the GII differ from those measured by the IHDI, the associated loss in achievement can be higher than the loss in human development captured by the IHDI.

3 Foster, López-Calva, and Szekely 2005. See also Alkire and Foster (2010).

4 The measure is the general mean of general means, a class of measures derived from Atkinson's (1983) seminal work on the measurement of inequality. Its basic desirable properties are path independence (the order of aggregation across populations and dimensions can be altered without affecting the value of the IHDI) and subgroup consistency. See *Technical note 2* for further details.

5 Calculating the IHDI requires setting a parameter that captures how much people dislike inequality. The parameter can range from 0 to infinity; we use a value of 1. This fairly mild adjustment for inequality moderately penalizes inequality in each dimension; see *Technical note 2* for more details. The choice of parameter involves a normative judgement analogous to that for other policy-relevant norms—for example, in establishing a threshold for relative and absolute poverty. It also reflects judgement about how much inequality matters. The academic literature addresses both theoretical and empirical issues (see Atkinson 1983 and Pirttilä and Uusitalo 2010). Another strand of the literature attempts to distinguish between inequality that is justified and inequality that is not (see Roemer 1998). Social preferences for redistribution have been examined based on the tax and transfer systems in place (see Bourguinon and Spadaro 2005).

6 Because of the multiplicative form of the HDI and the IHDI, the loss in HDI due to inequality (1 − IHDI/HDI) falls between the minimum and the maximum loss in dimensions.

7 Narayana 2008.

8 That is, the implicit welfare function is separable for the various dimensions of the IHDI (Atkinson and Bourguignon 2000).

9 Anand and Sen 1995.

10 See Charmes and Wieringa (2003), who review the GDI and GEM to construct the African Gender and Development index for the Economic Commission for Africa, and Klasen (2006) on the GDI and GEM.

11 Hawken and Munck (2009) and Klasen and Schüler (2010) provide useful reviews.

12 Various other gender indices have adopted this approach—including Social Watch's Gender Equity Index and the World Economic Forum's Global Gender Gap Index.

13 See *Technical note 3*. The aversion towards gender inequality parameter is set at 2 while the aversion towards overlapping deprivation is set at 1.

14 Seth 2009.

15 While indicators in other dimensions are compared between men and women, indicators of reproductive health are compared to thresholds of no maternal death and no teenage pregnancy.

16 The risk of maternal death is five times higher in teen births, in part because girls' bodies are not yet fully developed (see Rowbottom 2007). We use the adolescent fertility rate for girls ages 15–19. Fertility for girls below age 18 would be preferable, but these data are not available.

17 ILO 2010c. This figure differs from the global female labour force participation rate of 56.8 percent presented in statistical table 4 because of different schema used to weight country-specific female labour force participation rates.

18 Desai 2010.

19 The GDI relied on the gender ratio of nonagricultural wages, but the nonagricultural formal sector is limited in size in many developing countries and the gap may not have been representative of the overall picture.

20 This is not driven solely by the fact that both measures of inequality are (negatively) correlated with HDI: the correlation between the residuals of both inequality measures on the HDI is 0.48, which is significant at 1 percent.

21 Compared with *HDR* 2009 (UNDP–HDRO 2009; see inside back cover for a list of *HDRs*), the total coverage is lower than that for the GDI (155) but well above that for the GEM (109). As noted earlier, the previous approach relied heavily on imputations, which is not the case for the GII. The countries lacking sufficient data to adjust for the GII have HDI ranks from 6 (Lichtenstein) to 164 (Guinea-Bissau).

22 This is echoed in Pogge (2009: 21): "A credible index of development must be sensitive to whether an increase in literacy goes to landowners or the landless, an improvement in medical care goes to children or to aged, an increase in enrolment to privileged university students or to children in slums, an increase in life expectancy to the elite or to the marginalized, enhanced physical security to males or to females."

23 Alkire and Foster 2009; Alkire and Santos 2010; Bourguignon and Chakravarty 2003; Brandolini and D'Alessio 2009.

24 Anand and Sen 1997.

25 See for example, Kanbur and Squire (2001) and Micklewright and Stewart (2001).

26 Population figures refer to 2010. This assumes that the poverty rates in the year of the most recent survey (which goes back as far as 2000) adequately reflect poverty today. Because none of these surveys post-dates the more recent economic crisis, these may well be underestimates.

27 The average HDI of countries where the MPI headcount exceeded $1.25 a day poverty rate was 0.49; the average for countries where income poverty exceeded the MPI headcount was 0.60.

28 Income poverty estimates of less than $1.25 a day exclude the following countries because of lack of data: Belize, Czech Republic, Guyana, Iraq, Mauritius, Myanmar, Occupied Palestinian Territories, Somalia, Suriname, Syrian Arab Republic, Trinidad and Tobago, United Arab Emirates and Zimbabwe. Excluding these countries, the total number of multidimensionally poor people is 1,719 million, which is still between the two income poverty estimates. For the income poverty estimates of less than $2 a day the countries excluded because of lack of data are Guinea, Guyana, Haiti, Iraq, Lao PDR, Mauritania, Mauritius, Myanmar, Namibia, Somalia, Syrian Arab Republic, Trinidad and Tobago, United Arab Emirates and Zimbabwe. Excluding these countries, the total number of multidimensionally poor people is 1,699.5 million, which again is between the two income poverty estimates.

29 This terminology follows government categories, which are defined officially and vary by state.

30 Some experts have argued that inequality among poor people should be reflected in a measure of poverty, but this requires using cardinal measures, and the MPI would be sensitive to the scale in which these measures are defined. See Alkire and Foster (2009) for a discussion.

Chapter 6

1 Asher and Daponte 2010.

2 An alternative approach using the projections for component variables produced by international organizations and independent forecasters yielded similar projections. See Asher and Daponte (2010).

3 Maddison 2007.

4 Nelson and others 2009.

5 Cline 2008.

6 Rodríguez 2007.

7 Deaton 2010; Ravallion 1996.

8 Rodrik and Hausmann 2003; Rodrik 2007. See also box 3.1 in chapter 3.

9 Easterly 2002.

10 Ostrom 1996; Parks and others 1999; Pestoff 2009.

11 Drèze and Sen 2002; Sen 1985b.

12 UNDP 2010.

13 Walton 2010.

14 Rodrik 2003.

15 Evans 2010.

16 Pritchett, Woolcock, and Andrews 2010.

17 Pritchett, Woolcock, and Andrews 2010.

18 Panagariya 2008; Damodaran 2008.

19 Vaughan 2003.

20 Watson and Yohannes 2005.

21 Iglehart 2010.

22 The White House 2010.

23 Di Tella and Dubra 2009.

24 See Rajan and Zingales (2003) on the threat of oligarchic capitalism, and Walton (2010) for an overview.

25 These principles are associated with the work of Sen (1999), Unger (1998), and Jayadev (2010).

26 Birdsall 2008.

27 World Bank 2010e. The size of the carbon market ($144 billion) exceeds total official development assistance for 2009 ($136 billion).

28 See www.oslocfc2010.no.

29 Ethiopia's figure is for 2002, the latest year available.

30 UNAIDS 2008; The Global Fund 2009.

31 Wolf 2007; Asiedu and Nandwa 2007; d'Aiglepierre and Wagner 2010.

32 Levine 2004.

33 OECD/DAC 2010b.

34 Sachs and others 2004. In particular, aid provided for military and political considerations or other geopolitically motivated reasons tends to be negatively associated with growth (Minoiu and Reddy 2010).

35 Easterly 2006; Moyo 2009.

36 World Bank 2010d.

37 See OECD (2008a), which is based on a survey of 33 OECD partner countries.

38 For example, see www.aidtransparency.net.

39 This is shown by the burgeoning literature in the field, published in such scholarly journals as the *Journal of Human Development and Capabilities* or presented at the annual meetings of the Human Development and Capabilities Association. For an anthology of some key contributions, see Fukuda-Parr and Shiva Kumar (2003).

40 Living Standards Measurement Study surveys have been conducted in 40 countries since 1980 (www.surveynetwork.org); Demographic and Health Surveys are available for 82 countries (www.measuredhs.com/countries); and Multiple Indicator Cluster Surveys are available for more than 70 countries (www.childinfo.org/mics_available.html).

41 The Missing Dimensions programme of the Oxford Poverty and Human Development Initiative is seeking to rectify this gap for empowerment, work quality, physical safety, dignity and other areas (www.ophi.org).

42 OECD 2010.

43 Naturally, this should build on the existing literature (such as Ranis, Stewart, and Ramirez 2000; Bourguignon and others 2008; and Kenny 2008). Various global and National HDRs describe the causal chains through which economic growth addresses core human priorities—for example, by creating jobs for poor people, empowering women within the household and contributing revenue for social investment, social protection and redistribution.

44 For basic expositions, see Jones (2002) and Barro and Sala-i-Martin (2003). Most theoretical and empirical growth analysis is based on variants of the Ramsey-Cass-Koopmans model in which a representative agent maximizes a discounted sum of the utility of consumption.

45 See, for example, Diener and Seligman (2004) and Gough and McGregor (2007).

46 Neumayer 2010b.

47 Southgate 1990; Mink 1993.

48 Comin, Hobjin, and Rovito 2008; Córdoba and Ripoll 2008; Duarte and Restuccia 2006.

49 Barro 1991; Barro and Lee 1994.

50 Ibrahim and Alkire 2007; Alsop and Heinsohn 2005; Narayan 2005.

51 The sample was drawn from civil society organizations that have consultative status with the United Nations. The survey, prepared in three languages, had 644 respondents and a response rate of 29 percent. The best represented region was Western Europe (30 percent of respondents), followed by North America (26 percent) and Africa (17 percent).

52 Eyben 2004

53 Bassel 2008a, 2008b.

54 Gaye and Jha 2010; PNUD México 2003; PNUD Argentina 2002.

55 Nussbaum 2000; Osmani and Sen 2003; Klasen 2002; Robeyns 2003.

56 Stuckler, Basu, and McKee 2010; Mejía and St-Pierre 2008; Piketty 2000.

57 Bourguignon and Verdier 2000; Acemoglu and Robinson 2002.

58 Ivanov and Peleah 2010.

59 The relationship between competition and growth is complex and potentially nonlinear. See Aghion and Griffith (2005).

60 According to results from the Gallup World Poll, less than half of people around the world feel that the area where they live is becoming more liveable, only 4 in 10 feel that economic conditions in their country are getting better, and just half are satisfied with environmental preservation efforts.

61 Stiglitz and Members of the UN Commission of Financial Experts 2010.

62 Hoddinott and Quisumbing 2010.

63 Anand and Sen 2000a; Sen 2009b.

64 See www.earthsummit2012.org/.

65 King 1964.

References

Ablett, J., and I. Slengesol. 2000. *Education in Crisis: The Impact and Lessons of the East Asia Financial Shock 1997–1999*. Paris: United Nations Educational, Scientific and Cultural Organization.

Abraham, A., and J. P. Platteau. 2004. "Participatory Development: When Culture Creeps In." In *Culture and Public Action*, eds. V. Rao and M. Walton. Stanford, CA: Stanford University Press.

Acemoglu, D., S. Johnson, and J. Robinson. 2001. "The Colonial Origins of Comparative Development: An Empirical Investigation." *American Economic Review* 91(5): 1369–1401.

———. 2003. "An African Success Story: Botswana." In *In Search of Prosperity: Analytical Narratives on Economic Growth*, ed. D. Rodrik. Princeton, NJ: Princeton University Press.

Acemoglu, D., and J. Robinson. 2002. "The Political Economy of the Kuznets Curve." *Review of Development Economics* 6(2): 183–203.

ACHR (Asian Centre for Human Rights). 2008. *South Asia: Human Rights Index 2008*. New Delhi: Asian Centre for Human Rights.

Adamolekun, L., G. Lusignan, and A. Atomate (Eds.). 1997. *Civil Service Reform in Francophone Africa: Proceedings of a Workshop, Abidjan, January 23–26, 1996*. World Bank Technical Paper 357, Africa Region Series. Washington, DC: World Bank.

ADB (Asian Development Bank). 2007. *Key Indicators for Asia and the Pacific 2007: Inequality in Asia*. Manila.

Agarwal, B. 2001. "Participatory Exclusions, Community Forestry, and Gender: An Analysis for South Asia and a Conceptual Framework." *World Development* 29(10): 1623–48.

———. 2003. "Gender and Land Rights Revisited: Exploring New Prospects via the State, Family and Market." In *Agrarian Change, Gender and Land Rights*, ed. S. Razavi. Oxford, UK: Blackwell Publishing Ltd.

Agarwal, B., and P. Panda. 2007. "Toward Freedom from Domestic Violence: The Neglected Obvious." *Journal of Human Development and Capabilities* 8(3): 359–88.

Aghion, P., and R. Griffith. 2005. *Competition and Growth: Reconciling Theory and Evidence*. Cambridge, MA: MIT Press.

Akram, T. 2004. "Ranking Countries and Other Essays." Columbia University, New York.

Alderman, H., P. F. Orazem, and E. M. Paterno. 2001. "School Quality, School Cost, and the Public/Private School Choices of Low-Income Households in Pakistan." *Journal of Human Resources* 36(2): 304–26.

Alesina, A., S. Özler, N. Roubini, and P. Swagel. 1996. "Political Instability and Economic Growth." *Journal of Economic Growth* 1(2): 189–211.

Alkire, S. 2003. "A Conceptual Framework for Human Security." CRISE Working Paper 2. Centre for Research on Inequality, Human Security and Ethnicity, Oxford, UK.

———. 2007. "The Missing Dimensions of Poverty Data: Introduction to the Special Issue." *Oxford Development Studies* 35(4): 347–59.

———. 2010. "Conceptual Overview of Human Development: Definitions, Critiques, and Related Concepts." Human Development Research Paper 1. UNDP–HDRO, New York.

Alkire, S., and J. Foster. 2009. "Counting and Multidimensional Poverty Measurement." OPHI Working Paper 7. Oxford Poverty and Human Development Initiative, Oxford, UK.

———. 2010. "Designing the Inequality-Adjusted Human Development Index (HDI)." Human Development Research Paper 28. UNDP–HDRO, New York.

Alkire, S., and M. Santos. 2010. "Acute Multidimensional Poverty: A New Index for Developing Countries." Human Development Research Paper 11. UNDP–HDRO, New York.

Allendorf, K. 2007. "Do Women's Land Rights Promote Empowerment and Child Health in Nepal?" *World Development* 35(11): 1975–88.

Alsop, R., and N. Heinsohn. 2005. "Measuring Empowerment in Practice: Structuring Analysis and Framing Indicators." Policy Research Working Paper 3510. World Bank, Washington, DC.

Alvarez, M., J. A. Cheibub, F. Limongi, and A. Przeworski. 1996. "Classifying Political Regimes." *Studies in Comparative International Development* 31(2): 3–36.

Amnesty International. 2009a. *Nigeria: Petroleum, Pollution and Poverty in the Niger Delta*. London.

———. 2009b. "The Dealth Penalty in 2009." London. www.amnesty.org/en/death-penalty/death-sentences-and-executions-in-2009. Accessed 7 June 2010.

———. 2010. *Uganda: Antihomosexuality Bill is Inherently Discriminatory and Threatens Broader Human Rights*. London.

Anand, S., and P. Segal. 2008. "What Do We Know about Global Income Inequality?" *Journal of Economic Literature* 46(1): 57–94.

Anand, S., and A. Sen. 1995. "Gender Inequality in Human Development: Theories and Measurement." Human Development Report Office Occasional Paper 19. United Nations Development Programme, New York.

———. 1997. "Concepts of Human Development and Poverty: A Multidimensional Perspective." Human Development Report 1997 Papers: Poverty and Human Development. United Nations Development Programme, New York.

———. 2000a. "Human Development and Economic Sustainability." *World Development* 28(12): 2029–49.

———. 2000b. *Human Development and Human Rights*. Oxford, UK: Oxford University Press.

———. 2000c. "The Income Component of the Human Development Index." *Journal of Human Development and Capabilities* 1(1): 83–106.

Andrews, M. 2008. "The Good Governance Agenda: Beyond Indicators without Theory." *Oxford Development Studies* 36(4): 379–407.

Andrews, M., A. Grinsted, A. Nucifora, and R. Seligmann. 2010. "Public Institutional Reform in Mozambique: But with Limits." Working Paper. Harvard Kennedy School of Government, Cambridge, MA, and Center for Global Development, Washington, DC.

Asher, J., and B. Daponte. 2010. "A Hypothetical Cohort Model of Human Development." Human Development Research Paper 40. UNDP–HDRO, New York.

Asiedu, E., and B. Nandwa. 2007. "On the Impact of Foreign Aid in Education on Growth: How Relevant Is the Heterogeneity of Aid Flows and the Heterogeneity of Aid Recipients?" *Review of World Economics* 143(4): 631–49.

Aslund, A. 2001. "The Myth of Output Collapse after Communism." Carnegie Endowment for International Peace, Washington, DC. www.carnegieendowment.org/publications/index.cfm?fa=view&id=611. Accessed 25 June 2010.

Atkinson, A. 1970. "On the Measurement of Inequality." *Journal of Economic Theory* 2(3): 244–63.

———. 1983. *The Economics of Inequality*, 2nd edition. Oxford, UK: Clarendon Press.

Atkinson, A., and F. Bourguignon (Eds.). 2000. *Handbook of Income Distribution*, 1st edition. Amsterdam: Elsevier.

Atkinson, A., and J. Micklewright. 1992. *Economic Transformation in Eastern Europe and the Distribution of Income*. Cambridge, UK: Cambridge University Press.

Baird, S., J. Friedman, and N. Schady. 2007. "Aggregate Income Shocks and Infant Mortality in the Developing World." Policy Research Working Paper 4346. World Bank, Washington, DC.

Baland, J. M., and J. P. Platteau. 1996. *Halting Degradation of Natural Resources: Is There a Role for Rural Communities?* Rome: Food and Agriculture Organization.

Barbone, L., L. Cord, K. Hull, and J. Sandefur. 2007. "Democracy and Poverty Reduction: Explorations on the Sen Conjecture." In *Political Institutions and Development: Failed Expectations and Renewed Hopes*, eds. N. Dinello and V. Popov. Cheltenham, UK: Edward Elgar Publishing Ltd.

Bardhan, P. 2006. "Globalization and Rural Poverty." *World Development* 34(8): 1393–1404.

Bardhan, P., and D. Mookherjee. 2000. "Capture and Governance at Local and National Levels." *American Economic Review* 90(2): 135–39.

Barrett, C. B., and D. G. Maxwell. 2005. *Food Aid After Fifty Years: Recasting Its Role*. London: Routledge.

Barro, R. J. 1991. "Economic Growth in a Cross Section of Countries." *Quarterly Journal of Economics* 106(2): 407–43.

Barro, R. J., and J. W. Lee. 1994. "Sources of Economic Growth." *Carnegie-Rochester Conference Series on Public Policy* 40(1): 1–46.

———. 2010. *A New Data Set of Educational Attainment in the World, 1950–2010*. NBER Working Paper 15902. Cambridge, MA: National Bureau of Economic Research.

Barro, R. J., and X. Sala-i-Martin. 2003. *Economic Growth*, 2nd edition. Cambridge, MA: MIT Press.

Barros, R. P., F. Ferreira, J. R. Molinas Vega, and J. Saavedra Chanduvi. 2008. *Measuring Inequality of Opportunities in Latin America and the Caribbean*. Basingstroke, UK, and Washington, DC: Palgrave MacMillan and World Bank.

Bassel, L. 2008a. "Citizenship as Interpellation: Refugee Women and the State." *Government and Opposition* 43(2): 293–314.

———. 2008b. "Silencing to Protect: The Debate Over Women's Rights in France and Canada." In *Silencing Human Rights: Critical Engagements with a Contested Project*, eds. G. K. Bhambra and R. Shilliam. Basingstoke, UK: Palgrave Macmillan.

———. 2010. "Intersectional Politics at the Boundaries of the Nation State." *Ethnicities* 10(2): 155–80.

Bebenroth, R., D. Dietrich, and U. Vollmer. 2009. "Bank Regulation and Supervision in Bank-Dominated Financial Systems: A Comparison Between Japan and Germany." *European Journal of Law and Economics* 27(2): 177–209.

Beck, T., G. Clarke, A. Groff, P. Keefer, and P. Walsh. 2001. "New Tools in Comparative Political Economy: The Database of Political Institutions." *World Bank Economic Review* 15(1): 165–76.

Behrman, J., A. Murphy, A. Quisumbing, and K. Yount. 2009. "Are Returns to Mothers' Human Capital Realized in the Next Generation? The Impact of Mothers' Intellectual Capital and Long-Run Nutritional Status on Children's Human Capital in Guatemala." IFPRI Discussion Paper 850. International Food Policy Research Institute, Washington, DC.

Bénabou, R. 2000. "Unequal Societies: Income Distribution and the Social Contract." *The American Economic Review* 90(1): 96–129.

Benavot, A., and J. Resnik. 2006. "Lessons from the Past: A Comparative Socio-Historical Analysis of Primary and Secondary Education." In *Educating all Children: A Global Agenda*, eds. J. E. Cohen, D. E. Bloom, and M. B. Malin. Cambridge, MA: American Academy of Arts and Sciences.

Besley, T., R. Pande, and V. Rao. 2005. "Political Selection and the Quality of Government: Evidence from South India." CEPR Discussion Paper 5201. Center for Economic and Policy Research, Washington, DC.

Bessell, S. 2009a. "Indonesian Children's Views and Experiences of Work and Poverty." *Social Policy and Society* 8(4): 527–40.

———. 2009b. "Strengthening Fiji's Education System: A View from Key Stakeholders." *Pacific Economic Bulletin* 24(3): 58–70.

Bhagwati, J., and P. Desai. 1970. *India: Planning for Industrialization*. Oxford, UK: Oxford University Press.

Binder, M., and G. Georgiadis. 2010. "Determinants of Human Development: Insights from State-Dependent Panel Models." Human Development Research Paper 24. UNDP–HDRO, New York.

Birdsall, N. 2008. *Put Double Majority Voting Back on the Table at the IMF*. Washington, DC: Center for Global Development.

Blanchard, O. 2008. "Reforming Labor Market Institutions: Unemployment Insurance and Employment Protection." In *Washington Consensus Reconsidered: Towards a New Global Governance*, eds. N. Serra and J. E. Stiglitz. New York: Oxford University Press.

Boden, T. A., G. Marland, and R. J. Andres. 2009. "Global, Regional, and National Fossil-Fuel CO_2 Emissions." Carbon Dioxide Information Analysis Center, Oak Ridge National Laboratory, TN. http://cdiac.ornl.gov/trends/emis/tre_coun.html. Accessed 15 May 2010.

Boone, P., and Z. Zhan. 2006. "Lowering Child Mortality in Poor Countries: The Power of Knowledgeable Parents." CEP Discussion Papers 751. Centre for Economic Performance, London.

Bornstein, D. 2005. *The Price of a Dream: The Story of the Grameen Bank*. Oxford, UK: Oxford University Press.

Bourguignon, F. 2004. *The Poverty-Growth-Inequality Triangle*. New Delhi: Indian Council for Research on International Economic Relations.

Bourguignon, F., A. Bénassy-Quéré, S. Dercon, A. Estache, J. W. Gunning, R. Kanbur, S. Klasen, S. Maxwell, J. P. Platteau, and A. Spadaro. 2008. "Millennium Development Goals at Midpoint: Where Do We Stand and Where Do We Need to Go?" Background paper for the 2009 *European Report on Development*. European Commission, Brussels.

Bourguignon, F., and S. Chakravarty. 2003. "The Measurement of Multidimensional Poverty." *Journal of Economic Inequality* 1(1): 25–49.

Bourguinon, F., and A. Spadaro. 2005. "Tax-Benefit Revealed Social Preferences: Are Tax Authorities Non-Paretian?" Paris-Jourdan Sciences Economiques Working Paper 22. Paris-Jourdan Sciences Economiques, Paris..

Bourguignon, F., and T. Verdier. 2000. "Oligarchy, Democracy, Inequality and Growth." *Journal of Development Economics* 62(2): 285–313.

Bradsher, K. 2010. "Foreign Companies Chafe at China's Restrictions." *The New York Times*. May 16.

Brainerd, E. 2010. "Human Development in Eastern Europe and the CIS since 1990." Human Development Research Paper 16. UNDP–HDRO, New York.

Brainerd, E., and D. Cutler. 2005. "Autopsy on an Empire: Understanding Mortality in Russia and the Former Soviet Union." *Journal of Economic Perspectives* 19(1): 107–30.

Brandolini, A., and G. D'Alessio. 2009. "Measuring Well-Being in the Functioning Space." In *Debating Global Society: Reach and Limits of the Capability Approach*, ed. E. Chiappero-Martinetti. Milan, Italy: Feltrinelli Foundation.

Brown, G., A. Langer, and F. Stewart. 2008. "A Typology of Post-Conflict Environments: An Overview." CRISE Working Paper 53. Centre for Research on Inequality, Human Security and Ethnicity, Oxford, UK.

Brun, J. F., G. Chambas, and F. Mourji. 2009. "Guaranteeing Fiscal Space for Human Development in Morocco." In *Fiscal Space: Policy Options for Financing Human Development*, eds. R. Roy and A. Heuty. London: Earthscan.

Bryce, J., S. Arifeen, G. Pariyo, C. Lanata, D. Gwatkin, and J. P. Habicht. 2003. "Reducing Child Mortality: Can Public Health Deliver?" *The Lancet* 362 (9378): 159–64.

Budlender, D. 2008. *The Statistical Evidence on Care and Non-Care Work across Six Countries*. Gender and Development Programme Paper 4. Geneva: United Nations Research Institute for Social Development.

Burd-Sharps, S., K. Lewis, P. Guyer, and T. Lechterman. 2010. "Twenty Years of Human Development in Six Affluent Countries: Australia, Canada, Japan, New Zealand, United Kingdom, and United States." Human Development Research Paper 27. UNDP–HDRO, New York.

Burd-Sharps, S., K. Lewis, and E. B. Martins (Eds.). 2008. *The Measure of America: American Human Development Report 2008–2009*. New York: Columbia University Press.

Caldas, S. J. 1993. "Reexamination of Input and Process Factor Effects on Public School Achievement." *Journal of Educational Research* 86(4): 206–14.

Calvo, S. G. 2010. "The Global Financial Crisis of 2008–10: A View from the Social Sectors." Human Development Research Paper 18. UNDP–HDRO, New York.

Canning, D. 2010. "Progress in Health Around the World." Human Development Research Paper 43. UNDP–HDRO, New York.

Cartwright, N. 2009. "What Are Randomised Controlled Trials Good For?" *Philosophical Studies* 147(1): 59–70.

Casabonne, U., and C. Kenny. 2009. *The Best Things in Life are (Nearly) Free: Technology, Knowledge and Global Health*. Washington, DC: World Bank.

Chahine, J. 2005. "Lebanon Slips in Human Development Index—UN Report Identifies Three Pillars of Cooperation in Urgent Need of Committment." *The Daily Star*. 9 September.

Charmes, J., and S. Wieringa. 2003. "Measuring Women's Empowerment: An Assessment of the Gender-Related Development Index and the Gender Empowerment Measure." *Journal of Human Development and Capabilities* 4(3): 419–35.

Charumilind, C., R. Kali, and Y. Wiwattanakantang. 2006. "Connected Lending: Thailand Before the Financial Crisis." *Journal of Business* 79(1): 181–218.

Chattopadhyay, R., and E. Duflo. 2004. "Women as Policy Makers: Evidence from a Randomized Policy Experiment in India." *Econometrica* 72(5): 1409–43.

Cheibub, J. A., J. Gandhi, and J. R. Vreeland. 2009. "Democracy and Dictatorship Revisited Dataset." University of Illinois at Urbana-Champaign. netfiles.uiuc.edu/cheibub/www/DD_page.html. Accessed 15 April 2010.

Chen, Y., and H. Li. 2009. "Mother's Education and Child Health: Is There a Nurturing Effect?" *Journal of Health Economics* 28(2): 413–26.

Chen, S., and M. Ravallion. 2008. "The Developing World is Poorer Than We Thought, But No Less Successful in the Fight Against Poverty." Policy Research Working Paper 4703. Washington, DC: Development Research Group, World Bank.

China NDRC (National Development and Reform Commission). 2006. "The Outline of the 11th Five-year Plan for National Economic and Social Development of the People's Republic of China." en.ndrc.gov.cn/hot/t20060529_71334.htm. Accessed 15 July 2010.

Clemens, M. A. 2004. "The Long Walk to School: International Education Goals in Historical Perspective." Working Paper 37. Center for Global Development, Washington, DC.

Cline, W. 2008. *Global Warming and Agriculture: Impact Estimates by Country*. Washington, DC: Center for Global Development and Peterson Institute for International Economics.

Coale, A. 1991. "Excess Female Mortality and the Balance of the Sexes in the Population: An Estimate of 'Missing Females.'" *Population and Development Review* 17(3): 517–23.

Collier, P., and A. Hoeffler. 2007. "Civil War." In *Handbook of Defense Economics: Defense in a Globalized World*, eds. T. Sandler and K. Hartley. Amsterdam: Elsevier.

Comin, D., B. Hobijn, and E. Rovito. 2008. "Technology Usage Lags." *Journal of Economic Growth* 13(4): 237–56.

Commander, S. 2010. "Employment Risk and Policy." Human Development Research Paper 30. UNDP–HDRO, New York.

Commission on Growth and Development. 2008. *The Growth Report: Strategies for Sustained Growth and Inclusive Development.* Washington, DC: World Bank.

Commission on Human Security. 2003. *Human Security Now.* New York: Commission on Human Security.

Cook, A., and B. Daponte. 2008. "A Demographic Analysis of the Rise in the Prevalence of the US Population Overweight and/or Obese." *Population Research and Policy Review* 27(4): 403–26.

Cooke, M., F. Mitrou, D. Lawrence, E. Guimond, and D. Beavon. 2007. "Indigenous Well-Being in Four Countries: An Application of the UNDP's Human Development Index to Indigenous Peoples in Australia, Canada, New Zealand, and the United States." *BioMed Central International Health and Human Rights* 7(9): 1–11.

Cord, L., M. Verhoeven, C. Blomquist, and B. Rijkers. 2009. "The Global Economic Crisis: Assessing Vulnerability with a Poverty Lens." Policy Note. World Bank, Washington, DC.

Córdoba, J., and M. Ripoll. 2008. "Endogenous TFP and Cross-country Income Differences." *Journal of Monetary Economics* 55(6): 1158–70.

Cornia, G. 2010. "Income Distribution under Latin America's New Left Regimes." *Journal of Human Development and Capabilities* 11(1): 85–114.

Cornia, G., and J. Court. 2001. *Inequality, Growth, and Poverty in an Era of Liberalization and Globalization.* Helsinki: United Nations University, World Institute for Development Economics Research.

Cornia, G. A., S. Rosignoli, and L. Tiberti. 2007. *Globalisation and Health: Impact Pathways and Recent Evidence.* Santa Cruz, CA: University of California Santa Cruz, Center for Global, International and Regional Studies.

Council of Europe, CDEG (Steering Committee for Equality between Women and Men). 2009. "Sex-Disaggregated Statistics on the Participation of Women and Men in Political and Public Decision-Making in Council of Europe Member States: Situation as at 1 September 2008." Council of Europe, Strasbourg, France.

CPJ (Committee to Protect Journalists). 2009. "Attacks on the Press Report 2009." New York. www.cpj.org/attacks/. Accessed 15 May 2010.

CRED (Centre for Research on the Epidemiology of Disasters). 2010. "EM-DAT: The International Disaster Database." Université catholique de Louvain, Belgium. www.emdat.be/advanced-search-details. Accessed 15 April 2010.

Crocker, D. A. 2007. "Deliberative Participation in Local Development." *Journal of Human Development and Capabilities* 8(3): 431–55.

Cubero, R., and I. V. Hollar. 2010. "Equity and Fiscal Policy: The Income Distribution Effects of Taxation and Social Spending in Central America." IMF Working Paper 112. International Monetary Fund, Washington, DC.

Cuno, K., and M. Desai. 2009. *Family, Gender, and Law in a Globalizing Middle East and South Asia.* Syracuse, NY: Syracuse University Press.

Cutler, D., A. Deaton, and A. Lleras-Muney. 2006. "The Determinants of Mortality." *Journal of Economic Perspectives* 20(3): 97–120.

Cutler, D., and A. Lleras-Muney. 2006. "Education and Health: Evaluating Theories and Evidence." In *Making Americans Healthier: Social and Economic Policy as Health Policy,* eds. R. F. Schoeni, J. S. House, G. A. Kaplan, and H. Pollack. New York: Russell Sage Foundation.

Cutler, D., and G. Miller. 2005. "The Role of Public Health Improvements in Health Advances: The Twentieth-Century United States." *Demography* 42(1): 1–22.

d'Aiglepierre, R., and L. Wagner. 2010. "Aid and Universal Primary Education." Working Paper 201022. National Center for Scientific Research, Universite d'Auvergne, France.

Damodaran, H. 2008. *India's New Capitalists: Caste, Business, and Industry in a Modern Nation.* New York: Palgrave Macmillan.

Daponte, B., and R. Garfield. 2000. "The Effect of Economic Sanctions on the Mortality of Iraqi Children Prior to the 1991 Persian Gulf War." *American Journal of Public Health* 90(4): 546–52.

Dasgupta, A., and V. A. Beard. 2007. "Community Driven Development, Collective Action and Elite Capture in Indonesia." *Development and Change* 38(2): 229–49.

Davies, V. 2007. "Capital Flight and War." Post-Conflict Transitions Working Paper 13. University of Oxford, Centre for the Study of African Economies and Department of Economics, Oxford, UK.

Davies, R., M. Brumm, M. Manga, R. Rubiandini, R. Swarbrick, and M. Tingay. 2008. "The East Java Mud Volcano (2006 to Present): An Earthquake or Drilling Trigger?" *Earth and Planetary Science Letters* 272(3–4): 627–38.

de Quadros, C. A., J. M. Olivé, C. Nogueira, P. Carrasco, and C. Silveira. 1998. "Expanded Program on Immunization." In *Maternal Health and Child Health Activities at the Local Level: Toward the Goals of the World Summit for Children,* eds. Y. Benguigui, S. Land, J. M. Paganini, and J. Yunes. Washington, DC: Pan American Health Organization.

De, A., and J. Drèze. 1999. *Public Report on Basic Education in India.* New Delhi: Oxford University Press.

Deaton, A. 2002. "Policy Implications of the Gradient of Health and Wealth." *Health Affairs* 21(2): 13–30.

———. 2007. "Global Patterns of Income and Health: Facts, Interpretations, and Policies." WIDER Annual Lecture 10. United Nations University, World Institute for Development Economics Research, Helsinki.

———. 2008. "Income, Health, and Well-Being Around the World: Evidence from the Gallup World Poll." *Journal of Economic Perspectives* 22(2): 53–72.

———. 2009. *Instruments of Development: Randomization in the Tropics, and the Search for the Elusive Keys to Economic Development.* NBER Working Paper 14690. Cambridge, MA: National Bureau of Economic Research.

———. 2010. "Instruments, Randomization, and Learning about Development." *Journal of Economic Literature* 48(2): 424–55.

della Paolera, G., and A. M. Taylor (Eds.). 2003. *A New Economic History of Argentina.* New York: Cambridge University Press.

Denison, E. 1967. *Why Growth Rates Differ: Postwar Experience in Nine Western Countries.* Washington, DC: The Brookings Institution Press.

Desai, M. 2010. "Hope in Hard Times: Women's Empowerment and Human Development." Human Development Research Paper 14. UNDP–HDRO, New York.

Di John, J. 2009. *From Windfall to Curse? Oil and Industrialization in Venezuela, 1920 to the Present.* University Park, PA: Penn State University Press.

Di Tella, R., and J. Dubra. 2009. *The Interruption of a Policy for Less Corruption in the Health Sector, and Better Health Care in Argentina.* Cambridge, MA: Harvard Business School.

Diaw, A., S. Guérineau, and S. G. Jeanneney. 2009. "Securing Fiscal Space for the Millennium Development Goals in Senegal." In *Fiscal Space: Policy Options for Financing Human Development,* eds. R. Roy and A. Heuty. London: Earthscan.

Diener, E., and R. Biswas-Diener. 2000. "New Directions in Subjective Well-Being Research: The Cutting Edge." *Indian Journal of Clinical Psychology* 27: 21–33.

Diener, E., R. Lucas, U. Schimmack, and J. Helliwell. 2009. *Well-Being for Public Policy.* Oxford, UK: Oxford University Press.

Diener, E., and M. Seligman. 2004. "Beyond Money: Toward an Economy of Well-Being." *Psychological Science in the Public Interest* 5(1): 1–31.

Donner, J. 2008. "Research Approaches to Mobile Use in the Developing World: A Review of the Literature." *The Information Society* 24(3): 140–59.

Drèze, J., and R. Khera. 2010. "India's National Rural Employment Guarantee Act." UNDP–HDRO, New York.

Drèze, J., and A. Sen. 1989. *Hunger and Public Action.* Oxford, UK: Clarendon Press.

———. 2002. *India: Development and Participation.* New Delhi: Oxford University Press.

Duarte, M., and D. Restuccia. 2006. "The Productivity of Nations." *Federal Reserve Bank of Richmond Economic Quarterly* 92(3): 195–223.

Duflo, E. 2001. "Schooling and Labor Market Consequences of School Construction in Indonesia: Evidence from an Unusual Policy Experiment." *American Economic Review* 91(4): 795–813.

———. 2003. "Grandmothers and Granddaughters: Old-Age Pensions and Intrahousehold Allocation in South Africa." *World Bank Economic Review* 17(1): 1–25.

Duflo, E., R. Hanna, and S. Ryan. 2009. "Incentives Work: Getting Teachers to Come to School." Applied Economics Workshop. University of Chicago Booth School of Business, Chicago, IL.

Durlauf, S., P. A. Johnson, and J. Temple. 2005. "Growth Econometrics." In *Handbook of Economic Growth,* eds. P. Aghion and S. Durlauf. Amsterdam: Elsevier.

Easterlin, R. A. 1995. "Will Raising the Incomes of All Increase the Happiness of All?" *Journal of Economic Behavior and Organization* 27(1): 35–47.

Easterly, W. 1999. "Life During Growth." *Journal of Economic Growth* 4(3): 239–76.

———. 2002. *The Elusive Quest for Growth: Economists' Adventures and Misadventures in the Tropics.* Cambridge, MA: MIT Press.

———. 2006. *White Man's Burden: Why the West's Efforts to Aid the Rest Have Done so Much Ill and So Little Good.* New York: The Penguin Press.

———. 2009. "How the Millennium Development Goals are Unfair to Africa." *World Development* 37(1): 26–35.

ECLAC (Economic Commission for Latin America and the Caribbean). 2010. "Gender Equality Observatory for Latin America and the Caribbean." Santiago. www.eclac.cl/oig/default.asp?idioma=IN. Accessed 12 August 2010.

The Economist. 1990. "United Nations Development Programme Includes Human Development Index in 1990 Report." *The Economist.* 26 May.

———. 1991. "Measuring Human Development." *The Economist.* 25 May.

———. 2007. "Slimy Business: The Mud Does Not Stick." *The Economist.* 29 November.

————. 2010. "The Worldwide War on Baby Girls." *The Economist.* 4 March.

Edmonds, E. 2005. "Does Child Labor Decline with Improving Economic Status?" *Journal of Human Resources* 40(1): 77–99.

Edwards, M., and J. Gaventa. 2001. *Global Citizen Action.* Boulder, CO: Lynne Rienner Publishers.

EEA (European Environment Agency). 2008. "EN15 Accidental Oil Spills from Marine Shipping." Copenhagen. http://themes. eea.europa.eu/Sectors_and_activities/energy/indicators/ EN15%2C2008.11. Accessed 18 June 2010.

Eicher, T., and S. Turnovsky (Eds.). 2003. *Inequality and Growth: Theory and Policy Implications.* Cambridge, MA: MIT Press.

Elson, D. 2006. "The Changing Economic and Political Participation of Women: Hybridization, Reversals and Contradictions in the Context of Globalization." GEM-IWG Working Paper 8. Salt Lake City, UT: International Working Group on Gender, Macroeconomics, and International Economics.

Elson, R. E. 2001. *Suharto: A Political Biography.* Cambridge, MA: Cambridge University Press.

Eurostat. 2010. "European Union Statistics on Income and Living Conditions." European Commission, Brussels. http://epp.eurostat.ec.europa. eu/portal/page/portal/microdata/eu_silc. Accessed 15 April 2010.

Evans, P. 2010. "The Challenge of 21st Century Development: Building Capability-Enhancing States." Global Event Working Paper. United Nations Development Programme, New York.

Eyben, R. 2004. "Who Owns a Poverty Reduction Strategy? A Case Study of Power, Instruments and Relationships in Bolivia." In *Inclusive Aid: Changing Power and Relationships in International Development*, eds. L. Groves and R. Hinton. London: Earthscan.

Faguet, J. P. 2002. "Does Decentralization Increase Government Responsiveness to Local Needs? Evidence from Bolivia." Policy Research Working Paper 2516. World Bank, Washington, DC.

Fallon, P., S. Aiyar, L. Cui, M. Hussain, L. Redifer, N. Staines, and R. Stern. 2004. "Review of Recent IMF Experience in Post-Conflict Economies." International Monetary Fund, Washington, DC.

FAO (Food and Agriculture Organization). 2010a. "FAO Stat." Rome. http://faostat.fao.org/. Accessed 19 May 2010.

————. 2010b. "Food Security Statistics." Rome. www.fao.org/ economic/ess/food-security-statistics/en/. Accessed 30 June 2010.

Ferreira, F., and N. Schady. 2008. "Aggregate Economic Shocks, Child Schooling and Child Health." Policy Research Working Paper 4701. World Bank, Washington, DC.

Filmer, D., and L. Pritchett. 1999. "The Impact of Public Spending on Health: Does Money Matter?" *Social Science and Medicine* 49(10): 1309–23.

Fiszbein, A., N. Schady, F. Ferreira, M. Grosh, N. Keleher, P. Olinto, and E. Skoufias. 2009. *Conditional Cash Transfers: Reducing Present and Future Poverty.* Washington, DC: World Bank.

Fogel, R. W. 2004. *The Escape from Hunger and Premature Death, 1700–2100: Europe, America, and the Third World.* Cambridge, UK: Cambridge University Press.

Foster, J., L. López-Calva, and M. Szekely. 2005. "Measuring the Distribution of Human Development: Methodology and an Application to Mexico." *Journal of Human Development* 6(1): 5–25.

Franco, A., C. Alvarez-Dardet, and M. Ruiz. 2004. "Effect of Democracy on Health: Ecological Study." *British Medical Journal* 329(7480): 1421–23.

Frankel, J. 2010. "Mauritius: A Success Story." Presentation at Harvard Kennedy School MPA/ID 10th Anniversary. 15 May, Cambridge, MA.

Freeman, R. 1998. "War of the Models: Which Labour Market Institutions for the 21st Century?" *Labour Economics* 5(1): 1–24.

Friedman, S. 2006. "Participatory Governance and Citizen Action in Post-Apartheid South Africa." International Institute for Labour Studies Discussion Paper 164. International Labour Organization, Geneva.

Fuchs, T., and L. Woessmann. 2007. "What Accounts for International Differences in Student Performance: A Re-Examination Using PISA Data." *Empirical Economics* 32(2–3): 433–64.

Fuentes-Nieva, R., and I. Pereira. 2010. "The Disconnect Between Indicators of Sustainability and Human Development." Human Development Research Paper 34. UNDP–HDRO, New York.

Fuentes-Nieva, R., and P. Seck (Eds.). 2010. *Risk, Shocks and Human Development: On the Brink.* Basingstoke, UK: Palgrave Macmillan.

Fukuda-Parr, S. 2003. "The Human Development Paradigm: Operationalizing Sen's Ideas on Capabilities." *Feminist Economics* 9(2–3): 301–17.

————. 2007. "Has the Human Development Approach Influenced Policy? The Case of World Bank Flagship Reports." *Indian Journal of Human Development* 1(1): 153–60.

Fukuda-Parr, S., and A. K. Shiva Kumar. 2003. *Readings in Human Development.* New York: Oxford University Press.

Gallego, F. 2010. "Historical Origins of Schooling: The Role of Democracy and Political Decentralization." *Review of Economics and Statistics* 92(2): 228–43.

Gallup World Poll. 2010. "Gallup." Washington, DC. www.gallup. com/home.aspx. Accessed 7 June 2010.

Ganatra, B. 2008. "Maintaining Access to Safe Abortion and Reducing Sex Ratio Imbalances in Asia." *Reproductive Health Matters* 16(31): 90–98.

Gargarella, R. 2002. "'Too Far Removed from the People': Access to Justice for the Poor: The Case of Latin America." Universidad Torcuato Di Tella, Buenos Aires.

Gasper, D. 2005. "Securing Humanity: Situating 'Human Security' as Concept and Discourse." *Journal of Human Development and Capabilities* 6(2): 221–45.

Gauri, V. 2002. "Brazil: Maternal and Child Health." Report 23811. World Bank, Washington, DC.

Gauri, V., and P. Khaleghian. 2002. "Immunization in Developing Countries: Its Organizational and Political Determinants." *World Development* 30(12): 2109–32.

Gaye, A., and S. Jha. 2010. "A Review of Conceptual and Measurement Innovations in National and Regional Human Development Reports, 1998–2009." Human Development Research Paper 21. UNDP–HDRO, New York.

Georgiadis, G., J. Pineda, and F. Rodríguez. 2010. "Has the Preston Curve Broken Down?" Human Development Research Paper 32. UNDP–HDRO, New York.

Gertner, J. 2010. "The Rise and Fall of the G.D.P." *The New York Times.* May 16.

GFN (Global Footprint Network). 2009. "The Ecological Footprint Atlas." Oakland, CA. www.footprintnetwork.org/atlas. Accessed 15 June 2010.

Ghai, D. P., A. R. Khan, E. L. H. Lee, and T. Alfthan. 1980. *The Basic-Needs Approach to Development: Some Issues Regarding Concepts and Methodology.* Geneva: International Labour Office.

Gibney, M., L. Cornett, and R. Wood. 2010. "Political Terror Scale 1976–2008." Political Terror Scale. www.politicalterrorscale.org/. Accessed 7 June 2010.

Gidwitz, Z., M. Heger, J. Pineda, and F. Rodríguez. 2010. "Understanding Performance in Human Development: A Cross-National Study." Human Development Research Paper 42. UNDP–HDRO, New York.

Gittings, J. 1990. "New Economic Indicator Puts Rich Countries under Microscope." *The Guardian.* 25 May.

Glewwe, P. 1999. *The Economics of School Quality Investments in Developing Countries.* New York: Palgrave Macmillan.

Glewwe, P., and M. Kremer. 2006. "Schools, Teachers, and Education Outcomes in Developing Countries." In *Handbook of the Economics of Education*, eds. E. A. Hanushek and F. Welch. Amsterdam: Elsevier.

The Global Fund (The Global Fund to Fight AIDS, Tuberculosis and Malaria). 2009. "Global Fund ARV Fact Sheet." Geneva.

Gough, I., and J. A. McGregor (Eds.). 2007. *Wellbeing in Developing Countries: New Approaches and Research Strategies.* Cambridge, UK: Cambridge University Press.

Graham, C. 2010. "The Challenges of Incorporating Empowerment into the HDI: Some Lessons from Happiness Economics and Quality of Life Research." Human Development Research Paper 13. UNDP–HDRO, New York.

Graham, W., D. Braunholtz, and O. Campbell. 2010. "New Modelled Estimates of Maternal Mortality." *The Lancet* 375(9730): 1963.

Gray, G., and M. Purser. 2010. "Human Development Trends since 1970: A Social Convergence Story." Human Development Research Paper 2. UNDP–HDRO, New York.

Greaney, V., S. R. Khandker, and M. Alam. 1999. *Bangladesh: Assessing Basic Learning Skills.* Dhaka: University Press.

Grimm, M., and I. Günther. 2004. *How to Achieve Pro-Poor Growth in a Poor Economy: The Case of Burkina Faso.* Göttingen, Germany: University of Göttingen.

Gupta, K., and P. P. Yesudian. 2006. "Evidence of Women's Empowerment in India: A Study of Socio-Spatial Disparities." *GeoJournal* 65(4): 365–80.

Gupta, S., M. Verhoeven, and E. Tiongson. 2003. "Public Spending on Health Care and the Poor." *Health Economics* 12(8): 685–96.

Gwatkin, D., S. Rutstein, K. Johnson, E. Suliman, A. Wagstaff, and A. Amouzou. 2007. "Socio-Economic Differences in Health, Nutrition, and Population within Developing Countries: An Overview." Country Reports on HNP (Health, Nutrition and Population) and Poverty. World Bank, Washington, DC.

Hall, G., and H. A. Patrinos (Eds.). 2010. *Indigenous Peoples, Poverty and Development.* Washington, DC: World Bank.

Hamel, J. Y. 2010. "ICT4D and the Human Development and Capability Approach." Human Development Research Paper 37. UNDP–HDRO, New York.

Hanlon, J., A. Barrientos, and D. Hulme. 2010. *Just Give Money to the Poor: The Development Revolution from the Global South.* Sterling, VA: Kumarian Press.

Hanushek, E. A. 1995. "Interpreting Recent Research on Schooling in Developing Countries." *World Bank Research Observer* 10(2): 227–46.

Haq, K., and R. Ponzio (Eds.). 2008. *Pioneering the Human Development Revolution: An Intellectual Biography of Mahbub ul Haq.* New York: Oxford University Press.

Harding, R., and L. Wantchekon. 2010. "The Political Economy of Human Development." Human Development Research Paper 29. UNDP–HDRO, New York.

Harper, C., N. Jones, A. McKay, and J. Espey. 2009. "Children in Times of Economic Crisis: Past Lessons, Future Policies." ODI Background Note. Overseas Development Institute, London.

Harttgen, K., and S. Klasen. 2010. "A Household-Based Human Development Index." Human Development Research Paper 22. UNDP–HDRO, New York.

Hausmann, R., and F. Rodríguez. Forthcoming. *Venezuela: Anatomy of a Collapse.* Cambridge, MA: Harvard Kennedy School of Government.

Hausmann, R., F. Rodríguez, and R. Wagner. 2008. "Growth Collapses." In *Money, Crises and Transition: Essays in Honor of Guillermo A. Calvo,* eds. C. M. Reinhart, C. Végh, and A. Velasco. Cambridge, MA: MIT Press.

Hausmann, R., D. Rodrik, and A. Velasco. 2008. "Growth Diagnostics." In *The Washington Consensus Reconsidered: Towards a New Global Governance,* eds. N. Serra and J. E. Stiglitz. Oxford, UK: Oxford University Press.

Hawken, A., and G. Munck. 2009. "Cross-National Indices with Gender-Differentiated Data: What Do They Measure? How Valid Are They?" Technical Background Paper for the forthcoming UNDP Asia Pacific Human Development Report on Gender. United Nations Development Programme, New York.

Helpman, E. 1998. *General Purpose Technologies and Economic Growth.* Cambridge, MA: MIT Press.

Herrero, C., R. Martínez, and A. Villar. 2010. "Improving the Measurement of Human Development." Human Development Research Paper 12. UNDP–HDRO, New York.

Heston, A., R. Summers, and B. Aten. 2009. "Penn World Table Version 6.3." University of Pennsylvania, Center for International Comparisons of Production, Income and Prices, Philadelphia, PA. http://pwt.econ.upenn.edu/php_site/pwt_index.php. Accessed 15 July 2010.

Heyzer, N., and M. Khor. 1999. "Globalization and the Way Forward." *Development Outreach,* Summer 1999. www.devoutreach.com/summer99/GlobalizationandtheWayForward/tabid/819/Default.aspx. Accessed 1 February 2009.

Hidalgo, C. 2010. "Graphical Statistical Methods for the Representation of the Human Development Index and its Components." Human Development Research Paper 39. UNDP–HDRO, New York.

Hobbes, T. 1651. *Leviathan, or, the Matter, Forme, and Power of a Commonwealth Ecclesiastical and Civil.* Oxford, UK: Oxford University Press (Printed in 1996).

Hoddinott, J., and A. Quisumbing. 2010. "Methods for Microeconometric Risk and Vulnerability Assessment." In *Risk, Shocks and Human Development: On the Brink,* eds. R. Fuentes-Nieva and P. Seck. Basingstoke, UK: Palgrave Macmillan.

Hogan, M., K. Foreman, M. Naghavi, S. Ahn, M. Wang, S. Makela, A. Lopez, R. Lozano, and C. Murray. 2010. "Maternal Mortality for 181 Countries, 1980–2008: A Systematic Analysis of Progress Towards Millennium Development Goal 5." *The Lancet* 375(9726): 1609–23.

Horváth, B., A. Ivanov, and M. Peleah. 2010. "The Human Development Impact of the Global Crisis in Central, Eastern and Southern Europe and the CIS." Working Paper. United Nations Development Programme Bratislava Regional Center, Bratislava.

Houweling, T., C. Ronsmans, O. Campbell, and A. Kunst. 2007. "Huge Poor–Rich Inequalities in Maternity Care: An International Comparative Study of Maternity and Child Care in Developing Countries." *Bulletin of the World Health Organization* 85(10): 733–820.

Hulme, D., and S. Fukuda-Parr. 2009. "International Norm Dynamics and 'the End of Poverty': Understanding the Millennium Development Goals (MDGs)." Brooks World Poverty Institute Working Paper 96. University of Manchester, UK.

Hulme, D., and K. Moore. 2008. "Assisting the Poorest in Bangladesh: Learning from BRAC's 'Targeting the Ultra Poor' Programme." In *Social Protection for the Poor and Poorest: Concepts, Policies and Politics,* eds. A. Barrientos and D. Hulme. New York: Palgrave Macmillan.

Huntington, S. 1991. *The Third Wave: Democratization in the Late Twentieth Century.* Norman, OK: University of Oklahoma Press.

Hurt, L. S., C. Ronsmans, and S. Saha. 2004. "Effects of Education and Other Socioeconomic Factors in Middle Age Mortality in Rural Bangladesh." *Journal of Epidemiology and Community Health* 58(4): 315–20.

Ibrahim, S., and S. Alkire. 2007. "Agency and Empowerment: A Proposal for Internationally Comparable Indicators." *Oxford Development Studies* 35(4): 379–403.

IDMC (Internal Displacement Monitoring Centre). 2010. "Internal Displacement Monitoring Centre." Geneva. www.internal-displacement.org. Accessed 15 April 2010.

IEA (International Energy Agency). 2009. *World Energy Outlook 2009.* Paris: Organisation for Economic Co-operation and Development and IEA.

Iglehart, J. 2010. "Historic Passage—Reform at Last." *The New England Journal of Medicine* 362(14): 48.

ILO (International Labour Organization). 2009. *World of Work Report: The Global Jobs Crisis.* Geneva: International Labour Office.

———. 2010a. "Accelerating a Job-Rich Recovery in G20 Countries: Building on Experience." Report to G20 Labour and Employment Ministers. International Labour Office, Washington, DC.

———. 2010b. *Global Employment Trends.* Geneva: International Labour Office.

———. 2010c. *Key Indicators on the Labour Market,* 6th edition. Geneva: International Labour Office.

———. 2010d. "LABORSTA Database." Employment by Occupation Data. International Labour Office, Geneva. http://laborsta.ilo.org/. Accessed 15 January 2010.

Imai, K., and J. Weinstein. 2000. "Measuring the Economic Impact of Civil War." CID Working Paper 51. Harvard University, Center for International Development, Cambridge, MA.

IMF (International Monetary Fund). 2009. *World Economic Outlook: Sustaining the Recovery.* Washington, DC.

———. 2010a. *Government Finance Statstics.* Washington, DC.

———. 2010b. *World Economic Outlook Update: An Update of the Key WEO Projections.* Washington, DC.

IPU (Inter-Parliamentary Union). 2010. "Women in Parliaments: World and Regional Averages." Geneva. www.ipu.org/wmn-e/world.htm. Accessed 7 June 2010.

Ishida, H., W. Muller, and J. M. Ridge. 1995. "Class Origin, Class Destination, and Education: A Cross-National Study of Ten Industrial Nations." *American Journal of Sociology* 101(1): 145–93.

ITOPF (International Tank Owners Pollution Federation Limited). 2010. "ITOPF-Data and Statistics." London. www.itopf.com/information-services/data-and-statistics/index.html. Accessed 17 June 2010.

ITU (International Telecommunication Union). 2009. "ICT Indicators Database 2009." *International Telecommunication Union.* www.itu.int/ITU-D/ict/publications/world/world.html. Accessed 20 July 2010.

Ivanov, A., and M. Peleah. 2010. "From Centrally Planned to Human Development." Human Development Research Paper 38. UNDP–HDRO, New York.

Jayadev, A. 2010. "Global Governance and Human Development: Promoting Democratic Accountability and Institutional Experimentation." Human Development Research Paper 6. UNDP–HDRO, New York.

Jayadev, A., and F. Rodríguez. 2010. "The Declining Labor Share of Income." Human Development Research Paper 36. UNDP–HDRO, New York.

Joe, W., U.S. Mishra, and K. Navaneetham. 2009. "Inequalities in Childhood Malnutrition in India: Some Evidence on Group Disparities." *Journal of Human Development and Capabilities* 10(3): 417–39.

Johannes, T. A., T. Akwi, and P. E. Anzah. 2006. "The Distributive Impact of Fiscal Policy in Cameroon: Tax and Benefit Incidence." PMMA Working Paper 16. Ottawa: International Research Centre.

Jolly, R. 2010. "The UN and Development Policies." UN Intellectual History Project Briefing Note 7. United Nations, New York.

Jolly, R., L. Emmerij, and T. G. Weiss. 2009. *UN Ideas That Changed the World.* Bloomington, IN: Indiana University Press.

Jones, C. 2002. *Introduction to Economic Growth.* New York: W.W. Norton.

Jones, G., R. Steketee, R. Black, Z. Bhutta, and S. Morris. 2003. "How Many Child Deaths Can We Prevent This Year?" *The Lancet* 362(9377): 65–71.

Journal of Human Development and Capabilities. 2003. "Special Issue on New Insecurities." *Journal of Human Development and Capabilities* 4(2).

Kabeer, N. 1999. "Resources, Agency, Achievement: Reflections on the Measurement of Women's Empowerment." *Development as Change* 30(3): 435–64.

Kahneman, D. 1999. "Objective Happiness." In *Well-Being: The Foundations of Hedonic Psychology,* eds. D. Kahneman, E. Diener, and N. Schwarz. New York: Russell Sage Foundation.

Kahneman, D., E. Diener, and N. Schwarz (Eds.). 1999. *Well-Being: The Foundations of Hedonic Psychology.* New York: Russell Sage Foundation.

Kahneman, D., and A. B. Krueger. 2006. "Developments in the Measurement of Subjective Well-Being." *Journal of Economic Perspectives* 20(1): 3–24.

Kaletsky, A. 1990. "UN Adds a Human Element to Economics: Controversial New Way to Measure Development." *The Financial Times.* 25 May.

Kamal, N., and K. M. Zunaid. 2006. "Education and Women's Empowerment in Bangladesh." Working Paper 11. Centre for Health, Population and Development at Independent University Bangladesh, Dhaka.

Kanbur, R., and L. Squire. 2001. "The Evolution of Thinking about Poverty: Exploring the Interactions." In *Frontiers of Development Economics: The Future in Perspective,* eds. G. Meier and J. E. Stiglitz. New York: Oxford University Press.

Kant, I. 1785. *Grundlegung zur Metaphysik der Sitten*. Hamburg, Germany: Felix Meiner Verlag (Printed in 1952).

Kasirye, I. 2010. "What Are the Successful Strategies for Reducing Malnutrition among Young Children in East Africa?" Human Development Research Paper 15. UNDP–HDRO, New York.

Kenny, C. 2008. "The Global Expansion of Primary Education." http://charleskenny.blogs.com/weblog/files/the_global_expansion.pdf. Accessed 7 June 2010.

———. 2009. "There's More to Life than Money: Exploring the Levels/Growth Paradox in Health and Education." *Journal of International Development* 21(1): 24–41.

———. Forthcoming. *Getting Better: Why Global Development is Succeeding—And How We Can Improve the World Even More*. New York: Basic Books.

Khang, Y., J. W. Lynch, and G. A. Kaplan. 2004. "Health Inequalities in Korea: Age- and Sex-Specific Educational Differences in the 10 Leading Causes of Death." *International Journal of Epidemiology* 33(2): 299–308.

King Jr., M. L. 1964. *Why Can't We Wait*. New York: Signet Classics.

Klasen, S. 2000. "Does Gender Inequality Reduce Growth and Development? Evidence from Cross-Country Regressions." Collaborative Research Center 386, Discussion Paper 212. Institute for Statistics, Munich, Germany.

———. 2002. "Low Schooling for Girls, Slower Growth for All? Cross-Country Evidence on the Effect of Gender Inequality in Education on Economic Development." *World Bank Economic Review* 16(3): 345–73.

———. 2006. "Special Issue: Revisiting the Gender-Related Development Index and Gender Empowerment Measure." *Journal of Human Development and Capabilities* 7(2).

Klasen, S., and D. Schüler. 2010. "Reforming the Gender-Related Development Index (GDI) and the Gender Empowerment Measure (GEM): Implementing Some Specific Proposals." IAI Discussion Paper 186. Ibero America Institute for Economic Research, Göttingen, Germany.

Klasen, S., and C. Wink. 2009. "A Turning-Point in Gender Bias in Mortality? An Update on the Number of Missing Women." In *Gender and Discrimination: Health, Nutritional Status and the Role of Women in India*, eds. M. Pal, P. Bharati, B. Ghosh, and T. S. Vasulu. New Delhi: Oxford University Press.

Knowles, C., E. Pernia, and M. Racelis. 1999. "Social Consequences of the Financial Crisis in Asia: The Deeper Crisis." Economic and Development Resource Center Briefing Note 16. Asian Development Bank, Manila.

Kovacevic, M. 2010a. "Measurement of Inequality in Human Development—A Review." Human Development Research Paper 35. UNDP–HDRO, New York.

———. 2010b. "Review of Critiques to HDI and Potential Improvements." Human Development Research Paper 33. UNDP–HDRO, New York.

Krueger, A. 2008. "Comments on Economic Growth and Subjective Well-Being: Reassessing the Easterlin Paradox." *Brookings Papers on Economic Activity* 1: 95–100.

Krugman, P. 2007. *The Conscience of a Liberal*. New York: W.W. Norton.

Kruk, M., S. Galea, M. Prescott, and L. Freedman. 2007. "Health Care Financing and Utilization of Maternal Health Services in Developing Countries." *Health Policy and Planning* 22(5): 303–10.

Kudamatsu, M. 2007. "Has Democratization Reduced Infant Mortality in Sub-Saharan Africa? Evidence from Micro Data." Discussion Paper 685. Institute of Social and Economic Research, Osaka University, Japan.

Kumar, A. 2010. "A Review of Human Development Trends in South Asia 1990–2009." Human Development Research Paper 44. UNDP–HDRO, New York.

Kuznets, S. 1955. "Economic Growth and Income Inequality." *American Economic Review* 45(1): 1–28.

Lacina, B., and N. P. Gleditsch. 2005. "Monitoring Trends in Global Combat: A New Dataset of Battle Deaths." *European Journal of Population* 21(2–3): 145–66.

Lake, D. A., and M. Baum. 2001. "The Invisible Hand of Democracy: Political Control and the Provision of Public Services." *Comparative Political Studies* 34(6): 587–621.

Legovini, A. 2006. "Measuring Women's Empowerment in Ethiopia: The Women's Development Initiatives Project." In *Empowerment in Practice: From Analysis to Implementation*, eds. R. Alsop, M. Bertelsen, and J. Holland. Washington, DC: World Bank.

Leith, J. C. 2005. *Why Botswana Prospered*. Québec, Canada: McGill's-Queens University Press.

Levine, R. 2004. *Millions Saved: Proven Successes in Global Health*. Washington, DC: Center for Global Development.

Li, H., and L. Meng. 2005. *The Human Cost of China's Industrial Growth*. College Park, MD: University of Maryland, Department of Economics.

Lindauer, D., and L. Pritchett. 2002. "What's the Big Idea? The Third Generation of Policies for Economic Growth." *Economica* 3(1): 1–39.

LIS (Luxembourg Income Study). 2009. "Luxembourg Income Study Project." www.lisproject.org/techdoc.htm. Accessed 7 June 2010.

Little, I., T. Scitovsky, and M. Scott. 1970. *Industry and Trade in Some Developing Countries*. Oxford, UK: Oxford University Press.

Liu, M. 2010. "Human Development in East and Southeast Asian Economies: (1990–2010)." Human Development Research Paper 17. UNDP–HDRO, New York.

Lokshin, M., and M. Ravallion. 2005. "Self-Rated Power and Welfare in Russia." In *Empowerment: Cross-Disciplinary Perspectives Measuring*, ed. D. Narayan. Washington, DC: World Bank.

López-Calva, L., and N. Lustig (Eds.). 2010. *Declining Inequality in Latin America: A Decade of Progress?* New York: United Nations Development Programme.

Lustig, N. 2000. "Crises and the Poor: Socially Responsible Macroeconomics." *Economía* 1(1): 1–19.

Ma, X. 2001. "Stability of Socio-Economic Gaps in Mathematics and Science Achievement among Canadian Schools." *Canadian Journal of Education* 26(1): 97–118.

Maddison, A. 2007. *Contours of the World Economy, 1–2030 AD*. Paris: Organisation for Economic Co-operation and Development.

———. 2010. *Historical Statistics of the World Economy: 1–2008 AD*. Paris: Organisation for Economic Co-operation and Development.

Mansuri, G., and V. Rao. 2010. *Localizing Development: Has the Participatory Approach Worked?* Washington, DC: World Bank.

Marglin, S. 2008. *The Dismal Science: How Thinking Like an Economist Undermines Community*. New York: Faber and Faber Ltd.

Marone, H., N. Thelen, and N. Gulasan. 2009. "The Economic Crisis: Assessing Vulnerability in Human Development." UNDP/ODS Working Paper. United Nations Development Programme, Office of Development Studies, New York.

Marshall, M., and K. Jaggers. 2010. "Polity IV Project, Political Regime Characteristics and Transitions, 1800–2008." Integrated Network for Societal Conflict Research Program. University of Maryland, Center for International Development and Conflict Management, College Park, MD.

Maundu, J. 1988. "Family Background and Student Achievement." *Kenyan Journal of Education* 4(1): 53–87.

Mayer-Foulkes, D. 2010. "Divergences and Convergences in Human Development." Human Development Research Paper 20. UNDP–HDRO, New York.

McGuire, J. 2010. "Political Factors and Health Outcomes: Insights from Argentina's Provinces." Human Development Research Paper 25. UNDP–HDRO, New York.

McLeod, D., and M. Dávalos. 2008. "Sustainable Post-Conflict Employment Creation: From Stabilization to Poverty Reduction." UNDP Poverty Group Paper. United Nations Development Programme, New York.

Measure DHS. 2010. "Demographic and Health Surveys." www.measuredhs.com/. Accessed 10 May 2010.

Mejía, D., and M. St-Pierre. 2008. "Unequal Opportunities and Human Capital Formation." *Journal of Development Economics* 86(2): 395–413.

Micklewright, J., and K. Stewart. 2001. "Poverty and Social Exclusion in Europe: European Comparisons and Impact of Enlargement." *New Economy* 8(2): 104–09.

Miguel, E., and M. Kremer. 2004. "Worms: Identifying Impacts on Education and Health in the Presence of Treatment Externalities." *Econometrica* 72(1): 159–217.

Milanovic, B. 1998. *Income, Inequality, and Poverty During the Transition from Planned to Market Economy*. Washington, DC: World Bank.

———. 2009. "Global Inequality Recalculated: The Effect of New 2005 PPP Estimates on Global Inequality." Policy Research Working Paper 5061. World Bank, Washington, DC.

Miller, C. 2008. "Evaluation of Mchinji Cash Transfer." Research and Policy to Promote Child and Health Development. http://childresearchpolicy.org/mchinjicashtransfer.html. Accessed 18 May 2010.

Mink, S. D. 1993. "Poverty, Population and the Environment." Discussion Paper 189. World Bank, Washington, DC.

Minoiu, C., and S. Reddy. 2007. "Aid Does Matter, After All: Revisiting the Relationship Between Aid and Growth." *Challenge* 50(2): 39–58.

———. 2010. "Development Aid and Economic Growth: A Positive Long-Run Relation." *Quarterly Review of Economics and Finance* 50(1): 27–39.

Minujina, A., and E. Delamonica. 2003. "Mind the Gap! Widening Child Mortality Disparities." *Journal of Human Development and Capabilities* 4(3): 397–418.

Mody, A. 2010. "Who Fell in 2009: Those with Current Account Deficits or with Extra Froth?" Vox, London. http://voxeu.org/index.php?q=node/4507. Accessed 7 June 2010.

Mookherjee, D. 2005. "Is There Too Little Theory in Development Economics Today?" *Economic and Political Weekly* 40(40): 4328–33.

Moreno, M., and F. Rodríguez. 2009. "Plenty of Room? Fiscal Space in a Resource-Abundant Economy: The Case of Venezuela." In *Fiscal Space: Policy Options for Financing Human Development*, eds. R. Roy and A. Heuty. London: Earthscan.

Moreno-Lopez, P., L. Bandiera, M. Prasad, S. Zeikate, B. Mukho-padhyay, K. Kalonji, F. Painchaud, A. Unigovskaya, J. De, and S. Mockler. 2009. *Heavily Indebted Poor Countries (HIPC) Initiative and Multilateral Debt Relief Initiative (MDRI)—Status of Implementation*. Washington, DC: International Development Association and International Monetary Fund.

Moyo, D. 2009. *Dead Aid: Why Aid is Not Working and How There is a Better Way for Africa*. New York: Farrar, Straus and Giroux.

Munck, G., and J. Verkuilen. 2002. "Conceptualizing and Measuring Democracy." *Comparative Political Studies* 35(1): 5–34.

Mwabu, G., and A. Fosu. 2010. "Human Development in Africa." Human Development Research Paper 8. UNDP–HDRO, New York.

Myrdal, G. 1957. *Economic Theory and Underdeveloped Regions*. London: Duckworth.

Narayan, D. 2005. *Measuring Empowerment: Cross-Disciplinary Perspectives*. Washington, DC: World Bank.

Narayan, D., R. Chambers, M. Kaul Shah, and P. Petesch. 1999. *Voices of the Poor: Global Synthesis*. Washington, DC: World Bank.

Narayan, D., R. Patel, K. Schafft, A. Rademacher, and S. Koch-Schulte. 2000. *Voices of the Poor: Can Anyone Hear Us?* Oxford, UK: Oxford University Press.

Narayan, D., and P. Petesch. 2007. *Moving Out of Poverty: Cross-Disciplinary Perspectives on Mobility*. Washington, DC: World Bank.

Narayana, D. 2008. "Intensifying Infant Mortality Inequality in India and a Reversal by Policy Intervention." *Journal of Human Development and Capabilities* 9(2): 265–81.

Nath, S., K. Sylva, and J. Grimes. 1997. "Raising Basic Education Levels for the Children of Rural Bangladesh: The Impact of a Non-Formal Education Programme." *International Review of Education* 45(1): 5–26.

Nattrass, N., and J. Seekings. 2001. "Democracy and Distribution in Highly Unequal Economies: The Case of South Africa." *Journal of Modern African Studies* 39(3): 471–98.

Nayyar, D. 2008. "Learning to Unlearn from Development." *Oxford Development Studies* 36(3): 259–80.

Nelson, G., M. Rosegrant, J. Koo, R. Robertson, T. Sulser, T. Zhu, C. Ringler, S. Msangi, A. Palazzo, M. Batka, M. Magalhaes, R. Valmonte-Santos, M. Ewing, and D. Lee. 2009. *Climate Change: Impact on Agriculture and Costs of Adaptation*. Washington, DC: International Food Policy Research Institute.

Nelson, J., and D. Prescott. 2008. *Business and the Millennium Development Goals: A Framework for Action*, 2nd edition. New York: United Nations Development Programme and International Business Leaders Forum.

Neumayer, E. 2010a. "Human Development and Sustainability." Human Development Research Paper 5. UNDP–HDRO, New York.

———. 2010b. *Weak Versus Strong Sustainability. Exploring the Limits of Two Opposing Paradigms*, 3rd edition. Northampton, UK: Edward Elgar Publishing Ltd.

Nielson, H. D. 2009. *Moving Towards Free Primary Education: Policy Issues and Implementation Challenges*. New York: United Nations Children's Fund and World Bank.

NOIA (National Ocean Industries Association). 2006. "Oil in the Sea III: Inputs, Fates and Effects." Washington, DC. www.noia.org/website/article.asp?id=129. Accessed 18 June 2010.

Nussbaum, M. 2000. *Women and Human Development: The Capabilities Approach*. Cambridge, UK: Cambridge University Press.

———. 2005. "Women's Bodies: Violence, Security, Capabilities." *Journal of Human Development and Capabilities* 6(2): 167–83.

O'Brien, D. 2010. *When Women Matter: Linking Women's Descriptive and Substantive Representation*. St. Louis, MO: Center for New Institutional Social Sciences.

Ocampo, J. A., R. Vos, and J. K. Sundaram. 2007. *Growth Divergences: Explaining Differences in Economic Performance*. New York: Zed Books for the United Nations.

OECD (Organisation for Economic Co-operation and Development). 2008a. *2008 Survey on Monitoring the Paris Declaration: Making Aid More Effective by 2010*. Paris.

———. 2008b. *Growing Unequal? Income Distribution and Poverty in OECD Countries*. Paris.

———. 2009. "LMF5: Gender Pay Gaps for Full-Time Workers and Earnings Differentials by Educational Attainment." Paris. www.oecd.org/dataoecd/29/63/38752746.pdf. Accessed 25 April 2010.

———. 2010. "Measuring the Progress of Societies." Paris. www.oecd.org/pages/0,3417,en_40033426_40033828_1_1_1_1,00.html. Accessed 15 August 2010.

OECD/DAC (Organisation for Economic Co-operation and Development Development Assistance Committee). 2010a. "Creditor Reporting System Database." www.oecd.org/dac/stats/idsonline. Accessed 15 May 2010.

———. 2010b. "Development Aid Rose in 2009 and Most Donors Will Meet 2010 Aid Targets." *Newsroom*. 14 April. www.oecd.org/document/11/0,3343,en_21571361_44315115_44981579_1_1_1_1,00.html. Accessed 24 June 2010.

Oeppen, J., and J.W. Vaupel. 2002. "Broken Limits to Life Expectancy." *Science* 296(5570): 1029–32.

Olavarria-Gambi, M. 2003. "Poverty Reduction in Chile: Has Economic Growth Been Enough?" *Journal of Human Development and Capabilities* 4(1): 103–23.

Olshansky, S., D. Passaro, R. Hershow, J. Layden, B. Carnes, J. Brody, L. Hayfick, R. Butler, D. Allison, and D. Ludwig. 2005. "A Potential Decline in Life Expectancy in the United States in the 21st Century." *New England Journal of Medicine* 352(11): 1138–45.

Oman Ministry of National Economy. 2003. *Oman Human Development Report 2003*. Muscat.

Osmani, S. R. 2005. "Poverty and Human Rights: Building on the Capability Approach." *Journal of Human Development and Capabilities* 6(2): 205–19.

Osmani, S. R., and A. Sen. 2003. "The Hidden Penalties of Gender Inequality: Fetal Origins of Ill-Health." *Economics and Human Biology* 1(1): 105–21.

Ostrom, E. 1996. "Crossing the Great Divide: Coproduction, Synergy, and Development." *World Development* 24(6): 1073–87.

Ottoson, D. 2009. *State-Sponsored Homophobia: A World Survey of Laws Prohibiting Same Sex Activity Bewteen Consenting Adults*. Brussels: International Lesbian, Gay, Bisexual, Trans and Intersex Association.

Oxfam International. 2007. "Africa's Missing Billions: International Arms Flows and the Cost of Conflict." Briefing Paper 107. Oxford, UK.

Pagliani, P. 2010. "Influence of Regional, National, and Sub-national HDRs." Human Development Research Paper 19. UNDP–HDRO, New York.

Panagariya, A. 2008. *India: the Emerging Giant*. Oxford, UK: Oxford University Press.

Parks, R., P. Baker, L. Kiser, R. Oakerson, E. Ostrom, V. Ostrom, S. Percy, M. Vandivort, G. Whitaker, and R. Wilson. 1999. "Consumers as Coproducers of Public Services: Some Economic and Institutional Considerations." In *Polycentricity and Local Public Economies: Readings from the Workshop in Political Theory and Policy Analysis*, ed. M. D. McGinnes. Ann Arbor, MI: University of Michigan Press.

Pestoff, V. 2009. "Towards a Paradigm of Democratic Participation: Citizen Participation and Co-Production of Personal Social Services in Sweden." *Annals of Public and Cooperative Economics* 80(2): 197–224.

Piketty, T. 2000. "Theories of Persistent Inequality and Intergenerational Mobility." In *Handbook of Income Distribution*, 1st edition, eds. A. Atkinson and F. Bourguignon. Amsterdam: Elsevier.

Pineda, J., and F. Rodríguez. 2006. "The Political Economy of Investment in Human Capital." *Economics of Governance* 7(2): 167–93.

———. 2010. "Curse or Blessing? Natural Resources and Human Development." Human Development Research Paper 4. UNDP–HDRO, New York.

Pinkovskiy, M., and X. Sala-i-Martin. 2009. *Parametric Estimations of the World Distribution of Income*. NBER Working Paper 15433. Cambridge, MA: National Bureau of Economic Research.

———. 2010. *African Poverty is Falling…Much Faster Than You Think!* NBER Working Paper 15775. Cambridge, MA: National Bureau of Economic Research.

Pirttilä, J., and R. Uusitalo. 2010. "A 'Leaky Bucket' in the Real World: Estimating Inequality Aversion Using Survey Data." *Economica* 77(305): 60–76.

PNUD Argentina (Programa de las Naciones Unidas para el Desarrollo). 2002. *Aportes para el Desarrollo Humano de la Argentina 2002: Un Enfoque Integral*. Buenos Aires.

PNUD Mexico (Programa de las Naciones Unidas para el Desarrollo). 2003. *Informe Sobre Desarrollo Humano México 2002*. Mexico City: Mundi-Prensa México.

PNUD Tunisie (Le Programme des Nations Unies pour le développement). 2001. *Rapport sur le Developpement Humain en Tunisie*. Tunis.

Pogge, T. 2009. *Developing Morally Plausible Indices of Poverty and Gender Equity: A Research Program*. New York: New York University Institute for Public Knowledge.

Polanyi, K. 2002. "The Great Transformation." In *Readings in Economic Sociology*, ed. N. W. Biggart. Oxford, UK: Blackwell Publishers Ltd.

Prahalad, C. K. 2004. *The Fortune at the Bottom of the Pyramid*. Upper Saddle River, NJ: Wharton School Publishing.

Prasad, N. 2008. "Policies for Redistribution: The Use of Taxes and Social Transfers." ILO Discussion Paper DP/194/2008. International Labour Office, Geneva.

Preston, S. H. 1975. "The Changing Relation Between Mortality and Level of Economic Development." *Population Studies* 29(2): 231–48.

Pritchett, L. 1997. "Divergence, Big Time." *The Journal of Economic Perspectives* 11(3): 3–17.

———. 2002. *When Will They Ever Learn? Why All Governments Produce Schooling*. Cambridge, MA: Harvard Kennedy School of Government and Center for Global Development.

———. 2006. "Does Learning to Add up Add up? The Returns to Schooling in Aggregate Data." In *Handbook of the Economics of Education*, eds. E. A. Hanushek and F. Welch. Amsterdam: Elsevier.

———. 2010. "Birth Satisfaction Units (BSU): Measuring Cross-National Differences in Human Well-Being." Human Development Research Paper 3. UNDP–HDRO, New York.

Pritchett, L., and R. Murgai. 2007. "Teacher Compensation: Can Decentralization to Local Bodies Take India from Perfect Storm Through Troubled Waters to Clear Sailing?" In *India Policy Forum 2006–07*, eds. S. Bery, B. P. Bosworth, and A. Panagariya. New Dehli and Washington, DC: National Council of Applied Economic Research and Brookings Institution.

Pritchett, L., and L. Summers. 1996. "Wealthier is Healthier." *Journal of Human Resources* 31(4): 841–68.

Pritchett, L., and M. Viarengo. 2010. "Explaining the Cross-National and Time Series Variation in Life Expectancy: Income, Women's Education, Shifts, and What Else?" Human Development Research Paper 31. UNDP–HDRO, New York.

Pritchett, L., M. Woolcock, and M. Andrews. 2010. "Capability Traps? The Mechanisms of Persistent Implementation Failure." World Development Report Working Paper 11. World Bank, Washington, DC.

Przeworski, A. 2004. "Democracy and Economic Development." In *The Evolution of Political Knowledge*, eds. E. Mansfield and R. Sisson. Columbus, OH: Ohio State University Press.

Przeworski, A., M. Alvarez, J. A. Cheibub, and F. Limongi. 2000. *Democracy and Development: Political Institutions and Well-Being in the World, 1950–1990*. Cambridge, UK: Cambridge University Press.

Qian, Y. 2003. "How Reform Worked in China." In *In Search of Prosperity*, ed. D. Rodrik. Princeton, NJ: Princeton University Press.

Rajan, R., and A. Subramanian. 2008. "Aid and Growth: What Does the Cross-Country Evidence Really Show?" *The Review of Economics and Statistics* 90(4): 643–65.

Rajan, R., and L. Zingales. 2003. *Saving Capitalism from the Capitalists: Unleashing the Power of Financial Markets to Create Wealth and Spread Opportunity*. Princeton, NJ: Princeton University Press.

Rajaratnam, J., J. Marcus, A. Fraxman, H. Wang, A. Levin-Rector, L. Dwyer, M. Costa, A. Lopez, and C. Murray. 2010. "Neonatal, Postneonatal, Childhood, and Under-5 Mortality for 187 Countries, 1970–2010: A Systematic Analysis of Progress Towards Millennium Development Goal 4." *The Lancet* 375(9730): 1988–2008.

Ranis, G., and F. Stewart. 2000. "Strategies for Success in Human Development." *Journal of Human Development* 1(1): 49–70.

———. 2010. "Success and Failure in Human Development, 1970–2007." Human Development Research Paper 10. UNDP–HDRO, New York.

Ranis, G., F. Stewart, and A. Ramirez. 2000. "Economic Growth and Human Development." *World Development* 28(2): 197–220.

Ranis, G., F. Stewart, and E. Samman. 2006. "Human Development: Beyond the Human Development Index." *Journal of Human Development* 7(3): 323–58.

Ravallion, M. 1996. "How Well Can Method Substitute for Data? Five Experiments in Poverty Analysis." *The World Bank Research Observer* 11(2): 199–221.

Rawls, J. 1971. *A Theory of Justice*. Cambridge, MA: Harvard University Press.

Raworth, K., and D. Stewart. 2002. "Critiques of the Human Development Index: A Review." In *Readings in Human Development, Concepts, Measures and Policies for a Development Paradigm*, eds. S. Fukuda-Parr and A. K. Shiva Kumar. New York: Oxford University Press.

Reinhart, C. M., and K. Rogoff. 2009. *This Time is Different. Eight Hundred Years of Financial Folly*. Princeton, NJ: Princeton University Press.

Reporters Without Borders. 2009. "Press Freedom Index." http://en.rsf.org/press-freedom-index-2009,1001.html. Accessed 15 April 2010.

Richardson, H. S. 2006. *Democratic Autonomy: Public Reasoning about the Ends of Policy*. Oxford, UK: Oxford University Press.

Ridde, V., and A. Diarra. 2009. "A Process Evaluation of User Fees Abolition for Pregnant Women and Children under Five in Two Districts in Niger (West Africa)." *BioMed Central Health Services Research* 9(89).

Riley, J. C. 2001. *Rising Life Expectancy: A Global History*. Cambridge, UK: Cambridge University Press.

———. 2005. *Poverty and Life Expectancy*. Cambridge, UK: Cambridge University Press.

Risse, M. 2009. "Immigration, Ethics and the Capabilities Approach." Human Development Research Paper 2009/34. UNDP–HDRO, New York.

Robalino, D., M. Vodopivec, and A. Bodor. 2009. "Savings for Unemployment in Good and Bad Times: Options for Developing Countries." IZA Discussion Paper 4516. World Bank and Institute for the Study of Law, Washington, DC.

Robeyns, I. 2003. "Sen's Capability Approach and Gender Inequality: Selecting Relevant Capabilities." *Feminist Economics* 9(2–3): 61–92.

Rodríguez, F. 2006. "The Anarchy of Numbers: Understanding the Evidence on Venezuelan Economic Growth." *Canadian Journal of Development Studies* 27(4): 503–29.

———. 2007. "Cleaning Up the Kitchen Sink: Growth Empirics When the World is Not Simple." Working Paper. Wesleyan University, Middletown, CT.

Rodrik, D. 1998. "Why Do More Open Economies have Bigger Governments?" *Journal of Political Economy* 106(5): 997–1032.

——— (Ed.) 2003. *In Search of Prosperity: Analytic Narratives on Economic Growth*. Princeton, NJ: Princeton University Press.

———. 2006. "Goodbye Washington Consensus, Hello Washington Confusion? A Review of the World Bank's Economic Growth in the 1990s: Learning from a Decade of Reform." *Journal of Economic Literature* 44(4): 973–87.

———. 2007. *One Economics, Many Recipes: Globalizations, Institutions, and Economic Growth*. Princeton, NJ: Princeton University Press.

Rodrik, D., and R. Hausmann. 2003. "Economic Development as Self-Discovery." *Journal of Development Economics* 72(2): 603–33.

Roemer, J. E. 1998. *Equality of Opportunity*. Cambridge, MA: Harvard University Press.

Rowbottom, S. 2007. *Giving Girls Today and Tomorrow: Breaking the Cycle of Adolescent Pregnancy*. New York: United Nations Population Fund.

Royston, P., and D. G. Altman. 1994. "Regression Using Fractional Polynomials of Continuous Covariates: Parsimonious Parametric Modelling." *Applied Statistics* 43(3): 429–67.

Sachs, J. D., J. W. McArthur, G. Schmidt-Traub, M. Kruk, C. Bahadur, M. Faye, and G. McCord. 2004. "Ending Africa's Poverty Trap." *Brookings Papers on Economic Activity* 35(1): 217–30.

Salehi-Isfahani, D. 2010. "Human Development in the Middle East and North Africa." Human Development Research Paper 26. UNDP–HDRO, New York.

Schor, J. B. 1992. *The Overworked American: The Unexpected Decline of Leisure*. New York: Basic Books.

Schultz, G. F. 1993. "Socioeconomic Advantage and Achievement Motivation: Important Mediators of Academic Performance in Minority Children in Urban Schools." *The Urban Review* 25(3): 221–32.

Sen, A. 1983. *Poverty and Famines: An Essay on Entitlement and Deprivation*. New York: Oxford University Press.

———. 1985a. *Commodities and Capabilities*. Amsterdam: Elsevier.

———. 1985b. "Well-Being, Agency and Freedom: The Dewey Lectures 1984." *The Journal of Philosophy* 82(4): 169–221.

———. 1999. *Development as Freedom*. Oxford, UK: Oxford University Press.

———. 2002. *Rationality and Freedom*. Cambridge, MA: Harvard University Press.

———. 2003. "Missing Women Revisited." *British Medical Journal* 327(7427): 1297–98.

———. 2004. "Elements of a Theory of Human Rights." *Philosophy and Public Affairs* 32(4): 315–56.

———. 2005. "Human Rights and Capabilities." *Journal of Human Development and Capabilities* 6(2): 151–166.

———. 2009a. "Foreword." In *Handbook of Human Development*, eds. S. Fukuda-Parr and A. K. Shiva Kumar. New Delhi: Oxford University Press.

———. 2009b. *The Idea of Justice*. London: Penguin.

Sen, G., A. Iyer, and C. Mukherjee. 2009. "A Methodology to Analyse the Intersections of Social Inequalities in Health." *Journal of Human Development and Capabilities* 10(3): 397–415.

Seneviratne, K. 1999. "Has Asia Succumbed to Western Agenda?" *The Straits Times*. October 26.

Seth, S. 2009. "Inequality, Interactions, and Human Development." *Journal of Human Development and Capabilities* 10(3): 375–96.

Shiva Kumar, A. K. 2007. "Why Are Levels of Child Malnutrition High?" *The Hindu*. June 22.

Shryock, H., and J. Siegel. 1980. *The Methods and Materials of Demography*. Washington, DC: U.S. Government Printing Office.

SIPRI (Stockholm International Peace Research Institute). 2010a. *Correspondence on Arms Transfers*. Stockholm.

———. 2010b. *Correspondence on Military Expenditure*. Stockholm.

Sirimanne, S. 2009. *Emerging Issue: The Gender Perspectives of the Financial Crisis*. New York: Commission on the Status of Women.

Skoufias, E. 2003. "Economic Crisis and Natural Disasters: Coping Strategies and Policy Implications." *World Development* 31(7): 1087–1102.

Soares, R. R. 2007. "On the Determinants of Mortality Reductions in the Developing World." *Population and Development Review* 33(2): 247–87.

Southgate, D. 1990. "The Causes of Land Degradation along Spontaneously Expanding Agricultural Frontiers in the Third World." *Land Economics* 66(1): 93–101.

Srinivasan, T. N. 1994. "Human Development: A New Paradigm or Reinvention of the Wheel?" *The American Economic Review* 84(2): 238–43.

Staines, N. 2004. "Economic Performance Over the Conflict Cycle." IMF Working Paper 95. International Monetary Fund, Washington, DC.

Stasavage, D. 2005. "Democracy and Education Spending in Africa." *American Journal of Political Science* 49(2): 343–58.

Stern, N. 2006. *The Economics of Climate Change: The Stern Review.* Cambridge, MA: Cambridge University Press.

Stevenson, B., and J. Wolfers. 2008. "Economic Growth and Subjective Well-Being: Reassessing the Easterlin Paradox." *Brookings Papers on Economic Activity* 1: 1–87.

Stewart, F. 2009. "Horizontal Inequality: Two Types of Trap." *Journal of Human Development and Capabilities* 10(3): 315–40.

———. 2010. "Power and Progress: The Swing of the Pendulum." *Journal of Human Development and Capabilities* 11(3): 371–95.

Stewart, F., G. Brown, and L. Mancini. 2005. "Why Horizontal Inequalities Matter: Some Implications for Measurement." CRISE Working Paper 19. Centre for Research on Inequality, Human Security and Ethnicity, Oxford, UK.

Stewart, K. 2010. "Human Development in Europe." Human Development Research Paper 7. UNDP–HDRO, New York.

Stiglitz, J. E. and Members of the UN Commission of Financial Experts. 2010. *The Stiglitz Report: Reforming the International Monetary and Financial Systems in the Wake of the Global Crisis.* New York: The New Press.

Stiglitz, J. E., A. Sen, and J. Fitoussi. 2009. "Report by the Commission on the Measurement of Economic Performance and Social Progress." Commission on the Measurement of Economic Performance and Social Progress, Paris.

The Straits Times. 1990. "S'pore trails Hong Kong and Seoul in Human Resources Development." *The Straits Times.* May 29.

Strauss, J., and D. Thomas. 1998. "Health, Nutrition, and Economic Development." *Journal of Economic Literature* 36(2): 766–817.

———. 2008. "Health Over the Life Course." In *Handbook of Development Economics,* 4th edition, eds. T. Schultz and J. Strauss. Amsterdam: Elsevier.

Stuckler, D., S. Basu, and M. McKee. 2010. "Drivers of Inequality in Millennium Development Goal Progress: A Statistical Analysis." *PLoS Medicine* 7(3).

Subramanian, A., and R. Devesh. 2003. "Who Can Explain the Mauritian Miracle: Meade, Romer, Sachs, or Rodrik?" In *In Search of Prosperity: Analytic Narratives on Economic Growth,* ed. D. Rodrik. Princeton, NJ: Princeton University Press.

Tajbakhsh, S., and A. M. Chenoy. 2007. *Human Security: Concepts and Implications.* New York: Routledge.

Tansel, A. 2002. "Determinants of School Attainment of Boys and Girls in Turkey: Individual, Household and Community Factors." *Economics of Education Review* 21(5): 455–70.

Tanzi, V., and L. Schuknecht. 2000. *Public Spending in the 20th Century: A Global Perspective.* Cambridge, UK: Cambridge University Press.

Tavares, J., and R. Wacziarg. 2001. "How Democracy Affects Growth." *European Economic Review* 45(8): 1341–78.

Thede, N. 2009. "Decentralization, Democracy and Human Rights: A Human Rights-Based Analysis of the Impact of Local Democratic Reforms on Development." *Journal of Human Development and Capabilities* 10(1): 103–23.

Thomas, V., Y. Wang, and X. Fan. 2001. "Measuring Education Inequality: Gini Coefficients of Education." Policy Research Working Paper 2525. World Bank, Washington, DC.

Treisman, D. 2010. "Death and Prices: The Political Economy of Russia's Alcohol Crisis." *Economics of Transition* 18(2): 281–331.

Tsai, M. 2006. "Does Political Democracy Enhance Human Development in Developing Countries? A Cross-National Analysis." *American Journal of Economics and Sociology* 65(2): 233–68.

Twaweza. 2010. "Twaweza: Ni Sisi [We Can Make It Happen: It's Us]." Dar es Salaam. twaweza.org/. Accessed 7 June 2010.

UCDP and PRIO (Uppsala Conflict Data Program and International Peace Research Institute). 2009. "UCDP/PRIO Armed Conflict Dataset." Centre for the Study of Civil War, Oslo. www.prio.no/CSCW/Datasets/Armed-Conflict/UCDP-PRIO/. Accessed 7 June 2010.

UIA (Union of International Associations). 2010. "UIA Databases." www.uia.be/. Accessed 7 June 2010.

ul Haq, M. 1973. "System is to Blame for the 22 Wealthy Families." *The London Times.* March 22.

———. 1995. *Reflections on Human Development.* New York: Oxford University Press.

UN (United Nations). 2000. "We Can End Poverty 2015: Millennium Development Goals." New York. www.un.org/millenniumgoals/. Accessed 20 November 2009.

———. 2009. *The Millennium Development Goals Report 2009.* New York: United Nations.

———. 2010a. "Human Security Report of the Secretary-General." Sixty-fourth Session, Agenda Items 48 and 114, A/64/701. UN General Assembly, New York.

———. 2010b. "Progress to Date and Remaining Gaps in the Implementation of the Outcomes of the Major Summits in the Area of Sustainable Development and Analysis of the Themes for the Conference." Item of the Provisional Agenda, A/CONF.216/PC/2. UN General Assembly, New York.

UN Statistics Division (United Nations Statistics Division). 2010. United Nations Commodity Trade Statistics Database—UN Comtrade. New York. comtrade.un.org/db/dqBasicQuery.aspx. Accessed 3 August 2010.

UNAIDS (Joint United Nations Programme on HIV/AIDS). 2008. *Report on the Global AIDS Epidemic.* Geneva.

UNDESA (United Nations Department of Economic and Social Affairs). 2004. *World Youth Report 2003: The Global Situation of Young People.* New York.

———. 2006. *World Economic and Social Survey 2006: Diverging Growth and Development.* New York.

———. 2009a. "Population Ageing and Development 2009." New York. www.un.org/esa/population/publications/ageing/ageing2009.htm. Accessed 19 May 2010.

———. 2009b. "Rethinking Poverty." *Report on the World Social Situation.* New York.

———. 2009c. "World Fertility Patterns 2009." New York. www.un.org/esa/population/publications/worldfertility2009/worldfertility2009.htm. Accessed 7 June 2010.

———. 2009d. *World Population Prospects: The 2008 Revision.* New York.

———. 2010. "World Urbanization Prospects: The 2009 Revision Population Database." New York. esa.un.org/wup2009/unup/. Accessed 25 June 2010.

UNDESA-DAW-CSW (United Nations Department of Economic and Social Affairs, Division for the Advancement of Women, Commission on the Status of Women. 2010. "Review of the Implementation of the Beijing Declaration and Plan for Action."

New York. www.un.org/womenwatch/daw/beijing15/. Accessed 7 June 2010.

UNDP (United Nations Development Programme). 1998. *Human Development Report Zimbabwe.* New York.

———. 2003. *Avoiding the Dependency Trap.* New York.

———. 2008. "Post-Conflict Economic Recovery: Enabling Local Ingenuity." *Crisis Prevention and Recovery Report 2008.* New York: Bureau of Crisis Prevention and Recovery.

———. 2009. *Arab Human Development Report 2009: Challenges to Human Security in Arab Countries.* New York: Regional Bureau for Arab States.

———. 2010. *What Will It Take to Achieve the Millennium Development Goals?—An International Assessment.* New York.

UNDP (United Nations Development Programme) Armenia. 2007. *National Human Development Report 2006: Educational Transformations in Armenia.* Yerevan.

UNDP (United Nations Development Programme) China and China Institute for Reform and Development. 2008. *Human Development Report China 2007/08: Access for All: Basic Public Services for 1.3 Billion People.* Beijing: China Translation and Publishing Corporation.

UNDP (United Nations Development Programme) China and Renmin University of China. 2010. *China Human Development Report 2009/10: China and a Sustainable Future: Towards a Low Carbon Economy and Society.* Beijing: China Translation & Publishing Corporation.

UNDP (United Nations Development Programme) Evaluation Office. 2009. *Assessment of Development Results: Evaluation of UNDP Contribution—Peru.* New York.

UNDP (United Nations Development Programme) Nepal. 2002. *Nepal Human Development Report 2001: Poverty Reducation and Goverance.* Kathmandu.

———. 2004. *Nepal Human Development Report 2004: Empowerment and Poverty Reduction.* Kathmandu.

———. 2009. *Nepal Human Development Report 2009: State Transformation and Human Development.* Kathmandu.

UNDP (United Nations Development Programme) Zambia. 1997. *Zambia Human Development Report 1997: Poverty.* Lusaka.

UNDP (United Nations Development Programme)–Human Development Report Office. 1990–2009. *Human Development Reports 1990–2009.* New York: Oxford University Press through 2005; and Palgrave Macmillan since 2006.

UNEP-WCMC (United Nations Environment Programme—World Conservation Monitoring Centre). 2006. *World Database on Protected Areas.* Cambridge, UK: United Nations Environmental Programme.

UNESCO (United Nations Educational, Scientific and Cultural Organization). 2004. *EFA Global Monitoring Report 2005: Education For All: The Quality Imperative.* Paris.

———. 2006. *Teachers and Education Quality: Monitoring Global Needs for 2015.* Montreal, Canada: Institute for Statistics.

———. 2009. *EFA Global Monitoring Report 2009: Overcoming Inequality: Why Governance Matters.* Paris.

———. 2010. *EFA Global Monitoring Report 2010: Reaching the Marginalized.* Paris.

UNESCO (United Nations Educational, Scientific and Cultural Organization) Institute for Statistics. 2009. "Global

Education Digest 2008." New York. www.uis.unesco.org/ev_en.php?ID=7660_201&ID2=DO_TOPIC. Accessed 7 June 2010.

———. 2010a. *Correspondence on Education Indicators.* Montreal, Canada.

———. 2010b. "UNESCO Institute for Statistics Data Site." New York. http://stats.uis.unesco.org/unesco. Accessed May 2010.

Unger, R. M. 1998. *Democracy Realized: The Progressive Alternative.* London: Verso.

UNHCR (United Nations High Commissioner for Refugees). 1997. *The State of the World's Refugees 1997: A Humanitarian Agenda.* Geneva.

———. 2010. *Correspondence on Refugees.* Geneva.

UNICEF (United Nations Children's Fund). 2000–2008. *Multiple Indicators Cluster Surveys.* New York.

———. 2008. *Progress for Children: A Report Card on Maternal Mortality.* New York.

———. 2010a. "Protecting Salaries of Frontline Teachers and Health Workers." Social and Economic Policy Working Briefs. New York.

———. 2010b. *Recovery with a Human Face: A Coordinated Strategy of Policy Advocacy and Partnerships for Children in Response to the Global Financial Crisis and Economic Slowdown.* New York.

———. 2010c. *The State of the World's Children.* New York.

UNIFEM (United Nations Development Fund for Women). 2010. "Who Answers to Women? Gender and Accountability." *Progress of the World's Women 2008/2009.* New York.

United States Census Bureau. 2008. "U.S. Income Statistics." www.census.gov/hhes/www/income/data/statistics/index.html. Accessed 27 July 2010.

UNODC (United Nations Office on Drugs and Crime). 2010. "UNODC Homicide Statistics." Vienna. www.unodc.org/unodc/en/data-and-analysis/homicide.html. Accessed 15 May 2010.

UNRISD (United Nations Research Institute for Social Development). 2010. "Why Care Matters for Social Development." Research and Policy Brief 9. Geneva.

UNU-WIDER (United Nations University, World Institute for Development Economics Research). 2008. World Income Inequality Database, Version 2.0c, May 2008. Helsinki. www.wider.unu.edu/research/Database/en_GB/database/.

van der Hoeven, R. 2010. "Employment, Inequality and Globalization: A Continuous Concern," *Journal of Human Development and Capabilities* 11(1): 1–9.

Vaughan, S. 2003. *Ethnicity and Power in Ethiopia.* Edinburgh, UK: University of Edinburgh.

Veblen, T. 2007. *Theory of the Leisure Class.* Oxford, UK: Oxford University Press.

Vitols, S. 2003. "From Banks to Markets: The Political Economy of Liberalization of the German and Japanese Financial Systems." In *The End of Diversity? Prospects for German and Japanese Capitalism*, eds. K. Yamamura and W. Streeck. Ithaca, NY: Cornell University Press.

Vizard, P. 2006. *Poverty and Human Rights: Sen's 'Capability Perspective' Explored.* Oxford, UK: Oxford University Press.

Vollmer, S., and M. Ziegler. 2009. "Political Insitutions and Human Development: Does Democracy Fulfill its 'Constructive' and 'Instrumental' Role?" Policy Research Working Paper 4818. World Bank, Washington, DC.

von Braun, J., and U. Grote. 2000. "Does Decentralization Serve the Poor?" International Monetary Fund Conference on Fiscal Decentralization, Washington, DC.

Vroman, W., and V. Brsusentsev. 2009. "Unemployment Compensation in a Worldwide Recession." Urban Institute and University of Delaware, Washington, DC, and Dover, DE.

Wade, R. 1992. "East Asia's Economic Success: Conflicting Perspectives, Partial Insights, Shaky Evidence." *World Politics* 44(2): 270–320.

Walker, S., S. Chang, C. Powell, E. Simonoff, and S. Grantham-McGregor. 2007. "Early Childhood Stunting is Associated with Poor Psychological Functioning in Late Adolescence and Effects are Reduced by Psychosocial Stimulation." *Journal of Nutrition* 137(2): 2464–69.

Walton, M. 2010. "Capitalism, the State, and the Underlying Drivers of Human Development." Human Development Research Paper 9. UNDP–HDRO, New York.

Watson, D., and L. Yohannes. 2005. "Capacity Building for Decentralised Education Service Delivery in Ethiopia: A Case Study Prepared for the Project 'Capacity, Change and Performance.'" Discussion Paper 57H. European Centre for Development Policy Management, Maastricht, the Netherlands.

Watson, P. 1995. "Explaining Rising Mortality Among Men in Eastern Europe." *Social Science and Medicine* 41(7): 923–34.

WCED (World Commission on Environment and Development). 1987. *Our Common Future.* WCED Report. Oxford, UK: Oxford University Press.

Whitehead, L. 2002. *Democratization: Theory and Experience.* Oxford, UK: Oxford University Press.

The White House. 2010. "Health Care." Washington, DC. www.whitehouse.gov/issues/health-care. Accessed 12 May 2010.

WHO (World Health Organization). 2000–2008. *World Health Surveys.* Geneva.

———. 2005. *WHO Multi-Country Study on Women's Health and Domestic Violence Against Women: Summary Report of Initial Results on Prevalence, Health Outcomes and Women's Responses.* Geneva.

———. 2008. "Global Burden of Disease Series: 2004 Update." Geneva. www.who.int/healthinfo/global_burden_disease. Accessed 15 July 2010.

———. 2010. "World Health Statistics 2010." *World Health Organization Statistical Information System.* Geneva. www.who.int/whosis/whostat/2010/en/index.html. Accessed 29 June 2010.

WHO and UNICEF (World Health Organization and United Nations Children's Fund). 2010. "Joint Monitoring Programme for Water Supply and Sanitation." Geneva. www.wssinfo.org/. Accessed 15 July 2010.

Williamson, J. 1989. "What Washington Means by Policy Reform." In *Latin American Adjustment: How Much has Happened*, ed. J. Williamson. Washington, DC: Peterson Institute for International Economics.

Wolf, S. 2007. "Does Aid Improve Public Service Delivery?" *Review of World Economics* 143(4): 650–72.

Wolfers, J. 2009. "What Does the Human Development Index Measure?." *The New York Times.* 22 May.

Wood, M., J. Hales, S. Purdon, T. Sejersen, and O. Hayllar. 2009. "A Test for Racial Discrimination in Recruitment Practices in British Cities." DWP Research Report 607. Government of the United Kingdom, Department of Work and Pensions, London.

Wooldridge, J. 2002. *Econometric Analysis of Cross Section and Panel Data.* Cambridge, MA: MIT Press.

World Bank. 2000. *World Development Report 2000/2001: Attacking Poverty.* New York: Oxford University Press.

———. 2005a. *Economic Growth in the 1990s: Learning from a Decade of Reform.* Washington, DC.

———. 2005b. *World Development Report: Equity and Development.* Washington, DC.

———. 2009a. *Burkina Faso Population Growth, Competitiveness and Diversification: Country Economic Memorandum.* Washington, DC.

———. 2009b. "Financial Crisis Highlights Need for More Social Safety Nets, Including Conditional Cash Transfers." Press release, 10 February. World Bank. Washington, DC.

———. 2009c. *Global Monitoring Report 2009: A Development Emergency.* Washington, DC.

———. 2009d. *Timor-Leste: An Analysis of Early Grade Reading Acquisition.* Timor-Leste.

———. 2010a. *Environmental Economics and Indicators: Green Accounting.* Washington, DC.

———. 2010b. "Global Economic Prospects—Summer 2010." Washington, DC. www.worldbank.org. Accessed 15 July 2010.

———. 2010c. *International Income Distribution Database.* Washington, DC.

———. 2010d. "Poverty Reduction Supports Credits: An Evaluation of World Bank Support." IEG Study Series. Washington, DC: Independent Evaluation Group.

———. 2010e. *State and Trends of the Carbon Market 2010.* Washington, DC.

———. 2010f. *Women, Business and the Law Report: Measuring Legal Gender Parity for Entrepreneurs and Workers in 128 Economies.* Washington, DC.

———. 2010g. *World Development Indicators 2010.* Washington, DC.

Wrigley, E. and R. Schofield. 1989. *The Population History of England, 1541–1871: A Reconstruction.* Cambridge, UK: Cambridge University Press.

Yates, R. 2006. *International Experiences in Removing User Fees for Health Services—Implications for Mozambique.* London: UK Department for International Development, Health Resource Centre.

Zaridze, D., D. Maximovitch, A. Lazarev, V. Igitov, A. Boroda, J. Boreham, P. Boyle, R. Peto, and P. Boffetta. 2009. "Alcohol Poisoning is a Main Determinant of Recent Mortality Trends in Russia: Evidence from a Detailed Analysis of Mortality Statistics and Autopsies." *International Journal of Epidemiology* 38(1): 143–53.

Statistical Annex

Readers guide

The 17 statistical tables provide an assessment of country achievements in key aspects of human development, including several composite indices estimated by the Human Development Report Office (HDRO) and a series of new indicators related to sustainability and empowerment. The methods underlying the composite indices are detailed in *Technical notes 1–4*; key aspects of other indicators are detailed below.

The tables include data for as many of the 192 UN member states as possible, as well as Hong Kong Special Administrative Region of China and the Occupied Palestinian Territories. Countries and areas are ranked by their 2010 Human Development Index (HDI) value. *Key to countries* on the inside back cover of the Report lists countries alphabetically with their HDI ranks. Data in the tables are those available to the HDRO as of 15 May 2010, unless otherwise specified.

Six new statistical tables cover broad themes of empowerment, sustainability and vulnerability, human security, perceptions of individual well-being, measures of civic and community well-being, and decent work. Two tables reflect the enabling environment for improved human well-being in terms of financial flows and in terms of economy and infrastructure.

All the indicators are available online in several formats: individually, in predefined tables and via a query tool that allows users to design their own tables. Interactive media, including maps of all the human development indices and selected animations, are available. There are also more descriptive materials such as country factsheets as well as further technical details on how to calculate the indices. These materials are available in English (http://hdr.undp.org/en/statistics), French (http://hdr.undp.org/fr/statistiques) and Spanish (http://hdr.undp.org/es/estadisticas).

Sources and definitions

The HDRO is primarily a user, not a producer, of statistics. It relies on international data agencies with the mandate, resources and expertise to collect and compile international data on specific indicators. Where specific data are not available from our traditional data suppliers, data from other credible sources are used.

Sources for all data used in compiling the statistical tables are given at the end of each table with full references in the *References*. The source notes show the original data components used in calculations by the HDRO. Definitions of key indicators are included in *Definitions of statistical terms*. Other relevant information appears in the notes at the end of each table. For more detailed technical information about the indicators, the relevant websites of the source agencies should be consulted, links to which can be found at http://hdr.undp.org/en/statistics.

Coverage of the Human Development Index

Data availability determines HDI country coverage. To enable cross-country comparisons, the HDI is, to the extent possible, calculated based on data from leading international data agencies and other credible data sources available at the time of writing. However, for a number of countries data are missing from these agencies for one or more of the four HDI component indicators. Where reliable data are unavailable and there is significant uncertainty about the validity of data estimates, countries are excluded to ensure the credibility of the HDI and the *HDR* family of indices.

For example, gross national income (GNI) per capita is calculated using data from the

World Bank (2010g) and the International Monetary Fund (IMF 2010b). Four countries have information on the other three HDI components but not on GNI: Cuba, Iraq, Marshall Islands and Palau. Cuba, Marshall Islands and Palau do not participate in the International Comparisons Program, which provides the widely used estimates of purchasing power parity (PPP), and Iraq lacks information about GDP for the last 10 years.

To illustrate the options and problems that arise in attempting to reliably estimate GNI per capita in PPP terms, we use Cuba as an example. One well known approach to estimating GNI—used by the Center for International Comparisons of Production, Income and Prices at the University of Pennsylvania (Heston and others 2009)—is a regression that relies on data from the salaries of international civil servants converted using the official exchange rate. However, because the markets in which foreigners purchase goods and services tend to be separated from the rest of the economy, these data can be a weak guide to the prices citizens face in practice. The Center for International Comparisons of Production, Income and Prices recognizes this problem, rating its own estimate of Cuba's GDP as a "D" (the lowest grade). An alternative estimate uses the exchange rate faced by ordinary Cubans and the PPP conversion of an economy with similar attributes, but this method goes against the principle of using a country's legally recognized exchange rate and prices to convert its national aggregates to an international currency. Another option is to not apply any PPP correction factor to the official exchange rate for convertible pesos. Both of these options yield far lower estimated income than the PPP correction does. The wide variation in income estimates arising from these different techniques indicates that no single robust method exists in the absence of reliable data. Thus Cuba and several other countries are not included in this year's HDI ranking. Various other indicators are listed for Cuba, including the nonincome HDI, where it ranks 17th of 174 countries.

The HDI in 2010 can be calculated for 169 countries (168 UN member countries plus Hong Kong Special Administrative Region of China). Micronesia has entered the HDI table for the first time this year, and Zimbabwe has reentered. Dropping from the table this year are Antigua and Barbuda, Bhutan, Cuba, Dominica, Eritrea, Grenada, Lebanon, Oman, Saint Kitts and Nevis, Saint Lucia, Saint Vincent and the Grenadines, Samoa, Seychelles and Vanuatu.

Comparisons over time and across editions of the Report

The HDI is an important tool for monitoring long-term trends in human development. To facilitate trend analyses across countries, the HDI is calculated at five-year intervals for the period 1980–2010. Presented in table 2, these estimates are based on a consistent methodology (described in *Technical note 1*) using the data available at the time of writing. The HDI values and ranks presented in this Report are not comparable to those published in earlier editions. An alternative HDI measure, the hybrid HDI, based on indicators that are available over a longer time span, is used in chapters 2 and 3 to analyse long-term trends.

International data agencies continually improve their data series, including periodically updating historical data. The year-to-year changes in the HDI values and rankings across editions of the Report often reflect these revisions to data rather than real changes in a country. In addition, occasional changes in country coverage can affect the HDI ranking of a country. Thus, for example, a country's HDI rank could drop considerably between two consecutive Reports, but when comparable revised data are used to reconstruct the HDI, the HDI rank and value may actually show an improvement. For this reason, statistical table 2 should be used to see trends.

The HDI values and ranks presented in this Report are not comparable to estimates published in earlier editions of the Report—to look at trends over time, readers must refer to table 2.

Inconsistencies between national and international estimates

When compiling data series, international agencies apply international standards and harmonization procedures to make national data comparable across countries. When data for a country are missing, an international agency may produce an estimate if other relevant information is available. In some cases international data series may not incorporate the most recent national data. All these factors can lead to substantial differences between national and international estimates.

When data inconsistencies have arisen, the HDRO has helped bring national and international data authorities together to address them. In many cases this has led to better statistics becoming available. The HDRO continues to advocate for improving international data and actively supports efforts to enhance data quality. And it works with national agencies and international bodies to improve data consistency through more systematic reporting and monitoring of data quality.

Country groupings and aggregates

In addition to country-level data, several aggregates are shown in the tables. These are generally weighted averages that are calculated for the country groupings described below. In general, an aggregate is shown for a country grouping only when data are available for at least half the countries and represent at least two-thirds of the available weight in that classification. The HDRO does not impute missing data for the purpose of aggregation. Therefore, unless otherwise specified, aggregates for each classification represent only the countries for which data are available. Occasionally aggregates are those from the original source rather than weighted averages; these values are indicated with a superscript "T."

Human development classification

In the past, HDI classification was based on preset cut-off points of HDI values. This year the classifications are based on quartiles and denoted very high, high, medium and low HDI. Because there are 169 countries, one group must have one more country than others; the high HDI group was assigned the extra country.

Regional groupings

This edition divides countries into two main groups, developed and developing, based on HDI classification, and shows other key groupings, such as Least Developed Countries, as defined by the United Nations. Countries in the top quartile of the distribution, those with very high HDI, are classified as developed, and the rest as developing. The developed group is further classified into Organisation for Economic Co-operation and Development (OECD) members and non-OECD members (which includes Monaco and San Marino, even though an HDI value is not available), while the developing group is further classified into Arab States, East Asia and the Pacific, Europe and Central Asia, Latin America and the Caribbean, South Asia and Sub-Saharan Africa, following UNDP Regional Bureau classifications (see *Country groupings*).

Country notes

Data for China do not include Hong Kong Special Administrative Region of China, Macao Special Administrative Region of China or Taiwan Province of China, unless otherwise noted. Data for Sudan are often based on information collected from the northern part of the country only.

Symbols

A dash between two years, as in 2005–2010, indicates that the data presented are the most recent year available in the period specified, unless otherwise noted. Growth rates are usually average annual rates of growth between the first and last years of the period shown.

A slash between years such as 2005/2010 indicates average for the years shown, unless otherwise noted.

The following symbols are used in the tables:

..	Not available
0 or 0.0	Nil or negligible
—	Not applicable
<	Less than

Primary data sources for the Human Development Index

Life expectancy at birth

The life expectancy at birth estimates are from *World Population Prospects 1950–2050: The 2008 Revision* (UNDESA 2009d), the official source of UN population estimates and projections. They are prepared biennially by the United Nations Department of Economic and Social Affairs Population Division using data from national vital registration systems, population censuses and surveys.

UNDESA (2009d) classifies countries where HIV prevalence among people ages 15–49 was 1 percent or higher during 1980–2007 as affected by the HIV epidemic, and their mortality is projected by modelling the course of the epidemic and projecting the yearly incidence of HIV infection. Also considered among the affected countries are those where HIV prevalence has always been lower than 1 percent and where more than 500,000 people were living with HIV in 2007 (Brazil, China, India, the Russian Federation and the United States). This brings the number of countries considered to be affected by HIV to 58.

Expected years of schooling

The Report uses data on expected years of schooling from the United Nations Educational, Scientific and Cultural Organization (UNESCO) Institute for Statistics. The estimates are based on enrolment by age at all levels of education and population of official school age for all levels of education by age.

Cross-country comparison of expected years of schooling should be made with caution because the length of the school year and the quality of education are not the same in every country and because the indicator does not directly take into account the effects of repetition (some countries have automatic promotion while others do not). The coverage of different types of continuing education and training also varies across countries. Thus, where possible, the indicator should be interpreted in the context of complementary indicators, such as repetition rates, as well as indicators of quality.

Mean years of schooling

In the absence of mean years of schooling data from the UNESCO Institute for Statistics, the Report uses estimates from Barro and Lee (2010) that are based on population censuses and household survey data compiled by UNESCO, Eurostat and other sources to provide benchmarks for school attainment by gender and age group. They are presented in six categories: no formal education, incomplete primary, complete primary, first cycle of secondary, second cycle of secondary, and tertiary. Barro and Lee use country-specific information about duration of schooling at each level to calculate the estimates.

Gross national income per capita

Data on gross national income (GNI) per capita are from the World Bank's (2010g) World Development Indicators database. To better compare standards of living across countries, data must be converted into purchasing power parity (PPP) terms to eliminate differences in national price levels. The GNI estimates are based on price data from the latest round of the International Comparison Program (ICP), which was conducted in 2005 and covered 146 countries and areas. For more than 20 countries not included in the ICP surveys, the World Bank derives estimates through econometric regressions, and we rely on those here where available.

Underlying data for measures of inequality

Inequality in the underlying distributions of mean years of schooling and income are estimated from the most recent national household surveys available from international databases: Luxembourg Income Study; EU Statistics on Income and Living Conditions; United Nations Children's Fund Multiple Indicator Cluster Surveys; Measure DHS; the UN University's World Income Inequality Database; and, the World Bank's International Income Distribution Database. Inequality in the distribution of life expectancy is estimated from life tables produced by the United Nations Population Division.

Human development statistical tables

Composite measures

Dimensions of human development

Cross-cutting themes

Key to HDI countries and ranks, 2010

Afghanistan	155
Albania	64
Algeria	84
Andorra	30
Angola	146
Argentina	46
Armenia	76
Australia	2
Austria	25
Azerbaijan	67
Bahamas	43
Bahrain	39
Bangladesh	129
Barbados	42
Belarus	61
Belgium	18
Belize	78
Benin	134
Bolivia, Plurinational State of	95
Bosnia and Herzegovina	68
Botswana	98
Brazil	73
Brunei Darussalam	37
Bulgaria	58
Burkina Faso	161
Burundi	166
Cambodia	124
Cameroon	131
Canada	8
Cape Verde	118
Central African Republic	159
Chad	163
Chile	45
China	89
Colombia	79
Comoros	140
Congo	126
Congo, Democratic Republic of the	168
Costa Rica	62
Côte d'Ivoire	149
Croatia	51
Cyprus	35
Czech Republic	28
Denmark	19
Djibouti	147
Dominican Republic	88
Ecuador	77
Egypt	101
El Salvador	90
Equatorial Guinea	117
Estonia	34
Ethiopia	157
Fiji	86
Finland	16
France	14
Gabon	93
Gambia	151
Georgia	74
Germany	10
Ghana	130
Greece	22
Guatemala	116
Guinea	156
Guinea-Bissau	164
Guyana	104
Haiti	145
Honduras	106
Hong Kong, China (SAR)	21
Hungary	36
Iceland	17
India	119
Indonesia	108
Iran, Islamic Republic of	70
Ireland	5
Israel	15
Italy	23
Jamaica	80
Japan	11
Jordan	82
Kazakhstan	66
Kenya	128
Korea, Republic of	12
Kuwait	47
Kyrgyzstan	109
Lao People's Democratic Republic	122
Latvia	48
Lesotho	141
Liberia	162
Libyan Arab Jamahiriya	53
Liechtenstein	6
Lithuania	44
Luxembourg	24
Madagascar	135
Malawi	153
Malaysia	57
Maldives	107
Mali	160
Malta	33
Mauritania	136
Mauritius	72
Mexico	56
Micronesia, Federated States of	103
Moldova, Republic of	99
Mongolia	100
Montenegro	49
Morocco	114
Mozambique	165
Myanmar	132
Namibia	105
Nepal	138
Netherlands	7
New Zealand	3
Nicaragua	115
Niger	167
Nigeria	142
Norway	1
Pakistan	125
Panama	54
Papua New Guinea	137
Paraguay	96
Peru	63
Philippines	97
Poland	41
Portugal	40
Qatar	38
Romania	50
Russian Federation	65
Rwanda	152
São Tomé and Príncipe	127
Saudi Arabia	55
Senegal	144
Serbia	60
Sierra Leone	158
Singapore	27
Slovakia	31
Slovenia	29
Solomon Islands	123
South Africa	110
Spain	20
Sri Lanka	91
Sudan	154
Suriname	94
Swaziland	121
Sweden	9
Switzerland	13
Syrian Arab Republic	111
Tajikistan	112
Tanzania, United Republic of	148
Thailand	92
The former Yugoslav Republic of Macedonia	71
Timor-Leste	120
Togo	139
Tonga	85
Trinidad and Tobago	59
Tunisia	81
Turkey	83
Turkmenistan	87
Uganda	143
Ukraine	69
United Arab Emirates	32
United Kingdom	26
United States	4
Uruguay	52
Uzbekistan	102
Venezuela, Bolivarian Republic of	75
Viet Nam	113
Yemen	133
Zambia	150
Zimbabwe	169

TABLE 1

Human Development Index and its components

HDI rank	Human Development Index (HDI) value[a]	Life expectancy at birth (years)	Mean years of schooling (years)	Expected years of schooling (years)	Gross national income (GNI) per capita (PPP 2008 $)	GNI per capita rank minus HDI rank	Nonincome HDI value
	2010	2010	2010	2010[b]	2010	2010	2010
VERY HIGH HUMAN DEVELOPMENT							
1 Norway	0.938	81.0	12.6	17.3	58,810	2	0.954
2 Australia	0.937	81.9	12.0	20.5	38,692	11	0.989
3 New Zealand	0.907	80.6	12.5	19.7	25,438	30	0.979
4 United States	0.902	79.6	12.4	15.7	47,094	5	0.917
5 Ireland	0.895	80.3	11.6	17.9	33,078	20	0.936
6 Liechtenstein	0.891	79.6[c]	10.3[d]	14.8	81,011[e,f]	−5	0.861
7 Netherlands	0.890	80.3	11.2	16.7	40,658	4	0.911
8 Canada	0.888	81.0	11.5	16.0	38,668	6	0.913
9 Sweden	0.885	81.3	11.6	15.6	36,936	8	0.911
10 Germany	0.885	80.2	12.2	15.6	35,308	9	0.915
11 Japan	0.884	83.2	11.5	15.1	34,692	11	0.915
12 Korea, Republic of[g]	0.877	79.8	11.6	16.8	29,518	16	0.918
13 Switzerland	0.874	82.2	10.3	15.5	39,849	−1	0.889
14 France	0.872	81.6	10.4	16.1	34,341	9	0.898
15 Israel	0.872	81.2	11.9	15.6	27,831	14	0.916
16 Finland	0.871	80.1	10.3	17.1	33,872	8	0.897
17 Iceland	0.869	82.1	10.4	18.2	22,917	20	0.928
18 Belgium	0.867	80.3	10.6	15.9	34,873	3	0.888
19 Denmark	0.866	78.7	10.3	16.9	36,404	−1	0.883
20 Spain	0.863	81.3	10.4	16.4	29,661	6	0.897
21 Hong Kong, China (SAR)	0.862	82.5	10.0	13.8	45,090	−11	0.860
22 Greece	0.855	79.7	10.5	16.5	27,580	8	0.890
23 Italy	0.854	81.4	9.7	16.3	29,619	4	0.882
24 Luxembourg	0.852	79.9	10.1	13.3	51,109	−18	0.836
25 Austria	0.851	80.4	9.8	15.0	37,056	−9	0.859
26 United Kingdom	0.849	79.8	9.5	15.9	35,087	−6	0.860
27 Singapore	0.846	80.7	8.8	14.4[h]	48,893	−19	0.831
28 Czech Republic	0.841	76.9	12.3	15.2	22,678	10	0.886
29 Slovenia	0.828	78.8	9.0	16.7	25,857	3	0.853
30 Andorra	0.824	80.8[c]	10.4[i]	11.5	38,056[j,k]	−15	0.817
31 Slovakia	0.818	75.1	11.6	14.9	21,658	12	0.854
32 United Arab Emirates	0.815	77.7	9.2	11.5	58,006	−28	0.774
33 Malta	0.815	80.0	9.9	14.4	21,004[l]	11	0.850
34 Estonia	0.812	73.7	12.0	15.8	17,168	13	0.864
35 Cyprus	0.810	80.0	9.9	13.8	21,962	6	0.840
36 Hungary	0.805	73.9	11.7	15.3	17,472	10	0.851
37 Brunei Darussalam	0.805	77.4	7.5	14.0	49,915	−30	0.769
38 Qatar	0.803	76.0	7.3	12.7	79,426[m]	−36	0.737
39 Bahrain	0.801	76.0	9.4	14.3	26,664	−8	0.809
40 Portugal	0.795	79.1	8.0	15.5	22,105	0	0.815
41 Poland	0.795	76.0	10.0	15.2	17,803	4	0.834
42 Barbados	0.788	77.7	9.3	13.4[n]	21,673	0	0.806
HIGH HUMAN DEVELOPMENT							
43 Bahamas	0.784	74.4	11.1[b,o]	11.6	25,201[p]	−9	0.788
44 Lithuania	0.783	72.1	10.9	16.0	14,824	7	0.832
45 Chile	0.783	78.8	9.7	14.5	13,561	11	0.840
46 Argentina	0.775	75.7	9.3	15.5	14,603	6	0.821

TABLE
1

HDI rank		Human Development Index (HDI) value[a]	Life expectancy at birth (years)	Mean years of schooling (years)	Expected years of schooling (years)	Gross national income (GNI) per capita (PPP 2008 $)	GNI per capita rank minus HDI rank	Nonincome HDI value
		2010	2010	2010	2010[b]	2010	2010	2010
47	Kuwait	0.771	77.9	6.1	12.5	55,719	−42	0.714
48	Latvia	0.769	73.0	10.4	15.4	12,944	13	0.822
49	Montenegro	0.769	74.6	10.6 [b,q]	14.4 [h]	12,491	16	0.825
50	Romania	0.767	73.2	10.6	14.8	12,844	13	0.820
51	Croatia	0.767	76.7	9.0	13.8	16,389	−2	0.798
52	Uruguay	0.765	76.7	8.4	15.7	13,808	3	0.810
53	Libyan Arab Jamahiriya	0.755	74.5	7.3	16.5	17,068	−5	0.775
54	Panama	0.755	76.0	9.4	13.5	13,347	4	0.796
55	Saudi Arabia	0.752	73.3	7.8	13.5	24,726	−20	0.742
56	Mexico	0.750	76.7	8.7	13.4	13,971	−3	0.785
57	Malaysia	0.744	74.7	9.5	12.5	13,927	−3	0.775
58	Bulgaria	0.743	73.7	9.9	13.7	11,139	10	0.795
59	Trinidad and Tobago	0.736	69.9	9.2	11.4	24,233	−23	0.719
60	Serbia	0.735	74.4	9.5	13.5	10,449	11	0.788
61	Belarus	0.732	69.6	9.3 [b,q]	14.6	12,926	1	0.763
62	Costa Rica	0.725	79.1	8.3	11.7	10,870	7	0.768
63	Peru	0.723	73.7	9.6	13.8	8,424	14	0.788
64	Albania	0.719	76.9	10.4	11.3	7,976	19	0.787
65	Russian Federation	0.719	67.2	8.8	14.1	15,258	−15	0.729
66	Kazakhstan	0.714	65.4	10.3	15.1	10,234	6	0.756
67	Azerbaijan	0.713	70.8	10.2 [b,o]	13.0	8,747	8	0.769
68	Bosnia and Herzegovina	0.710	75.5	8.7 [b,q]	13.0	8,222	12	0.771
69	Ukraine	0.710	68.6	11.3	14.6	6,535	20	0.794
70	Iran, Islamic Republic of	0.702	71.9	7.2	14.0	11,764	−3	0.725
71	The former Yugoslav Republic of Macedonia	0.701	74.5	8.2	12.3	9,487	3	0.742
72	Mauritius	0.701	72.1	7.2	13.0	13,344	−13	0.712
73	Brazil	0.699	72.9	7.2	13.8	10,607	−3	0.728
74	Georgia	0.698	72.0	12.1 [b,q]	12.6	4,902	26	0.805
75	Venezuela, Bolivarian Republic of	0.696	74.2	6.2	14.2	11,846	−9	0.716
76	Armenia	0.695	74.2	10.8	11.9	5,495	19	0.787
77	Ecuador	0.695	75.4	7.6	13.3	7,931	7	0.749
78	Belize	0.694	76.9	9.2	12.4	5,693	16	0.782
79	Colombia	0.689	73.4	7.4	13.3	8,589	−3	0.732
80	Jamaica	0.688	72.3	9.6	11.7	7,207	6	0.748
81	Tunisia	0.683	74.3	6.5	14.5	7,979	1	0.729
82	Jordan	0.681	73.1	8.6	13.1	5,956	10	0.755
83	Turkey	0.679	72.2	6.5	11.8	13,359	−26	0.679
84	Algeria	0.677	72.9	7.2	12.8	8,320	−6	0.716
85	Tonga	0.677	72.1	10.4	13.7	4,038	23	0.792

MEDIUM HUMAN DEVELOPMENT

HDI rank		HDI	Life exp	Mean yrs	Exp yrs	GNI	GNI rank	Nonincome
86	Fiji	0.669	69.2	11.0	13.0	4,315	21	0.771
87	Turkmenistan	0.669	65.3	9.9 [b,o]	13.0 [h]	7,052	1	0.719
88	Dominican Republic	0.663	72.8	6.9	11.9	8,273	−9	0.695
89	China	0.663	73.5	7.5	11.4	7,258	−4	0.707
90	El Salvador	0.659	72.0	7.7	12.1	6,498	0	0.711
91	Sri Lanka	0.658	74.4	8.2	12.0	4,886	10	0.738
92	Thailand	0.654	69.3	6.6	13.5 [n]	8,001	−11	0.683
93	Gabon	0.648	61.3	7.5	12.7	12,747	−29	0.637
94	Suriname	0.646	69.4	7.2 [b,q]	12.0	7,093	−7	0.681
95	Bolivia, Plurinational State of	0.643	66.3	9.2	13.7	4,357	11	0.724
96	Paraguay	0.640	72.3	7.8	12.0	4,585	9	0.714
97	Philippines	0.638	72.3	8.7	11.5	4,002	12	0.726
98	Botswana	0.633	55.5	8.9	12.4	13,204	−38	0.613
99	Moldova, Republic of	0.623	68.9	9.7	12.0	3,149	19	0.729
100	Mongolia	0.622	67.3	8.3	13.5	3,619	12	0.710
101	Egypt	0.620	70.5	6.5	11.0	5,889	−8	0.657
102	Uzbekistan	0.617	68.2	10.0 [b,q]	11.5	3,085	17	0.721
103	Micronesia, Federated States of	0.614	69.0	8.8 [b,o]	11.7 [r]	3,266 [s]	13	0.709
104	Guyana	0.611	67.9	8.5	12.2	3,302	11	0.702

HDI rank		Human Development Index (HDI) value[a]	Life expectancy at birth (years)	Mean years of schooling (years)	Expected years of schooling (years)	Gross national income (GNI) per capita (PPP 2008 $)	GNI per capita rank minus HDI rank	Nonincome HDI value
		2010	2010	2010	2010[b]	2010	2010	2010
105	Namibia	0.606	62.1	7.4	11.8	6,323	−14	0.629
106	Honduras	0.604	72.6	6.5	11.4	3,750	5	0.676
107	Maldives	0.602	72.3	4.7	12.4	5,408	−11	0.636
108	Indonesia	0.600	71.5	5.7	12.7	3,957	2	0.663
109	Kyrgyzstan	0.598	68.4	9.3	12.6	2,291	17	0.726
110	South Africa	0.597	52.0	8.2	13.4	9,812	−37	0.581
111	Syrian Arab Republic	0.589	74.6	4.9	10.5[r]	4,760	−9	0.627
112	Tajikistan	0.580	67.3	9.8	11.4	2,020	22	0.709
113	Viet Nam	0.572	74.9	5.5	10.4	2,995	7	0.646
114	Morocco	0.567	71.8	4.4	10.5	4,628	−10	0.594
115	Nicaragua	0.565	73.8	5.7	10.8	2,567	7	0.652
116	Guatemala	0.560	70.8	4.1	10.6	4,694	−13	0.583
117	Equatorial Guinea	0.538	51.0	5.4[b,q]	8.1	22,218	−78	0.454
118	Cape Verde	0.534	71.9	3.5[b,o]	11.2	3,306	−4	0.573
119	India	0.519	64.4	4.4	10.3	3,337	−6	0.549
120	Timor-Leste	0.502	62.1	2.8[b,o]	11.2	5,303	−23	0.485
121	Swaziland	0.498	47.0	7.1	10.3	5,132	−23	0.482
122	Lao People's Democratic Republic	0.497	65.9	4.6	9.2	2,321	3	0.548
123	Solomon Islands	0.494	67.0	4.5[b,o]	9.1	2,172	6	0.550
124	Cambodia	0.494	62.2	5.8	9.8	1,868	12	0.566
125	Pakistan	0.490	67.2	4.9	6.8	2,678	−4	0.523
126	Congo	0.489	53.9	5.9	9.3	3,258	−9	0.503
127	São Tomé and Príncipe	0.488	66.1	4.2[b,o]	10.2	1,918	8	0.553

LOW HUMAN DEVELOPMENT

HDI rank		HDI value	Life exp.	Mean yrs	Expected yrs	GNI per capita	GNI rank − HDI rank	Nonincome HDI
128	Kenya	0.470	55.6	7.0	9.6	1,628	10	0.541
129	Bangladesh	0.469	66.9	4.8	8.1	1,587	12	0.543
130	Ghana	0.467	57.1	7.1	9.7	1,385	14	0.556
131	Cameroon	0.460	51.7	5.9	9.8	2,197	−3	0.493
132	Myanmar	0.451	62.7	4.0	9.2	1,596	8	0.511
133	Yemen	0.439	63.9	2.5	8.6	2,387	−9	0.453
134	Benin	0.435	62.3	3.5	9.2	1,499	8	0.491
135	Madagascar	0.435	61.2	5.2[b,o]	10.2	953	22	0.550
136	Mauritania	0.433	57.3	3.7	8.1	2,118	−5	0.454
137	Papua New Guinea	0.431	61.6	4.3	5.2	2,227	−10	0.447
138	Nepal	0.428	67.5	3.2	8.8	1,201	12	0.506
139	Togo	0.428	63.3	5.3	9.6	844	22	0.557
140	Comoros	0.428	66.2	2.8[b,o]	10.7	1,176	12	0.507
141	Lesotho	0.427	45.9	5.8	10.3	2,021	−8	0.448
142	Nigeria	0.423	48.4	5.0[b,q]	8.9	2,156	−12	0.436
143	Uganda	0.422	54.1	4.7	10.4	1,224	5	0.491
144	Senegal	0.411	56.2	3.5	7.5	1,816	−7	0.433
145	Haiti	0.404	61.7	4.9	6.8[n]	949	13	0.493
146	Angola	0.403	48.1	4.4[b,o]	4.4	4,941	−47	0.353
147	Djibouti	0.402	56.1	3.8[b,q]	4.7	2,471	−24	0.394
148	Tanzania, United Republic of	0.398	56.9	5.1	5.3	1,344	−1	0.441
149	Côte d'Ivoire	0.397	58.4	3.3	6.3	1,625	−10	0.420
150	Zambia	0.395	47.3	6.5	7.2	1,359	−5	0.434
151	Gambia	0.390	56.6	2.8	8.6	1,358	−5	0.426
152	Rwanda	0.385	51.1	3.3	10.6	1,190	−1	0.432
153	Malawi	0.385	54.6	4.3	8.9	911	6	0.463
154	Sudan	0.379	58.9	2.9	4.4	2,051	−22	0.373
155	Afghanistan	0.349	44.6	3.3	8.0	1,419	−12	0.358
156	Guinea	0.340	58.9	1.6[b,t]	8.6	953	0	0.380
157	Ethiopia	0.328	56.1	1.5[b,o]	8.3	992	−2	0.357
158	Sierra Leone	0.317	48.2	2.9	7.2	809	4	0.360
159	Central African Republic	0.315	47.7	3.5	6.3	758	4	0.363
160	Mali	0.309	49.2	1.4	8.0	1,171	−7	0.312
161	Burkina Faso	0.305	53.7	1.3[b,q]	5.8	1,215	−12	0.303
162	Liberia	0.300	59.1	3.9	11.0	320	5	0.509

TABLE 1

Human Development Index and its components

TABLE 1

HDI rank	Human Development Index (HDI) value[a]	Life expectancy at birth (years)	Mean years of schooling (years)	Expected years of schooling (years)	Gross national income (GNI) per capita (PPP 2008 $)	GNI per capita rank minus HDI rank	Nonincome HDI value
	2010	2010	2010	2010[b]	2010	2010	2010
163 Chad	0.295	49.2	1.5 [b,o]	6.0	1,067	−9	0.298
164 Guinea-Bissau	0.289	48.6	2.3 [b,q]	9.1	538	1	0.362
165 Mozambique	0.284	48.4	1.2	8.2	854	−5	0.300
166 Burundi	0.282	51.4	2.7	9.6	402	0	0.400
167 Niger	0.261	52.5	1.4	4.3	675	−3	0.285
168 Congo, Democratic Republic of the	0.239	48.0	3.8	7.8	291	0	0.390
169 Zimbabwe	0.140	47.0	7.2	9.2	176	0	0.472
OTHER COUNTRIES OR TERRITORIES							
Antigua and Barbuda	..	..	..	..	17,924	..	..
Bhutan	..	66.8	..	11.3	5,607	..	0.260
Cuba	..	79.0	10.2	17.7	..	..	0.892
Dominica	..	..	..	12.5	8,549	..	..
Eritrea	..	60.4	..	5.5	643	..	..
Grenada	..	75.8	..	13.4	7,998	..	..
Iraq	..	68.5	5.6	9.7	..	..	0.600
Kiribati	..	..	..	12.3	3,715	..	..
Korea, Democratic People's Rep. of	..	67.7	..	..	..	..	..
Lebanon	..	72.4	..	13.5	13,475	..	..
Marshall Islands	..	..	9.8 [b,o]	13.0	..	..	0.766
Monaco	..	..	..	..	..	..	..
Nauru	..	..	..	8.5	..	..	..
Occupied Palestinian Territories	..	73.9	..	13.1	..	..	..
Oman	..	76.1	..	11.1	25,653	..	..
Palau	..	..	12.1 [b,o]	14.9	..	..	0.836
Saint Kitts and Nevis	..	..	..	12.3	14,196	..	..
Saint Lucia	..	74.2	..	13.0	8,652	..	..
Saint Vincent and the Grenadines	..	72.0	..	13.5	8,535	..	..
Samoa	..	72.2	..	12.2	4,126	..	..
San Marino	..	..	..	..	..	..	..
Seychelles	..	..	..	14.7	19,128	..	..
Somalia	..	50.4	..	1.8 [r]	..	..	..
Tuvalu	..	..	..	11.2	..	..	..
Vanuatu	..	70.8	..	10.4	3,908	..	..
Developed							
OECD	0.879	80.3	11.4	15.9	37,077	—	0.904
Non-OECD	0.844	80.0	10.0	13.9	42,370	—	0.845
Developing							
Arab States	0.588	69.1	5.7	10.8	7,861	—	0.610
East Asia and the Pacific	0.643	72.6	7.2	11.5	6,403	—	0.692
Europe and Central Asia	0.702	69.5	9.2	13.6	11,462	—	0.740
Latin America and the Caribbean	0.704	74.0	7.9	13.7	10,642	—	0.746
South Asia	0.516	65.1	4.6	10.0	3,417	—	0.551
Sub-Saharan Africa	0.389	52.7	4.5	9.0	2,050	—	0.436
Very high human development	0.878	80.3	11.3	15.9	37,225	—	0.902
High human development	0.717	72.6	8.3	13.8	12,286	—	0.749
Medium human development	0.592	69.3	6.3	11.0	5,134	—	0.634
Low human development	0.393	56.0	4.1	8.2	1,490	—	0.445
Least developed countries	0.386	57.7	3.7	8.0	1,393	—	0.441
World	0.624	69.3	7.4	12.3	10,631	—	0.663

NOTES

a See *Technical note 1* for details on how the HDI is calculated.

b Refers to an earlier year than that specified.

c To calculate the HDI, unpublished estimates from UNDESA (2009d) were used. The data are not published because the population is below 100,000.

d Assumes the same adult mean years of schooling as Switzerland.

e Based on the growth rate of GDP per capita in purchasing power parity (PPP) US dollars for Switzerland from IMF (2010a).

f Based on data on GDP from the United Nations Statistics Division's National Accounts: Main Aggregates Database, data on population from UNDESA (2009d) and the PPP exchange rate for Switzerland from World Bank (2010g).

g In keeping with common usage, the Republic of Korea is referred to as South Korea in the body of this Report.

h Based on cross-country regression.

i Assumes the same adult mean years of schooling as Spain.

j Based on the growth rate of GDP per capita in PPP US dollars for Spain from IMF (2010a).

k Based on data on GDP from the United Nations Statistics Division's National Accounts: Main Aggregates Database, data on population from UNDESA (2009d) and the PPP exchange rate for Spain from World Bank (2010g).

l 2007 prices.

m Based on the ratio of GNI in US dollars to GDP in US dollars from World Bank (2010g).

n UNESCO Institute for Statistics (2009).

o Based on data on years of schooling of adults from household surveys in the World Bank's International Income Distribution Database.

p Based on implied PPP conversion factors from IMF (2010a), data on GDP per capita in local currency unit and the ratio between GNI and GDP in US dollars from World Bank (2010g).

q Based on data from United Nations Children's Fund Multiple Indicator Cluster Surveys.

r Refers to primary and secondary education only from UNESCO Institute for Statistics (2010a).

s Based on the growth rate of GDP per capita in PPP US dollars for Fiji from IMF (2010a).

t Based on data from Measure DHS Demographic and Health Surveys.

SOURCES

Column 1: Calculated based on data from UNDESA (2009d), Barro and Lee (2010), UNESCO Institute for Statistics (2010a), World Bank (2010g) and IMF (2010a).

Column 2: UNDESA (2009d).

Column 3: Barro and Lee (2010).

Column 4: UNESCO Institute for Statistics (2010a).

Column 5: Based on data on GNI per capita and GDP per capita in PPP US dollars (current and constant prices) from World Bank (2010g) and implied growth rates of GDP per capita from IMF (2010a).

Column 6: Calculated based on GNI per capita rank and HDI rank.

Column 7: Calculated based on data in columns 2–4.

TABLE 2

Human Development Index trends, 1980–2010

HDI rank		Human Development Index (HDI) Value							HDI rank Change		Average annual HDI growth rate (%)			HDI improvement rank[a]
		1980	1990	1995	2000	2005	2009	2010	2005–2010	2009–2010	1980–2010	1990–2010	2000–2010	1980–2010
VERY HIGH HUMAN DEVELOPMENT														
1	Norway	0.788	0.838	0.869	0.906	0.932	0.937	0.938	0	0	0.58	0.56	0.34	34
2	Australia	0.791	0.819	0.887	0.914	0.925	0.935	0.937	0	0	0.57	0.67	0.25	35
3	New Zealand	0.786	0.813	0.846	0.865	0.896	0.904	0.907	0	0	0.48	0.55	0.47	47
4	United States	0.810	0.857	0.873	0.893	0.895	0.899	0.902	0	0	0.36	0.25	0.10	65
5	Ireland	0.720	0.768	0.799	0.855	0.886	0.894	0.895	0	0	0.72	0.76	0.45	26
6	Liechtenstein	..	..	..	..	0.875	0.889	0.891	5	0	..	..	..	..
7	Netherlands	0.779	0.822	0.853	0.868	0.877	0.888	0.890	3	0	0.44	0.40	0.25	59
8	Canada	0.789	0.845	0.857	0.867	0.880	0.886	0.888	0	0	0.39	0.25	0.24	64
9	Sweden	0.773	0.804	0.843	0.889	0.883	0.884	0.885	−3	0	0.45	0.48	−0.04	..
10	Germany	..	0.782	0.820	..	0.878	0.883	0.885	−1	0	..	0.62	..	61
11	Japan	0.768	0.814	0.837	0.855	0.873	0.881	0.884	1	0	0.47	0.41	0.33	56
12	Korea, Republic of	0.616	0.725	0.776	0.815	0.851	0.872	0.877	8	0	1.18	0.95	0.74	11
13	Switzerland	0.800	0.824	0.836	0.859	0.870	0.872	0.874	0	0	0.30	0.30	0.18	76
14	France	0.711	0.766	0.807	0.834	0.856	0.869	0.872	5	2	0.68	0.65	0.45	37
15	Israel	0.748	0.788	0.809	0.842	0.861	0.871	0.872	0	−1	0.51	0.51	0.35	50
16	Finland	0.745	0.782	0.810	0.825	0.863	0.869	0.871	−2	−1	0.52	0.54	0.54	49
17	Iceland	0.747	0.792	0.815	0.849	0.881	0.869	0.869	−10	0	0.50	0.46	0.23	55
18	Belgium	0.743	0.797	0.840	0.863	0.858	0.865	0.867	−1	0	0.51	0.42	0.05	52
19	Denmark	0.770	0.797	0.821	0.842	0.860	0.864	0.866	−3	0	0.39	0.41	0.27	69
20	Spain	0.680	0.729	0.789	0.828	0.848	0.861	0.863	1	0	0.79	0.84	0.42	24
21	Hong Kong, China (SAR)	0.693	0.774	0.797	0.800	0.842	0.857	0.862	2	0	0.73	0.53	0.75	31
22	Greece	0.707	0.753	0.761	0.784	0.839	0.853	0.855	3	0	0.63	0.64	0.86	43
23	Italy	0.703	0.764	0.795	0.825	0.838	0.851	0.854	4	0	0.65	0.56	0.35	42
24	Luxembourg	0.719	0.784	0.812	0.845	0.856	0.850	0.852	−6	0	0.57	0.42	0.08	48
25	Austria	0.727	0.777	0.801	0.826	0.841	0.849	0.851	−1	0	0.52	0.45	0.30	58
26	United Kingdom	0.737	0.770	0.824	0.823	0.845	0.847	0.849	−4	0	0.47	0.49	0.31	63
27	Singapore	..	..	..	..	0.826	0.841	0.846	1	0	..	..	..	..
28	Czech Republic	..	..	0.774	0.801	0.838	0.841	0.841	−2	0	..	..	0.50	..
29	Slovenia	..	..	0.743	0.780	0.813	0.826	0.828	0	0	..	..	0.59	..
30	Andorra	..	..	..	..	0.803	0.822	0.824	2	0	..	..	..	..
31	Slovakia	..	..	0.738	0.764	0.796	0.815	0.818	5	0	..	..	0.69	..
32	United Arab Emirates	0.627	0.693	0.732	0.756	0.794	0.812	0.815	5	1	0.87	0.81	0.76	23
33	Malta	0.683	0.735	0.754	0.783	0.806	0.813	0.815	−3	−1	0.59	0.51	0.39	57
34	Estonia	..	..	0.700	0.762	0.805	0.809	0.812	−3	0	..	..	0.63	..
35	Cyprus	0.662	0.723	0.766	0.768	0.793	0.809	0.810	4	0	0.67	0.57	0.54	44
36	Hungary	0.689	0.692	0.723	0.767	0.798	0.803	0.805	−1	1	0.52	0.76	0.48	66
37	Brunei Darussalam	..	0.773	0.787	0.792	0.801	0.804	0.805	−5	−1	..	0.20	0.16	..
38	Qatar	..	..	..	0.764	0.799	0.798	0.803	−5	0	..	..	0.49	..
39	Bahrain	0.615	0.694	0.738	0.765	0.793	0.798	0.801	−1	0	0.88	0.72	0.46	25
40	Portugal	0.625	0.694	0.745	0.774	0.775	0.791	0.795	3	1	0.80	0.68	0.27	36
41	Poland	..	0.683	0.710	0.753	0.775	0.791	0.795	3	−1	..	0.76	0.54	..
42	Barbados	..	..	..	..	0.775	0.787	0.788	−1	0	..	..	..	..
HIGH HUMAN DEVELOPMENT														
43	Bahamas	..	..	..	..	0.776	0.783	0.784	−3	0	..	..	..	..
44	Lithuania	..	0.709	0.677	0.730	0.775	0.782	0.783	−2	0	..	0.50	0.71	..
45	Chile	0.607	0.675	0.707	0.734	0.762	0.779	0.783	2	0	0.85	0.74	0.65	30
46	Argentina	0.656	0.682	0.709	0.734	0.749	0.772	0.775	4	0	0.56	0.64	0.55	70
47	Kuwait	0.675	..	0.760	0.763	0.764	0.769	0.771	−2	0	0.44	..	0.10	80

TABLE
2

HDI rank		Human Development Index (HDI) Value							HDI rank Change		Average annual HDI growth rate (%)			HDI improvement rank[a]
		1980	1990	1995	2000	2005	2009	2010	2005–2010	2009–2010	1980–2010	1990–2010	2000–2010	1980–2010
48	Latvia	0.651	0.679	0.652	0.709	0.763	0.769	0.769	−2	0	0.55	0.63	0.81	71
49	Montenegro	..	..	..	..	0.755	0.768	0.769	−1	0	..	..	..	..
50	Romania	..	0.688	0.674	0.690	0.733	0.764	0.767	1	1	..	0.54	1.06	..
51	Croatia	..	..	0.690	0.720	0.752	0.765	0.767	−2	−1	..	..	0.63	..
52	Uruguay	..	0.670	0.691	0.716	0.733	0.760	0.765	0	0	..	0.67	0.67	..
53	Libyan Arab Jamahiriya	..	..	..	..	0.726	0.749	0.755	3	1	..	..	..	..
54	Panama	0.613	0.644	0.672	0.703	0.724	0.751	0.755	4	−1	0.69	0.79	0.70	54
55	Saudi Arabia	0.556	0.620	0.649	0.690	0.732	0.748	0.752	−2	0	1.01	0.96	0.85	21
56	Mexico	0.581	0.635	0.660	0.698	0.727	0.745	0.750	−2	0	0.85	0.83	0.73	38
57	Malaysia	0.541	0.616	0.659	0.691	0.726	0.739	0.744	−2	1	1.06	0.94	0.73	19
58	Bulgaria	0.649	0.678	0.678	0.693	0.724	0.741	0.743	−1	−1	0.45	0.46	0.69	82
59	Trinidad and Tobago	0.656	0.660	0.662	0.685	0.713	0.732	0.736	1	1	0.38	0.54	0.71	84
60	Serbia	..	..	..	..	0.719	0.733	0.735	−1	−1	..	..	..	..
61	Belarus	..	..	..	..	0.706	0.729	0.732	1	0	..	..	..	..
62	Costa Rica	0.599	0.639	0.668	0.684	0.708	0.723	0.725	−1	0	0.63	0.63	0.59	68
63	Peru	0.560	0.608	0.644	0.675	0.695	0.718	0.723	4	0	0.85	0.87	0.69	41
64	Albania	..	0.647	0.633	0.670	0.700	0.716	0.719	−1	0	..	0.52	0.70	..
65	Russian Federation	..	0.692	0.644	0.662	0.693	0.714	0.719	3	0	..	0.19	0.82	..
66	Kazakhstan	..	0.650	0.620	0.614	0.696	0.711	0.714	−1	0	..	0.47	1.51	..
67	Azerbaijan	..	..	0.563	0.597	0.655	0.710	0.713	16	0	..	..	1.77	..
68	Bosnia and Herzegovina	..	..	..	..	0.698	0.709	0.710	−4	0	..	..	..	..
69	Ukraine	..	0.690	0.644	0.649	0.696	0.706	0.710	−3	0	..	0.14	0.89	..
70	Iran, Islamic Republic of	..	0.536	0.576	0.619	0.660	0.697	0.702	10	2	..	1.35	1.27	..
71	The former Yugoslav Republic of Macedonia	..	..	0.634	0.660	0.678	0.697	0.701	1	−1	..	..	0.61	..
72	Mauritius	0.525	0.602	0.631	0.657	0.685	0.697	0.701	−2	−1	0.96	0.76	0.64	28
73	Brazil	..	..	..	0.649	0.678	0.693	0.699	0	4	..	..	0.73	..
74	Georgia	..	..	..	..	0.679	0.695	0.698	−3	0	..	..	..	..
75	Venezuela, Bolivarian Republic of	0.611	0.620	0.633	0.637	0.666	0.696	0.696	3	−2	0.44	0.58	0.90	85
76	Armenia	..	..	0.571	0.620	0.669	0.693	0.695	0	0	..	..	1.15	..
77	Ecuador	0.576	0.612	0.630	0.642	0.676	0.692	0.695	−2	1	0.62	0.64	0.79	72
78	Belize	..	..	..	..	0.690	0.694	0.694	−9	−3	..	..	..	..
79	Colombia	0.537	0.579	0.612	0.637	0.658	0.685	0.689	2	1	0.83	0.87	0.79	46
80	Jamaica	0.589	0.620	0.648	0.665	0.676	0.686	0.688	−6	−1	0.52	0.52	0.35	83
81	Tunisia	0.436	0.526	0.568	0.613	0.650	0.677	0.683	5	0	1.49	1.30	1.07	7
82	Jordan	0.509	0.564	0.595	0.621	0.652	0.677	0.681	2	0	0.97	0.94	0.92	32
83	Turkey	0.467	0.552	0.583	0.629	0.656	0.674	0.679	−1	1	1.24	1.03	0.76	14
84	Algeria	0.443	0.537	0.564	0.602	0.651	0.671	0.677	1	1	1.42	1.16	1.18	9
85	Tonga	..	0.619	0.641	0.651	0.663	0.675	0.677	−6	−2	..	0.45	0.39	..

MEDIUM HUMAN DEVELOPMENT

HDI rank		1980	1990	1995	2000	2005	2009	2010	2005–2010	2009–2010	1980–2010	1990–2010	2000–2010	1980–2010
86	Fiji	0.551	0.612	0.636	0.651	0.667	0.667	0.669	−9	0	0.65	0.45	0.28	75
87	Turkmenistan	..	..	..	..	0.642	0.662	0.669	0	0	..	..	..	..
88	Dominican Republic	..	0.560	0.591	0.624	0.638	0.660	0.663	0	0	..	0.85	0.61	..
89	China	0.368	0.460	0.518	0.567	0.616	0.655	0.663	8	0	1.96	1.83	1.57	2
90	El Salvador	0.456	0.511	0.562	0.606	0.635	0.655	0.659	0	0	1.23	1.27	0.85	16
91	Sri Lanka	0.513	0.558	0.584	..	0.635	0.653	0.658	0	0	0.83	0.82	..	51
92	Thailand	0.483	0.546	0.581	0.600	0.631	0.648	0.654	1	0	1.01	0.90	0.86	29
93	Gabon	0.510	0.593	0.610	0.616	0.628	0.642	0.648	1	1	0.80	0.45	0.50	62
94	Suriname	..	..	..	..	0.636	0.643	0.646	−5	−1	..	..	..	..
95	Bolivia, Plurinational State of	..	..	..	0.593	0.631	0.637	0.643	−3	0	..	..	0.80	..
96	Paraguay	0.528	0.557	0.580	0.593	0.619	0.634	0.640	0	1	0.64	0.69	0.75	79
97	Philippines	0.523	0.552	0.569	0.597	0.619	0.635	0.638	−2	−1	0.66	0.72	0.67	78
98	Botswana	0.431	0.576	0.589	0.572	0.593	0.627	0.633	2	0	1.28	0.47	1.01	15
99	Moldova, Republic of	..	0.616	0.547	0.552	0.606	0.620	0.623	0	0	..	0.06	1.21	..
100	Mongolia	..	0.520	0.502	0.539	0.588	0.616	0.622	2	0	..	0.90	1.43	..
101	Egypt	0.393	0.484	0.523	0.566	0.587	0.614	0.620	2	0	1.52	1.23	0.90	8
102	Uzbekistan	..	..	..	..	0.588	0.612	0.617	−1	1	..	..	..	..
103	Micronesia, Federated States of	..	..	..	..	0.614	0.612	0.614	−5	−1	..	..	..	..
104	Guyana	0.500	0.472	0.522	0.552	0.585	0.605	0.611	1	0	0.67	1.29	1.02	81
105	Namibia	..	0.553	0.582	0.568	0.577	0.603	0.606	2	0	..	0.46	0.64	..
106	Honduras	0.436	0.495	0.523	0.552	0.579	0.601	0.604	0	0	1.09	0.99	0.91	27

Human Development Index trends, 1980–2010

HDI rank		Human Development Index (HDI) Value							HDI rank Change		Average annual HDI growth rate (%)			HDI improvement rank[a]
		1980	1990	1995	2000	2005	2009	2010	2005–2010	2009–2010	1980–2010	1990–2010	2000–2010	1980–2010
107	Maldives	..	..	..	0.513	0.560	0.595	0.602	4	0	..	..	1.60	..
108	Indonesia	0.390	0.458	0.508	0.500	0.561	0.593	0.600	2	2	1.43	1.35	1.82	12
109	Kyrgyzstan	..	0.577	0.515	0.550	0.572	0.594	0.598	0	−1	..	0.18	0.84	..
110	South Africa	..	0.601	0.634	..	0.587	0.594	0.597	−6	−1	..	−0.03	..	..
111	Syrian Arab Republic	0.470	0.519	0.546	..	0.576	0.586	0.589	−3	0	0.75	0.63	..	74
112	Tajikistan	..	0.592	0.501	0.493	0.550	0.576	0.580	0	0	..	−0.10	1.61	..
113	Viet Nam	..	0.407	0.457	0.505	0.540	0.566	0.572	1	0	..	1.70	1.24	..
114	Morocco	0.351	0.421	0.450	0.491	0.536	0.562	0.567	1	0	1.59	1.49	1.44	5
115	Nicaragua	0.440	0.454	0.473	0.512	0.545	0.562	0.565	−2	0	0.84	1.10	1.00	67
116	Guatemala	0.408	0.451	0.479	0.514	0.533	0.556	0.560	0	0	1.05	1.08	0.85	39
117	Equatorial Guinea	..	..	..	0.477	0.510	0.536	0.538	1	0	..	..	1.21	..
118	Cape Verde	..	..	..	0.500	0.519	0.531	0.534	−1	0	..	..	0.64	..
119	India	0.320	0.389	0.415	0.440	0.482	0.512	0.519	1	0	1.61	1.44	1.66	6
120	Timor-Leste	..	..	..	..	0.428	0.497	0.502	11	0	..	..	..	..
121	Swaziland	..	0.511	0.523	0.490	0.474	0.492	0.498	0	0	..	−0.13	0.17	..
122	Lao People's Democratic Republic	..	0.354	0.388	0.425	0.460	0.490	0.497	4	1	..	1.69	1.56	..
123	Solomon Islands	..	..	..	0.459	0.483	0.492	0.494	−4	−1	..	..	0.73	..
124	Cambodia	..	..	0.385	0.412	0.466	0.489	0.494	1	0	..	..	1.81	..
125	Pakistan	0.311	0.359	0.389	0.416	0.468	0.487	0.490	−2	0	1.52	1.55	1.64	10
126	Congo	0.462	0.499	0.469	0.458	0.470	0.483	0.489	−4	1	0.19	−0.10	0.65	90
127	São Tomé and Príncipe	..	..	..	..	0.466	0.485	0.488	−3	−1	..	..	..	..

LOW HUMAN DEVELOPMENT

HDI rank		1980	1990	1995	2000	2005	2009	2010	2005–2010	2009–2010	1980–2010	1990–2010	2000–2010	1980–2010
128	Kenya	0.404	0.437	0.435	0.424	0.443	0.464	0.470	−1	0	0.50	0.37	1.03	87
129	Bangladesh	0.259	0.313	0.350	0.390	0.432	0.463	0.469	1	0	1.99	2.03	1.86	3
130	Ghana	0.363	0.399	0.421	0.431	0.443	0.463	0.467	−2	0	0.84	0.79	0.82	77
131	Cameroon	0.354	0.418	0.408	0.415	0.437	0.456	0.460	−2	0	0.87	0.48	1.02	73
132	Myanmar	..	..	..	..	0.406	0.444	0.451	6	0	..	..	..	..
133	Yemen	..	..	..	0.358	0.403	0.431	0.439	8	2	..	..	2.04	..
134	Benin	0.264	0.305	0.347	0.386	0.418	0.432	0.435	0	0	1.67	1.78	1.19	4
135	Madagascar	..	..	..	0.399	0.420	0.436	0.435	−2	−2	..	..	0.86	..
136	Mauritania	..	0.337	0.368	0.390	0.411	0.429	0.433	0	0	..	1.25	1.05	..
137	Papua New Guinea	0.295	0.349	0.386	..	0.408	0.426	0.431	0	1	1.27	1.07	..	22
138	Nepal	0.210	0.316	0.344	0.375	0.400	0.423	0.428	5	2	2.37	1.52	1.34	1
139	Togo	0.347	0.361	0.374	0.399	0.414	0.425	0.428	−4	0	0.70	0.85	0.72	86
140	Comoros	..	..	..	..	0.423	0.426	0.428	−8	−3	..	..	..	..
141	Lesotho	0.397	0.451	0.452	0.423	0.404	0.423	0.427	−1	0	0.24	−0.27	0.10	91
142	Nigeria	..	..	..	..	0.402	0.419	0.423	0	0	..	..	..	..
143	Uganda	..	0.281	0.312	0.350	0.380	0.416	0.422	4	0	..	2.03	1.87	..
144	Senegal	0.291	0.331	0.338	0.360	0.388	0.408	0.411	0	1	1.15	1.08	1.34	40
145	Haiti	..	..	..	..	0.406	0.410	0.404	−6	−1	..	..	..	..
146	Angola	..	..	..	0.349	0.376	0.399	0.403	2	1	..	..	1.45	..
147	Djibouti	..	..	..	..	0.382	0.399	0.402	−1	−1	..	..	..	..
148	Tanzania, United Republic of	..	0.329	0.330	0.332	0.370	0.392	0.398	1	1	..	0.95	1.81	..
149	Côte d'Ivoire	0.350	0.360	0.369	0.379	0.383	0.394	0.397	−4	−1	0.42	0.48	0.47	89
150	Zambia	0.382	0.423	0.371	0.345	0.360	0.387	0.395	1	0	0.11	−0.34	1.35	92
151	Gambia	..	..	0.312	0.343	0.362	0.385	0.390	−1	0	..	..	1.29	..
152	Rwanda	0.249	0.215	0.192	0.277	0.334	0.379	0.385	2	0	1.45	2.92	3.31	13
153	Malawi	0.258	0.289	0.344	0.344	0.336	0.376	0.385	0	0	1.33	1.44	1.13	20
154	Sudan	0.250	0.282	0.310	0.336	0.360	0.375	0.379	−2	0	1.39	1.47	1.19	18
155	Afghanistan	..	..	..	..	0.307	0.342	0.349	1	0	..	..	..	..
156	Guinea	..	..	..	..	0.323	0.338	0.340	−1	0	..	..	..	..
157	Ethiopia	..	..	..	0.250	0.287	0.324	0.328	3	0	..	..	2.73	..
158	Sierra Leone	0.229	0.230	0.226	0.236	0.292	0.313	0.317	1	0	1.09	1.62	2.95	53
159	Central African Republic	0.265	0.293	0.294	0.299	0.299	0.311	0.315	−1	0	0.58	0.37	0.52	88
160	Mali	0.165	0.187	0.212	0.245	0.279	0.305	0.309	2	0	2.10	2.53	2.34	60
161	Burkina Faso	..	..	..	..	0.285	0.303	0.305	0	0	..	..	..	..
162	Liberia	0.295	..	..	0.294	0.264	0.294	0.300	2	0	0.05	..	0.20	93
163	Chad	..	..	..	0.269	0.299	0.293	0.295	−6	0	..	..	0.90	..
164	Guinea-Bissau	..	..	..	..	0.278	0.286	0.289	−1	0	..	..	..	..
165	Mozambique	0.195	0.178	0.186	0.224	0.263	0.280	0.284	0	0	1.25	2.34	2.37	33

TABLE 2

HDI rank		Human Development Index (HDI)							HDI rank		Average annual HDI growth rate			HDI improvement rank[a]
		Value							Change		(%)			
		1980	1990	1995	2000	2005	2009	2010	2005–2010	2009–2010	1980–2010	1990–2010	2000–2010	1980–2010
166	Burundi	0.181	0.236	0.216	0.223	0.239	0.276	0.282	1	0	1.47	0.87	2.33	17
167	Niger	0.166	0.180	0.192	0.212	0.241	0.258	0.261	−1	0	1.51	1.87	2.09	45
168	Congo, Democratic Republic of the	0.267	0.261	0.226	0.201	0.223	0.233	0.239	0	0	−0.37	−0.44	1.75	94
169	Zimbabwe	0.241	0.284	0.262	0.232	0.159	0.118	0.140	0	0	−1.81	−3.53	−5.05	95
Developed														
OECD		0.754	0.798	0.827	0.852	0.868	0.876	0.879	—	—	0.51	0.48	0.31	—
Non-OECD		0.701	0.761	0.779	0.799	0.829	0.840	0.844	—	—	0.62	0.51	0.54	—
Developing														
Arab States		0.396	0.470	0.505	0.525	0.562	0.583	0.588	—	—	1.32	1.12	1.14	—
East Asia and the Pacific		0.383	0.466	0.519	0.559	0.600	0.636	0.643	—	—	1.73	1.61	1.40	—
Europe and Central Asia		0.503	0.660	0.628	0.648	0.679	0.698	0.702	—	—	1.11	0.31	0.80	—
Latin America and the Caribbean		0.573	0.614	0.640	0.660	0.681	0.699	0.704	—	—	0.68	0.68	0.64	—
South Asia		0.315	0.387	0.415	0.440	0.481	0.510	0.516	—	—	1.65	1.44	1.61	—
Sub-Saharan Africa		0.293	0.354	0.358	0.315	0.366	0.384	0.389	—	—	0.94	0.46	2.10	—
Very high human development		0.753	0.797	0.827	0.851	0.867	0.875	0.878	—	—	0.51	0.48	0.31	—
High human development		0.556	0.633	0.634	0.659	0.692	0.712	0.717	—	—	0.85	0.62	0.84	—
Medium human development		0.361	0.440	0.480	0.510	0.555	0.586	0.592	—	—	1.65	1.49	1.49	—
Low human development		0.271	0.310	0.324	0.332	0.366	0.388	0.393	—	—	1.24	1.19	1.68	—
Least developed countries		0.251	0.292	0.311	0.325	0.357	0.382	0.386	—	—	1.44	1.40	1.72	—
World		0.455	0.526	0.554	0.570	0.598	0.619	0.624	—	—	1.05	0.85	0.89	—

TABLE
2

NOTE

a   Measured using deviation from fit (see chapter 2). Lower numbers indicate faster improvement.

SOURCES

Columns 1–7: Calculated based on data from UNDESA (2009d), Barro and Lee (2010), UNESCO Institute for Statistics (2010a), World Bank (2010g) and IMF (2010a).
Columns 8–13: Calculated based on Human Development Index values in the relevant years.

TABLE 3

Inequality-adjusted Human Development Index

HDI rank	Human Development Index (HDI)[a] Value	Inequality-adjusted HDI			Inequality-adjusted life expectancy at birth index[c]		Inequality-adjusted education index[d]		Inequality-adjusted income index[e]		Income Gini coefficient
		Value	Overall loss (%)	Change in rank[b]	Value	Loss (%)	Value	Loss (%)	Value	Loss (%)	
	2010	2010	2010	2010	2010	2010	2010	2010	2010	2010	2000–2010
VERY HIGH HUMAN DEVELOPMENT											
1 Norway	0.938	**0.876**	6.6	0	0.927	4.0	0.919	2.4	0.788	13.1 [f]	25.8
2 Australia	0.937	**0.864**	7.9	0	0.934	4.7	0.982	1.7	0.702	16.6 [f]	35.2
3 New Zealand	0.907	..	..	..	0.912	5.0	..	..	..	..	36.2
4 United States	0.902	**0.799**	11.4	−9	0.886	6.0	0.863	3.2	0.667	23.5 [f]	40.8
5 Ireland	0.895	**0.813**	9.2	−3	0.911	4.6	0.888	3.2	0.664	18.8 [f]	34.3
6 Liechtenstein	0.891	..	..	..	..	..	..	..	..	..	..
7 Netherlands	0.890	**0.818**	8.1	1	0.911	4.6	0.834	4.0	0.720	15.3 [f]	30.9
8 Canada	0.888	**0.812**	8.6	−2	0.918	5.0	0.834	3.2	0.698	17.1 [f]	32.6
9 Sweden	0.885	**0.824**	6.9	4	0.934	3.7	0.825	3.6	0.726	13.0 [f]	25.0
10 Germany	0.885	**0.814**	8.0	3	0.911	4.4	0.858	2.3	0.689	16.7 [f]	28.3
11 Japan	0.884	..	..	..	0.961	3.9	..	..	..	..	24.9
12 Korea, Republic of	0.877	**0.731**	16.7	−18	0.902	4.8	0.663	25.5	0.653	18.4 [f]	31.6
13 Switzerland	0.874	**0.813**	7.1	4	0.941	4.4	0.786	2.0	0.725	14.3 [f]	33.7
14 France	0.872	**0.792**	9.2	−3	0.932	4.5	0.751	9.1	0.709	13.9 [f]	32.7
15 Israel	0.872	**0.763**	12.5	−11	0.922	4.8	0.799	7.9	0.603	23.7 [f]	39.2
16 Finland	0.871	**0.806**	7.5	2	0.913	4.0	0.805	4.7	0.711	13.4 [f]	26.9
17 Iceland	0.869	**0.811**	6.6	5	0.948	3.5	0.854	2.6	0.659	13.4 [f]	..
18 Belgium	0.867	**0.794**	8.4	2	0.911	4.6	0.784	5.2	0.701	15.1 [f]	33.0
19 Denmark	0.866	**0.810**	6.5	6	0.884	4.8	0.813	3.0	0.738	11.3 [f]	24.7
20 Spain	0.863	**0.779**	9.7	0	0.928	4.4	0.781	5.7	0.653	18.5 [f]	34.7
21 Hong Kong, China (SAR)	0.862	..	..	..	0.950	4.1	..	..	..	..	43.4
22 Greece	0.855	**0.768**	10.2	−2	0.907	4.0	0.788	5.8	0.633	19.9 [f]	34.3
23 Italy	0.854	**0.752**	12.0	−5	0.931	4.3	0.706	11.8	0.645	19.4 [f]	36.0
24 Luxembourg	0.852	**0.775**	9.0	2	0.903	4.8	0.692	6.2	0.746	15.7 [f]	..
25 Austria	0.851	**0.787**	7.5	5	0.913	4.5	0.753	2.4	0.709	15.1 [f]	29.1
26 United Kingdom	0.849	**0.766**	9.7	1	0.900	4.9	0.766	2.1	0.653	21.0 [f]	36.0
27 Singapore	0.846	..	..	..	0.925	3.8	..	..	..	..	42.5
28 Czech Republic	0.841	**0.790**	6.1	8	0.862	4.3	0.859	1.3	0.667	12.2 [f]	25.8
29 Slovenia	0.828	**0.771**	6.9	5	0.891	4.3	0.750	4.0	0.685	12.2 [f]	31.2
30 Andorra	0.824	..	..	..	..	..	..	..	..	..	..
31 Slovakia	0.818	**0.764**	6.7	3	0.816	6.5	0.821	1.7	0.664	11.7 [f]	25.8
32 United Arab Emirates	0.815	..	..	..	0.846	7.4	..	..	..	..	..
33 Malta	0.815	..	..	..	0.897	5.6	..	..	..	..	..
34 Estonia	0.812	**0.733**	9.8	0	0.784	7.9	0.851	3.1	0.590	17.7 [f]	36.0
35 Cyprus	0.810	**0.716**	11.7	−1	0.901	5.1	0.626	15.7	0.650	13.8 [f]	..
36 Hungary	0.805	**0.736**	8.6	3	0.796	6.6	0.815	4.1	0.614	14.7 [g]	30.0
37 Brunei Darussalam	0.805	..	..	..	0.860	5.4	..	..	..	..	..
38 Qatar	0.803	..	..	..	0.820	7.4	..	..	..	..	41.1
39 Bahrain	0.801	..	..	..	0.816	8.1	..	..	..	..	..
40 Portugal	0.795	**0.700**	11.9	−1	0.891	4.8	0.670	5.7	0.575	23.9 [f]	38.5
41 Poland	0.795	**0.709**	10.8	1	0.829	6.4	0.728	7.1	0.590	18.4 [f]	34.9
42 Barbados	0.788	..	..	..	0.841	7.9	..	..	0.631	16.1 [g]	..
HIGH HUMAN DEVELOPMENT											
43 Bahamas	0.784	**0.671**	14.4	−4	0.777	9.7	0.665	7.9	0.586	24.5 [g]	..
44 Lithuania	0.783	**0.693**	11.5	1	0.752	8.8	0.804	4.3	0.551	20.6 [f]	35.8
45 Chile	0.783	**0.634**	19.0	−10	0.867	6.9	0.656	13.3	0.448	34.1 [f]	52.0
46 Argentina	0.775	**0.562**	27.5	−21	0.790	10.4	0.672	12.1	0.334	51.7 [f]	48.8

HDI rank	Human Development Index (HDI)[a] Value	Inequality-adjusted HDI			Inequality-adjusted life expectancy at birth index[c]		Inequality-adjusted education index[d]		Inequality-adjusted income index[e]		Income Gini coefficient
		Value	Overall loss (%)	Change in rank[b]	Value	Loss (%)	Value	Loss (%)	Value	Loss (%)	
	2010	2010	2010	2010	2010	2010	2010	2010	2010	2010	2000–2010
47 Kuwait	0.771	..	..	..	0.850	7.3	..	..	..	..	..
48 Latvia	0.769	0.684	11.0	2	0.768	8.5	0.778	3.3	0.536	20.5 [f]	36.3
49 Montenegro	0.769	0.693	9.9	4	0.801	7.3	0.711	9.6	0.584	12.6 [h]	36.9
50 Romania	0.767	0.675	12.1	3	0.751	10.9	0.693	13.1	0.590	12.2 [g]	32.1
51 Croatia	0.767	0.650	15.3	–2	0.844	6.0	0.636	10.4	0.512	27.8 [g]	29.0
52 Uruguay	0.765	0.642	16.1	–2	0.806	10.1	0.653	10.8	0.504	26.3 [f]	47.1
53 Libyan Arab Jamahiriya	0.755	..	..	..	0.759	12.1	..	..	..	..	..
54 Panama	0.755	0.541	28.3	–20	0.766	13.6	0.644	9.9	0.321	52.6 [f]	54.9
55 Saudi Arabia	0.752	..	..	..	0.737	12.7	..	..	..	..	..
56 Mexico	0.750	0.593	21.0	–8	0.787	12.3	0.564	17.9	0.469	31.6 [f]	51.6
57 Malaysia	0.744	..	..	..	0.797	8.0	..	..	0.488	28.7 [f]	37.9
58 Bulgaria	0.743	0.659	11.3	5	0.771	9.4	0.682	8.1	0.545	16.1 [g]	29.2
59 Trinidad and Tobago	0.736	0.621	15.5	–2	0.653	17.4	0.611	6.6	0.601	21.9 [h]	40.3
60 Serbia	0.735	0.656	10.8	6	0.783	9.0	0.640	11.1	0.562	12.2 [h]	28.2
61 Belarus	0.732	0.664	9.3	9	0.716	8.8	0.683	8.0	0.599	11.1 [g]	28.8
62 Costa Rica	0.725	0.576	20.6	–6	0.858	8.3	0.519	17.7	0.428	33.7 [f]	48.9
63 Peru	0.723	0.501	30.7	–26	0.709	16.5	0.510	30.2	0.348	42.7 [g]	50.5
64 Albania	0.719	0.627	12.7	4	0.802	10.9	0.601	12.7	0.512	14.4 [g]	33.0
65 Russian Federation	0.719	0.636	11.5	7	0.661	11.5	0.631	11.2	0.616	11.9 [g]	43.7
66 Kazakhstan	0.714	0.617	13.6	3	0.595	17.2	0.753	5.3	0.525	17.6 [h]	30.9
67 Azerbaijan	0.713	0.614	13.8	3	0.613	23.8	0.646	12.0	0.586	4.4 [g]	16.8
68 Bosnia and Herzegovina	0.710	0.565	20.4	–2	0.798	9.2	0.545	19.4	0.416	31.1 [g]	36.3
69 Ukraine	0.710	0.652	8.1	14	0.685	11.0	0.795	2.8	0.509	10.4 [f]	27.6
70 Iran, Islamic Republic of	0.702	..	..	..	0.680	17.3	..	..	..	..	38.3
71 The former Yugoslav Republic of Macedonia	0.701	0.584	16.7	4	0.773	10.4	0.527	17.5	0.489	21.8 [h]	42.8
72 Mauritius	0.701	..	..	..	0.731	11.4	..	..	..	..	..
73 Brazil	0.699	0.509	27.2	–15	0.698	16.6	0.470	25.7	0.401	37.6 [f]	55.0
74 Georgia	0.698	0.579	17.0	5	0.667	19.0	0.749	4.9	0.388	25.9 [h]	40.8
75 Venezuela, Bolivarian Republic of	0.696	0.549	21.2	–1	0.745	13.3	0.495	17.0	0.449	32.0 [f]	43.4
76 Armenia	0.695	0.619	11.0	12	0.727	15.3	0.675	6.5	0.483	10.8 [g]	30.2
77 Ecuador	0.695	0.554	20.2	3	0.745	15.2	0.501	21.8	0.458	23.4 [f]	54.4
78 Belize	0.694	0.495	28.7	–16	0.788	12.4	0.545	19.8	0.282	48.5 [g]	59.6
79 Colombia	0.689	0.492	28.6	–18	0.718	15.1	0.482	23.9	0.344	43.6 [f]	58.5
80 Jamaica	0.688	0.574	16.6	9	0.690	16.7	0.619	8.3	0.442	24.1 [g]	45.5
81 Tunisia	0.683	0.511	25.2	–6	0.751	12.7	0.378	38.7	0.469	21.8 [i]	40.8
82 Jordan	0.681	0.550	19.2	7	0.729	13.3	0.508	25.1	0.450	18.7 [g]	37.7
83 Turkey	0.679	0.518	23.6	1	0.690	16.5	0.405	27.4	0.498	26.5 [h]	41.2
84 Algeria	0.677	..	..	..	0.688	17.9	..	..	..	..	35.3
85 Tonga	0.677	..	..	..	0.705	14.5	0.721	5.1	..	..	..

MEDIUM HUMAN DEVELOPMENT

HDI rank	Value	Value	Overall loss (%)	Change in rank	Value	Loss (%)	Value	Loss (%)	Value	Loss (%)	Gini
86 Fiji	0.669	..	..	..	0.671	13.9	0.679	11.0	..	..	..
87 Turkmenistan	0.669	0.493	26.4	–12	0.520	27.5	0.647	10.2	0.355	38.7 [g]	40.8
88 Dominican Republic	0.663	0.499	24.8	–7	0.678	18.9	0.450	22.2	0.407	32.6 [f]	48.4
89 China	0.663	0.511	23.0	0	0.714	15.6	0.453	23.2	0.412	29.5 [i]	41.5
90 El Salvador	0.659	0.477	27.6	–14	0.687	16.5	0.415	32.5	0.382	32.7 [f]	46.9
91 Sri Lanka	0.658	0.546	17.1	11	0.756	12.3	0.519	17.9	0.414	20.8 [g]	41.1
92 Thailand	0.654	0.516	21.2	5	0.706	9.5	0.491	18.0	0.396	34.0 [g]	42.5
93 Gabon	0.648	0.512	21.0	5	0.446	31.9	0.575	7.3	0.523	22.1 [g]	41.5
94 Suriname	0.646	0.489	24.3	–7	0.651	16.7	0.475	20.1	0.378	34.9 [g]	52.8
95 Bolivia, Plurinational State of	0.643	0.398	38.0	–17	0.534	27.2	0.510	28.7	0.232	54.2 [f]	57.2
96 Paraguay	0.640	0.482	24.7	–6	0.663	19.9	0.494	19.8	0.342	33.4 [f]	53.2
97 Philippines	0.638	0.518	18.9	11	0.705	15.0	0.554	12.9	0.355	28.0 [g]	44.0
98 Botswana	0.633	..	..	..	0.417	25.9	..	..	..	..	61.0
99 Moldova, Republic of	0.623	0.539	13.5	16	0.673	13.1	0.635	7.5	0.367	19.4 [g]	37.4
100 Mongolia	0.622	0.527	15.2	16	0.579	22.6	0.635	5.8	0.399	16.4 [g]	36.6
101 Egypt	0.620	0.449	27.5	–7	0.641	19.8	0.304	43.6	0.465	15.9 [g]	32.1
102 Uzbekistan	0.617	0.521	15.7	17	0.565	25.9	0.672	1.4	0.372	17.9 [h]	36.7
103 Micronesia, Federated States of	0.614	0.375	39.0	–11	0.616	20.5	0.503	22.4	0.170	63.1 [f]	..
104 Guyana	0.611	0.497	18.6	7	0.567	25.2	0.588	9.6	0.369	20.3 [f]	43.2

TABLE 3

	Human Development Index (HDI)[a]	Inequality-adjusted HDI			Inequality-adjusted life expectancy at birth index[c]		Inequality-adjusted education index[d]		Inequality-adjusted income index[e]		Income Gini coefficient
HDI rank	Value	Value	Overall loss (%)	Change in rank[b]	Value	Loss (%)	Value	Loss (%)	Value	Loss (%)	
	2010	2010	2010	2010	2010	2010	2010	2010	2010	2010	2000–2010
105 Namibia	0.606	0.338	44.3	−15	0.503	24.5	0.429	27.8	0.178	68.3 [h]	74.3
106 Honduras	0.604	0.419	30.6	−4	0.669	19.7	0.379	31.0	0.291	39.7 [f]	55.3
107 Maldives	0.602	0.508	15.6	14	0.700	15.5	0.433	11.5	0.434	19.5 [g]	37.4
108 Indonesia	0.600	0.494	17.7	9	0.678	16.8	0.424	21.4	0.418	14.8 [g]	37.6
109 Kyrgyzstan	0.598	0.508	15.1	15	0.601	21.6	0.611	11.1	0.357	12.2 [g]	33.5
110 South Africa	0.597	0.411	31.2	−1	0.353	30.2	0.529	20.8	0.373	40.9 [h]	57.8
111 Syrian Arab Republic	0.589	0.467	20.8	4	0.769	11.1	0.312	31.5	0.424	18.3 [g]	
112 Tajikistan	0.580	0.469	19.1	6	0.517	31.0	0.608	9.4	0.328	15.3 [g]	33.6
113 Viet Nam	0.572	0.478	16.4	9	0.750	13.8	0.398	17.1	0.367	18.2 [g]	37.8
114 Morocco	0.567	0.407	28.1	2	0.671	18.3	0.246	42.7	0.409	20.7 [g]	40.9
115 Nicaragua	0.565	0.426	24.6	6	0.718	15.6	0.333	33.3	0.324	23.8 [g]	52.3
116 Guatemala	0.560	0.372	33.6	0	0.640	20.4	0.270	36.1	0.297	42.5 [f]	53.7
117 Equatorial Guinea	0.538	..	..	..	0.255	48.2	0.297	29.2	..	..	
118 Cape Verde	0.534	..	..	..	0.688	16.4	0.277	30.7	..	..	50.4
119 India	0.519	0.365	29.6	0	0.483	31.3	0.255	40.6	0.397	14.7 [g]	36.8
120 Timor-Leste	0.502	0.334	33.3	−4	0.438	34.3	0.197	44.3	0.433	19.2 [g]	31.9
121 Swaziland	0.498	0.320	35.7	−7	0.272	36.4	0.336	38.3	0.359	32.3 [g]	50.7
122 Lao People's Democratic Republic	0.497	0.374	24.8	5	0.526	27.6	0.287	30.5	0.345	15.5 [g]	32.6
123 Solomon Islands	0.494	..	..	..	0.557	25.2	0.284	30.2	..	..	..
124 Cambodia	0.494	0.351	28.8	3	0.445	33.4	0.331	31.1	0.295	21.4 [g]	44.2
125 Pakistan	0.490	0.336	31.5	1	0.501	32.9	0.196	46.4	0.385	10.6 [g]	31.2
126 Congo	0.489	0.334	31.8	0	0.312	41.9	0.330	30.0	0.360	22.0 [g]	47.3
127 São Tomé and Príncipe	0.488	..	..	..	0.479	34.4	0.324	22.7	..	..	50.6

LOW HUMAN DEVELOPMENT

128 Kenya	0.470	0.320	31.9	−1	0.354	37.2	0.369	29.2	0.252	28.8 [g]	47.7
129 Bangladesh	0.469	0.331	29.4	1	0.555	25.3	0.219	44.8	0.299	14.8 [g]	31.0
130 Ghana	0.467	0.349	25.4	7	0.354	39.7	0.487	7.5	0.246	25.4 [g]	42.8
131 Cameroon	0.460	0.304	33.9	−1	0.279	44.4	0.312	35.3	0.321	19.9 [g]	44.6
132 Myanmar	0.451	..	..	..	0.418	38.2	..	..	..	..	..
133 Yemen	0.439	0.289	34.2	−2	0.477	31.2	0.149	49.8	0.341	17.6 [g]	37.7
134 Benin	0.435	0.282	35.2	−5	0.404	39.7	0.202	44.1	0.276	19.2 [g]	38.6
135 Madagascar	0.435	0.308	29.2	3	0.415	36.4	0.320	30.8	0.220	19.3 [g]	47.2
136 Mauritania	0.433	0.281	35.1	−5	0.361	38.9	0.199	43.2	0.310	21.5 [g]	39.0
137 Papua New Guinea	0.431	..	..	..	0.470	28.5	..	..	..	..	50.9
138 Nepal	0.428	0.292	31.9	3	0.569	24.3	0.193	43.3	0.226	26.4 [g]	47.3
139 Togo	0.428	0.287	32.9	2	0.443	35.4	0.264	41.5	0.203	20.0 [g]	34.4
140 Comoros	0.428	0.240	43.9	−11	0.534	27.0	0.185	47.4	0.140	54.0 [h]	64.3
141 Lesotho	0.427	0.282	34.0	0	0.260	36.6	0.368	24.9	0.234	39.5 [h]	52.5
142 Nigeria	0.423	0.246	41.7	−6	0.220	51.1	0.228	46.0	0.298	25.1 [g]	42.9
143 Uganda	0.422	0.286	32.1	5	0.321	40.7	0.321	28.2	0.229	26.4 [g]	42.6
144 Senegal	0.411	0.262	36.2	0	0.359	37.4	0.172	47.3	0.293	21.1 [g]	39.2
145 Haiti	0.404	0.239	40.8	−7	0.443	32.9	0.219	40.7	0.141	47.9 [h]	59.5
146 Angola	0.403	0.242	39.9	−4	0.206	53.7	0.207	26.2	0.334	36.4 [g]	58.6
147 Djibouti	0.402	0.252	37.3	0	0.338	41.0	0.144	47.0	0.329	21.3 [g]	39.9
148 Tanzania, United Republic of	0.398	0.285	28.4	9	0.365	37.5	0.237	28.7	0.268	17.6 [g]	34.6
149 Côte d'Ivoire	0.397	0.254	36.1	3	0.361	40.5	0.160	44.8	0.281	20.5 [g]	48.4
150 Zambia	0.395	0.270	31.5	7	0.231	46.5	0.330	24.2	0.259	20.8 [g]	50.7
151 Gambia	0.390	0.238	39.0	−2	0.356	38.5	0.174	44.7	0.218	33.3 [g]	47.3
152 Rwanda	0.385	0.243	37.0	3	0.259	47.4	0.263	30.7	0.210	31.5 [g]	46.7
153 Malawi	0.385	0.261	32.1	8	0.327	40.3	0.256	34.7	0.213	19.7 [g]	39.0
154 Sudan	0.379	..	..	..	0.379	38.5	..	..	..	..	..
155 Afghanistan	0.349	..	..	..	0.161	58.8	0.199	39.3	..	..	..
156 Guinea	0.340	0.209	38.4	−1	0.341	44.5	0.135	42.6	0.199	26.8 [g]	43.3
157 Ethiopia	0.328	0.216	34.3	1	0.331	42.1	0.137	38.2	0.220	20.8 [g]	29.8
158 Sierra Leone	0.317	0.193	39.3	−1	0.248	44.5	0.150	48.2	0.192	22.2 [g]	42.5
159 Central African Republic	0.315	0.183	42.0	−3	0.220	49.8	0.163	45.9	0.170	28.1 [g]	43.6
160 Mali	0.309	0.191	38.3	0	0.231	50.1	0.133	36.9	0.227	25.4 [g]	39.0
161 Burkina Faso	0.305	0.195	36.2	3	0.296	44.5	0.108	37.3	0.231	25.3 [g]	39.6
162 Liberia	0.300	0.188	37.3	1	0.351	43.3	0.225	46.4	0.084	19.0 [g]	52.6

HDI rank	Human Development Index (HDI)[a] Value	Inequality-adjusted HDI			Inequality-adjusted life expectancy at birth index[c]		Inequality-adjusted education index[d]		Inequality-adjusted income index[e]		Income Gini coefficient
		Value	Overall loss (%)	Change in rank[b]	Value	Loss (%)	Value	Loss (%)	Value	Loss (%)	
	2010	2010	2010	2010	2010	2010	2010	2010	2010	2010	2000–2010
163 Chad	0.295	**0.179**	39.3	0	0.210	54.5	0.119	37.8	0.229	20.8 [g]	39.8
164 Guinea-Bissau	0.289	**0.166**	42.4	−2	0.215	52.5	0.172	40.3	0.124	32.5 [h]	35.5
165 Mozambique	0.284	**0.155**	45.3	−2	0.244	45.7	0.144	28.2	0.107	58.1 [g]	47.1
166 Burundi	0.282	**0.177**	37.0	2	0.259	47.8	0.206	36.3	0.104	24.9 [g]	33.3
167 Niger	0.261	**0.173**	33.9	2	0.274	46.8	0.109	31.3	0.173	21.1 [h]	43.9
168 Congo, Democratic Republic of the	0.239	**0.153**	36.2	0	0.209	52.9	0.244	29.1	0.070	22.1 [g]	44.4
169 Zimbabwe	0.140	**0.098**	29.9	0	0.281	34.2	0.416	20.1	0.008	34.5 [h]	50.1
Developed											
OECD	0.879	**0.789**	10.2	..	0.907	5.0	0.810	5.6	0.669	19.5	..
Non-OECD	0.844	**0.756**[j]	10.5	..	0.900[j]	5.3	0.790[j]	4.3	0.607[j]	21.8	..
Developing											
Arab States	0.588	**0.426**[j]	27.6	..	0.619[j]	21.6	0.289[j]	43.4	0.432[j]	17.7	..
East Asia and the Pacific	0.643	**0.505**[j]	21.5	..	0.699[j]	16.3	0.452[j]	21.2	0.407[j]	27.1	..
Europe and Central Asia	0.702	**0.607**	13.6	..	0.672	14.3	0.623	11.9	0.535	16.1	..
Latin America and the Caribbean	0.704	**0.527**	25.1	..	0.728	15.1	0.510	22.1	0.395	37.6	..
South Asia	0.516	**0.361**	30.2	..	0.499	30.4	0.246	41.3	0.383	14.5	..
Sub-Saharan Africa	0.389	**0.261**	32.8	..	0.294	43.8	0.254	34.1	0.238	26.0	..
Very high human development	0.878	**0.789**	10.2	..	0.907	5.0	0.810	5.7	0.668	19.5	..
High human development	0.717	**0.575**	19.8	..	0.718	13.8	0.561	17.6	0.472	28.1	..
Medium human development	0.592	**0.449**	24.3	..	0.611	22.4	0.369	29.3	0.401	21.9	..
Low human development	0.393	**0.267**	32.0	..	0.348	40.8	0.227	38.2	0.242	23.2	..
Least developed countries	0.386	**0.263**	31.9	..	0.375	39.0	0.209	38.0	0.232	22.3	..
World	0.624	**0.489**	21.7	..	0.630	21.3	0.436	28.2	0.425	22.7	..

NOTES

a See *Technical note 2* for details on how the Inequality-adjusted HDI (IHDI) is calculated.

b Change in rank is based on countries for which IHDI is calculated.

c Inequality adjustment is based on life tables produced by the United Nations Department of Economic and Social Affairs.

d Inequality adjustment is based on data from household surveys, including the Luxembourg Income Study, Eurostat's European Union Survey of Income and Living Conditions, the World Bank's International Income Distribution Database, the United Nations Children's Fund's (UNICEF) Multiple Indicator Cluster Survey, Measure DHS Demographic and Health Surveys and the World Health Organization's (WHO) World Health Survey.

e Inequality adjustment is based on data from household surveys, including the Luxembourg Income Study, Eurostat's European Union Survey of Income and Living Conditions, the World Bank's International Income Distribution Database, UNICEF's Multiple Indicators Cluster Survey, Measure DHS Demographic and Health Surveys and the United Nations University World Institute for Development Economics Research's (UNU-WIDER) World Income Inequality Database.

f Inequality is estimated from household disposable income per capita.

g Inequality is estimated from imputed income using the assets index matching methodology in Harttgen and Klasen (2010).

h Inequality is estimated from income deciles available from UNU-WIDER.

i Inequality is estimated from household consumption per capita.

j Based on less than half the countries.

SOURCES

Column 1: Calculated based on data from UNDESA (2009d), Barro and Lee (2010), UNESCO Institute for Statistics (2010a), World Bank (2010g) and IMF (2010a).

Column 2: Calculated as the geometric mean of the values in columns 5, 7 and 9 using the methodology in *Technical note 2*.

Columns 3, 6, 8 and 10: Calculated based on data from UN life tables, the Luxembourg Income Study, Eurostat's European Union Survey of Income and Living Conditions, the World Bank's International Income Distribution Database, UNICEF's Multiple Indicator Cluster Survey, Measure DHS Demographic and Health Surveys, the WHO's World Health Survey and UNU-WIDER's World Income Inequality Database using the methodology in *Technical note 2*.

Column 4: Calculated based on data in columns 1 and 2.

Column 5: Calculated based on data in column 6 and the unadjusted life expectancy index.

Column 7: Calculated based on data in column 10 and the unadjusted education index.

Column 9: Calculated based on data in column 9 and the unadjusted income index.

Column 11: World Bank (2010c).

TABLE 3

TABLE 4

Gender Inequality Index

HDI rank	Gender Inequality Index[a] Rank	Value	Maternal mortality ratio[b]	Adolescent fertility rate[c]	Seats in parliament (%) Female	Population with at least secondary education (% ages 25 and older) Female	Male	Labour force participation rate (%) Female	Male	Contraceptive prevalence rate, any method (% of married women ages 15–49)	Antenatal coverage of at least one visit (%)	Births attended by skilled health personnel (%)
	2008	2008	2003–2008[d]	1990–2008[d]	2008	2010	2010	2008	2008	1990–2008[d]	1990–2008[d]	2000–2008[d]
VERY HIGH HUMAN DEVELOPMENT												
1 Norway	5	0.234	7	8.6	36.1	99.3	99.1	77.3	82.6	88.4	..	..
2 Australia	18	0.296	4	14.9	29.7	95.1	97.2	69.9	83.0	70.8	..	99 [e]
3 New Zealand	25	0.320	9	22.6	33.6	71.6	73.5	72.1	84.5	..	..	94 [e]
4 United States	37	0.400	11	35.9	17.0 [f]	95.3	94.5	68.7	80.6	72.8	..	99
5 Ireland	29	0.344	1	15.9	15.5	82.3	81.5	62.8	80.7	89.0	..	100
6 Liechtenstein	..	..	..	..	24.0	..	..	..	..	..	..	..
7 Netherlands	1	0.174	6	3.8	39.1	86.3	89.2	73.4	85.4	67.0	..	100
8 Canada	16	0.289	7	12.8	24.9	92.3	92.7	74.3	82.7	74.0	..	100
9 Sweden	3	0.212	3	7.7	47.0	87.9	87.1	77.1	81.8	..	..	..
10 Germany	7	0.240	4	7.7	31.1	91.3	92.8	70.8	82.3	..	..	100 [g]
11 Japan	12	0.273	6	4.7	12.3	80.0	82.3	62.1	85.2	54.3	..	100
12 Korea, Republic of	20	0.310	14	5.5	13.7	79.4	91.7	54.5	75.6	80.2	..	100
13 Switzerland	4	0.228	5	5.5	27.2	62.9	74.5	76.6	87.8	..	..	100 [g]
14 France	11	0.260	8	6.9	19.6	79.6	84.6	65.8	74.9	71.0	..	..
15 Israel	28	0.332	4	14.3	14.2	78.9	77.2	61.1	70.1	..	..	..
16 Finland	8	0.248	7	11.4	41.5	70.1	70.1	73.9	77.7	..	..	100
17 Iceland	13	0.279	4	15.1	33.3	66.3	57.7	81.7	89.9	..	..	..
18 Belgium	6	0.236	8	7.7	36.2	75.7	79.8	60.9	73.5	74.6	..	..
19 Denmark	2	0.209	3	6.0	38.0	59.0	65.6	77.2	84.3	..	..	..
20 Spain	14	0.280	4	12.1	33.6	70.9	75.7	63.2	81.7	65.7	..	..
21 Hong Kong, China (SAR)	..	..	..	5.7	..	67.3	71.0	60.5	79.2	84.0	..	..
22 Greece	23	0.317	3	8.9	14.7	64.4	72.0	55.4	79.0	76.2	..	..
23 Italy	9	0.251	3	4.9	20.2	76.5	84.1	51.6	74.5	..	..	99 [e]
24 Luxembourg	24	0.318	12	12.3	23.3	66.4	73.9	58.1	73.9	..	..	100
25 Austria	19	0.300	4	12.8	26.6	67.3	85.9	68.3	81.0	..	..	..
26 United Kingdom	32	0.355	8	24.1	19.6	68.8	67.8	69.2	82.2	82.0	..	..
27 Singapore	10	0.255	14	4.5	24.5	57.3	64.8	60.6	81.8	..	..	100 [e]
28 Czech Republic	27	0.330	4	10.6	16.0	85.5	87.6	61.1	78.1	..	..	100
29 Slovenia	17	0.293	6	4.9	10.0	45.9	63.7	67.5	75.4	..	..	100
30 Andorra	..	..	..	..	25.0	50.8	50.9 [h]	..	..	..	..	..
31 Slovakia	31	0.352	6	20.7	19.3	80.8	87.1	61.3	76.5	..	..	100
32 United Arab Emirates	45	0.464	37	16.0	22.5	76.9	77.3	42.5	92.6	..	..	100
33 Malta	35	0.395	8	11.5	8.7	64.4	73.5	41.3	77.7	..	..	100 [g]
34 Estonia	39	0.409	25	21.4	20.8	94.4	94.6	70.2	78.6	..	..	100
35 Cyprus	15	0.284	10	6.1	14.3	64.0	75.2	64.5	78.5	..	..	100
36 Hungary	34	0.382	6	20.2	11.1	93.2	96.7	54.8	68.0	..	..	100
37 Brunei Darussalam	..	..	13	25.0	..	66.6	23.5	62.6	77.8	..	..	100
38 Qatar	94	0.671	12	15.9	0.0	62.1	54.7	49.3	93.1	..	..	100
39 Bahrain	55	0.512	32	16.7	13.8	57.0 [h]	74.7 [h]	33.5	86.5	..	..	99
40 Portugal	21	0.310	11	16.5	28.3	44.6	43.8	69.0	79.6	67.1	..	100
41 Poland	26	0.325	8	13.9	18.0	79.7	83.9	56.9	71.0	..	..	100
42 Barbados	42	0.448	16	42.7	13.7	89.5	87.6	76.5	84.9	..	100	100

HDI rank		Gender Inequality Index[a]		Maternal mortality ratio[b]	Adolescent fertility rate[c]	Seats in parliament (%)	Population with at least secondary education (% ages 25 and older)		Labour force participation rate (%)		Contraceptive prevalence rate, any method (% of married women ages 15–49)	Antenatal coverage of at least one visit (%)	Births attended by skilled health personnel (%)
		Rank	Value			Female	Female	Male	Female	Male			
		2008	2008	2003–2008[d]	1990–2008[d]	2008	2010	2010	2008	2008	1990–2008[d]	1990–2008[d]	2000–2008[d]

HIGH HUMAN DEVELOPMENT

43	Bahamas	..	..	16	53.0	25.0	..	..	74.3	82.8	..	98	99
44	Lithuania	33	0.359	11	21.9	17.7	91.9	95.7	65.5	71.6	..	..	100
45	Chile	53	0.505	16	59.6	12.7	67.3	69.8	48.1	78.9	64.2	..	100
46	Argentina	60	0.534	77	56.9	39.8	57.0	54.9	57.0	81.6	65.3	99	99
47	Kuwait	43	0.451	4	13.2	3.1[i]	52.2	43.9	45.6	84.5	..	..	100
48	Latvia	22	0.316	10	15.2	20.0	94.8	96.2	70.6	78.8	..	..	100
49	Montenegro	..	..	14	14.7	11.1	97.5[h]	98.8[h]	..	..	39.4	97	99[j]
50	Romania	49	0.478	24	31.2	9.8	83.8	90.5	55.3	70.7	70.0	94	99
51	Croatia	30	0.345	7	14.1	20.9	57.4	72.3	58.9	71.7	..	..	100
52	Uruguay	54	0.508	20	61.1	12.3	56.6	51.7	64.4	84.6	77.0	97	99
53	Libyan Arab Jamahiriya	52	0.504	97	3.2	7.7	55.6	44.0	25.1	81.1	..	..	100[j]
54	Panama	81	0.634	130	82.6	16.7	63.5	60.7	52.6	87.0	..	..	91
55	Saudi Arabia	128	0.760	18	26.1	0.0	50.3	57.9	21.8	81.8	23.8	..	96
56	Mexico	68	0.576	60	64.8	22.1	57.7	63.6	46.3	84.6	70.9	94	94
57	Malaysia	50	0.493	62	12.8	14.6	66.0	72.8	46.7	82.1	..	79	100
58	Bulgaria	36	0.399	11	42.2	21.7	69.1	70.6	63.4	73.8	..	..	99
59	Trinidad and Tobago	48	0.473	45	34.6	33.3	67.6	66.6	59.4	81.9	42.5	96	98
60	Serbia	..	..	14	22.1	21.6	61.7	70.7	..	..	41.2	98	99[j]
61	Belarus	..	..	18	21.3	32.5	..	..	68.1	74.1	72.6	99	100[j]
62	Costa Rica	51	0.501	30	67.0	36.8	54.4	52.8	48.8	84.2	..	90	94
63	Peru	74	0.614	240	54.7	29.2	64.1	78.6	61.3	77.6	71.3	91	73[j]
64	Albania	61	0.545	92	14.2	7.1	83.2	89.2	55.5	76.4	60.1	97	100
65	Russian Federation	41	0.442	28	25.1	11.5	90.6	71.3	68.7	76.3	..	..	100
66	Kazakhstan	67	0.575	140	30.7	12.3	92.2	95.1	73.9	80.4	50.7	100	100[j]
67	Azerbaijan	62	0.553	82	33.8	11.4	90.0[h]	96.0[h]	66.3	71.1	51.1	77	89[j]
68	Bosnia and Herzegovina	..	..	3	15.9	12.3	..	..	65.4	78.1	35.7	99	100[j]
69	Ukraine	44	0.463	18	28.3	8.2	91.5	96.1	62.3	72.6	66.7	99	99
70	Iran, Islamic Republic of	98	0.674	140	18.3	2.8	39.0	57.2	32.5	73.1	73.3	98	97
71	The former Yugoslav Republic of Macedonia	..	..	10	21.7	31.7	..	..	50.4	74.8	13.5	94	98[j]
72	Mauritius	46	0.466	15	39.3	17.1	45.2	52.9	46.3	80.3	75.8	..	99[e]
73	Brazil	80	0.631	110	75.6	9.4	48.8	46.3	64.0	85.2	..	98	97
74	Georgia	71	0.597	66	44.7	6.0	89.7[h]	92.7[h]	59.8	77.4	47.3	94	98
75	Venezuela, Bolivarian Republic of	64	0.561	57	89.9	18.6	33.4	29.6	54.0	82.7	..	94	95
76	Armenia	66	0.570	76	35.7	8.4	94.1	94.8	68.6	81.8	53.1	93	98
77	Ecuador	86	0.645	210	82.8	25.0	44.2	45.8	48.1	79.2	72.7	84	99[j]
78	Belize	73	0.600	52	78.7	11.1	35.2	32.8	49.0	83.7	34.3	94	96[j]
79	Colombia	90	0.658	130	74.3	9.7	49.5	48.5	43.3	79.8	78.2	94	96[j]
80	Jamaica	84	0.638	170	77.3	13.6	74.0	71.1	62.2	78.4	69.0	91	97[j]
81	Tunisia	56	0.515	100	6.9	19.9	33.5	48.0	27.7	74.2	60.2	96	90
82	Jordan	76	0.616	62	24.5	8.5	57.6	73.8	24.7	78.3	57.1	99	99
83	Turkey	77	0.621	44	38.8	9.1	27.1	46.8	26.9	74.6	71.0	92	83
84	Algeria	70	0.594	180	7.3	6.5	36.3	49.3	38.2	83.1	61.4	89	95
85	Tonga	..	..	..	22.8	3.1[k]	84.0	87.9	56.0	76.7	..	..	99

MEDIUM HUMAN DEVELOPMENT

86	Fiji	..	..	210	31.5	..	86.6	88.6	40.2	80.4	..	..	99
87	Turkmenistan	..	..	130	19.5	..	..	..	65.3	76.6	61.8	99	100
88	Dominican Republic	87	0.646	150	108.7	17.1	49.7	41.8	54.6	83.6	72.9	99	98
89	China	38	0.405	45	9.7	21.3	54.8	70.4	74.5	84.8	86.9	91	98
90	El Salvador	89	0.653	170	82.7	16.7	41.9	48.2	50.5	81.2	72.5	94	84[e]
91	Sri Lanka	72	0.599	58	29.8	5.8	56.0	57.6	38.5	80.3	68.0	99	99
92	Thailand	69	0.586	110	37.3	12.7	25.6	33.7	70.7	85.0	81.1	98	99
93	Gabon	99	0.678	520	89.9	16.1	53.8	34.7	71.1	82.9	32.7	94	86
94	Suriname	..	..	72	39.5	25.5	..	..	41.8	71.3	42.1	90	90[j]

TABLE
4

TABLE 4

HDI rank		Gender Inequality Index[a]		Maternal mortality ratio[b]	Adolescent fertility rate[c]	Seats in parliament (%)	Population with at least secondary education (% ages 25 and older)		Labour force participation rate (%)		Contraceptive prevalence rate, any method (% of married women ages 15–49)	Antenatal coverage of at least one visit (%)	Births attended by skilled health personnel (%)
		Rank	Value			Female	Female	Male	Female	Male			
		2008	2008	2003–2008[d]	1990–2008[d]	2008	2010	2010	2008	2008	1990–2008[d]	1990–2008[d]	2000–2008[d]
95	Bolivia, Plurinational State of	96	0.672	290	78.2	14.7	55.1	67.9	64.1	82.9	60.6	77	66
96	Paraguay	85	0.643	150	72.3	13.6	46.7	51.3	58.0	88.3	79.4	96	77
97	Philippines	78	0.623	230	45.0	20.2	65.9	63.7	50.2	80.6	50.6	91	62
98	Botswana	91	0.663	380	52.1	11.1	73.6	77.5	75.1	81.8	44.4	97	94[j]
99	Moldova, Republic of	40	0.429	22	33.8	21.8	85.8	92.3	53.4	55.6	67.8	98	100[j]
100	Mongolia	57	0.523	46	16.6	4.2	83.0	81.8	70.0	79.5	66.0	99	99
101	Egypt	108	0.714	130	39.0	3.7	43.4	61.1	24.4	76.4	60.3	74	79
102	Uzbekistan	..	..	24	12.9	16.4	..	..	61.7	73.7	64.9	99	100[j]
103	Micronesia, Federated States of	..	..	..	25.4	0.0	..	..	..	..	..	..	88
104	Guyana	92	0.667	470	62.7	30.0	42.6	43.7	49.2	85.4	34.2	81	83[j]
105	Namibia	75	0.615	210	74.4	26.9	49.6	46.1	53.5	63.6	55.1	95	81
106	Honduras	101	0.680	280	93.1	23.4	31.9	36.3	43.4	84.6	65.2	92	67[j]
107	Maldives	59	0.533	120	13.4	12.0	31.3	37.3	58.3	76.5	39.0	81	84
108	Indonesia	100	0.680	420	39.8	11.6	24.2	31.1	53.3	86.2	61.4	93	73[j]
109	Kyrgyzstan	63	0.560	150	32.3	25.6	81.0	81.2	60.9	83.8	47.8	97	98[j]
110	South Africa	82	0.635	400	59.2	33.9[i]	66.3	68.0	51.0	67.0	60.3	92	91
111	Syrian Arab Republic	103	0.687	130	61.1	12.4	24.7	24.1	22.0	82.1	58.3	84	93[j]
112	Tajikistan	65	0.568	170	28.4	19.6	93.2	85.8	59.1	79.8	37.9	89	83[j]
113	Viet Nam	58	0.530	150	16.6	25.8	24.7	28.0	74.2	80.6	79.0	91	88[j]
114	Morocco	104	0.693	240	18.9	6.2	20.1	36.4	28.7	83.6	63.0	68	63
115	Nicaragua	97	0.674	170	112.7	18.5	30.8	44.7	48.6	81.9	72.4	90	74
116	Guatemala	107	0.713	290	107.2	12.0	16.0	21.2	50.0	89.9	43.3	84	41
117	Equatorial Guinea	..	..	680	122.8	6.0	..	..	39.4	94.0	10.1	86	63[j]
118	Cape Verde	..	..	210	94.9	18.1	..	..	56.2	82.7	61.3	98	78[j]
119	India	122	0.748	450	68.1	9.2	26.6	50.4	35.7	84.5	56.3	74	47[j]
120	Timor-Leste	..	..	380	53.8	29.2	..	..	61.6	84.8	10.0	61	19
121	Swaziland	93	0.668	390	83.9	22.1	49.9	46.1	55.2	75.8	50.6	85	74[j]
122	Lao People's Democratic Republic	88	0.650	660	37.4	25.2	22.9	36.8	81.4	80.6	32.2	35	20[j]
123	Solomon Islands	..	..	220	41.8	0.0	..	..	24.6	50.4	..	74	43[e]
124	Cambodia	95	0.672	540	39.2	15.8	11.6	20.6	75.6	85.5	40.0	69	44
125	Pakistan	112	0.721	320	45.7	21.2	23.5	46.8	21.8	86.7	29.6	61	39
126	Congo	121	0.744	740	112.8	9.2	43.8	48.7	62.4	83.6	44.3	86	86[j]
127	São Tomé and Príncipe	..	..	..	66.1	7.3	..	..	46.9	78.5	29.3	98	81

LOW HUMAN DEVELOPMENT

HDI rank		Gender Inequality Index[a]		Maternal mortality ratio[b]	Adolescent fertility rate[c]	Seats in parliament (%)	Population with at least secondary education		Labour force participation rate (%)		Contraceptive prevalence rate, any method	Antenatal coverage of at least one visit (%)	Births attended by skilled health personnel (%)
128	Kenya	117	0.738	560	103.5	9.8	20.1	38.6	77.6	88.9	39.3	92	42
129	Bangladesh	116	0.734	570	71.6	6.3	30.8	39.3	61.4	85.5	55.8	51	18[j]
130	Ghana	114	0.729	560	64.0	7.9	33.9	83.1	75.2	75.6	23.5	90	57
131	Cameroon	129	0.763	1000	127.5	13.9	21.1	34.9	54.0	82.2	29.2	82	63
132	Myanmar	..	..	380	18.4	..	18.0	17.6	64.2	86.7	37.0	76	57
133	Yemen	138	0.853	430	68.1	0.7	7.6	24.4	20.1	74.3	27.7	47	36
134	Benin	127	0.759	840	111.8	10.8	11.3	25.9	68.1	79.0	17.0	84	78[j]
135	Madagascar	..	..	510	132.8	9.4	..	..	86.0	89.3	27.1	80	51[j]
136	Mauritania	118	0.738	820	90.0	19.9	8.0	20.8	60.4	82.2	9.3	75	61[j]
137	Papua New Guinea	133	0.784	470	55.0	0.9	12.4	24.4	72.1	74.2	..	79	39[e]
138	Nepal	110	0.716	830	101.4	33.2	17.9	39.9	65.9	81.9	48.0	44	19
139	Togo	115	0.731	510	64.8	11.1	15.3	45.1	64.6	86.4	16.8	84	62[j]
140	Comoros	..	..	400	45.7	3.0	..	..	74.6	85.9	25.7	75	62[j]
141	Lesotho	102	0.685	960	73.5	25.8	24.3	20.3	71.9	78.7	37.3	90	55[j]
142	Nigeria	..	..	1100	126.6	7.3	..	..	39.5	74.8	14.7	58	39[j]
143	Uganda	109	0.715	550	150.0	30.7	9.1	20.8	80.5	91.2	23.7	94	42
144	Senegal	113	0.727	980	104.4	29.2	10.9	19.4	65.3	89.9	11.8	87	52[j]
145	Haiti	119	0.739	670	46.4	5.2	22.5	36.3	58.4	83.0	32.0	85	26[j]
146	Angola	..	..	1400	123.7	37.3	..	..	76.3	89.2	6.2	80	47[j]
147	Djibouti	..	..	650	23.0	13.9	..	..	63.2	80.3	17.8	92	93[j]
148	Tanzania, United Republic of	..	..	950	130.4	30.4	..	..	88.8	91.1	26.4	76	46[j]

HDI rank	Gender Inequality Index[a] Rank	Gender Inequality Index[a] Value	Maternal mortality ratio[b]	Adolescent fertility rate[c]	Seats in parliament (%) Female	Population with at least secondary education (% ages 25 and older) Female	Population with at least secondary education (% ages 25 and older) Male	Labour force participation rate (%) Female	Labour force participation rate (%) Male	Contraceptive prevalence rate, any method (% of married women ages 15–49)	Antenatal coverage of at least one visit (%)	Births attended by skilled health personnel (%)
	2008	2008	2003–2008[d]	1990–2008[d]	2008	2010	2010	2008	2008	1990–2008[d]	1990–2008[d]	2000–2008[d]
149 Côte d'Ivoire	130	0.765	810	129.9	8.9	13.6	25.2	51.3	82.4	12.9	85	57
150 Zambia	124	0.752	830	141.8	15.2	25.7	44.2	60.4	78.7	40.8	94	47[j]
151 Gambia	120	0.742	690	88.1	9.4	16.5	31.6	71.2	85.1	17.5	98	57[j]
152 Rwanda	83	0.638	1300	36.7	50.9	7.4	8.0	87.9	85.9	36.4	96	52[j]
153 Malawi	126	0.758	1100	135.2	13.0	10.4	20.4	74.6	77.7	41.0	92	54
154 Sudan	106	0.708	450	56.8	16.8	12.8	18.2	32.3	74.0	7.6	64	49[j]
155 Afghanistan	134	0.797	1800	121.3	25.9	5.8	34.0	33.3	85.5	18.6	16	14
156 Guinea	..	..	910	152.3	..[m]	..	..	82.3	90.0	9.1	88	38[j]
157 Ethiopia	..	..	720	104.4	21.4	..	..	80.8	91.1	14.7	28	6
158 Sierra Leone	125	0.756	2100	126.0	13.2	9.5	20.4	67.1	68.1	8.2	87	42[j]
159 Central African Republic	132	0.768	980	106.6	10.5	10.3	26.2	71.6	86.9	19.0	69	54[j]
160 Mali	135	0.799	970	162.9	10.2	3.2	8.4	38.1	68.9	8.2	70	49[j]
161 Burkina Faso	..	..	700	130.9	15.3	..	..	79.7	91.5	17.4	85	54
162 Liberia	131	0.766	1200	141.6	13.8	15.7	39.2	69.1	76.8	11.4	79	46
163 Chad	..	..	1500	164.4	5.2	..	..	64.0	78.3	2.8	39	14
164 Guinea-Bissau	..	..	1100	129.2	10.0	..	..	61.2	85.4	10.3	78	39[j]
165 Mozambique	111	0.718	520	149.2	34.8	1.5	6.0	85.7	86.6	16.5	89	48[j]
166 Burundi	79	0.627	1100	18.6	31.7	5.2	9.2	91.5	88.3	19.7	92	34
167 Niger	136	0.807	1800	157.4	12.4	2.5	7.6	37.9	88.1	11.2	46	18
168 Congo, Democratic Republic of the	137	0.814	1100	201.4	7.7	10.7	36.2	57.4	86.8	20.6	85	74[j]
169 Zimbabwe	105	0.705	880	64.6	18.2	48.8	62.0	60.8	74.5	60.2	94	69

OTHER COUNTRIES OR TERRITORIES

Antigua and Barbuda	..	..	..	..	16.7	..	..	..	..	..	100	100
Bhutan	..	..	440	38.3	13.9	..	..	54.1	71.9	30.7	88	51
Cuba	47	0.473	45	45.2	43.2	73.9	80.4	48.6	77.0	72.6	100	100
Dominica	..	..	..	..	18.8	29.7[h]	23.2[h]	..	..	..	100	94
Eritrea	..	..	450	66.9	22.0	..	..	61.6	84.4	8.0	70	28[j]
Grenada	..	..	..	42.4	21.4	..	..	..	..	..	100	99
Iraq	123	0.751	300	85.5	25.5	22.0	42.7	14.2	71.5	49.8	84	89
Kiribati	..	..	..	..	4.4	..	..	..	..	36.1	..	90
Korea, Democratic People's Rep. of	..	..	370	0.0	20.1	..	..	60.7	80.7	68.6	..	97
Lebanon	..	..	150	16.2	4.7	..	..	24.1	74.8	58.0	96	98
Marshall Islands	..	..	..	..	3.0	..	..	..	..	..	81	95
Monaco	..	..	..	..	25.0	..	..	..	..	..	..	..
Nauru	..	..	..	..	0.0	..	..	..	..	35.6	95	97
Occupied Palestinian Territories	..	..	..	78.7	..	..	..	16.7	72.4	50.2	..	..
Oman	..	..	64	10.4	9.1	..	..	26.1	79.1	..	100	98
Palau	..	..	..	..	6.9	..	..	..	..	32.8	..	100
Saint Kitts and Nevis	..	..	..	..	6.7	..	..	..	..	..	100	100
Saint Lucia	..	..	..	61.6	17.2	..	..	55.3	80.4	..	99	98
Saint Vincent and the Grenadines	..	..	..	58.9	18.2	..	..	61.4	84.1	..	95	100
Samoa	..	..	..	27.6	8.2	..	..	41.8	79.5	..	..	100
San Marino	..	..	..	..	15.0	..	..	..	..	..	..	..
Seychelles	..	..	..	..	23.5	66.9[h]	66.6[h]	..	..	..	..	..
Somalia	..	..	1400	70.1	8.2	..	..	58.0	86.0	14.6	26	33[j]
Tuvalu	..	..	..	..	0.0	..	..	..	..	..	97	100
Vanuatu	..	..	..	47.0	3.9	..	..	79.7	88.6	..	84	93

TABLE
4

Gender Inequality Index

TABLE 4

HDI rank	Gender Inequality Index[a] Rank	Gender Inequality Index[a] Value	Maternal mortality ratio[b]	Adolescent fertility rate[c]	Seats in parliament (%) Female	Population with at least secondary education (% ages 25 and older) Female	Population with at least secondary education (% ages 25 and older) Male	Labour force participation rate (%) Female	Labour force participation rate (%) Male	Contraceptive prevalence rate, any method (% of married women ages 15–49)	Antenatal coverage of at least one visit (%)	Births attended by skilled health personnel (%)
	2008	2008	2003–2008[d]	1990–2008[d]	2008	2010	2010	2008	2008	1990–2008[d]	1990–2008[d]	2000–2008[d]
Developed												
OECD	—	0.317	8	19.4	20.6	84.0	86.6	65.5	80.1	..	..	99
Non-OECD	—	0.376	16	11.2	18.1	70.4	72.1	58.2	82.3	..	100	100
Developing												
Arab States	—	0.699	238	42.6	8.7	31.8	45.0	27.0	78.2	46.9	74	77
East Asia and the Pacific	—	0.467	126	18.1	19.8	48.2	61.4	70.1	84.5	..	91	91
Europe and Central Asia	—	0.498	41	28.2	12.5	78.0	74.0	58.6	75.0	63.0	95	96
Latin America and the Caribbean	—	0.609	122	72.6	17.5	51.3	52.7	55.3	83.3	..	95	91
South Asia	—	0.739	454	65.0	10.4	27.4	49.1	37.2	84.2	53.8	70	45
Sub-Saharan Africa	—	0.735	881	122.3	17.3	23.9	38.1	63.8	82.3	23.6	73	48
Very high human development	—	0.319	8	19.1	20.5	83.7	86.1	65.3	80.2	..	100	99
High human development	—	0.571	82	47.7	13.3	61.2	61.3	52.7	79.5	66.3	95	96
Medium human development	—	0.591	242	41.8	16.0	40.9	57.4	54.7	84.1	68.4	84	74
Low human development	—	0.748	822	108.9	14.4	19.0	32.0	61.3	83.4	27.8	66	39
Least developed countries	—	0.746	786	104.5	16.6	17.8	29.1	64.7	85.2	29.5	63	36
World	—	0.560	273	53.7	16.2	51.6	61.7	56.8	82.6	..	82	75

NOTES

a See *Technical note 3* for details on how the Gender Inequality Index is calculated.
b Defined as maternal deaths per 100,000 live births.
c Defined as the number of births per 1,000 women ages 15–19.
d Data refer to the most recent year available during the period specified.
e Institutional births.
f The denominator of the calculation refers to voting members of the House of Representatives only.
g World Health Organization estimate.
h United Nations Educational, Scientific and Cultural Organization Institute for Statistics estimate.

i No women were elected in the 2008 elections; however, two women were appointed to the cabinet in June 2008, and cabinet ministers also sit in parliament.
j Includes deliveries by cadres of health workers other than doctors, nurses and midwives.
k No women were elected in 2008; however, one woman was appointed to the cabinet, and cabinet ministers also sit in parliament.
l Does not include the 36 special rotating delegates appointed on an ad hoc basis; all percentages are calculated based on the 54 permanent seats.
m The parliament was dissolved following the December 2008 coup.

SOURCES

Columns 1 and 2: Calculated based on data from UNICEF (2010c), UNDESA (2009d), IPU (2010), Barro and Lee (2010) and ILO (2010d).
Columns 3 and 11: UNICEF (2010c).
Column 4: UNDESA (2009d).
Column 5: IPU (2010).
Columns 6 and 7: Barro and Lee (2010).
Columns 8 and 9: ILO (2010d).
Column 10: UN (2009).
Column 12: WHO (2010).

TABLE **5**

Multidimensional Poverty Index

HDI rank	Multidimensional Poverty Index[a,b] 2000–2008[e]	POPULATION IN MULTIDIMENSIONAL POVERTY		Population at risk of multidimensional poverty[b,c] (%) 2000–2008[e]	POPULATION WITH AT LEAST ONE SEVERE DEPRIVATION IN			POPULATION BELOW INCOME POVERTY LINE	
		Headcount[b] (%) 2000–2008[e]	Intensity of deprivation[b] (%) 2000–2008[e]		Education[d] (%) 2000–2008[e]	Health[d] (%) 2000–2008[e]	Living standards[d] (%) 2000–2008[e]	PPP $1.25 a day (%) 2000–2008[e]	National poverty line (%) 2000–2008[e]
VERY HIGH HUMAN DEVELOPMENT									
28 Czech Republic	**0.000**	0.0	46.7	3.1	0.0	3.1	0.0	..	..
29 Slovenia	..	0.0	0.0	0.4	0.0	3.1	0.0	<2	..
31 Slovakia	**0.000**	0.0	0.0	0.0	0.0	3.8	0.0	..	16.8
32 United Arab Emirates	**0.002**	0.6	35.3	2.0	0.6	5.4	0.0	..	..
34 Estonia	**0.026**	7.2	36.5	1.3	7.3	5.1	0.1	<2	..
36 Hungary	**0.003**	0.8	38.9	3.8	0.1	4.5	0.0	<2	..
41 Poland	..	..	..	..	..	..	..	<2	14.8
HIGH HUMAN DEVELOPMENT									
44 Lithuania	..	..	..	..	..	..	..	<2	..
45 Chile	..	..	..	..	..	..	..	<2	..
46 Argentina	**0.011**[f]	3.0[f]	37.7[f]	5.7[f]	15.4[f]	3.8[f]	4.7[f]	3.4	..
48 Latvia	**0.001**	0.3	46.7	1.3	0.1	1.6	1.1	<2	5.9
49 Montenegro	**0.006**	1.5	41.6	1.9	4.2	0.8	0.7	<2	..
50 Romania	..	..	..	2.8	..	..	..	<2	28.9
51 Croatia	**0.007**	1.6	41.6	..	2.3	2.4	0.4	<2	11.1
52 Uruguay	**0.006**	1.7	34.7	0.1	1.7	5.1	0.0	<2	..
54 Panama	..	..	..	..	..	..	..	9.5	36.8
56 Mexico	**0.015**	4.0	38.9	5.8	10.1	9.2	6.7	4.0	47.0
57 Malaysia	..	..	..	..	..	..	..	<2	..
58 Bulgaria	..	..	..	..	..	..	..	<2	12.8
59 Trinidad and Tobago	**0.020**	5.6	35.1	0.4	1.5	5.6	0.8	..	..
60 Serbia	**0.003**	0.8	40.0	3.6	5.2	0.4	0.8	<2	..
61 Belarus	**0.000**	0.0	35.1	0.8	2.0	3.1	0.1	<2	17.4
62 Costa Rica	..	..	..	..	..	..	..	<2	23.9
63 Peru	**0.085**	19.8	43.1	17.1	8.5	14.6	38.2	7.7	51.6
64 Albania	**0.004**	1.0	38.1	9.4	6.6	7.2	0.9	<2	18.5
65 Russian Federation	**0.005**	1.3	38.9	0.8	1.6	3.5	0.4	<2	19.6
66 Kazakhstan	**0.002**	0.6	36.9	5.0	1.3	9.8	1.1	<2	15.4
67 Azerbaijan	**0.021**	5.4	38.6	12.4	10.2	20.3	4.2	<2	49.6
68 Bosnia and Herzegovina	**0.003**	0.8	37.2	7.0	11.1	0.4	0.8	<2	19.5
69 Ukraine	**0.008**	2.2	35.7	1.2	6.2	2.1	0.2	<2	19.5
70 Iran, Islamic Republic of	..	..	..	..	..	..	..	<2	..
71 The former Yugoslav Republic of Macedonia	**0.008**	1.9	40.9	6.7	5.9	7.2	0.9	<2	21.7
73 Brazil	**0.039**	8.5	46.0	13.1	20.2	5.2	2.8	5.2	21.5
74 Georgia	**0.003**	0.8	35.2	5.3	2.4	5.9	4.6	13.4	54.5
75 Venezuela, Bolivarian Republic of	..	..	..	..	..	..	..	3.5	..
76 Armenia	**0.008**	2.3	36.5	5.5	9.5	14.6	0.8	3.7	50.9
77 Ecuador	**0.009**	2.2	41.6	2.1	2.3	4.6	3.9	4.7	38.3
78 Belize	**0.024**	5.6	42.6	7.6	8.5	13.3	7.0	..	..
79 Colombia	**0.041**	9.2	44.1	8.3	13.2	17.5	9.7	16.0	45.1
80 Jamaica	..	..	..	..	..	..	..	<2	18.7
81 Tunisia	**0.010**	2.8	37.1	4.9	1.1	13.1	6.9	2.6	..
82 Jordan	**0.010**	2.7	35.5	1.6	10.6	11.9	0.2	<2	14.2
83 Turkey	**0.039**	8.5	45.9	19.0	15.4	16.0	7.3	2.6	27.0

Multidimensional Poverty Index

HDI rank		Multidimensional Poverty Index[a,b]	POPULATION IN MULTIDIMENSIONAL POVERTY		Population at risk of multidimensional poverty[b,c]	POPULATION WITH AT LEAST ONE SEVERE DEPRIVATION IN			POPULATION BELOW INCOME POVERTY LINE	
			Headcount[b] (%)	Intensity of deprivation[b] (%)	(%)	Education[d] (%)	Health[d] (%)	Living standards[d] (%)	PPP $1.25 a day (%)	National poverty line (%)
		2000–2008[e]	2000–2008[e]	2000–2008[e]	2000–2008[e]	2000–2008[e]	2000–2008[e]	2000–2008[e]	2000–2008[e]	2000–2008[e]
MEDIUM HUMAN DEVELOPMENT										
88	Dominican Republic	0.048	11.1	43.3	13.2	17.5	13.1	13.2	4.4	48.5
89	China	0.056	12.5	44.9	6.3	10.9	11.3	12.4	15.9	2.8
90	El Salvador	..	..	..	..	..	..	..	6.4	30.7
91	Sri Lanka	0.021	5.3	38.7	14.4	0.5	9.8	26.4	14	22.7
92	Thailand	0.006	1.7	38.5	9.9	12.6	5.6	1.5	<2	..
93	Gabon	0.161	35.4	45.5	22.4	19.2	35.4	34.8	4.8	..
94	Suriname	0.044	7.5	58.8	5.2	18.8	15.9	2.3	..	..
95	Bolivia, Plurinational State of	0.175	36.3	48.3	21.6	37.8	31.4	38.0	11.7	37.7
96	Paraguay	0.064	13.3	48.5	15.0	7.5	13.1	32.4	6.5	..
97	Philippines	0.067	12.6	53.5	11.1	13.6	14.2	18.2	22.6	..
99	Moldova, Republic of	0.008	2.2	37.6	7.2	5.1	10.1	5.3	2.4	48.5
100	Mongolia	0.065	15.8	41.0	20.7	6.8	19.0	39.6	2.2	36.1
101	Egypt	0.026	6.4	40.4	6.9	18.0	16.9	0.9	<2	16.7
102	Uzbekistan	0.008	2.3	36.2	8.1	4.4	17.4	2.3	46.3	27.2
104	Guyana	0.055	13.8	39.7	6.5	4.7	12.4	10.8	..	..
105	Namibia	0.187	39.6	47.2	23.5	16.0	37.2	60.8	..	..
106	Honduras	0.160	32.6	48.9	17.8	46.6	21.1	30.8	18.2	50.7
108	Indonesia	0.095	20.8	45.9	12.2	12.6	14.4	31.2	29.4	16.7
109	Kyrgyzstan	0.019	4.9	38.8	9.2	18.7	2.1	8.3	3.4	43.1
110	South Africa	0.014	3.1	46.7	3.9	3.2	8.1	10.8	26.2	22.0
111	Syrian Arab Republic	0.021	5.5	37.5	7.1	20.4	13.6	1.3	..	..
112	Tajikistan	0.068	17.1	40.0	23.1	14.3	35.6	21.9	21.5	53.5
113	Viet Nam	0.075	14.3	52.5	12.0	12.3	10.8	30.1	21.5	28.9
114	Morocco	0.139	28.5	48.8	11.4	36.3	31.5	21.4	2.5	..
115	Nicaragua	0.211	40.7	51.9	15.7	36.4	25.9	54.1	15.8	45.8
116	Guatemala	0.127	25.9	49.1	9.8	26.8	15.0	40.5	11.7	51.0
118	Cape Verde	..	..	..	..	..	..	..	20.6	..
119	India	0.296	55.4	53.5	16.1	37.5	56.5	58.5	41.6	28.6
120	Timor-Leste	..	..	..	..	..	..	..	37.2	39.7
121	Swaziland	0.183	41.1	44.4	24.5	25.9	33.5	66.3	62.9	69.2
122	Lao People's Democratic Republic	0.267	47.3	56.5	14.1	43.9	22.3	59.7	44.0	33.5
124	Cambodia	0.263	53.9	48.9	20.2	40.9	36.0	78.4	25.8	30.1
125	Pakistan	0.275[g]	51.0[g]	54.0[g]	11.8[g]	51.2	29.2[g]	42.9	22.6	..
126	Congo	0.270	55.9	48.4	22.5	21.7	47.6	73.8	54.1	42.3
127	São Tomé and Príncipe	0.236	51.6	45.8	23.9	36.7	26.6	74.3	28.4	..
LOW HUMAN DEVELOPMENT										
128	Kenya	0.302	60.4	50.0	23.2	21.9	41.4	86.2	19.7	46.6
129	Bangladesh	0.291	57.8	50.4	21.2	31.4	53.1	76.3	49.6	40.0
130	Ghana	0.140	30.1	46.4	21.4	24.1	17.9	57.5	30	28.5
131	Cameroon	0.299	54.6	54.7	18.3	37.4	42.6	67.9	32.8	39.9
132	Myanmar	0.088	14.2	62.0	17.6	32.7	11.7	22.8	..	32.0
133	Yemen	0.283	52.5	53.9	13.0	54.5	34.4	38.2	17.5	..
134	Benin	0.412	72.0	57.3	13.2	62.8	51.7	79.1	47.3	39.0
135	Madagascar	0.413	70.5	58.5	14.8	55.4	49.6	83.7	67.8	68.7
136	Mauritania	0.352	61.7	57.1	15.1	55.3	44.1	66.8	21.2	46.3
138	Nepal	0.350	64.7	54.1	15.6	38.0	58.3	77.2	55.1	30.9
139	Togo	0.284	54.3	52.4	21.6	39.9	38.0	75.5	38.7	..
140	Comoros	0.408	73.9	55.3	16.0	60.1	45.7	90.3	46.1	..
141	Lesotho	0.220	48.1	45.8	27.5	29.7	22.1	82.4	43.4	56.3
142	Nigeria	0.368	63.5	57.9	15.7	42.4	59.5	72.1	64.4	..
143	Uganda	..	..	..	..	..	..	..	51.5	31.1
144	Senegal	0.384	66.9	57.4	11.6	66.9	54.3	54.9	33.5	..
145	Haiti	0.306	57.3	53.3	18.4	41.0	37.3	76.0	54.9	..
146	Angola	0.452	77.4	58.4	10.7	56.9	60.8	82.0	54.3	..
147	Djibouti	0.139	29.3	47.3	16.1	39.3	25.6	28.1	18.4	..

TABLE 5

HDI rank	Multidimensional Poverty Index[a,b]	POPULATION IN MULTIDIMENSIONAL POVERTY		Population at risk of multidimensional poverty[b,c]	POPULATION WITH AT LEAST ONE SEVERE DEPRIVATION IN			POPULATION BELOW INCOME POVERTY LINE	
		Headcount[b]	Intensity of deprivation[b]		Education[d]	Health[d]	Living standards[d]	PPP $1.25 a day	National poverty line
		(%)	(%)	(%)	(%)	(%)	(%)	(%)	(%)
	2000–2008[e]	2000–2008[e]	2000–2008[e]	2000–2008[e]	2000–2008[e]	2000–2008[e]	2000–2008[e]	2000–2008[e]	2000–2008[e]
148 Tanzania, United Republic of	0.367	65.3	56.3	23.0	34.0	35.5	90.6	88.5	35.7
149 Côte d'Ivoire	0.320	52.2	61.4	16.4	62.7	40.6	37.7	23.3	..
150 Zambia	0.325	63.7	51.1	17.8	30.1	51.3	78.3	64.3	68.0
151 Gambia	0.324	60.4	53.6	17.6	53.4	52.1	60.1	34.3	61.3
152 Rwanda	0.443	81.4	54.4	14.0	53.6	46.1	95.3	76.6	56.9
153 Malawi	0.384	72.3	53.2	19.8	43.6	45.2	93.9	73.9	52.4
155 Afghanistan	..	..	..	..	..	..	..		42.0
156 Guinea	0.505	82.4	61.3	9.4	74.8	60.8	84.4	70.1	..
157 Ethiopia	0.582	90.0	64.7	5.2	83.9	48.2	94.2	39	44.2
158 Sierra Leone	0.489	81.5	60.0	11.1	60.6	58.2	92.4	53.4	70.2
159 Central African Republic	0.512	86.4	59.3	7.6	72.7	56.2	92.3	62.4	..
160 Mali	0.564	87.1	64.7	7.3	81.1	65.8	86.8	51.4	..
161 Burkina Faso	0.536	82.6	64.9	8.6	80.4	62.9	81.6	56.5	46.4
162 Liberia	0.484	83.9	57.7	9.5	68.9	59.6	91.6	83.7	..
163 Chad	0.344	62.9	54.7	28.2	39.4	8.2	95.2	61.9	..
164 Guinea-Bissau	..	..	..	..	..	..	..	48.8	65.7
165 Mozambique	0.481	79.8	60.3	9.8	69.1	52.7	86.4	74.7	55.2
166 Burundi	0.530	84.5	62.7	12.2	71.6	35.5	97.3	81.3	..
167 Niger	0.642	92.7	69.3	4.0	87.1	64.9	93.0	65.9	..
168 Congo, Democratic Republic of the	0.393	73.2	53.7	16.1	48.4	48.2	85.5	59.2	71.3
169 Zimbabwe	0.174	38.5	45.2	24.6	15.1	29.6	64.5	..	..

OTHER COUNTRIES OR TERRITORIES

Bhutan	..	..	..	..	..	..	..	26.3	..
Iraq	0.059	14.3	41.3	14.3	32.0	20.0	5.2	..	..
Occupied Palestinian Territories	0.003	0.7	38.2	12.7	14.6	2.8	0.8	..	..
Seychelles	..	..	..	..	..	..	..	<2	..
Somalia	0.514	81.2	63.3	9.5	74.5	47.6	86.7	..	..

NOTES

a   See *Technical note 4* for details on how the Multidimensional Poverty Index is calculated.

b   Not all indicators were available for all countries; caution should thus be used in cross-country comparisons. Where data are missing, indicator weights are adjusted to total 100 percent. For details on countries missing data, see Alkire and Santos (2010).

c   People at risk of suffering multiple deprivations—that is, those suffering from overlapping deprivations in 2 of 10 indicators.

d   Percentage of the population suffering a deprivation in at least 1.5 of the weighted indicators in health, education or living standards. For details see Alkire and Santos (2010).

e   Data refer to the most recent year available during the period specified.

f   Estimates are for parts of the country only.

g   Estimates should be interpreted as a lower bound because data on nutrition were not available from the dataset used.

SOURCES

Columns 1, 2 and 4–7: Calculated based on data on household deprivation in health, education and living standards from various household surveys.

Column 3: Based on various household surveys (Measure DHS Demographic and Health Surveys, United Nations Children's Fund Multiple Indicator Cluster Surveys and World Health Organization World Health Surveys) conducted between 2000 and 2008.

Columns 8 and 9: World Bank (2010c).

TABLE 5

TABLE 6

Empowerment

		AGENCY		POLITICAL FREEDOM	CIVIL LIBERTIES			ACCOUNTABILITY		
		Satisfaction with freedom of choice (% satisfied)		Democracy	Human rights violations	Press freedom	Journalists imprisoned	Corruption victims (% of people who faced a bribe situation in the last year)	Democratic decentralization	Political engagement (% of people who voiced opinion to public officials)
HDI rank		Total	Female	Score (0–2)[a]	Score (1–5)[b]	(index)[c]	(number)[d]		Score (0–2)[e]	
		2009	2009	2008	2008	2009	2009	2008	2008	2008
VERY HIGH HUMAN DEVELOPMENT										
1	Norway	93	93	2	..	0.0	0	5	2	31
2	Australia	91	90	2	1	3.1	0	8	1	23
3	New Zealand	89	90	2	1	3.0	0	9	2	23
4	United States	83	85	2	3	4.0	0	9	2	32
5	Ireland	82	83	2	1	0.0	0	7	2	26
6	Liechtenstein	..	..	2	..	..	0	..	..	..
7	Netherlands	87	88	2	1	1.0	0	4	1	30
8	Canada	91	92	2	2	3.7	0	8	2	20
9	Sweden	90	81	2	1	0.0	0	6	2	29
10	Germany	85	86	2	1	3.5	0	4	2	35
11	Japan	70	75	2	1	3.3	0	3	2	22
12	Korea, Republic of	55	56	2	2	15.7	0	10	1	22
13	Switzerland	90	87	2	2	1.0	0	..	2	36
14	France	79	78	2	2	10.7	0	6	2	23
15	Israel	64	58	2	3[f]	23.8	0	11	..	18
16	Finland	92	93	2	1	0.0	0	9	1	19
17	Iceland	86	87	2	..	2.0	0	5	2	25
18	Belgium	86	85	2	2	2.5	0	6	..	23
19	Denmark	96	93	2	2	0.0	0	5	2	37
20	Spain	70	70	2	3	11.0	0	6	2	17
21	Hong Kong, China (SAR)	90	90	..	..	11.8	0	3	..	5
22	Greece	43	39	2	3	9.0	0	15	2	16
23	Italy	63	60	2	2	12.1	0	6	2	14
24	Luxembourg	93	90	2	..	4.0	0	4	..	36
25	Austria	85	86	2	1	3.0	0	5	..	36
26	United Kingdom	81	82	2	2	4.0	0	4	2	24
27	Singapore	73	73	1	1	45.0	0	1	0	12
28	Czech Republic	73	71	2	1	5.0	0	..	..	27
29	Slovenia	89	88	2	1	9.5	0	9	..	36
30	Andorra	..	..	2	..	..	0	..	..	..
31	Slovakia	49	51	2	1	11.0	0	..	2	14
32	United Arab Emirates	83	85	0	2	21.5	0	20	0	16
33	Malta	76	73	2	2	2.5	0	5	1	21
34	Estonia	53	53	2	2	0.5	0	9	..	16
35	Cyprus	74	73	2	1	5.5	0	18	2	16
36	Hungary	43	44	2	1	5.5	0	34	2	15
37	Brunei Darussalam	..	..	..	..	..	0	..	..	..
38	Qatar	77	72	0	2	24.0	0	8	1	24
39	Bahrain	..	89	0	2	36.5	0	20	1	..
40	Portugal	60	67	2	2	8.0	0	6	2	23
41	Poland	74	68	2	1	9.5	0	8	2	5
42	Barbados	..	..	2	..	..	0	..	..	..

		AGENCY		POLITICAL FREEDOM	CIVIL LIBERTIES			ACCOUNTABILITY		
		Satisfaction with freedom of choice (% satisfied)		Democracy	Human rights violations	Press freedom	Journalists imprisoned	Corruption victims	Democratic decentralization	Political engagement
								(% of people who faced a bribe situation in the last year)		(% of people who voiced opinion to public officials)
HDI rank		Total	Female	Score (0–2)[a]	Score (1–5)[b]	(index)[c]	(number)[d]		Score (0–2)[e]	
		2009	2009	2008	2008	2009	2009	2008	2008	2008

HIGH HUMAN DEVELOPMENT

43	Bahamas	..	..	2	2	..	0	..	..	..
44	Lithuania	45	47	2	1	2.3	0	21	2	11
45	Chile	72	74	2	2	10.5	0	8	1	26
46	Argentina	62	59	2	2	11.3	0	8	..	11
47	Kuwait	80	78	0	1	15.3	0	19	1	24
48	Latvia	39	41	2	2	3.0	0	22	..	17
49	Montenegro	47	50	1	2	17.0	0	..	..	13
50	Romania	54	52	2	3	12.5	0	36	2	9
51	Croatia	62	48	2	1	17.2	0	..	..	19
52	Uruguay	80	80	2	1	7.6	0	5	..	19
53	Libyan Arab Jamahiriya	..	..	0	3	64.5	0	..	2	..
54	Panama	68	64	2	..	14.5	0	6	1	30
55	Saudi Arabia	60	52	0	4	76.5	1	29	0	22
56	Mexico	66	66	2	4	48.3	0	11	2	22
57	Malaysia	83	83	1	2	44.3	0	4	..	11
58	Bulgaria	48	45	2	2	15.6	0	..	2	14
59	Trinidad and Tobago	81	83	2	3	7.0	0	4	..	12
60	Serbia	42	37	2	..	15.5	0	..	..	12
61	Belarus	56	57	0	3	59.5	0	22	0	11
62	Costa Rica	87	87	2	..	8.0	0	9	2	31
63	Peru	59	57	2	2	20.9	0	12	1	18
64	Albania	47	43	2	2	21.8	0	..	2	14
65	Russian Federation	50	51	1	4	60.9	1	21	..	13
66	Kazakhstan	71	69	1	3	49.7	1	23	..	11
67	Azerbaijan	45	45	1	2	53.5	6	36	1	25
68	Bosnia and Herzegovina	32	25	0	2	10.5	0	..	2	8
69	Ukraine	38	38	2	3	22.0	0	23	..	13
70	Iran, Islamic Republic of	57	59	0	4	104.1	23	19	1	19
71	The former Yugoslav Republic of Macedonia	42	51	2	2	8.8	0	..	2	12
72	Mauritius	..	..	2	..	14.0	0	..	2	..
73	Brazil	76	73	2	4	15.9	0	5	2	19
74	Georgia	43	40	2	3	18.8	0	2	..	23
75	Venezuela, Bolivarian Republic of	65	61	2	3	39.5	1	7	2	20
76	Armenia	39	39	2	3	31.1	0	17	2	12
77	Ecuador	73	71	2	2	20.0	0	7	2	15
78	Belize	62	62	2	..	..	0	..	0	22
79	Colombia	75	75	2	5	40.1	0	11	2	29
80	Jamaica	73	74	2	4	4.8	0	..	..	15
81	Tunisia	70	76	1	3	61.5	2	14	2	16
82	Jordan	75	76	0	4	31.9	0	5	1	14
83	Turkey	38	46	2	3	38.3	1	13	2	12
84	Algeria	50	58	1	3	49.6	0	28	1	16
85	Tonga	..	..	1	..	..	0	..	..	..

MEDIUM HUMAN DEVELOPMENT

86	Fiji	..	..	0	1	60.0	0	..	..	..
87	Turkmenistan	..	..	0	2	107.0	0	..	0	..
88	Dominican Republic	83	83	2	4	26.8	0	12	2	16
89	China	70	68	0	4	84.5	24	..	2	..
90	El Salvador	64	63	2	2	17.3	0	6	2	14
91	Sri Lanka	74	74	2	4	75.0	1	5	2	12
92	Thailand	84	86	2	3	44.0	0	13	2	29
93	Gabon	..	..	1	..	43.5	0	..	2	..
94	Suriname	..	..	2	1	10.6	0	..	..	..
95	Bolivia, Plurinational State of	74	69	2	3	24.2	0	18	2	27

TABLE
6

HDI rank	AGENCY: Satisfaction with freedom of choice (% satisfied)		POLITICAL FREEDOM: Democracy	CIVIL LIBERTIES: Human rights violations	Press freedom	Journalists imprisoned	ACCOUNTABILITY: Corruption victims (% of people who faced a bribe situation in the last year)	Democratic decentralization	Political engagement (% of people who voiced opinion to public officials)
	Total	Female	Score (0–2)[a]	Score (1–5)[b]	(index)[c]	(number)[d]		Score (0–2)[e]	
	2009	2009	2008	2008	2009	2009	2008	2008	2008
96 Paraguay	69	67	2	3	14.3	0	10	..	10
97 Philippines	87	87	2	4	38.3	0	13	2	24
98 Botswana	84	84	1	..	15.5	0	10	1	18
99 Moldova, Republic of	48	46	2	3	33.8	0	34	..	20
100 Mongolia	42	40	2	3	23.3	0	20	1	25
101 Egypt	60	55	1	4	51.4	3	24	0	12
102 Uzbekistan	76	71	1	3	67.7	7	12	1	23
103 Micronesia, Federated States of	..	..	2	..	..	0	..	..	..
104 Guyana	66	65	1	..	10.5	0	..	2	19
105 Namibia	76	75	1	1	9.0	0	..	..	23
106 Honduras	64	64	2	2	42.0	0	9	2	13
107 Maldives	..	..	2	1	14.0	0	..	..	..
108 Indonesia	75	75	2	3	28.5	0	4	2	11
109 Kyrgyzstan	63	64	2	1	40.0	0	24	1	12
110 South Africa	73	70	1	3	8.5	0	13	2	24
111 Syrian Arab Republic	72	66	0	4	78.0	1	24	..	10
112 Tajikistan	59	65	1	2	32.0	0	17	1	19
113 Viet Nam	73	74	0	3	81.7	1	9	2	16
114 Morocco	71	81	0	3	41.0	1	24	0	6
115 Nicaragua	74	76	2	2	16.8	0	13	2	14
116 Guatemala	63	63	2	2	29.5	0	12	0	23
117 Equatorial Guinea	..	..	1	3	65.5	0	..	0	..
118 Cape Verde	..	..	2	..	11.0	0	..	..	..
119 India	66	60	2	4	29.3	1	15	1	12
120 Timor-Leste	..	..	2	2	16.0	0	..	0	..
121 Swaziland	..	..	0	3	52.5	0	..	..	..
122 Lao People's Democratic Republic	84	84	0	1	92.0	0	15	1	42
123 Solomon Islands	..	..	2	1	..	0	..	..	..
124 Cambodia	93	91	1	2	35.2	1	11	..	14
125 Pakistan	31	40	2	4	65.7	0	9	1	15
126 Congo	52	55	1	3	34.3	0	43	..	25
127 São Tomé and Príncipe	..	..	2	..	..	0	..	..	..

LOW HUMAN DEVELOPMENT

HDI rank	Total	Female	Democracy	Human rights violations	Press freedom	Journalists imprisoned	Corruption victims	Democratic decentralization	Political engagement
128 Kenya	58	61	2	4	25.0	0	32	..	23
129 Bangladesh	62	62	0	4	37.3	0	9	0	7
130 Ghana	74	72	2	4	6.0	0	14	..	19
131 Cameroon	69	70	1	4	30.5	1	26	..	20
132 Myanmar	..	..	0	5	102.7	9	..	..	6
133 Yemen	62	54	1	4	83.4	2	41	1	9
134 Benin	67	66	2	2	16.0	0	20	2	21
135 Madagascar	33	29	2	..	45.8	0	12	2	10
136 Mauritania	69	76	0	3	28.5	1	18	..	28
137 Papua New Guinea	..	..	2	2	14.7	0	..	2	..
138 Nepal	58	57	2	4	35.6	0	8	2	11
139 Togo	24	23	1	2	15.5	0	22	2	19
140 Comoros	50	40			19.0	0	11	..	..
141 Lesotho	..	..	1	..	27.5	0	..	..	..
142 Nigeria	51	47	2	4	46.0	0	27	0	30
143 Uganda	76	78	1	3	21.5	0	23	..	21
144 Senegal	54	57	2	3	22.0	0	20	0	26
145 Haiti	42	40	1	2	15.0	0	20	..	26
146 Angola	69	70	0	..	36.5	0	33	..	39
147 Djibouti	65	65	0	..	31.0	0	13	..	29
148 Tanzania, United Republic of	54	58	1	2	15.5	0	27	..	32
149 Côte d'Ivoire	76	75	0	3	29.0	0	22	..	..
150 Zambia	71	68	1	..	26.8	0	17	1	16
151 Gambia	..	..	1	2	48.3	1	..	0	..

TABLE 6

		AGENCY		POLITICAL FREEDOM	CIVIL LIBERTIES			ACCOUNTABILITY		
		Satisfaction with freedom of choice (% satisfied)		Democracy	Human rights violations	Press freedom	Journalists imprisoned	Corruption victims	Democratic decentralization	Political engagement
								(% of people who faced a bribe situation in the last year)		(% of people who voiced opinion to public officials)
HDI rank		Total	Female	Score (0–2)[a]	Score (1–5)[b]	(index)[c]	(number)[d]		Score (0–2)[e]	
		2009	2009	2008	2008	2009	2009	2008	2008	2008
152	Rwanda	77	74	1	2	64.7	0	10	1	26
153	Malawi	88	88	2	2	15.5	0	10	0	26
154	Sudan	69	69	0	5	54.0	0	..	..	38
155	Afghanistan	63	56	1	5	54.3	0	31	0	22
156	Guinea	67	63	0	4	28.5	0	..	..	30
157	Ethiopia	35	37	1	3	49.0	4	14	1	17
158	Sierra Leone	72	73	2	3	34.0	0	15	0	41
159	Central African Republic	66	67	1	4	17.8	0	..	0	38
160	Mali	49	63	2	2	8.0	0	23	2	16
161	Burkina Faso	57	56	1	3	15.0	0	14	1	12
162	Liberia	72	71	2	2	15.5	0	29	..	28
163	Chad	52	41	1	5	44.5	0	16	0	22
164	Guinea-Bissau	..	..	2	1	23.5	0	..	..	..
165	Mozambique	51	49	1	3	19.0	0	20	1	15
166	Burundi	43	44	2	4	29.0	0	14	2	13
167	Niger	88	87	2	3	48.5	0	17	..	19
168	Congo, Democratic Republic of the	54	55	1	5	53.5	0	..	0	19
169	Zimbabwe	41	43	1	4	46.5	0	33	..	10

OTHER COUNTRIES OR TERRITORIES

	Total	Female	Score (0–2)[a]	Score (1–5)[b]	(index)[c]	(number)[d]	Corruption	Score (0–2)[e]	Political
Antigua and Barbuda	..	..	2	..	..	0	..	..	..
Bhutan	..	..	2	..	15.8	0	..	..	..
Cuba	26	28	0	3	94.0	22	..	1	40
Dominica	..	..	2	..	..	0	..	..	..
Eritrea	..	..	1	3	115.5	19	..	0	..
Grenada	..	..	2	..	..	0	..	..	..
Iraq	37	39	0	5	53.3	1	36	..	21
Kiribati	..	..	2	..	..	0	..	..	..
Korea, Democratic People's Rep. of	..	..	0	..	112.5	0	..	2	..
Lebanon	66	64	0	3	15.4	0	30	1	12
Marshall Islands	..	..	2	..	..	0	..	..	..
Monaco	..	..	..	..	..	0	..	..	..
Nauru	..	..	2	..	..	0	..	..	..
Occupied Palestinian Territories	46	47	..	5 [g]	69.8	0	15	..	20
Oman	..	..	0	1	29.5	0	..	0	..
Palau	..	..	2	..	..	0	..	..	..
Saint Kitts and Nevis	..	..	2	..	..	0	..	..	..
Saint Lucia	..	..	2	..	..	0	..	2	..
Saint Vincent and the Grenadines	..	..	2	..	..	0	..	..	..
Samoa	..	..	1	..	..	0	..	0	..
San Marino	..	..	2	..	..	0	..	..	..
Seychelles	..	..	1	..	16.0	0	..	..	..
Somalia	..	..	0	5	77.5	0	..	..	..
Tuvalu	..	..	2	..	..	0	..	..	..
Vanuatu	..	..	2	..	..	0	..	2	..

NOTES

a 0 is nondemocratic, 1 is democratic with no alternation, 2 is democratic.
b 1 is fewest human rights violations, 5 is most human rights violations.
c A lower score indicates more freedom of the press.
d Data refer to verified cases of journalists having been imprisoned as of December 1, 2009. Countries with a value of 0 did not have any verified cases as of that date.

e 0 is no local elections, 1 is legislature elected but executive appointed, 2 is legislature and executive locally elected.
f Refers to Israel's pre-1967 borders and does not include Occupied Territories (Gaza and the West Bank).

g Refers to violence committed within the Occupied Palestinian Territories by Israeli forces. Violence committed in West Bank by actors working with or for the Palestinian National Authority receives a score of 4.

SOURCES
Columns 1, 2, 7 and 9: Gallup World Poll database (2010).
Column 3: Cheibub, Gandhi, and Vreeland (2010).
Column 4: Gibney, Cornett, and Woods (2010).
Column 5: Reporters Without Borders (2009).
Column 6: CPJ (2009).
Column 8: Beck and others (2001).

TABLE 6

TABLE 7

Sustainability and vulnerability

HDI rank	Adjusted net savings[a] (% of GNI) 2008	Ecological footprint of consumption (hectares per capita) 2006	SHARE OF TOTAL PRIMARY ENERGY SUPPLY		Carbon dioxide emissions per capita (tonnes)		Protected area (% terrestrial area) 2009	Population living on degraded land (%) 2010	POPULATION WITHOUT ACCESS TO IMPROVED SERVICES		Deaths due to indoor and outdoor air and water pollution[d] (per million people) 2004	Population affected by natural disasters[e] (average per year, per million people) 2000–2009
			Fossil fuels[b] (%) 2007	Renewable sources[c] (%) 2007	1990	2006			Water (%) 2008	Sanitation (%) 2008		
VERY HIGH HUMAN DEVELOPMENT												
1 Norway	16.2	4.2	69	31	7.4	8.6	14.4	0	0	0	65	49
2 Australia	15.0	..	94	6	17.4	18.1	10.5	9	0	0	35	458
3 New Zealand	..	7.6	67	33	6.7	7.4	25.9	5	0	..	0	189
4 United States	0.9	9.0	86	5	19.0	19.0	14.8	1	1	0	135	7,322
5 Ireland	7.5	8.2	91	3	8.8	10.4	1.0	0	0	1	0	46
6 Liechtenstein	..	..	..	..	..	..	42.4	..	..	..	0	..
7 Netherlands	−1.2	4.6	93	4	11.2	10.3	12.4	5	0	0	203	0
8 Canada	7.6	5.8	76	16	16.2	16.7	8.0	3	0	0	84	63
9 Sweden	20.5	..	33	31	6.0	5.6	11.3	0	0	0	55	4
10 Germany	..	4.0	81	9	12.1[f]	9.7	40.5	8	0	0	124	449
11 Japan	15.3	4.1	83	3	9.5	10.1	16.3	0	0	0	194	1,378
12 Korea, Republic of	21.1	3.7	82	1	5.6	9.9	2.4	3	2	0	150	1,232
13 Switzerland	..	5.6	52	21	6.3	5.6	22.8	0	0	0	108	108
14 France	9.8	4.6	51	7	7.0	6.2	15.1	4	0	0	81	108
15 Israel	11.3	5.4	96	4	7.4	10.3	18.7	13	0	0	213	9
16 Finland	16.0	5.5	50	24	10.2	12.7	9.1	0	0	0	19	8
17 Iceland	..	..	19	81	8.1	7.4	9.7	0	0	0	0	44
18 Belgium	..	5.7	73	4	10.8	10.3	0.9	10	0	0	203	27
19 Denmark	13.8	7.2	82	18	9.8	9.9	5.0	9	0	0	111	0
20 Spain	10.1	5.6	83	7	5.9	8.0	8.6	1	0	0	137	20
21 Hong Kong, China (SAR)	..	..	95	0	4.8	5.5	41.8	..	..	..	0	83
22 Greece	−4.8	5.8	94	5	7.2	8.7	13.8	1	0	2	226	195
23 Italy	8.6	4.9	91	7	7.5	8.1	9.9	2	0	..	137	127
24 Luxembourg	..	..	89	3	26.0	24.5	19.8	..	0	0	0	0
25 Austria	17.6	4.9	73	26	7.9	8.6	22.9	3	0	0	147	820
26 United Kingdom	3.9	6.1	90	..	10.0	9.4	24.4	3	0	0	189	683
27 Singapore	34.7	4.5	100	0	15.6	12.8	5.4	..	0	0	262	52
28 Czech Republic	13.4	5.3	83	5	12.7	11.3	15.1	4	0	2	167	2,344
29 Slovenia	18.1	3.9	69	10	6.4[f]	7.6	12.1	8	1	0	150	33
30 Andorra	..	..	..	..	..	..	6.0	..	0	0	0	..
31 Slovakia	−81.1	4.9	71	6	8.4[f]	7.0	23.5	9	0	0	74	219
32 United Arab Emirates	..	10.3	100	0	29.4	32.8	5.6	2	0	3	51	..
33 Malta	..	..	100	0	6.3	6.3	17.3	..	0	0	0	..
34 Estonia	9.0	6.4	90	10	16.4[f]	13.1	20.0	5	2	5	74	8
35 Cyprus	−2.8	..	97	3	6.8	9.2	11.0	11	0	0	242	0
36 Hungary	5.0	3.2	79	5	6.0	5.7	5.1	17	0	0	208	509
37 Brunei Darussalam	..	..	100	0	25.0	15.5	42.9	0	..	..	0	..
38 Qatar	..	9.7	100	0	25.2	56.2	0.7	0	0	0	0	..
39 Bahrain	15.6	..	100	0	24.1	28.8	1.4	0	..	..	0	..
40 Portugal	4.1	4.4	79	18	4.4	5.7	5.9	2	1	0	191	1,560
41 Poland	9.2	3.9	94	6	9.1	8.3	21.8	13	0	10	162	61
42 Barbados	..	..	..	..	4.0	4.6	0.1	..	0	0	0	0

HDI rank	Adjusted net savings[a] (% of GNI) 2008	Ecological footprint of consumption (hectares per capita) 2006	SHARE OF TOTAL PRIMARY ENERGY SUPPLY		Carbon dioxide emissions per capita (tonnes)		Protected area (% terrestrial area) 2009	Population living on degraded land (%) 2010	POPULATION WITHOUT ACCESS TO IMPROVED SERVICES		Deaths due to indoor and outdoor air and water pollution[d] (per million people) 2004	Population affected by natural disasters[e] (average per year, per million people) 2000–2009
			Fossil fuels[b] (%) 2007	Renewable sources[c] (%) 2007	1990	2006			Water (%) 2008	Sanitation (%) 2008		
HIGH HUMAN DEVELOPMENT												
43 Bahamas	..	..	..	..	7.6	6.5	13.7	..	..	0	0	6,666
44 Lithuania	6.6	3.3	62	9	6.0	4.2	4.5	5	..	..	204	0
45 Chile	−0.4	3.1	78	22	2.7	3.7	16.5	1	4	4	161	4,774
46 Argentina	7.7	3.0	90	7	3.5	4.4	5.4	2	3	10	349	1,963
47 Kuwait	9.7	7.9	100	0	19.0	31.2	1.6	1	1	0	115	0
48 Latvia	14.8	4.6	64	30	5.1[f]	3.3	17.8	2	1	22	0	5
49 Montenegro	..	..	..	..	..	..	13.3	8	2	8	0	273
50 Romania	13.7	2.7	83	13	6.8	4.6	7.1	13	..	28	460	1,072
51 Croatia	11.3	3.3	87	7	3.7[f]	5.2	7.3	18	1	1	225	52
52 Uruguay	7.2	..	62	38	1.3	2.1	0.3	6	0	0	421	4,824
53 Libyan Arab Jamahiriya	..	3.2	99	1	9.2	9.2	0.1	8	..	3	310	..
54 Panama	18.9	3.2	75	25	1.3	2.0	18.7	4	7	31	189	2,950
55 Saudi Arabia	−1.8	3.5	100	0	13.2	15.8	31.3	4	..	..	108	61
56 Mexico	9.0	3.2	89	9	4.6	4.1	11.1	4	6	15	174	6,587
57 Malaysia	..	..	95	5	3.1	7.2	17.9	1	0	4	60	1,667
58 Bulgaria	2.9	3.3	78	5	8.7	6.3	9.1	8	0	0	437	203
59 Trinidad and Tobago	−19.2	..	100	0	13.9	25.3	31.2	..	6	8	0	146
60 Serbia	..	..	89	11	..	..	6.0	19	1	8	0	176
61 Belarus	19.8	4.2	92	5	9.6	7.1	7.3	5	0	7	10	0
62 Costa Rica	9.1	2.7	47	53	1.0	1.8	20.9	1	3	5	118	11,383
63 Peru	7.0	1.8	70	30	1.0	1.4	13.6	1	18	32	244	18,032
64 Albania	8.5	2.6	68	21	2.3	1.4	9.8	6	3	2	97	21,349
65 Russian Federation	1.6	4.4	89	3	13.9[f]	10.9	9.0	3	4	13	241	1,531
66 Kazakhstan	2.5	4.4	99	1	15.9[f]	12.6	2.5	24	5	3	358	571
67 Azerbaijan	−0.1	2.3	98	2	5.9[f]	4.2	7.2	4	20	55	525	474
68 Bosnia and Herzegovina	..	3.4	91	9	1.2[f]	7.0	0.6	6	1	5	79	10,832
69 Ukraine	8.5	2.7	82	9	11.9	6.9	3.5	6	2	5	313	1,561
70 Iran, Islamic Republic of	..	2.7	99	1	4.0	6.6	7.1	25	..	..	134	58,770
71 The former Yugoslav Republic of Macedonia	9.0	..	85	8	5.6[f]	5.3	4.9	7	0	11	148	60,392
72 Mauritius	8.5	..	..	..	1.4	3.1	4.5	..	1	9	81	220
73 Brazil	5.2	..	53	44	1.4	1.9	28.0	8	3	20	269	3,908
74 Georgia	−0.3	..	70	30	2.9[f]	1.2	3.7	2	2	5	421	18,916
75 Venezuela, Bolivarian Republic of	6.5	2.3	88	12	6.2	6.3	53.8	2	..	..	69	506
76 Armenia	18.1	1.6	71	6	1.1[f]	1.5	8.0	10	4	10	1,045	10,704
77 Ecuador	0.4	1.9	87	13	1.6	2.4	25.1	2	6	8	124	9,126
78 Belize	8.8	..	..	..	1.7	2.9	28.0	1	1	10	0	54,328
79 Colombia	1.5	1.9	71	29	1.6	1.4	20.4	2	8	26	168	11,288
80 Jamaica	..	..	90	10	3.4	4.5	18.9	3	6	17	340	17,504
81 Tunisia	7.0	1.9	86	14	1.6	2.3	1.3	37	6	15	174	362
82 Jordan	3.6	2.0	98	2	3.2	3.6	9.4	22	4	2	204	2,639
83 Turkey	8.3	2.8	90	10	2.6	3.6	1.9	5	1	10	427	957
84 Algeria	21.4	1.9	100	0	3.1	4.0	6.3	29	17	5	324	622
85 Tonga	..	..	..	..	0.8	1.3	14.5	..	..	0	0	18,168
MEDIUM HUMAN DEVELOPMENT												
86 Fiji	−7.1	3.7	..	..	1.1	1.9	1.3	..	..	..	0	6,720
87 Turkmenistan	..	3.8	100	0	7.2[f]	9.0	3.0	11	..	2	691	0
88 Dominican Republic	−0.3	1.4	81	20	1.3	2.1	22.1	7	14	17	256	3,319
89 China	35.1	1.8	87	12	2.1	4.6	16.6	9	11	45	693	96,359
90 El Salvador	−0.1	..	42	58	0.5	1.0	0.8	6	13	13	215	39,965
91 Sri Lanka	10.4	0.9	46	55	0.2	0.6	20.8	21	10	9	315	31,444
92 Thailand	18.0	1.7	81	19	1.8	4.3	19.6	17	2	4	345	46,173
93 Gabon	3.6	..	40	60	6.6	1.6	14.9	0	13	67	372	1,357
94 Suriname	..	..	..	..	4.5	5.4	11.4	0	7	16	0	6,744
95 Bolivia, Plurinational State of	−4.7	2.4	82	18	0.8	1.2	18.2	2	14	75	633	17,895

TABLE 7

HDI rank		Adjusted net savings[a] (% of GNI)	Ecological footprint of consumption (hectares per capita)	SHARE OF TOTAL PRIMARY ENERGY SUPPLY		Carbon dioxide emissions per capita (tonnes)		Protected area (% terrestrial area)	Population living on degraded land (%)	POPULATION WITHOUT ACCESS TO IMPROVED SERVICES		Deaths due to indoor and outdoor air and water pollution[d] (per million people)	Population affected by natural disasters[e] (average per year, per million people)
				Fossil fuels[b] (%)	Renewable sources[c] (%)					Water (%)	Sanitation (%)		
		2008	2006	2007	2007	1990	2006	2009	2010	2008	2008	2004	2000–2009
96	Paraguay	9.0	3.4	15	85	0.5	0.7	5.5	1	14	30	224	10,590
97	Philippines	22.3	..	57	43	0.7	0.8	10.9	2	9	24	322	60,119
98	Botswana	37.2	3.9	69	23	1.6	2.6	30.9	22	5	40	771	7,925
99	Moldova, Republic of	17.3	1.7	90	2	4.8[f]	2.0	1.4	22	10	21	340	86,995
100	Mongolia	3.0	..	96	3	4.5	3.6	13.4	31	24	50	318	120,113
101	Egypt	2.1	1.4	96	4	1.4	2.2	5.9	25	1	6	345	2
102	Uzbekistan	−14.1	1.7	99	1	5.3[f]	4.3	2.3	27	13	0	715	2,431
103	Micronesia, Federated States of	..	..	..	..	..	..	4.0	..	..	..	0	10,768
104	Guyana	14.4	..	..	..	1.6	2.0	4.9	0	6	19	262	59,712
105	Namibia	9.9	3.0	68	21	0.0	1.4	14.5	28	8	67	152	42,577
106	Honduras	13.1	2.2	55	45	0.5	1.0	18.2	15	14	29	385	18,638
107	Maldives	..	..	..	..	0.7	2.9	..	..	9	2	0	4,901
108	Indonesia	−2.4	..	69	31	0.8	1.5	14.1	3	20	48	505	4,935
109	Kyrgyzstan	10.4	1.3	61	39	2.5	1.1	6.9	10	10	7	736	518
110	South Africa	−3.5	2.7	88	10	9.1	8.6	6.9	17	9	23	350	33,998
111	Syrian Arab Republic	−15.2	1.6	98	2	2.9	3.5	0.6	33	11	4	222	8,263
112	Tajikistan	18.8	0.9	62	38	3.9[f]	1.0	4.1	10	30	6	1,302	100,709
113	Viet Nam	9.7	1.0	51	49	0.3	1.2	6.2	8	6	25	438	25,632
114	Morocco	19.8	1.3	94	4	0.9	1.5	1.6	39	19	31	186	1,156
115	Nicaragua	..	2.3	41	59	0.6	0.8	36.7	14	15	48	316	10,527
116	Guatemala	5.3	1.7	46	54	0.6	0.9	30.6	9	6	19	468	27,087
117	Equatorial Guinea	−38.5	..	..	..	0.4	8.8	19.2	0	..	..	1,182	155
118	Cape Verde	..	..	..	..	0.2	0.6	2.5	..	16	46	213	11,020
119	India	24.2	0.8	70	29	0.8	1.3	5.3	10	12	69	954	55,557
120	Timor-Leste	..	..	..	..	..	0.2	6.1	..	31	50	316	93
121	Swaziland	7.1	..	..	..	0.5	0.9	3.0	0	31	45	718	156,115
122	Lao People's Democratic Republic	17.1	1.0	..	..	0.1	0.2	16.3	4	43	47	847	24,535
123	Solomon Islands	54.7	1.7	..	..	0.5	0.4	0.1	..	..	..	433	2,050
124	Cambodia	..	0.9	29	71	0.0	0.3	24.0	39	39	71	1,304	62,992
125	Pakistan	6.1	0.7	62	37	0.6	0.9	10.3	4	10	55	896	8,953
126	Congo	−57.1	1.0	39	58	0.5	0.4	9.5	0	29	70	898	862
127	São Tomé and Príncipe	..	..	..	..	0.6	0.7	..	..	11	74	666	..

LOW HUMAN DEVELOPMENT

128	Kenya	10.2	..	20	80	0.2	0.3	11.6	31	41	69	1,106	94,526
129	Bangladesh	23.7	..	66	34	0.1	0.3	1.6	11	20	47	821	49,538
130	Ghana	−6.6	1.6	32	68	0.3	0.4	14.0	1	18	87	1,283	3,238
131	Cameroon	..	1.1	27	73	0.1	0.2	9.2	15	26	53	1,832	168
132	Myanmar	..	1.0	31	68	0.1	0.2	6.3	19	29	19	883	5,989
133	Yemen	..	1.0	99	1	0.8[f]	1.0	0.5	32	38	48	1,102	135
134	Benin	..	1.0	37	62	0.1	0.4	23.8	2	25	88	2,037	3,832
135	Madagascar	7.0	1.2	..	..	0.1	0.1	2.9	0	59	89	1,967	23,628
136	Mauritania	..	3.1	..	..	1.4	0.5	0.5	24	51	74	1,273	37,166
137	Papua New Guinea	3.1	1.7	..	..	0.5	0.7	3.1	0	60	55	737	5,078
138	Nepal	30.5	..	11	89	0.0	0.1	17.0	2	12	69	877	9,611
139	Togo	..	..	13	85	0.2	0.2	11.3	5	40	88	1,403	2,991
140	Comoros	7.0	..	..	..	0.1	0.1	0.0	..	5	64	664	47,708
141	Lesotho	19.4	..	..	..	..	..	0.5	64	15	71	304	52,807
142	Nigeria	..	1.6	19	81	0.5	0.7	12.8	12	42	68	2,120	432
143	Uganda	3.3	..	..	..	0.0	0.1	9.7	23	33	52	1,692	10,899
144	Senegal	12.2	1.2	53	47	0.4	0.4	24.1	16	31	49	1,911	7,394
145	Haiti	..	0.5	28	72	0.1	0.2	0.3	15	37	83	1,080	12,150
146	Angola	−42.6	0.9	34	66	0.4	0.6	12.4	3	50	43	5,225	5,421
147	Djibouti	..	0.9	..	..	0.7	0.6	0.0	8	8	44	885	94,144
148	Tanzania, United Republic of	..	1.0	10	90	0.1	0.1	27.7	25	46	76	1,392	13,303
149	Côte d'Ivoire	1.7	0.9	23	77	0.5	0.4	22.6	1	20	77	1,884	39
150	Zambia	−0.7	1.2	11	89	0.3	0.2	36.0	5	40	51	1,961	36,424
151	Gambia	3.9	1.1	..	..	0.2	0.2	1.5	18	8	33	1,283	2,059

TABLE
7

HDI rank	Adjusted net savings[a] (% of GNI)	Ecological footprint of consumption (hectares per capita)	SHARE OF TOTAL PRIMARY ENERGY SUPPLY		Carbon dioxide emissions per capita (tonnes)		Protected area (% terrestrial area)	Population living on degraded land (%)	POPULATION WITHOUT ACCESS TO IMPROVED SERVICES		Deaths due to indoor and outdoor air and water pollution[d] (per million people)	Population affected by natural disasters[e] (average per year, per million people)
			Fossil fuels[b] (%)	Renewable sources[c] (%)					Water (%)	Sanitation (%)		
	2008	2006	2007	2007	1990	2006	2009	2010	2008	2008	2004	2000–2009
152 Rwanda	20.1	..	..	..	0.1	0.1	10.0	10	35	46	3,345	21,544
153 Malawi	25.1	..	..	..	0.1	0.1	15.0	19	20	44	2,395	70,315
154 Sudan	−13.1	2.2	26	74	0.2	0.3	4.9	40	43	66	979	20,408
155 Afghanistan	..	..	..	..	0.2	0.0	0.4	11	52	63	5,125	23,278
156 Guinea	−11.3	1.5	..	..	0.2	0.1	6.8	1	29	81	1,759	3,227
157 Ethiopia	8.9	..	9	92	0.1	0.1	18.4	72	62	88	2,571	37,289
158 Sierra Leone	−1.0	0.8	..	..	0.1	0.2	5.0	0	51	87	5,623	457
159 Central African Republic	−4.6	1.4	..	..	0.1	0.1	14.7	0	33	66	1,812	510
160 Mali	..	1.9	..	..	0.1	0.0	2.4	60	44	64	3,367	9,531
161 Burkina Faso	..	1.4	..	..	0.1	0.1	13.9	73	24	89	3,130	2,504
162 Liberia	..	1.2	..	..	0.2	0.2	18.1	0	32	83	3,287	1,080
163 Chad	−49.9	1.8	..	..	0.0	0.0	9.4	45	50	91	2,547	31,625
164 Guinea-Bissau	16.6	1.0	..	..	0.2	0.2	16.1	1	39	79	3,269	11,817
165 Mozambique	−4.6	..	5	95	0.1	0.1	15.8	2	53	83	1,428	47,950
166 Burundi	..	..	..	..	0.1	0.0	4.9	19	28	54	3,519	51,177
167 Niger	..	1.7	..	..	0.1	0.1	6.8	25	52	91	5,445	50,079
168 Congo, Democratic Republic of the	−2.5	0.7	4	96	0.1	0.0	10.0	0	54	77	3,260	1,288
169 Zimbabwe	..	1.0	28	70	1.6	0.8	28.0	29	18	56	889	75,240

OTHER COUNTRIES OR TERRITORIES

HDI rank	Adjusted net savings[a] (% of GNI)	Ecological footprint of consumption (hectares per capita)	Fossil fuels[b] (%)	Renewable sources[c] (%)	1990	2006	Protected area (% terrestrial area)	Population living on degraded land (%)	Water (%)	Sanitation (%)	Air/water pollution	Natural disasters
Antigua and Barbuda	..	..	..	..	4.9	5.1	7.0	..	..	..	0	32,725
Bhutan	50.4	..	..	..	0.2	0.6	28.4	0	8	35	789	0
Cuba	..	2.3	87	13	3.1	2.6	6.3	17	6	9	233	97,163
Dominica	..	..	..	..	0.9	1.7	21.7	..	..	..	0	12,965
Eritrea	..	0.8	27	74	..	0.1	5.0	59	39	86	1,231	87,758
Grenada	..	..	..	..	1.3	2.3	1.7	..	..	3	0	65,910
Iraq	..	1.3	99	0	2.8	3.2	0.1	5	21	27	1,244	276
Kiribati	..	..	..	..	0.3	0.3	22.0	..	..	..	0	0
Korea, Democratic People's Rep. of	..	1.4	88	12	12.2	3.6	4.0	3	0	..	436	7,874
Lebanon	0.1	2.1	93	5	3.1	3.8	0.5	1	0	..	149	460
Marshall Islands	..	..	..	..	1.0	1.6	3.1	..	6	27	0	1,465
Monaco	..	..	..	..	..	..	23.7	..	0	0	0	..
Nauru	..	..	..	..	14.4	14.1	..	..	..	..	0	..
Occupied Palestinian Territories	..	..	..	..	..	0.8	..	..	9	11	0	0
Oman	..	3.5	100	0	5.6	16.3	10.7	6	12	..	117	783
Palau	..	..	..	..	15.7	5.8	2.0	..	..	..	0	..
Saint Kitts and Nevis	..	..	..	..	1.6	2.7	3.6	..	1	4	0	..
Saint Lucia	..	..	..	..	-1.2	2.3	14.3	..	2	..	0	0
Saint Vincent and the Grenadines	7.6	..	..	..	0.7	1.7	10.9	..	..	..	0	1,557
Samoa	..	..	..	..	0.8	0.9	3.4	..	..	0	0	3,277
San Marino	..	..	..	..	..	..	..	..	..	..	0	..
Seychelles	..	..	..	..	1.6	8.6	42.0	..	..	..	0	22,448
Somalia	..	1.5	..	..	0.0	0.0	0.6	26	70	77	3,490	67,697
Tuvalu	..	..	..	..	..	..	0.4	..	3	16	0	..
Vanuatu	..	..	..	..	0.5	0.4	4.3	..	17	48	0	36,308

TABLE 7

NOTES

a Includes particulate emissions damage.

b Fossils fuels include coal and coal products, crude, natural gas liquids, feedstocks, petroleum products and natural gas.

c Renewables sources include hydropower, geothermal power, combustible renewables, waste, solar and wind, and exclude nuclear energy.

d Includes deaths from diarrhoea attributable to water, sanitation and hygiene; deaths from acute respiratory infections (children under age 5), chronic obstructive pulmonary disease (adults over age 30) and lung cancer (adults over age 30) attributable to indoor smoke; and deaths from respiratory infections and diseases, lung cancer and selected cardiovascular diseases attributable to outdoor air pollution.

e Natural disasters include droughts, earthquakes, epidemics, extreme temperatures, floods, insect infestation, storms, volcanoes and wildfires.

f Data refer to a year other than that specified.

SOURCES

Column 1: World Bank (2010a).
Column 2: GFN (2009).
Columns 3 and 4: Calculated based on data on total primary energy supply source from IEA (2009).

Columns 5 and 6: Boden, Marland, and Andres (2009).
Column 7: UNEP-WCMC (2006).
Column 8: FAO (2010a).
Columns 9 and 10: WHO and UNICEF (2010).

Column 11: Calculated based on data from WHO (2008) and UNDESA (2009d).
Column 12: Calculated based on data from CRED EM-DAT (2010) and UNDESA (2009d).

TABLE 8

Human security

HDI rank	Conventional arms transfers[a] (1990 $ millions) Exports	Conventional arms transfers[a] (1990 $ millions) Imports	Refugees by country of origin (thousands)	Internally displaced persons[b] (thousands)	Civil war Fatalities (average per year of conflict per million inhabitants)	Civil war Intensity Score (0–2)[c]	Prevalence of undernourishment (% of total population) 1990–1992[d]	Prevalence of undernourishment (% of total population) 2004–2006[d]	Intensity of food deprivation (average % shortfall in minimum dietary energy requirements) 1990/1992	Intensity of food deprivation (average % shortfall in minimum dietary energy requirements) 2004/2006
	2008	2008	2008	2008	1990/2008	2008	1990–1992[d]	2004–2006[d]	1990/1992	2004/2006
VERY HIGH HUMAN DEVELOPMENT										
1 Norway	2	536	0.0	..	..	0	<5	<5	..	..
2 Australia	6	380	0.0	..	..	0	<5	<5	..	..
3 New Zealand	..	2	0.0	..	..	0	<5	<5	..	..
4 United States	6,093	808	2.1	..	..	0	<5	<5	..	..
5 Ireland	1	21	0.0	..	..	0	<5	<5	..	..
6 Liechtenstein	..	..	..	..	..	0	..	..	..	..
7 Netherlands	554	132	0.0	..	..	0	<5	<5	..	..
8 Canada	236	427	0.1	..	..	0	<5	<5	..	..
9 Sweden	457	64	0.0	..	..	0	<5	<5	..	..
10 Germany	..	..	0.2	..	..	0	<5	<5	..	..
11 Japan	..	584	0.2	..	..	0	<5	<5	..	..
12 Korea, Republic of	80	1,821	1.1	..	..	0	<5	<5	7	7
13 Switzerland	467	14	0.0	..	..	0	<5	<5	..	..
14 France	1,831	7	0.1	..	..	0	<5	<5	..	..
15 Israel	271	665	1.5	..	78.5	1	<5	<5	..	..
16 Finland	67	152	0.0	..	..	0	<5	<5	..	..
17 Iceland	..	..	0.0	..	..	0	<5	<5	..	..
18 Belgium	228	177	0.1	..	..	0	<5	<5	..	..
19 Denmark	15	90	0.0	..	..	0	<5	<5	..	..
20 Spain	603	361	0.0	..	0.9	0	<5	<5	..	..
21 Hong Kong, China (SAR)	..	..	0.0	..	..	0	..	..	..	..
22 Greece	..	563	0.1	..	..	0	<5	<5	..	..
23 Italy	424	189	0.1	..	..	0	<5	<5	..	..
24 Luxembourg	..	..	..	..	..	0	<5	<5	..	..
25 Austria	16	220	0.0	..	..	0	<5	<5	..	..
26 United Kingdom	1,027	506	0.2	..	1.3	0	<5	<5	..	..
27 Singapore	1	1,123	0.1	..	..	0	..	..	..	..
28 Czech Republic	33	20	1.4	..	..	0	<5	<5	7	10
29 Slovenia	..	..	0.1	..	..	0	<5	<5	7	10
30 Andorra	..	..	0.0	..	..	0	..	..	..	..
31 Slovakia	8	..	0.3	..	..	0	<5	<5	7	5
32 United Arab Emirates	..	748	0.3	..	..	0	<5	<5	6	20
33 Malta	..	..	0.0	..	..	0	<5	<5	..	..
34 Estonia	..	50	0.2	..	..	0	<5	<5	10	9
35 Cyprus	..	..	0.0	200.5 [e]	..	0	<5	<5	6	10
36 Hungary	..	5	1.6	..	..	0	<5	<5	6	..
37 Brunei Darussalam	..	..	0.0	..	..	0	<5	<5	8	..
38 Qatar	..	..	0.1	..	..	0	..	..	..	..
39 Bahrain	..	19	0.1	..	..	0	..	..	..	..
40 Portugal	87	159	0.0	..	..	0	<5	<5	..	..
41 Poland	76	623	2.4	..	..	0	<5	<5	6	10
42 Barbados	..	13	0.0	..	..	0	<5	<5	7	8

LIMITATIONS TO FREEDOM FROM FEAR

LIMITATIONS TO FREEDOM FROM WANT

		LIMITATIONS TO FREEDOM FROM FEAR						LIMITATIONS TO FREEDOM FROM WANT			
		Conventional arms transfers[a] (1990 $ millions)		Refugees by country of origin	Internally displaced persons[b]	Civil war		Prevalence of undernourishment		Intensity of food deprivation	
		Exports	Imports			Fatalities	Intensity				
						(average per year of conflict per million inhabitants)	Score (0–2)[c]	(% of total population)		(average % shortfall in minimum dietary energy requirements)	
HDI rank				(thousands)	(thousands)						
		2008	2008	2008	2008	1990/2008	2008	1990–1992[d]	2004–2006[d]	1990/1992	2004/2006

HIGH HUMAN DEVELOPMENT

HDI rank	Country	Exports	Imports	Refugees	IDP	Fatalities	Intensity	1990–1992	2004–2006	1990/1992	2004/2006
43	Bahamas	..	..	0.0	..	..	0	7	6	9	12
44	Lithuania	..	26	0.5	..	..	0	<5	<5	8	10
45	Chile	133	577	1.0	..	..	0	7	<5	9	11
46	Argentina	..	21	1.0	..	..	0	<5	<5	7	11
47	Kuwait	..	5	0.9	..	..	0	20	<5	12	7
48	Latvia	..	44	0.8	..	..	0	<5	<5	7	0
49	Montenegro	..	..	1.3	..	..	0	..	..	..	..
50	Romania	..	70	4.8	..	..	0	<5	<5	7	13
51	Croatia	..	99	97.0	2.4	269.4	0	..	<5	10	4
52	Uruguay	..	65	0.2	..	..	0	5	<5	8	0
53	Libyan Arab Jamahiriya	9	..	2.1	..	..	0	<5	<5	7	4
54	Panama	..	..	0.1	..	..	0	18	17	13	11
55	Saudi Arabia	..	115	0.7	..	..	0	<5	<5	8	7
56	Mexico	..	..	6.2	5.5	0.7	0	<5	<5	10	12
57	Malaysia	..	541	0.6	..	..	0	<5	<5	7	7
58	Bulgaria	8	123	3.0	..	..	0	<5	<5	9	10
59	Trinidad and Tobago	..	..	0.2	..	23.2	0	11	10	11	15
60	Serbia	..	..	185.9	250[f]	..	0	..	..	..	..
61	Belarus	292	..	5.4	..	..	0	<5	<5	6	18
62	Costa Rica	..	..	0.4	..	..	0	<5	<5	8	8
63	Peru	..	2	7.3	150	21.9	1	28	13	14	14
64	Albania	..	13	15.0	..	..	0	<5	<5	10	8
65	Russian Federation	6,026	..	103.1	18–82[g]	40.2	1	<5	<5	8	11
66	Kazakhstan	..	25	4.8	..	..	0	<5	<5	6	10
67	Azerbaijan	..	21	16.3	573–603[h]	236.6	0	27	11	12	7
68	Bosnia and Herzegovina	..	..	74.4	125	3,458.2	0	<5	<5	9	7
69	Ukraine	269	..	28.4	..	..	0	<5	<5	7	7
70	Iran, Islamic Republic of	2	91	69.1	..	1.1	1	<5	<5	9	12
71	The former Yugoslav Republic of Macedonia	..	..	7.5	<1	60.6	0	<5	<5	10	8
72	Mauritius	..	..	0.0	..	..	0	7	6	10	12
73	Brazil	72	212	1.4	..	..	0	10	6	13	12
74	Georgia	..	77	12.6	247–249[i]	289.0	1	47	12	14	9
75	Venezuela, Bolivarian Republic of	3	764	5.8	..	5.3	0	10	12	10	10
76	Armenia	..	..	16.3	8.4	..	0	46	23	14	13
77	Ecuador	..	140	1.1	..	..	0	24	13	12	5
78	Belize	..	..	0.0	..	..	0	5	<5	9	25
79	Colombia	..	92	373.5	3,304–4,916[j]	44.7	2	15	10	13	9
80	Jamaica	..	2	0.8	..	..	0	11	5	10	9
81	Tunisia	..	7	2.3	..	..	0	<5	<5	7	10
82	Jordan	28	136	1.9	..	..	0	<5	<5	9	6
83	Turkey	43	578	214.4	954–1,200[k]	28.2	1	<5	<5	8	9
84	Algeria	..	1,518	9.1	..	134.8	1	<5	..	10	10
85	Tonga	..	..	0.0	..	..	0	..	..	..	..

MEDIUM HUMAN DEVELOPMENT

86	Fiji	..	..	1.9	..	..	0	8	<5	10	2
87	Turkmenistan	..	..	0.7	l	..	0	9	6	10	9
88	Dominican Republic	..	..	0.3	..	..	0	27	21	13	12
89	China	544	1,481	175.2	..	..	0	15	10	14	13
90	El Salvador	..	..	5.2	..	210.2	0	9	10	11	11
91	Sri Lanka	..	..	137.8	380	193.8	2	27	21	15	14
92	Thailand	..	12	1.8	..	5.5	1	29	17	15	11
93	Gabon	..	21	0.1	..	..	0	5	<5	8	8

TABLE 8

Human security

HDI rank	Conventional arms transfers[a] (1990 $ millions) Exports	Conventional arms transfers[a] (1990 $ millions) Imports	Refugees by country of origin (thousands)	Internally displaced persons[b] (thousands)	Civil war Fatalities (average per year of conflict per million inhabitants)	Civil war Intensity Score (0–2)[c]	Prevalence of undernourishment (% of total population) 1990–1992[d]	Prevalence of undernourishment (% of total population) 2004–2006[d]	Intensity of food deprivation (average % shortfall in minimum dietary energy requirements) 1990/1992	Intensity of food deprivation (average % shortfall in minimum dietary energy requirements) 2004/2006
	2008	2008	2008	2008	1990/2008	2008				
94 Suriname	..	..	0.1	..	..	0	11	7	10	10
95 Bolivia, Plurinational State of	..	3	0.5	..	..	0	24	23	13	15
96 Paraguay	..	..	0.1	..	..	0	16	12	12	12
97 Philippines	..	10	1.4	125–188	8.0	1	21	15	15	14
98 Botswana	..	..	0.0	..	..	0	20	26	13	13
99 Moldova, Republic of	20	..	5.6	..	170.7	0	<5	<5	9	9
100 Mongolia	..	14	1.3	..	..	0	30	29	14	14
101 Egypt	..	214	6.8	..	2.2	0	<5	<5	10	13
102 Uzbekistan	..	..	6.3	3	6.1	0	5	13	8	13
103 Micronesia, Federated States of	..	..	..	..	..	0	..	..	..	..
104 Guyana	..	..	0.7	..	..	0	18	6	12	13
105 Namibia	..	66	1.0	..	..	0	29	19	14	8
106 Honduras	..	..	1.1	..	..	0	19	12	15	13
107 Maldives	..	..	0.0	..	..	0	9	7	10	5
108 Indonesia	..	241	19.3	70–120	2.2	0	19	16	13	13
109 Kyrgyzstan	16	..	2.5	..	..	0	17	<5	12	4
110 South Africa	161	387	0.5	..	..	0	<5	<5	..	..
111 Syrian Arab Republic	..	292	15.2	433 m	..	0	<5	<5	9	7
112 Tajikistan	..	..	0.5	..	815.4	0	34	26	13	10
113 Viet Nam	..	250	328.2	..	..	0	28	13	16	16
114 Morocco	..	49	3.5	..	..	0	5	<5	11	13
115 Nicaragua	..	..	1.5	..	..	0	52	21	21	18
116 Guatemala	..	..	5.9	.. n	44.5	0	14	16	12	12
117 Equatorial Guinea	..	41	0.4	..	..	0	..	..	..	..
118 Cape Verde	..	..	0.0	..	..	0	12	14	11	9
119 India	11	1,810	19.6	500	4.1	1	24	22	17	15
120 Timor-Leste	..	..	0.0	<1	..	0	18	23	..	..
121 Swaziland	..	..	0.0	..	..	0	12	18	11	12
122 Lao People's Democratic Republic	..	7	8.6	..	4.6	0	27	19	16	15
123 Solomon Islands	..	..	0.1	..	..	0	25	9	13	8
124 Cambodia	..	..	17.3	..	13.6	0	38	25	16	14
125 Pakistan	..	939	32.4	1,250 o	11.4	2	22	23	16	16
126 Congo	..	..	19.9	7.8	582.3	0	40	21	17	14
127 São Tomé and Príncipe	..	..	0.0	..	..	0	15	5	11	7

LOW HUMAN DEVELOPMENT

HDI rank	Exports 2008	Imports 2008	Refugees 2008	IDP 2008	Fatalities 1990/2008	Intensity 2008	Undern. 1990–1992	Undern. 2004–2006	Food dep. 1990/1992	Food dep. 2004/2006
128 Kenya	..	..	9.7	400 p	..	0	33	30	15	13
129 Bangladesh	..	12	10.1	60–500	0.2	0	36	26	18	17
130 Ghana	..	..	13.2	..	..	0	34	8	15	9
131 Cameroon	..	1	13.9	..	..	0	34	23	15	9
132 Myanmar	..	..	184.4	470 q	42.1	1	44	17	17	17
133 Yemen	..	45	1.8	250	257.3	0	30	32	15	16
134 Benin	..	..	0.3	..	..	0	28	19	15	12
135 Madagascar	..	..	0.3	..	..	0	32	35	16	15
136 Mauritania	..	..	45.6	..	..	0	10	8	12	7
137 Papua New Guinea	..	..	0.0	..	10.7	0	..	..	..	..
138 Nepal	..	..	4.2	50–70	45.1	0	21	16	14	11
139 Togo	..	..	16.8	<2	44.1	0	45	37	18	16
140 Comoros	..	5	0.4	..	101.4	0	40	51	16	19
141 Lesotho	..	..	0.0	..	60.4	0	15	15	13	6
142 Nigeria	..	17	14.2	.. r	1.0	0	15	8	13	11
143 Uganda	..	3	7.5	437 s	25.1	0	19	15	14	11
144 Senegal	..	1	16.0	24–40	14.3	0	28	25	14	10
145 Haiti	..	..	23.1	..	52.9	0	63	58	24	23
146 Angola	..	20	171.4	20	313.7	0	66	44	24	17
147 Djibouti	..	..	0.7	..	209.7	0	60	31	22	12

TABLE 8

HDI rank	Conventional arms transfers[a] (1990 $ millions) Exports	Conventional arms transfers[a] (1990 $ millions) Imports	Refugees by country of origin (thousands)	Internally displaced persons[b] (thousands)	Civil war Fatalities (average per year of conflict per million inhabitants)	Civil war Intensity Score (0–2)[c]	Prevalence of undernourishment (% of total population) 1990–1992[d]	Prevalence of undernourishment (% of total population) 2004–2006[d]	Intensity of food deprivation (average % shortfall in minimum dietary energy requirements) 1990/1992	Intensity of food deprivation (average % shortfall in minimum dietary energy requirements) 2004/2006
	2008	2008	2008	2008	1990/2008	2008	1990–1992	2004–2006	1990/1992	2004/2006
148 Tanzania, United Republic of	..	..	1.3	..	..	0	28	35	15	16
149 Côte d'Ivoire	..	..	22.2	..[l]	24.4	0	15	14	13	11
150 Zambia	..	..	0.2	..	..	0	40	45	18	19
151 Gambia	..	..	1.4	..	..	0	20	29	14	14
152 Rwanda	..	6	72.5	..	279.4	0	45	40	20	19
153 Malawi	..	..	0.1	..	..	0	45	29	20	17
154 Sudan	..	128	419.2	4,900 [t]	47.9	1	31	20	15	14
155 Afghanistan	..	..	2,833.1	240	299.1	2	..	..	..	..
156 Guinea	..	..	9.5	..	70.0	0	19	16	15	7
157 Ethiopia	..	..	63.9	200–400	38.6	2	71	44	25	18
158 Sierra Leone	..	..	32.5	..	336.1	0	45	46	22	22
159 Central African Republic	..	..	125.1	162	29.2	0	47	41	19	16
160 Mali	..	2	1.8	..	9.4	1	14	10	13	12
161 Burkina Faso	..	..	0.7	..	..	0	14	9	13	10
162 Liberia	..	..	75.2	..[u]	660.9	0	30	38	18	18
163 Chad	..	89	55.1	168	97.8	1	59	38	22	17
164 Guinea-Bissau	..	..	1.1	..	798.8	0	20	31	14	14
165 Mozambique	..	..	0.2	..	260.3	0	59	37	22	16
166 Burundi	..	..	281.6	100	111.5	1	44	63	18	21
167 Niger	..	7	0.8	6.5 [v]	18.9	1	38	28	18	15
168 Congo, Democratic Republic of the	..	..	368.0	19,000 [w]	331.4	1	29	75	15	25
169 Zimbabwe	..	..	16.8	570–1,000	..	0	40	39	19	17

TABLE 8

NOTES

a Indicates the monetary value of voluntary transfers by a supplier of weapons with a military purpose destined for the armed forces, paramilitary forces or intelligence agencies of another country. Data indicate only the volume of international arms transfers, not the actual financial value of such transfers, and may underestimate actual transfers of conventional weapons.

b Estimates are from the Internal Displacement Monitoring Centre, based on various sources, and are associated with a high level of uncertainty.

c 0 is no civil war, 1 is minor civil war (fewer than 1,000 deaths), 2 is major civil war (at least 1,000 deaths).

d Data refer to the most recent year available during the period specified.

e Includes more than 200,000 Greek and Turkish Cypriots displaced in 1974.

f Includes 207,000 registered internally displaced persons in Serbia, 20,000 unregistered Roma and 20,000 displaced persons in Kosovo.

g Includes internally displaced persons from Chechnya and North Ossetia with forced migrant status in and outside the North Caucasus, as well as internally displaced persons registered by the government.

h Includes internally displaced persons from Nagorno Karabakh and the seven occupied territories only.

i Some internally displaced persons displaced in 2008 have not yet been registered. According to the national law, returned and relocated internally displaced persons retain their status.

j Higher value is cumulative since 1985.

k Based on Hacettepe University survey commissioned by the government.

l Undetermined because there are no statistics on returns.

m Includes 433,000 people displaced from the Golan Heights in 1967.

n At the end of 2007 the government had not agreed on criteria to include internally displaced persons in a national reparation programme, and it is unclear how many people can still be considered displaced.

o Conflict-induced displacement has taken place in the North West Frontier Province, Balochistan and Waziristan, but no estimates are available due to lack of access.

p Takes into account the Kenyan government's return programme, which claims that some 172,000 people displaced during the post-election violence in December 2007 have returned as of May 2008.

q Rural areas of eastern Myanmar only.

r No reliable estimates exist on internally displaced persons in Nigeria, nor is there a general agreement on their numbers.

s Does not include internally displaced persons in urban areas or those in the Karamoja region but does include returnees receiving ongoing assistance and protection.

t Includes 2.7 million internally displaced persons in Darfur, 1.7 million in the Greater Khartoum area, 390,000 in Southern Sudan and 60,000 in Southern Kordofan.

u According to the government, all internally displaced persons have achieved durable solutions (integrated into their new locations); approximately 23,000 people are believed to remain in former internally displaced persons camps.

v Does not include estimated 4,500 internally displaced persons believed to have returned to the town of Iferouane.

w Includes estimated number of people displaced in the eastern part of the country during the 2009 fighting between militia and Congolese armed forces supported by the United Nations.

SOURCES

Columns 1 and 2: SIPRI (2010a).
Column 3: UNHCR (2010).
Column 4: IDMC (2010).
Column 5: Calculated based on data from Lacina and Gleditsch (2005) and UNDESA (2009d).
Column 6: UCDP and PRIO (2009).
Columns 7–10: FAO (2010a).

TABLE 9

Perceptions of individual well-being and happiness

HDI rank		Overall life satisfaction[a] (0, least satisfied, 10, most satisfied)		SATISFACTION WITH PERSONAL DIMENSIONS OF WELL-BEING			ELEMENTS OF HAPPINESS (% answering "'yes'" to having the element)						Negative experience index
				Job[a] (% of employed respondents who are satisfied)	Personal health[a] (% of all respondents who are satisfied)	Standard of living[a] (% of all respondents who are satisfied)	Purposeful life		Treated with respect		Social support network		(0, most negative, 100, least negative)
		Total	Female				Total	Female	Total	Female	Total	Female	
		2006–2009[b]	2006–2009[b]	2006–2009[b]	2006–2009[b]	2006–2009[b]	2006–2009[b]	2006–2009[b]	2006–2009[b]	2006–2009[b]	2006–2009[b]	2006–2009[b]	2006–2009[b]
VERY HIGH HUMAN DEVELOPMENT													
1	Norway	8.1	8.2	..	82	91	85	90	90	90	93	92	16
2	Australia	7.9	8.0	91	82	85	87	89	89	88	94	95	22
3	New Zealand	7.8	8.0	90	85	79	87	90	90	88	94	95	24
4	United States	7.9	7.9	86	83	75	94	95	89	88	91	90	28
5	Ireland	8.1	8.1	95	90	79	87	91	93	93	96	97	23
6	Liechtenstein	..	..	..	..	..	..	..	..	..	..	..	..
7	Netherlands	7.8	7.8	92	85	91	70	79	93	92	94	93	16
8	Canada	8.0	8.2	90	85	87	91	92	93	94	94	93	25
9	Sweden	7.9	7.9	93	80	89	85	91	93	92	91	89	16
10	Germany	7.2	7.4	88	82	88	85	87	90	88	91	91	22
11	Japan	6.8	7.0	73	68	64	76	77	60	65	89	92	21
12	Korea, Republic of	6.3	6.5	68	71	71	80	81	63	67	79	82	23
13	Switzerland	8.0	8.0	93	89	89	82	84	94	91	94	94	21
14	France	7.1	7.1	87	84	72	84	85	93	93	91	91	29
15	Israel	7.1	7.1	80	80	71	88	88	81	77	85	95	33
16	Finland	8.0	8.2	90	84	84	81	86	91	92	94	95	15
17	Iceland	7.8	7.9	..	84	82	..	..	97	95	98	98	17
18	Belgium	7.3	7.3	89	88	84	73	78	92	90	92	92	24
19	Denmark	8.2	8.3	94	84	93	89	91	94	93	95	93	15
20	Spain	7.6	7.6	86	84	78	86	88	97	96	92	91	29
21	Hong Kong, China (SAR)	6.0	..	81	80	78	60	64	83	86	82	82	26
22	Greece	6.8	6.8	80	82	57	90	91	92	91	79	76	23
23	Italy	6.7	6.7	82	85	77	91	91	93	93	87	87	27
24	Luxembourg	7.7	7.8	..	87	92	..	..	94	93	94	95	24
25	Austria	7.8	7.8	91	85	86	72	73	92	89	93	85	18
26	United Kingdom	7.4	7.5	87	85	88	79	84	90	90	96	97	24
27	Singapore	6.7	6.7	88	95	79	90	89	81	83	84	83	19
28	Czech Republic	6.9	6.8	80	77	65	68	72	64	77	86	92	23
29	Slovenia	7.1	7.0	88	78	70	63	65	91	86	91	89	26
30	Andorra	6.8	..	..	..	..	..	..	..	..	..	..	..
31	Slovakia	5.8	..	76	72	47	85	87	78	79	93	94	27
32	United Arab Emirates	7.3	..	84	93	78	95	94	94	95	86	84	28
33	Malta	7.1	7.1	..	83	65	..	..	93	92	90	92	31
34	Estonia	5.6	5.6	79	64	46	72	73	79	80	85	85	20
35	Cyprus	7.1	7.1	89	89	84	95	94	88	89	81	80	33
36	Hungary	5.7	5.6	83	69	43	88	86	88	87	90	92	26
37	Brunei Darussalam	..	..	..	..	..	..	..	..	..	..	..	..
38	Qatar	6.7	7.0	89	93	86	..	..	93	89	91	87	26
39	Bahrain	..	..	..	86	66	..	..	90	92	90	91	37
40	Portugal	5.9	5.7	90	80	47	92	90	93	95	87	83	28
41	Poland	6.5	6.6	82	72	67	87	91	91	91	89	94	20
42	Barbados	..	..	..	..	..	..	..	..	..	..	..	..

		Overall life satisfaction[a] (0, least satisfied, 10, most satisfied)		SATISFACTION WITH PERSONAL DIMENSIONS OF WELL-BEING			ELEMENTS OF HAPPINESS (% answering "'yes'" to having the element)						Negative experience index
				Job[a]	Personal health[a]	Standard of living[a]	Purposeful life		Treated with respect		Social support network		
HDI rank		Total	Female	(% of employed respondents who are satisfied)	(% of all respondents who are satisfied)	(% of all respondents who are satisfied)	Total	Female	Total	Female	Total	Female	(0, most negative, 100, least negative)
		2006–2009[b]	2006–2009[b]	2006–2009[b]	2006–2009[b]	2006–2009[b]	2006–2009[b]	2006–2009[b]	2006–2009[b]	2006–2009[b]	2006–2009[b]	2006–2009[b]	2006–2009[b]
HIGH HUMAN DEVELOPMENT													
43	Bahamas	..	..	..	..	..	..	..	..	..	..	..	..
44	Lithuania	5.8	5.8	78	64	33	78	77	54	52	83	85	22
45	Chile	6.3	6.2	81	73	68	90	88	93	91	83	83	27
46	Argentina	7.1	7.1	83	87	70	93	95	96	95	91	91	21
47	Kuwait	6.6	..	89	89	77	97	98	91	93	86	83	24
48	Latvia	5.4	5.4	79	63	33	79	81	80	81	78	78	24
49	Montenegro	5.2	..	63	72	45	84	93	76	81	81	82	27
50	Romania	5.9	6.0	74	65	42	74	73	89	87	79	82	25
51	Croatia	6.0	..	78	77	48	83	83	74	76	90	83	28
52	Uruguay	6.8	6.7	79	84	67	87	89	94	94	91	93	23
53	Libyan Arab Jamahiriya	..	..	..	78	64	..	..	64	55	..	..	..
54	Panama	7.8	7.8	91	85	73	98	98	93	93	90	90	15
55	Saudi Arabia	7.7	7.6	92	84	77	95	93	77	69	91	86	19
56	Mexico	7.7	7.9	88	82	69	93	93	91	91	86	84	20
57	Malaysia	6.6	6.6	86	87	68	95	94	88	86	79	79	15
58	Bulgaria	4.4	..	73	67	29	77	75	77	78	81	78	20
59	Trinidad and Tobago	7.0	..	76	82	40	97	97	93	94	85	87	19
60	Serbia	5.6	..	73	73	35	84	82	77	76	82	76	28
61	Belarus	5.5	5.5	66	55	34	70	73	71	71	88	87	20
62	Costa Rica	8.5	8.5	88	90	83	97	97	94	94	90	89	21
63	Peru	5.9	5.8	74	72	54	96	95	89	88	79	78	28
64	Albania	4.6	..	72	75	43	78	91	68	80	79	77	20
65	Russian Federation	5.9	5.9	74	56	36	79	78	83	83	88	90	16
66	Kazakhstan	6.1	6.1	82	68	51	88	85	81	81	88	86	13
67	Azerbaijan	5.3	5.2	73	68	42	87	86	79	81	72	67	21
68	Bosnia and Herzegovina	5.8	..	76	75	39	80	85	67	72	74	72	25
69	Ukraine	5.3	5.2	71	55	23	74	73	78	77	81	81	17
70	Iran, Islamic Republic of	5.6	5.8	71	82	55	87	87	81	81	62	65	32
71	The former Yugoslav Republic of Macedonia	4.7	..	71	82	34	93	92	81	82	78	72	22
72	Mauritius	..	..	..	..	..	..	..	..	..	..	..	..
73	Brazil	7.6	7.6	86	82	74	96	97	94	95	91	91	24
74	Georgia	4.3	4.3	63	50	22	86	85	83	83	54	56	22
75	Venezuela, Bolivarian Republic of	7.8	7.7	86	90	80	100	100	92	92	94	94	19
76	Armenia	5.0	5.1	61	53	31	93	94	89	88	67	68	31
77	Ecuador	6.4	6.3	80	76	57	98	97	93	92	78	74	27
78	Belize	6.6	6.6	79	83	69	90	91	75	77	83	86	24
79	Colombia	7.3	7.3	82	84	69	98	98	96	96	88	87	25
80	Jamaica	6.7	..	82	88	50	98	98	80	81	91	92	18
81	Tunisia	5.9	5.9	73	85	72	..	..	91	89	86	90	30
82	Jordan	5.7	5.8	80	89	72	90	90	89	90	90	88	28
83	Turkey	5.5	5.5	71	76	44	85	85	68	75	64	73	28
84	Algeria	5.6	5.9	66	87	61	..	..	84	86	87	90	33
85	Tonga	..	..	..	..	..	..	..	..	..	..	..	..
MEDIUM HUMAN DEVELOPMENT													
86	Fiji	..	..	..	..	..	..	..	..	..	..	..	..
87	Turkmenistan	7.2	7.3	..	85	78	96	96	84	83	92	94	15
88	Dominican Republic	7.6	7.4	69	80	57	96	94	92	95	84	87	32
89	China	6.4	..	78	80	60	..	..	87	86	79	78	17
90	El Salvador	6.7	6.7	82	80	60	97	97	89	90	72	72	25
91	Sri Lanka	4.7	4.8	86	77	58	91	91	76	75	82	84	24
92	Thailand	6.3	6.3	91	79	63	95	94	75	80	86	87	16
93	Gabon	..	..	..	..	..	..	..	..	..	..	..	..

TABLE 9

HDI rank		Overall life satisfaction[a] (0, least satisfied, 10, most satisfied)		SATISFACTION WITH PERSONAL DIMENSIONS OF WELL-BEING			ELEMENTS OF HAPPINESS (% answering "yes" to having the element)						Negative experience index
				Job[a] (% of employed respondents who are satisfied)	Personal health[a] (% of all respondents who are satisfied)	Standard of living[a] (% of all respondents who are satisfied)	Purposeful life		Treated with respect		Social support network		(0, most negative, 100, least negative)
		Total	Female				Total	Female	Total	Female	Total	Female	
		2006–2009[b]	2006–2009[b]	2006–2009[b]	2006–2009[b]	2006–2009[b]	2006–2009[b]	2006–2009[b]	2006–2009[b]	2006–2009[b]	2006–2009[b]	2006–2009[b]	2006–2009[b]
94	Suriname	..	..	..	..	..	..	..	..	..	..	..	..
95	Bolivia, Plurinational State of	6.5	6.4	83	79	67	94	93	90	91	82	81	32
96	Paraguay	6.9	6.9	85	84	63	93	93	96	96	89	90	16
97	Philippines	5.5	5.5	83	77	68	96	96	94	95	77	76	34
98	Botswana	4.7	4.4	58	67	41	92	91	83	85	83	81	23
99	Moldova, Republic of	5.7	5.6	68	60	39	79	77	73	73	83	84	27
100	Mongolia	5.7	5.6	78	69	50	96	96	66	70	91	92	15
101	Egypt	5.8	6.2	84	86	82	86	87	90	84	74	75	33
102	Uzbekistan	6.0	6.0	86	79	69	97	97	92	91	90	89	14
103	Micronesia, Federated States of	..	..	..	..	..	..	..	..	..	..	..	..
104	Guyana	6.5	6.6	84	87	64	95	98	77	79	84	85	28
105	Namibia	5.2	..	84	87	61	98	98	86	88	83	86	16
106	Honduras	7.0	7.0	84	83	65	95	94	91	92	81	83	24
107	Maldives	..	..	..	..	..	..	..	..	..	..	..	..
108	Indonesia	5.7	5.6	63	83	62	95	95	92	94	78	78	13
109	Kyrgyzstan	5.0	4.9	78	74	48	91	92	86	85	85	85	16
110	South Africa	5.0	4.7	66	79	42	97	96	83	83	88	89	24
111	Syrian Arab Republic	5.9	6.1	..	89	67	..	..	91	92	84	85	31
112	Tajikistan	5.1	4.9	78	75	69	91	90	76	77	65	67	21
113	Viet Nam	5.4	5.4	72	79	59	98	98	92	90	79	77	17
114	Morocco	5.8	6.0	69	88	71	90	91	89	87	85	87	19
115	Nicaragua	7.1	7.1	80	80	62	98	97	91	93	83	83	28
116	Guatemala	7.2	..	92	88	76	97	96	91	91	83	81	23
117	Equatorial Guinea	..	..	..	..	..	..	..	..	..	..	..	..
118	Cape Verde	..	..	..	..	..	..	..	..	..	..	..	..
119	India	5.5	5.4	74	85	61	91	90	72	79	66	65	26
120	Timor-Leste	..	..	..	..	..	..	..	..	..	..	..	..
121	Swaziland	..	..	..	..	..	..	..	..	..	..	..	..
122	Lao People's Democratic Republic	6.2	6.3	91	89	80	98	98	43	42	81	83	..
123	Solomon Islands	..	..	..	..	..	..	..	..	..	..	..	..
124	Cambodia	4.9	4.9	80	69	51	81	79	87	85	82	79	19
125	Pakistan	5.4	5.5	77	75	53	72	73	89	81	44	50	32
126	Congo	3.6	..	67	62	32	..	..	80	82	55	57	25
127	São Tomé and Príncipe	..	..	..	..	..	..	..	..	..	..	..	..

LOW HUMAN DEVELOPMENT

HDI rank		Total	Female	Job	Personal health	Standard of living	Total	Female	Total	Female	Total	Female	Negative
128	Kenya	3.7	3.6	57	70	25	98	98	78	81	79	80	19
129	Bangladesh	5.3	5.4	76	73	63	94	92	87	86	53	51	22
130	Ghana	4.7	4.7	54	66	34	98	97	88	85	63	61	22
131	Cameroon	3.9	4.0	63	69	40	93	91	85	87	73	74	23
132	Myanmar	..	..	68	75	59	90	89	53	55	89	86	..
133	Yemen	4.8	..	74	80	53	88	87	84	90	75	73	35
134	Benin	3.0	2.9	53	63	23	96	95	79	80	38	34	24
135	Madagascar	3.7	3.7	46	76	24	96	95	77	75	77	74	19
136	Mauritania	5.0	5.0	57	79	47	93	93	85	85	81	80	19
137	Papua New Guinea	..	..	..	..	..	..	..	..	..	..	..	..
138	Nepal	5.3	5.5	80	84	51	93	93	48	44	80	80	21
139	Togo	2.6	2.7	31	40	11	99	99	54	55	28	24	30
140	Comoros	..	..	..	67	23	..	..	87	89	62	62	16
141	Lesotho	..	..	..	..	..	..	..	..	..	..	..	..
142	Nigeria	3.8	4.9	65	80	40	92	90	81	80	72	69	23
143	Uganda	4.5	4.7	53	64	35	96	96	79	83	85	85	31
144	Senegal	4.5	4.6	39	68	27	89	88	85	80	81	80	22
145	Haiti	3.9	..	51	51	35	81	81	66	64	64	65	27

TABLE 9

HDI rank	Overall life satisfaction[a] (0, least satisfied, 10, most satisfied)		SATISFACTION WITH PERSONAL DIMENSIONS OF WELL-BEING			ELEMENTS OF HAPPINESS (% answering "'yes'" to having the element)						Negative experience index
			Job[a]	Personal health[a]	Standard of living[a]	Purposeful life		Treated with respect		Social support network		
			(% of employed respondents who are satisfied)	(% of all respondents who are satisfied)	(% of all respondents who are satisfied)							(0, most negative, 100, least negative)
	Total	Female				Total	Female	Total	Female	Total	Female	
	2006–2009[b]	2006–2009[b]	2006–2009[b]	2006–2009[b]	2006–2009[b]	2006–2009[b]	2006–2009[b]	2006–2009[b]	2006–2009[b]	2006–2009[b]	2006–2009[b]	2006–2009[b]
146 Angola	4.3	4.2	72	67	54	90	89	83	83	58	59	27
147 Djibouti	5.7	5.7	89	86	77	..	..	84	84	90	90	12
148 Tanzania, United Republic of	2.4	2.4	45	67	21	95	88	74	77	76	87	22
149 Côte d'Ivoire	4.5	4.5	..	68	17	98	99	89	89	67	67	16
150 Zambia	4.3	4.2	48	78	34	93	94	83	83	62	76	18
151 Gambia	..	..	..	..	..	..	..	..	..	..	..	..
152 Rwanda	4.2	4.1	41	64	37	88	95	77	75	56	56	13
153 Malawi	6.2	5.9	62	77	64	99	99	88	90	72	70	14
154 Sudan	5.0	..	65	77	64	97	97	89	90	89	90	28
155 Afghanistan	4.1	4.1	71	79	53	83	83	64	59	54	51	24
156 Guinea	4.5	..	68	75	27	96	96	86	87	58	59	26
157 Ethiopia	4.2	..	50	79	33	89	87	74	47	76	77	21
158 Sierra Leone	3.6	3.7	49	47	19	98	98	81	80	59	59	37
159 Central African Republic	4.6	..	78	81	31	96	96	74	74	56	60	28
160 Mali	3.8	3.9	30	71	30	99	98	86	91	75	74	13
161 Burkina Faso	3.6	3.7	46	70	27	94	91	83	81	73	74	24
162 Liberia	3.4	3.4	47	70	46	100	99	82	80	58	58	27
163 Chad	5.4	5.0	78	69	52	93	83	79	74	57	67	20
164 Guinea-Bissau	..	..	..	..	..	..	..	..	..	..	..	..
165 Mozambique	3.8	3.9	74	82	46	93	92	89	90	75	77	22
166 Burundi	2.9	2.8	43	55	24	..	..	81	83	32	30	16
167 Niger	3.8	3.7	54	82	52	99	99	93	94	77	79	14
168 Congo, Democratic Republic of the	4.4	3.6	60	74	40	98	..	79	69	67	71	23
169 Zimbabwe	2.8	2.8	49	72	27	91	92	81	84	81	81	22

OTHER COUNTRIES OR TERRITORIES

Cuba	..	..	68	76	..	96	96	88	88	93	93	28
Iraq	5.5	5.3	64	66	41	..	..	84	82	84	84	36
Lebanon	4.7	4.9	69	80	58	86	86	90	92	73	74	39
Occupied Palestinian Territories	5.0	5.0	..	78	43	77	80	89	88	74	71	45
Somalia	..	..	..	87	73	..	..	74	74	88	89	9

TABLE
9

NOTES

a For details on satisfaction questions see the Gallup World Poll (www.gallup.com).

b Data refer to the most recent year available during the period specified.

SOURCE

Columns 1–12: Gallup World Poll database (2010).

Civic and community well-being

		CRIME AND SAFETY				SATISFACTION WITH MEASURES OF WELL-BEING (% satisfied)					
HDI rank		Homicide rate (per 100,000 people)	Robbery rate (per 100,000 people)	Assault victims (% reporting having been a victim)	Perception of safety[a] (%)	Community[b]	Affordable housing[b]	Healthcare quality[b]	Education system and schools[b]	Air quality[b]	Water quality[b]
		2003–2008[c]	2003–2008[c]	2006–2009[c]	2006–2009[c]	2006–2009[c]	2006–2009[c]	2006–2009[c]	2006–2009[c]	2006–2009[c]	2006–2009[c]

VERY HIGH HUMAN DEVELOPMENT

1	Norway	0.6	34	3	81	..	42	80	75	89	95
2	Australia	1.2	78	4	63	..	42	79	68	89	88
3	New Zealand	1.3	53	1	57	..	55	80	73	91	85
4	United States	5.2	142	2	75	75	70	76	70	85	87
5	Ireland	2.0	56	3	62	73	56	68	75	94	86
6	Liechtenstein	2.8	3	..	..	..	..	..	..	..	..
7	Netherlands	1.0	84	3	74	..	51	89	70	76	93
8	Canada	1.7	97	3	76	73	62	70	71	83	89
9	Sweden	0.9	97	4	69	..	51	77	67	84	95
10	Germany	0.8	61	3	72	78	70	86	59	87	95
11	Japan	0.5	3	1	73	70	71	67	53	79	81
12	Korea, Republic of	2.3	10	3	60	68	60	64	51	78	83
13	Switzerland	0.7	56	3	76	..	54	92	75	82	96
14	France	1.4	172	5	59	76	57	83	70	78	86
15	Israel	2.4	40	4	70	..	45	71	57	57	53
16	Finland	2.5	32	3	75	..	63	66	64	81	91
17	Iceland	0.0	14	3	77	..	65	88	87	85	97
18	Belgium	1.8	1,837	6	64	..	52	91	77	69	85
19	Denmark	1.4	62	1	83	..	71	86	74	93	96
20	Spain	0.9	1,067	6	58	69	26	77	58	76	80
21	Hong Kong, China (SAR)	0.6	..	1	85	..	68	65	52	..	71
22	Greece	1.1	26	3	60	63	63	51	50	74	69
23	Italy	1.2	122	4	61	64	42	64	61	71	83
24	Luxembourg	1.5	68	3	76	..	52	90	73	78	89
25	Austria	0.5	62	4	75	..	57	93	73	80	94
26	United Kingdom	4.8	282	2	64	77	59	88	70	87	93
27	Singapore	0.4	22	0	98	89	54	89	94	97	99
28	Czech Republic	2.0	45	6	60	..	42	68	71	66	80
29	Slovenia	0.5	19	3	79	69	26	79	75	76	85
30	Andorra	1.3	..	..	..	..	..	..	..	..	..
31	Slovakia	1.7	25	2	47	..	38	58	53	62	78
32	United Arab Emirates	0.9	13	2	91	71	53	82	83	72	73
33	Malta	1.0	36	4	66	..	41	69	63	41	65
34	Estonia	6.3	68	5	60	60	44	45	59	75	67
35	Cyprus	1.0	8	4	65	60	42	67	62	67	67
36	Hungary	1.5	31	5	61	..	47	66	60	75	78
37	Brunei Darussalam	0.5	1	..	..	..	..	..	..	..	..
38	Qatar	1.0	..	4	87	70	49	85	77	81	80
39	Bahrain	0.8	39	5	79	71	61	84	88	72	62
40	Portugal	1.2	195	7	62	..	35	64	69	88	88
41	Poland	1.2	55	1	61	..	0	49	66	77	75
42	Barbados	8.7	..	..	..	..	..	..	..	..	..

HDI rank	CRIME AND SAFETY				SATISFACTION WITH MEASURES OF WELL-BEING (% satisfied)					
	Homicide rate (per 100,000 people)	Robbery rate (per 100,000 people)	Assault victims (% reporting having been a victim)	Perception of safety[a] (%)	Community[b]	Affordable housing[b]	Healthcare quality[b]	Education system and schools[b]	Air quality[b]	Water quality[b]
	2003–2008[c]	2003–2008[c]	2006–2009[c]	2006–2009[c]	2006–2009[c]	2006–2009[c]	2006–2009[c]	2006–2009[c]	2006–2009[c]	2006–2009[c]
HIGH HUMAN DEVELOPMENT										
43 Bahamas	13.7	..	..	..	..	..	..	..	..	..
44 Lithuania	8.6	104	4	29	51	20	37	40	66	71
45 Chile	8.1	180	13	42	65	46	47	61	60	85
46 Argentina	5.2	859	16	39	58	29	58	51	72	74
47 Kuwait	1.1	..	5	86	62	61	72	62	37	52
48 Latvia	4.4	64	8	44	56	43	32	42	75	65
49 Montenegro	3.7	13	5	70	..	38	66	72	70	69
50 Romania	2.2	12	4	51	57	23	49	58	70	67
51 Croatia	1.6	28	9	73	..	39	66	67	83	81
52 Uruguay	5.8	277	11	46	74	41	77	76	87	94
53 Libyan Arab Jamahiriya	2.2	..	..	..	..	..	..	..	..	..
54 Panama	13.3	38	11	47	67	54	64	70	82	74
55 Saudi Arabia	0.9	..	6	77	63	58	65	67	55	52
56 Mexico	11.6	505	12	44	64	41	58	72	73	66
57 Malaysia	2.3	82	6	49	83	70	89	93	83	86
58 Bulgaria	2.3	38	4	56	..	59	33	45	60	57
59 Trinidad and Tobago	39.7	..	7	42	..	45	57	70	76	74
60 Serbia	3.4	37	12	70	..	30	51	64	63	58
61 Belarus	5.6	69	2	48	57	30	32	57	66	64
62 Costa Rica	8.3	527	16	44	73	57	72	84	84	87
63 Peru	3.2	156	15	43	52	39	46	51	61	62
64 Albania	3.3	5	1	54	..	57	38	49	58	53
65 Russian Federation	14.2	173	3	31	45	24	29	42	54	42
66 Kazakhstan	10.6	72	4	52	53	35	39	54	61	60
67 Azerbaijan	2.0	7	2	71	56	57	41	59	65	55
68 Bosnia and Herzegovina	1.8	20	6	69	..	43	53	59	76	77
69 Ukraine	6.3	59	4	31	45	29	17	38	53	44
70 Iran, Islamic Republic of	2.9	..	7	55	..	0	60	51	67	58
71 The former Yugoslav Republic of Macedonia	2.0	25	6	60	..	40	53	63	66	60
72 Mauritius	3.8	98	..	..	..	..	..	..	..	..
73 Brazil	22.0	..	10	40	57	45	39	53	70	78
74 Georgia	7.6	62	1	79	64	51	47	60	68	66
75 Venezuela, Bolivarian Republic of	52.0	..	11	23	61	35	67	78	70	60
76 Armenia	2.5	11	2	75	54	33	44	55	63	65
77 Ecuador	18.1	399	20	38	60	40	50	71	63	64
78 Belize	34.3	182	14	43	..	40	43	58	71	63
79 Colombia	38.8	..	13	45	66	46	64	73	69	73
80 Jamaica	59.5	..	4	46	..	50	71	69	86	89
81 Tunisia	1.5	..	5	81	69	74	71	72	65	59
82 Jordan	1.7	14	3	84	65	53	73	67	58	45
83 Turkey	2.9	10	8	42	..	63	59	50	63	53
84 Algeria	0.6	72	15	39	55	37	50	61	57	61
85 Tonga	..	..	..	..	..	..	..	..	..	..
MEDIUM HUMAN DEVELOPMENT										
86 Fiji	2.8	..	..	..	..	..	..	..	..	..
87 Turkmenistan	2.9	3	..	..	..	..	..	..	81	71
88 Dominican Republic	21.5	556	7	38	..	42	52	74	72	65
89 China	1.2	..	3	74	67	67	57	61	73	74
90 El Salvador	51.8	92	13	43	69	57	64	78	80	68
91 Sri Lanka	7.4	..	4	72	77	36	75	83	89	86
92 Thailand	5.9	107	3	65	..	87	87	88	82	84
93 Gabon	..	..	..	..	..	..	..	..	..	..
94 Suriname	13.7	..	..	..	..	..	..	..	..	..
95 Bolivia, Plurinational State of	10.6	..	20	37	64	43	52	77	75	80

TABLE
10

Civic and community well-being

HDI rank		CRIME AND SAFETY				SATISFACTION WITH MEASURES OF WELL-BEING (% satisfied)					
		Homicide rate (per 100,000 people)	Robbery rate (per 100,000 people)	Assault victims (% reporting having been a victim)	Perception of safety[a] (%)	Community[b]	Affordable housing[b]	Healthcare quality[b]	Education system and schools[b]	Air quality[b]	Water quality[b]
		2003–2008[c]	2003–2008[c]	2006–2009[c]	2006–2009[c]	2006–2009[c]	2006–2009[c]	2006–2009[c]	2006–2009[c]	2006–2009[c]	2006–2009[c]
96	Paraguay	12.2	31	12	40	65	54	55	75	88	83
97	Philippines	6.4	10	5	66	76	52	80	82	87	84
98	Botswana	11.9	..	13	39	..	65	64	68	84	69
99	Moldova, Republic of	5.1	25	6	37	49	26	41	58	59	56
100	Mongolia	7.9	31	6	40	..	21	45	60	51	63
101	Egypt	0.8	1	4	73	63	39	61	61	76	74
102	Uzbekistan	3.2	..	1	66	79	70	75	81	87	81
103	Micronesia, Federated States of	..	..	..	..	..	..	..	..	..	..
104	Guyana	20.7	..	10	47	..	42	63	61	79	54
105	Namibia	17.9	..	14	33	..	52	57	75	76	82
106	Honduras	60.9	..	14	48	67	50	59	73	82	75
107	Maldives	2.6	196		..	..	..	..	..	..	..
108	Indonesia	0.7	..	3	83	67	40	74	78	76	82
109	Kyrgyzstan	7.8	43	3	52	64	57	55	68	86	70
110	South Africa	36.5	..	15	20	60	39	50	66	74	70
111	Syrian Arab Republic	3.0	4	5	84	62	59	67	67	64	59
112	Tajikistan	2.3	3	2	73	63	52	50	68	83	47
113	Viet Nam	1.9	..	2	80	71	59	68	83	73	79
114	Morocco	0.4	74	5	75	51	46	34	44	67	65
115	Nicaragua	13.0	441	13	49	64	40	60	71	82	65
116	Guatemala	45.2	..	15	41	69	50	65	80	78	64
117	Equatorial Guinea	..	..	..	..	..	..	..	..	..	..
118	Cape Verde	11.4	..	..	..	..	..	..	..	..	..
119	India	2.8	2	3	74	..	62	59	72	86	67
120	Timor-Leste	..	..	..	..	..	..	..	..	..	..
121	Swaziland	12.6	..	..	..	..	..	..	..	..	..
122	Lao People's Democratic Republic	..	..	3	79	..	44	72	83	89	83
123	Solomon Islands	..	10	..	..	..	..	..	..	..	..
124	Cambodia	3.2	..	1	60	82	41	86	98	96	88
125	Pakistan	6.8	..	5	44	53	47	36	54	80	63
126	Congo	..	..	11	41	..	28	24	41	65	33
127	São Tomé and Príncipe	..	..	..	..	..	..	..	..	..	..

LOW HUMAN DEVELOPMENT

HDI rank											
128	Kenya	3.6	9	14	35	51	54	44	64	79	45
129	Bangladesh	2.6	..	3	82	72	68	54	79	92	80
130	Ghana	1.7	..	10	69	53	50	44	53	79	62
131	Cameroon	2.3	..	8	47	55	53	50	70	77	51
132	Myanmar	..	..	1	81	..	54	..	..	88	91
133	Yemen	4.0	..	10	65	49	..	28	45	73	47
134	Benin	..	..	8	63	..	48	40	46	78	56
135	Madagascar	..	..	2	57	..	75	44	64	81	53
136	Mauritania	..	..	10	65	44	40	24	42	64	57
137	Papua New Guinea	..	..	..	..	..	..	..	..	..	..
138	Nepal	2.2	1	5	43	64	62	57	77	81	71
139	Togo	..	..	10	42	..	27	20	30	52	34
140	Comoros	..	..	9	78	44	21	13	39	77	66
141	Lesotho	36.7	53	..	..	..	..	..	..	..	..
142	Nigeria	1.3	..	17	51	35	31	24	0	68	36
143	Uganda	8.7	13	24	51	49	37	38	49	83	53
144	Senegal	1.1	..	10	63	41	55	16	30	69	44
145	Haiti	..	..	33	44	..	18	22	35	43	37
146	Angola	5.0	..	38	53	..	38	49	62	60	47
147	Djibouti	..	..	11	84	56	43	41	72	69	63
148	Tanzania, United Republic of	7.7	..	21	46	..	28	26	55	62	34
149	Côte d'Ivoire	0.4	3	6	47	41	54	21	26	75	52

TABLE 10

182

HUMAN DEVELOPMENT REPORT **2010**

HDI rank	CRIME AND SAFETY				SATISFACTION WITH MEASURES OF WELL-BEING (% satisfied)						
	Homicide rate (per 100,000 people)	Robbery rate (per 100,000 people)	Assault victims (% reporting having been a victim)	Perception of safety[a] (%)	Community[b]	Affordable housing[b]	Healthcare quality[b]	Education system and schools[b]	Air quality[b]	Water quality[b]
	2003–2008[c]	2003–2008[c]	2006–2009[c]	2006–2009[c]	2006–2009[c]	2006–2009[c]	2006–2009[c]	2006–2009[c]	2006–2009[c]	2006–2009[c]
150 Zambia	..	..	11	49	..	45	44	55	79	54
151 Gambia	0.4	..	..	..	..	..	..	..	..	..
152 Rwanda	4.2	..	6	80	60	42	68	75	78	55
153 Malawi	..	..	14	55	65	57	62	67	91	62
154 Sudan	..	7	12	79	59	54	50	58	73	57
155 Afghanistan	..	..	16	37	48	35	32	58	69	61
156 Guinea	0.4	2	12	48	..	36	27	55	55	38
157 Ethiopia	6.4	..	16	49	..	25	17	43	77	29
158 Sierra Leone	2.6	3	26	53	..	21	19	34	64	28
159 Central African Republic	..	..	10	69	..	34	34	35	77	40
160 Mali	..	..	5	77	..	55	27	30	67	36
161 Burkina Faso	0.5	..	7	60	..	44	32	48	68	38
162 Liberia	..	..	24	34	..	21	20	32	69	39
163 Chad	..	..	19	28	..	23	34	48	45	31
164 Guinea-Bissau	..	..	..	..	..	..	..	..	..	..
165 Mozambique	5.1	..	24	52	..	60	66	76	79	71
166 Burundi	..	..	11	63	54	32	43	79	85	52
167 Niger	..	..	5	73	56	65	34	55	94	60
168 Congo, Democratic Republic of the	..	..	13	47	..	25	29	28	54	42
169 Zimbabwe	8.7	71	12	41	51	59	32	31	80	62

OTHER COUNTRIES OR TERRITORIES

Bhutan	1.4	..	..	..	..	..	..	..	..	..
Cuba	..	..	6	51	..	14	60	78	53	59
Iraq	..	..	10	34	44	31	35	55	45	26
Lebanon	0.6	4	4	56	55	69	67	70	41	37
Monaco	0.0	12	..	..	..	..	..	..	..	..
Occupied Palestinian Territories	3.9	..	6	47	54	54	57	59	52	49
Oman	0.9	9	..	..	..	..	..	..	..	..
Saint Kitts and Nevis	35.2	..	..	..	..	..	..	..	..	..
Saint Lucia	16.0	..	..	..	..	..	..	..	..	..
Seychelles	8.4	..	..	..	..	..	..	..	..	..
Somalia	..	..	13	74	51	49	31	56	90	65

TABLE
10

NOTES

a Refers to people answering "yes" to the question: "Do you feel safe walking alone at night?"

b For details on satisfaction questions see the Gallup World Poll (www.gallup.com).

c Data refer to the most recent year available during the period specified.

SOURCES

Columns 1 and 2: UNODC (2010).
Columns 3–10: Gallup World Poll database (2010).

TABLE 11

Demographic trends

HDI rank	Total (millions) 1990	2010	2030	Avg annual growth (%) 1990–1995	2010–2015	Urban (% of total)[a] 1990	2010	Median age (years) 1990	2010	Dependency ratio (per 100 people ages 15–64) 1990	2010	Total fertility rate (births per woman) 1990–1995	2010–2015	Sex ratio at birth (male births per 100 female births)[b] 1990	2010
VERY HIGH HUMAN DEVELOPMENT															
1 Norway	4.2	4.9	5.5	0.5	0.7	72.0	79.4	35.4	38.9	54.4	51.0	1.9	1.9	105.2	105.4
2 Australia	17.1	21.5	25.7	1.2	1.0	85.4	89.1	32.2	37.8	49.8	48.8	1.9	1.9	105.2	105.3
3 New Zealand	3.4	4.3	5.0	1.7	0.9	84.7	86.2	31.0	36.6	51.9	49.7	2.1	2.0	105.1	105.8
4 United States	254.9	317.6	370.0	1.2	0.9	75.3	82.3	32.8	36.6	51.7	49.6	2.0	2.0	104.9	105.1
5 Ireland	3.5	4.6	5.6	0.5	1.3	56.9	61.9	29.1	34.6	63.1	47.3	2.0	1.9	105.7	106.4
6 Liechtenstein	0.0	0.0	0.0	1.3	0.8	16.9	14.3	..	..	..	..	..	..	..	..
7 Netherlands	15.0	16.7	17.5	0.7	0.3	68.7	82.9	34.5	40.8	45.1	49.2	1.6	1.8	104.7	105.2
8 Canada	27.7	33.9	40.1	1.1	0.9	76.6	80.6	32.9	39.9	47.0	43.8	1.7	1.6	104.9	105.1
9 Sweden	8.6	9.3	10.1	0.6	0.4	83.1	84.7	38.3	40.9	55.6	53.4	2.0	1.9	105.4	105.7
10 Germany	79.4	82.1	77.9	0.5	−0.2	73.1	73.9	37.7	44.3	45.0	51.1	1.3	1.3	105.5	105.4
11 Japan	123.2	127.0	117.4	0.4	−0.2	63.1	66.8	37.4	44.7	43.5	55.7	1.5	1.3	105.0	105.5
12 Korea, Republic of	43.0	48.5	49.1	0.8	0.3	73.8	83.0	27.0	37.9	44.1	37.4	1.7	1.3	112.6	110.0
13 Switzerland	6.7	7.6	8.1	0.9	0.4	73.2	73.6	36.9	41.9	46.2	48.0	1.5	1.5	104.4	105.1
14 France	56.8	62.6	66.5	0.4	0.4	74.1	85.3	34.9	40.1	52.1	54.7	1.7	1.9	104.9	104.3
15 Israel	4.5	7.3	9.2	3.5	1.4	90.4	91.9	25.8	29.7	67.7	60.8	2.9	2.6	104.9	105.9
16 Finland	5.0	5.3	5.5	0.5	0.3	79.4	85.1	36.4	42.0	48.6	50.9	1.8	1.9	104.5	104.6
17 Iceland	0.3	0.3	0.4	1.0	1.4	90.8	93.4	30.0	35.1	55.3	47.2	2.2	2.1	104.8	106.0
18 Belgium	9.9	10.7	11.3	0.3	0.3	96.4	97.4	36.3	41.3	49.3	51.9	1.6	1.8	105.5	104.8
19 Denmark	5.1	5.5	5.6	0.3	0.2	84.8	86.9	37.1	40.8	48.4	53.2	1.8	1.9	105.5	105.8
20 Spain	38.8	45.3	49.8	0.3	0.8	75.4	77.4	33.7	40.2	50.2	47.3	1.3	1.6	105.8	106.4
21 Hong Kong, China (SAR)	5.7	7.1	8.2	1.7	0.9	99.5	100.0	31.0	41.9	42.8	32.3	1.3	1.0	107.8	108.1
22 Greece	10.2	11.2	11.2	1.0	0.1	58.8	61.4	36.1	41.6	49.1	48.2	1.4	1.4	105.6	106.6
23 Italy	57.0	60.1	59.5	0.1	0.2	66.7	68.4	37.1	43.3	46.2	52.9	1.3	1.4	105.9	105.5
24 Luxembourg	0.4	0.5	0.6	1.4	1.1	81.0	85.2	36.4	39.3	44.5	46.3	1.7	1.7	104.4	106.5
25 Austria	7.7	8.4	8.6	0.7	0.2	65.8	67.6	35.7	41.8	48.0	47.7	1.5	1.4	105.3	105.4
26 United Kingdom	57.2	61.9	68.0	0.3	0.5	78.1	79.6	35.8	39.9	53.2	51.4	1.8	1.9	104.6	105.0
27 Singapore	3.0	4.8	5.5	2.9	0.9	100.0	100.0	29.3	40.6	37.1	34.7	1.8	1.3	107.4	107.3
28 Czech Republic	10.3	10.4	10.5	0.0	0.2	75.2	73.5	35.2	39.6	51.5	41.5	1.7	1.5	104.9	105.7
29 Slovenia	1.9	2.0	2.0	0.4	0.2	50.4	49.5	34.1	41.7	47.1	43.3	1.4	1.5	105.1	105.3
30 Andorra	0.1	0.1	0.1	4.1	1.5	94.7	88.0	..	..	..	..	..	..	..	..
31 Slovakia	5.3	5.4	5.3	0.4	0.1	56.5	55.0	31.3	37.2	55.2	37.8	1.9	1.4	104.3	105.5
32 United Arab Emirates	1.9	4.7	6.6	5.3	2.0	79.1	84.1	27.4	31.7	45.2	25.2	3.9	1.9	104.1	105.3
33 Malta	0.4	0.4	0.4	1.0	0.3	90.4	94.7	33.0	39.0	51.3	42.9	2.0	1.3	105.7	106.0
34 Estonia	1.6	1.3	1.3	−1.7	0.0	71.1	69.5	34.4	39.6	51.0	48.0	1.6	1.8	105.0	105.6
35 Cyprus	0.7	0.9	1.1	1.4	1.0	66.8	70.3	30.9	36.5	58.1	44.2	2.4	1.6	107.1	106.8
36 Hungary	10.4	10.0	9.5	−0.1	−0.2	65.8	68.1	36.4	39.8	50.6	45.2	1.7	1.4	104.7	105.9
37 Brunei Darussalam	0.3	0.4	0.5	2.8	1.7	65.8	75.7	23.4	27.8	59.2	42.4	3.1	2.0	108.4	106.7
38 Qatar	0.5	1.5	2.0	2.4	1.6	92.2	95.8	29.6	30.1	40.5	20.5	4.1	2.3	103.8	105.4
39 Bahrain	0.5	0.8	1.1	3.2	1.8	88.1	88.6	25.9	28.1	50.8	39.3	3.4	2.1	107.5	105.2
40 Portugal	10.0	10.7	10.6	0.1	0.1	47.9	60.7	34.2	41.0	51.0	49.3	1.5	1.4	105.2	106.0
41 Poland	38.1	38.0	36.2	0.3	−0.1	61.3	61.0	32.3	38.2	54.3	39.4	1.9	1.3	105.0	105.7
42 Barbados	0.3	0.3	0.3	−0.1	0.2	32.7	44.5	28.4	37.8	51.5	37.9	1.6	1.6	102.8	103.4
HIGH HUMAN DEVELOPMENT															
43 Bahamas	0.3	0.3	0.4	1.9	1.1	79.8	84.1	23.1	29.7	59.0	47.1	2.6	2.0	103.8	104.3
44 Lithuania	3.7	3.3	2.9	−0.4	−0.7	67.6	67.0	32.7	39.8	50.3	44.9	1.8	1.4	104.3	105.3
45 Chile	13.2	17.1	19.8	1.8	0.9	83.3	89.0	25.7	32.1	56.4	46.0	2.6	1.9	103.6	103.8
46 Argentina	32.5	40.7	47.3	1.4	0.9	87.0	92.4	27.6	30.4	65.4	55.2	2.9	2.2	103.4	103.6

HDI rank		Total (millions)			Average annual growth (%)		Urban (% of total)[a]		Median age (years)		Dependency ratio (per 100 people ages 15–64)		Total fertility rate (births per woman)		Sex ratio at birth (male births per 100 female births)[b]	
		1990	2010	2030	1990–1995	2010–2015	1990	2010	1990	2010	1990	2010	1990–1995	2010–2015	1990	2010
47	Kuwait	2.1	3.1	4.3	−4.3	2.0	98.0	98.4	22.8	30.6	60.9	34.5	3.2	2.1	103.3	102.7
48	Latvia	2.7	2.2	2.0	−1.3	−0.4	69.3	67.7	34.6	40.0	49.9	45.5	1.6	1.5	104.3	105.5
49	Montenegro	0.6	0.6	0.6	1.2	0.0	48.0	61.5	30.0	35.9	53.0	47.1	1.8	1.7	106.4	107.9
50	Romania	23.2	21.2	19.5	−0.5	−0.4	53.2	57.5	32.6	38.5	51.4	43.0	1.5	1.4	104.2	105.9
51	Croatia	4.5	4.4	4.2	0.7	−0.2	54.0	57.7	35.8	41.6	46.7	47.7	1.5	1.5	104.9	105.8
52	Uruguay	3.1	3.4	3.6	0.7	0.3	89.0	92.5	30.7	33.7	60.4	57.2	2.5	2.0	104.4	104.7
53	Libyan Arab Jamahiriya	4.4	6.5	8.5	2.0	1.8	75.7	77.9	17.9	26.2	84.4	52.5	4.1	2.5	104.4	104.9
54	Panama	2.4	3.5	4.5	2.0	1.5	53.9	74.8	21.9	27.3	67.1	55.4	2.9	2.4	104.0	104.5
55	Saudi Arabia	16.3	26.2	36.5	2.3	1.9	76.6	82.1	19.4	24.6	79.2	53.6	5.5	2.8	102.2	102.1
56	Mexico	83.4	110.6	126.5	1.9	0.9	71.4	77.8	19.8	27.6	75.0	52.7	3.2	2.0	104.0	104.3
57	Malaysia	18.1	27.9	35.3	2.6	1.5	49.8	72.2	21.5	26.3	69.7	51.3	3.5	2.4	106.4	105.8
58	Bulgaria	8.8	7.5	6.5	−1.1	−0.6	66.4	71.5	36.6	41.7	50.3	45.1	1.5	1.5	104.9	105.7
59	Trinidad and Tobago	1.2	1.3	1.4	0.7	0.4	8.5	13.9	23.5	30.8	65.9	37.9	2.1	1.7	103.0	103.1
60	Serbia	9.6	9.9	9.6	1.3	−0.1	50.4	56.1	33.6	37.6	48.9	46.9	2.0	1.6	107.6	107.8
61	Belarus	10.3	9.6	8.6	0.0	−0.5	66.0	74.7	33.0	38.2	50.9	39.0	1.7	1.3	105.1	106.1
62	Costa Rica	3.1	4.6	5.8	2.4	1.3	50.7	64.4	22.5	28.2	69.0	46.6	3.0	1.9	105.1	104.8
63	Peru	21.8	29.5	36.0	1.9	1.1	68.9	76.9	20.5	25.6	73.2	56.0	3.6	2.4	103.4	104.2
64	Albania	3.3	3.2	3.4	−1.0	0.5	36.4	51.9	23.8	30.0	61.6	48.5	2.8	1.9	108.2	107.0
65	Russian Federation	148.1	140.4	128.9	0.1	−0.3	73.4	73.2	33.3	38.1	49.4	38.7	1.6	1.5	104.4	105.5
66	Kazakhstan	16.5	15.8	17.2	−0.7	0.7	56.3	58.5	26.0	29.4	59.5	44.5	2.6	2.2	103.6	105.2
67	Azerbaijan	7.2	8.9	10.3	1.5	1.1	53.8	51.9	23.2	28.4	62.6	43.9	2.9	2.1	106.5	115.6
68	Bosnia and Herzegovina	4.3	3.8	3.5	−5.1	−0.2	39.3	48.6	29.7	39.3	43.5	41.0	1.5	1.2	103.3	106.7
69	Ukraine	51.6	45.4	40.2	−0.2	−0.6	66.8	68.8	35.1	39.5	50.6	41.8	1.6	1.5	105.1	105.5
70	Iran, Islamic Republic of	56.7	75.1	89.9	1.8	1.1	56.3	70.8	17.4	26.8	92.9	40.2	4.0	1.7	104.7	105.2
71	The former Yugoslav Republic of Macedonia	1.9	2.0	2.0	0.6	0.0	57.8	59.3	29.5	36.0	50.6	41.9	2.1	1.5	106.0	107.9
72	Mauritius	1.1	1.3	1.4	1.3	0.6	43.9	41.8	24.9	32.6	50.9	42.2	2.3	1.9	102.7	103.7
73	Brazil	149.6	195.4	217.1	1.6	0.7	73.9	86.5	22.5	29.0	65.9	47.9	2.6	1.7	103.5	104.2
74	Georgia	5.5	4.2	3.8	−1.5	−0.7	55.0	52.8	31.2	37.6	51.4	44.9	2.1	1.6	105.5	110.7
75	Venezuela, Bolivarian Republic of	19.7	29.0	37.1	2.3	1.5	84.3	93.4	21.0	26.1	71.7	54.1	3.3	2.4	104.2	104.5
76	Armenia	3.5	3.1	3.2	−1.9	0.3	67.4	64.2	27.0	32.0	56.2	45.5	2.4	1.8	103.2	116.5
77	Ecuador	10.3	13.8	16.7	2.1	1.2	55.1	67.0	20.1	25.4	75.9	59.5	3.4	2.4	103.6	104.4
78	Belize	0.2	0.3	0.4	3.0	1.9	47.5	52.3	17.9	22.3	90.0	62.9	4.4	2.7	103.1	102.6
79	Colombia	33.2	46.3	57.3	1.9	1.3	68.3	75.1	21.5	26.8	69.1	52.4	3.0	2.3	104.1	104.3
80	Jamaica	2.4	2.7	2.9	0.8	0.4	49.4	52.0	21.9	26.3	73.7	57.9	2.8	2.3	103.5	105.1
81	Tunisia	8.2	10.4	12.1	1.7	1.0	58.0	67.3	20.7	29.1	74.5	42.0	3.1	1.8	106.2	106.7
82	Jordan	3.3	6.5	8.6	5.6	1.4	72.2	78.5	16.3	22.8	100.0	60.4	5.1	2.8	106.7	104.4
83	Turkey	56.1	75.7	90.4	1.7	1.1	59.2	69.7	21.5	28.3	67.3	47.8	2.9	2.1	103.5	104.1
84	Algeria	25.3	35.4	44.7	2.2	1.5	52.1	66.5	18.2	26.2	87.4	46.3	4.1	2.3	104.6	104.6
85	Tonga	0.1	0.1	0.1	0.6	0.1	22.7	23.4	19.7	21.3	78.1	76.3	4.5	3.6	107.0	106.5

MEDIUM HUMAN DEVELOPMENT

HDI rank		Total (millions)			Average annual growth (%)		Urban (% of total)[a]		Median age (years)		Dependency ratio (per 100 people ages 15–64)		Total fertility rate (births per woman)		Sex ratio at birth (male births per 100 female births)[b]	
86	Fiji	0.7	0.9	0.9	1.2	0.5	41.6	51.9	21.3	25.0	69.4	55.9	3.4	2.6	106.3	106.3
87	Turkmenistan	3.7	5.2	6.3	2.6	1.2	45.1	49.5	19.7	24.7	79.4	49.6	4.0	2.3	103.2	103.2
88	Dominican Republic	7.4	10.2	12.4	1.9	1.2	55.2	69.2	20.3	25.0	73.2	59.3	3.3	2.5	103.7	104.1
89	China	1,142.1[c]	1,354.1[c]	1,462.5[c]	1.2	0.6	26.4	47.0	25.0	34.2	51.2	39.1	2.0	1.8	110.4	121.2
90	El Salvador	5.3	6.2	7.2	1.4	0.6	49.2	64.3	19.2	23.9	83.6	63.5	3.7	2.2	103.5	104.5
91	Sri Lanka	17.3	20.4	22.2	1.1	0.7	18.6	14.3	24.3	30.6	59.9	47.1	2.5	2.2	103.5	103.7
92	Thailand	56.7	68.1	73.5	1.2	0.5	29.4	34.0	24.6	33.2	53.0	41.2	2.1	1.9	104.5	104.6
93	Gabon	0.9	1.5	2.0	3.2	1.8	69.1	86.0	19.6	21.6	88.5	66.4	5.1	3.0	101.9	102.1
94	Suriname	0.4	0.5	0.6	1.4	0.8	60.0	69.4	23.0	27.6	61.2	53.9	2.6	2.3	106.4	107.2
95	Bolivia, Plurinational State of	6.7	10.0	13.0	2.3	1.6	55.6	66.6	19.2	21.9	80.8	68.2	4.8	3.1	103.6	104.1
96	Paraguay	4.2	6.5	8.5	2.4	1.6	48.7	61.5	19.3	23.1	83.3	63.2	4.3	2.8	103.5	103.9
97	Philippines	62.4	93.6	124.4	2.3	1.7	48.6	48.9	19.3	23.2	78.3	60.7	4.1	2.9	104.5	105.0
98	Botswana	1.4	2.0	2.4	2.7	1.3	41.9	61.1	17.3	22.8	90.9	58.2	4.3	2.7	101.5	101.8
99	Moldova, Republic of	4.4	3.6	3.2	−0.1	−0.6	46.8	47.0	29.9	35.2	56.8	38.4	2.1	1.5	104.3	105.8
100	Mongolia	2.2	2.7	3.2	0.5	1.1	57.0	62.0	18.8	26.3	84.2	42.1	3.5	1.9	102.3	104.1
101	Egypt	57.8	84.5	110.9	2.0	1.7	43.5	43.4	18.9	23.9	85.2	58.1	3.9	2.7	104.4	104.7
102	Uzbekistan	20.5	27.8	33.9	2.2	1.2	40.2	36.3	19.4	24.5	81.5	49.3	3.9	2.2	103.5	103.9
103	Micronesia, Federated States of	0.1	0.1	0.1	2.1	0.5	25.8	22.7	17.6	20.8	91.2	67.3	4.8	3.2	108.0	107.2
104	Guyana	0.7	0.8	0.7	0.3	−0.2	29.6	28.6	20.8	27.4	69.9	54.5	2.6	2.2	102.8	103.4

TABLE
11

Demographic trends

		Total (millions)			Average annual growth (%)		Urban (% of total)[a]		Median age (years)		Dependency ratio (per 100 people ages 15–64)		Total fertility rate (births per woman)		Sex ratio at birth (male births per 100 female births)[b]	
HDI rank		1990	2010	2030	1990–1995	2010–2015	1990	2010	1990	2010	1990	2010	1990–1995	2010–2015	1990	2010
105	Namibia	1.4	2.2	3.0	2.7	1.7	27.7	38.0	17.8	21.1	88.9	66.8	4.9	3.1	100.8	101.3
106	Honduras	4.9	7.6	10.5	2.6	1.9	40.5	51.6	17.1	20.9	95.4	69.8	4.9	3.0	103.6	104.2
107	Maldives	0.2	0.3	0.4	2.8	1.5	25.8	40.1	16.3	24.4	99.3	46.0	5.3	1.9	104.0	103.0
108	Indonesia	177.4	232.5	271.5	1.5	1.0	30.6	44.3	21.7	28.2	65.6	48.7	2.9	2.0	103.5	104.1
109	Kyrgyzstan	4.4	5.6	6.5	0.9	1.1	37.8	34.6	21.6	25.1	74.1	51.7	3.6	2.4	102.9	104.8
110	South Africa	36.7	50.5	54.7	2.4	0.5	52.0	61.7	20.1	24.9	72.7	53.6	3.3	2.4	101.5	101.6
111	Syrian Arab Republic	12.7	22.5	30.6	2.8	1.7	48.9	55.7	15.7	22.5	104.3	61.2	4.9	2.9	104.1	104.5
112	Tajikistan	5.3	7.1	9.6	1.7	1.9	31.7	26.3	18.3	20.7	88.6	66.5	4.9	3.1	102.9	104.2
113	Viet Nam	66.2	89.0	105.4	1.9	1.0	20.3	30.4	20.0	28.5	78.9	45.8	3.3	2.0	104.0	105.9
114	Morocco	24.8	32.4	39.3	1.7	1.2	48.4	58.2	19.7	26.2	77.3	50.2	3.7	2.3	103.7	103.7
115	Nicaragua	4.1	5.8	7.4	2.4	1.5	52.3	57.3	16.8	22.0	96.6	64.2	4.5	2.6	103.4	104.3
116	Guatemala	8.9	14.4	21.7	2.3	2.4	41.1	49.5	17.1	18.8	95.1	85.0	5.5	3.7	104.1	103.8
117	Equatorial Guinea	0.4	0.7	1.1	3.5	2.4	34.8	39.7	21.2	19.3	76.1	77.3	5.9	5.1	100.5	101.3
118	Cape Verde	0.4	0.5	0.6	2.3	1.3	44.1	61.1	16.3	21.3	106.9	65.5	4.9	2.5	101.2	101.6
119	India	862.2	1,214.5	1,484.6	2.0	1.3	25.6	30.0	21.1	25.0	71.5	55.6	3.9	2.5	107.7	108.5
120	Timor-Leste	0.7	1.2	2.1	2.7	3.4	20.8	28.1	19.4	17.4	72.1	91.2	5.7	6.0	106.2	104.7
121	Swaziland	0.9	1.2	1.5	2.3	1.4	22.9	21.4	15.9	19.3	103.2	73.0	5.3	3.2	101.1	101.2
122	Lao People's Democratic Republic	4.2	6.4	8.9	2.7	1.8	15.4	33.2	17.9	20.6	89.4	68.1	5.8	3.2	103.5	104.3
123	Solomon Islands	0.3	0.5	0.8	2.9	2.2	13.7	18.6	17.0	20.3	93.4	71.8	5.5	3.5	109.0	108.9
124	Cambodia	9.7	15.1	20.1	3.2	1.7	12.6	20.1	17.9	22.3	90.0	56.6	5.6	2.7	102.9	104.1
125	Pakistan	115.8	184.8	265.7	2.4	2.1	30.6	35.9	18.2	21.3	89.2	68.6	5.7	3.6	105.9	105.8
126	Congo	2.4	3.8	5.5	2.6	2.3	54.3	62.1	17.8	19.5	91.4	78.6	5.2	3.9	101.8	101.7
127	São Tomé and Príncipe	0.1	0.2	0.2	1.9	1.7	43.7	62.2	16.7	19.3	104.1	79.2	5.2	3.4	102.4	102.1

LOW HUMAN DEVELOPMENT

128	Kenya	23.4	40.9	63.2	3.2	2.6	18.2	22.2	15.5	18.4	106.8	83.3	5.6	4.5	101.5	101.5
129	Bangladesh	115.6	164.4	203.2	2.0	1.3	19.8	28.1	18.1	24.5	85.4	53.4	4.0	2.2	103.2	103.6
130	Ghana	15.0	24.3	34.9	2.8	2.0	36.4	51.5	17.7	20.6	89.1	71.8	5.3	4.0	104.2	104.5
131	Cameroon	12.2	20.0	28.6	2.8	2.1	40.7	58.4	17.3	19.2	95.7	79.6	5.7	4.2	101.6	101.6
132	Myanmar	40.8	50.5	59.4	1.4	1.0	24.7	33.7	21.3	27.9	71.0	47.2	3.1	2.2	101.1	101.2
133	Yemen	12.3	24.3	39.4	4.6	2.7	20.9	31.8	14.3	17.8	116.0	84.2	7.7	4.7	104.6	103.9
134	Benin	4.8	9.2	15.4	3.5	2.9	34.5	42.0	17.2	18.4	96.5	85.8	6.6	5.1	103.1	103.8
135	Madagascar	11.3	20.1	31.5	3.0	2.5	23.6	30.2	17.4	18.4	91.8	83.6	6.1	4.3	100.3	101.4
136	Mauritania	2.0	3.4	4.8	2.7	2.1	39.7	41.4	17.5	20.1	89.7	72.1	5.7	4.1	106.6	106.3
137	Papua New Guinea	4.1	6.9	10.1	2.6	2.2	15.0	12.5	18.6	20.0	78.2	72.3	4.7	3.8	106.3	107.8
138	Nepal	19.1	29.9	40.6	2.5	1.7	8.9	18.6	18.6	21.6	84.0	66.6	4.9	2.7	106.0	105.2
139	Togo	3.9	6.8	10.1	2.4	2.3	30.1	43.4	16.9	19.8	96.4	75.8	6.0	3.9	100.2	100.6
140	Comoros	0.4	0.7	1.0	2.4	2.1	27.9	28.2	16.8	21.1	97.0	69.9	5.1	3.6	102.7	103.4
141	Lesotho	1.6	2.1	2.4	1.5	0.8	14.0	26.9	17.2	19.8	97.1	76.2	4.7	3.1	101.3	101.4
142	Nigeria	97.3	158.3	226.7	2.5	2.1	35.3	49.8	17.1	18.6	95.0	83.5	6.4	4.8	101.6	102.6
143	Uganda	17.7	33.8	60.8	3.3	3.2	11.1	13.3	15.9	15.6	103.1	105.1	7.1	5.9	101.4	101.7
144	Senegal	7.5	12.9	19.5	2.8	2.4	38.9	42.4	16.5	18.0	97.2	84.2	6.5	4.5	102.0	102.3
145	Haiti	7.1	10.2	13.2	2.0	1.5	28.5	52.1	18.5	21.6	88.5	67.5	5.2	3.2	103.6	104.1
146	Angola	10.7	19.0	30.4	3.2	2.7	37.1	58.5	16.2	17.4	100.5	89.2	7.1	5.3	99.7	99.9
147	Djibouti	0.6	0.9	1.2	2.1	1.6	75.7	76.2	17.8	21.5	86.5	63.6	5.9	3.5	101.7	102.2
148	Tanzania, United Republic of	25.5	45.0	75.5	3.3	2.9	18.9	26.4	16.9	17.5	94.7	91.8	6.1	5.3	101.2	101.9
149	Côte d'Ivoire	12.6	21.6	32.6	3.4	2.3	39.7	50.6	17.7	19.5	90.3	79.6	5.9	4.2	100.7	101.0
150	Zambia	7.9	13.3	20.9	2.8	2.4	39.4	35.7	17.0	16.8	94.0	97.0	6.3	5.3	101.3	101.4
151	Gambia	0.9	1.8	2.7	3.8	2.5	38.3	58.2	18.7	18.8	84.0	81.6	6.0	4.6	101.1	101.8
152	Rwanda	7.2	10.3	16.1	-5.5	2.7	5.4	18.9	15.4	18.7	107.5	81.2	6.2	5.1	98.9	98.9
153	Malawi	9.5	15.7	25.9	1.4	2.7	11.6	19.8	16.7	16.8	97.7	96.2	6.8	5.1	101.5	102.2
154	Sudan	27.1	43.2	61.0	2.6	2.0	26.6	40.1	17.8	20.3	88.8	73.4	5.8	3.7	103.8	104.1
155	Afghanistan	12.6	29.1	50.6	7.3	3.2	18.1	22.6	16.8	16.9	94.0	92.8	8.0	6.3	106.1	106.0
156	Guinea	6.1	10.3	16.9	3.9	2.7	28.0	35.4	17.7	18.5	91.6	84.9	6.6	5.0	104.3	104.4
157	Ethiopia	48.3	85.0	131.6	3.3	2.5	12.6	16.7	17.4	18.0	92.0	86.5	7.0	4.8	100.8	101.6
158	Sierra Leone	4.1	5.8	8.9	-0.5	2.3	32.9	38.4	18.7	18.2	82.4	82.9	5.5	5.0	98.1	100.7
159	Central African Republic	2.9	4.5	6.1	2.6	1.8	36.8	38.9	18.4	19.5	88.9	79.3	5.7	4.3	99.9	100.0
160	Mali	8.7	13.3	20.5	2.0	2.4	23.3	35.9	17.3	17.6	91.6	86.5	6.3	5.2	101.7	102.2
161	Burkina Faso	8.8	16.3	27.9	2.8	3.1	13.8	25.7	16.2	16.7	99.7	93.9	6.7	5.6	103.5	103.8
162	Liberia	2.2	4.1	6.5	-2.2	2.6	40.9	47.8	17.5	18.5	92.7	83.9	6.4	4.7	100.2	102.1

TABLE 11

186 HUMAN DEVELOPMENT REPORT 2010

	HDI rank	Total (millions)			Average annual growth (%)		Urban (% of total)[a]		Median age (years)		Dependency ratio (per 100 people ages 15–64)		Total fertility rate (births per woman)		Sex ratio at birth (male births per 100 female births)[b]	
		1990	2010	2030	1990–1995	2010–2015	1990	2010	1990	2010	1990	2010	1990–1995	2010–2015	1990	2010
163	Chad	6.1	11.5	19.0	3.1	2.6	20.8	27.6	17.0	17.1	97.5	93.9	6.7	5.8	100.9	101.0
164	Guinea-Bissau	1.0	1.6	2.5	2.6	2.3	28.1	30.0	18.6	18.7	81.3	85.4	5.9	5.4	100.5	100.8
165	Mozambique	13.5	23.4	33.9	3.3	2.1	21.1	38.4	16.5	17.9	99.2	89.3	6.1	4.6	100.3	101.3
166	Burundi	5.7	8.5	11.9	1.6	2.0	6.3	11.0	17.4	20.3	93.9	68.7	6.5	4.0	100.6	100.9
167	Niger	7.9	15.9	32.6	3.3	3.7	15.4	17.1	15.4	15.0	104.8	108.8	7.8	6.9	104.0	104.3
168	Congo, Democratic Republic of the	37.0	67.8	108.6	3.9	2.6	27.8	35.2	16.4	16.6	99.6	96.2	7.1	5.5	100.8	100.7
169	Zimbabwe	10.5	12.6	17.9	2.3	2.1	29.0	38.3	16.8	19.0	96.1	77.3	4.8	3.1	100.8	101.0

OTHER COUNTRIES OR TERRITORIES

		1990	2010	2030	1990–1995	2010–2015	1990	2010	1990	2010	1990	2010	1990–1995	2010–2015	1990	2010
	Antigua and Barbuda	0.1	0.1	0.1	1.9	1.0	35.4	30.3	..	..	..	..	..	..	..	..
	Bhutan	0.5	0.7	0.9	−1.5	1.7	16.4	34.7	18.7	24.2	85.2	53.2	5.4	2.4	102.3	103.0
	Cuba	10.6	11.2	11.0	0.6	0.0	73.4	75.2	28.2	38.3	45.5	42.1	1.7	1.5	106.4	106.8
	Dominica	0.1	0.1	0.1	0.0	0.1	67.7	67.2	..	..	..	..	..	..	..	..
	Eritrea	3.2	5.2	8.1	0.3	2.8	15.8	21.6	16.5	19.1	95.8	78.6	6.1	4.2	100.6	102.4
	Grenada	0.1	0.1	0.1	0.8	0.4	33.4	39.3	20.4	25.0	88.0	52.4	3.5	2.2	104.2	104.9
	Iraq	18.1	31.5	48.9	3.0	2.6	69.7	66.2	17.0	19.3	95.6	78.3	5.8	3.7	105.8	106.0
	Kiribati	0.1	0.1	0.1	1.5	1.5	35.0	43.9	..	..	..	..	..	..	..	..
	Korea, Democratic People's Rep. of	20.1	24.0	25.3	1.5	0.3	58.4	60.2	26.2	34.0	44.6	44.9	2.4	1.9	104.7	105.4
	Lebanon	3.0	4.3	4.9	3.2	0.8	83.1	87.2	21.9	29.2	69.3	47.2	3.0	1.9	103.3	104.0
	Marshall Islands	0.0	0.1	0.1	1.5	1.9	65.1	71.8	..	..	..	..	..	..	..	..
	Monaco	0.0	0.0	0.0	0.9	0.3	100.0	100.0	..	..	..	..	..	..	..	..
	Nauru	0.0	0.0	0.0	1.7	0.6	100.0	100.0	..	..	..	..	..	..	..	..
	Occupied Palestinian Territories	2.2	4.4	7.3	3.9	2.9	67.9	74.1	16.4	17.6	100.4	90.1	6.5	4.5	103.2	104.5
	Oman	1.8	2.9	4.0	3.3	1.9	66.1	73.0	18.3	24.3	85.4	51.5	6.3	2.8	104.4	104.9
	Palau	0.0	0.0	0.0	2.7	0.5	69.6	83.4	..	..	..	..	..	..	..	..
	Saint Kitts and Nevis	0.0	0.1	0.1	1.1	1.2	34.6	32.4	..	..	..	..	..	..	..	..
	Saint Lucia	0.1	0.2	0.2	1.2	0.9	29.4	28.0	21.4	27.5	78.8	48.4	3.2	1.9	97.9	102.7
	Saint Vincent and the Grenadines	0.1	0.1	0.1	0.1	0.0	41.4	49.3	20.4	27.8	78.9	49.8	2.9	2.1	101.3	102.0
	Samoa	0.2	0.2	0.2	0.8	0.2	21.2	20.2	18.5	19.6	81.1	77.2	4.7	3.6	108.7	108.0
	San Marino	0.0	0.0	0.0	1.2	0.6	90.4	94.1	..	..	..	..	..	..	..	..
	Seychelles	0.1	0.1	0.1	1.0	0.3	49.3	55.3	..	..	..	..	..	..	..	..
	Somalia	6.6	9.4	15.7	−0.2	2.7	29.7	37.5	17.6	17.6	90.0	90.8	6.5	6.2	100.6	101.2
	Tuvalu	0.0	0.0	0.0	0.7	0.4	40.7	50.4	..	..	..	..	..	..	..	..
	Vanuatu	0.1	0.2	0.4	2.8	2.4	18.7	25.6	18.1	20.5	90.5	71.2	4.8	3.6	108.5	106.1

Developed

		1990	2010	2030	1990–1995	2010–2015	1990	2010	1990	2010	1990	2010	1990–1995	2010–2015	1990	2010
	OECD	911.0	1,026.3	1,093.3	0.7	0.4	72.0	77.1	34.5	39.9	49.1	49.7	1.7	1.6	105.4	105.5
	Non-OECD	19.3	29.7	36.3	2.5	1.2	89.9	91.7	29.2	35.5	49.9	39.6	2.2	1.9	106.2	106.5

Developing

		1990	2010	2030	1990–1995	2010–2015	1990	2010	1990	2010	1990	2010	1990–1995	2010–2015	1990	2010
	Arab States	226.4	348.2	477.9	2.4	1.9	49.2	55.3	18.2	23.1	87.8	61.9	4.7	2.6	104.2	104.3
	East Asia and the Pacific	1,606.6	1,974.3	2,204.3	1.3	0.8	28.1	45.3	24.0	32.2	56.2	42.5	2.3	2.8	108.5	116.0
	Europe and Central Asia	399.6	410.3	416.4	0.3	0.2	62.8	64.4	30.0	34.3	55.8	43.5	2.1	1.6	104.4	105.6
	Latin America and the Caribbean	437.2	582.7	683.6	1.7	1.0	70.3	79.5	21.9	27.7	70.3	53.2	3.0	2.2	103.8	104.2
	South Asia	1,200.0	1,719.1	2,158.2	2.1	1.4	26.5	31.7	20.3	24.5	75.8	56.8	4.1	2.5	106.8	107.5
	Sub-Saharan Africa	483.1	808.8	1,228.6	2.8	2.4	28.3	37.0	17.2	18.5	94.2	84.8	6.1	3.6	101.3	101.9
	Very high human development	930.3	1,056.0	1,129.5	0.7	0.5	72.3	77.5	34.4	39.8	49.1	49.4	1.7	1.8	105.5	105.6
	High human development	873.1	1,052.4	1,175.1	1.2	0.7	67.8	75.8	25.3	30.4	65.0	47.2	2.7	1.8	104.2	104.8
	Medium human development	2,739.1	3,597.3	4,239.7	1.6	1.1	28.5	39.9	22.5	28.6	64.3	49.5	3.0	2.7	107.8	112.2
	Low human development	673.6	1,099.0	1,626.5	2.7	2.2	24.2	33.4	17.4	19.6	92.3	79.0	5.7	4.1	102.1	102.5
	Least developed countries	524.8 [T]	854.7 [T]	1,271.6 [T]	2.7	2.2	21.0	29.1	17.6	19.9	91.1	77.9	5.6	4.1	102.2	102.5
	World	5,290.4 [T]	6,908.7 [T]	8,308.9 [T]	1.6	1.1	42.6	50.5	24.4	29.1	65.4	54.0	3.1	2.3	106.0	108.4

TABLE
11

NOTES

a Because data are based on national definitions of what constitutes a city or metropolitan area, cross-country comparison should be made with caution.

b The natural sex ratio at birth is commonly assumed and empirically confirmed to be 105 male births to 100 female births.

c Includes Taiwan Province of China.

T Data are aggregates provided by the original data source.

SOURCES

Columns 1–5 and 8–15: UNDESA (2009d).

Columns 6 and 7: UNDESA (2010).

TABLE **12** Decent work

HDI rank	Employment to population ratio (% of population ages 15–64)		Formal employment		Vulnerable employment[a]		Employed people living on less than $1.25 a day (% of total employment)	Unemployment rate by level of education (% of labour force with given level of attainment)		Child labour (% of children ages 5–14)	Mandatory paid maternity leave[b] (calendar days)
			(% of total employment)	Ratio of female to male rates	(% of total employment)	Ratio of female to male rates		Primary or less	Secondary or above		
	1991	2008	2000–2008[c]	2000–2008[c]	2000–2008[c]	2000–2008[c]	2000–2008[c]	2000–2008[c]	2000–2008[c]	1999–2007[c]	2007–2009[c]
VERY HIGH HUMAN DEVELOPMENT											
1 Norway	57.7	62.3	94.3	1.05	5.7	0.42	..	6.0	3.8	..	126
2 Australia	55.6	59.4	90.7	1.05	9.3	0.61	..	7.4	6.2	..	0
3 New Zealand	55.4	62.7	87.9	1.05	11.9	0.68	..	6.1	6.0	..	98
4 United States	59.4	59.2	92.8 [d]	1.03 [d]	..	..	..	..	..	..	0
5 Ireland	43.5	57.8	88.3	1.14	11.7	0.31	..	7.6	7.0	..	182
6 Liechtenstein	..	..	..	..	..	..	..	..	..	..	..
7 Netherlands	51.4	59.3	90.5	1.02	9.4	0.80	..	8.0	7.8	..	112
8 Canada	57.8	61.2	89.6	1.04	10.4	0.71	..	12.1	10.2	..	119
9 Sweden	62.0	57.6	93.4	1.05	6.6	0.51	..	12.7	8.8	..	98
10 Germany	53.8	51.7	93.1	1.01	6.8	0.85	..	16.8	12.1	..	98
11 Japan	61.3	54.2	88.7	0.98	10.8	1.20	..	4.4	..	..	98
12 Korea, Republic of	58.6	58.1	74.9	0.94	25.2	1.18	..	2.1	7.1	..	60 [e]
13 Switzerland	65.0	61.2	89.8	0.99	10.1	1.09	..	6.8	5.7	..	112 [f]
14 France	47.2	47.9	94.1	1.02	5.9	0.69	..	12.3	12.5	..	112
15 Israel	45.2	50.4	91.5	1.04	7.4	0.59	..	14.0	19.1	..	84
16 Finland	57.2	54.7	91.0	1.05	9.0	0.59	..	12.3	10.5	..	263
17 Iceland	70.9	71.2	90.9	1.08	8.7	0.39	..	5.1	4.1	..	180
18 Belgium	43.8	46.5	90.0	1.03	10.0	0.78	..	11.0	10.0	..	105
19 Denmark	59.4	60.3	95.0	1.03	5.0	0.52	..	7.2	7.8	..	126
20 Spain	41.2	48.6	88.1	1.04	11.8	0.73	..	10.5	13.4	..	112
21 Hong Kong, China (SAR)	61.8	56.6	92.8	1.06	7.1	0.45	..	5.6	6.3	..	70 [f]
22 Greece	44.3	48.4	73.1	1.01	27.0	0.99	..	7.5	16.1	..	119 [e]
23 Italy	42.6	43.6	81.4	1.07	18.6	0.75	..	7.3	10.0	..	150
24 Luxembourg	49.3	51.2	95.9	0.98	5.2	1.06	..	..	..	..	..
25 Austria	51.8	54.5	91.1	1.01	9.0	0.95	..	8.8	6.1	..	112
26 United Kingdom	55.6	56.3	89.2	1.08	10.5	0.50	..	9.4	8.0	..	365 [e]
27 Singapore	63.7	61.6	89.8	1.06	10.2	0.59	..	..	..	..	84 [e]
28 Czech Republic	58.2	54.3	87.5	1.08	12.5	0.56	..	20.2	6.3	..	196
29 Slovenia	54.5	54.1	89.1	1.03	11.0	0.79	..	7.9	9.5	..	365
30 Andorra	..	..	..	..	..	..	..	..	..	..	..
31 Slovakia	54.5	52.6	89.3	1.09	10.6	0.44	..	46.6	13.0	..	196
32 United Arab Emirates	71.3	75.9	98.4	1.01	1.6	0.29	..	2.4	7.9	..	45 [f]
33 Malta	42.5	45.2	91.0	1.07	9.2	0.50	..	8.5	2.7	..	..
34 Estonia	61.2	54.5	95.5	1.02	5.8	0.48	..	10.3	7.1	..	140
35 Cyprus	59.9	57.5	85.5	1.06	14.4	0.69	..	4.4	7.5	..	..
36 Hungary	47.5	44.8	92.9	1.03	7.1	0.67	..	17.3	9.5	..	168
37 Brunei Darussalam	62.2	63.3	..	..	..	..	..	..	..	..	..
38 Qatar	73.0	76.9	99.5	1.01	0.4	0.00	..	..	..	..	..
39 Bahrain	61.0	61.0	..	..	..	..	..	..	..	5	..
40 Portugal	57.6	55.7	81.5	0.99	18.5	1.06	..	8.0	15.6	3	120
41 Poland	53.0	48.2	81.2	1.03	18.9	0.89	..	15.5	14.9	..	112 [e]
42 Barbados	54.8	64.4	85.6	1.11	14.0	0.55	..	..	..	..	..

HDI rank	Employment to population ratio (% of population ages 15–64)		Formal employment		Vulnerable employment[a]		Employed people living on less than $1.25 a day (% of total employment)	Unemployment rate by level of education (% of labour force with given level of attainment)		Child labour (% of children ages 5–14)	Mandatory paid maternity leave[b] (calendar days)
			(% of total employment)	Ratio of female to male rates	(% of total employment)	Ratio of female to male rates		Primary or less	Secondary or above		
	1991	2008	2000–2008c	2000–2008c	2000–2008c	2000–2008c	2000–2008c	2000–2008c	2000–2008c	1999–2007c	2007–2009c
HIGH HUMAN DEVELOPMENT											
43 Bahamas	62.6	65.4	84.4 d	1.07 d	..	..	..	..	..	..	..
44 Lithuania	53.7	50.2	90.7	1.04	9.4	0.72	..	7.3	7.2	..	126
45 Chile	50.6	49.6	75.2	1.02	24.8	0.94	..	4.9	15.6	3	126
46 Argentina	53.0	56.5	79.9	1.06	20.1	0.78	3.5	9.9	18.1	7	90
47 Kuwait	61.9	65.3	..	..	..	..	..	..	..	..	70 f
48 Latvia	57.6	55.0	93.2	1.03	6.8	0.70	..	10.3	9.6	..	112
49 Montenegro	..	..	80.5 d	1.11 d	..	..	..	..	..	4	365 e
50 Romania	55.6	48.1	68.7	0.99	31.2	1.03	..	7.1	9.8	1	126
51 Croatia	49.9	45.9	83.8	0.98	16.2	1.12	1.3	10.7	16.5	..	365
52 Uruguay	52.7	56.4	74.7	1.02	25.1	0.92	..	10.0	15.9	8	84
53 Libyan Arab Jamahiriya	45.3	48.6	..	..	..	..	..	..	..	..	..
54 Panama	49.5	58.7	72.3	1.09	27.7	0.78	11.8	5.4	15.7	3	98 e
55 Saudi Arabia	50.4	50.9	..	..	..	..	..	..	..	..	70 f
56 Mexico	56.5	57.1	70.5	0.94	29.5	1.16	0.8	2.9	8.7	16	84
57 Malaysia	59.7	60.5	77.6	1.02	22.3	0.93	0.6	..	..	..	60 f
58 Bulgaria	45.2	46.3	91.3	1.03	8.7	0.77	..	17.5	8.2	..	135
59 Trinidad and Tobago	44.5	60.7	83.4	1.05	15.6	0.76	..	..	..	1	..
60 Serbia	..	..	77.3	1.06	22.7	0.83	..	..	..	10	365
61 Belarus	57.5	52.3	..	..	..	..	..	..	..	5	126
62 Costa Rica	56.3	57.2	80.2	1.00	19.7	1.02	2.9	5.2	7.0	5	120 e
63 Peru	53.4	68.8	60.1	0.79	39.6	1.41	9.0	..	..	19	90
64 Albania	48.9	46.2	..	..	..	..	1.3	15.8	29.0	12	..
65 Russian Federation	56.8	56.7	94.1	1.01	5.8	0.90	..	13.2	11.8	..	140
66 Kazakhstan	62.7	63.5	63.3	0.93	35.8	1.16	3.8	10.3	16.8	2	126 f
67 Azerbaijan	56.5	60.0	46.8	0.57	53.2	1.63	..	11.3	11.3	7	126 e
68 Bosnia and Herzegovina	42.3	41.5	72.9 d	1.01 d	..	..	..	31.2	..	5	365
69 Ukraine	56.9	53.5	80.7 d	0.97 d	..	..	..	6.7	14.6	7	126
70 Iran, Islamic Republic of	45.9	48.9	56.8	0.72	42.7	1.41	1.9	8.3	33.2	..	90
71 The former Yugoslav Republic of Macedonia	37.1	34.8	77.8	1.05	22.2	0.84	..	..	..	6	..
72 Mauritius	55.5	53.8	82.4	1.04	16.8	0.82	..	8.0	15.3	..	..
73 Brazil	55.7	63.9	68.1	1.02	27.2	0.82	6.2	8.4	13.3	6	120
74 Georgia	57.4	54.3	37.8	0.97	62.2	1.02	17.4	7.1	30.3	18	126
75 Venezuela, Bolivarian Republic of	51.4	61.3	63.5	0.98	29.8	1.18	4.4	..	..	8	126 e
76 Armenia	38.0	38.1	..	..	..	..	18.9	..	..	4	140
77 Ecuador	51.6	60.5	66.2	0.83	33.8	1.41	5.8	..	..	8	84
78 Belize	47.3	56.9	76.4	1.04	23.5	0.87	..	12.1	16.5	40	..
79 Colombia	52.1	62.0	58.9	1.01	40.9	0.99	21.3	..	..	5	84
80 Jamaica	60.7	56.2	64.3	1.11	35.4	0.82	..	..	..	6	56 f
81 Tunisia	40.5	41.0	64.3 d	..	..	..	3.9	..	..	..	..
82 Jordan	35.7	37.9	..	..	..	..	..	..	..	..	70 f
83 Turkey	52.5	42.3	64.6	0.73	35.3	1.61	3.9	9.0	22.4	5	112
84 Algeria	39.2	49.4	64.8	0.76	34.9	1.53	..	19.0	45.3	5	98
85 Tonga	..	..	..	..	..	..	..	..	..	..	..
MEDIUM HUMAN DEVELOPMENT											
86 Fiji	53.5	56.3	59.7	0.95	39.0	1.01	..	..	..	..	..
87 Turkmenistan	55.6	58.3	..	..	..	..	..	..	..	..	..
88 Dominican Republic	43.5	53.3	57.6	1.36	42.4	0.62	4.9	12.3	35.3	10	84 f
89 China	75.1	71.0	..	..	..	..	18.3	..	..	..	90 f
90 El Salvador	58.6	54.3	59.0	0.66	35.5	1.51	15.6	..	..	6	84 f
91 Sri Lanka	51.3	54.7	59.3	0.91	40.7	1.14	17.8	4.0	20.0	8	84 f
92 Thailand	77.3	71.5	46.6	0.90	53.3	..	..	..	..	8	45 f
93 Gabon	58.1	58.2	..	..	..	..	6.3	..	..	..	..
94 Suriname	45.3	46.5	..	..	..	..	..	..	..	6	..
95 Bolivia, Plurinational State of	61.4	70.7	38.1	0.63	61.6	1.31	22.5	..	..	22	60

TABLE
12

Decent work

HDI rank	Employment to population ratio (% of population ages 15–64)		Formal employment		Vulnerable employment[a]		Employed people living on less than $1.25 a day (% of total employment)	Unemployment rate by level of education (% of labour force with given level of attainment)		Child labour (% of children ages 5–14)	Mandatory paid maternity leave[b] (calendar days)
			(% of total employment)	Ratio of female to male rates	(% of total employment)	Ratio of female to male rates		Primary or less	Secondary or above		
	1991	2008	2000–2008c	2000–2008c	2000–2008c	2000–2008c	2000–2008c	2000–2008c	2000–2008c	1999–2007c	2007–2009c
96 Paraguay	61.1	72.8	53.2	0.89	46.8	1.13	7.3	4.6	13.6	15	84
97 Philippines	59.1	60.1	55.3	0.95	44.7	1.07	27.2	2.7	16.4	12	60
98 Botswana	46.7	46.0	75.9	0.96	11.7	2.29	..	..	..	..	84 f
99 Moldova, Republic of	58.1	44.7	67.6	1.09	32.4	0.84	11.1	..	..	32	126 e
100 Mongolia	50.2	51.6	39.9	1.12	59.7	0.93	30.5	..	..	18	120
101 Egypt	42.6	43.2	75.2	0.71	24.8	2.13	2.7	..	..	7	90 e
102 Uzbekistan	53.8	57.5	..	..	..	..	59.7	..	..	..	126 e
103 Micronesia, Federated States of	..	..	..	..	..	..	..	..	..	..	..
104 Guyana	51.4	57.8	..	..	..	..	..	..	..	16	..
105 Namibia	45.4	42.9	78.4	0.89	21.1	1.66	..	..	..	13	90
106 Honduras	58.9	56.3	89.7	1.06	48.9	1.08	21.4	..	..	16	70 e
107 Maldives	44.9	57.3	27.2	1.16	50.3	0.69	..	..	..	..	..
108 Indonesia	63.0	61.8	36.9	0.81	63.1	1.13	27.8	6.2	31.5	4	90 f
109 Kyrgyzstan	58.0	58.3	51.9	1.01	47.3	0.99	27.2	2.6	43.0	4	126
110 South Africa	39.4	41.1	97.1	0.99	2.7	1.50	44.4	23.4	34.8	..	112
111 Syrian Arab Republic	46.6	44.8	57.5	0.81	42.4	1.28	..	..	..	4	60 f
112 Tajikistan	53.8	55.4	..	..	..	..	28.6	..	..	10	..
113 Viet Nam	74.8	69.4	26.1	0.71	73.9	1.13	24.2	..	..	16	120
114 Morocco	45.9	46.1	47.1	0.67	51.1	1.40	3.4	8.8	54.2	8	98
115 Nicaragua	57.2	58.3	54.7	0.99	44.9	1.02	19.4	..	..	15	84 f
116 Guatemala	55.1	62.4	34.2	0.74	55.0	1.20	14.6	..	..	29	84 f
117 Equatorial Guinea	61.4	62.6	..	..	..	..	..	..	..	28	..
118 Cape Verde	56.7	55.7	41.4	0.74	39.6	1.23	26.6	..	..	3	..
119 India	58.3	55.6	..	..	..	..	51.4	..	..	12	84 f
120 Timor-Leste	63.8	66.8	..	..	..	..	63.2	..	..	4	..
121 Swaziland	54.2	50.4	..	..	..	..	83.8	..	..	9	..
122 Lao People's Democratic Republic	80.2	77.7	..	..	..	..	45.7	..	..	11	90 e
123 Solomon Islands	67.1	64.5	..	..	..	..	..	..	..	..	..
124 Cambodia	77.2	74.6	13.1	0.71	86.7	1.07	45.7	..	..	45	90 f
125 Pakistan	47.5	51.5	38.2	0.59	61.8	1.29	28.9	5.1	11.6	..	84 f
126 Congo	65.5	64.6	..	..	..	..	66.7	..	..	25	..
127 São Tomé and Príncipe	..	..	..	..	..	..	..	..	..	8	..
LOW HUMAN DEVELOPMENT											
128 Kenya	73.4	73.0	..	..	..	..	22.9	..	..	26	90 f
129 Bangladesh	74.0	67.9	14.2	0.80	85.0	1.02	56.9	..	..	13	112 f
130 Ghana	68.4	65.2	..	..	..	..	37.6	..	..	34	84 f
131 Cameroon	59.1	59.1	20.8	0.31	75.9	1.36	39.9	..	..	31	98
132 Myanmar	74.2	74.4	..	..	..	..	..	..	..	..	..
133 Yemen	38.3	39.0	..	..	..	..	26.0	..	..	23	60 f
134 Benin	70.1	71.6	..	..	..	..	55.6	..	..	46	98
135 Madagascar	79.3	83.3	..	..	82.2	1.08	76.7	..	..	32	98 e
136 Mauritania	66.5	47.2	..	..	..	..	24.6	..	..	16	98
137 Papua New Guinea	69.9	70.2	..	..	..	..	..	..	..	..	108
138 Nepal	59.6	61.5	28.4	0.44	71.6	1.34	67.6	..	..	31	52 f
139 Togo	65.9	64.6	..	..	..	..	45.9	..	..	29	98 e
140 Comoros	70.0	69.4	..	..	..	..	64.6	..	..	27	..
141 Lesotho	48.3	54.1	..	..	..	..	61.0	..	..	23	84
142 Nigeria	52.7	51.8	..	..	..	..	72.2	..	..	13	84 f
143 Uganda	81.8	83.0	14.8	0.34	85.2	1.19	55.7	..	..	36	60 f
144 Senegal	66.8	66.0	..	..	..	..	44.4	..	..	22	98
145 Haiti	56.0	55.4	..	..	..	..	66.9	..	..	21	..
146 Angola	76.5	76.4	..	..	..	..	59.9	..	..	24	56
147 Djibouti	..	..	..	..	..	..	..	..	..	8	..
148 Tanzania, United Republic of	87.4	78.0	12.3	0.40	87.7	1.13	90.0	..	..	36	84 f
149 Côte d'Ivoire	62.5	60.4	..	..	..	..	26.3	..	..	35	98
150 Zambia	57.0	61.2	19.1	0.35	79.3	1.23	76.6	..	..	12	84 f
151 Gambia	73.2	72.1	..	..	..	..	42.7	..	..	25	..

TABLE 12

HDI rank		Employment to population ratio (% of population ages 15–64)		Formal employment		Vulnerable employment[a]		Employed people living on less than $1.25 a day (% of total employment)	Unemployment rate by level of education (% of labour force with given level of attainment)		Child labour (% of children ages 5–14)	Mandatory paid maternity leave[b] (calendar days)
				(% of total employment)	Ratio of female to male rates	(% of total employment)	Ratio of female to male rates		Primary or less	Secondary or above		
		1991	2008	2000–2008[c]	2000–2008[c]	2000–2008[c]	2000–2008[c]	2000–2008[c]	2000–2008[c]	2000–2008[c]	1999–2007[c]	2007–2009[c]
152	Rwanda	86.6	80.3	..	..	..	..	79.5	..	..	35	98[e]
153	Malawi	71.7	72.1	..	..	..	..	79.8	..	..	26	56[f]
154	Sudan	46.1	47.3	..	..	..	..	..	..	..	13	56[f]
155	Afghanistan	54.1	55.2	..	..	..	..	..	..	..	30	..
156	Guinea	82.1	81.2	..	..	..	..	73.9	..	..	25	98[e]
157	Ethiopia	71.3	80.6	47.0	0.86	51.8	1.16	45.8	..	..	53	90[f]
158	Sierra Leone	63.6	64.8	81.9	0.92	..	..	67.1	..	..	48	..
159	Central African Republic	73.3	72.6	..	..	..	..	71.1	..	..	47	..
160	Mali	49.3	47.0	13.6[d]	0.75[d]	..	..	60.6	..	..	34	98
161	Burkina Faso	81.6	81.9	..	..	..	..	60.7	..	..	47	98
162	Liberia	65.7	65.9	..	..	..	..	86.2	..	..	21	..
163	Chad	66.6	69.7	..	..	..	..	72.1	..	..	53	98
164	Guinea-Bissau	66.3	66.9	..	..	..	..	55.3	..	..	39	..
165	Mozambique	79.9	77.9	..	..	..	..	81.2	..	..	22	..
166	Burundi	84.9	84.2	..	..	..	..	87.2	..	..	19	..
167	Niger	59.4	59.8	..	..	..	..	76.6	..	..	43	98[f]
168	Congo, Democratic Republic of the	67.8	66.7	..	..	..	..	69.6	..	..	32	105[e]
169	Zimbabwe	70.1	64.9	38.2	0.45	61.9	1.58	..	..	..	13	..

OTHER COUNTRIES OR TERRITORIES

		1991	2008	2000–2008[c]	2000–2008[c]	2000–2008[c]	2000–2008[c]	2000–2008[c]	2000–2008[c]	2000–2008[c]	1999–2007[c]	2007–2009[c]
	Bhutan	53.3	61.1	40.8	0.35	52.3	1.94	31.7	..	..	19	..
	Cuba	52.4	54.4	83.1[d]	1.22[d]	..	..	..	..	..	..	..
	Dominica	..	..	73.3	1.13	25.9	0.70	..	..	..	..	..
	Eritrea	65.8	65.6	..	..	..	..	..	..	..	..	..
	Iraq	36.8	37.1	..	..	..	..	..	..	..	11	..
	Korea, Democratic People's Rep. of	62.1	63.9	..	..	..	..	..	..	..	..	..
	Lebanon	43.8	45.9	..	..	..	..	..	..	..	7	49[e]
	Occupied Palestinian Territories	30.1	30.2	63.9	0.85	36.1	1.29	..	24.7	41.8	..	..
	Oman	52.6	51.4	89.6	0.98	..	..	..	..	..	..	42
	Saint Kitts and Nevis	..	..	88.4	1.04	8.5	0.70	..	..	..	..	..
	Saint Lucia	..	..	69.5	1.12	28.7	0.80	..	..	..	..	..
	Samoa	..	..	53.5	1.32	..	..	..	..	..	..	..
	San Marino	..	..	90.4[d]	1.05[d]	..	..	..	..	..	..	..
	Somalia	65.6	66.5	..	..	..	..	..	..	..	49	..
	Tuvalu	..	..	97.9	1.01	2.0	0.81	..	..	..	..	..

NOTES

a Percentage of employed people engaged as unpaid family workers and own-account workers.

b Number of days of maternity leave paid by the government, unless otherwise noted. Refers to women in formal employment.

c Data refer to the most recent year available during the period specified.

d Does not include data on employers.

e Benefits paid by both the government and the employer.

f Benefits paid by the employer.

SOURCES

Columns 1–9: ILO (2010d).
Column 10: UNICEF (2010c).
Column 11: World Bank (2010f).

TABLE
12

TABLE 13
Education

		ACHIEVEMENTS IN EDUCATION		ACCESS TO EDUCATION					EFFICIENCY OF PRIMARY EDUCATION		QUALITY OF PRIMARY EDUCATION	
		Adult literacy rate	Population with at least secondary education	Primary enrolment ratio (% of primary school-age population)		Secondary enrolment ratio (% of secondary school-age population)		Tertiary enrolment ratio (% of tertiary school-age population)	Dropout rate, all grades	Repetition rate, all grades	Pupil–teacher ratio	Primary school teachers trained to teach
HDI rank		(% ages 15 and older)	(% ages 25 and older)	Gross	Net	Gross	Net	Gross	(% of primary school cohort)	(% of total primary enrolment in previous year)	(number of pupils per teacher)	(%)
		2005–2008ª	2010	2001–2009ª	2001–2009ª	2001–2009ª	2001–2009ª	2001–2009ª	2005–2008ª	2005–2008ª	2005–2008ª	2005–2008ª
VERY HIGH HUMAN DEVELOPMENT												
1	Norway	..	87.3	98.4	98.4	112.5	96.6	75.9	0.2	..	..	..
2	Australia	..	73.4	104.9	97.0	147.9	87.5	75.0	..	..	15.8	..
3	New Zealand	..	67.9	101.2	99.2	120.4	90.8	79.1	..	..	17.1	..
4	United States	..	89.7	98.0	91.5	94.3	88.2	81.6	1.5	..	14.3	..
5	Ireland	..	64.1	105.4	96.9	113.4	88.1	61.2	..	0.7	17.8	..
6	Liechtenstein	..	..	109.6	89.3	106.1	65.2	31.2	18.2	..	9.5	..
7	Netherlands	..	67.4	106.8	98.5	119.5	88.6	60.1	1.7 b	..	..	..
8	Canada	..	79.6	107.1	99.5	101.3	..	62.3 b	..	..	..	..
9	Sweden	..	80.3	94.2	93.8	103.1	99.1	74.5	0.1	..	10.7	..
10	Germany	..	97.2 b,c	105.7	98.2	100.6	..	..	4.4	1.3	18.0	..
11	Japan	..	71.9	102.2	100.0	100.7	98.0	57.9	..	..	18.8	..
12	Korea, Republic of	..	75.3	103.7	98.6	97.5	96.4	96.1	1.6	0.0	24.1	..
13	Switzerland	..	71.0	102.4	93.5	95.7	84.7	47.2	..	1.5	18.1	..
14	France	..	55.7	110.2	98.5	113.3	98.3	54.7	2.0 b	4.2	20.3	..
15	Israel	..	61.8	110.9	97.1	91.5	87.6	60.4	0.4	1.5	17.2	..
16	Finland	..	70.5	97.6	96.3	111.3	96.8	93.8	0.2	0.4	15.9	..
17	Iceland	..	54.8	97.2	97.1	110.0	90.3	72.3	..	..	..	..
18	Belgium	..	47.7	102.3	97.8	109.5	86.9	62.1	12.8	3.4	12.6	..
19	Denmark	..	68.1	99.0	95.6	119.2	89.6	80.3	7.9 b	..	..	..
20	Spain	97.6	46.9	105.4	99.7	119.1	94.3	68.5	0.1	..	13.1	..
21	Hong Kong, China (SAR)	..	62.7	101.0	93.5	82.9	75.2	34.3	0.0	0.9	..	95.1
22	Greece	97.0	47.4	101.2	99.4	101.8	91.0	90.8	1.8	0.7	10.1	..
23	Italy	98.8	46.7	103.8	98.6	99.9	92.4	67.1	0.4	0.2	10.4	..
24	Luxembourg	..	78.1 b,c	100.3	95.5	95.4	83.0	10.0	13.5	3.8	13.1	..
25	Austria	..	70.1	101.5	97.9	99.9	..	50.3	2.2	1.2 b	12.9	..
26	United Kingdom	..	58.2	104.0	97.2	97.4	91.3	59.0	..	..	20.1	..
27	Singapore	94.5	59.1	..	..	..	..	..	..	0.3	19.5	97.1
28	Czech Republic	..	99.8 b,c	102.1	92.2	95.0	..	54.3	1.1	0.6	17.3	..
29	Slovenia	99.7	94.3 b,c	102.9	95.6	93.5	88.5	85.5	1.1	0.6	17.1	..
30	Andorra	..	50.9 b,c	86.7	80.1	82.2	71.4	11.0	..	2.8	..	100.0
31	Slovakia	..	98.8 b,c	101.9	91.8	92.8	..	50.1	2.6 b	3.0	18.6	..
32	United Arab Emirates	90.0	..	107.9	91.6	93.8	83.8	25.2	0.0	1.9	17.2	100.0
33	Malta	92.4	44.2	99.0	91.4	98.1	82.0	33.0	1.0 b	0.8	12.1	..
34	Estonia	99.8	87.3 b,c	99.2	94.4	99.7	89.9	65.0	1.7	0.9	..	..
35	Cyprus	97.8	58.7	102.5	99.0	97.8	95.1	36.2	1.6	0.4	15.0	..
36	Hungary	99.0	46.7	97.9	88.8	96.7	90.5	67.2	1.0	1.7	10.6	..
37	Brunei Darussalam	95.0	..	106.7	93.3	96.7	88.2	16.0	1.6	0.8	10.1	84.3
38	Qatar	93.1	54.1 b,c	108.6	94.1	93.2	79.2	11.0	3.3	0.6	..	52.3
39	Bahrain	90.8	48.1	105.3	97.9	96.8	89.4	29.9	1.3 b	2.0	..	..
40	Portugal	94.6	27.5	115.2	98.9	101.3	87.9	56.9	..	10.2	11.7	..
41	Poland	99.5	60.6	97.1	95.6	99.8	93.8	66.9	2.7	0.7	11.0	..
42	Barbados	..	58.8	..	..	..	..	..	6.1	..	13.5	61.0

		ACHIEVEMENTS IN EDUCATION		ACCESS TO EDUCATION					EFFICIENCY OF PRIMARY EDUCATION		QUALITY OF PRIMARY EDUCATION	
		Adult literacy rate	Population with at least secondary education	Primary enrolment ratio (% of primary school-age population)		Secondary enrolment ratio (% of secondary school-age population)		Tertiary enrolment ratio (% of tertiary school-age population)	Dropout rate, all grades	Repetition rate, all grades	Pupil–teacher ratio	Primary school teachers trained to teach
		(% ages 15 and older)	(% ages 25 and older)	Gross	Net	Gross	Net	Gross	(% of primary school cohort)	(% of total primary enrolment in previous year)	(number of pupils per teacher)	(%)
HDI rank		2005–2008[a]	2010	2001–2009[a]	2001–2009[a]	2001–2009[a]	2001–2009[a]	2001–2009[a]	2005–2008[a]	2005–2008[a]	2005–2008[a]	2005–2008[a]
HIGH HUMAN DEVELOPMENT												
43	Bahamas	..	89.6 [b,c]	102.4	90.5	93.7	86.1	..	9.1	..	15.8	91.1
44	Lithuania	99.7	88.6 [b,c]	96.1	91.3	99.1	92.1	75.9	2.0	0.7	9.7	..
45	Chile	98.6	51.8	105.6	94.4	90.6	85.3	52.1	5.1	2.4	26.2	..
46	Argentina	97.7	44.6	114.6	98.5	85.3	79.4	68.1	5.1	6.1	14.8	..
47	Kuwait	94.5	56.9	95.5	87.6	90.8	79.9	17.6	0.5	0.9	9.1	100.0 [b]
48	Latvia	99.8	97.9 [b,c]	96.8	90.1	114.5	..	69.2	4.3	3.3	12.8	..
49	Montenegro	..	98.2 [b,c]	..	..	..	..	..	..	..	..	..
50	Romania	97.6	79.1 [b,c]	104.7	93.9	87.5	73.0	58.3	6.7	1.7	16.3	..
51	Croatia	98.7	78.0 [b,c]	98.6	90.2	93.6	88.3	47.0	0.2	0.3	17.3	100.0 [b]
52	Uruguay	98.2	44.6	114.3	97.5	92.0	67.7	64.3	6.3	7.0	15.5	..
53	Libyan Arab Jamahiriya	88.4	..	110.3	..	93.5	..	55.7 [b]	..	..	..	..
54	Panama	93.5	48.3	111.1	98.3	71.2	65.6	45.0	14.8	5.3	24.2	91.3
55	Saudi Arabia	85.5	48.8 [b,c]	98.4	84.5	94.6	73.0	29.9	3.6	3.3	..	91.5
56	Mexico	92.9	40.3	112.9	97.9	87.4	70.9	26.3	8.5	3.6	28.0	95.4
57	Malaysia	92.1	50.5	97.9	97.5	69.1	68.7	29.7	7.8	..	17.5 [b]	..
58	Bulgaria	98.3	87.6 [b,c]	101.1	94.6	105.2	87.5	49.7	6.3	1.8	16.1	..
59	Trinidad and Tobago	98.7	48.6	103.4	91.8	88.8	73.9	11.6	4.2	6.6	17.2	86.6
60	Serbia	..	..	100.6	97.0	90.5	89.6	48.7	1.6	0.6	..	100.0
61	Belarus	99.7	..	99.2	94.4	95.3	86.8	72.8	0.5	0.0	..	99.9
62	Costa Rica	96.0	29.9	109.9	..	89.2	..	25.3	5.7	7.0	19.0	86.0
63	Peru	89.6	50.5	112.8	96.8	97.6	75.9	34.5	17.0	7.2	20.9	..
64	Albania	99.0	75.7 [b,c]	102.1	90.8	77.7	73.8	19.3 [b]	10.1 [b]	2.1 [b]	..	..
65	Russian Federation	99.5	..	96.8	..	84.0	..	75.0	4.8	0.4	..	..
66	Kazakhstan	99.7	82.1 [b,c]	108.8	89.3	94.9	86.9	41.0	1.0	0.1	..	..
67	Azerbaijan	99.5	92.8 [b,c]	116.2	96.0	105.6	98.3	15.8	1.6	0.3	..	99.9
68	Bosnia and Herzegovina	97.6	..	111.0	..	89.1	..	33.5	..	0.1	..	..
69	Ukraine	99.7	88.2 [b,c]	98.4	88.9	94.4	85.0	79.4	2.7	0.1	..	99.8
70	Iran, Islamic Republic of	82.3	29.5	128.4	99.7	79.7	75.1	36.1	12.2 [b]	1.8	20.0 [b]	100.0 [b]
71	The former Yugoslav Republic of Macedonia	97.0	47.8 [b,c]	92.8	86.5	84.2	81.6	35.5	2.5	0.1	..	..
72	Mauritius	87.5	36.3	99.4	93.1	87.6	80.1	16.0	2.1	4.0	21.7	100.0 [b]
73	Brazil	90.0	21.9	129.6	92.6	100.1	77.0	30.0	24.4 [b]	18.7	23.0	..
74	Georgia	99.7	91.0 [b,c]	107.4	98.7	90.0	80.8	34.3	4.9	0.3	12.5	95.0
75	Venezuela, Bolivarian Republic of	95.2	27.7	103.1	90.1	81.1	69.5	78.1	19.3	3.4	16.2	83.5
76	Armenia	99.5	91.1 [b,c]	79.6	74.0	88.1	85.7	34.2	2.3	0.2	..	77.5
77	Ecuador	84.2	37.0	118.5	96.9	69.6	59.2	35.3	18.6	2.5	22.6	100.0
78	Belize	..	24.5 [b,c]	120.5	97.7	75.0	63.4	11.2	9.5	8.2	24.5	42.8
79	Colombia	93.4	31.3	119.9	90.0	90.6	71.2	35.4	12.2	3.5	29.4	100.0
80	Jamaica	85.9	42.1	90.1	85.1	90.2	76.7	19.3 [b]	12.8 [b]	3.0	29.1	79.5
81	Tunisia	78.0	23.1	107.6	97.7	90.2	65.8	31.6	5.9	8.5	17.3	..
82	Jordan	92.2	54.2	96.3	89.1	86.3	83.7	37.7	0.9	0.6	12.2	..
83	Turkey	88.7	22.3	97.6	93.9	82.1	71.2	37.1	5.8	2.1	..	..
84	Algeria	72.6	25.9	107.5	94.9	83.2	66.3	23.9	7.1	7.8	..	98.9
85	Tonga	99.0	..	111.8	99.0	102.7	66.2	6.4 [b]	9.1	5.2	..	..
MEDIUM HUMAN DEVELOPMENT												
86	Fiji	..	41.9	94.2	91.2	80.9	79.1	15.4	5.4	1.7	26.1	97.8
87	Turkmenistan	99.5	..	..	..	..	..	..	..	..	..	..
88	Dominican Republic	88.2	27.6	104.3	80.0	74.9	57.7	33.3 [b]	31.2	3.4	19.6	89.2
89	China	93.7	38.4	112.1	..	74.0	..	22.1	0.4	0.3	18.3	..
90	El Salvador	84.0	19.4	115.0	94.0	63.6	55.0	24.6	24.3	6.1	33.3	93.2
91	Sri Lanka	90.6	44.9	105.1	99.7	87.0	..	..	2.0	0.8	22.5 [b]	..
92	Thailand	93.5	20.6	..	..	..	..	..	..	..	9.2	21.2

TABLE
13

HDI rank		ACHIEVEMENTS IN EDUCATION		ACCESS TO EDUCATION					EFFICIENCY OF PRIMARY EDUCATION		QUALITY OF PRIMARY EDUCATION	
		Adult literacy rate	Population with at least secondary education	Primary enrolment ratio (% of primary school-age population)		Secondary enrolment ratio (% of secondary school-age population)		Tertiary enrolment ratio (% of tertiary school-age population)	Dropout rate, all grades	Repetition rate, all grades	Pupil–teacher ratio	Primary school teachers trained to teach
		(% ages 15 and older)	(% ages 25 and older)	Gross	Net	Gross	Net	Gross	(% of primary school cohort)	(% of total primary enrolment in previous year)	(number of pupils per teacher)	(%)
		2005–2008[a]	2010	2001–2009[a]	2001–2009[a]	2001–2009[a]	2001–2009[a]	2001–2009[a]	2005–2008[a]	2005–2008[a]	2005–2008[a]	2005–2008[a]
93	Gabon	87.0	..	134.3	80.3	53.1	..	7.1[b]	44.5[b]	34.4	36.0[b]	100.0[b]
94	Suriname	90.7	..	113.8	90.1	75.4	64.6	12.3[b]	32.3	17.2	13.2	100.0
95	Bolivia, Plurinational State of	90.7	29.3	108.3	93.7	81.8	69.9	38.3	19.8	2.5	25.1	90.6[b]
96	Paraguay	94.6	26.4	108.3	92.4	65.9	57.7	25.5	20.9	4.1	16.6[b]	..
97	Philippines	93.6	53.6	108.2	90.4	81.4	59.9	27.8	26.8	2.3	33.7	100.0[b]
98	Botswana	83.3	24.7	109.7	87.2	80.2	56.5	5.2	13.2	4.7	25.4	94.3
99	Moldova, Republic of	98.3	..	89.2	83.3	83.1	79.1	39.9	4.4	0.1	..	..
100	Mongolia	97.3	80.2[b,c]	101.5	88.7	95.1	82.0	49.8	5.1	0.2	31.6	99.0
101	Egypt	66.4	36.1	99.7	93.6	79.3	71.2	31.2	3.2	3.1	21.9[b]	99.9[b]
102	Uzbekistan	99.3	..	94.4	89.9	102.4	91.7	9.9	1.3	0.0	..	100.0
103	Micronesia, Federated States of	..	..	110.3	..	90.5	..	14.1[b]	..	..	..	..
104	Guyana	..	40.0	108.7	94.7	102.1	..	11.5	41.2[b]	0.7	25.6	58.5
105	Namibia	88.2	..	112.4	89.0	65.8	54.4	8.9	23.4	18.1	29.4	95.0
106	Honduras	83.6	17.1	116.0	96.6	64.5	..	18.7	23.8	5.3	33.3	36.4
107	Maldives	98.4	..	112.0	96.2	83.7	69.4	..	..	4.3	13.3	67.9
108	Indonesia	92.0	26.8	120.9	94.8	75.8	69.7	18.0	19.9	2.9	21.4	93.5[b]
109	Kyrgyzstan	99.3	89.2[b,c]	94.7	83.5	85.1	80.5	52.0	1.7	0.1	..	64.4
110	South Africa	89.0	57.9	104.5	87.5	95.1	71.9	..	23.0[b]	8.0	..	78.7[b]
111	Syrian Arab Republic	83.6	33.5	124.4	94.5	74.0	67.7	..	3.3	7.5	..	88.4
112	Tajikistan	99.7	92.4[b,c]	102.2	97.3	84.4	82.5	20.2	0.5	0.3	22.2	88.3
113	Viet Nam	92.5	..	104.1	94.0	66.9	62.3	9.7[b]	7.9	1.0	20.9	98.6
114	Morocco	56.4	..	106.9	89.5	55.8	34.5	12.3	23.8	11.9	29.9	100.0[b]
115	Nicaragua	78.0	25.4	116.9	91.8	67.9	45.2	18.0[b]	51.6	11.0	29.2	72.7
116	Guatemala	73.8	15.3	113.6	95.1	56.6	39.9	17.7	35.3	12.4	29.4	..
117	Equatorial Guinea	93.0	..	98.7	66.4	26.2	21.6	3.3[b]	67.4[b]	24.3	54.5[b]	30.9
118	Cape Verde	84.1	..	101.3	84.4	67.7	56.7	11.9	12.9	11.6	24.4[b]	84.7
119	India	62.8	22.2	113.1	89.8	57.0	..	13.5	34.2	3.4	40.7	..
120	Timor-Leste	..	..	106.6	75.9	54.7	31.4	15.2	..	12.5	37.4	..
121	Swaziland	86.5	32.6	107.9	82.8	53.3	28.6	4.4	26.3	18.0	32.4	94.0
122	Lao People's Democratic Republic	72.7	..	111.8	82.4	43.9	36.0	13.4	33.2	16.8	..	96.9
123	Solomon Islands	76.6[b]	..	107.3	67.0	34.8	30.2	..	..	..	48.5	98.2
124	Cambodia	77.0	..	115.9	88.6	40.4	34.1	7.0	45.6	11.2	48.5	98.2
125	Pakistan	53.7	16.8	84.8	66.1	32.9	32.5	5.2	30.3	4.4	40.7	85.1
126	Congo	..	34.8	114.0	58.9	43.1	..	3.9[b]	29.8	22.4	51.8	89.0
127	São Tomé and Príncipe	88.3	..	133.3	96.1	51.3	38.1	4.1	26.1	24.2	30.8	..

LOW HUMAN DEVELOPMENT

128	Kenya	86.5	15.5	111.5	81.5	58.3	49.1	4.1	16.4[b]	5.8	46.5	98.4
129	Bangladesh	55.0	16.7	93.8	88.0	44.1	41.5	7.0	45.2	13.2	43.7	54.4
130	Ghana	65.8	28.7	101.8	73.9	54.1	46.4	6.2	40.0[b]	6.5	32.2	49.1
131	Cameroon	75.9	13.1	110.9	88.3	37.3	..	7.8	43.3	16.8	..	61.8
132	Myanmar	91.9	16.6	115.0	..	49.3	46.4	10.7	26.1	0.4	28.8	99.0
133	Yemen	60.9	..	85.4	72.7	45.7	37.4	10.2	40.5[b]	5.7	..	..
134	Benin	40.8	9.8	116.6	92.8	36.3	19.6	5.8	36.9[b]	14.3	44.6	71.8
135	Madagascar	70.7	..	151.7	98.5	30.1	23.8	3.4	57.5	19.7	47.2	52.1
136	Mauritania	56.8	..	98.2	79.7	23.3	16.3	3.8	18.1	2.0	37.2	100.0[b]
137	Papua New Guinea	59.6	8.3	54.9	..	..	..	2.0[b]	..	..	..	..
138	Nepal	57.9	15.4	124.0	78.8	43.5	..	5.6[b]	38.4	16.8	37.8	66.4
139	Togo	64.9	14.1	105.0	83.5	41.3	22.5	5.3	55.5	23.7	37.6	14.6
140	Comoros	73.6	..	121.5	72.9	45.8	..	2.7[b]	28.3[b]	24.4	30.2	57.4
141	Lesotho	89.5	13.1	107.7	72.7	39.9	25.2	3.6	54.2	21.0	37.0	71.4
142	Nigeria	60.1	..	93.1	61.4	30.5	25.8	10.1	25.1[b]	2.9	46.3	51.2
143	Uganda	74.6	11.0	120.2	97.1	25.3	19.2	3.7	67.6	11.0	49.9	89.4

TABLE 13

HDI rank	Adult literacy rate (% ages 15 and older) 2005–2008[a]	Population with at least secondary education (% ages 25 and older) 2010	Primary enrolment ratio Gross 2001–2009[a]	Primary enrolment ratio Net 2001–2009[a]	Secondary enrolment ratio Gross 2001–2009[a]	Secondary enrolment ratio Net 2001–2009[a]	Tertiary enrolment ratio Gross 2001–2009[a]	Dropout rate, all grades 2005–2008[a]	Repetition rate, all grades 2005–2008[a]	Pupil–teacher ratio 2005–2008[a]	Primary school teachers trained to teach (%) 2005–2008[a]
144 Senegal	41.9	8.6	83.5	72.9	30.6	25.1	8.0	41.6	7.7	36.4	90.5[b]
145 Haiti	61.0[b]	13.3	..	..	..	..	..	..	..	..	..
146 Angola	69.6	..	..	..	17.3	..	2.8	..	..	..	..
147 Djibouti	..	..	55.5	45.3	29.5	24.4	2.6	..	10.6	..	80.3
148 Tanzania, United Republic of	72.6	6.0[b,c]	110.2	99.3	6.1	..	1.5	17.2	4.2	52.2	100.0[b]
149 Côte d'Ivoire	54.6	..	74.5	56.0	26.3	21.2	8.4	10.5	18.0	41.9	100.0[b]
150 Zambia	70.7	25.7	119.1	95.2	51.8	49.0	2.4[b]	21.4	5.9	63.4	100.0
151 Gambia	45.3	11.0	86.2	68.7	50.8	41.8	1.2[b]	29.7	5.4	34.4	74.7[b]
152 Rwanda	70.3	3.3	150.9	95.9	21.9	..	4.0	69.1[b]	17.7	70.2	94.2
153 Malawi	72.8	4.6	120.2	90.6	29.4	25.0	..	64.3	20.1	..	..
154 Sudan	69.3	11.5	74.0	39.2	38.0	..	5.9[b]	6.9	4.9	36.7	61.0
155 Afghanistan	..	6.4	106.1	..	28.6	26.8	1.3[b]	..	16.3	..	..
156 Guinea	..	..	89.9	71.3	35.8	27.7	9.2	45.1	15.4	44.1	82.1
157 Ethiopia	35.9[b]	..	97.8	78.2	33.4	25.3	3.6	59.7	5.0	59.3	89.7
158 Sierra Leone	39.8	9.1	157.7	..	34.6	24.9	2.0[b]	..	9.9	44.2	49.4
159 Central African Republic	54.6	9.3	77.4	59.1	11.9	..	2.3	54.4	25.6	100.2	..
160 Mali	26.2	3.7	91.3	71.5	34.8	28.6	5.4	20.9	14.2	51.4	50.1
161 Burkina Faso	28.7	..	78.5	63.3	19.8	15.4	3.1	28.9	10.5	48.9	87.7
162 Liberia	58.1	12.8	90.6	75.2	31.6	19.5	17.4[b]	..	6.7	23.9	40.2
163 Chad	32.7	..	82.7	61.0	19.0	10.5	1.9	70.2	21.8	176.2	35.5
164 Guinea-Bissau	51.0	..	119.7	52.1	35.9	9.7	2.9	..	18.7	88.1	35.1
165 Mozambique	54.0	3.2	114.2	79.9	20.6	6.2	1.5	56.3	5.5	64.1	67.0
166 Burundi	65.9	..	135.6	99.4	17.9	..	2.5	46.3	33.8	52.0	87.4
167 Niger	28.7	2.9	62.4	54.0	11.0	8.9	1.3	33.2	6.4	40.7	98.4
168 Congo, Democratic Republic of the	66.6	19.5	90.4	32.4	34.8	..	5.0	20.5	15.3	39.0	93.3
169 Zimbabwe	91.4	33.4	103.6	89.9	41.0	38.0	3.8[b]	..	..	..	..

OTHER COUNTRIES OR TERRITORIES

Antigua and Barbuda	99.0[b]	..	102.5	74.0	105.2	..	..	2.6[b]	5.6	17.1	52.9
Bhutan	52.8	..	109.1	87.4	61.7	47.5	6.6	9.9	6.4	29.9	91.5
Cuba	99.8	68.8[b,c]	101.9	98.8	91.4	84.3	121.5	4.4	0.5	9.6	100.0[b]
Dominica	..	26.5[b,c]	81.6	72.3	104.8	68.1	..	9.2	3.9	16.7	59.4
Eritrea	65.3	..	52.3	38.9	30.5	26.0	2.0	26.7	15.4	47.4	89.3
Grenada	..	..	102.6	93.4	107.7	88.6	..	17.4[b]	2.9	22.6	73.5
Iraq	77.6	26.3	98.0	87.3	46.8	39.6	15.7	29.9[b]	8.0	20.5	100.0[b]
Kiribati	..	..	112.8	97.4	87.9	68.3	..	18.6[b]	..	..	85.4
Lebanon	89.6	..	101.1	88.3	81.6	74.6	51.5	6.9	8.8	17.8	13.3
Marshall Islands	..	..	93.0	66.3	66.4	44.9	17.0[b]	..	..	16.9[b]	..
Monaco	..	..	127.7	..	153.4	..	..	..	..	..	..
Nauru	..	..	78.8	72.3	46.1	..	..	74.6[b]	..	..	74.2
Occupied Palestinian Territories	94.1	47.3[b,c]	80.4	73.3	92.4	88.6	47.2	0.9	0.5	29.0	100.0
Oman	86.7	..	75.0	68.3	88.1	78.2	26.3	0.5	1.1	14.3	100.0[b]
Palau	..	..	98.8	..	96.9	..	40.2[b]	..	4.7	..	..
Saint Kitts and Nevis	..	..	85.3	70.6	88.2	78.7	..	32.0	1.5	16.1	63.6
Saint Lucia	..	..	98.0	91.5	93.2	79.6	14.8	4.0[b]	2.4	21.4	87.8
Saint Vincent and the Grenadines	..	..	109.0	94.6	108.2	90.3	..	20.9	4.6	17.0	83.0
Samoa	98.7	..	99.5	90.6	78.3	64.2	7.4[b]	4.1	1.2	23.8	..
Seychelles	91.8	66.8[b,c]	125.3	99.4	111.8	94.3	..	1.6	..	13.1	77.9[b]
Tuvalu	..	..	105.6	..	..	..	..	37.4[b]	..	..	..
Vanuatu	81.3	..	108.7	97.3	40.1	38.1	4.8[b]	26.6	13.6	..	100.0

TABLE 13

HDI rank	ACHIEVEMENTS IN EDUCATION		ACCESS TO EDUCATION					EFFICIENCY OF PRIMARY EDUCATION		QUALITY OF PRIMARY EDUCATION	
	Adult literacy rate	Population with at least secondary education	Primary enrolment ratio (% of primary school-age population)		Secondary enrolment ratio (% of secondary school-age population)		Tertiary enrolment ratio (% of tertiary school-age population)	Dropout rate, all grades	Repetition rate, all grades	Pupil–teacher ratio	Primary school teachers trained to teach
	(% ages 15 and older)	(% ages 25 and older)	Gross	Net	Gross	Net	Gross	(% of primary school cohort)	(% of total primary enrolment in previous year)	(number of pupils per teacher)	(%)
	2005–2008[a]	2010	2001–2009[a]	2001–2009[a]	2001–2009[a]	2001–2009[a]	2001–2009[a]	2005–2008[a]	2005–2008[a]	2005–2008[a]	2005–2008[a]
Developed											
OECD	..	73.8	101.7	95.6	101.1	91.8	71.4	2.9	..	..	..
Non-OECD	..	61.7	108.4	95.6	93.6	86.7	43.0	3.0	1.2	..	..
Developing											
Arab States	72.1	..	96.4	80.9	68.8	60.4	22.7	9.5	5.7	..	..
East Asia and the Pacific	..	..	112.2	93.3	72.8	62.6	20.9	21.3	..	..	..
Europe and Central Asia	97.5	65.1	98.5	92.3	89.3	82.1	54.2	3.3	0.9	..	..
Latin America and the Caribbean	91.1	32.5	116.5	94.4	89.8	72.5	36.7	17.8	9.2	..	..
South Asia	62.4	21.6	108.2	86.9	53.5	42.0	12.8	24.1	5.0	..	..
Sub-Saharan Africa	62.4	..	101.8	73.6	34.4	29.5	5.5	36.5	9.4	..	..
Very high human development	..	73.6	101.9	95.6	100.9	91.7	70.8	3.0	1.7	..	..
High human development	92.3	41.0	111.9	94.4	88.9	74.9	43.2	7.3	6.5	..	..
Medium human development	80.7	..	110.2	88.5	64.7	57.0	17.6	22.6	2.9	..	..
Low human development	61.2	14.3	99.9	73.4	34.7	30.9	6.0	40.4	9.6	..	..
										..	
Least developed countries	59.9	..	101.6	75.5	34.1	30.8	5.4	39.1	11.0	..	..
World	..	..	106.9	86.1	66.4	60.2	25.7	18.0	5.1	..	..

NOTES

a Data refer to the most recent year available during the period specified.

b Refers to an earlier year than that specified.

c UNESCO Institute for Statistics (2010a).

SOURCES

Columns 1 and 3–11: UNESCO Institute for Statistics (2010a).

Column 2: Barro and Lee (2010).

TABLE
13

TABLE 14

Health

		RESOURCES			RISK FACTORS					MORTALITY				
					Infants lacking immunization against		HIV prevalence							
		Expenditure on health	Physician	Hospital beds	DTP	Measles	Youth (% ages 15–24)		Adult (% ages 15–49)	Infant	Under-five	Adult (per 1,000 people)		Age-standardized death rates from non-communicable diseases
HDI rank		Per capita (PPP $)	(per 10,000 people)		(% of one-year-olds)		Female	Male	Total	(per 1,000 live births)		Female	Male	(per 100,000 people)
		2007	2000–2009[a]		2008		2007			2008	2008	2008	2008	2004

VERY HIGH HUMAN DEVELOPMENT

1	Norway	4,763	39	39	6	7	0.1	0.1	0.1	3	4	53	81	391
2	Australia	3,357	10	39	8	6	<0.1	0.2	0.2	5	6	46	81	355
3	New Zealand	2,497	21	62	11	14	..	0.1	0.1	5	6	57	88	398
4	United States	7,285	27	31	4	8	0.3	0.7	0.6	7	8	79	135	450
5	Ireland	3,424	31	53	7	11	0.1	0.2	0.2	3	4	56	90	459
6	Liechtenstein	..	..	..	..	..	..	..	..	2	2	..	..	..
7	Netherlands	3,509	39	48	3	4	0.1	0.2	0.2	4	5	57	78	425
8	Canada	3,900	19	34	6	6	0.2	0.4	0.4	6	6	53	87	374
9	Sweden	3,323	36	..	2	4	0.1	0.1	0.1	2	3	48	76	372
10	Germany	3,588	35	83	10	5	0.1	0.1	0.1	4	4	54	101	429
11	Japan	2,696	21	139	2	3	..	..	..	3	4	43	87	284
12	Korea, Republic of	1,688	17	86	6	8	<0.1	<0.1	<0.1	5	5	43	108	470
13	Switzerland	4,417	40	55	5	13	0.5	0.4	0.6	4	5	44	76	360
14	France	3,709	37	72	2	13	0.2	0.4	0.4	3	4	55	119	387
15	Israel	2,181	36	58	7	16	0.1	<0.1	0.1	4	5	46	87	368
16	Finland	2,840	33	68	1	3	<0.1	0.1	0.1	3	3	57	129	405
17	Iceland	3,323	38	75	2	4	0.1	0.2	0.2	2	3	46	66	375
18	Belgium	3,323	42	53	1	7	0.1	0.2	0.2	4	5	61	110	437
19	Denmark	3,513	32	35	25	11	0.1	0.2	0.2	4	4	67	112	495
20	Spain	2,671	38	34	3	2	0.2	0.6	0.5	4	4	43	102	379
21	Hong Kong, China (SAR)	..	..	..	..	..	..	..	..	..	..	..	..	..
22	Greece	2,727	54	48	1	1	0.1	0.2	0.2	3	4	44	105	436
23	Italy	2,686	37	39	4	9	0.2	0.4	0.4	3	4	42	80	372
24	Luxembourg	5,734	29	63	1	4	0.1	0.2	0.2	2	3	56	101	419
25	Austria	3,763	38	78	17	17	0.1	0.2	0.2	3	4	50	99	409
26	United Kingdom	2,992	21	39	8	14	0.1	0.3	0.2	5	6	59	96	441
27	Singapore	1,643	15	32	3	5	0.1	0.2	0.2	2	3	47	82	345
28	Czech Republic	1,626	36	81	1	3	..	<0.1	..	3	4	65	143	559
29	Slovenia	2,099	24	47	3	4	..	..	<0.1	3	4	55	132	480
30	Andorra	3,004	37	26	1	2	..	..	..	3	4	44	99	373
31	Slovakia	1,555	31	68	1	1	..	..	<0.1	7	8	73	195	628
32	United Arab Emirates	982	15	19	8	8	..	..	..	7	8	60	78	410
33	Malta	4,053	34	78	28	22	0.1	0.1	0.1	6	6	44	77	433
34	Estonia	1,094	33	56	5	5	0.7	1.6	1.3	4	6	84	249	664
35	Cyprus	3,034	23	37	3	13	..	..	..	4	4	39	84	412
36	Hungary	1,388	28	71	1	1	<0.1	0.1	0.1	5	7	101	233	693
37	Brunei Darussalam	1,176	11	26	1	3	..	..	..	6	7	80	106	473
38	Qatar	3,075	28	25	6	8	..	..	..	9	10	53	77	512
39	Bahrain	1,199	30	20	3	1	..	..	..	10	12	82	116	678
40	Portugal	2,284	34	35	3	3	0.3	0.5	0.5	3	4	52	128	456
41	Poland	1,035	20	52	1	2	0.1	0.1	0.1	6	7	77	205	583
42	Barbados	1,263	..[b]	76	7	8	0.6	1.3	1.2	10	11	108	168	531

HDI rank		Expenditure on health Per capita (PPP $) 2007	Physician (per 10,000 people) 2000–2009a	Hospital beds (per 10,000 people) 2000–2009a	DTP (% of one-year-olds) 2008	Measles (% of one-year-olds) 2008	Youth (% ages 15–24) Female 2007	Youth (% ages 15–24) Male 2007	Adult (% ages 15–49) Total 2007	Infant (per 1,000 live births) 2008	Under-five 2008	Adult (per 1,000 people) Female 2008	Adult (per 1,000 people) Male 2008	Age-standardized death rates from non-communicable diseases (per 100,000 people) 2004
		RESOURCES			RISK FACTORS					MORTALITY				
					Infants lacking immunization against		HIV prevalence							

HIGH HUMAN DEVELOPMENT

43	Bahamas	1,987	..	32	7	10	1.5	3.2	3.0	9	13	127	206	509
44	Lithuania	1,109	40	81	4	3	0.1	0.1	0.1	6	7	114	314	635
45	Chile	863	11	23	4	8	0.2	0.3	0.3	7	9	60	116	458
46	Argentina	1,322	32 b	41	4	1	0.3	0.6	0.5	15	16	86	160	515
47	Kuwait	814	18	18	1	1	..	..	..	9	11	51	68	454
48	Latvia	1,071	30	76	3	3	0.5	0.9	0.8	8	9	115	311	710
49	Montenegro	1,107	20	40	5	11	..	..	..	7	8	90	173	..
50	Romania	592	19	65	3	3	0.2	0.2	0.1	12	14	90	220	706
51	Croatia	1,398	26	53	4	4	..	..	<0.1	5	6	65	163	578
52	Uruguay	916	37	29 c	6	5	0.3	0.6	0.6	12	14	85	158	521
53	Libyan Arab Jamahiriya	453	12	37	2	2	..	..	..	15	17	97	170	654
54	Panama	773	15	22	18	15	0.6	1.1	1.0	19	23	83	140	417
55	Saudi Arabia	768	16	22	2	3	..	..	..	18	21	103	186	678
56	Mexico	819	29	17 c	2	4	0.2	0.3	0.3	15	17	89	154	501
57	Malaysia	604	7	18	10	5	0.3	0.6	0.5	6	6	97	177	623
58	Bulgaria	835	37	64	5	4	..	..	..	9	11	91	214	733
59	Trinidad and Tobago	1,178	12 b	27	10	9	1.0	0.3	1.5	31	35	107	219	751
60	Serbia	769	20	54	5	8	0.1	0.1	0.1	6	7	91	183	..
61	Belarus	704	49	112	3	1	0.1	0.3	0.2	11	13	111	330	854
62	Costa Rica	899	13	13	10	9	0.2	0.4	0.4	10	11	68	124	439
63	Peru	327	..	15	10	10	0.3	0.5	0.5	22	24	95	118	534
64	Albania	505	11	29	1	2	..	..	..	13	14	91	141	752
65	Russian Federation	797	43	97	2	1	0.6	1.3	1.1	12	13	147	396	904
66	Kazakhstan	405	39	77	1	1	0.1	0.2	0.1	27	30	186	432	1,145
67	Azerbaijan	284	38	79	30	34	0.1	0.3	0.2	32	36	138	228	856
68	Bosnia and Herzegovina	767	14	30	9	16	..	..	<0.1	13	15	68	147	670
69	Ukraine	475	31	87	10	6	1.5	1.5	1.6	14	16	151	399	881
70	Iran, Islamic Republic of	689	9	14	1	2	0.1	0.2	0.2	27	32	95	152	687
71	The former Yugoslav Republic of Macedonia	669	25	46	5	2	..	..	<0.1	10	11	80	151	737
72	Mauritius	502	11	33	1	2	1.0	1.8	1.7	15	17	104	214	731
73	Brazil	837	17	24	3	1	0.6	1.0	0.6	18	22	106	210	625
74	Georgia	384	45	33	8	4	0.1	0.1	0.1	26	30	85	232	554
75	Venezuela, Bolivarian Republic of	697	19	13	53	18	..	..	..	16	18	93	195	441
76	Armenia	246	37	41	11	6	0.1	0.2	0.1	21	23	101	240	1,064
77	Ecuador	434	15	6 c	25	34	0.2	0.4	0.4	21	25	121	207	484
78	Belize	279	11	12 c	6	4	1.5	0.5	2.1	17	19	129	223	677
79	Colombia	516	14	10	8	8	0.3	0.7	0.6	16	20	75	162	483
80	Jamaica	357	9	17 c	13	12	0.9	1.7	1.6	26	31	130	220	605
81	Tunisia	463	13	20	1	2	<0.1	0.1	0.1	18	21	72	132	537
82	Jordan	434	26	18	3	5	..	..	..	17	20	116	179	711
83	Turkey	677	15	28	4	3	..	..	..	20	22	73	138	701
84	Algeria	338	12	17	7	12	0.1	0.1	0.1	36	41	119	144	565
85	Tonga	167	3	24	1	1	..	..	..	17	19	228	143	658

MEDIUM HUMAN DEVELOPMENT

86	Fiji	169	5	21	1	6	..	0.1	0.1	16	18	156	249	767
87	Turkmenistan	153	24	41	4	1	..	..	<0.1	43	48	212	377	1,100
88	Dominican Republic	411	19	10 c	23	21	0.6	0.3	1.1	27	33	127	188	794
89	China	233	14	30	3	6	0.1	0.1	0.1	18	21	84	140	627
90	El Salvador	402	12	8 c	6	5	0.5	0.9	0.8	16	18	136	301	518
91	Sri Lanka	179	6	31	2	2	..	<0.1	..	13	15	93	315	681
92	Thailand	286	3	22	1	2	1.2	1.2	1.4	13	14	140	276	516
93	Gabon	650	3	13 c	62	45	3.9	1.3	5.9	57	77	301	353	716
94	Suriname	527	5	31	16	14	1.4	2.7	2.4	25	27	128	218	728

TABLE 14

198   HUMAN DEVELOPMENT REPORT **2010**

HDI rank	Expenditure on health Per capita (PPP $) 2007	Physician (per 10,000 people) 2000–2009[a]	Hospital beds (per 10,000 people) 2000–2009[a]	DTP (% of one-year-olds) 2008	Measles (% of one-year-olds) 2008	HIV Youth Female 2007	HIV Youth Male 2007	HIV Adult Total 2007	Infant (per 1,000 live births) 2008	Under-five 2008	Adult Female (per 1,000 people) 2008	Adult Male (per 1,000 people) 2008	Age-standardized death rates from non-communicable diseases (per 100,000 people) 2004
95 Bolivia, Plurinational State of	200	12	11	17	14	0.1	0.2	0.2	46	54	163	230	765
96 Paraguay	253	11	13	24	23	0.3	0.7	0.6	24	28	105	170	602
97 Philippines	130	12	5	9	8	..	..	..	26	32	117	227	620
98 Botswana	762	4	18	4	6	15.3	5.1	23.9	26	31	394	419	594
99 Moldova, Republic of	281	27	61	5	6	0.2	0.4	0.4	15	17	141	312	963
100 Mongolia	138	26	60	4	3	..	0.1	0.1	34	41	145	291	923
101 Egypt	310	24	21	3	8	..	..	..	20	23	151	222	891
102 Uzbekistan	121	26	48	2	2	0.1	0.1	0.1	34	38	140	223	880
103 Micronesia, Federated States of	373	6	33	21	8	..	..	..	32	39	156	187	682
104 Guyana	197	5	19	7	5	1.7	0.5	2.5	47	61	226	291	835
105 Namibia	467	3	27[c]	17	27	10.3	3.4	15.3	31	42	290	356	513
106 Honduras	235	6	7[c]	7	5	0.4	0.7	0.7	26	31	129	227	761
107 Maldives	514	9	26	2	3	..	..	..	24	28	72	100	953
108 Indonesia	81	1	6	23	17	0.1	0.3	0.2	31	41	185	226	690
109 Kyrgyzstan	130	23	51	5	1	0.1	0.2	0.1	33	38	184	343	1,012
110 South Africa	819	8	28	33	38	12.7	4.0	18.1	48	67	479	563	867
111 Syrian Arab Republic	154	5	15	18	19	..	..	..	14	16	120	179	679
112 Tajikistan	93	20	61	14	14	0.1	0.4	0.3	54	64	162	185	884
113 Viet Nam	183	6	28	7	8	0.3	0.6	0.5	12	14	110	192	611
114 Morocco	202	6	11	1	4	0.1	0.1	0.1	32	36	88	147	655
115 Nicaragua	232	4	9[c]	4	1	0.1	0.3	0.2	23	27	123	209	705
116 Guatemala	334	..	6[c]	15	4	1.5	..	0.8	29	35	159	302	515
117 Equatorial Guinea	543	3	19[c]	67	49	2.5	0.8	3.4	90	148	356	366	938
118 Cape Verde	148	6	21	2	4	..	..	..	24	29	115	274	591
119 India	109	6	9	34	30	0.3	0.3	0.3	52	69	173	250	713
120 Timor-Leste	116	1	..	21	27	..	..	..	75	93	204	275	663
121 Swaziland	287	2	21	5	5	22.6	5.8	26.1	59	83	616	631	707
122 Lao People's Democratic Republic	84	3	12	39	48	0.1	0.2	0.2	48	61	288	317	828
123 Solomon Islands	123	1	14	22	40	..	..	..	30	36	136	182	694
124 Cambodia	108	2	..	9	11	0.3	0.8	0.8	69	90	216	294	832
125 Pakistan	64	8	6	27	15	0.1	0.1	0.1	72	89	190	216	717
126 Congo	90	1	16	11	21	2.3	0.8	3.5	80	127	374	389	716
127 São Tomé and Príncipe	183	5	32	1	7	..	..	..	64	98	227	271	788

LOW HUMAN DEVELOPMENT

128 Kenya	72	1	14	15	10	..	..	..	81	128	364	382	729
129 Bangladesh	42	3	4	5	11	..	..	..	43	54	230	247	730
130 Ghana	113	1	9	13	14	1.3	0.4	1.9	51	76	247	298	699
131 Cameroon	104	2	15	16	20	4.3	1.2	5.1	82	131	403	405	840
132 Myanmar	21	4	6	15	18	0.6	0.7	0.7	71	98	304	368	775
133 Yemen	104	3	7	31	38	..	..	..	53	69	185	249	941
134 Benin	70	1	5	33	39	0.9	0.3	1.2	76	121	291	312	835
135 Madagascar	41	2	3	18	19	0.1	0.2	0.1	68	106	240	286	799
136 Mauritania	47	1	4	26	35	0.5	0.9	0.8	75	118	262	318	812
137 Papua New Guinea	65	1	..	48	46	0.7	0.6	1.5	53	69	235	292	772
138 Nepal	53	2	50	18	21	0.3	0.5	0.5	41	51	273	281	769
139 Togo	68	1	9	11	23	2.4	0.8	3.3	64	98	296	351	818
140 Comoros	37	2	22	19	24	<0.1	0.1	<0.1	75	105	231	286	713
141 Lesotho	92	1	13	17	15	14.9	5.9	23.2	63	79	633	758	581
142 Nigeria	131	4	5	46	38	2.3	0.8	3.1	96	186	399	424	909
143 Uganda	74	1	4	36	32	3.9	1.3	5.4	85	135	424	451	786
144 Senegal	99	1	3[c]	12	23	0.8	0.3	1.0	57	108	247	293	852
145 Haiti	58	..	13	47	42	1.4	0.6	2.2	54	72	229	306	740
146 Angola	131	1	8	19	21	0.3	0.2	2.1	130	220	383	460	1,071
147 Djibouti	148	2	..	11	27	2.1	0.7	3.1	76	95	283	335	862
148 Tanzania, United Republic of	63	<0.5	11	16	12	0.9	0.5	6.2	67	104	444	475	851

TABLE 14

		RESOURCES			RISK FACTORS					MORTALITY				
					Infants lacking immunization against		HIV prevalence							
		Expenditure on health	Physician	Hospital beds	DTP	Measles	Youth (% ages 15–24)		Adult (% ages 15–49)	Infant	Under-five	Adult (per 1,000 people)		Age-standardized death rates from non-communicable diseases
HDI rank		Per capita (PPP $)	(per 10,000 people)		(% of one-year-olds)		Female	Male	Total	(per 1,000 live births)		Female	Male	(per 100,000 people)
		2007	2000–2009ᵃ		2008		2007			2008	2008	2008	2008	2004
149	Côte d'Ivoire	67	1	4	26	37	2.4	0.8	3.9	81	114	354	367	946
150	Zambia	79	1	19	20	15	11.3	3.6	15.2	92	148	498	538	833
151	Gambia	71	<0.5	11	4	9	0.6	0.2	0.9	80	106	253	300	830
152	Rwanda	95	<0.5	16	3	8	1.4	0.5	2.8	72	112	281	330	878
153	Malawi	50	<0.5	11	9	12	8.4	2.4	11.9	65	100	468	498	796
154	Sudan	71	3	7	14	21	1.0	0.3	1.4	70	109	304	335	986
155	Afghanistan	83	2	4	15	25	..	..	..	165	257	398	543	1,309
156	Guinea	62	1	3	34	36	1.2	0.4	1.6	90	146	320	352	844
157	Ethiopia	30	<0.5	2ᶜ	19	26	1.5	0.5	2.1	69	109	286	329	817
158	Sierra Leone	32	<0.5	4	40	40	1.3	0.4	1.7	123	194	368	422	1,033
159	Central African Republic	30	1	12	46	38	5.5	1.1	6.3	115	173	467	448	868
160	Mali	67	1	6	32	32	1.1	0.4	1.5	103	194	365	412	967
161	Burkina Faso	72	1	9	21	25	0.9	0.5	1.6	92	169	361	388	924
162	Liberia	39	<0.5	7	36	36	1.3	0.4	1.7	100	145	328	353	931
163	Chad	72	<0.5	4	80	77	2.8	2.0	3.5	124	209	429	465	910
164	Guinea-Bissau	33	<0.5	10	37	24	1.2	0.4	1.8	117	195	370	436	925
165	Mozambique	39	<0.5	8	28	23	8.5	2.9	12.5	90	130	458	485	777
166	Burundi	51	<0.5	7	8	16	1.3	0.4	2.0	102	168	401	425	919
167	Niger	35	<0.5	3	34	20	0.5	0.9	0.8	79	167	340	374	1,030
168	Congo, Democratic Republic of the	17	1	8	31	33	..	..	..	126	199	373	443	921
169	Zimbabwe	20	2	30	38	34	7.7	2.9	15.3	62	96	752	812	816

OTHER COUNTRIES OR TERRITORIES

		2007	2000–2009ᵃ		2008		2007			2008	2008	2008	2008	2004
	Antigua and Barbuda	946	..	17	1	1	..	..	..	11	12	160	192	674
	Bhutan	188	<0.5	17	4	1	<0.1	0.1	0.1	54	81	197	256	708
	Cuba	917	64	60	1	1	0.1	0.1	0.1	5	6	81	122	437
	Dominica	550	..	38	4	1	..	..	..	9	11	119	209	580
	Eritrea	20	1	12	3	5	0.9	0.3	1.3	41	58	197	266	686
	Grenada	591	..	26	1	1	..	..	..	13	15	209	245	827
	Iraq	78	5	13	38	31	..	..	..	36	44	179	377	1,018
	Kiribati	358	2	15	18	28	..	..	..	38	48	175	321	730
	Korea, Democratic People's Rep. of	..	33	132	8	2	..	..	..	42	55	161	229	642
	Lebanon	921	33	34	26	47	0.1	0.1	0.1	12	13	131	191	715
	Marshall Islands	357	5	..	7	6	..	..	..	30	36	384	427	961
	Monaco	2,139	..	..	1	1	..	..	..	3	4	53	118	321
	Nauru	812	8	35	1	1	..	..	..	36	45	303	448	1,093
	Occupied Palestinian Territories	..	..	..	..	..	..	..	..	24	27	..	..	..
	Oman	688	18	20	8	1	..	..	..	10	12	84	155	664
	Palau	812	16	50	8	3	..	..	..	13	15	112	232	735
	Saint Kitts and Nevis	863	11	55	1	1	..	..	..	14	16	95	180	691
	Saint Lucia	608	..	28	4	1	..	..	..	13	13	94	193	522
	Saint Vincent and the Grenadines	474	8	30	1	1	..	..	..	12	13	169	305	674
	Samoa	237	3	10	54	55	..	..	..	22	26	203	235	766
	San Marino	2,810	..	..	13	27	..	..	..	1	2	48	59	357
	Seychelles	1,094	15	39	1	1	..	..	..	11	12	109	232	650
	Somalia	..	<0.5ᵇ	..	69	76	0.3	0.6	0.5	119	200	373	459	1,148
	Tuvalu	150	9	56	1	7	..	..	..	30	36	279	257	979
	Vanuatu	145	1	37	24	35	..	..	..	27	33	162	202	749

TABLE 14

HDI rank	RESOURCES			RISK FACTORS					MORTALITY				
				Infants lacking immunization against		HIV prevalence							
	Expenditure on health	Physician	Hospital beds	DTP	Measles	Youth (% ages 15–24)		Adult (% ages 15–49)	Infant	Under-five	Adult (per 1,000 people)		Age-standardized death rates from non-communicable diseases
	Per capita (PPP $)	(per 10,000 people)		(% of one-year-olds)		Female	Male	Total	(per 1,000 live births)		Female	Male	(per 100,000 people)
	2007	2000–2009[a]		2008		2007			2008	2008	2008	2008	2004
Developed													
OECD	4,222	..	63	4	7	..	..	..	5	6	60	114	418
Non-OECD	1,807	..	40	6	11	..	..	..	5	6	54	93	416
Developing													
Arab States	287	..	16	15	19	..	..	..	38	50	161	231	810
East Asia and the Pacific	207	..	20	8	9	..	..	..	23	28	110	170	636
Europe and Central Asia	623	..	52	5	4	..	..	..	20	22	127	296	847
Latin America and the Caribbean	732	..	24	10	7	..	..	..	19	23	102	185	560
South Asia	123	..	17	28	25	..	..	..	56	73	181	248	724
Sub-Saharan Africa	127	..	19	29	28	..	..	..	86	144	381	420	859
Very high human development	4,172	..	49	5	7	..	..	..	5	6	60	114	418
High human development	721	..	34	6	5	..	..	..	18	21	106	216	666
Medium human development	179	..	20	20	18	..	..	..	38	49	140	206	678
Low human development	66	..	13	25	26	..	..	..	83	134	339	376	851
Least developed countries	54	..	18	22	24	..	..	..	82	126	318	360	851
World	869	..	30	18	17	..	..	..	44	63	154	221	662

NOTES

a   Data refer to the most recent year available during the period specified.

b   Refers to an earlier year than that specified.

c   Public sector only.

SOURCES

Columns 1–5, 11 and 12: WHO (2010).

Columns 6–8: UNICEF (2010c).

Columns 9 and 10: UNDESA (2009d).

Column 13: WHO (2008).

TABLE
14

TABLE 15

Enabling environment: financial flows and commitments

		PUBLIC EXPENDITURE (% of GDP)				Tax revenue	Gross fixed capital formation	FOREIGN DIRECT INVESTMENT	OFFICIAL DEVELOPMENT ASSISTANCE			REMITTANCE INFLOWS	
	Education	Health	Research and development	Military	Debt service (% of GNI)	(% of GDP)	(% of GDP)	Net inflows (% of GDP)	Total (% of GNI)	Per capita ($)	Allocated to social sectors[a] (% of total aid)	Total (% of GDP)	Per capita ($)
HDI rank	2000–2007[b]	2000–2007[b]	2000–2007[b]	2008	2008	2008	2008	2008	2008	2008	2008	2008	2008

VERY HIGH HUMAN DEVELOPMENT

1 Norway	6.7	7.5	1.7	1.3	..	28.1	20.8	−0.3	[0.88]	..	..	0.2	144
2 Australia	4.7	6.0	2.2	1.8	..	23.1	28.3	4.7	[0.32] c	..	..	0.5	220
3 New Zealand	6.2	7.1	1.3	1.1	..	31.7	23.3	4.2	[0.30] c	..	..	0.5	147
4 United States	5.5	7.1	2.7	4.3	..	10.3	18.4	2.2	[0.19] c	..	..	0.0	10
5 Ireland	4.9	6.1	1.3	0.6	..	25.4	26.3	−7.4	[0.59] c	..	..	0.2	146
6 Liechtenstein	..	..	..	..	..	..	..	..	..	..	..	..	..
7 Netherlands	5.5	7.3	1.8	1.4	..	23.6	20.5	−0.3	[0.80] c	..	..	0.4	201
8 Canada	4.9	7.1	2.0	1.3	..	14.2	22.6	3.0	[0.32] c	..	..	..	..
9 Sweden	6.7	7.4	3.7	1.3	..	..	19.5	8.7	[0.98] c	..	..	0.2	89
10 Germany	4.4	8.0	2.6	1.3	..	11.8	19.2	0.6	[0.38] c	..	..	0.3	135
11 Japan	3.4	6.5	3.4	0.9	..	..	23.4	0.5	[0.19] c	..	..	0.0	15
12 Korea, Republic of	4.2	3.5	3.5	2.8	..	16.6	29.3	0.2	..	..	..	0.3	63
13 Switzerland	5.3	6.4	2.9	0.8	..	10.2	22.0	1.3	[0.42] c	..	..	0.4	288
14 France	5.6	8.7	2.1	2.3	..	21.8	21.9	3.5	[0.39] c	..	..	0.6	255
15 Israel	6.4	4.5	4.7	7.0	..	25.3	18.5	4.8	..	..	..	0.7	195
16 Finland	5.9	6.1	3.5	1.3	..	21.7	20.6	−2.8	[0.44] c	..	..	0.3	156
17 Iceland	7.5	7.7	2.8	0.0	..	24.6	23.9	4.2	..	..	..	0.2	112
18 Belgium	6.1	7.0	1.9	1.2	..	25.6	22.7	19.8	[0.48] c	..	..	2.1	973
19 Denmark	7.9	8.2	2.6	1.4	..	35.6	21.5	0.9	[0.82] c	..	..	0.3	162
20 Spain	4.4	6.1	1.3	1.2	..	10.6	29.4	4.4	[0.45] c	..	..	0.7	258
21 Hong Kong, China (SAR)	3.3	..	0.8	..	..	..	19.7	29.3	..	..	..	0.2	51
22 Greece	4.0	5.8	0.5	3.6	..	19.9	19.3	1.5	[0.21] c	..	..	0.8	239
23 Italy	4.3	6.7	1.1	1.7	..	22.6	20.9	0.7	[0.22] c	..	..	0.1	52
24 Luxembourg	3.7	6.5	1.7	..	..	24.5	20.1	215.6	[0.97] c	..	..	3.2	3,527
25 Austria	5.4	7.7	2.5	0.9	..	20.1	22.4	3.5	[0.43] c	..	..	0.8	389
26 United Kingdom	5.6	6.9	1.8	2.5	..	28.6	16.7	3.5	[0.43] c	..	..	0.3	128
27 Singapore	2.8	1.0	2.6	4.1	..	14.6	28.5	12.5	..	..	..	..	..
28 Czech Republic	4.6	5.8	1.6	1.3	..	14.8	23.9	5.0	..	..	..	0.7	136
29 Slovenia	5.2	5.6	1.5	1.5	..	20.0	27.5	3.5	..	..	..	0.6	170
30 Andorra	3.2	5.3	..	..	..	..	..	..	..	..	..	..	..
31 Slovakia	3.6	5.2	0.5	1.5	..	13.5	26.1	3.3	..	..	..	2.0	365
32 United Arab Emirates	0.9	1.9	..	..	..	..	20.4	..	..	..	..	..	..
33 Malta	4.8	5.8	0.6	0.7	..	28.6	19.4	12.7	..	..	..	0.6	121
34 Estonia	5.0	4.1	1.1	2.2	..	16.8	29.3	8.3	..	..	..	1.7	297
35 Cyprus	7.1	3.0	0.4	1.8	..	56.7	23.3	15.5	..	..	..	1.1	323
36 Hungary	5.4	5.2	1.0	1.2	..	23.6	20.1	40.6	..	..	..	1.7	262
37 Brunei Darussalam	3.7	1.9	0.0	3.9	..	..	13.0	0.8	..	..	..	..	..
38 Qatar	3.3	2.9	..	..	..	23.1	30.2	..	..	..	..	..	..
39 Bahrain	2.9	2.6	..	3.0	..	1.5	31.9	8.2	0.0	0.0	..	..	..
40 Portugal	5.3	7.1	1.2	2.0	..	22.2	21.7	1.5	[0.27] c	..	..	1.7	382
41 Poland	4.9	4.6	0.6	2.0	11.2	18.4	22.0	2.8	..	..	..	2.0	274
42 Barbados	6.7	4.4	..	..	..	35.6	22.5	6.8	..	18.6	87.3	4.6	658

HDI rank	PUBLIC EXPENDITURE (% of GDP)						Gross fixed capital formation	FOREIGN DIRECT INVESTMENT	OFFICIAL DEVELOPMENT ASSISTANCE			REMITTANCE INFLOWS	
	Education	Health	Research and development	Military	Debt service (% of GNI)	Tax revenue (% of GDP)	(% of GDP)	Net inflows (% of GDP)	Total (% of GNI)	Per capita ($)	Allocated to social sectors[a] (% of total aid)	Total (% of GDP)	Per capita ($)
	2000–2007[b]	2000–2007[b]	2000–2007[b]	2008	2008	2008	2008	2008	2008	2008	2008	2008	2008
HIGH HUMAN DEVELOPMENT													
43 Bahamas	3.6	3.7	..	..	..	16.7	37.8	9.9	..	..	..	..	..
44 Lithuania	4.7	4.5	0.8	1.5	20.6	17.4	24.4	3.7	..	..	..	3.1	435
45 Chile	3.4	3.7	0.7	3.5	9.8	19.8	24.0	9.9	0.0	4.4	63.9	0.0	0
46 Argentina	4.9	5.1	0.5	0.8	3.0	14.2	23.3	3.0	0.0	3.3	69.5	0.2	17
47 Kuwait	3.8	1.7	0.1	3.2	..	0.9	18.9	0.0	..	..	..	..	..
48 Latvia	5.0	3.6	0.6	1.9	18.1	15.0	30.2	4.0	..	..	..	1.8	265
49 Montenegro	..	5.1	1.2	1.8	1.4	..	27.7	19.2	2.4	171.5	52.8	..	..
50 Romania	4.4	3.8	0.5	1.5	9.3	17.9	31.1	6.9	..	..	..	4.7	436
51 Croatia	3.9	6.6	0.9	1.9	..	20.4	27.6	6.9	0.6	89.7	31.3	2.3	361
52 Uruguay	2.8	5.9	0.4	1.3	4.7	17.2	18.7	6.9	0.1	10.0	59.1	0.3	32
53 Libyan Arab Jamahiriya	2.7[d]	1.9	..	1.3	..	..	27.9	4.4	0.1	9.6	81.0	0.0	3
54 Panama	3.8	4.3	0.2	0.0	7.2	9.3	22.2	10.4	0.1	8.4	50.7	0.9	58
55 Saudi Arabia	5.7	2.7	0.0	8.2	..	..	19.3	4.8	0.0	0.0	..	0.0	9
56 Mexico	4.8	2.7	0.5	0.5	3.9	11.7	22.1	2.1	0.0	1.4	66.0	2.4	247
57 Malaysia	4.5	1.9	0.6	2.0	4.1	16.6	21.7	3.3	0.1	5.9	52.5	0.9	71
58 Bulgaria	4.1	4.2	0.5	2.4	10.3	24.2	33.4	18.4	..	..	..	5.3	346
59 Trinidad and Tobago	4.2	2.7	0.1	..	..	25.9	25.3	3.8	0.1	9.1	63.2	0.5	82
60 Serbia	4.5	6.1	0.3	2.4	9.6	22.0	20.4	6.0	2.1	142.4	51.5	11.1	753
61 Belarus	5.2	4.9	1.0	1.5	2.0	25.5	32.7	3.6	0.2	11.4	81.3	0.7	46
62 Costa Rica	5.0	5.9	0.4	0.0	5.4	15.8	24.2	6.8	0.2	14.6	31.8	2.0	134
63 Peru	2.7	2.5	0.1	1.1	4.1	15.4	26.1	3.2	0.4	16.1	57.9	1.9	85
64 Albania	2.9	2.9	..	2.0	1.3	17.3	32.4	7.6	3.0	122.8	55.7	12.2	476
65 Russian Federation	3.9	3.5	1.1	3.5	4.1	15.7	22.0	4.3	..	..	..	0.4	43
66 Kazakhstan	2.8	2.5	0.2	1.2	29.2	12.7	31.3	11.0	0.3	21.2	43.0	0.1	12
67 Azerbaijan	1.9	1.0	0.2	3.8	0.7	16.7	20.1	0.0	0.6	27.1	39.9	3.4	179
68 Bosnia and Herzegovina	..	5.6	0.0	1.4	2.3	21.0	24.4	5.7	2.5	128.0	62.0	14.8	725
69 Ukraine	5.3	4.0	0.9	2.7	10.1	17.8	25.6	6.1	0.3	13.3	56.2	3.2	125
70 Iran, Islamic Republic of	4.8	3.0	0.7	2.7	1.0	7.3	25.8	0.6	0.0[e]	1.4	84.5	0.4	16
71 The former Yugoslav Republic of Macedonia	3.5	4.7	0.2	1.8	5.1	19.7	23.9	6.3	2.3	108.1	52.8	4.3	199
72 Mauritius	3.6	2.0	0.4	0.2	1.7	18.2	24.6	4.1	1.2	86.3	21.5	2.3	179
73 Brazil	5.2	3.5	1.0	1.5	3.6	16.4	19.0	2.9	0.0	2.4	67.4	0.3	27
74 Georgia	2.9	1.5	0.2	8.5	1.5	23.8	22.5	12.2	7.0	203.6	27.5	5.7	170
75 Venezuela, Bolivarian Republic of	3.7	2.7	..	1.4	1.9	15.5	19.8	0.1	0.0	2.1	75.7	0.0	5
76 Armenia	3.0	2.1	0.2	3.3	3.0	17.0	40.0	7.8	2.4	98.3	43.3	8.9	345
77 Ecuador	1.0	2.3	0.2	2.8	5.0	..	23.8	1.8	0.5	17.1	53.8	5.2	210
78 Belize	5.1	2.6	..	1.1	8.2	22.9	25.5	14.0	2.1	81.4	19.0	5.8	243
79 Colombia	3.9	5.1	0.2	3.7	3.4	12.6	..	4.3	0.4	21.8	70.7	2.0	109
80 Jamaica	6.2	2.4	0.1	0.6	7.9	25.4	..	9.8	0.6	29.5	33.1	14.9	811
81 Tunisia	7.2	3.0	1.0	1.3	5.6	22.8	25.3	6.5	1.3	46.4	38.5	4.9	191
82 Jordan	4.9[d]	5.4	0.3	5.9	12.2	18.3	25.6	9.3	3.5	125.6	43.5	17.9	642
83 Turkey	2.9	3.4	0.7	2.2	7.4	18.6	19.9	2.5	0.3	27.4	27.3	0.2	18
84 Algeria	4.3	3.6	0.1	3.0	0.8	46.5	27.0	1.6	0.2	9.2	49.0	1.3	64
85 Tonga	4.7	3.1	..	..	1.9	..	17.1	2.2	9.6	257.0	70.3	35.8	961
MEDIUM HUMAN DEVELOPMENT													
86 Fiji	6.2	2.8	..	1.3	0.7	22.7	16.0	8.9	1.3	53.9	62.1	3.4	143
87 Turkmenistan	..	1.4	..	..	1.2	..	6.5	5.3	0.1	3.6	74.0	..	..
88 Dominican Republic	2.2	1.9	..	0.6	3.3	15.9	18.2	6.3	0.3	15.5	43.5	7.8	357
89 China	1.9[d]	1.9	1.5	2.0	0.8	9.4	42.0	3.4	0.0	1.1	49.1	1.1	37
90 El Salvador	3.6	3.6	0.1[d]	0.5	4.6	13.9	15.0	3.5	1.1	38.1	55.7	17.2	620
91 Sri Lanka	..	2.0	0.2	3.6	3.1	14.2	25.3	1.9	1.8	36.2	28.4	7.3	146
92 Thailand	4.9	2.7	0.2	1.5	6.3	16.5	27.4	3.6	−0.3	..	42.7	0.7	28
93 Gabon	3.8	3.0	..	..	4.7	..	24.4	0.1	0.4	37.6	65.4	0.1	8
94 Suriname	..	3.6	..	..	..	..	25.1	−7.7	3.7	195.2	30.1	0.1	4
95 Bolivia, Plurinational State of	6.3	3.4	0.3	1.5	5.9	17.0	17.2	3.1	3.9	64.9	53.5	6.9	118

TABLE
15

HDI rank		PUBLIC EXPENDITURE (% of GDP)					Tax revenue	Gross fixed capital formation	FOREIGN DIRECT INVESTMENT	OFFICIAL DEVELOPMENT ASSISTANCE			REMITTANCE INFLOWS	
		Education	Health	Research and development	Military	Debt service			Net inflows	Total	Per capita	Allocated to social sectors[a]	Total	Per capita
						(% of GNI)	(% of GDP)	(% of GDP)	(% of GDP)	(% of GNI)	($)	(% of total aid)	(% of GDP)	($)
		2000–2007[b]	2000–2007[b]	2000–2007[b]	2008	2008	2008	2008	2008	2008	2008	2008	2008	2008
96	Paraguay	4.0	2.4	0.1	0.8	2.9	12.5	19.6	2.0	0.8	21.4	42.0	3.1	81
97	Philippines	2.6	1.3	0.1	0.8	6.6	14.1	14.7	0.8	0.0	0.7	34.1	11.2	206
98	Botswana	8.1	4.3	0.4	2.7	0.5	..	23.4	0.8	5.6	377.0	35.8	0.9	59
99	Moldova, Republic of	8.2	5.2	0.5	0.6	7.5	20.5	34.1	11.7	4.5	82.3	51.5	31.4	522
100	Mongolia	5.1	3.5	0.2	..	1.4	23.2	35.7	13.0	4.8	93.7	39.4	3.8	76
101	Egypt	3.8	2.4	0.2	2.3	1.9	15.4	22.4	5.9	0.8	16.5	37.0	5.4	107
102	Uzbekistan	..	2.3	..	..	2.5	..	23.0	3.3	0.7	6.9	50.2	..	..
103	Micronesia, Federated States of	7.3	12.6	..	..	..	..	..	..	35.9	855.8	53.3	..	..
104	Guyana	6.1	7.2	..	..	2.3	..	39.7	14.5	14.5	217.8	54.6	24.1	365
105	Namibia	6.5	3.2	..	3.5	..	27.2	23.4	6.1	2.4	98.0	66.3	0.2	6
106	Honduras	..	4.1	0.0	0.8	2.8	15.8	32.2	6.6	4.1	77.9	43.1	21.5	392
107	Maldives	8.1	6.4	..	..	5.4	21.0	53.5	1.2	4.5	175.0	47.8	0.2	10
108	Indonesia	3.5	1.2	0.0	1.0	4.8	12.3	27.6	1.8	0.2	5.4	37.8	1.3	30
109	Kyrgyzstan	6.6	3.5	0.3	3.7	6.6	16.8	22.7	4.6	8.3	68.2	63.0	24.4	234
110	South Africa	5.1	3.6	1.0	1.3	1.7	27.7	23.2	3.5	0.4	23.1	66.8	0.3	17
111	Syrian Arab Republic	4.9	1.6	..	3.4	..	..	16.4	3.1	0.3	6.4	50.7	1.5	41
112	Tajikistan	3.5	1.1	0.1	..	2.7	9.8	19.3	7.3	5.8	42.5	55.2	49.6	372
113	Viet Nam	5.3	2.8	0.2	2.4	1.5	..	36.0	10.6	2.9	29.6	35.7	7.9	84
114	Morocco	5.7	1.7	0.6	3.4	4.8	27.5	33.1	2.8	1.4	39.0	47.6	7.8	218
115	Nicaragua	3.1	4.5	0.0	0.7	4.3	17.0	29.4	9.5	11.5	130.4	43.0	12.4	144
116	Guatemala	3.2	2.1	..	0.4	4.6	11.3	17.7	2.1	1.4	39.2	43.0	11.4	326
117	Equatorial Guinea	0.6	1.7	..	..	..	..	28.2	..	0.3	57.0	80.0	..	..
118	Cape Verde	5.7	3.4	..	0.5	2.0	23.9	46.6	13.3	12.8	437.1	37.6	9.7	311
119	India	3.2	1.1	0.8	2.6	2.7	12.9	34.8	3.6	0.2	1.8	50.4	4.3	44
120	Timor-Leste	7.1	11.5	..	4.7	..	..	21.8	..	9.5	252.3	69.9	..	..
121	Swaziland	7.9	3.8	..	..	1.7	27.6	16.5	0.4	2.5	57.6	58.0	3.5	86
122	Lao People's Democratic Republic	2.3	0.8	0.0	0.4	3.8	10.1	37.1	4.1	10.0	79.8	44.7	0.0	0
123	Solomon Islands	2.2 [d]	4.3	..	..	2.8	..	13.4	11.8	35.1	439.8	79.3	3.2	41
124	Cambodia	1.6	1.7	0.0	1.1	0.4	8.2	19.4	7.9	8.1	50.5	60.5	3.1	22
125	Pakistan	2.9	0.8	0.7	2.6	1.8	9.8	20.4	3.3	0.9	9.3	55.1	4.3	42
126	Congo	1.8	1.7	..	1.1	1.3	6.2	20.5	24.5	6.0	139.5	15.8	0.1	4
127	São Tomé and Príncipe	..	5.3	..	..	1.9	..	..	18.9	26.3	293.9	43.2	1.1	13

LOW HUMAN DEVELOPMENT

HDI rank		Education	Health	R&D	Military	Debt service	Tax revenue	GFCF	FDI net	ODA Total	ODA per cap	ODA social	Rem Total	Rem per cap
128	Kenya	7.0	2.0	..	1.9	1.3	18.9	19.4	0.3	4.0	35.3	51.9	5.6	44
129	Bangladesh	2.4	1.1	..	1.0	1.2	8.8	24.2	1.2	2.4	12.9	31.8	11.3	56
130	Ghana	5.4	4.3	..	0.7	1.6	22.9	35.9	12.7	8.1	55.4	45.4	0.8	5
131	Cameroon	2.9	1.3	..	1.5	1.6	..	17.1	0.2	2.3	27.8	22.9	0.6	8
132	Myanmar	1.3	0.2	0.2	..	..	3.3	11.7	..	..	10.8	24.1	..	3
133	Yemen	5.2	1.5	..	4.2	1.2	..	23.1	5.8	1.3	13.3	62.6	5.3	62
134	Benin	3.6	2.5	..	1.1	1.5	17.3	20.7	1.8	9.6	74.0	48.5	4.1	31
135	Madagascar	2.9	2.7	0.1	1.1	0.3	11.4	35.6	15.6	9.5	44.0	40.5	0.1	1
136	Mauritania	4.4	1.6	..	3.7	4.4	..	25.9	3.6	..	97.1	38.5	0.1	1
137	Papua New Guinea	..	2.6	..	0.4	12.7	21.0	18.1	−0.4	4.1	47.2	61.3	0.2	2
138	Nepal	3.8	2.0	..	2.0	1.3	10.4	21.1	0.0	5.6	25.1	46.2	21.6	95
139	Togo	3.7	1.5	..	1.9	6.8	16.3	22.3	2.3	11.7	51.0	33.7	9.8	44
140	Comoros	7.6	1.9	..	..	2.3	..	16.1	1.5	7.0	58.2	60.4	2.3	22
141	Lesotho	12.4	3.6	0.1	1.6	1.8	58.9	28.3	13.4	7.0	71.0	71.9	27.0	214
142	Nigeria	..	1.7	..	0.8	0.3	..	..	1.8	0.7	8.5	72.9	4.8	66
143	Uganda	3.8	1.6	0.4	2.3	0.5	12.8	23.3	5.5	11.7	52.3	44.2	5.1	23
144	Senegal	5.1	3.2	0.1	1.6	1.4	16.1	30.2	5.3	8.1	86.6	42.9	9.7	105
145	Haiti	..	1.2	..	0.0	..	..	..	0.4	13.1	93.2	50.6	19.6	143
146	Angola	2.6	2.0	..	3.0	2.3	..	12.4	2.0	0.5	20.5	69.1	0.1	5
147	Djibouti	8.7	5.5	..	3.7	2.8	..	38.9	28.9	12.7	142.2	40.3	3.5	36
148	Tanzania, United Republic of	6.8	3.5	..	1.1	0.3	..	16.4	3.6	11.7	54.9	51.3	0.1	0
149	Côte d'Ivoire	4.6	1.0	..	1.5	4.7	15.6	10.1	1.7	2.7	29.9	45.6	0.8	9
150	Zambia	1.4	3.6	0.0	2.0	1.3	17.1	22.7	6.6	8.4	86.0	58.3	0.5	5
151	Gambia	2.0	2.6	..	..	3.3	..	24.8	8.9	12.8	56.5	15.7	8.2	40

TABLE 15

HDI rank	PUBLIC EXPENDITURE (% of GDP)							FOREIGN DIRECT INVESTMENT	OFFICIAL DEVELOPMENT ASSISTANCE			REMITTANCE INFLOWS	
	Education	Health	Research and development	Military	Debt service (% of GNI)	Tax revenue (% of GDP)	Gross fixed capital formation (% of GDP)	Net inflows (% of GDP)	Total (% of GNI)	Per capita ($)	Allocated to social sectors[a] (% of total aid)	Total (% of GDP)	Per capita ($)
	2000–2007[b]	2000–2007[b]	2000–2007[b]	2008	2008	2008	2008	2008	2008	2008	2008	2008	2008
152 Rwanda	4.1	4.9	..	1.5	0.4	..	24.1	2.3	21.1	95.7	60.5	1.5	7
153 Malawi	4.2	5.9	..	..	0.8	..	24.2	0.9	21.5	63.9	56.1	0.0	0
154 Sudan	..	1.3	0.3	..	0.8	..	20.2	4.6	4.6	57.6	27.5	5.5	75
155 Afghanistan	..	1.8	..	1.9	0.1	5.8	27.6	2.8	45.8	..	47.7	..	..
156 Guinea	1.7	0.6	..	..	4.2	..	15.5	10.1	7.6	32.4	33.0	1.9	7
157 Ethiopia	5.5	2.2	0.2	1.4	0.4	10.2	20.1	0.4	12.5	41.2	42.9	1.5	5
158 Sierra Leone	3.8	1.4	..	2.4	0.3	10.8	14.7	−0.2	19.2	66.0	53.1	7.7	27
159 Central African Republic	1.3	1.4	..	1.6	1.8	6.2	11.6	6.1	13.2	58.0	30.9	..	..
160 Mali	3.8	2.9	..	1.9	0.8	15.6	23.3	1.5	11.4	75.8	51.5	3.9	27
161 Burkina Faso	4.6	3.4	0.1	1.4	0.6	12.5	20.8	1.7	12.6	65.6	41.4	0.6	4
162 Liberia	2.7	2.8	..	0.6	135.2	..	16.4	17.1	185.0	329.9	13.7	6.9	15
163 Chad	1.9	2.7	..	6.6	2.1	..	14.1	9.9	6.2	37.6	24.9	..	..
164 Guinea-Bissau	5.2[d]	1.6	..	..	4.0	..	23.9	3.5	31.2	83.3	49.1	7.0	19
165 Mozambique	5.0	3.5	0.5	0.8	0.5	..	18.5	6.0	22.9	91.5	49.3	1.2	5
166 Burundi	7.2	5.2	..	4.0	3.7	..	16.4	0.3	43.9	63.0	35.4	0.3	0
167 Niger	3.7	2.8	..	..	0.5	11.5	18.9	2.7	11.3	41.3	45.2	1.5	5
168 Congo, Democratic Republic of the	..	1.2	0.5	1.4	6.2	6.3	23.9	8.6	15.6	25.1	46.8	..	..
169 Zimbabwe	4.6	4.1	..	..	7.3	..	21.0	3.0	..	49.0	35.1	..	..

OTHER COUNTRIES OR TERRITORIES

Antigua and Barbuda	3.9	3.2	..	..	..	..	73.7	20.8	0.7	91.3	82.9	1.0	141
Bhutan	5.1	3.3	..	..	6.3	7.9	46.4	2.3	6.2	125.4	46.5	..	..
Cuba	13.6	9.9	0.4	..	..	..	..	..	..	11.3	50.4	..	..
Dominica	4.8	3.9	..	..	5.4	..	32.7	14.6	6.3	312.4	15.4	1.3	62
Eritrea	2.0	1.5	..	..	0.9	..	10.6	2.2	8.7	28.6	54.1	0.5	1
Grenada	5.2	3.6	..	..	3.9	..	29.8	25.3	5.5	300.4	35.6	4.3	263
Iraq	..	1.9	..	5.4	..	..	..	..	..	..	18.1	..	0
Kiribati	17.9	16.1	..	..	..	..	..	..	13.9	269.0	57.7	6.6	93
Korea, Democratic People's Rep. of	..	3.0	..	..	..	..	..	..	..	9.1	11.2	..	..
Lebanon	2.0	3.9	..	3.9	15.6	16.3	30.7	12.3	4.0	259.9	45.3	24.5	1,712
Marshall Islands	12.3	14.3	..	..	..	..	..	..	27.3	887.0	43.6	..	..
Monaco	..	2.9	..	..	..	..	..	..	..	..	..	..	..
Nauru	..	..	..	..	..	..	..	..	..	3,124.0	39.4	..	..
Occupied Palestinian Territories	..	..	..	..	..	..	25.7	1.2	0.0	675.2	66.7	14.6	160
Oman	4.0	1.9	..	7.7	..	7.4	12.6	7.5	..	11.4	83.0	0.1	16
Palau	10.3	8.5	..	..	..	..	..	..	23.4	2,147.0	6.4	..	..
Saint Kitts and Nevis	9.9	3.4	..	..	8.8	22.2	41.6	16.1	9.1	924.8	5.0	0.8	91
Saint Lucia	6.3	3.4	0.4[d]	..	5.2	..	25.9	10.5	2.0	112.3	35.4	0.3	16
Saint Vincent and the Grenadines	7.0	3.3	0.2	..	4.9	..	37.9	20.0	4.7	243.6	33.3	1.8	101
Samoa	5.4	4.2	..	..	2.7	..	..	1.1	7.8	219.2	64.5	25.8	755
San Marino	..	6.1	..	..	..	22.4	..	..	..	..	..	..	..
Seychelles	5.0	3.6	0.4	1.3	12.6	26.0	28.3	43.7	1.6	134.2	37.4	1.4	138
Somalia	..	..	..	..	..	..	..	..	..	84.7	16.8	..	..
Tuvalu	..	..	..	..	..	..	..	..	..	1,662.0	41.3	..	..
Vanuatu	6.9	2.7	..	..	0.8	..	24.2	5.8	16.2	398.6	36.9	1.2	30

NOTES

a Data refer to allocation of aid to social infrastructure and services including health, education, water, sanitation, government, civil society and other services, expressed as a percentage of total official development assistance received. Differences in allocation of funds exist between countries.

b Data refer to the most recent year available during the period specified.

c Since 1970 developed countries committed to spending 0.7 percent of gross national income on official development assistance. Values in brackets refer to official development assistance disbursed by donor countries.

d Refers to an earlier year than that specified.

e Refers to 2007.

SOURCES

Column 1: UNESCO Institute for Statistics (2010a).

Columns 2, 3, 5–8, 12 and 13: World Bank (2010g).

Column 4: SIPRI (2010b).

Columns 9–11: OECD-DAC (2010a).

TABLE

15

TABLE 16

Enabling environment: economy and infrastructure

		ECONOMY					PHYSICAL INFRASTRUCTURE				MEDIA INFRASTRUCTURE		
		GDP		GDP per capita		Consumer price index	Road density	Rail lines	Air transport (freight)	Population without electricity	Daily newspapers	Radio coverage	Television coverage
HDI rank		($ billions)	(PPP $ billions)	($)	Average annual growth rate (%)	Average annual change (%)	(km of road per sq. km of land area)	(km)	(million tonnes per km)	(% of population)	(per thousand people)	(% of population)	(% of population)
		2008	2008	2008	1970–2008	2000–2008	2004–2007[a]	2004–2008[a]	2005–2008[a]	2008	2004	2005	2005
VERY HIGH HUMAN DEVELOPMENT													
1	Norway	451.8	280.0	94,759	2.6	1.7	29	4,114	..	..	516	100	98
2	Australia	1,015.2	831.2	47,370	1.9	3.0	..	9,661	2,212	..	155	100	100
3	New Zealand	129.9	116.4	30,439	1.2	2.7	35	..	921	..	182	100	100
4	United States	14,591.4	14,591.4	46,350	1.9	2.8	68	227,058	39,314	..	193	..	..
5	Ireland	267.6	185.2	60,460	3.5	3.6	..	1,919	..	..	182	..	..
6	Liechtenstein	..	..	..	3.2	..	..	..	..	..	..	..	..
7	Netherlands	871.0	673.6	52,963	1.9	2.0	372	2,896	4,903	..	307	100	100
8	Canada	1,501.3	1,301.7	45,070	1.9	2.2	14	57,216	1,389	..	175	92	95
9	Sweden	479.0	340.8	51,950	1.6	1.5	95	9,830	..	..	481	100	100
10	Germany	3,649.5	2,904.6	44,446	1.9	1.7	181	33,862	8,353	..	267	..	..
11	Japan	4,910.8	4,358.5	38,455	2.1	–0.1	316	20,048	8,173	..	551	..	..
12	Korea, Republic of	929.1	1,344.4	19,115	5.6	3.1	103	3,381	8,727	..	..	100	100
13	Switzerland	491.9	324.4	64,327	1.1	1.0	173	3,499	1,182	..	420	100	99
14	France	2,856.6	2,121.7	44,508	1.8	1.9	172	29,901	6,188	..	163	100	100
15	Israel	202.1	204.0	27,652	1.9	1.7	81	1,005	902	0.0	..	..	..
16	Finland	272.7	192.3	51,323	2.2	1.5	23	5,919	543	..	431	100	100
17	Iceland	16.7	11.7	52,479	2.5	4.9	13	..	..	..	552	100	100
18	Belgium	504.2	377.3	47,085	2.0	2.2	499	3,513	982	..	165	..	..
19	Denmark	341.3	202.4	62,118	1.6	2.0	168	2,133	..	..	353	100	100
20	Spain	1,604.2	1,442.9	35,215	2.1	3.2	..	15,046	1,306	..	144	..	..
21	Hong Kong, China (SAR)	215.4	306.5	30,863	4.6	0.0	184	..	..	..	..	48	23
22	Greece	355.9	329.9	31,670	2.0	3.3	89	2,552	78	..	..	98	98
23	Italy	2,303.1	1,871.7	38,492	1.7	2.3	162	16,862	1,279	..	137	100	100
24	Luxembourg	53.7	38.6	109,903	2.9	2.4	201	275	..	..	255	100	100
25	Austria	413.5	316.1	49,599	2.2	2.0	128	5,755	421	..	311	100	98
26	United Kingdom	2,674.1	2,178.2	43,541	1.9	3.0	172	16,321	6,284	..	290	..	..
27	Singapore	181.9	238.5	37,597	5.0	1.3	472	..	..	0.0	361	..	..
28	Czech Republic	215.5	256.9	20,673	0.2	2.5	163	9,487	27	..	183	..	..
29	Slovenia	54.6	56.3	27,019	2.4	4.4	191	1,228	..	..	..	..	..
30	Andorra	..	..	..	0.8	..	..	..	..	..	..	..	..
31	Slovakia	98.5	119.7	18,212	0.9	5.1	89	3,592	46	..	126	..	..
32	United Arab Emirates	..	..	..	4.2	..	5	..	..	0.0	..	100	100
33	Malta	..	..	..	4.3	2.5	705	..	..	..	..	100	100
34	Estonia	23.4	27.7	17,454	0.7	4.3	128	816	1	..	191	92	76
35	Cyprus	24.9	21.3	31,410	3.4	2.8	132	..	..	..	..	75	75
36	Hungary	154.7	198.6	15,408	2.2	5.5	210	7,942	..	..	217	100	100
37	Brunei Darussalam	..	..	..	0.2	0.1	63	..	..	0.0	68	..	..
38	Qatar	..	..	..	0.0	7.3	68	..	..	0.0	..	100	..
39	Bahrain	21.9	27.0	28,240	1.0	1.8	..	..	..	0.0	..	..	..
40	Portugal	243.5	247.0	22,923	2.5	2.9	90	2,842	347	..	..	83	100
41	Poland	527.9	658.6	13,845	2.7	2.4	83	19,627	79	..	114	92	99
42	Barbados	3.7	..	14,426	1.8	3.7	372	..	..	..	..	..	..

		ECONOMY					PHYSICAL INFRASTRUCTURE				MEDIA INFRASTRUCTURE		
		GDP		GDP per capita		Consumer price index	Road density	Rail lines	Air transport (freight)	Population without electricity	Daily newspapers	Radio coverage	Television coverage
HDI rank		($ billions)	(PPP $ billions)	($)	Average annual growth rate (%)	Average annual change (%)	(km of road per sq. km of land area)	(km)	(million tonnes per km)	(% of population)	(per thousand people)	(% of population)	(% of population)
		2008	2008	2008	1970–2008	2000–2008	2004–2007[a]	2004–2008[a]	2005–2008[a]	2008	2004	2005	2005
HIGH HUMAN DEVELOPMENT													
43	Bahamas	..	..	..	..	2.2	..	..	1	..	..	..	..
44	Lithuania	47.3	59.6	14,098	–0.5	2.5	124	1,765	1	..	108	100	100
45	Chile	169.5	242.4	10,084	2.8	3.2	..	5,898	1,308	1.8	51	..	98
46	Argentina	328.5	570.4	8,236	1.2	10.3	..	35,753	132	2.8	36	..	..
47	Kuwait	148.0	..	54,260	–1.2	3.0	32	..	..	0.0	..	..	..
48	Latvia	33.8	37.1	14,908	1.3	6.1	108	2,263	..	..	154	..	..
49	Montenegro	4.9	8.3	7,859	0.0	..	..	..	..	..	..	..	..
50	Romania	200.1	289.3	9,300	3.3	12.5	..	10,784	6	..	70	90	100
51	Croatia	69.3	78.3	15,637	2.1	2.8	51	2,722	2	..	..	..	..
52	Uruguay	32.2	42.5	9,654	2.2	9.5	102	2,993	..	0.0	..	98	98
53	Libyan Arab Jamahiriya	93.2	101.9	14,802	–1.3	–0.5	..	..	0	0.0	..	..	..
54	Panama	23.1	42.4	6,793	2.8	2.1	..	..	..	11.8	65	..	..
55	Saudi Arabia	468.8	590.8	19,022	1.1	1.7	10	2,758	1,383	0.8	..	..	..
56	Mexico	1,088.1	1,549.5	10,232	1.7	4.5	18	26,677	483	..	..	98	92
57	Malaysia	221.8	383.7	8,209	4.4	2.3	28	1,665	2,444	0.7	109	..	..
58	Bulgaria	49.9	89.9	6,546	3.3	6.3	37	4,159	2	..	79	..	..
59	Trinidad and Tobago	24.1	33.5	18,108	2.1	6.1	..	..	49	0.0	..	..	..
60	Serbia	50.1	77.6	6,811	–0.7	16.6	..	4,058	..	..	..	..	..
61	Belarus	60.3	118.8	6,230	1.2	20.2	46	5,491	1	..	81	..	..
62	Costa Rica	29.7	50.7	6,564	1.9	11.3	72	..	11	0.0	65	..	..
63	Peru	129.1	245.2	4,477	1.1	2.3	6	2,020	230	22.5	..	..	..
64	Albania	12.3	22.9	3,911	2.2	2.9	..	423	..	..	..	98	95
65	Russian Federation	1,679.5	2,258.5	11,832	–0.8	12.6	5	84,158	2,400	..	92	..	..
66	Kazakhstan	133.4	177.4	8,513	0.2	8.3	3	14,205	16	..	..	..	..
67	Azerbaijan	46.1	76.1	5,315	1.1	10.0	68	2,099	12	..	..	100	100
68	Bosnia and Herzegovina	18.5	30.5	4,906	10.9	..	43	1,016	..	..	..	..	..
69	Ukraine	180.4	336.4	3,899	–1.9	9.8	28	21,676	63	..	131	48	62
70	Iran, Islamic Republic of	..	..	..	0.2	15.0	10	7,335	97	1.6	..	..	..
71	The former Yugoslav Republic of Macedonia	9.5	19.1	4,664	1.3	2.3	54	699	..	..	89	..	..
72	Mauritius	9.3	15.7	7,345	4.0	6.3	99	..	191	0.0	77	100	100
73	Brazil	1,575.2	1,976.6	8,205	2.2	7.3	20	29,817	1,807	2.2	36	90	90
74	Georgia	12.8	21.4	2,970	0.3	7.1	29	1,513	..	..	4	90	90
75	Venezuela, Bolivarian Republic of	314.2	357.8	11,246	0.1	20.6	..	336	2	1.1	93	..	..
76	Armenia	11.9	18.7	3,873	0.7	3.8	25	845	..	..	8	..	..
77	Ecuador	54.7	108.0	4,056	2.2	7.0	15	..	5	8.2	..	..	..
78	Belize	1.4	2.2	4,218	2.1	3.2	..	..	..	..	..	..	..
79	Colombia	243.8	395.7	5,416	2.0	5.9	15	1,663	1,100	6.7	23	..	91
80	Jamaica	14.6	20.7	5,438	0.3	11.4	201	..	..	7.4	..	..	..
81	Tunisia	40.3	82.1	3,903	3.1	3.2	12	2,218	..	1.0	..	..	..
82	Jordan	21.2	32.3	3,596	1.6	4.2	9	251	141	0.0	..	100	97
83	Turkey	734.9	991.7	9,942	2.4	18.6	55	8,699	481	..	..	..	..
84	Algeria	166.5	276.0	4,845	1.1	2.8	5	3,572	17	0.6	..	..	..
85	Tonga	0.3	0.4	2,687	2.7	9.1	..	..	..	..	..	..	..
MEDIUM HUMAN DEVELOPMENT													
86	Fiji	3.6	3.7	4,253	1.5	3.3	..	..	96	..	53	..	..
87	Turkmenistan	15.3	33.4	3,039	0.3	..	..	3,181	11	..	9	..	..
88	Dominican Republic	45.5	80.8	4,576	3.0	16.0	..	..	..	4.0	39	70	..
89	China	4,327.0	7,903.2	3,267	7.9	2.2	36	60,809	11,386	0.6	74	94	96
90	El Salvador	22.1	41.7	3,605	1.1	3.9	..	..	18	14.7	38	..	..
91	Sri Lanka	40.6	91.9	2,013	3.4	11.0	..	1,463	..	23.4	..	..	..
92	Thailand	272.4	544.5	4,043	4.4	3.0	35	4,429	2,289	0.6	..	..	..
93	Gabon	14.5	21.1	10,037	0.5	1.5	3	810	68	62.1	..	..	..

TABLE 16

	ECONOMY				Consumer price index	PHYSICAL INFRASTRUCTURE				MEDIA INFRASTRUCTURE		
	GDP		GDP per capita			Road density	Rail lines	Air transport (freight)	Population without electricity	Daily newspapers	Radio coverage	Television coverage
HDI rank	($ billions)	(PPP $ billions)	($)	Average annual growth rate (%)	Average annual change (%)	(km of road per sq. km of land area)	(km)	(million tonnes per km)	(% of population)	(per thousand people)	(% of population)	(% of population)
	2008	2008	2008	1970–2008	2000–2008	2004–2007[a]	2004–2008[a]	2005–2008[a]	2008	2004	2005	2005
94 Suriname	3.0	3.8	5,888	0.9	14.3	..		28	..	..	..	..
95 Bolivia, Plurinational State of	16.7	41.4	1,720	0.9	4.9	6	2,866	9	22.7	..	..	..
96 Paraguay	16.0	29.3	2,561	1.5	8.7	..		0	4.8	..	..	..
97 Philippines	166.9	317.1	1,847	1.4	5.5	..	479	277	13.8	79	..	..
98 Botswana	13.4	26.1	6,982	5.9	8.7	4	888	0	52.1	41	..	..
99 Moldova, Republic of	6.0	10.6	1,694	0.2	11.3	38	1,156	..	..	..	..	..
100 Mongolia	5.3	9.4	1,991	2.3	8.1	..	1,810	6	34.1	20	95	67
101 Egypt	162.3	442.0	1,991	2.5	7.2	9	5,063	195	0.6	..	94	92
102 Uzbekistan	27.9	72.5	1,023	−0.4		..	4,230	72	..	..	..	..
103 Micronesia, Federated States of	0.3	0.3	2,334	1.1	..	..		..	..	..	..	..
104 Guyana	1.2	2.3	1,513	1.6	6.6	..		..	..	..	..	..
105 Namibia	8.8	13.6	4,149	0.5	5.4	..		0	65.7	28	..	..
106 Honduras	13.3	28.8	1,823	1.4	7.9	..		..	28.7	..	..	..
107 Maldives	1.3	1.7	4,135	5.0	..	..		..	..	..	..	..
108 Indonesia	510.7	907.3	2,246	4.3	9.3	20	3,370	395	35.7	..	..	..
109 Kyrgyzstan	5.1	11.6	958	−1.4	6.1	..	417	2	..	1	..	..
110 South Africa	276.4	492.2	5,678	0.6	4.3	..	24,487	761	24.2	30	..	..
111 Syrian Arab Republic	55.2	94.2	2,682	2.2	5.9	21	2,139	14	7.1	..	88	95
112 Tajikistan	5.1	13.0	751	−2.5	13.0	..	616	5	..	..	..	..
113 Viet Nam	90.6	240.1	1,051	4.2	7.1	49	3,147	296	10.9	..	..	..
114 Morocco	88.9	136.8	2,769	2.4	1.9	13	1,989	55	2.8	..	..	..
115 Nicaragua	6.6	15.2	1,163	−0.2	8.6	14		..	28.2	..	..	..
116 Guatemala	39.0	65.1	2,848	1.2	7.5	..		..	19.7	..	..	..
117 Equatorial Guinea	18.5	22.3	28,103	8.5	5.6	..		..	..	..	..	..
118 Cape Verde	1.6	1.6	3,193	2.3	2.1	..		2	..	..	90	70
119 India	1,159.2	3,356.3	1,017	3.6	4.8	1,001	63,327	1,234	34.2	71	99	..
120 Timor-Leste	0.5	0.9	453	1.0	5.2	..		..	81.9	..	..	..
121 Swaziland	2.8	5.7	2,429	3.7	6.9	..	300	..	..	24	..	..
122 Lao People's Democratic Republic	5.5	13.2	893	3.4	9.0	13		3	43.5	3	..	..
123 Solomon Islands	0.6	1.3	1,263	0.7	9.1	..		1	..	11	..	..
124 Cambodia	10.4	28.4	711	1.9	5.6	22	650	1	76.9	..	..	85
125 Pakistan	164.5	421.3	991	2.4	7.1	34	7,791	320	39.8	50	99	..
126 Congo	10.7	14.3	2,966	2.0	3.1	5	795	..	74.7	..	..	..
127 São Tomé and Príncipe	0.2	0.3	1,090	0.7	..	..		0	..	..	..	..

LOW HUMAN DEVELOPMENT

128 Kenya	30.4	60.1	783	0.5	10.7	11	1,917	295	84.6	..	..	..
129 Bangladesh	79.6	213.5	497	1.8	6.7	..	2,835	84	59.3	..	..	..
130 Ghana	16.7	34.1	713	1.1	16.4	25	953	..	47.1	..	..	..
131 Cameroon	23.4	41.9	1,226	1.2	2.3	11	977	26	70.2	..	65	50
132 Myanmar	..	..	..	..	23.7	4		3	86.4	..	90	..
133 Yemen	26.6	55.3	1,160	2.2	11.7	14		33	62.0	4	..	..
134 Benin	6.7	12.8	771	0.6	3.0	17	758	..	80.8	0	..	..
135 Madagascar	9.5	20.1	495	−1.2	10.8	..	854	12	85.8	..	..	..
136 Mauritania	2.9	..	889	0.6	7.5	1	728	0	..	..	61	19
137 Papua New Guinea	8.2	14.3	1,253	1.8	5.9	..		22	..	9	..	..
138 Nepal	12.6	31.8	438	1.7	5.5	12		7	55.9	..	70	..
139 Togo	2.9	5.4	449	−0.4	2.7	..		..	83.6	..	..	..
140 Comoros	0.5	0.8	824	0.1	..	..		..	..	..	..	..
141 Lesotho	1.6	3.2	791	2.8	7.8	..		..	82.9	..	..	..
142 Nigeria	207.1	317.2	1,370	1.0	12.9	21	3,528	10	53.3	..	..	..
143 Uganda	14.3	36.9	453	0.9	6.0	..	259	..	91.9	..	80	40
144 Senegal	13.3	21.9	1,087	0.2	2.2	..		0	60.6	9	..	..
145 Haiti	7.2	11.1	729	−0.6	18.0	..		..	60.8	..	60	80
146 Angola	84.9	104.8	4,714	1.4	47.0	..		71	71.6	2	..	..

TABLE 16

208 HUMAN DEVELOPMENT REPORT 2010

		ECONOMY					PHYSICAL INFRASTRUCTURE				MEDIA INFRASTRUCTURE		
		GDP		GDP per capita		Consumer price index	Road density	Rail lines	Air transport (freight)	Population without electricity	Daily newspapers	Radio coverage	Television coverage
		($ billions)	(PPP $ billions)	($)	Average annual growth rate (%)	Average annual change (%)	(km of road per sq. km of land area)	(km)	(million tonnes per km)	(% of population)	(per thousand people)	(% of population)	(% of population)
HDI rank		2008	2008	2008	1970–2008	2000–2008	2004–2007[a]	2004–2008[a]	2005–2008[a]	2008	2004	2005	2005
147	Djibouti	0.9	1.8	1,030	−2.1	..	..	781	..	..	..	..	..
148	Tanzania, United Republic of	20.5	53.7	496	0.9	6.0	..	2,600	1	86.6	2	80	20
149	Côte d'Ivoire	23.4	34.0	1,137	−1.1	3.0	25	639	..	50.5	..	..	..
150	Zambia	14.3	17.1	1,134	−1.1	16.6	..	1,273	0	78.4	5	..	..
151	Gambia	0.8	2.3	489	0.4	8.1	33	..	..	..	..	100	75
152	Rwanda	4.5	10.0	458	1.2	8.5	57	..	..	..	..	100	..
153	Malawi	4.3	11.9	288	1.9	12.7	..	797	2	87.6	..	..	..
154	Sudan	55.9	89.0	1,353	1.9	8.2	..	4,578	47	65.3	..	100	..
155	Afghanistan	10.6	32.0	366	1.9	12.9	6	..	..	85.6	..	..	..
156	Guinea	3.8	10.4	386	0.7	..	..	..	..	..	..	..	..
157	Ethiopia	25.6	70.1	317	1.3	11.1	3	..	228	85.1	5	..	..
158	Sierra Leone	2.0	4.3	352	0.2	..	..	..	..	..	..	..	..
159	Central African Republic	2.0	3.2	458	−0.8	3.0	..	..	..	..	..	..	..
160	Mali	8.7	14.3	688	1.4	2.2	1	..	..	..	..	..	..
161	Burkina Faso	7.9	17.7	522	2.0	2.9	34	622	0	90.6	..	..	..
162	Liberia	0.8	1.5	222	−2.0	..	..	..	..	..	..	..	..
163	Chad	8.4	14.6	770	0.9	2.2	3	..	..	..	..	..	..
164	Guinea-Bissau	0.4	0.8	273	1.7	2.3	..	..	..	..	..	..	..
165	Mozambique	9.8	18.7	440	2.2	11.5	..	3,116	7	86.2	3	..	..
166	Burundi	1.2	3.1	144	−0.3	8.5	48	..	..	..	..	..	..
167	Niger	5.4	10.0	364	−1.3	2.4	1	..	..	..	0	100	..
168	Congo, Democratic Republic of the	11.7	20.2	182	−3.0	26.9	..	4,007	..	88.7	..	75	90
169	Zimbabwe	..	..	..	−0.5	497.7	..	2,583	7	62.6	..	..	..

OTHER COUNTRIES OR TERRITORIES

	($ billions)	(PPP $ billions)	($)	Growth %	CPI %	Road density	Rail lines	Air transport	Pop. w/o elec.	Daily newspapers	Radio coverage	Television coverage
Antigua and Barbuda	1.2	1.8	14,048	3.7	..	..	..	..	..	..	..	..
Bhutan	1.3	3.3	1,869	4.5	4.4	..	..	..	..	..	100	20
Cuba	..	..	..	..	..	..	5,076	32	2.7	65	..	98
Dominica	0.4	0.6	4,883	3.4	2.1	..	..	..	..	..	..	..
Eritrea	1.7	3.2	336	0.9	..	..	..	..	69.0	..	..	..
Grenada	0.6	0.9	6,162	3.8	3.1	..	..	..	..	..	..	..
Iraq	..	..	..	..	..	..	2,032	..	14.0	..	..	..
Kiribati	0.1	0.2	1,414	0.1	..	..	..	..	..	..	..	..
Korea, Democratic People's Rep. of	..	..	..	..	..	21	..	..	74.3	..	..	..
Lebanon	29.3	49.4	6,978	4.0	..	67	..	..	0.0	54	..	..
Marshall Islands	0.2	..	2,655	−0.1	..	..	..	0	..	0	..	..
Monaco	..	..	..	..	..	3,850	..	..	..	..	..	..
Occupied Palestinian Territories	..	..	..	..	3.9	..	..	..	..	10	..	..
Oman	..	..	..	3.4	2.3	16	..	..	3.6	..	100	100
Palau	0.2	..	8,911	−0.1	..	..	..	..	..	..	..	..
Saint Kitts and Nevis	0.5	0.8	11,046	3.7	3.8	..	..	..	..	..	..	..
Saint Lucia	1.0	1.7	5,854	3.0	2.5	..	..	..	..	..	98	..
Saint Vincent and the Grenadines	0.6	1.0	5,480	3.9	3.2	..	..	..	..	..	95	100
Samoa	0.5	0.8	2,926	1.4	6.1	..	..	2	..	..	..	..
San Marino	..	..	..	..	2.3	..	..	..	..	..	100	100
Seychelles	0.8	1.9	9,580	3.2	4.4	..	..	27	..	..	..	..
Somalia	..	..	..	−1.4	..	..	..	..	..	..	..	..
Vanuatu	0.6	0.9	2,521	1.6	2.4	..	..	..	..	14	..	..

TABLE 16

HDI rank	ECONOMY				Consumer price index	PHYSICAL INFRASTRUCTURE				MEDIA INFRASTRUCTURE		
	GDP		GDP per capita			Road density	Rail lines	Air transport (freight)	Population without electricity	Daily newspapers	Radio coverage	Television coverage
	($ billions)	(PPP $ billions)	($)	Average annual growth rate (%)	Average annual change (%)	(km of road per sq. km of land area)	(km)	(million tonnes per km)	(% of population)	(per thousand people)	(% of population)	(% of population)
	2008	2008	2008	1970–2008	2000–2008	2004–2007ª	2004–2008ª	2005–2008ª	2008	2004	2005	2005
Developed												
OECD	41,979.1	37,872.1	40,976	2.4	..	3,838	516,479	92,753	..	254	..	..
Non-OECD	..	..	..	2.2	..	6,060			..	..	..	..
Developing												
Arab States	1,357.1	1,951.6	4,774	−1.1	..	..	..	..	15.2	..	..	..
East Asia and the Pacific	5,625.7	10,369.7	3,032	1.7	..	..	..	..	..	..	..	..
Europe and Central Asia	3,414.5	4,852.7	8,361	0.1	..	..	176,175	..	..	..	..	..
Latin America and the Caribbean	4,202.9	5,963.9	7,567	2.0	..	..	..	..	..	..	..	..
South Asia	1,469.6	4,151.8	954	3.8	..	..	..	..	36.9	..	..	..
Sub-Saharan Africa	928.5	1,595.1	1,233	2.7	..	..	..	..	..	..	..	..
Very high human development	42,652.4	38,697.1	40,748	2.3	..	6,048	518,300	..	..	254	..	..
High human development	8,552.4	11,832.1	8,937	1.1	..	1,332	289,531	..	..	..	..	..
Medium human development	7,635.8	15,560.3	2,200	2.7	..	..	..	17,542	..	..	..	..
Low human development	771.2	1,425.9	781	−0.4	..	..	..	..	..	..	..	..
Least developed countries	503.2	1,000.8	664	2.0	..	..	..	..	..	..	..	..
World	60,042.1	68,323.9	9,120	2.1	..	..	..	..	..	..	..	..

NOTE

a   Data refer to the most recent year available during the period specified.

SOURCES

Columns 1–3 and 6–8: World Bank (2010g).
Column 4: Calculated based on data from World Bank (2010g) and IMF (2010a).
Column 5: Calculated based on data on the consumer price index from World Bank (2010g).
Column 9: Calculated based on data on population without electricity from IEA (2009) and data on population from UNDESA (2009d).
Columns 10–12: UNESCO Institute for Statistics (2010b).

TABLE
16

TABLE 17

Access to information and communication technology

HDI rank	TELEPHONES		Population covered by mobile phone network	INTERNET		Broadband subscriptions[a]	ACCESSIBILITY AND COST	Mobile phone connection charge	Fixed-line phone connection charge	Price of a 3-minute local fixed-line phone call
	Mobile and fixed-line phone subscriptions			Users			Personal computers			
	(per 100 people)	(% growth, population-based)	(%)	(per 100 people)	(% growth, population-based)	(per 100 people)	(per 100 people)	($)	($)	(US cents)
	2008	2000–2008	2008	2008	2000–2008	2008	2006–2008[b]	2006–2008[b]	2006–2008[b]	2006–2008[b]

VERY HIGH HUMAN DEVELOPMENT

1 Norway	150	27	..	82.5	228	33.3	62.7	17.6	175.5	22
2 Australia	147	66	99	70.8	66	24.4	..	24.3	49.5	25
3 New Zealand	149	87	97	71.4	64	21.6	53.0	24.6	36.6	0 c
4 United States	140	41	100	75.9	87	23.5	78.7	0.0	39.0	24
5 Ireland	171	77	99	62.7	310	20.1	58.1	14.5	178.5	11
6 Liechtenstein	150	78	95	66.0	96	55.0	..	33.1	35.5	15
7 Netherlands	170	36	98	87.0	106	35.1	90.9	14.6	69.6	10
8 Canada	121	37	98	75.3	94	29.6	94.4	0.0	92.8	0 c
9 Sweden	176	34	98	87.7	100	41.2	87.8	15.2	102.4	8
10 Germany	191	60	99	75.5	151	27.5	65.5	14.6	87.8	12
11 Japan	124	23	100	75.2	152	23.7	..	0.0	373.8	..
12 Korea, Republic of	138	27	94	75.8	94	32.1	58.1	0.0	54.4	0
13 Switzerland	180	37	100	75.9	66	34.2	97.6	45.2	39.7	23
14 France	149	46	99	67.9	396	28.5	65.2	22.0	80.5	20
15 Israel	167	65	100	47.9	175	23.9	..	57.6	56.3	..
16 Finland	160	29	100	82.5	127	30.5	..	26.2	142.9	22
17 Iceland	169	30	99	90.0	127	32.9	53.1	28.4	33.0	7
18 Belgium	152	52	100	68.1	142	28.0	..	12.5	96.6	24
19 Denmark	170	29	114	83.3	118	37.1	55.1	19.4	186.3	14
20 Spain	153	65	99	55.4	349	20.2	40.0	0.0	117.6	10
21 Hong Kong, China (SAR)	225	67	100	67.0	152	28.1	69.3	..	0.0	0 c
22 Greece	176	69	100	43.1	379	13.5	9.4	7.3	51.1	13
23 Italy	186	60	100	41.8	88	18.9	..	13.2	140.6	16
24 Luxembourg	198	72	100	79.2	280	29.8	67.7	0.0	84.2	10
25 Austria	169	40	99	71.2	120	20.7	..	0.0	244.5	14
26 United Kingdom	180	40	100	76.0	195	28.2	80.2	0.0	229.8	13
27 Singapore	170	68	100	69.6	148	21.7	76.0	5.0	37.8	2
28 Czech Republic	154	94	100	57.8	500	17.1	..	0.0	34.8	20
29 Slovenia	152	53	100	55.7	275	21.2	42.7	25.4	130.9	12
30 Andorra	..	..	99	70.5	..	24.5	..	..	52.8	..
31 Slovakia	122	125	100	66.0	604	11.2	58.2	14.0	55.7	48
32 United Arab Emirates	242	344	100	65.2	282	12.4	33.1	44.9	49.0	3
33 Malta	152	95	100	48.3	287	24.8	..	0.0	34.6	3
34 Estonia	225	180	100	66.2	127	23.7	25.5	4.7	0.0	13
35 Cyprus	163	113	100	38.8	179	16.4	38.3	37.5	147.1	7
36 Hungary	153	122	99	58.5	719	17.5	25.6	7.5	196.1	26
37 Brunei Darussalam	115	158	..	55.3	623	3.6	..	..	35.3	6
38 Qatar	152	593	100	34.0	1,353	8.1	15.7	54.9	54.9	..
39 Bahrain	214	341	100	51.9	907	14.2	74.6	16.0	53.2	5
40 Portugal	179	74	99	42.1	168	15.3	18.2	..	126.2	18
41 Poland	141	203	99	49.0	567	12.6	16.9	2.1	96.7	19
42 Barbados	218	265	100	73.7	1,780	64.8	..	25.0	49.0	0 c

Access to information and communication technology

	TELEPHONES			INTERNET				ACCESSIBILITY AND COST		
	Mobile and fixed-line phone subscriptions		Population covered by mobile phone network	Users		Broadband subscriptions[a]	Personal computers	Mobile phone connection charge	Fixed-line phone connection charge	Price of a 3-minute local fixed-line phone call
HDI rank	(per 100 people)	(% growth, population-based)	(%)	(per 100 people)	(% growth, population-based)	(per 100 people)	(per 100 people)	($)	($)	(US cents)
	2008	2000–2008	2008	2008	2000–2008	2008	2006–2008[b]	2006–2008[b]	2006–2008[b]	2006–2008[b]
HIGH HUMAN DEVELOPMENT										
43 Bahamas	145	236	100	31.5	711	10.1	..	50.0	..	..
44 Lithuania	173	235	100	54.4	703	17.8	24.5	2.1	106.1	15
45 Chile	109	173	100	32.5	113	8.5	..	1.9	92.1	9
46 Argentina	141	291	94	28.1	331	8.0	..	48.4	47.7	2
47 Kuwait	126	284	100	36.7	601	1.4	..	17.3	130.1	0[c]
48 Latvia	127	152	99	60.4	809	8.9	32.8	2.0	..	14
49 Montenegro	176	..	99	47.2	..	10.0	..	7.3	..	100
50 Romania	137	364	98	28.8	679	11.7	19.3	5.6	0.0	23
51 Croatia	175	176	100	50.5	632	11.9	..	20.3	123.6	13
52 Uruguay	134	233	100	40.2	282	7.3	..	46.1	52.1	10
53 Libyan Arab Jamahiriya	93	809	71	5.1	3,130	0.2	..	3.8	38.1	..
54 Panama	131	429	83	27.5	383	5.8	2.8	30.0	30.6	9
55 Saudi Arabia	163	837	98	31.5	1,612	4.2	68.3	26.7	80.0	4
56 Mexico	90	265	100	22.2	368	7.0	14.1	0.0	116.8	15
57 Malaysia	118	228	92	55.8	203	4.9	23.1	2.5	15.0	4
58 Bulgaria	166	252	100	34.7	517	11.1	11.0	..	18.0	12
59 Trinidad and Tobago	136	279	100	17.0	127	4.6	13.2	0.0	23.9	12
60 Serbia	173	..	93	44.9	..	4.6	19.3	3.6	89.7	1
61 Belarus	122	321	99	32.1	1,553	4.9	..	1.5	28.2	1
62 Costa Rica	74	199	69	32.3	540	2.4	..	5.5	39.7	2
63 Peru	83	697	95	24.7	791	2.5	..	13.7	122.1	5
64 Albania	..	..	99	23.9	21,329	2.0	4.6	0.0	143.0	4
65 Russian Federation	172	587	95	31.9	1,450	6.6	13.3	9.6	281.7	3
66 Kazakhstan	117	791	94	10.9	1,582	4.3	..	5.7	117.3	1
67 Azerbaijan	91	541	99	28.2	20,206	0.7	8.0	4.9	97.3	0[c]
68 Bosnia and Herzegovina	112	382	99	34.7	3,169	5.0	6.4	11.2	52.6	7
69 Ukraine	149	513	100	10.5	1,294	3.5	4.6	22.9	31.6	3
70 Iran, Islamic Republic of	94	532	95	32.0	3,483	0.4	10.4	30.8	106.1	1
71 The former Yugoslav Republic of Macedonia	145	375	100	41.5	1,596	8.9	36.8	14.3	34.9	7
72 Mauritius	110	204	99	22.2	225	7.2	17.4	3.5	40.4	8
73 Brazil	100	254	91	37.5	1,341	5.3	..	18.7	62.7	15
74 Georgia	78	379	98	23.8	4,352	2.2	27.2	6.7	120.7	24
75 Venezuela, Bolivarian Republic of	120	319	90	25.7	776	4.7	..	2.3	31.0	9
76 Armenia	120	572	88	6.2	378	0.2	..	3.3	39.2	5
77 Ecuador	100	688	84	28.8	2,057	0.3	13.0	5.0	67.2	3
78 Belize	59	237	..	10.6	110	2.6	15.3	25.0	50.0	11
79 Colombia	110	423	83	38.5	1,874	4.2	11.2	0.0	36.6	13
80 Jamaica	113	259	101	57.3	1,856	3.6	..	0.0	9.1	3
81 Tunisia	95	813	100	27.1	973	2.2	9.8	4.1	16.2	2
82 Jordan	99	494	99	27.0	1,187	2.2	7.2	0.0	50.5	6
83 Turkey	113	141	100	34.4	916	7.8	..	16.8	5.8	13
84 Algeria	..	..	82	11.9	2,633	1.4	..	7.7	46.5	7
85 Tonga	73	669	90	8.1	250	0.7	..	8.5	61.8	9
MEDIUM HUMAN DEVELOPMENT										
86 Fiji	86	415	65	12.2	758	1.9	..	6.2	57.7	8
87 Turkmenistan	32	334	14	1.5	1,150	0.1	..	..	..	..
88 Dominican Republic	82	412	..	21.6	556	2.3	..	0.7	28.9	10
89 China	74	329	97	22.5	1,233	6.2	5.6	9.9	..	3
90 El Salvador	131	486	95	10.6	829	2.0	..	0.0	40.0	6
91 Sri Lanka	72	1,104	95	5.8	850	0.5	..	5.5	129.2	5
92 Thailand	102	698	38	23.9	600	1.4	..	1.5	119.6	9
93 Gabon	92	734	79	6.2	500	0.2	3.4	..	104.1	15
94 Suriname	97	328	..	9.7	327	1.1	..	0.0	..	..
95 Bolivia, Plurinational State of	57	405	46	10.8	775	0.7	..	0.0	41.4	7

TABLE 17

212

HUMAN DEVELOPMENT REPORT **2010**

		TELEPHONES			INTERNET				ACCESSIBILITY AND COST		
		Mobile and fixed-line phone subscriptions		Population covered by mobile phone network	Users		Broadband subscriptions[a]	Personal computers	Mobile phone connection charge	Fixed-line phone connection charge	Price of a 3-minute local fixed-line phone call
HDI rank		(per 100 people)	(% growth, population-based)	(%)	(per 100 people)	(% growth, population-based)	(per 100 people)	(per 100 people)	($)	($)	(US cents)
		2008	2000–2008	2008	2008	2000–2008	2008	2006–2008[b]	2006–2008[b]	2006–2008[b]	2006–2008[b]
96	Paraguay	103	484	..	14.3	2,136	1.4	..	..	80.2	7
97	Philippines	80	659	99	6.2	265	1.2	7.2	0.9	44.9	0[c]
98	Botswana	85	355	99	6.2	140	0.5	6.2	2.9	37.1	17
99	Moldova, Republic of	97	389	98	23.4	1,516	3.2	11.4	4.3	173.2	3
100	Mongolia	74	622	66	12.5	1,000	1.4	24.6	..	43.8	..
101	Egypt	65	678	95	16.6	2,916	0.9	3.9	4.0	74.0	2
102	Uzbekistan	53	746	93	9.0	1,938	0.2	3.1	7.0	12.0	..
103	Micronesia, Federated States of	39	343	..	14.5	300	0.1	..	50.0	24.0	0[c]
104	Guyana	..	..	..	26.9		0.3	..	22.1	2.5	0
105	Namibia	56	520	95	5.3	278	0.0	23.9	5.9	35.5	18
106	Honduras	96	1,450	90	13.1	1,177	..	2.5	5.0	25.8	8
107	Maldives	158	1,405	100	23.5	1,096	5.2	20.2	7.7	134.4	6
108	Indonesia	75	1,555	90	7.9	847	0.2	2.0	..	..	3
109	Kyrgyzstan	74	927	24	16.1	1,576	0.1	..	10.0	79.7	8
110	South Africa	102	272	100	8.6	75	0.9	..	18.0	51.5	18
111	Syrian Arab Republic	52	547	96	17.3	12,156	0.1	8.8	5.7	28.7	..
112	Tajikistan	58	1,703	..	8.8	19,900	0.1	..	3.7	..	..
113	Viet Nam	116	2,881	70	24.2	10,286	2.4	9.5	3.1	25.0	2
114	Morocco	82	585	98	33.0	5,121	1.5	5.7	2.6	77.4	26
115	Nicaragua	60	1,242	..	3.3	270	0.6	..	..	101.8	4
116	Guatemala	120	969	76	14.3	2,350	0.6	..	13.3	82.7	9
117	Equatorial Guinea	54	3,107	..	1.8	1,614	0.0	..	..	..	..
118	Cape Verde	70	370	96	20.6	1,185	1.5	14.0	26.6	29.1	6
119	India	34	979	61	4.5	850	0.5	3.2	2.3	6.9	2
120	Timor-Leste	..	..	..	..	..	0.0	..	20.0	36.2	31
121	Swaziland	49	788	91	6.9	700	0.1	3.7	11.5	25.8	5
122	Lao People's Democratic Republic	35	3,914	..	8.5	8,691	0.1	..	5.2	36.4	7
123	Solomon Islands	7	330	..	2.0	400	0.3	..	36.2	..	..
124	Cambodia	29	2,551	87	0.5	1,133	0.1	0.4	10.1	50.6	3
125	Pakistan	56	2,632	90	11.1	..	0.1	..	7.1	10.7	3
126	Congo	51	1,888	53	4.3	19,275	..	..	..	..	..
127	São Tomé and Príncipe	35	1,129	20	15.5	282	0.5	..	..	29.5	11

LOW HUMAN DEVELOPMENT

128	Kenya	43	3,848	83	8.7	3,260	0.0	..	34.7	33.2	12
129	Bangladesh	29	5,870	90	0.3	456	0.0	2.3	2.2	29.2	1
130	Ghana	50	3,319	73	4.3	3,223	0.1	1.1	7.0	42.8	16
131	Cameroon	33	3,107	58	3.8	1,712	..	..	5.6	89.3	25
132	Myanmar	2	314	10	0.2	..	0.0	0.9	..	..	..
133	Yemen	21	1,172	68	1.6	2,367	..	2.8	6.0	85.1	1
134	Benin	41	3,255	80	1.8	967	0.0	0.7	5.6	215.7	3
135	Madagascar	26	4,134	23	1.7	954	0.0	..	2.0	34.5	35
136	Mauritania	67	6,227	62	1.9	1,100	0.2	4.5	11.1	18.5	22
137	Papua New Guinea	10	799	..	1.8	167	..	..	0.0	3.7	4
138	Nepal	17	1,706	10	1.7	898	0.0	..	7.2	25.8	1
139	Togo	26	1,722	85	5.4	250	0.0	..	3.3	111.7	14
140	Comoros	19	1,706	40	3.6	1,441	..	..	0.0	120.6	15
141	Lesotho	32	1,375	55	3.6	1,733	0.0	..	6.1	40.8	18
142	Nigeria	43	10,921	83	15.9	29,878	0.0	..	84.4	75.9	14
143	Uganda	28	4,526	100	7.9	6,150	0.0	1.7	4.1	69.7	21
144	Senegal	46	1,134	85	8.4	2,450	0.4	..	5.6	22.3	22
145	Haiti	33	2,495	..	10.1	4,900	..	5.1	..	..	..
146	Angola	38	7,493	40	3.1	3,567	0.1	0.6	..	60.0	27
147	Djibouti	15	1,186	85	2.3	1,253	0.3	3.8	28.1	56.2	8
148	Tanzania, United Republic of	31	4,522	65	1.2	1,200	0.0	..	5.8	16.7	22
149	Côte d'Ivoire	52	1,367	59	3.2	1,550	0.1	..	19.1	22.3	20
150	Zambia	29	1,892	50	5.5	3,400	0.0	..	..	13.3	70

TABLE
17

	TELEPHONES			INTERNET			ACCESSIBILITY AND COST			
	Mobile and fixed-line phone subscriptions		Population covered by mobile phone network	Users		Broadband subscriptions[a]	Personal computers	Mobile phone connection charge	Fixed-line phone connection charge	Price of a 3-minute local fixed-line phone call	
HDI rank	(per 100 people)	(% growth, population-based)	(%)	(per 100 people)	(% growth, population-based)	(per 100 people)	(per 100 people)	($)	($)	(US cents)
	2008	2000–2008	2008	2008	2000–2008	2008	2006–2008[b]	2006–2008[b]	2006–2008[b]	2006–2008[b]
151 Gambia	73	3,023	85	6.9	852	0.0	3.5	..	28.0	7
152 Rwanda	14	2,268	92	3.1	5,900	0.0	0.3	3.2	46.5	18
153 Malawi	13	1,949	93	2.1	2,007	0.0	..	3.1	..	7
154 Sudan	30	2,916	66	10.2	46,567	0.1	10.7	2.4	0.0	6
155 Afghanistan	..	..	75	1.7	..	..	0.4	24.8	31.4	41
156 Guinea	39	5,713	80	0.9	1,025	..	..	..	36.9	..
157 Ethiopia	4	1,042	10	0.4	3,500	..	0.7	47.7	31.8	2
158 Sierra Leone	19	3,264	70	0.3	178	..	..	..	..	..
159 Central African Republic	4	1,050	19	0.4	850	..	..	2.2	79.1	13
160 Mali	28	6,994	22	1.6	1,233	0.0	0.8	2.2	86.3	12
161 Burkina Faso	18	3,337	61	0.9	1,456	0.0	0.6	6.7	55.8	14
162 Liberia	19	8,851	..	0.5	3,900	..	..	..	..	..
163 Chad	17	11,460	24	1.2	4,233	..	..	..	101.6	..
164 Guinea-Bissau	32	4,438	65	2.4	1,137	..	..	..	..	..
165 Mozambique	20	3,178	44	1.6	1,650	0.1	..	0.2	18.8	26
166 Burundi	6	1,307	80	0.8	1,200	..	0.9	2.9	9.7	..
167 Niger	13	8,801	45	0.5	1,900	..	..	11.2	33.5	17
168 Congo, Democratic Republic of the	..	..	..	..	..	..	..	..	..	..
169 Zimbabwe	16	288	75	11.4	2,742	0.1	7.6	..	..	..

OTHER COUNTRIES OR TERRITORIES

Antigua and Barbuda	202	190	100	75.0	1,200	14.5	20.7	..	68.5	..
Bhutan	41	1,869	21	6.6	1,900	0.3	2.5	1.7	13.8	3
Cuba	13	190	77	12.9	2,317	0.0	5.6	120.0	..	..
Dominica	161	370	..	37.6	338	15.4	..	..	55.6	7
Eritrea	3	388	80	4.1	3,900	..	1.0	91.1	65.0	4
Grenada	86	148	..	23.2	484	9.8	..	13.0	85.2	6
Iraq	61	2,652	72	1.0	..	..	..	..	159.4	1
Kiribati	5	37	..	2.1	33	..	..	..	..	..
Korea, Democratic People's Rep. of	5	136	0	0.0	..	..	..	..	..	3
Lebanon	52	65	100	22.5	215	5.0	10.2	47.0	29.9	8
Marshall Islands	9	21	..	3.7	175	..	..	..	..	..
Monaco	..	..	..	..	..	41.9	..	..	..	..
Occupied Palestinian Territories	38	236	95	9.0	922	2.4	..	..	..	..
Oman	125	810	96	20.0	559	1.2	16.9	26.0	26.0	65
Palau	96	..	95	..	..	0.5	..	..	..	..
Saint Kitts and Nevis	204	334	..	32.5	492	21.7	..	..	..	..
Saint Lucia	124	307	..	58.8	1,142	9.1	..	0.0	46.3	6
Saint Vincent and the Grenadines	140	461	100	60.5	1,786	8.6	..	0.0	37.0	7
Samoa	85	1,287	..	5.0	800	0.1	2.3	17.6	20.2	6
San Marino	146	..	98	54.8	..	15.7	79.0	..	141.4	6
Seychelles	133	140	98	39.0	445	4.1	21.6	9.1	55.4	8
Somalia	8	592	..	1.1	580	..	..	..	..	..
Tuvalu	..	..	..	..	..	4.6	..	..	75.3	..
Vanuatu	20	562	50	7.3	325	0.1	..	45.2	88.8	30

NOTES

a Number of subscriptions to digital subscriber lines, cable modems or other fixed broadbands expressed per 100 people. Includes digital subscriber line/analog subscriber line connections with speeds of 56 kilobits per second and higher.

b Data refer to the most recent year available during the period specified.

c Locals calls are free.

SOURCES

Column 1: Calculated based on data on cellular subscribers and telephone lines from World Bank (2010c).

Columns 2 and 5: Calculated based on data on cellular subscribers and telephone lines from World Bank (2010c) and data on population from UNDESA (2009d).

Columns 3 and 6–10: ITU (2009).

Column 4: World Bank (2010c).

TABLE
17

Technical notes

Calculating the human development indices—graphical presentation

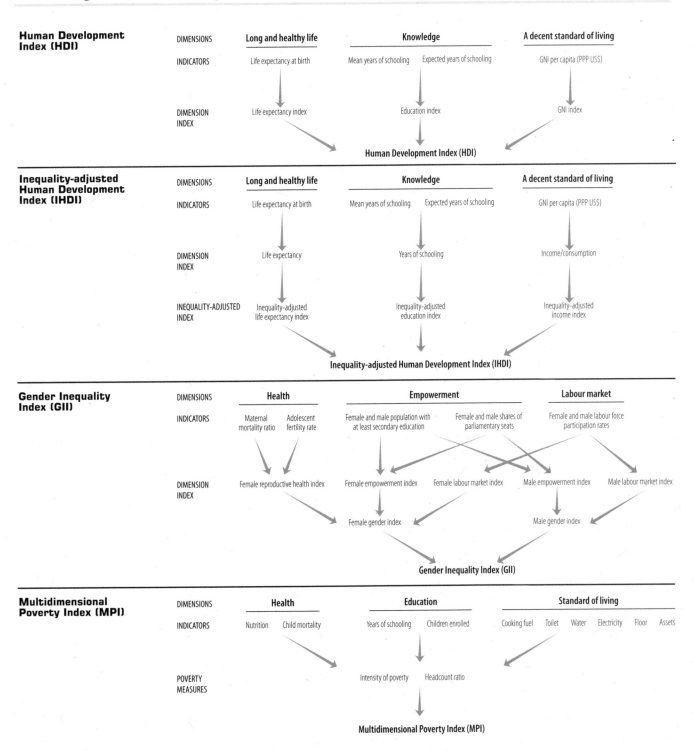

Human Development Index (HDI)

DIMENSIONS: Long and healthy life | Knowledge | A decent standard of living

INDICATORS: Life expectancy at birth | Mean years of schooling | Expected years of schooling | GNI per capita (PPP US$)

DIMENSION INDEX: Life expectancy index | Education index | GNI index

Human Development Index (HDI)

Inequality-adjusted Human Development Index (IHDI)

DIMENSIONS: Long and healthy life | Knowledge | A decent standard of living

INDICATORS: Life expectancy at birth | Mean years of schooling | Expected years of schooling | GNI per capita (PPP US$)

DIMENSION INDEX: Life expectancy | Years of schooling | Income/consumption

INEQUALITY-ADJUSTED INDEX: Inequality-adjusted life expectancy index | Inequality-adjusted education index | Inequality-adjusted income index

Inequality-adjusted Human Development Index (IHDI)

Gender Inequality Index (GII)

DIMENSIONS: Health | Empowerment | Labour market

INDICATORS: Maternal mortality ratio | Adolescent fertility rate | Female and male population with at least secondary education | Female and male shares of parliamentary seats | Female and male labour force participation rates

DIMENSION INDEX: Female reproductive health index | Female empowerment index | Female labour market index | Male empowerment index | Male labour market index

Female gender index | Male gender index

Gender Inequality Index (GII)

Multidimensional Poverty Index (MPI)

DIMENSIONS: Health | Education | Standard of living

INDICATORS: Nutrition | Child mortality | Years of schooling | Children enrolled | Cooking fuel | Toilet | Water | Electricity | Floor | Assets

POVERTY MEASURES: Intensity of poverty | Headcount ratio

Multidimensional Poverty Index (MPI)

Technical note 1. Calculating the Human Development Index

The Human Development Index (HDI) is a summary measure of human development. It measures the average achievements in a country in three basic dimensions of human development: a long and healthy life, access to knowledge and a decent standard of living. The HDI is the geometric mean of normalized indices measuring achievements in each dimension.

Data sources

- Life expectancy at birth: UNDESA (2009d)
- Mean years of schooling: Barro and Lee (2010)
- Expected years of schooling: UNESCO Institute for Statistics (2010a)
- Gross national income (GNI) per capita: World Bank (2010g) and IMF (2010a)

Creating the dimension indices

The first step is to create subindices for each dimension. Minimum and maximum values (goalposts) need to be set in order to transform the indicators into indices between 0 and 1. Because the geometric mean is used for aggregation, the maximum value does not affect the relative comparison (in percentage terms) between any two countries or periods of time. The maximum values are set to the actual observed maximum values of the indicators from the countries in the time series, that is, 1980–2010. The minimum values will affect comparisons, so values that can be appropriately conceived of as subsistence values or "natural" zeros are used. Progress is thus measured against minimum levels that a society needs to survive over time. The minimum values are set at 20 years for life expectancy, at 0 years for both education variables and at $163 for per capita gross national income (GNI). The life expectancy minimum is based on long-run historical evidence from Maddison (2010) and Riley (2005).[1] Societies can subsist without formal education, justifying the education minimum. A basic level of income is necessary to ensure survival: $163 is the lowest value attained by any country in recorded history (in Zimbabwe in 2008) and corresponds to less than 45 cents a day, just over a third of the World Bank's $1.25 a day poverty line.

Goalposts for the Human Development Index in this Report

Dimension	Observed maximum	Minimum
Life expectancy	83.2 (Japan, 2010)	20.0
Mean years of schooling	13.2 (United States, 2000)	0
Expected years of schooling	20.6 (Australia, 2002)	0
Combined education index	0.951 (New Zealand, 2010)	0
Per capita income (PPP $)	108,211 (United Arab Emirates, 1980)	163 (Zimbabwe, 2008)

Having defined the minimum and maximum values, the subindices are calculated as follows:

$$\text{Dimension index} = \frac{\text{actual value} - \text{minimum value}}{\text{maximum value} - \text{minimum value}}. \quad (1)$$

For education, equation 1 is applied to each of the two subcomponents, then a geometric mean of the resulting indices is created and finally, equation 1 is reapplied to the geometric mean of the indices, using 0 as the minimum and the highest geometric mean of the resulting indices for the time period under consideration as the maximum. This is equivalent to applying equation 1 directly to the geometric mean of the two subcomponents. Because each dimension index is a proxy for capabilities in the corresponding dimension, the transformation function from income to capabilities is likely to be concave (Anand and Sen 2000c). Thus, for income the natural logarithm of the actual minimum and maximum values is used.

Aggregating the subindices to produce the Human Development Index

The HDI is the geometric mean of the three dimension indices:

$$(I_{Life}^{1/3} \cdot I_{Education}^{1/3} \cdot I_{Income}^{1/3}). \quad (2)$$

Expression 2 embodies imperfect substitutability across all HDI dimensions. It thus addresses one of the most serious criticisms of the linear aggregation formula, which allowed for perfect substitution across dimensions. Some substitutability is inherent in the definition of any index that increases with the values of its components.

Example: China

Indicator	Value
Life expectancy at birth (years)	73.5
Mean years of schooling (years)	7.5
Expected years of schooling (years)	11.4
GNI per capita (PPP US$)	7,263

Note: Values are rounded.

$$\text{Life expectancy index} = \frac{73.5 - 20}{83.2 - 20} = 0.847$$

$$\text{Mean years of schooling index} = \frac{7.5 - 0}{13.2 - 0} = 0.568$$

$$\text{Expected years of schooling index} = \frac{11.4 - 0}{20.6 - 0} = 0.553$$

$$\text{Education index} = \frac{\sqrt{0.568 \cdot 0.553} - 0}{0.951 - 0} = 0.589$$

$$\text{Income index} = \frac{\ln(7,263) - \ln(163)}{\ln(108,211) - \ln(163)} = 0.584$$

$$\text{Human Development Index} = \sqrt[3]{0.847 \cdot 0.589 \cdot 0.584} = 0.663$$

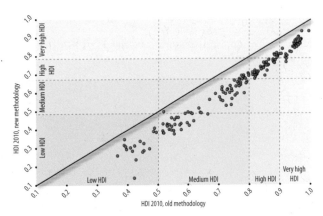

FIGURE T1.1 Human Development Index 2010: new and old methodologies

Source: HDRO calculations using data from the HDRO database.

Overall effects of the Human Development Index methodological improvements

The methodological improvements in the HDI, using new indicators and the new functional form, result in substantial changes (figure T1.1). Adopting the geometric mean produces lower index values, with the largest changes occurring in countries with uneven development across dimensions. The geometric mean has only a moderate impact on HDI ranks. Setting the upper bounds at actual maximum values has less impact on overall index values and has little further impact on ranks.

Analysis of historical trends in this Report

The analysis of historical trends in chapters 2 and 3 uses a different version of the HDI, the hybrid HDI, which applies the same aggregation formula as the new HDI to the set of indicators and sources used in previous Reports (since 1995) in order to allow more extensive analysis over time. Linear interpolation was used to fill missing values when both earlier and later values

were present. When unavailable for the whole time period, gross enrolment ratios were projected using the last available value (for forward projections) and the first available value (for backward projections). A sensitivity analysis showed that the results of the analysis were robust to alternative extrapolation techniques. See Gidwitz and others (2010) for further details on the construction of this data set.

The analysis in chapters 2 and 3 also uses the deviation from fit criterion to comparatively evaluate changes over time in the hybrid HDI. This measure evaluates the progress of countries compared with the average progress of countries with a similar initial HDI level. It is calculated as the residual of a second degree fractional polynomial regression of the annual percentage growth rate of the HDI on the logarithm of its initial HDI value. Statistical table 2 reports the country rank in the deviation from fit for the HDI for 1980–2010. See Royston and Altman (1994) for a description of regression models based on fractional polynomial functions of a continuous covariate.

Technical note 2. Calculating the Inequality-adjusted Human Development Index

The Inequality-adjusted Human Development Index (IHDI) adjusts the Human Development Index (HDI) for inequality in distribution of each dimension across the population. It is based on a distribution-sensitive class of composite indices proposed by Foster, Lopez-Calva, and Szekely (2005), which draws on the Atkinson (1970) family of inequality measures. It is computed as a geometric mean of geometric means, calculated across the population for each dimension separately (for details, see Alkire and Foster 2010). The IHDI accounts for inequalities in HDI dimensions by "discounting" each dimension's average value according to its level of inequality. The IHDI equals the HDI when there is no inequality across people but is less than the

HDI as inequality rises. In this sense, the IHDI is the actual level of human development (accounting for this inequality), while the HDI can be viewed as an index of "potential" human development (or the maximum level of HDI) that could be achieved if there was no inequality. The "loss" in potential human development due to inequality is given by the difference between the HDI and the IHDI and can be expressed as a percentage.

Data sources

Since the HDI relies on country-level aggregates such as national accounts for income, the IHDI must draw on alternative sources of data to obtain the distribution of each dimension.

The distributions have different units—income and years of schooling are distributed across individuals, while expected length of life is distributed across age intervals. Available distributional data are not necessarily for the same individuals or households.

The inequality in distribution of the HDI dimensions is estimated for:

- Life expectancy, which uses data from abridged life tables provided by UNDESA (2009d). This distribution is available across age intervals (0–1, 1–5, 5–10, … , 85+), with the mortality rates and average age at death specified for each interval.

- Years of schooling and household income (or consumption), which use household survey data harmonized in international databases: Luxembourg Income Study, Eurostat's European Union Survey of Income and Living Conditions, the World Bank's International Income Distribution Database, the United Nations Children's Fund's Multiple Indicators Cluster Survey, the US Agency for International Development's Demographic and Health Survey, the World Health Organization's World Health Survey and the United Nations University's World Income Inequality Database.

- The inequality in standard of living dimension, which uses disposable household income per capita, household consumption per capita or income imputed based on an asset index matching methodology (Harttgen and Klasen 2010).

For a full account of data sources used for estimating inequality, see Kovacevic (2010a).

Computing the Inequality-adjusted Human Development Index

There are three steps to computing the IHDI.

Step 1. Measuring inequality in underlying distributions

The IHDI draws on the Atkinson (1970) family of inequality measures and sets the aversion parameter ε equal to 1.[2] In this case the inequality measure is A = 1– g/μ, where g is the geometric mean and μ is the arithmetic mean of the distribution. This can be written:

$$A_x = 1 - \frac{\sqrt[n]{X_1 \ldots X_n}}{\bar{X}} \qquad (1)$$

where $\{X_1, \ldots , X_n\}$ denotes the underlying distribution in the dimensions of interest. A_x is obtained for each variable (life expectancy, years of schooling and disposable income or consumption per capita) using household survey data and the life tables.[3]

The geometric mean in equation 1 does not allow zero values. For mean years of schooling one year is added to all valid observations to compute the inequality. Income per capita outliers—extremely high incomes as well as negative and zero incomes—were dealt with by truncating the top 0.5 percentile of the distribution to reduce the influence of extremely high incomes and by replacing the negative and zero incomes with the minimum value of the bottom 0.5 percentile of the distribution of positive incomes.

For more details on measuring inequality in the distribution of the HDI indicators, see Alkire and Foster (2010).

Step 2. Adjusting the dimension indices for inequality

The mean achievement in a dimension, $\bar{X}$, is adjusted for inequality as follows:

$$\bar{X}^* = \bar{X}(1 - A_x) = \sqrt[n]{X_1 \ldots X_n} .$$

Thus $\bar{X}^*$, the geometric mean of the distribution, reduces the mean according to the inequality in distribution, emphasizing the lower end of the distribution.

The inequality-adjusted dimension indices, I_{I_x}, are obtained from the HDI dimension indices, I_X, by multiplying them by $(1 - A_x)$, where A_x is the corresponding Atkinson measure:

$$I_{I_x} = (1 - A_x) \cdot I_X .$$

The inequality-adjusted income index, $I^*_{I_{Income}}$, is based on the unlogged gross national income (GNI) index, I^*_{Income}. This enables the IHDI to account for the full effect of income inequality.

Step 3. Computing the Inequality-adjusted Human Development Index

The IHDI is the geometric mean of the three dimension indices adjusted for inequality. First, the IHDI that includes the unlogged income index (IHDI*) is calculated:

$$IHDI^* = \sqrt[3]{I_{I_{Life}} \cdot I_{I_{Education}} \cdot I^*_{I_{Income}}} =$$

$$\sqrt[3]{(1 - A_{Life}) \cdot I_{Life} \cdot (1 - A_{Education}) \cdot I_{Education} \cdot (1 - A_{Income}) \cdot I^*_{Income}} .$$

The HDI based on unlogged income index (HDI^*) is then calculated. This is the value that $IHDI^*$ would take if all achievements were distributed equally:

$$HDI^* = \sqrt[3]{I_{I_{Life}} \cdot I_{I_{Education}} \cdot I^*_{I_{Income}}} \,.$$

The percentage loss to the HDI^* due to inequalities in each dimension is calculated as:

$$Loss = 1 - \frac{IHDI^*}{HDI^*} = 1 - \sqrt[3]{(1 - A_{Life}) \cdot (1 - A_{Education}) \cdot (1 - A_{Income})}.$$

Assuming that the percentage loss due to inequality in income distribution is the same for both average income and its logarithm, the IHDI is then calculated as:

$$IHDI = \left(\frac{IHDI^*}{HDI^*} \right) \cdot HDI$$

which is equivalent to

$$IHDI = \sqrt[3]{(1 - A_{Life}) \cdot (1 - A_{Education}) \cdot (1 - A_{Income})} \cdot HDI.$$

Notes on methodology and limits

The IHDI is based on an index that satisfies subgroup consistency. This ensures that improvements or deteriorations in distribution of human development within a certain group of society (while human development remains constant in the other groups) will be reflected in changes in the overall measure of human development. This index is also path independent, which means that the order in which data are aggregated across individuals, or groups of individuals, and across dimensions yields the same result—so there is no need to rely on a particular sequence or a single data source. This allows estimation for a large number of countries.

Although the IHDI is about human development losses from inequality, the measurement of inequality in any dimension implicitly conflates inequity and inequality due to chance, choice and circumstances. It does not address the ethical and policy-relevant issues around whether these aspects should be distinguished (see Roemer 1998 and World Bank 2005b for applications in Latin America).

The main disadvantage of the IHDI is that it is not association sensitive, so it does not capture overlapping inequalities. To make the measure association sensitive, all the data for each individual must be available from a single survey source, which is not currently possible.

Example: Slovenia

	Indicator	Dimension index	Inequality measure (A1)	Inequality-adjusted index
Life expectancy	78.8	0.930	0.043	$(1-0.043) \cdot 0.930 = 0.890$
Mean years of schooling	9	0.682		
Expected years of schooling	16.7	0.811		
Education index		0.782	0.040	$(1-0.040) \cdot 0.782 = 0.751 \cdot$
Logarithm of GNI	10.16	0.780		
GNI	25,857	0.238	0.122	$(1-0.122) \cdot 0.238 = 0.209$

	Human Development Index	Inequality-adjusted Human Development Index	Percent loss
HDI with unlogged income	$\sqrt[3]{0.930 \cdot 0.782 \cdot 0.238} = 0.557$	$\sqrt[3]{0.890 \cdot 0.751 \cdot 0.209} = 0.519$	$1-0.519/0.557 = 0.068$
HDI	$\sqrt[3]{0.930 \cdot 0.782 \cdot 0.780} = 0.828$	$(0.519 / 0.557) \cdot 0.828 = 0.772$	

Note: Values are rounded.

Technical note 3. Calculating the Gender Inequality Index

The Gender Inequality Index (GII) reflects women's disadvantage in three dimensions—reproductive health, empowerment and the labour market—for as many countries as data of reasonable quality allow. The index shows the loss in human development due to inequality between female and male achievements in these dimensions. It ranges from 0, which indicates that women and men fare equally, to 1, which indicates that women fare as poorly as possible in all measured dimensions.

The GII is computed using the association-sensitive inequality measure suggested by Seth (2009). The index is based on the general mean of general means of different orders—the first aggregation is by the geometric mean across dimensions; these means, calculated separately for women and men, are then aggregated using a harmonic mean across genders.

Data sources

- Maternal mortality ratio (MMR): United Nations Children's Fund (2010c)
- Adolescent fertility rate (AFR): United Nations Department of Economic and Social Affairs (2009d)
- Share of parliamentary seats held by each sex (PR): Inter-parliamentary Union's Parline database (2010)

- Attainment at secondary and higher education (*SE*) levels: Barro and Lee (2010)
- Labour market participation rate (*LFPR*): International Labour Organization (2010d)

Computing the Gender Inequality Index

There are five steps to computing the GII.

Step 1. Treating zeros and extreme values

The maternal mortality ratio is truncated symmetrically at 10 (minimum) and at 1,000 (maximum). The maximum of 1,000 is based on the normative assumption that countries where the maternal mortality ratio exceeds 1,000 are not different in their ability to create conditions and support for maternal health. Similarly, it is assumed that countries with 1–10 deaths per 100,000 births are essentially performing at the same level.

The female parliamentary representation of countries reporting 0 percent is coded as 0.1 percent because the geometric mean cannot have zero values and because these countries do have some kind of political influence by women.

Step 2. Aggregating across dimensions within each gender group, using geometric means

Aggregating across dimensions for each gender group by the geometric mean makes the GII association sensitive (see Seth 2009).

For women and girls, the aggregation formula is

$$G_F = \sqrt[3]{\left(\frac{1}{MMR} \cdot \frac{1}{AFR}\right)^{1/2} \cdot (PR_F \cdot SE_F)^{1/2} \cdot LFPR_F},$$

and for men and boys the formula is

$$G_M = \sqrt[3]{1 \cdot (PR_M \cdot SE_M)^{1/2} \cdot LFPR_M}.$$

Step 3. Aggregating across gender groups, using a harmonic mean

The female and male indices are aggregated by the harmonic mean to create the equally distributed gender index

$$HARM\,(G_F, G_M) = \left[\frac{(G_F)^{-1} + (G_M)^{-1}}{2}\right]^{-1}.$$

Using the harmonic mean of geometric means within groups captures the inequality between women and men and adjusts for association between dimensions.

Step 4. Calculating the geometric mean of the arithmetic means for each indicator

The reference standard for computing inequality is obtained by aggregating female and male indices using equal weights (thus treating the genders equally) and then aggregating the indices across dimensions:

$$G_{\overline{F,M}} = \sqrt[3]{\overline{Health} \cdot \overline{Empowerment} \cdot \overline{LFPR}}$$

where $\overline{Health} = \left(\sqrt{\frac{1}{MMR} \cdot \frac{1}{AFR}} + 1\right)/2,$

$$\overline{Empowerment} = \left(\sqrt{PR_F \cdot SE_F} + \sqrt{PR_M \cdot SE_M}\right)/2 \text{ and}$$

$$\overline{LFPR} = \frac{LFPR_F + LFPR_M}{2}.$$

$\overline{Health}$ should not be interpreted as an average of corresponding female and male indices but as half the distance from the norms established for the reproductive health indicators—fewer maternal deaths and fewer adolescent pregnancies.

Step 5. Calculating the Gender Inequality Index

Comparing the equally distributed gender index to the reference standard yields the GII,

$$1 - \frac{Harm\,(G_F, G_M)}{G_{\overline{F,M}}}.$$

Example: Brazil

| | Reproductive health | | Empowerment | | Labour market |
	Maternal mortality ratio	Adolescent fertility rate	Parliamentary representation	Attainment at secondary and higher education	Labour market participation rate
Female	110	75.6	0.094	0.488	0.640
Male	na	na	0.906	0.463	0.852
(F+M)/2	$\left(\sqrt{(1/110)\cdot(1/75.6)}+1\right)/2=0.50$		$\left(\sqrt{0.094\cdot0.488}+\sqrt{0.906\cdot0.463}\right)/2=0.431$		$(0.640+0.852)/2=0.746$

na is not applicable.

Using the above formulas, it is straightforward to obtain:

$$G_F \quad 0.115 = \sqrt[3]{\sqrt{\left(\frac{1}{110}\cdot\frac{1}{75.6}\right)}\cdot\sqrt{0.094\cdot0.488}\cdot0.640}$$

$$G_{\bar{F},\bar{M}} \quad 0.546 = \sqrt[3]{0.505\cdot0.431\cdot0.746}$$

$$G_M \quad 0.820 = \sqrt[3]{1\cdot\sqrt{0.906\cdot0.463}\cdot0.852}$$

$$\text{GII} \quad 1-0.201/0.546 = 0.632.$$

$$Harm\,(G_F, G_M) \quad 0.201 = \left[\frac{1}{2}\left(\frac{1}{0.115}+\frac{1}{0.820}\right)\right]^{-1}$$

Technical note 4. Calculating the Multidimensional Poverty Index

The Multidimensional Poverty Index (MPI) identifies multiple deprivations at the individual level in health, education and standard of living. It uses micro data from household surveys, and—unlike the Inequality-adjusted Human Development Index—all the indicators needed to construct the measure must come from the same survey.

Each person in a given household is classified as poor or nonpoor depending on the number of deprivations his or her household experiences. These data are then aggregated into the national measure of poverty.

Methodology

Each person is assigned a score according to his or her household's deprivations in each of the 10 component indicators, (d). The maximum score is 10, with each dimension equally weighted (thus the maximum score in each dimension is 3⅓). The health and education dimensions have two indicators each, so each component is worth 5/3 (or 1.67). The standard of living dimension has six indicators, so each component is worth 5/9 (or 0.56).

The health thresholds are having at least one household member who is malnourished and having had one or more children die. The education thresholds are having no household member who has completed five years of schooling and having at least one school-age child (up to grade 8) who is not attending school. The standard of living thresholds relate to not having electricity, not having access to clean drinking water, not having access to adequate sanitation, using "dirty" cooking fuel (dung, wood or charcoal), having a home with a dirt floor, and owning no car, truck or similar motorized vehicle, and owning at most one of these assets: bicycle, motorcycle, radio, refrigerator, telephone or television.

To identify the multidimensionally poor, the deprivation scores for each household are summed to obtain the household deprivation, c. A cut-off of 3, which is the equivalent of one-third of the indicators, is used to distinguish between the poor and nonpoor.[4] If c is 3 or greater, that household (and everyone in it) is multidimensionally poor. Households with a deprivation count between 2 and 3 are vulnerable to or at risk of becoming multidimensionally poor.

The MPI value is the product of two measures: the multidimensional headcount ratio and the intensity (or breadth) of poverty.

The headcount ratio, H, is the proportion of the population who are multidimensionally poor:

$$H = \frac{q}{n}$$

where q is the number of people who are multidimensionally poor and n is the total population.

The intensity of poverty, A, reflects the proportion of the weighted component indicators, d, in which, on average, poor people are deprived. For poor households only, the deprivation scores are summed and divided by the total number of indicators and by the total number of poor persons:

$$A = \frac{\sum_1^q c}{qd}$$

where c is the total number of weighted deprivations the poor experience and d is the total number of component indicators considered (10 in this case).

Example using hypothetical data

	Household				
Indicators	1	2	3	4	Weights
Household size	4	7	5	4	
Health					
At least one member is malnourished	0	0	1	0	5/3=1.67
One or more children have died	1	1	0	1	5/3=1.67
Education					
No one has completed five years of schooling	0	1	0	1	5/3=1.67
At least one school-age child not enrolled in school	0	1	0	0	5/3=1.67
Living conditions					
No electricity	0	1	1	1	5/9=0.56
No access to clean drinking water	0	0	1	0	5/9=0.56
No access to adequate sanitation	0	1	1	0	5/9=0.56
House has dirt floor	0	0	0	0	5/9=0.56
Household uses "dirty" cooking fuel (dung, firewood or charcoal)	1	1	1	1	5/9=0.56
Household has no car and owns at most one of: bicycle, motorcycle, radio, refrigerator, telephone or television	0	1	0	1	5/9=0.56
Results					
Weighted count of deprivation, c (sum of each deprivation multiplied by its weight)	2.22	7.22	3.89	5.00	
Is the household poor ($c > 3$)?	No	Yes	Yes	Yes	

Note: 1 indicates deprivation in the indicator; 0 indicates non-deprivation.

Weighted count of deprivations in household 1:

$$\left(1 \cdot \frac{5}{3}\right) + \left(1 \cdot \frac{5}{9}\right) = 2.22$$

Headcount ratio

$$(H) = \left(\frac{7 + 5 + 4}{4 + 7 + 5 + 4}\right) = 0.80$$

(80 percent of people live in poor households)

Intensity of poverty

$$(A) = \frac{(7.22 \cdot 7) + (3.89 \cdot 5) + (5.00 \cdot 4)}{(7 + 5 + 4) \cdot 10} = 0.56$$

(the average poor person is deprived in 56 percent of the weighted indicators).

$$\mathrm{MPI} = H \cdot A = 0.450$$

In sum, the basic intuition is that the MPI represents the share of the population that is multidimensionally poor, adjusted by the intensity of the deprivations suffered.

NOTES

1 Lower values have occurred during some crisis situations (such as the Rwandan genocide) but were obviously not sustainable.

2 The inequality aversion parameter guides the degree to which lower achievements are emphasized and higher achievements are de-emphasized

3 A_x is estimated from survey data using the survey weights,

$$\hat{A}_x = 1 - \frac{X_1^{w_1} \dots X_n^{w_n}}{\sum_1^n w_i X_i}, \text{ where } \sum_1^n w_i = 1.$$

4 Technically this would be 3.33. Because of the weighting structure, the same households are identified as poor if a cut-off of 3 is used.

Definitions of statistical terms

Adjusted net savings Rate of savings in an economy after taking into account investments in human capital, depletion of natural resources and damage caused by pollution, expressed as a percentage of gross national income (GNI). Negative adjusted net saving implies that total wealth is declining and that the economy is on an unsustainable path.

Births attended by skilled health personnel Percentage of deliveries attended by personnel (including doctors, nurses and midwives) trained to give the necessary care to women during pregnancy, labour and the postpartum period. Excludes traditional birth attendants, whether trained or not.

Civil war, fatalities Average number of fatalities resulting from civil war per year of conflict, expressed per million people. For countries with multiple wars, the best estimates for the total number of battle deaths from conflict are used.

Civil war, intensity Score indicating the level of intensity of civil war conflict. A score of 0 indicates no conflict; 1 is a sign of minor civil war where the number of deaths in a year is less than 1,000; 2 indicates a major civil war where the number of deaths in a year is at least 1,000.

Consumer price index Average price of a basket of goods and services purchased by households; the basket varies by country and may be fixed or may change at specified intervals. Changes in the consumer price index indicate the change in the real value (purchasing power) of money.

Contraceptive prevalence rate, any method Percentage of women of reproductive age (ages 15–49) who are using, or whose partners are using, any form of contraception, whether modern or traditional.

Debt service, public expenditure on Sum of principal repayments and interest actually paid in foreign currency, goods or services on long-term debt (having a maturity of more than one year), interest paid on short-term debt and repayments to the International Monetary Fund, expressed as a percentage of GNI.

Degraded land, people living on Percentage of people living on severely and very severely degraded land. Land degradation is based on four aspects of ecosystem services: biomass, soil health, water quantity and biodiversity. Severe degradation indicates that biotic functions are largely destroyed and that land is nonreclaimable at the farm level. Very severe degradation indicates that biotic functions are fully destroyed and that land is nonreclaimable.

Democratic decentralization measure Score published by the Database of Political Institutions indicating whether elections were held for the legislature and executive at the lowest subnational (municipal) level. Scores range from 0 (no local elections) to 2 (legislators and executives are locally elected).

Dependency ratio Ratio of the population ages 0–14 and ages 65 and older to the working-age population (ages 15–64), expressed as dependants per 100 people ages 15–64.

Ecological footprint of consumption Amount of biologically productive land and sea area that a country requires to produce the resources it consumes and to absorb the waste it generates, expressed in hectares per capita.

Enrolment ratio, gross Total enrolment in a given level of education, regardless of age, expressed as a percentage of the official school-age population for the same level of education.

Enrolment ratio, net Enrolment in a given level of education of the official age for that level, expressed as a percentage of the total population of the same age group.

Expected years of schooling Number of years of schooling that a child of school entrance age can expect to receive if prevailing patterns of age-specific enrolment rates were to stay the same throughout the child's life.

Fertility rate, adolescent Number of births to women ages 15–19, expressed per 1,000 women of the same age.

Fertility rate, total Number of children that would be born to each woman if she were to live to the end of her child-bearing years and bear children at each age in accordance with prevailing age-specific fertility rates.

Food deprivation, intensity of Average shortfall in kilocalories suffered by malnourished people, expressed as a percentage of the minimum daily requirement of dietary energy intake. The lower the value, the less intense food deprivation is.

Foreign direct investment, net inflows Net inflows of investment to acquire a lasting management interest (10 percent or more of voting stock) in an enterprise operating in an economy other than that of the investor. It is the sum of equity capital, reinvestment of earnings, other long-term capital and short-term capital, expressed as a percentage of GDP.

Formal employment Wage and salaried workers, plus employers, expressed as a percentage of total employment.

GDP (gross domestic product) Sum of value added by all resident producers in the economy plus any product taxes (less subsidies) not included in the valuation of output, calculated without making deductions for depreciation of fabricated capital assets or for depletion and degradation of natural resources. Value added is the net output of an industry after adding up all outputs and subtracting intermediate inputs. When expressed in US dollar terms, it is converted using the average official exchange rate reported by the International Monetary Fund. An alternative conversion factor is applied if the official exchange rate is judged to diverge by an exceptionally large margin from the rate effectively applied to transactions in foreign currencies and traded products. When expressed in purchasing power parity (PPP) US dollar terms, it is converted to international dollars using PPP rates. An international dollar has the same purchasing power over GDP that the US dollar has in the United States.

GDP per capita Gross domestic product (GDP) in US dollar terms, divided by mid-year population. When expressed as an average annual growth rate, the least squares annual growth rate is used with constant GDP per capita data in local currency units.

Gender Inequality Index A composite index measuring loss in achievements in three dimensions of human development—reproductive health, empowerment and labour market, due to inequality between genders. For details on how the index is calculated, see *Technical note 4*.

Gini coefficient, income Measure of the deviation of the distribution of income (or consumption) among individuals or households within a country from a perfectly equal distribution. A Lorenz curve plots the cumulative percentages of total income received against the cumulative number of recipients, starting with the poorest individual or household. The Gini index measures the area between the Lorenz curve and a hypothetical line of absolute equality, expressed as a percentage of the maximum area under the line. A value of 0 represents absolute equality, a value of 100 absolute inequality.

GNI (gross national income) per capita Sum of value added by all resident producers in the economy plus any product taxes (less subsidies) not included in the valuation of output plus net receipts of primary income (compensation of employees and property income) from abroad, divided by midyear population. Value added is the net output of an industry after adding up all outputs and subtracting intermediate inputs. When expressed in PPP US dollar terms, it is converted to international dollars using PPP rates. An international dollar has the same purchasing power over GDP that a US dollar has in the United States.

Human Development Index (HDI) A composite index measuring average achievement in three basic dimensions of human development—a long and healthy life, knowledge and a decent standard of living. For details on how the index is calculated, see *Technical note 1*.

Human Development Index—hybrid An index that uses the same functional form as the HDI but uses literacy and gross enrollment to build the education index and GDP per capita for the income indicator. This index is used in the trends analysis presented in chapters 2 and 3.

Human Development Index, Inequality-adjusted Human development index value adjusted for inequalities in the three basic dimensions of human development. For details on how the measure is calculated, see *Technical note 2*.

Human rights violations Score published by the Database of Political Institutions (which calls it the Political Terror Scale) measuring human rights violations, as classified in Gibney, Cornett, and Wood (2010) and based on sanctioned killing, torture, disappearance and political imprisonment. The score is based on expert coding of the scope (type), intensity (frequency) and range of violence.

Income poverty line, population below Percentage of the population living below the specified poverty line (PPP $1.25 a day and the national poverty line). The national poverty line is the poverty line deemed appropriate for a country by its authorities. National estimates are based on population-weighted subgroup estimates from household surveys.

Labour force participation rate Percentage of the working-age population (ages 15–64) that actively engages in the labour market, by either working or actively looking for work.

Life expectancy at birth Number of years a newborn infant could expect to live if prevailing patterns of age-specific mortality rates at the time of birth were to stay the same throughout the infant's life.

Life satisfaction, overall Score based on responses to a question about satisfaction with life in a Gallup World Poll.

Literacy rate, adult Percentage of people ages 15 and older who can, with understanding, both read and write a short simple statement on their everyday life.

Mean years of schooling Average number of years of education received by people ages 25 and older in their lifetime based on education attainment levels of the population converted into years of schooling based on theoretical durations of each level of education attended.

Military, public expenditure on All expenditures of the defence ministry and other ministries on recruiting and training military personnel and on the construction and purchase of military supplies and equipment, expressed as a percentage of GDP.

Mortality rate, adult Probability per 1,000 that a 15-year-old person will die before reaching age 60.

Mortality rate, infant Probability of dying between birth and exactly age 1, expressed per 1,000 live births.

Mortality rate, under-five Probability per 1,000 that a newborn baby will die before reaching age five, if subject to current age-specific mortality rates.

Mortality ratio, maternal Number of maternal deaths, expressed per 100,000 live births. Maternal death is defined as the death of a woman while pregnant or within 42 days after terminating a pregnancy, regardless of the length and site of the pregnancy, due to any cause related to or aggravated by the pregnancy itself or its care but not due to accidental or incidental causes.

Multidimensional poverty, headcount Percentage of the population that suffers deprivation in at least 3 of the 10 weighted indicators used to construct the Multidimensional Poverty Index.

Multidimensional Poverty Index The share of the population that is multidimensionally poor adjusted by the intensity of the deprivations.

Multidimensional poverty, intensity of deprivation Average percentage of deprivation experienced by people in multidimensional poverty.

Negative experience index Scale indicating the percentage of survey respondents in a Gallup World Poll who experienced a negative emotion such as physical pain, worry, sadness, stress, depression and anger the day before the survey. Responses were coded 1 for "yes" and 0 for "no" and then averaged and multiplied by 100.

Nonincome HDI value Value of Human Development Index computed from life expectancy and education index only.

Official development assistance Disbursements of loans made on concessional terms (net of repayments of principal) and grants by official agencies of the members of the Development Assistance Committee (DAC), by multilateral institutions and by non-DAC countries to promote economic development and welfare in countries and territories in part I of the DAC list of aid recipients, expressed as a percentage of the recipient country's GNI. It includes loans with a grant element of at least 25 percent (calculated at a discount rate of 10 percent).

Physician density Number of medical doctors (physicians), including generalist and specialist medical practitioners, expressed per 10,000 people.

Political engagement Percentage of respondents who answered "yes" to the Gallup World Poll question, "Have you voiced your opinions to a public official in the past month?"

Political freedom, democracy Score on the Democracy and Dictatorship measure of political regimes, which distinguishes between regimes in which executive and legislative offices are filled through contested elections and those in which they are not.

Repetition rate, primary Number of primary school students enrolled in the same grade that they attended in the previous school year, expressed as a percentage of total enrolments in the school in the previous year.

Seats in parliament held by gender Percentage of seats held by a respective gender in a lower or single house or an upper house or senate, where relevant.

Tax revenue Total receipts from compulsory transfers to the central government for public purposes, including income and property taxes and excluding fines, penalties and most social security contributions, expressed as a percentage of GDP.

Trained teachers, primary Percentage of primary school teachers who have received the minimum organized teacher training (pre-service or in-service) required for teaching at the primary level of education.

Undernourishment, prevalence of Percentage of the population whose dietary energy consumption is continuously below a minimum dietary energy requirement for maintaining a healthy life and carrying out light physical activity with an acceptable bodyweight for attained height.

Unemployment rate Percentage of the labour force (the employed and unemployed population) ages 15 years and older who are not in paid employment nor self-employed but who are available for work and have taken specific steps to seek paid employment or self-employment.

Vulnerable employment Percentage of employed people engaged as unpaid family workers and own-account workers.

Country groupings

Developed countries

Developed Organisation for Economic Co-operation and Development (OECD)
(28 countries)

Australia
Austria
Belgium
Canada
Czech Republic
Denmark
Finland
France
Germany
Greece
Hungary
Iceland
Ireland
Italy
Japan
Korea, Republic of
Luxembourg
Netherlands
New Zealand
Norway
Poland
Portugal
Slovakia
Spain
Sweden
Switzerland
United Kingdom
United States

Developed non-OECD
(16 countries or areas)

Andorra
Bahrain
Barbados
Brunei Darussalam
Cyprus
Estonia
Hong Kong, China (SAR)
Israel
Liechtenstein
Malta
Monaco
Qatar
San Marino
Singapore
Slovenia
United Arab Emirates

Developing countries

Arab States
(17 countries or areas)

Algeria
Djibouti
Egypt
Iraq
Jordan
Kuwait
Lebanon
Libyan Arab Jamahiriya
Morocco
Occupied Palestinian Territories
Oman
Saudi Arabia
Somalia
Sudan
Syrian Arab Republic
Tunisia
Yemen

East Asia and the Pacific
(24 countries)

Cambodia
China
Fiji
Indonesia
Kiribati
Korea, Democratic People's Rep. of
Lao People's Democratic Republic
Malaysia
Marshall Islands
Micronesia, Federated States of
Mongolia
Myanmar
Nauru
Palau
Papua New Guinea
Philippines
Samoa
Solomon Islands
Thailand
Timor-Leste
Tonga
Tuvalu
Vanuatu
Viet Nam

Europe and Central Asia
(23 countries)

Albania
Armenia
Azerbaijan
Belarus
Bosnia and Herzegovina
Bulgaria
Croatia
Georgia
Kazakhstan
Kyrgyzstan
Latvia
Lithuania
Moldova, Republic of
Montenegro
Romania
Russian Federation
Serbia
Tajikistan
The former Yugoslav Republic of Macedonia
Turkey
Turkmenistan
Ukraine
Uzbekistan

Developing countries

Latin America and the Caribbean
(32 countries)

Antigua and Barbuda
Argentina
Bahamas
Belize
Bolivia, Plurinational State of
Brazil
Chile
Colombia
Costa Rica
Cuba
Dominica
Dominican Republic
Ecuador
El Salvador
Grenada
Guatemala
Guyana
Haiti
Honduras
Jamaica
Mexico
Nicaragua
Panama
Paraguay
Peru
Saint Kitts and Nevis
Saint Lucia
Saint Vincent and the Grenadines
Suriname
Trinidad and Tobago
Uruguay
Venezuela, Bolivarian Republic of

South Asia
(9 countries)

Afghanistan
Bangladesh
Bhutan
India
Iran, Islamic Republic of
Maldives
Nepal
Pakistan
Sri Lanka

Sub-Saharan Africa
(45 countries)

Angola
Benin
Botswana
Burkina Faso
Burundi
Cameroon
Cape Verde
Central African Republic
Chad
Comoros
Congo
Congo, Democratic Republic of the
Côte d'Ivoire
Equatorial Guinea
Eritrea
Ethiopia
Gabon
Gambia
Ghana
Guinea
Guinea-Bissau
Kenya
Lesotho
Liberia
Madagascar
Malawi
Mali
Mauritania
Mauritius
Mozambique
Namibia
Niger
Nigeria
Rwanda
São Tomé and Príncipe
Senegal
Seychelles
Sierra Leone
South Africa
Swaziland
Tanzania, United Republic of
Togo
Uganda
Zambia
Zimbabwe

Least Developed Countries
(23 countries)

Afghanistan
Bhutan
Burkina Faso
Burundi
Central African Republic
Chad
Congo, Democratic Republic of the
Eritrea
Ethiopia
Guinea
Guinea-Bissau
Haiti
Kiribati
Liberia
Malawi
Mali
Mozambique
Niger
Samoa
Sierra Leone
Somalia
Tuvalu
Vanuatu